REGULATING THE RISK OF UNEMPLOYMENT

This book has been published thanks to the European research project RECWOWE (Reconciling Work and Welfare in Europe), 2006–2011, co-funded by the European Commission, under 6th Framework Programme for Research – Socio-Economic Sciences and Humanities (contract nr 028339-2) in the Directorate-General for Research. The information and views set out in this book are those of the authors and do not necessarily reflect the official opinion of the European Union. Neither the European Union institutions and bodies nor any person acting on their behalf may be held responsible for the use which may be made of the information contained therein.

REGULATING THE RISK OF UNEMPLOYMENT

National adaptations to post-industrial labour markets in Europe

JOCHEN CLASEN
DANIEL CLEGG (EDITORS)

OXFORD

UNIVERSITY PRESS

Great Clarendon Street, Oxford, OX2 6DP,
United Kingdom

Oxford University Press is a department of the University of Oxford.
It furthers the University's objective of excellence in research, scholarship,
and education by publishing worldwide. Oxford is a registered trade mark of
Oxford University Press in the UK and in certain other countries

© Jochen Clasen and Daniel Clegg 2011

The moral rights of the authors have been asserted

First published 2011

Published in the United States of America by Oxford University Press
198 Madison Avenue, New York, NY 10016, United States of America

British Library Cataloguing in Publication Data

Data available

Library of Congress Cataloging in Publication Data

Data available

ISBN 978-0-19-959229-6

Acknowledgements

This book was written in the framework of the European Commission FP6 Network of Excellence *Reconciling Work and Welfare in Europe* (RECWOWE). We have benefited greatly from the opportunities afforded by RECWOWE to meet and develop our collective work. Two dedicated workshops, funded by RECWOWE and held in spring 2009 and 2010 at the University of Edinburgh, were crucial in the development of our common framework for analysis. We were also able to host sessions for the project at the annual RECWOWE Integration Weeks in Utrecht (June 2009) and Nantes (June 2010). We would like to extend our thanks to the coordinators of RECWOWE, Denis Bouget and Bruno Palier, as well as the management team at the MSH in Nantes, for the energy and commitment they have shown to make the network such a valuable forum for the development of new research agendas.

As editors we have been privileged to work with such an excellent and dedicated team of authors, all of whom engaged with and helped us to improve our analytical framework. A special word of thanks goes to Johan De Deken, who in addition to his contributions to Chapters 6 and 15 undertook the very large task of reconciling national data from many of the country studies with available comparative datasets of benefit claimants to generate the original data tables reproduced in Annex B.

We have received valuable comments and feedback on our work for this project from a range of scholars, too numerous to mention in person. We are extremely grateful to all the external participants in the aforementioned meetings, as well as the organizers and participants in workshops or seminars at the University of Southern Denmark in Odense, the European University Institute in Florence, Sciences Po – Collège Universitaire de Menton, and the Akademie für Politische Bildung in Tutzing, Munich, where findings from the project were presented. Finally, we would like to thank Michael Edwards and particularly Evgeniya Plotnikova for excellent research assistance.

Jochen Clasen and Daniel Clegg

Table of Contents

List of Figures

List of Tables

List of Appendices

List of Abbreviations

ADG	Arbeitsamt der Deutschsprachigen Gemeinschaft (employment office of the German community)
ALMP	Active Labour Market Policy
APE	Aides à la Promotion de l'emploi (subsidized employment scheme in Wallonia)
ASC-GESCO	Agent Contractuels Subventionnés – Gesubsidieerde Contractuelen (subsidised employment scheme in the non-profit sector in Brussels and Flanders)
BGDA-ORBEM	Brusselse Gewestelijke Dienst voor Arbeidsbemiddeling – Office Régional Bruxellois de l'Emploi (Brussels region employment office)
CBP	Conventioneel Brugpensioen – Prépension Conventionelle (conventional bridging pension)
CSIAS/SKOS	Swiss Conference for Social Assistance
DAC-TCT	Derde Arbeiscircuit – Troisième Circuit de Travail (subsidised employment scheme in the non-profit sector)
EBP	Bijzonder Brugpensioen Prépension Spéciale (exceptional bridging pension)
EES	European Employment Strategy
ERP	Brugrustpensioen – Prépension de Retraite (early retirement pension)
FFBSS	Fonds voor Financieel Evenwicht van de Sociale Zekerheid – Fonds pour l'Équilibre Financier de la Sécurité Sociale (fund for the financial balance in social security)
FOREM	Walloon public employment and vocational training service – Service Public Wallon de l'Emploi et de la Formation
KSZ-BCSS	Kruispantbank van de Sociale Zekerheid–Banque Carrefour de la Sécurite Sociale (information database for social security)
LEA	Local Employment Agencies – Plaatselijke Werkgelegenheidsagentschappen – Agences Locales pour l'Emploi
MIG	Minimum Income Guarantee – leefloon – revenu d'intégration
MSAO	Municipal Social Assistance Office – Openbaar Centrum voor Maatschappelijk Welzijn – Centre Public d'Aide Sociale
NEO	National Employment Office – Rijksdienst voor Arbeidsvoorziening – Office National de l'Emploi
NSSO	National Social Security Office – Rijksdienst voor Sociale Zekerheid – Office National de Sécurité Sociale

OFAS	Federal Social Insurance Office, Switzerland
OFS	Swiss Federal Statistical Office
RAV/ORP	Regional Placement Offices, Switzerland
SBP	Statutory Bridging Pension – Wettelijk Brugpensioen – Prépension Légale
SECO	State Secretariat for Economic Affairs, Switzerland
SLFS	Swiss Labour Force Statistics
SWF	Fondsen voor Bestaanszekerheid – Fonds de Sécurité d'Existence (sectoral welfare funds)
UI	Unemployment Insurance
VDAB	Vlaamse Dienst voor Arbeidsbemiddeling (Flemish public employment and vocational training Service)

List of Annexes

List of Contributors

Jørgen Goul Andersen is Professor of Political Science, Aalborg University, Denmark. His research interests include social and labour market policy, welfare state change, political economy, and political behaviour. He has authored or edited some thirty-five books, including The Changing Face of Welfare (with A.-M. Guillemard, P.H. Jensen, and B. Pfau-Effinger), Policy Press, 2005. He has directed several large national and international research projects funded by research councils, the Danish government, the Rockwool Foundation, and others.

Giuliano Bonoli is Professor of Social Policy at the Swiss Graduate School of Public Administration at the University of Lausanne, Switzerland. He has published some fifty articles and chapters in edited books, as well as a few books. Among these is Bonoli, G. (2000) *The Politics of Pension Reform. Institutions and Policy Change in Western Europe*, Cambridge University Press.

Cyrielle Champion is a PhD candidate and research assistant at the Swiss Graduate School for Public Administration (IDHEAP), Lausanne, Switzerland. Her main research interests are focused on comparative unemployment and labour market policy as well as the transformations in the governance of European welfare states.

Jochen Clasen is Professor of Comparative Social Policy at the University of Edinburgh. His research interests cover labour market policy, social security, welfare state theory, and comparative methodology. Recent publications include 'Investigating welfare state change. The dependent variable problem in comparative analysis' (edited with N. A. Siegel) Edward Elgar, 2007; 'Converging Worlds of Welfare? British and German Social Policy in the 21st Century' (ed; Oxford University Press, 2011); and 'Exit Bismarck, Enter Dualism? Assessing Contemporary German Labour Market Policy' (with Alexander Goerne) in *Journal of Social Policy*, 40, 4, 2011.

Daniel Clegg is Senior Lecturer in Social Policy in the School of Social and Political Science at the University of Edinburgh, and a member of the executive committee of the network of excellence 'Reconciling Work and Welfare in Europe' (FP6, 2006–11). His research focuses on unemployment benefit and labour market policy reforms in developed welfare states. He has authored many book chapters and journal articles on these themes. His recent publications include 'Labour Market Policy and the Crisis: The UK in Comparative Perspective' (*Journal of Poverty and Social Justice*, 2010) and 'Welfare Institutions and the Mobilisation of Consent: Union Responses to Labour Market Activation Policies in France and the Netherlands' (with Christa van Wijnbergen, *European Journal of Industrial Relations*, 2011).

Johan J. De Deken is a Lecturer at the Department of Sociology at the University of Amsterdam. Previously, he taught at the Humboldt University in Berlin. His recent publications include 'Social expenditure under scrutiny: the problems of using aggregate spending data for assessing welfare state dynamics' in J. Clasen and N.A. Siegel (eds) Investigating Welfare State Change. The 'Dependent Variable Problem' in Comparative Analysis (Edward Elgar, 2007); 'Belgium' in P. de Beer and T. Schils (eds) The Labour Market Triangle. Employment Protection, Unemployment Compensation and Activation in Europe (Edward Elgar, 2009); and 'Belgium: The Paradox of Persisting Voluntarism in a Corporatist Welfare State' in B. Ebbinghaus (ed) The Varieties of Pension Governance. Pension Privatization in Europe (Oxford University Press, 2011).

Irene Dingeldey leads the research unit 'Changes in the Working Society' at the Institute of Work and Labour at Bremen University. She holds a PhD in social sciences and has published on Industrial Relations in Great Britain, family tax systems, marginal part time employment, and labour market policies in Germany and other European countries. Her current research interests include new forms of governance and welfare state change in Germany, the United Kingdom, and Denmark. Articles have been published in *Politische Vierteljahresschrift* (1996, 2008), *Journal of Social Policy* (2001), *Aus Politik und Zeitgeschichte* (1998, 2001, 2006, 2010), *Österreichische Zeitschrift für Politikwissenschaft* (2003), *Feminist Economics* (2004), *Berliner Journal für Soziologie*, and *European Journal of Political Research* (2007).

Anil Duman is an Assistant Professor currently at Central European University, Budapest. Her research interests include social policy, inequality, and labour market. The most recent publications have appeared in *European Journal of Industrial Relations*, *International Journal of Education Economics*, and *International Journal of Social Economics*.

Werner Eichhorst is Deputy Director of Labor Policy at the Institute for the Study of Labor (IZA) in Bonn, Germany. His main research area is the comparative analysis of labour market institutions and performance as well as the political economy of labour market reform strategies. At the IZA, he is responsible for international and European policy-oriented research activities.

Marcel Hoogenboom is Assistant Professor of sociology at the Department of Interdisciplinary Social Sciences, Utrecht University in the Netherlands. His research interests include the history of the welfare state and the restructuring under the influence of late modernity processes. Among his recent publications are: Bannink, D. and Hoogenboom, M. (2007), 'Hidden Change. Disaggregation of Welfare State Regimes for Greater Insight into Welfare State Change', in: *Journal of European Social Policy*, 17, 1, 19–32; and Hoogenboom, M., Bannink, D. and Trommel, W. (2010), 'From local to global, and back', *Business History*, 52, 6, 933–55.

Ondřej Hora is Assistant Professor at School of Social Studies Masaryk University in Brno and Research Fellow at Research Institute for Labour and Social Affairs. His work focuses on labour market, unemployment, active labour market programmes, and social protection schemes for unemployed people. He is co-editor of the book "Rodina, děti a zaměstnání v České společnosti" Albert, Brno, 2008.

Matteo Jessoula is Assistant Professor at the Department of Social and Political Studies of the University of Milan. His work focuses on pensions, labour market policy, and social assistance. His recent publications include *Pension Policy* (Il Mulino, in Italian) and '*Selective Flexicurity' in Segmented Labour Markets: the Case of Italian 'Mid-Siders'* (with P. Graziano and I. Madama) in *Journal of Social Policy*. He is co-editor (with Karl Hinrichs) of *Labour Market Flexibility and Pension Reforms: Flexible Today, Secure Tomorrow?* (Palgrave, 2011).

Regina Konle-Seidl is a Senior Researcher at the Institute for Employment (IAB) in Nuremberg, Germany. She works in the research area on 'International Comparisons and European Integration'. Her research focuses on international comparisons of labour market institutions and labour market reforms, activating labour market policies, and governance of employment services.

Alison Koslowski is a Lecturer in Social Policy at the School of Social and Political Science, University of Edinburgh. Her current research considers the social stratification associated with welfare markets and personal income protection.

Paul Marx joined the IZA in Bonn in October 2008 as a Resident Research Affiliate. His research interests are related to comparative labour market analysis, economic history, and the development of standard employment in Germany.

F. Javier Mato is Associate Professor, Department of Applied Economics of the University of Oviedo. He holds a PhD in Economics (Oviedo) and an MSc in European Social Policy (LSE). One of his main research interests is the evaluation of labour market policies. His latest publications include: 'A non-experimental evaluation of training programmes: regional evidence for Spain', *Annals of Regional Science* 43 (2009, co-authored with B. Cueto) and 'Training in Spain from a comparative perspective', *Papeles de Economía Española*, 124 (2010, in Spanish).

Ágota Scharle is an Economist and senior research partner at the Budapest Institute for Policy Analysis. Her main research interests are the effects of taxes and benefits on labour supply and income redistribution. She is editor of the Working Papers in Public Finance and has recently published in the *Journal of Comparative Policy Analysis*.

Ola Sjöberg is Professor of Sociology at the Swedish Institute for Social Research, Stockholm University. His main research interests are comparative welfare state and labour market research. Recent publications include Social Insurance as a Collective Resource (*Social Forces*), Ambivalent Attitudes, Contradictory Institutions (*International Journal of Comparative Sociology*), and Corporate Governance and Earnings Inequality in the OECD Countries 1979–2000 (*European Sociological Review*).

Tomáš Sirovátka is Professor of Social Policy at the Faculty of Social Studies, Masaryk University in Brno. He has contributed to comparative books on employment and social policies in post-communist countries – recently (with Mirka Rakoczyova) in Cerami, A., Vanhuysse, P. (eds) Post-Communist Welfare Pathways (Palgrave, 2009) – and in several journals including the *Journal of Comparative Policy Analysis, European Journal of Social Security, International Review of Sociology, International Journal of Sociology and Social Policy, Social Policy and Administration, Journal of Marriage and the Family, Czech Sociological Review*, and *Prague Economic Papers*.

Patrik Vesan is Assistant Professor at the Faculty of Political Sciences and International Relations of the University of Valle d'Aosta. His main research interests include labour market and local development policies as well as European governance. He has published several book chapters on Italian labour market policy and two research reports on flexicurity and the quality of work and employment in Europe commissioned by the European Foundation for the Improvement of Living and Working Conditions.

1

Unemployment protection and labour market change in Europe: towards 'triple integration'?

Jochen Clasen and Daniel Clegg

Like the welfare states in which they are embedded, European unemployment protection systems are products of the industrial era (Alber, 1981). Their original institutional templates were premised upon and articulated with the normally stable employment relationships that characterized manufacturing-dominated economies. Since peaking somewhere around the middle of the 1960s in most places, however, the share of manufacturing employment has been in steady decline in Europe in recent decades, as domestic markets for manufactured goods have neared saturation point and the international division of labour has shifted. The potential for employment growth in the European economy today appears to reside overwhelmingly in the service sector, which is purported to flourish where there is flexibility, rather than stability, of employment relationships (Esping Andersen and Regini, 2000; Schmid, 2002). Unemployment protection systems that continue to reflect their industrial heritage will arguably be inadequately equipped to provide efficient and effective risk coverage in labour markets dominated by service employment, and may furthermore help to render structural the regular risks of temporary economic exclusion that they were designed to protect individuals against. Adapting unemployment protection to labour market change thus represents a major social and economic challenge for European welfare states.

In the large comparative literature on welfare state development in recent decades, there are few comprehensive studies of unemployment protection systems as a whole, and fewer still that focus explicitly on the relationship between the regulation of the risk of unemployment and labour market change. This volume represents an attempt to remedy this situation. Its main aim is to investigate how, and how far, unemployment protection systems in Europe are changing towards a model premised on service employment or, more broadly, on a post-industrial economy. Its contributions focus mainly on reforms and adjustments in unemployment protection systems between the early 1990s and the present, a period that opened as it closed, namely with a major recession and fast-rising unemployment. The volume's twelve national case studies document the

structural shifts in national systems of unemployment protection in the intervening period, while a further three chapters address specific issues in unemployment
protection in broader comparative perspective.

The aim of this introductory chapter is to lay out the common analytical
framework of the volume, and thereby set the scene for the chapters that follow.
In a necessarily somewhat stylized fashion, the chapter focuses on the broad
historical evolution of the relationship between the regulation of the risk of
unemployment and the functioning of labour markets. The first section expands
on the industrial heritage of the traditional model of unemployment protection that
developed in European countries, suggesting that – notwithstanding the distributive
conflict that has always surrounded issues of unemployment protection – its key
institutional features ensured a relatively virtuous interaction between the social
protection of workers and the promotion of the conditions for successful industrial
production. The second section then goes on to discuss how this model was
progressively undermined by reactions to fast-rising unemployment, not only
resulting most immediately from the massive demand-shocks of the 1970s but also
reflecting deeper-seated changes in European economies. Though initial political
reactions to these circumstances varied cross-nationally, they all led, we argue, to a
blurring of the previously clear boundaries between insurance and poverty relief as
well as the growth of 'unemployment protection by other means'. The third section
draws out a number of trends and themes from labour market reforms since the early
1990s that are, in our view, suggestive of the gradual emergence of a new model
of unemployment support, based on a reworked articulation between economic
production and social protection. We capture these developments through the
concept of 'triple integration', with integration referring here not to the perhaps
more familiar issue of the integration of individuals in work, but rather to *three
processes of institutional realignment* that tend towards the creation of an integrated
benefit-and-service system adapted to the profile of economic risks that characterize
post-industrial labour markets. The final section briefly summarizes the contributions to the remainder of the volume.

1.1 THE INDUSTRIAL HERITAGE

Though governments already disposed of a panoply of policy instruments for
helping and supporting the unemployed, what we think of today as labour market
policy was not in fact a major sector of welfare state activity in the first decades
after the Second World War in many European countries. In the context of
a buoyant labour market regulated through an active Keynesian macroeconomic
policy, unemployment was generally kept low and individuals – specifically men,
in general – were largely assumed to be capable of managing their own transitions
between jobs, and between employment and temporary periods of non-employment.
In Central and Eastern European countries in the Soviet sphere of influence,
the command economy eradicated the risk of unemployment altogether (Standing,
1999: 51–7).

In Western Europe, the core institution for regulating the risk of unemployment in this period was unemployment benefit, and notably contributory unemployment insurance. National-level unemployment insurance systems were established in most European countries (including in Central and Eastern Europe) in the first half of the twentieth century, in the wake of the pioneering British scheme introduced in 1911 (Alber, 1981). In most countries, these were compulsory social insurance systems, though some European countries maintained – and maintain to this day – voluntary systems run by trade unions and subsidized by the state under the so-called Ghent system (Clasen and Viebrock, 2008). In both types of system, payment of contributions while in work ensured that individuals were protected against risks of cyclical and frictional unemployment through benefits that replaced a part of their previous salary for a set period. In most countries, secondary systems of unemployment assistance or social assistance also existed, paying benefits to those with inadequate contribution histories to be entitled to unemployment insurance and/or those who failed to find work before their regular benefit entitlement expired. These secondary systems always paid benefits at a lower level, usually on a means-tested basis (Kvist, 1998; Van Langendonck, 1997).

These benefit systems existed alongside, and were sometimes articulated with, labour market offices or labour exchanges that existed to provide intermediation services, through the publication of job offers, for example. Generally, however, manpower or active labour market policies (ALMPs) were not traditionally a major instrument for regulating the risk of unemployment in the European context. A partial exception to this rule was the case of Sweden, where public works programmes had continued to be the privileged labour market policy instrument in the pre-war period, setting the scene for the development of the retraining policies that were at the heart of the famous Rehn–Meidner model, in which context they helped the labour market reallocation of workers made redundant by less competitive firms being deliberately priced out of the market through a solidaristic wage policy (Rehn, 1985; Weir and Skocpol, 1985). Though the repute of the Swedish model – and its active promotion by the Organisation for Economic Cooperation and Development (OECD) – encouraged some other states to experiment with similar approaches in the late 1960s (Bonoli, this volume), the principal way of regulating unemployment in the European context was compensating it financially.

This compensatory approach should not, however, be construed as entirely 'passive'. On the contrary, the payment of unemployment benefit served a number of 'productive functions' in a labour market dominated by industrial employment and where the stability of employment relationships was generally seen as economically valuable (Clasen, 1999). By providing better risk protection to those who had previously been in long-term employment relationships, contributory unemployment insurance not only responded to 'moral economy' imperatives but also encouraged people to enter into such relationships in the first place and thus helped to stabilize the standard employment relationships on which intensive industrial production was built (Atkinson and Micklewright, 1990). By giving people the 'breathing space' necessary to find employment corresponding to their skills and interests if made redundant, unemployment insurance can also improve job matching in the labour market, militating against inefficient turnover (Acemoglu and Shimer, 2000). Finally, the existence of relatively generous wage-related unemployment insurance, accompanied by restrictive regulations surrounding the work unemployed people could be expected to search for, arguably also diminished the disincentives individuals might face to make otherwise risky investments in the highly specific skills that industrial producers required their workforces to have (Estevez-Abe et al., 2001; Sjöberg, 2008). These properties, combined with the countercyclical role that unemployment benefits could play in stabilizing aggregate demand during temporary downturns, meant that unemployment benefit provision was a small but important pillar on which the industrial-era model of economic organization was built – even if this was not always recognized by employers, who often fought bitterly against unemployment benefits being introduced or improved.

It may be reasonably objected that the above characterization unduly downplays the great diversity of unemployment protection arrangements in Europe, which like other areas of social protection are to a large extent the fruit of political struggles and contingent process of institutional evolution that played out very differently across the continent. Some have suggested that West European unemployment protection arrangements clustered into the now familiar three or four 'worlds' or 'models' of welfare capitalism (Esping-Andersen, 1990; Gallie and Paugam, 2000; Palme et al., 2010), characterized by very different institutional structures that reflected varying socio-economic and distributive logics. Others point out that in many contexts, economic risks were mainly managed not through national unemployment insurance, but instead through functionally equivalent institutions, such as labour market regulations and collective agreements (Bonoli, 2003). Predominantly industrial economies also came in distinctly different varieties, structuring the development of institutional complementarities with rather different labour market and social policies (Wood, 2001).

We fully acknowledge institutional variations in the regulation of the risk of unemployment in Europe, and indeed shed further light on them in the empirical chapters of this volume. Regarding modes of access to benefits, however, we would nonetheless want to emphasize that there was in fact far less cross-national diversity than in other areas of social protection, such as pensions and health care. Possibly because of its centrality to the functioning of labour markets, at least in capitalist Western Europe, unemployment benefit systems have always rested on some relatively standard institutional characteristics and underlying socio-economic logics. Unemployment benefit systems were thus never formally universalistic, but always based on some combination of contributory and means-tested access, even if the financing and governance of these different benefit tiers showed greater cross-national variation (Schmid and Reissert, 1996). With respect to socio-economic logics, even the most residual of European unemployment protection systems was at least partly premised on an 'industrial achievement' logic of upholding and supporting stable employment relationships. The introduction of the British unemployment insurance system was, for example, from the outset explicitly presented as a measure of 'industrial organization' that would help to encourage good work habits (Beveridge, 1909).

1.2 A POLICY LOGIC UNRAVELS

The economic functionality of the contributory benefit-centred model of risk regulation was, however, closely tied to a labour market structure that was destined to disappear. Initially largely masked by the more immediately obvious impacts of the mid-decade demand shocks that saw unemployment increase markedly, the 1970s also witnessed the acceleration of some secular economic trends that would completely change the context of labour market policy making. Industrial employment began to rapidly shrink as a share of all employment, as developed economies became increasingly service-based (see Statistical Annex, Tables A.1 and A.2). Somewhat later, and with considerable cross-national variation, female labour market participation also began to increase everywhere, as the male-breadwinner model crumbled under the impact of economic and social change (Statistical Annex, Table A.4).

Though there is controversy over the extent of the effect (Kenworthy, 2008), it is generally accepted that the scope for productivity increases is considerably lower in service-based economies. Thus, flexibility rather than stability becomes the key to efficient production and the establishment of a virtuous cycle of falling prices, buoyant consumer demand, and output expansion (Esping-Andersen, 1999; Iversen and Wren, 1998). While in high-skill segments of the labour market this flexibility can be secured thanks to highly polyvalent workers, in low-skill segments numerical and wage flexibility tend to dominate, leading to downward pressure on wages and/or terms of employment. An increase in fixed-term and involuntary part-time employment is another common result (Kalleberg, 2009; Schmid, 2002). Due to the degradation in the employment norm, however, the risk of a 'collision' between the benefit system and the low end of the labour market increases under such conditions. The danger is that there will be limited demand for low-skilled workers on the terms they expect, and limited supply on the terms that will be offered. In this context, the risk of unemployment is no longer only cyclical or frictional, but at the bottom end of the labour market also increasingly structural.

The initial reaction of Western European welfare states to this transformed risk profile, in a period broadly between the late 1970s and the early 1990s, differed in certain respects cross-nationally, but also shared some key similarities. Despite pressure on public budgets, in many countries, unemployment benefit provision for the core workforce was largely spared from cuts, and was sometimes even improved (Blöndal and Pearsson, 1995). In these countries, the sharp increase in unemployment at the time was understood as a transitory crisis rather than a structural phenomenon, and the expansion of unemployment benefits was seen – in the conventional Keynesian paradigm – as a way of both cushioning its social consequences and maintaining the conditions for demand-led recovery (Palier, 2010*a*). Elsewhere, where Keynesianism was weakly institutionalized or where monetarist principles were gaining ground, unemployment benefits were often a rather easy target for fiscal consolidation, leading to cuts in the level and duration of unemployment insurance benefits. While growing recourse to means-tested unemployment or social assistance for those with no personal savings was a deliberate effect of policy change in the latter group of countries, it was also evident even in the former, as a result of tendentially lengthening unemployment durations and an increasing number of people working in atypical forms of employment that did not allow them to build up entitlement to contributory benefits (Eardley et al., 1996; Van Oorschott and Schell, 1991).

Everywhere, in this period the broader social benefit system was also explicitly or implicitly used to move unemployed people out of the labour market altogether. Whether through early retirement benefits, disability benefits, family policies such as long-term leave schemes, specific new social assistance schemes (e.g. for lone mothers), or simply 'inactive' receipt of unemployment benefits,[1] exit routes out of the labour market were opened for a variety of groups of potential but 'peripheral' workers. Some of the reasons for the sharp growth of claimant numbers in various non-employment benefits in the 1980s related to social change (i.e. increased single-parenthood, cf. Lewis, 1997) and the emergence of new psycho-social risks (i.e. growing numbers of people incapable for work due to mental health problems, cf. Kemp, 2008), but a large part was also due to these benefit systems coming to function as parallel systems of social support for groups of working-age people who found themselves excluded from the labour market due to, for example, low or redundant skills (Blöndal and Pearsson, 1995; Erlinghagen and Knuth, 2010). For governments, such 'labour shedding' strategies had the obvious benefit of allowing them to, in some cases (such as early retirement), trumpet advances in social rights, while simultaneously limiting open unemployment (Ebbinghaus, 2006).

Masking open unemployment was also one of the motives behind a third trend in regulatory practices around unemployment issues in this period – the massive expansion in ALMPs. However, unlike the human capital enhancing policies of the earlier period, the new wave of ALMPs were mainly oriented to directly providing (usually temporary) employment to individuals, particularly in the public and para-public sector. As Bonoli (this volume) describes, massive schemes of this kind were established in a number of countries in this period. The once much vaunted Swedish ALMP was also largely turned into a vast public works programme. Young people were the main beneficiaries of such measures, though large programmes of this kind often existed for the long-term unemployed too.

Thus, as a result of changes in the labour market as well as initial political reactions to the new environment, the logics and divisions of labour that had characterized institutional arrangements for regulating the risk of unemployment in industrial labour markets had to a large extent unravelled by the 1980s. While systems of unemployment insurance for core workers were often left largely unchanged, their productive functions and protective capacities had been undermined by the sharp reduction in stable employment opportunities for lower-skilled workers. Large systems of secondary support for those facing the greatest barriers to labour market (re-)integration had grown up alongside them, organized around unemployment or social assistance schemes that had originally been intended to be merely marginal. Largely for political reasons, the relationships between the

---

[1] In many countries it was possible, particularly for older unemployed people, to receive unemployment benefits for a longer period and with less administrative 'hassle' by leaving the unemployment register, and thus no longer being counted as unemployed. Elsewhere, the payment of unemployment benefit support was decoupled from the process of registering as unemployed.

provision of benefits and the work of the public employment services had been weakened, and in many countries the latter now devoted most of its resources to the provision of large employment programmes to occupy the unemployed. Finally, benefit schemes that had been originally designed for groups that were not expected to be active in the labour market had come increasingly to serve as 'pressure valves' for the challenges of managing the risk of unemployment in a transformed economic context, and served to draw people into labour market inactivity and what more and more came to be seen as 'welfare dependency'.

1.3 TOWARDS UNEMPLOYMENT PROTECTION FOR A TRANSFORMED LABOUR MARKET?

Against the backdrop of this stylized reconstruction of the post-war history of unemployment protection, we argue that it is possible to identify a distinctively new phase of policy development that has been taking shape across developed countries from around the middle of the 1990s. While the thrust of policy change in this phase has certainly been to reverse some of the consequences of political reactions to labour market change in the 1980s – the closure of exit routes from the labour market being probably the best example – we suggest that this is far more than a return to the status quo ante. Where the regulation of the risk of unemployment in the old welfare state was designed essentially to provide an institutional undergirding to an economy organized around stable labour market attachments, the common quest is today for policies that can help to enforce flexible labour relations, and thereby encourage service sector expansion. This, however, entails a fundamental reworking of the institutional structures through which unemployment protection was conventionally organized. We see this process of institutional change, which we call 'triple integration', as having three principal dimensions.

The first of these can be called *unemployment benefit homogenization*, or alternatively standardization. This refers to the process whereby social rights, expressed here in terms of the level and/or the duration of entitlement to unemployment benefits, tend to become less dependent on previous labour market achievements and positions than in the past. In the service economy, the stable labour market attachment that rigidly contributory (and thus transparently 'acquired') rights to unemployment insurance encourage is no longer seen as something to be explicitly promoted, and the flexible attachment that they explicitly disadvantage no longer as something to be discouraged. The rationale for rewarding good contributors with better benefits, and punishing those with unstable labour market attachments, thus disappears. Further, calibrating an unemployed individuals' reservation wage – and job-search regime – on their previous employment is increasingly seen to generate disincentives for occupational mobility, and thus to be counterproductive in a flexible labour market.

In concrete policy terms, unemployment benefit homogenization can involve making insurance benefits less status confirming by lowering their generosity, weakening their 'earnings relatedness', or even substituting earnings-related with flat-rate payments. It might also involve disconnecting an individual's contribution record and their benefit rights altogether. At a minimum, we would expect the 'gap' between insurance-based (primary) and other (secondary) benefits for the unemployed to diminish, which may in some circumstances lead to pressures for the introduction of a single scheme for all the unemployed. Unemployment benefit homogenization need not mean the abolition of insurance-type protection altogether, however. A lower level of relevance of the 'earnings relatedness' of unemployment insurance, whether in terms of the diminishing relevance of the earnings relation within an encompassing unemployment insurance scheme, or the restriction of generous earnings related benefits to a decreasing minority of the unemployed, would be an indication of this trend.

The second dimension of integration that we identify can be referred to as *risk re-categorization*, and involves processes at the frontiers between (provisions for) the risk of unemployment and other groups in the working-age population. At a minimum, this dimension entails reversing the process of the narrowing of unemployment as an administrative risk category that characterized the 'labour shedding' policies of the 1980s, a process that is often driven by cost considerations; a 'broadening' of unemployment, therefore. But more than simply returning the 'hidden' unemployed to their 'rightful' category, trends here also involve challenging the very distinctions between the long-established risk categories around which social provisions for working-age people have long been organized.

It is perhaps appropriate here to clarify the rationale for our use of the notion 'unemployment' in the title of this volume and throughout its contributions. Unemployment is of course a social construction, and the very notion is closely linked to the emergence, and bound up with the functioning, of industrial-era labour markets (Gautié, 2002; Salais et al., 1986). Particularly visible in this second of our analytical dimensions, our framework is built on the assumption that the notion of unemployment, at least in its traditional understanding, is gradually becoming less important as an operational concept in social and labour market policy. Because of the limited productivity increases referred to earlier, the growth potential of a service-based economy depends largely on its capacity to mobilize as much of the potentially active population as possible, including groups – such as those with young children, with health problems and with milder forms of disability – whose integration in the labour market would not previously have been a priority, and whose social support would not have been 'work-focussed'. Today, we expect that it would become much more so, with the implication that the identification of the unemployed as a *specific* group within the non-employed population of working age becomes ever less meaningful for the purposes of benefits and other types of social support. Nonetheless, this process is far from complete, and its progress in different national contexts is best tapped by retaining a focus on unemployment while being sensitive to its shifting boundaries. Besides its continuing social and political saliency, then, it is above all for analytical reasons that unemployment remains a crucial concept and lens for viewing changes in the regulation of labour market risks, even as it is being 'diluted'.

In policy terms, risk re-categorization can be manifested in several ways. Benefit levels across unemployment and other working-age risk categories might be harmonized, and obligations – particularly regarding job search – might be built into programmes for working-age groups other than the unemployed, thereby blurring the boundaries between benefit programmes as the basis for logics of state intervention. A more extreme version of risk re-categorization could involve the wholesale abolition of certain benefit schemes and the transfer of their recipients to unemployment support. Most radical of all would be the establishment of a single benefit scheme for all people of working age, in which benefit rights would be similar but job-search obligations and access to additional support services calibrated on the particular needs of individual claimants.

A rather different but analytically related aspect of risk re-categorization involves the frontiers between the risk of unemployment and the once 'non-risk' of employment. As in the industrial labour market being in work was usually a guarantee of a living wage and an indicator of social integration, the primary focus of benefit policies and other state interventions was logically on those who were out of work. Today, with the steep increase in in-work poverty in many countries (Bonoli, 2005; Lohmann and Marx, 2008), these assumptions seem less justified. While specific measures may be put in place to support the incomes of the working-poor through the tax or benefit system, another policy option might be to extend entitlement to certain out-of-work benefits, as well as some of the labour market support services that accompany them, to those in precarious positions in the labour market. In this way, employment status can be expected to become a less important operational category in the targeting of labour market policies of different kinds.

Turning to our third and final dimension of change, a process of so-called benefit *activation* has been witnessed across many welfare states since the early 1990s, in recognition of the greater difficulties that low-skilled people now have in making transitions from unemployment to work, as well as the disincentives they may face to do so. Thanks to a large specific literature on this trend in social and labour market policy (e.g. Barbier and Ludwig-Mayerhofer, 2004; Eichhorst et al., 2008), this last dimension of institutional change in unemployment protection is by now very well documented, and requires less full elaboration here. While activation can mean a number of things for different authors and in different national contexts, our principal concern is the institutional articulation – and possibly integration – of labour market programmes and job-search support for those out of the labour market with the provision of benefit support. Relevant institutional trends would include the modification of regulations concerning the explicit obligations of benefit recipients to engage in activation measures, as well as the development of common administrative units ('single gateways') in charge of both 'active' and 'passive' labour market support. In line with the arguments developed above, these units could in principle be expected to responsible for benefits and services not only for the unemployed but also for other groups of working-age benefit claimants too ('one-stop shops'). Other trends in ALMP, such as the development of increasingly 'work first' forms of programme provision, that target rapid return to normal unsubsidized employment, are also congruent with our framework, and are explored in both the national case studies and in Chapter 16.

Table 1.1 depicts these three processes of integration that we see as characterizing institutional change in contemporary unemployment protection. Suffice to say, following through fully on these overlapping policy shifts would amount to a considerable structural transformation for any unemployment protection system, requiring the integration of previously distinct logics of contributory and

Table 1.1. Triple integration in contemporary labour market policy

Process of integration	Possible policy implications
Unemployment benefit homogenization	• Fewer tiers of unemployment protection • Emergence of dominant tier of unemployment provision • Diminishing differences between benefit tiers
Risk re-categorization	• Diminishing differences in entitlement and conditionality between unemployment and other benefit schemes • Transferring claimants to unemployment benefit systems • Merging benefit programmes • Creating a single benefit for working-age people
Activation	• Merging employment services (active LMP) and unemployment benefit provision (passive LMP) • Tightening requirements to engage in supported job search • Providing labour market advice and support systems for unemployed and other working-age benefit groups ('one-stop shops')

Source: Authors.

non-contributory benefit provision, of different and until recently separate working-age risk categories, and finally of 'active' and 'passive' forms of support for the unemployed. Contributions to this volume will seek to assess how frequent such thoroughgoing institutional transformations have actually been in the unemployment protection systems of European countries in the last two decades.

1.4 THE PLAN OF THE BOOK

The core of this volume consists of twelve national case studies tracking developments in the regulation of the risk of unemployment in European countries over the last two decades. Even though we have emphasized the underlying cross-national commonalities in unemployment protection systems and their articulation with labour markets, the cases included in the book have been selected to maximize variation in institutional structures and economic contexts within Europe. They include unemployment protection systems traditionally embedded in very different welfare systems, including liberal (the United Kingdom), conservative-corporatist (Belgium, France, Germany, and the Netherlands), and social democratic (Denmark and Sweden), the latter two also representing instances of voluntary state-subsidized (or 'Ghent') systems of unemployment insurance. We also include two cases from Southern Europe, where unemployment protection remained underdeveloped in the late 1970s due to strong familialism (Italy) and late democratization (Spain), and two Central and Eastern European countries, in which unemployment protection reform since 1990 has been part of a broader process of transition to a democracy and a market economy (Czech Republic and Hungary). Our final case, Switzerland, also represents an outlier, on the one hand having had very low unemployment during the 1980s, and on the other not being a member of the European Union, unlike all the other cases analysed.

The national case study chapters are structured according to a relatively standardized format. As well as discussing the nationally specific institutional heritage of unemployment protection and its articulation with broader economic and social policy, the first section of each chapter describes initial adaptation of the unemployment protection system to rising unemployment, in most cases in the 1980s.[2] The core of each of the chapters then analyses the subsequent reforms of unemployment protection systems, with particular reference to the three dimensions of institutional integration outlined above.

The heart of the analysis in each of the national case study chapters thus focuses on roughly twenty years of reform, between the early 1990s and 2010. This two-decade time frame has not been selected for convenience alone, however. It was in the beginning of this period that, in many countries, the limits of earlier policies in the realm of unemployment protection became more and more evident, and the role of social policy reform in the development of dynamic and inclusive labour markets came to be emphasized, especially by the European Commission. Starting from the 1993 White Paper 'Growth, Competitiveness and Employment', the Commission has become an increasingly visible actor in the field of social and labour market policy, and since the launch of the integrated strategy for employment in 1994, and European Employment Strategy in 1997, has furthermore actively tried to steer policy development at Member State level in the area of unemployment protection. For many countries, until the end of the 2000s, this period as a whole was also one of relatively dynamic economic performance and employment growth, which if not a result of regulatory change may at least have enhanced the scope for more structural reforms of the type promoted at the European level. The context of course changed considerably with the global economic crisis in 2008, and most of the chapters devote some consideration to the extent and nature of the impact this has had on the structural reform dynamics in motion prior to its onset.

The country studies conclude with some reflection on the political and institutional factors that have shaped the pattern policy change in each national context. As the principal aim of this volume is descriptive and analytical rather than explanatory, testing the influence of particular factors on the development of unemployment protection policy in a systematic way would have been beyond its scope. The chapters nonetheless throw up a number of regularities with respect to the drivers of and constraints upon the adaptation of unemployment protection policies to post-industrial risk structures. These are discussed together in the concluding chapter of the volume, which also offers a tentative categorization of national reform trajectories in this field over the period as a whole.

Our point of departure for this study was the assumption that, notwithstanding the impact of contingent political and institutional factors on domestic reform patterns, changing labour market risks profiles are encouraging modifications to unemployment protection arrangements right across Europe. We very much acknowledge, however, that the causal relationships between labour market

---

[2] As in the cases of the Czech Republic and Hungary and, for different reasons, Sweden and Switzerland, unemployment rates increased sharply only in the early-to-mid-1990s, these case studies adopt a slightly different temporal frame.

change and unemployment protection run in both directions, and therefore anticipate that the patterns of unemployment protection reforms revealed by the analyses in the volume will have effects of their own on the structure and functioning of European labour markets. This theme is taken up explicitly in Chapter 14, the first of the comparative chapters in the volume, which examines how patterns of transitions between unemployment, inactivity, and work are changing across a number of European countries. Using labour force data, the chapter seeks to explore not only whether unemployment protection reforms are making European labour markets more inclusive but also whether they are encouraging the growth of precarious forms of labour market attachment.

As our framework suggests and the national chapters amply detail, changes in the regulation of the risk of unemployment since the 1980s have also often involved shifts in the distribution of non-employed people of working age be-tween different systems of benefit support. Even at the macro level, however, tracking the changing composition of working-age benefit receipt across countries is seriously complicated by the absence of valid and reliable comparative data. Chapter 15 examines the comparative data sources in this area, illustrates some of these problems, and finally explores the potential for making more meaningful comparisons around this issue across a number of countries using national administrative data.

Though the principal focus of this volume is on unemployment protection in the strict sense, developments in this field relate to and are increasingly articulated with – as the case studies all emphasize – policy changes in the area of ALMP. In view of this, Chapter 16 complements the analysis of unemployment protection by providing a more macro-level and comparative assessment of policy develop-ment in this whole area over the long term. Notwithstanding mediation by policy legacies and national-level institutional factors, this analysis demonstrates how strongly policy developments in this field have apparently been shaped by changes in economic problem profiles and risks, or at least in policymakers understanding of these. In this sense, it nicely underscores the argument of the volume as a whole.

Part I

National Developments

2

The United Kingdom: towards a single working-age benefit system

Jochen Clasen

2.1 INTRODUCTION

In cross-national European comparisons, the United Kingdom has often been portrayed as the prototypical 'liberal' welfare state. While this has always been questionable for any analyses which go beyond income transfers, it is certainly the case that British social security is firmly guided by the aim of targeting resources rather than providing income maintenance on a comprehensive scale. However, 'liberal' income provision can be designed in different ways, embracing or eschewing means testing, for example, or giving contributory (social insurance) principles a major or minor role. In other words, there is ample scope for change which this chapter on unemployment protection will illustrate. While maintaining its overall 'liberal' character, underlying principles as well as institutional parameters have been modified considerably and are in the process of undergoing further significant change with the next few years.

The analytical perspective which was outlined in the previous chapter helps to capture the nature of this change, as well as its scale. As will be shown, benefit homogenization started already in the 1980s and continued thereafter. Activation policies began in the early 1990s and were strongly expanded with the introduction, and perpetual reforming, of New Deal programmes after 1998. Finally, since the early 2000s, and partly still unfolding, governments have aimed to rectify policies of the 1980s which facilitated labour market exit and narrowed unemployment as an administrative category. The integration of potentially all working-age benefit claimants into the labour market has become a dominant policy aim of the previous as well as the current government.

One factor which has facilitated the considerable scale and speed of reform, as well as a fairly linear reform trajectory, is the decline of the relevance of social insurance, at least for persons of working age. To explain this decline with reference to the inherent tension between the contributory principle and liberal social protection would be failing to acknowledge the role of programmatic political change. Until fairly recently, the prospect for social insurance as a means of income maintenance in the United Kingdom appeared fairly open. Earnings-related benefits were introduced in the 1960s for sickness and unemployment benefits. Even two decades ago, that is, before Labour became New Labour, the centre-left seemed still keen on reinvigorating the contributory principle as a form of redistributive justice and involvement of average and better earners in the welfare state. Moreover, even under the current Conservative–Liberal Democrat coalition government the role of social insurance for working-age people has not (or at least not yet) be completely rejected, although it has become vastly overshadowed by the notion that benefits should be targeted at low-income groups only. Also a second principle, that is, that all working-age people should be in employment and, if not, receive state support only under the condition that they seek and enter paid work, seems fully in accordance with current government thinking. However, such a reading would ignore a shift in political thinking on the part of the Conservative Party, most notably regarding the 'proper role' of lone parents who were once regarded as carers first and foremost but now as employees.

In short, looking back over the past three decades or so, there has been considerable change within both parties regarding the perception of employment and unemployment, as well as the principles which should underpin public support to people out of work. As Section 2.2 shows this is perhaps most evident within what we have called 'benefit homogenization' in the previous chapter and which in the United Kingdom can be traced back to the 1980s. Comparing the main characteristics of unemployment protection as they existed in 1990 with those of 2010, Section 2.3 illustrates the scale of change and identifies instances of integration within all three analytical dimensions. The most recent trend towards 'risk re-categorization' can be seen partly as a spillover from accelerated activation efforts since the late 1990s and stubbornly high numbers of people out of work and in receipt of different types of transfers. However, as discussed in Section 2.4, reforms which led to more integration have not simply been prompted by economic and labour market developments but required political reorientations within both major political parties and the emergence of an implicit cross-party consensus. A major reform proposed by the Conservative–Liberal Democrat coalition government in 2010 illustrates this. The creation of a single working-age benefit system is now firmly on the political agenda. Perhaps less comprehensive than has been claimed, it nevertheless represents a major step in the process of triple integration in the United Kingdom.

2.2 ECONOMIC AND POLICY CONTEXT

Two factors left profound marks on the development of British social policy during the 1980s. In 1979, Margaret Thatcher and the Conservative Party won the general election, ousting the previous Labour government and receiving further legislative remits to significantly shape and change the political landscape after subsequent elections in 1983 and 1987. Thatcher's neo-liberal approach was strongly guided by a commitment to reduce the scope of the public sector and encourage private ownership. The welfare state was regarded as overly bureaucratic and as undermining economic incentives (Timmins, 2001). Lowering levels of income taxation and reducing public borrowing remained major policy objectives throughout the decade, which influenced several rounds of generally incremental reform and cutbacks in social security and other social policy domains (see Glennerster and Hills, 1998; Hills, 1998).

The second factor was the economic recession in the late 1970s and the steep rise in unemployment in the early 1980s (see Statistical Annex, Tables A.3 and A.5). The number of claims made for unemployment benefit almost trebled between 1979 and the mid-1980s (see Figure 2.1). It should be noted that the scale of employment loss was politically reinforced, not only due to the emphasis on tackling inflation at the expense of unemployment but also as a consequence of the government actively promoting the decline of some industrial sectors, notably mining. There was significant deindustrialization during the 1970s and 1980s (see Statistical Annex, Table A.1), which contributed to a steep decline in male employment from 85 per cent in the late 1970s to almost 75 per cent by the mid-1980s. Foregone tax revenue as well as high annual social security expenditure in the early 1980s (Levell et al., 2009: 71) added problem pressure on a government intent on reducing public spending.

A prominent motive within the government's unemployment policy was its 'obsession' (Timmins, 2001: 375) with work incentives and the perceived need to widen the gap between benefits and earnings. Real wages at the lower end of the earnings spectrum were falling, partly because of higher indirect taxation and national insurance contributions. This reinforced the perceived urgency for cutbacks, which were implemented in the form of the temporary suspension of benefit indexation, the introduction of benefit taxation, the removal of partial insurance benefits for claimants with shorter contribution records, and, most relevant in the context of this chapter, the abolition of the earnings-related element of unemployment benefit.

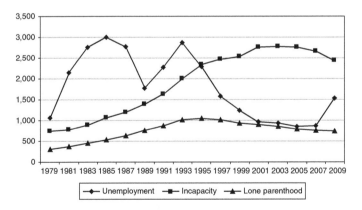

Figure 2.1. Working-age claimant data (thousands), major groups only*

Notes: Unemployment: claimants of contribution-based and means-tested benefits, including 'credits' only (ca. 10 per cent); Incapacity: Incapacity Benefit (excluding claims under twenty-eight weeks), Severe Disablement Allowance, and Employment Support Allowance. *: Excluded are 'carers' and other groups.
Sources: Unemployment: ONS, time series data, seasonally adjusted. Disability: DWP, tabulation tools, time series; from 2000: DWP Quarterly Statistical Summary, August 2009 (February figures). Lone parents: DWP Quarterly Statistical Summary (2000–8: May figures; 2009 February figures); 1980s figures: December or May; 1990s: calculated based on: research.dwp.gove.uk/asd/asd4/table_c1.xls. Data for 1985 (lone parenthood claimants) has been estimated as the average between the numbers for 1984 and 1986.

During the 1960s, originally flat-rate benefits had become partially wage related. However, low benefit levels and restrictive access to earnings-related additions made it feasible for the Conservative government to terminate the experiment of wage-replacement benefits in the early 1980s (Clasen, 1994). Since contribution conditions were tightened, the scope of unemployment insurance substantially weakened (see Appendix 2.A).[1] In the early 1980s, more than half of all registered unemployed persons received unemployment benefit as a right based on contributions. By the end of the decade, the share had declined to little more than a quarter (see also Table 2.2 below). In short, a trend towards benefit homogenization can already be identified for the 1980s in two respects. While the gap between insurance and assistance support narrowed in terms of benefit generosity, means-tested rather than insurance-based support was becoming the dominant type of unemployment benefit.

There was no such integration between unemployment protection and other working-age benefit schemes. On the contrary, during the first half of the 1980s, the boundaries between unemployment and other causes for benefit entitlement became more sharply defined. Most notably, some groups became excluded from the status of unemployment, and thus considered to be outside the reach of the usual rights and obligations applicable to jobseekers. In 1981, unemployed persons over the age of 60 were granted a higher benefit level (the long-term supplementary benefit rate) in return for ceasing to register as job-seeking, thereby effectively transferring this group from unemployment and into (quasi) retirement. In the mid-1980s, almost all persons under the age of 18 were barred from eligibility to unemployment benefit and by the late 1980s this applied to all students.

The latter policy might be regarded as an attempt to reduce labour supply, which was pursued in many European countries too at the time. However, public 'pension pathways' (Ebbinghaus, 2006) via de facto or actual early retirement schemes were available only to a limited extent in the United Kingdom. The moderate flat-rate basic state pension, even combined with low levels of earnings-related pension benefits (SERPS), provided few incentives for employees to retire early.

Some workers made use of the job release scheme (JRS). Introduced in 1977 and initially restricted to persons just one year prior to retirement in high unemployment regions, eligibility conditions were relaxed and coverage widened in the early 1980s (Banks et al., 2008; Casey and Wood, 1994). However, the scheme provided a relatively modest flat-rate benefit and was thus attractive mainly to lower-paid workers. Take-up amongst low- and semi-skilled manual workers was highest, but as a whole the scheme represented a form of pre-retirement for merely about 5 per cent of men aged 60–64 in the mid-1980s (Ebbinghaus, 2006: 148).

For other employees occupational pensions were an alternative to public provision given that most schemes allowed members to draw a benefit once they reached the age of 55. However, this option applied mainly to employees with better paid and

---

[1] For a more detailed account of social security reforms affecting unemployed people during the 1980s, see Atkinson and Micklewright (1989) and Clasen (2005: 76–9).

more secure jobs. As a whole, these limited statutory and occupational pathways into early retirement help explain the comparatively high levels of long-term unemployment in the 1980s (see Statistical Annex, Table A.6), particularly amongst British men over the age of 55 in the 1980s, which is remarkable given that employment for this group was well above many other European countries (Ebbinghaus, 2006: 94–100). Open unemployment would probably have been higher still had it not been for disability benefits. The number of claimants in receipt of long-term sickness or disability benefits rose steadily during the first half of the 1980s and continued to do so even after 1986 when unemployment declined (see Figure 2.1). Much of this rise reflected an increase in benefit receipt amongst older men who were previously engaged in manual work (Alcock et al., 2003). In the late 1980s, four-fifths of all claimants of contributory invalidity benefits were men and half of all claimants were aged 60 or over (Disney and Webb, 1991). The value of disability benefit was about 50 per cent higher than unemployment benefit and the assessment of eligibility conditions took account of not only medical but also 'socio-economic' factors such as age, skill, and experience (Lonsdale, 1993). Thus, it seems safe to argue that at least for some, and particularly older men, disability benefit receipt became a functional equivalent to unemployment protection during the 1980s.

Another response to unemployment in the early 1980s was the introduction and expansion of training schemes and public employment programmes. Traditionally leaving training to employers and maintaining a low profile in active labour market policy (ALMP), British spending on both of these domains reached a level commensurable to average government outlays elsewhere in the EU, even if adjusted by unemployment (Clasen, 2005: 61). However, in the early 1990s, the Conservative government scaled down spending on ALMP generally and training expenditure in particular (see Statistical Annex, Tables A.10 and A.11).

It should be noted that there was little integration between training and other 'active' labour market schemes and benefit provision. In fact, as an example of what in hindsight might be called 'deactivation', some policies were introduced which separated both functions further. For example, during the first half of the 1980s, unemployed benefit claimants were allowed to 'sign on' (confirm their status as unemployed) every two weeks rather than weekly as before, or only every three months for some groups such as people with health problems. The operations of unemployment benefit offices on the one hand and public employment services on the other were geographically and administratively separate, and unemployment benefit claimants were no longer required to be registered with Job Centres (Finn et al., 2005).

In sum, as a result of benefit retrenchment in general and cutbacks to unemployment insurance protection in particular, the overall character of unemployment protection became less differentiated in the 1980s, most notably due to the abolition of earnings-related benefits and, as will be discussed below, the emergence of a dominant (means-tested) benefit tier for the unemployed. However, similar trends of integration cannot be identified, either regarding unemployment as a risk category or in terms of a tighter connection between ALMP and benefit provision. On the contrary, work conditionality became more narrowly restricted by unemployment status, thereby diminishing the reach of unemployment protection, while job-search support became administratively removed from benefit provision.

2.3 SYSTEM DESCRIPTION

Unemployment protection in the United Kingdom has become de facto a single-tier system while technically remaining a two-tier one consisting of a contributory and a means-tested component. In a major reform in 1996, the Jobseeker's Allowance (JSA) was introduced, which amalgamated unemployment benefit and means-tested Income Support (social assistance) for unemployed persons. JSA consists of two separate benefit types: contributory-based JSA (CB JSA) and means-tested (officially 'income-based') JSA.[2] As an insurance benefit, contributory JSA is technically separate from non-contributory transfers. As was the case with unemployment benefit before, it is paid out of the National Insurance Fund (NIF), which is the common source for all contributory benefits, most notably the basic state pension. NIF benefit spending is financed by mandatory contributions levied on employees and employers. However, unlike in many other European countries, the central government has full control over the NIF which effectively serves, and is generally perceived, as just another form of revenue and expenditure alongside general taxation. The British government is not impeded by institutional obstacles which would prevent raising contributions to the fund for purposes other than insurance-based spending.

Unusually in the international context, the levels of unemployment insurance (CB JSA) and unemployment assistance (Income Support and later IB JSA) have never diverged much. In 1990, assistance and insurance rates varied by a small margin (see Table 2.1) but have been fully identical for many years. Moreover, since rates are linked to inflation rather than earnings, the generosity of unemployment protection has been declining. Relative to average full-time adult earnings, the value of unemployment benefit dropped from about 20 per cent in the late 1970s to about 14 per cent by 1990. In 2010, it was equivalent to 11 per cent of average earnings.

Qualifying conditions for the contributory component of JSA have not changed during the past twenty years. Somewhat more complex, they basically require two years' employment history or benefit credits.[3] In return, the maximum entitlement to contributory JSA is only six months, after having been halved in 1996.

Changing labour market conditions generally and more frequent interruptions in working careers in particular might be among the factors which led to the further decline in coverage of unemployment insurance amongst persons out of work which had already begun in the 1980s. However, stricter eligibility requirements and the reduction of the maximum benefit entitlement have reinforced this erosion during the 1990s (Clasen, 2009*a*). Most recently the increase in unemployment levels after 2008 has raised recipient benefit coverage somewhat. It has

---

[2] The official term for means-tested benefits became 'income-based' benefits after 1998. The previous Conservative government had already changed Unemployment Benefit to Jobseeker's Allowance, and the Labour government was equally keen on semantically highlighting the relevance of paid work within social policy, transforming the previous Department of Social Security (DSS) into the Department for Work and Pensions (DWP) in 2001 and Incapacity Benefit into the Employment and Support Allowance (ESA) in 2008.

[3] Twenty-five weekly contributions to National Insurance Fund paid and 100 credited within previous two years (for more details see CPAG, 2009).

Table 2.1. Basic features of unemployment protection (the United Kingdom)

	1990	2010
Benefit	Unemployment benefit (contributory) – UB; Income Support (means tested) – IS	Jobseeker's Allowance (contributory) CB JSA; IB JSA Jobseeker's Allowance (income based);
Benefit level[a]	UB (single person): 14.2% of average earnings; IS: 13.9%	11% of average earnings
Benefit structure	Flat rate (lower rates for under-25-year-olds if on IS)	Flat rate (lower rate for under-25-year-olds of either JSA type)
Entitlement	UB: 12 months; IS unlimited if circumstances unchanged	6 months (CB JSA); IB JSA unlimited if circumstances unchanged
Qualifying conditions (for UB; CB JSA)	Two years of sufficient National Insurance contributions	As of 1990
Job-seeking requirements:[b] (a): availability	(a) for each day of claim (UB); 24 hours per week (IS)	(a) 40 hours per week; after 13 weeks: travel to and from work up to 3 hours;
(b): seeking work	(b) actively seeking work each week	(b) three 'steps' to actively looking for work each week;
(c): jobseeker's agreement	(c) voluntary	(c) mandatory; from 2013 'work for your benefit' for long-term unemployed (JSA claim for 2 years).

[a] *Source*: DWP Historical abstract of statistics (2003).
[b] Finn and Schulte (2008: 306) and DWP (2008*b*).

Table 2.2. Beneficiary rates

	1976	1983	1988	1996	2005	2009
UB or JSA (contributory)	54	56	28	15	17	21
IS or JSA (means-tested)	38	34	56	65	75	77

Sources: Own calculations based on DSS, Social Security Statistics (various years), and DWP (2010*a*: table C1) (for 1991 onwards) – benefit claimants divided by annual claimant count; 1996 onwards: claimants with CB JSA and IB JSA, respectively, divided by claimant count (forecast for 2009).

made insurance-based support more important too, though it remains marginal compared with means-tested protection (Table 2.2).

The relatively minor role played by unemployment insurance is also reflected in the share of spending on contributory JSA, which was less than 20 per cent of total JSA expenditure in 2007–8 (Levell et al., 2009: 5). However, it needs to be noted that the JSA regime is far from being the only or even the most important source of income for unemployed persons. Due to the modest rates, it has always been common for recipients of unemployment benefits, and particularly those with a non-working partner or dependants, to be claiming additional benefits. Indeed, the receipt of income-based JSA automatically qualifies for a range of other means-tested transfers, such as free school meals for children, free prescriptions, and exemptions from other health costs and from paying a local tax (council tax benefit). It also serves as a 'passport' for the receipt of the maximum level of housing benefit. Thus, rather than focusing on a single benefit type it can be argued that unemployment protection in the United Kingdom consists of a range of transfers for the majority of unemployed persons. Housing benefit in particular plays a major role. In 2009, just over 3 million working-age persons claiming JSA or other main working-age benefits received an average award of £86 per week in housing benefit, which was well above the (single person) JSA rate of £65 per week (DWP, 2010b). Thus, as a share of total transfer income received by individual claimants and their families it is often more important than JSA.

The introduction of JSA was accompanied by reduced contributory benefit levels for the under-25-year-olds. Lower benefit rates for this age group had already applied to persons in receipt of social assistance prior to 1996. The extension of this to all younger claimants irrespective of benefit type can be seen as yet another step towards homogenization between insurance and assistance.

Several other changes introduced during the past twenty years have made British unemployment protection more conditional, and at the same time integrated benefit receipt (and delivery) more closely with active labour market programmes. Some commentators have emphasized 1986 as a 'turning point' towards activation with the introduction of compulsory 'restart' (job search) interviews for claimants after six months of unemployment (e.g. Finn et al., 2005: 5). Perhaps an even earlier indicator can be identified for 1989 when unemployed benefit claimants became required to be 'actively' seeking work on a weekly basis and lost the right to refuse job offers based on low pay after thirteen weeks of unemployment (see Appendix 2.A).

Ever since the introduction of JSA benefit, claimants (of either type) have been required to sign agreements with the employment office and JSA officials became permitted to issue a 'Jobseeker's Direction', that is, requiring individuals to take certain steps to 'improve their employability'. The definition of 'actively seeking work' was tightened under the JSA regime and more frequent compulsory interviews introduced (Clasen, 2009a: 76). At different stages, different labour market schemes became compulsory and different types of help available. This became formalized with the introduction of a range of 'New Deal' programmes under the Labour government after 1997. Since then, after a certain period of unemployment, claimants have had to be transferred to a number of alternatives to benefit receipt, such as training, education, or temporary employment. Having undergone a number of revisions since the late 1990s, the so-called 'Flexible New Deal' was introduced in 2009, which abolished differential treatments for the under- and over-25-year-olds in exchange for a more 'personalized' support. It involved a transfer of the responsibility for unemployed jobseekers from Jobcentre Plus to public, voluntary, or private providers which are paid by results and receive bonuses for claimants' speedy labour market integration. Claimants enter contracts with their providers (personal action plans), which may include participation in mandatory work-related activities. Since 2010, long-term JSA claimants (over twenty-four months; or earlier in some pilot areas at the discretion of advisers) have been required to enter a 'work for your benefit' phase of up to six months of full-time employment aimed at improving skills and 'work habits' in return for their benefit (DWP, 2008b).[4] At the time of writing (November 2010), the new coalition government between the Conservative and Liberal Democrat parties is in the process of rolling out its 'Work Programme' which will supersede the Flexible New Deal. In line with the coalition's plans (Cabinet Office, 2010), the overall orientation has not changed but the 'Work Programme' emphasizes even more the marketization of the delivery of employment programmes, provides suppliers with more discretion, and restructures the performance-related pay system. It also involves mandatory 'community activities' for claimants who have been unemployed for two years during a three-year period.

In short, from the perspective of individual unemployed persons, benefit entitlement during the past two decades has become increasingly conditional on participating in work-related activities. A similar trend can be identified in terms of administration. Having become more coordinated, the responsibility for ALMP and benefit delivery remained initially separate, even within the JSA regime. However, already in the early 1990s, some steps towards coordination were taken and since 2002 both functions have become fully integrated within the same agency, that is, the network of Jobcentre Plus offices. Moreover, since 2006, Jobcentre Plus has been responsible not only for benefit and employment programmes for claimants of JSA but for all working-age benefit claimants.

Indeed, one of the characteristics of British policy under the previous Labour government, and continued under the new government (see below), has been to shift the policy focus from unemployment in a narrow sense to a broader notion of worklessness (Clasen, 2005). In other words, policies since the 1990s have widened the target group for employment-related programmes and thus started to blur the distinction between unemployment and other causes for working-age benefit receipt. Reversing policies pursued during the 1980s, this policy has two components. First, it includes groups who previously remained outside the regulation of unemployment, such as lone parents and claimants' partners. Since 2001, unemployed couples without children have been required to jointly claim JSA, that is, both partners have to register as job seeking and fulfil benefit conditions. Prior to 2008, lone parents were entitled to benefit support without work conditionality attached as long as their youngest child was no older than 16. On the basis of the expansion of financial support for and availability of childcare (Millar, 2008), lone parents whose youngest child was 12 or older were transferred from Income Support (which is not based on job search in return for benefit eligibility) to JSA in 2008. Since October 2010, the same has applied to lone parents whose youngest child is seven or older (for details see Finn and Gloster, 2010).

Second, short of a full transfer to JSA, voluntary New Deal programmes for persons with disabilities and unemployed aged 50 and over became gradually more work oriented and conditional. From 2001 onwards, the so-called 'work-focused interviews' were introduced for lone parents and incapacity benefit claimants. Since 2005, most claimants have had to agree to an action plan which might include referral to a non-mandatory employment programme

---

[4] For more details on New Deal programmes and reforms of activation requirements in recent years, see Finn and Schulte (2008), DWP (2008a, 2008b), and Griggs et al. (2011).

(Finn and Schulte, 2008: 313). In 2008, the Employment and Support Allowance (ESA) replaced Incapacity Benefits (and Income Support paid on grounds of incapacity) for new claimants and by 2013 all claimants with a disability will have been transferred to ESA. Responding to a persistently high number of benefit claims on the grounds of long-term sickness and disability even at a time of declining unemployment (see Figure 2.1), the previous Labour government implemented a much more employment-focused 'capability' test as a condition for ESA receipt, and introduced a wage subsidy ('return to work credit') for a maximum of twelve months for ESA claimants who enter employment. Moreover, modelled on JSA, the ESA combined contributory and means-tested benefits within a single programme and aligned incapacity benefit levels with JSA rates, thereby inflicting significant reductions in rates for all but a few claimants with a sufficient contributory record (Williams, 2009). Most recently, as part of a major benefit retrenchment in response to public deficits, in October 2010, the new coalition government announced that receipt of ESA for those who are deemed to be capable of working (and thus receive the 'work-related' ESA) will be limited to one year, after which claimants would be referred to the (lower) JSA.

For the regulation of social security as a whole, the ESA is yet another indication of the increasing irrelevance of the contributory principle and the overriding focus on work conditionality as, apart from need, the only criterion determining social rights. In fact, an explicit short-term goal of the Labour government was to abolish social assistance (Income Support) altogether and move all working-age groups to either ESA or JSA (DWP, 2008*a*: 32). This is much in line with the new Conservative–Liberal Democrat coalition which intends to integrate benefit schemes even more comprehensively. In a consultation paper (DWP, 2010*c*), it pointed to 'welfare dependency' as a main problem which is to be tackled by a 'strong system of conditionality' (ibid.: 5) embedded within a 'single welfare to work programme' (Cabinet Office, 2010). A structural reform aims to merge several working-age benefits into a single payment so that the level of conditionality would no longer be determined by the benefit but by 'the reason for receiving benefit, creating a single progression to higher levels of conditionality' (DWP, 2010*c*: 29). Concretely, this would mean that some claimants would have no conditionality attached to benefit eligibility (e.g. those with severe health problems), others a medium-level work-related conditionality (e.g. lone parents and those with some form of disability), and others still a full work conditionality in terms of job-search plans or 'mandatory work activity'.

The reform towards what has been called 'universal credit' was announced in November 2010 (DWP, 2010*d*). It envisages an amalgamation of not only benefit schemes but also the so-called tax credits, that is, subsidies for persons on low wages and, often, part-time work. The coalition government considers the growing reliance on tax credits as a major problem. Indeed, within ten years the proportion of households in receipt of tax credits has trebled (Evans and Williams, 2009: 68). Disregarding the so-called family element of child tax credits (which used to include also better earners), about 16 per cent of all working households were dependent on state subsidies in the form of tax credits in 2009. From another perspective, about a third of all children lived in families whose wages are supported by tax credits. The combined real expenditure on benefits and tax credits rose from £63 billion in 1996–7 to over £87 billion by 2009–10 (DWP, 2010c: 8).

It should be pointed out that 'universal credit' would not be all-encompassing since contributory benefits (JSA and ESA) would continue to exist, because the government 'recognises the importance of Beveridge's insurance based principle ...' (DWP, 2010d: 46). Stopping short of spelling out what concretely this recognition is based on, the 'universal credit' nevertheless represents a major structural reform. Between 2013 and 2017, it will merge a range of current benefit programmes (including housing benefits, local tax benefits) into a single integrated scheme and would 'remove the distinction between in- and out-of-work benefits' and apply 'conditionality in a way that pushes individuals to increase their work to levels that are appropriate to their own particular circumstances' (DWP, 2010c: 29). Concretely, this could involve requiring jobseekers not only to look for full-time work but to 'push' those who have found a (subsidized) job to 'extend their working hours and/or increase their earnings until they were working full time or until they were off benefits altogether' (ibid.).

In sum, assessing the current system of unemployment protection in a narrow sense and the regulation of working-age benefit receipt more broadly, one instance of policy continuation and two policy reversals can be identified. First, the process of benefit homogenization which had already started in the 1980s continued with the creation of the JSA system in 1996. While nominally maintaining a distinction between contributory and means-tested support, due to the marginalization of the former component, de facto JSA represents a single-benefit system not only by name. Second, 'active' and 'passive' support have become much more closely connected and integrated within the same agency. Finally, the boundaries of unemployment protection have been extended to previously exempt groups, while the receipt of other working-age beneficiaries benefits has become more conditional on employment-related criteria. As a whole, policies have followed a path of 'triple integration', preparing the ground for the introduction of a single working-age benefit system which, in a slightly less ambitious form, had already been envisaged by the previous Labour government (DWP, 2008b).

2.4 ANALYSING REFORM TRAJECTORIES

British unemployment insurance, as British social insurance more generally, constitutes a weak citizenship model (Crouch, 1999). Benefits have at best been mildly earnings related and thus have never been regarded as a 'social wage' as in continental and Nordic countries. Ruling out possible trade-offs between wage moderation for improved benefit rights, a clear separation between social protection and benefits on the one hand and industrial relations and wages on the other is a characteristic of British social policy (Rhodes, 2000).

Hence, British workers would not conceive of unemployment benefits as 'deferred wages', whether insurance based or means tested. As the previous section has shown, this traditionally lower degree of 'industrialism' within British unemployment protection might help explain why in all three analytical dimensions there has been a considerable degree of restructuring within a relatively short period of time, thereby producing a system which is substantially different now than it was twenty years ago. Moreover, official documentations by the previous Labour government (DWP, 2008*a*, 2008*b*, 2009), as well as those by the new coalition government (DWP, 2010*c*, 2010*d*), indicate a continuation of the same policy path pursued since the 1990s. The rise in unemployment after 2008 has not dimmed the vision of a single-benefit regime for working-age persons.

However, while the process of triple integration seems entirely congruent with current government policies, it would be wrong to explain the former with the latter. Instead, in the early 1990s, there was nothing to suggest that either the Labour Party or the then ruling Conservative Party were aiming to shape the future of unemployment protection with a set of policies which have all but become consensual across both major parties by 2010. Looking back over the past twenty years, this section reviews some of the causes of major reforms which have transformed the fairly disjointed and narrow system of unemployment protection of the 1980s into a not only more integrated but also more encompassing policy structure today. In line with the three dimensions outlined in the introductory chapter, I review the process of benefit homogenization first, followed by the increasingly tight connectedness between benefit provision and labour market programmes (activation), and finally the transition of unemployment as a narrow risk category to more broadly defined worklessness.

2.4.1 Integrating benefit support – the waning relevance of the contributory principle

In the current system of unemployment protection (JSA) benefit, homogenization has all but been achieved. Admittedly, the division between unemployment insurance and assistance has never been as pronounced in the United Kingdom as in many other European countries. However, the contributory principle was clearly more prominent in the early 1980s than it is today. Moreover, while the notion of insurance has been invigorated within recent pension policy (Bridgen and Meyer, 2010), for working-age persons it has all but become irrelevant. The government has repeatedly justified such a stance with reference to two reports which proposed that social rights for working-age persons should not be determined by benefit received but merely by personal circumstances and individual need for help with employment support. Indicating a broad cross-party consensus on this issue, one of these reports was published by a centre-left research institute (Sainsbury and Stanley, 2007), and the other by David Freud, who has since become Minister for Welfare Reform within the Conservative–Liberal Democrat coalition government (Freud, 2007).

As discussed, due to a growing proportion of unemployed persons receiving the same type of transfer, and a diminishing distance between insurance and assistance support, a process of benefit homogenization began in the 1980s. At that time the aims of deregulating labour markets, creating wider wage dispersion, enhancing work incentives, and cutting social security spending were strong policy motives under the Thatcher government. Institutionally unimpeded and ideologically driven, benefit restrictions were not necessarily unpopular at times of rising unemployment in the early 1980s and in the early 1990s. At both periods, real wages, particularly at the lower end of the scale, were falling and governments fuelled debates on benefit fraud and workshyness, portraying antisocial behaviour on the part of welfare state claimants as part of the unemployment problem (Clasen, 2005).

By the early 1990s, wage and income inequality had significantly widened (Evans and Williams, 2009) and employment protection as well as the role of trade unions considerably weakened. The continuing decline in benefit levels relative to average wages was not a cause for concern for the Conservative government since the relevant comparison was 'between the rates of benefit and the level of wages paid in the kinds of jobs which claimants are likely to obtain' (Deacon, 1997: 38).

However, while principally in line with government preferences, the growth of means testing potentially undermined work incentives due to the interaction between benefits and wages at the lower end of the labour market. As a response, in the early 1990s, in-work benefits (for parents) were made more attractive and small-scale job subsidies introduced (Meager, 1997). This strategy began to connect unemployment benefit claimants more closely with labour market policy which, under the Conservative government, culminated with the introduction of the Jobseeker's Allowance in 1996. The reform was expected to save expenditure, with about a quarter of a million people becoming worse off due to benefit exclusion or reduction (Unemployment Unit, 1995). As discussed, the common JSA framework represented a further demotion of insurance-based support and thus progress towards homogenization.

In short, responding to contingent economic and labour market changes and driven by a preference for containing social spending and targeting public support, the homogenization of benefit support can be linked to a broader deregulatory and cost-containment agenda pursued by Conservative governments in the 1980s and 1990s. More unexpected might be the fact that the Labour government after 1997 simply continued along the same path.

Even in the early 1990s, one of the Labour Party's core social policy objectives had still been to turn back the expansion of means testing, which was regarded as sapping self-esteem and diminishing work incentives (Field, 2002: 98). However, by the time Labour entered government, the party had undergone a programmatic change in social and labour market policy (Clasen, 2009b). Under Tony Blair, the Labour government was anxious not to raise public expenditure or place any financial burdens on employers. An explicit aim was to maintain the 'most lightly regulated labour market of any leading economy of the world' (Cm 3968, 1998) which became regarded as providing the United Kingdom with a competitive advantage in a more internationalized economy (Wood, 2001). Such an approach also included the acceptance of targeted (and thus means-tested) support at the expense of social insurance. One of the strongest proponents of means testing was Gordon Brown as the Chancellor of Exchequer in the Blair government. Once remaining critics of means testing had left the Cabinet and the Treasury had been established as the main actor in welfare reform, any prospect of strengthening the insurance principle had disappeared (Clasen, 2005).

2.4.2 Activating claimants and integrating policy

The second analytical dimension relates to the integration between benefit receipt on the one hand and work conditionality and participation in employment programmes on the other. As discussed, during the 1980s both were administratively divided, and some claimant groups exempted from job-search requirements. Towards the end of that decade, a policy reversal can be identified. Already in 1986 a compulsory 'Restart' interview for the unemployed, after six months out of work, was introduced. In 1990, such interviews became more frequent and a Restart course was made obligatory for long-term unemployed and those who rejected job offers. The integration between benefit receipt and job-search requirements became more prescriptive under the 'stricter benefit regime' of the JSA in 1996. Under the subsequent Labour government, both aspects became much more closely articulated and coordinated, particularly once the administrative functions were merged within Jobcentre Plus.

More recent reforms and plans included tougher sanctions for people failing to attend interviews as well as 'skills checks' or mandatory transfer of long-term benefit claimants to full-time community-based work experience to improve their 'employability and work habits' (DWP, 2008a: 37). This process of 'deepening the conditionality principle' has been accompanied by more flexibility in the sense of the involvement of the voluntary and private providers, as well as more discretionary powers for personal advisers both under Labour's 'Flexible New Deal' and its successor, the coalition government's 'Work Programme'.

Prior to 2009, different mandatory New Deal programmes existed for different claimant groups, subject to different conditionality criteria regarding the mandatory transfer from benefit to training or employment programmes (see Finn and Schulte, 2008). Under the short lifespan of the 'Flexible New Deal', this differentiation was replaced and schemes became integrated. Rather than benefit status or age, the two criteria influencing the type of job-search activity claimants were offered (and had to accept) were length of unemployment spell and a 'personalized' discretionary assessment on the part of their personal advisers. Prior to Labour's defeat at the 2010 general election, plans had envisaged even more discretionary powers for advisers and tougher conditionality. This applied to unemployed who had claimed JSA for two years or more who were to be required to 'work for their benefit'. This step was justified with references to other countries where similar approaches had arguably been successful, such as Australia ('work for the dole') and also Denmark and the Netherlands (DWP, 2008a: 44). As discussed above, the current coalition government has adopted a similar policy with its 'mandatory community activity' plan for the same claimant group.

In short, as far as activation and conditionality within unemployment protection are concerned, a clear trend can be identified. If anything, under the Labour government after 1997, as well as under the current coalition, policy delivery has not only become more outsourced but also more coordinated, while job-search requirements became more explicit and prescriptive especially for long-term unemployed. A broad if implicit political consensus on activation can be traced back to the mid-1990s when the problem of 'welfare dependency', as well as a need to expand supply-side labour market policies, was emphasized by both the government and the opposition.

There are three factors which help explain Labour's shift from a labour demand to labour supply approach and thus growing bipartisan agreement on activation. First, the assumption that raising the number of 'employable' benefit claimants would increase the effective competition for jobs and contribute to non-inflationary employment growth gained prominence within the Labour Party by the mid-1990s. The introduction of stricter work tests and mandatory training or other appropriate measures was assumed to improve the employability of particularly long-term jobseekers and increase the actual supply of labour (Layard, 2000). Any deadweight associated with job-search support and short-term training or work experience schemes measures were likely to be compensated by employment generating wage moderation effects. It should be pointed out that the new emphasis on ALMP under Labour did not correspond to an increase in spending. Instead, it was the mix of programmes which changed, with expenditure on administration and job search growing and becoming much more prominent than spending on training or subsidized employment (Clasen, 2005: 61–2; OECD, 2008). The government portrayed this 'work first' approach as the appropriate model for British ALMP (DWP, 2003).

Second, while the stock of youth unemployment declined after 1993, the risk of unemployment before the age of 25 actually increased, as well as the average duration of unemployment spells for young men. This seems to have been a major reason for Labour to introduce mandatory job-search and employment schemes for younger unemployed persons (Stafford, 2003). In turn the government attributed the steady decline in long-term unemployment after 1997 to its more employment-oriented benefit policy. The rise in youth unemployment since 2008 has been used by the coalition government as justification for the need for an even earlier referral of younger unemployed claimants to a 'welfare-to-work' programme (Cabinet Office, 2010).

A third factor relates to timing. After the mid-1990s, a move towards more conditional benefit receipt became a chance of political credit claiming. In the early 1990s, when unemployment was high, Conservative governments had been reluctant to embark on anything which could have been construed as adopting US-imported 'workfare' policies. This seemed justified in the light of opinion polls at the time, suggesting that a majority of the British population had regarded unemployed people as victims of external circumstances. However, after 1997 there was a sharp rise of those who perceived unemployed persons as passive and benefits as too generous and discouraging active job search (Hills, 2004). Also, the steady increase in employment and decline in unemployment since the mid-1990s (see Statistical Annex, Tables A.4 and A.5) provided a more favourable context for a more activation-oriented unemployment support system (Clasen, 2000).

2.4.3 Widening unemployment as a risk category

A third trend of integration manifested itself as a U-turn of policies pursued in the 1980s which excluded groups from job-search conditionality. As discussed, this reversal affected lone parents with younger children who were transferred from claiming social assistance (Income Support) to JSA. The previous Labour government aimed to extend this transfer to all lone parents 'when resources allow' (DWP, 2008a: 55). Moreover, previously outside JSA work conditionality, the Labour government intended to include people aged over 60 within the New Deal programme, albeit on a voluntary basis (DWP, 2008a: 51). Finally, the previous government brought in a much more work-focused disability benefit regime under the Employment Support Allowance (ESA). In fact, the ESA was regarded as merely a temporary scheme, in time to be replaced by a single working-age benefit system including ESA and JSA claimants into a single system with increased 'personalized' work conditionality. The plan was to allocate all claimants to one of three groups depending on individual work readiness. Following recommendations along these lines made in an influential report (Gregg, 2008), the government intended to pilot such an approach from 2010 onwards (DWP, 2008b). As discussed above, the 'universal credit' reform under the new coalition government is broadly in line and extends such plans by integrating out-of-work and in-work support within the same programme.

All of the above has to be set against the background of a steep rise in the number of people in receipt of benefit and not classified as unemployed, such as lone parents and persons claiming sickness or disability benefits (see Figure 2.1). The steady increase in the number of economically inactive persons had become a concern already in the second half of the 1990s (HM Treasury and DWP, 2001) and inactivity especially amongst men with no or low qualifications a major issue in public policy (Nickell and Quintini, 2002). The decline in unemployment for this particular group after the mid-1990s was matched by an increase in labour market inactivity of roughly the same rate. In other words, the labour market recovery until the mid-2000s failed to have an effect on the growth of incapacity-related benefit receipt and did not prevent low-skilled men from dropping out of the labour market altogether. In fact, there are indications that the introduction of the JSA in 1996 pushed men of core working age from unemployment into inactivity rather than into employment (Clasen et al., 2006).

These trends have been used by the government as justification for the portrayal of the benefit system as having encouraged dependency for groups such as lone parents and disabled people (DWP, 2008a: 24). The New Deal programmes, as well as other policies such as help with childcare costs and also more generous tax credits for low-income earners, have arguably helped to lower the number of annual claims for working-age benefits between 1997 and 2007 by about 1 million (DWP, 2008a: 27). Most of this is due to the increase of lone parents in work. By contrast, incapacity benefit receipt continued to rise and declined only slightly after 2005 (Figure 2.1). The Labour government argued that between 80 and 90 per cent of those who enter incapacity benefit expect to return to work (DWP, 2008a: 31). Consequently, the replacement of incapacity benefits with the more work-focused ESA was justified as responding to demand. Furthermore, Labour's plan of a single-benefit system for all working-age benefits was arguably aimed at 'reducing complexity' on the one hand and 'increasing flexibility' on the other (DWP, 2008a: 107).

The reform plans by the new coalition government may have used a somewhat different wording, but fully subscribe to the idea of a single working-age benefit. If implemented, it would not only integrate distinct benefit schemes but further accelerate the trend towards social rights which will be determined almost entirely by personal circumstances, individual employability, and work readiness. Unemployment as an (administrative) category would have been radically redefined and social citizenship no longer defined as a 'basic status, which in turn is the basis of entitlement', but 'something that has to be developed or achieved' (Plant, 2003: 153).

2.5 CONCLUSION

There is one characteristic within the design and development of the British welfare state which sets it apart from most other European countries, that is, the emphasis on flat-rate rather than earnings-related benefits. While other nations strengthened the 'earnings relatedness' within their social insurance programmes in the 1950s and 1960s, and thus gave average and better earners a larger stake in social security, the parallel move in the United Kingdom remained tentative, which subsequently facilitated its termination in the 1980s. Since then the idea of acquiring individual entitlements based on social insurance contributions, irrespective of need, has gradually but steadily disappeared, at least for citizens below retirement age. This trend has been politically facilitated by decades of cuts and retrenchment in contributory benefits, reinforced after Labour's acceptance of means testing as the dominant distributive principle. As a consequence, the expansion of needs-based social protection created fiscal pressure as well as disincentive problems for claimants intent on moving from receiving benefit into paid work. The further advancement of all three dimensions of the 'triple integration' process can partly be seen as a response to such problems.

Apart from growing problem pressure manifest in a stubbornly high number of working age people in receipt of benefits, political reorientations within both major political parties paved the way for what has become a consensus on the creation of a social protection system which should be not only more work oriented but also more integrated. The prospective introduction of 'universal credit' from 2013 will accelerate this trend by merging a range of working-age benefits into a single scheme for people out of work as well as in subsidized employment. Since contributory benefits are not intended to be incorporated, the 'universal credit' will not be an exclusive single-benefit programme for all. However, it is a major step in that direction. Once implemented, the question remains for how much longer the remnants of Beveridge's ideas of insurance-based social rights will survive for British citizens below retirement age.

Appendix 2.A Major reforms in unemployment protection in the United Kingdom

Year	Measure
1981	Higher means-tested Supplementary Benefit (SB) for unemployed over-60-year-olds who chose to retire early.
1982	Abolition of earnings-related supplement (ERS). Unemployment Insurance Benefit (UB) made subject to income taxation. Most unemployed continue to 'sign on' fortnightly at UB offices but decision to register at separate Job Centre becomes voluntary.
1984	Abolition of child additions (except for claimants over pension age) in UB.
1985	Exemption from disqualification provisions in UB for those accepting voluntary redundancy.
1986	Increase in maximum disqualification period in UB from 6 to 13 weeks. Abolition of one-fourth and one-half UB rates for those with incomplete contribution records. With introduction of Income Support (IS), as replacement for SB, introduction of a lower benefit rates for under-25-year-olds (18–25). Introduction of 'Restart' programme, with compulsory job-search reviews after 6 months of unemployment; more regular, availability for work' testing.
1988	Tighter contribution requirement for UB. Increase in disqualification period for UB from 13 to 26 weeks. Exclusion of 16-and 17-year-olds from IS, except in special circumstances.
1989	Introduction of 'Actively Seeking Work' test. After 13 weeks of unemployment, conditions defining suitable work (i.e. of possibility to place limitations on 'suitable' or 'acceptable' work) abandoned.
1990	Introduction of Employment Service 'back to work plans'. Reductions in IS made possible for unemployed claimants failing to attend Restart interviews.
1992	Further tightening of disqualification conditions in UB. Reduction of UB for recipients of occupational pensions over 55.
1996	Merger of UB and IS for the unemployed into Jobseeker's Allowance (JSA), consisting of 'contributory JSA' and 'income-based JSA'. Reduction of maximum duration of contributory (insurance) benefit from 1 year to 6 months. Reduction of benefit rate for claimants aged 18–24 (by 20%). Removal of all remaining dependant additions which existed under UB. Reduction of contributory benefit rights for unemployed recipients of occupational pensions of all ages. • requirement to sign a jobseeker's agreement; • introduction of 'Jobseeker's Direction' (allowing officials to issue directions regarding appearance etc. of jobseekers); • 'permitted period' of 13 weeks for restriction of job search. Introduction of 'project work' pilots for long-term unemployed, based on 13 weeks' compulsory supervised job search followed by 13 weeks' work experience.
1998	With introduction of New Deal programmes for young people under 25 (NDYP) and long-term unemployed (NDLTU) obligatory transfer of benefit claimants into 'options'. New Deal for Lone Parents (NDLP) (voluntary job-related interview).
1999	Voluntary New Deal for Partners (NDP): joint claim required for those with partners claiming JSA for over 6 months (for those without children and under 25). Voluntary New Deal for those over 50. Introduction of front-line Personal Advisers (PA), individualizing employment assistance.

2000	Creation of fully private sector model-based Employment Zones in 15 of the most disadvantaged labour market areas in which participation in New Deal programmes for over-25-year-olds becomes mandatory after 18 months (or 12 months in seven zones).
2001	NDLTU revamped as ND 25+ (compulsory after 18 months' unemployment within past 21 months; gateway period introduced, as well as subsequent 'intensive Activity Period' of 13–26 weeks). Introduction of NDDP – New Deal for disabled people (voluntary).
2002	Creation of Jobcentre Plus, joining up the administration of the benefit system and employment services. NDLP: introduction of work-focused interview with personal adviser every 6 months. NDP: mandatory for JSA claimants under 45 years of age (if no children).
2003	Pathways to Work replaces NDDP – requirement to complete action plan with personal adviser.
2004	Entry into NDYP and ND25+ already after 3 months of unemployment piloted in certain areas.
2006	Introduction of nationwide Jobcentre Plus.
2008–10	Lone parents switched from Income Support to JSA if youngest child is over 12 years old; (10 years old from 2009; 7 years old from 2010).
2008	Introduction of ESA (Employment and Support Allowance), all claimants on IB to switch to ESA by 2013.
2009	Flexible New Deal to take over from NDYP and ND25+; no differentiation by age; public, voluntary, or private providers take over from Jobcentre Plus after 12 months on JSA, payment by results.
2010	Pilots for 'personalized conditionality' (especially for ESA claimants and lone parents) and for 'Work for your Benefit' scheme for JSA claimants after 2 years on benefit.
2010	Replacement of the Flexible New Deal with the new (coalition) government's Work Programme; White Paper on 'Universal Credit' published.

Source: *Journal of Social Policy 'Social Policy Review'*; CPAG 'Welfare Rights Bulletin' (1980–2003); Clasen (2005), Finn (2005), and DWP (2008*a*, 2008*b*).

3

France: integration versus dualization

Daniel Clegg

3.1 INTRODUCTION

In the last two decades of the twentieth century the development of unemployment protection policy in France followed a dualistic logic. While those with longer work records could continue to rely on relatively generous wage-related support if they became unemployed, an increasing number of other workers came to depend on alternative, less generous provisions, often not designed with the risk of unemployment in mind. Insurance-based and assistance-based benefits for the unemployed were both largely passive, their delivery not strongly articulated with the activities of the Public Employment Services (PES). Since the beginning of the new millennium, however, an emphasis on activation that germinated in the expanding social assistance margins of the French social protection system has gradually gained ground more widely, and has in turn stimulated efforts to reconnect and synchronize provisions for different groups in the unemployed population. While the interests and strategies of powerful policy actors ensure dualistic tendencies remain strongly embedded in French unemployment protection policy, they are thus increasingly challenged by integrative policy logics that are encouraging the development of a more unified benefit-and-service system for all the non-employed.

This chapter traces the conflict between the logics of dualization and integration in reforms to the regulation of the unemployment risk in France over the last two decades. The argument is organized in three parts. To place later developments in context, Section 3.2 first describes how France's unemployment and labour market policies were initially restructured in the 1980s in the face of pressures of high unemployment and broader economic change. Section 3.3 then analyses the evolution of unemployment protection between 1990 and 2010 in detail, focusing in particular on the three analytical dimensions outlined in the introductory chapter to this volume. Section 3.4 offers an explanatory interpretation of the trends observed, emphasizing in particular how in the French case the dualistic reform strategy of the 1980s and 1990s in fact sowed the seeds of its own later – though as yet only partial – reversal.

3.2 ORGANIZING LABOUR SHEDDING: FRENCH LABOUR MARKET POLICIES IN THE 1980s

In France as elsewhere, the early 1980s was a period of slow growth and far-reaching economic restructuring, with unemployment rising extremely fast as vast numbers of workers were made redundant from traditional industries (see Statistical Annex, Tables A.3 and A.5). The initial response of French governments was to endeavour to redistribute employment opportunities though the reduction of labour supply, especially among older workers. Early retirement benefit schemes had been initiated by conservative governments in the early 1970s, but were vastly expanded by the socialist government elected in 1981 (IGAS, 2004: 156–7). Although driven partly by successive governments, this policy of 'labour shedding' was largely organized and financed through the unemployment insurance system, which was formally under the managerial control of trade unions and employer representatives. Along with fast-rising unemployment, the policy contributed to mounting deficits in the dedicated unemployment insurance fund, UNEDIC (*Union national interprofessionnelle pour l'emploi dans l'industrie et le commerce*). A major financial crisis was averted in 1979 only by the then conservative government agreeing to subsidize the previously entirely contribution-financed fund out of general taxation. When massive deficits reappeared in 1982, however, the socialist government – on the cusp of its historic 'turn to rigour' – refused to increase the share of the tax subsidy, while the social partners objected to modifying contribution rates to fund measures that they had not themselves decided upon (Clegg, 2005: 159–63).

To find a way out of the budgetary crisis, between 1982 and 1984, the government and the social partners negotiated a new division of labour in the sphere of labour market policy (ibid.; Clegg and Palier, 2007). The government agreed to relieve UNEDIC of the burden of financing the largest early retirement schemes, the cost of which were fully transferred to the state budget. In 1983 – to honour a pledge included in Mitterrand's election manifesto two years earlier – the state retirement age was also lowered from 65 to 60, freeing UNEDIC of the need to provide unemployment benefits to many older workers. More significantly for present purposes, though, the new division of labour additionally introduced a separation between 'insurance' and 'solidarity' benefits for the unemployed. Insurance benefits would continue to provide earnings-related support for the unemployed, but with entitlement more closely linked to the contribution record of the claimants than in the past. These would be financed uniquely from social contributions, and regulated through periodic collective agreements negotiated between the social partners and extended by law. Solidarity benefits would for their part provide benefits to those who were not, or were no longer, eligible for insurance as a result of their contribution record or unemployment duration. These benefits were to be financed out of general taxation, and regulated by the state. Through this explicit partition of unemployment insurance (UI) and unemployment assistance (UA), the 'logic of integration' that had characterized much of the post-war history of French unemployment protection was thus superseded, under pressure of rising unemployment and mounting costs, by a 'logic of segmentation' (Daniel, 2000).

Though the socialist government embraced budgetary rigour after 1983, it fell far short of a fully fledged neo-liberal conversion. Even the conservative Chriac government elected in 1986 soon toned down its initially bold deregulatory rhetoric when it observed how little appetite there appeared to be for this among the French electorate. Resistance to structural reform, particularly of the labour market, remained high in France throughout the 1980s (Smith, 2004). As a consequence, France maintained one of the most regulated labour markets in Europe which, allied to substantial non-wage labour costs and a relatively high minimum wage, tended to impede job creation, particularly in low-skill sectors of the economy (Cahuc and Kramarz, 2005; Malo et al., 2000). The social effects of the high unemployment that resulted were cushioned by the continued use of the social protection system for labour shedding, or what in France was more commonly known as the 'social treatment of unemployment' (Daguerre and Palier, 2004; see also Levy, 2000; Vail, 2010).

Though French governments gradually ran down tax-funded early retirement measures in the 1980s, these were soon replaced by new schemes managed by the social partners through UNEDIC (see Section 3.3). As a result, early exit continued to grow in France even as it started to stabilize in other European countries (Ebbinghaus, 2006: 105). Unemployment benefits proper played a role in encouraging this too. In UI, age-related eligibility criteria allowed older workers with good contribution records to receive benefits right up to retirement age. In 1984, a mechanism called *dispense de recherche d'emploi* (DRE) was also introduced, freeing older unemployed people receiving either UI or UA of the need to register with the PES, and therefore ensuring that they were no longer counted in the politically sensitive national unemployment statistics. By 1990, more than 225,000 people received unemployment benefits with a DRE (see Figure 3.3).

The desire to massage unemployment figures was also one of the prime motivations behind another popular strategy for the social treatment of unemployment in the 1980s – the vast expansion of job-creation schemes. Targeted first at young people and later at the long-term unemployed, a series of special employment programmes was introduced during the decade, providing the unemployed with jobs in the public and para-public sectors on a temporary and usually part-time basis (Erhel, 2009; Meyer, 1999). Initially smaller programmes also existed offering social contribution exemptions to private firms hiring from specific target groups among the unemployed, though these were always more controversial with the trade unions, who saw them as 'a gift to employers' and a means of deregulating the labour market by the back door. As such schemes expanded nonetheless, they arguably did tend to gradually undermine the role played by full-time permanent employment paid at minimum wage level in setting the minimum norm for work in low-skill sectors of the labour market, and thus helped legitimize greater use of non-subsidized precarious employment contracts (Castel, 2007).

Although the social protection system expanded vastly in the 1980s to cushion the effects of high unemployment, its net still had holes through which many victims of economic change fell. During the 1980s, media attention came to focus more and more on the so-called 'new poor', a term that covered groups of individuals who were being thrown into poverty as a result of the prolonged economic crisis and an absence of adequate non-contributory social protection

(Paugam, 1993). The UA scheme introduced for the long-term unemployed in 1984 was of only limited help, as it had prior work conditions that were actually more demanding than those in UI, and which many unemployed people – and especially those previously employed in the growing precarious sector of the labour market – therefore failed to meet.

Francois Mitterrand made the plight of the new poor one of the central themes in his re-election campaign, and pledged to introduce a general, national social assistance (SA) scheme. Though France had a localized system of discretionary 'social aid' and a number of categorical means-tested benefits covering different social risks, there had previously been widespread hostility across the political spectrum to the introduction of a general SA scheme (Belorgey, 1988; Clegg, 2002). Following Mitterrand's re-election in 1988, the *Revenu Minimum d'Insertion* (RMI) was introduced, providing a means-tested minimum income to all over-25s not in work. The insertion element of the RMI referred to a clause whereby the benefit was in principle paid on the basis of a 'reciprocal engagement' by the state and the claimant to take measures to promote the latter's social or professional integration.

While this may suggest an emphasis on activation, social protection was not – yet – conceived in these terms in France. The insertion requirement in SA was essentially a myth, intended more to legitimize the introduction of generalized SA than to actually guide the administrative treatment of minimum income recipients (Clegg and Palier, 2012, forthcoming). No recipients of SA were obliged to register with the PES as a condition for receipt of benefit. Unless they benefited from a DRE, recipients of UI and UA were, and in principle also had to accept offers of suitable work or face the risk of total suspension of their benefit. Signing on (*pointage*) was, however, more a simple bureaucratic requirement than part of an active employment policy, and sanctions were rarely applied (Barbier and Kaufmann, 2008: 109). In UI, the principle of benefit being an earned return on contributions paid was strong; the prevailing understanding was that 'one contributes to be covered against a risk; when that risk materialises, one must be compensated' (Borgetto, 2009: 1045).

Underscoring the limited emphasis on activation was the traditional lack of any real institutional articulations between the administration of non-employment benefits and the administration of job-search and employment policy. Scope for greater cooperation was long limited by the different legal statuses of the organizations that administered French labour market policy (CERC, 2005: 23–5). While the PES was a national structure controlled by the state, UNEDIC was a formally private organization under the managerial control of the social partners, and entirely financed out of social contributions. As for insertion policies designed for recipients of SA, these were mainly organized on a decentralized level by local authorities, who co-financed them along with the state.

3.3 RE-REGULATING THE RISK OF UNEMPLOYMENT IN FRANCE, 1990–2010

In 1990, France thus had a three-tiered structure of benefit for unemployed, comprising UI, UA (with separate benefit schemes for the long-term unemployed and labour market entrants), and SA, though the latter was not formally an unemployment benefit. Also defined out of the official scope of unemployment were large numbers of individuals receiving early retirement benefits and those participating in large labour market programmes. None of the systems of benefit provision for the unemployed was closely articulated with the work of PES. The labour market policy administration was characterized by internal divisions resulting from different modes of governance (social partners, state, local authorities) and of financing (social contributions, general taxation, local taxation).

Structurally, French labour market policy appears to have changed little between 1990 and 2010. The benefit system in 2010 remained three-tiered, and although unemployment and SA benefits had lost some value relative to the minimum wage, overall benefits were paid at broadly similar levels to twenty years previously. A majority of other key institutional parameters are also suggestive of stability rather than transformation (see Table 3.1; most significant formal changes are in bold text). Nonetheless, as this section shows, the 1990s and 2000s saw substantial changes in the role and understanding of different unemployment benefits, a gradual strengthening of the conceptual and organizational articulation between active measures and a range of benefits, as well as shifts in the boundaries between active and inactive groups of benefit claimants. In this process, and formal institutional stability notwithstanding, policy logics that were initially perpetuated and even intensified latterly came to be seriously challenged.

3.3.1 Benefits: dualization and beyond

After a transitory economic boom at the end of the 1980s, at the beginning of the 1990s, France experienced a severe recession, plunging UNEDIC into deficit again. In 1992, the social partners responded by negotiating consequential changes in the eligibility and entitlement parameters for UI. The existing UI benefits were replaced with a new single 'degressive' benefit (*Allocation Unique Degressive*, AUD), under which the level of benefits was periodically reduced over the course of an unemployment spell, initially at a rate of around 17 per cent every four months (and faster for those under 25). The minimum duration of contribution for access to UI was also increased, from three to four months in the last eight. Finally, the duration of benefit was sharply reduced for those with only six months of contributions in the last year, from fifteen months for under-50s and twenty-one months for over-50s to seven months for the unemployed of all ages. Of the large number of unemployed people who found themselves excluded from UI with the introduction of AUD – beneficiary rates declined sharply after the reform (see Figure 3.1) – a disproportionate number were younger people and those previously employed on fixed-term contracts (Daniel and Tuchszirer, 1999: 307).

This reform and its further tightening in 1993 had a spectacular effect on UNE-DIC's finances, which were in surplus by 8.7 billion French francs (FF) in 1993 and 22.4 billion FF by 1995, even though unemployment had continued to rise up the end of 1993 and had remained stable thereafter (see Statistical Annex, Table A.5).

Table 3.1. Unemployment benefit entitlements and key institutional features of French labour market policy, 1990–2010

	1990		2000	
BENEFITS				
Unemployment insurance				
Benefit amount (% gross reference salary)	From 57.4 to 75%		From 57.4 to 75%	
Financing	Contributions		Contributions	
Governance	Social partners		Social partners	
Lead delivery agency	Assedic (+ANPE)		**Pôle Emploi**	
Unemployment assistance				
Benefit amount (monthly maximum in	ASS	AI	ASS	ATA
euros/% gross minimum wage)	317/39	203/25	461/34	325/24
Financing	General taxation		General taxation	
Governance	Central state		Central state	
Lead delivery agency	Assedic (+ANPE)		**Pôle Emploi**	
Social assistance				
Benefit amount (Monthly maximum	RMI		RSA	
(single person) in euros/% gross	317/39		460/34	
minimum wage)				
Financing	General + local taxation		General + local taxation	
Governance	Central state + local authorities		Central state + local authorities	
Lead administrative agency	CAF (Family benefit fund) + local partnerships		**CAF (family benefit fund) + Pôle Emploi**	
SERVICES				
Placement services and employment policies for unemployed				
Financing	General taxation		**General taxation + local taxation + contributions**	
Governance	Central state		Central state	
Lead administrative agency	ANPE		**Pôle Emploi**	

Source: DREES; UNECDIC; INSEE.

Rather than repairing all the cuts introduced in 1992, however, in their subsequent negotiations on UI the social partners agreed on a series of changes that mainly improved the situation of those *already* eligible for benefit (ibid.: 306; see also Appendix 3.A). In 1995, a new early retirement benefit was introduced, open to those with forty years of contributions and meeting certain age conditions. The following year, instead of extending benefit duration or relaxing contributory requirements, the new collective agreement instead slightly improved replacement rates and slowed down the application of the degressivity mechanism, which now operated every six months instead of every four. In 1999, the beneficiary rate of UI actually reached a decade low of 42.1 per cent.

For many of those excluded from UI as a result of these parametric choices, UA offered little help. The scheme for labour market entrants (*Allocation d'Insertion*, AI) was closed-off to its main group of beneficiaries – young people – in 1991, the then socialist government deeming that it was preferable for young unemployed people to be enrolled in more active labour market measures. The number of beneficiaries fell by 75 per cent, or around 100,000 people, between 1990 and

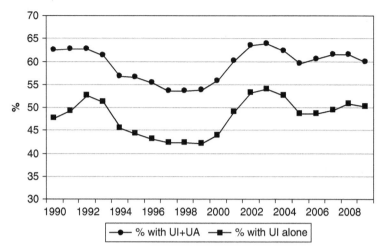

Figure 3.1. Unemployment benefit recipients as % unemployed, 1990–2010
Source: Caseload Annex (France).

1992.[1] As for the UA scheme for the long-term unemployed (*Allocation Spécifique de Solidarité*, ASS), it, as mentioned, had rather stricter contribution requirements than UI, demanding five years of contributions in the last ten. Though in 1992 the social affairs inspectorate warned of the risk of a 'very serious social regression' if these were not relaxed (IGAS, 1992), the government paid no heed. In fact, contribution requirements were further strengthened in 1997,[2] when the means test was also made stricter.

Although the number of special employment measures was expanded and diversified in the early 1990s – the stock of people in the main public sector scheme, CES, increased from 150,000 in 1989 to 350,000 in 1993 (Meyer, 1999: 86) – many of the unemployed were therefore left with no source of income, and forced to fall back on the still relatively new SA scheme. It was into SA, rather than UA, that the majority of the needy unemployed no longer eligible for UI were transferred (Figure 3.2).

Largely as a result of this, the SA caseload more than doubled between 1990 and 1995, and continued to grow rapidly up to the turn of the millennium. One consequence was that the profile of the beneficiaries of SA quickly diverged from the image of the 'socially excluded' that had been very present at the time of the introduction of the RMI. In reality, the new entrants were increasingly young and socially integrated, but out of work (Clary, 1995; Cordazzo, 2003). Another consequence, more widely debated, was the growing cost of the tax-financed RMI: while 5 billion French francs (€0.76 billion) were allocated from

---

[1] In 2006, AI was replaced by the temporary waiting allowance (*Allocation Temporaire d'Attente*, ATA), the main beneficiaries of which are asylum seekers and those coming out of prison.

[2] Instead of five years' contributions, it was henceforth necessary to have actually worked for five years; periods of, for example, insured unemployment for which contributions were paid were thus no longer counted.

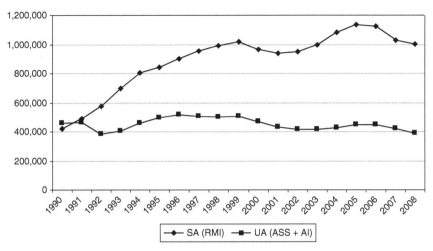

Figure 3.2. Beneficiaries of SA and UA, 1980–2008

Source: see Caseload Annex (France).

the state budget for the new scheme in 1989, the cost had more than quadrupled to 21.4 billion FF (€3.26 billion) by the time of the 1997 budget (Lafore, 1996).

The main dynamic in French unemployment benefit reforms in the 1990s was thus a sort of dualization in provision (cf. Clegg, 2007; Palier, 2010*b*); on the one hand there was an increasingly 'exclusive' UI system, paying still relatively generous earnings-related benefits to those with better contribution records, and on the other, SA for those who could not qualify for UI and had low incomes. In between, UA continued to exist but was allowed to atrophy. Only the UA scheme for the long-term unemployed was of any quantitative significance by the end of 1990s, but its restrictive contribution conditions meant that it was a scheme that was largely reserved for unemployed people aged 50 and above (Gilles and Loisy, 2005).[3]

This developmental dynamic was partially arrested in the early 2000s, when beneficiary rates for UI recovered substantially, and reliance on SA declined concomitantly. Between December 1999 and December 2003, UI beneficiary rates increased by around 12 per cent (cf. Figure 3.1), while the SA caseload fell for the first time since the introduction of the RMI in 1988 (cf. Figure 3.2). Part of the reason for this was the effect of the period of strong employment growth from the late 1990s, which had an automatic entitlement effect in UI. But part was also a result of changes in the eligibility and entitlement parameters of UI agreed in 2001. This was the year when a generalized system of activation was introduced into UI for the first time, on the back of proposals put forward by the employers' association (see below). To leverage the agreement of at least some of the trade union confederations for this activation principle, however, the employers agreed

---

[3] The conservative Raffarin government in fact attempted to limit the maximum duration of ASS receipt to two years in 2003, but this measure was withdrawn by President Chirac following his party's poor showing in local elections in early 2004.

Table 3.2. Evolution of contribution conditions and benefit durations in UI

	1992–2001	2001–2	2003–5	2006–8	2009–
Minimum contribution requirement	4 months in last 8	4 months in last 18	6 months in last 22	6 months in last 22	4 months in last 28
Minimum benefit duration	4 months	4 months	7 months	7 months	4 months
Maximum benefit duration	30 months (over-50s = 45 months)	30 months (over-50s = 45 months)	23 months (over-50s = 36 months)	23 months (over-50s = 36 months)	24 months (over-50s = 36 months)

Source: UNEDIC.

to a relaxation of the restrictive measures that had been introduced over the previous decade. Minimum contribution conditions were substantially reduced – from four months of contribution in the previous eight to four months in the previous eighteen – and the degressivity mechanism scrapped altogether. As a result of the first measure in particular, 'bad contributors' (*les précaires*) were for the first time in a decade the major winners in a parametric reform of UI.

The social partners partially retreated from this new concern for opening UI to less good contributors in the mid-2000s, only to return to it at the end of the decade, this time in a rapidly worsening employment context (see Table 3.2). As a result of the combined effects of rising unemployment, the relatively disappointing results of the activation measures introduced in 2001, and an imbalance between the extensions to benefits and reductions in UI contribution rates decided in the previous collective agreement, UNEDIC found itself facing yet another difficult budgetary situation by the 2003. The agreements of 2004 and then 2006 responded by altogether removing the bottom tier of entitlement for UI; henceforth only those who had contributed for at least six months, albeit in a still lengthy reference period of twenty-two months, could access UI. In these reforms, however, the cuts were more equally shared than in 1992; the duration of benefits was reduced from thirty months (or forty-five for over-50s) to twenty-three months for those with contribution records of fourteen months in the last two years, and from forty-five months to thirty-six months for over-50s with twenty-seven months of contributions in the last three years. From 2009, moreover, provided an individual has worked a minimum of four months in the last two years, the duration of benefit payment is strictly equal to the duration of contribution before entering employment, up to a maximum twenty-five months for under-50s and thirty-six months for over-50s. The biggest winners in this reform were those with four or five months' contribution records; the biggest losers were those with contribution records of between sixteen and twenty-two months for under-25s and between twenty-seven and thirty-five months for over-50s (Cornilleau and Elbaum, 2009).

Reforms of UI in France are chronically pro-cyclical, because the social partners' ability to balance their budget is the guarantor of the long-term viability of the autonomous system that both the unions and employers support. Incentives are strong for them to cut benefits back in periods of rising unemployment, and increase them as unemployment declines (ibid.). This pattern held across the period between 1990 and 2010; what varied was the distribution of costs and benefits during the periods of belt-tightening and expansion, respectively. In the early 1990s, it was above all 'bad contributors' who saw their already minimal benefit entitlements cut when times were tough; but by the late 2000s, it was those with better levels of protection on whom the biggest losses were being imposed.

3.3.2 From insertion to activation

It was in SA that the concern with the development of more vigorous policies for reintegrating claimants of non-employment benefits back into the labour market developed first in France. As described above, the introduction of a general SA scheme in 1988 had been accompanied with an essentially rhetorical requirement for benefit to be articulated with measures of social or professional reinsertion. Unsurprisingly, early evaluations of the new SA showed that this aspect of the scheme functioned poorly (Vanlerenberghe, 1992). Very few claimants signed, or were even made aware of, insertion contracts (Lefèvre and Zoyem, 1999). Even as the profile of SA claimants changed due to reforms in unemployment benefit, insertion measures that were organized remained most often related to social, rather than professional, insertion, focusing on issues such as health and housing (Castra, 2003). And claimants often reported that the signature of an insertion contract had not been helpful to them, especially when it focused on reintegration in work (Zoyem, 2001).

By the late 1990s, however, the succession of negative evaluations – as well as the growing size and cost of a scheme that was originally intended to be marginal – resulted in pressure for reform of the insertion dimension of SA (Clegg and Palier, 2012, forthcoming). First, under the socialist-led Jospin government in 1998, the possibilities to cumulate receipt of SA with income from work for a limited period were considerably extended, amidst a growing concern about the disincentives to work facing recipients of SA and the more general need to 'make work pay' in a labour market characterized by a growing number of temporary and part-time jobs.[4] Then, in 2004 and with the conservatives back in office, a reform of the SA scheme greatly increased the emphasis on professional relative to social forms of insertion activity for claimants (Lafore, 2004: 25), and introduced a new special employment contract specifically reserved for SA recipients. The same reform also decentralized the financing and administration of SA to local authorities. Though SA was largely caught up in the general decentralizing ardour of the Raffarin government, a supplementary argument was that with the costs of benefit provision falling on local authorities, they would have incentives to organize more energetic and work-focused insertion activities.

By this time, an emphasis on the articulation between benefit provision and support for return to the labour market had begun to characterize debates around

---

[4] Attesting to the same preoccupation, the socialist government introduced a work-conditioned negative income tax in 2001, the *Prime pour l'emploi* (PPE).

UI too. In 2000, the employers' association – largely in response to the socialist-led government's high-profile legislation on the 35-hour working week, and in the context of a shift in power between different federations within the main employers' confederation (see Section 3.4) – launched an ambitious structural reform agenda called the *réfondation sociale*, in which the thoroughgoing activation of unemployment benefits was a showpiece proposal. Ostensibly designed to embarrass the government, the employers' strategy also directly menaced the survival of the social partner-managed UNEDIC, which the employers threatened to suspend their participation in if negotiations over their reform projects were not successfully concluded. Largely to head off this risk (Freyssinet, 2002), and also in return for some concessions on the generosity of benefits (see above), a number of the unions reached agreement with the employers over a new UI system. From 2001 the main UI benefit was as a result recast as a 'return-to-work benefit' (*allocation de retour à l'emploi* – ARE), and eligibility was henceforth conditioned not only on the payment of contributions but also on claimants signing and respecting an individualized project for help with the return to work (*plan d'aide au retour à l'emploi*, PARE).

At the demand of the government, who were concerned about the possible emergence of parallel employment service networks for the insured and other jobseekers, responsibility for the implementation and monitoring of the PARE was ultimately vested in the PES rather than in UNEDIC, as the social partners had originally planned. The local offices of the UI system continued to deliver benefits separately from placement services and the administration of employment policy instruments. Criticisms were soon voiced as to the impact of this multi-agency delivery structure on the effectiveness of the new activation policy (Cour des Comptes, 2006; Marimbert, 2004), and the old idea of a merger between the PES and UNEDIC gradually returned to the top of the policy agenda. After a number of years of experimentations with more-or-less effective 'reinforced co-operations' between the local-level offices of the two organizations (Vericel, 2006), the merger was finally implemented in February 2008, nine months after the election of Nicolas Sarkozy – who had pledged this reform in his manifesto – as president. Though out of a concession to the social partners the UI system was not totally absorbed by the state-run PES – the social partners retaining notably responsibility for fixing the eligibility and entitlement parameters of UI through collective agreements – the new state-run *Pôle Emploi* is now responsible for the integrated delivery of unemployment benefits, placement services, and employment policies (Willmann, 2009). This reform considerably weakened the organizational strength of UNEDIC, which henceforth has between 100 and 200 employees nationwide as opposed to around 14,000 previously.

The period since the election of Sarkozy has seen the activation emphasis in French labour market policy considerably reinforced in other respects, too. In August 2008, a new 'law on the rights and responsibilities of jobseekers' was adopted (Rousseau, 2009). With limited emphasis on the rights of jobseekers – which in any case remain formally a prerogative of the social partners, at least as far as UI is concerned – the law reformed both the definition of reasonable work offers that jobseekers are required to accept and the regime of sanctions that can be imposed if they fail to do so, or more generally do not comply with the terms of their jobseeker's agreement, now known as the 'Personalized Project for Access to

Employment' (PPAE). In respect of both reasonable work definitions and the sanction regime, the legislation represented less a tightening of rules than a greater specification and diversification of them, based on the understanding that it was the bluntness of pre-existing rules that led to them being routinely ignored in administrative practice. For example, where previously the only administrative sanction was total eviction from the jobseekers register resulting in complete suspension of benefits for those obliged to sign on, the new sanction regime allows the possibility for partial and/or temporary reductions in benefit entitlements for those failing to discharge their responsibilities as jobseekers.

Since July 2009, this regime also applies to the vast majority of SA claimants. This follows from a reform of SA that replaced the pre-existing RMI with a new Active Solidarity Income (*Revenu de Solidarité Active*, RSA). The most high-profile aspect of the RSA is that SA in France can henceforth be received either as an out-of-work benefit ('RSA *socle*') or in-work, as a permanent subsidy to low-paying employment ('RSA *activité*'). The reform was explicitly focused on trying to help the situation of the working poor and, in so doing, on increasing the differential between incomes for those in and out of work – but with the obvious risk of encouraging the further expansion of part-time and temporary work (Lafore, 2009). But the RSA also substantially strengthened the activation emphasis in SA for those out of the labour market (Clegg and Palier, 2012, forthcoming). The reform established an even clearer hierarchy between professional and social forms of insertion activity in which all SA claimants should be engaged; social forms of insertion should henceforth be clearly reserved for the minority of beneficiaries with such serious problems that they could not immediately consider a return to work-related activity of any kind, and should then explicitly be a first step in a process ultimately leading to professional insertion. Furthermore, professional insertion for SA claimants will not, as in the past, be organized independently of other employment policies; instead, the majority of recipients of the RSA will now be obliged to register as jobseekers and to sign a PPAE specifying their rights and responsibilities, as for any other jobseeker.

The reform that introduced the RSA also substantially streamlined France's battery of special employment measures; in place of a range of measures managed by different administrations and targeted on different (if partially overlapping) groups of benefit claimants, there will now be a single insertion contract (*contrat unique d'insertion*) that can be used to support the return-to-work of all jobseekers, irrespective of their benefit status. Having become considerably more active since the late 1990s, French policies towards the unemployed have thus in the late 2000s become – at least in their active dimensions – significantly more integrated too.

3.3.3 Exit routes: from cheapening to closure

A further implication of the new SA scheme introduced in 2009 was a considerably expanded definition of those who are considered as jobseekers, and are subject to the obligation to look for work. Under the RMI, registration at the PES was voluntary; with the RSA it became obligatory for all but a very small minority of SA claimants. Furthermore, the RSA replaced not only the RMI but also the means-tested benefit for single parents, *Allocation de Parent Isolé*. Most of the 200,000 beneficiaries of this scheme are also now required to actively seek work. The RSA is also far more explicit than the RMI it replaced that obligations to seek work apply to all working-age members of the claimant household. Finally, it is not merely those out of work who are required to actively seek employment; recipients of the RSA-*activité* with low pre-transfer incomes from work must, theoretically, remain in contact with the PES and demonstrate that they are taking steps to find more work (ibid.).

This expansion was rendered possible by the adoption from 2009 of a new procedure for tracking the unemployment rate. Where previously the national unemployment rate was based on a combination of the national labour force survey and the jobseekers register, reconciled according to a statistical adjustment procedure (*calage*), the politically sensitive monthly unemployment rate is now based only the former. This change was justified on technical grounds, by the increasing difficulty of using the two sources due to growing discrepancies between them. But it also meant that 'the public authorities are now free to take in hand people "encountering employment difficulties" without fear that measures taken to increase the employment rate will lead to an aggravation of the unemployment statistics' (Rousseau, 2009: 1104).

The broader concern for bringing people back into the labour market and closing off 'exit routes' in the benefit system had, however, been building up for some time. Despite France having a legal retirement age of 60 up until 2010, around 300,000 people were still benefiting from early retirement measures in 1990 (IRES, 2004), and early retirement was further expanded in response to the recession of the early 1990s. Thereafter, governments tried to run down use of these instruments, mainly for fiscal consolidation reasons. Even then their attempts were partially counteracted by the decisions of the social partners, who used the UI system to keep a certain number of exit routes open. For example, the ARPE (*Allocation de remplacement pour l'emploi*) early retirement scheme – contribution-financed and managed through UNEDIC – was introduced in late 1995, and grew up to a peak of 100,000 beneficiaries in 2000.

Since the turn of the millennium, early retirement measures of all kinds (tax- and contribution-financed) have declined steadily, irrespective of the employment context. Initially, however, the driver of reform appeared to be less that of closing off exit routes out of the labour market than of making labour shedding cheaper by subsidizing it less generously. Accordingly, from around the time that numbers of early retirement pensions began their steady decline, the number of DRE for those on unemployment benefits began to climb just as rapidly (cf. Figure 3.3). By 2006 there were more than 400,000 people in receipt of unemployment benefits, but not obliged to register with the PES and not, therefore, counted among the unemployed. This ensured that even though numbers of early retirement benefits fell in the 2000s, France's activity rates among over-55s remained among the lowest in Europe (see Statistical Annex, Table A.7).

The law on the rights and responsibilities of jobseekers in 2008 marked a break with this policy. It legislated for the progressive suppression of DRE; though those who currently benefit from the measure will not be brought back into the labour market, the age at which it is possible to have a DRE will be gradually raised until 2012, when the measure will be formally withdrawn to new entrants. In parallel,

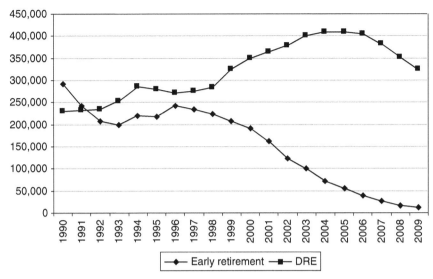

Figure 3.3. Annual stocks of early retirement and DRE

Source: see Caseload Annex (France).

the government has also promised that extra resources will be guaranteed to the PES to provide 'reinforced support' for over-50s seeking work.

3.4 FROM DUALIZATION TO TRIPLE INTEGRATION? UNDERSTANDING CHANGE IN FRENCH LABOUR MARKET POLICY

As the preceding discussion has shown, there has been considerable change in French labour market policy, and in the regulation of the risk of unemployment, since 1990. Across the period as a whole, however, two rather contradictory trends are visible (see Table 3.3). Up to at least the end of the 1990s, the main dynamic of change was towards the dualization of policies for the non-employed. Reforms in benefits created an ever-sharper distinction between insurance-based provision for good contributors and general assistance for those with weaker labour market attachment; the intervening benefit tier of UA atrophied. The definition of unemployment as a risk category focused ever more narrowly on core workers in receipt of UI, with other groups of workers coming to rely on benefits without a formal link to employment. And even when activation policies developed, they did so initially in a dualized form, with different arrangements for SA claimants on the one hand and UI recipients on the other, and without the PES having strong linkages to either of the main benefit systems for the non-employed.

During the 2000s, however, this dualizing tendency in French labour market policy was increasingly challenged, and by the end of the decade reforms had been adopted that were suggestive of its at least partial reversal across all the policy

Table 3.3. The re-regulation of the risk of unemployment in France, 1990–2010

Dimension	Dynamic of change
Unemployment protection as a social right	Dualization (1990–2001)
	Sharper distinction between UI for good contributors and SA for bad
	Integration (2001–3, 2008–)
	Relaxation of contributory conditions in UI
Unemployment as an administrative risk category	Dualization (1990–2008)
	Opening and maintenance of exit routes out of labour market
	Integration (2008–)
	End of DRE for UI/UA claimants
	SA claimants registered as jobseekers
	API integrated in SA
	Jobseeking requirements for all adults in households receiving SA
Jobseekers in post-industrial labour markets	Dualization (1990–2008)
	Activation in SA only (1990–2000)
	Different activation policies for SA and UI
	Integration (2008–)
	Partial merger of UI administration and PES
	Integration of activation policies for SA claimants in work of PES
	Single set of 'rights and responsibilities' for all jobseekers

dimensions considered here. The 2009 UI agreement thus relaxed the contributory conditions for benefit, confirming a still tentative retreat from the specialization between insurance and assistance that was first hinted at by reforms in the early 2000s. A series of reforms in 2008 and 2009 also partially reconnected and considerably rationalized the labour market policy administration, with *Pôle Emploi* now delivering both benefits and labour market services to UI claimants, as well as organizing the professional insertion of SA recipients, on the basis of a universal set of job-search rules that apply to all jobseekers. And these changes also drew SA claimants and single-parents back into the formal category of jobseekers, which will be further enlarged by the closure that is underway of exit routes out of the labour market for older workers.

How can these patterns of policy change be accounted for? Much of the dualistic dynamic in policy development up to the late 1990s can be explained by the exceptionally strong regulatory role of the social partners in French UI, which as mentioned is – uniquely for a basic UI scheme – governed through periodic collective agreements at the national level. Condemned by common organizational interests to find a mutually acceptable way of adapting this institutional arrangement to cost pressures, the employers' associations and the unions repeatedly found common cause in status-maintaining recalibrations that mainly benefited their core constituencies of large manufacturing firms and well-integrated older workers, respectively. The limited legitimacy of French governments to intervene decisively to enforce alternative policy directions in unemployment protection was only compounded by the dynamics of partisan competition, which meant the social partners could always rely on the support of the parliamentary opposition for attempts to head off any 'statist takeover' of their regulatory prerogatives in this area. In this context, governments concerned about issues of social cohesion could at best temper dualistic policy adjustment at the margins, for which their main instrument was the development of subsidized employment contracts for particularly disadvantaged groups in the labour market (Clegg, 2005).

While Palier and Thelen (2010) see the dualization of policies for the unemployed as a structural feature of the adjustment of the coordinated market economies of continental European countries to enhanced competitive pressures, it was thus particularly pronounced in the French case as a result of the institutional configuration of unemployment protection and the incentives and constraints this generated for different policy actors (cf. also Clegg, 2011, forthcoming). Furthermore, though an apparent 'complementarity' developed between the dualistic regulation of the unemployment risk and the use of non-standard employment arrangements, in France the former was not driven by the latter, as Palier and Thelen's account of dualization suggests. On the contrary, the rapid growth in 'precarious' forms of employment that started from the late 1980s was arguably driven by the dualistic reforms to unemployment protection institutions enacted earlier in the decade, nicely illustrating how the regulation of the risk of unemployment shapes, as much as it is shaped by, the development of employment norms.

How then can we explain that this path of institutional development was at least partially reversed in the 2000s? Part of the story is about growth of tensions and conflicts within the organizations that represent socio-economic interests in France, especially on the employers' side. The late 1990s saw the traditional monopoly of the large metalworking federation over social policy issues within the main French employers' association increasingly challenged by representatives of firms with very different interests (Woll, 2006).[5] The employers' aggressive promotion of activation going into the renegotiation of the UI agreement in 2000–1 reflected the growing influence of service-sector employers, and also opened the possibility for unconventional bargains – trading more aggressive activation for the expanded entitlement and looser eligibility requirements – to be struck with the unions (Clegg, 2010: 93–4).

Much of the impetus for the broader change of policy direction has come from strategic action by government, however. Given the apparently sharp break from 2008 in the developmental trends across all the dimensions analysed here, it is hard not to attribute particular causal significance in this regard to the election the previous year of Nicolas Sarkozy, who ran for president on a boldly proclaimed programme of 'rupture' with what he saw as three decades of failed policies in the socio-economic sphere. Sarkozy certainly showed considerable reformist zeal in the field of labour market policy, and a willingness to intervene more assertively than before in areas of labour market policy under the formal control of the social partners, such as UI (Freyssinet, 2010). He was also rather adroit in neutralizing the influence of potential opponents of reform,[6] a process in which he was abetted

---

[5] These power shifts were symbolized in the name of the confederation being changed in 1998 from the traditional *Conseil National du Patronat Français* (CNPF) to the *Mouvement des Entreprises de France* (MEDEF).

[6] Sarkozy bombarded the social partners with reform projects on many fronts, limiting their capacity to effectively organize opposition on any one. He is also widely credited with having publicized a system of fraudulent usage of social insurance and training funds, in the process discrediting especially the aforementioned federation of metalworking employers, who opposed many of his labour market reforms.

by the Socialist Party, who through their internal conflicts effectively managed to neutralize themselves.

At the same time, the role of Sarkozy's willingness to break with conventional governmental thinking in French labour market policy should not be over-played. Reforms such as the introduction of the RSA built on and amplified earlier policy developments that had been implemented under previous governments, both conservative and socialist. The RSA was indeed devised and championed by a former civil servant who had been closer to the socialists than to the right before entering Sarkozy's first government, and in 2007 the policy featured not only in Sarkozy's manifesto but also that of his socialist opponent (Damon, 2009). Other proposals, such as the merger between UNEDIC and the PES, had been on the policy agenda for a long time and had been gathering momentum even before Sarkozy's election (Barbier, 2007; Rousseau, 2008). In short, the reforms of 2008 and 2009 are the manifestation of an ideational shift on labour market policy issues that had been underway in France for some time.

This has obviously intersected with the broader evolution of international ideas and paradigms regarding social and labour market policy. Recent reforms in this field have all been preceded by reports making reference to international 'best practice' and European orientations. The increased emphasis on acti-vation in French labour market policy is clearly congruent with the guidelines of the European Employment Strategy, for example (Palier and Petrescu, 2007). But at least in French social policy it is hard to attribute causal policy influence to the discourses and reform agendas promoted by international organizations or the EU. Rather, French policymakers appear to make use of international guidelines, recommendations, and best practices to help lever the reforms that they have already decided, independently, to pursue (cf. Erhel et al., 2005).

To fully understand the paradigm shift in French labour market policy in the 2000s, it is instead necessary to appreciate how the dualization of unemployment protection was itself a vector for ideas and policy practices that would ultimately come to destabilize this adjustment trajectory from within. The notion of activa-tion was not simply imported into France; it already existed, in a 'Gallicised' form, in the insertion dimension of SA policy. As described above, this was initially a rather hollow legitimating device, introduced to build acceptance for the intro-duction of a (cheaper) type of social benefit that was alien to, and indeed pushed against the fundamental principles of, the work-related social insurance benefits around which the French welfare model was built; insertion was, in other words, an alibi for dualizing reforms. But having been introduced for these reasons, the rhetoric of returning social benefit claimants to the labour market soon developed a transformational potential of its own. In response to negative evaluation reports, insertion was first refocused and reinvigorated in SA policy, shedding many of its social aspects and increasingly emphasizing labour market integration (Clegg and Palier, 2012, forthcoming). This helped popularize the notion of activation and encouraged its extension to the realm of UI, after which multiple activation policies for different groups of benefit claimants coexisted in parallel. Official appraisals soon came in turn to identify this as a source of poor outcomes (e.g. CERC, 2005), and made a case on grounds of efficiency and effectiveness for reforms that pushed ever more clearly against the pre-existing policy logic and division of institutional labour in French unemployment policy, such as the merger of UNEDIC and the PES and the reconnection of SA to general employment policy. While political leaders and other policy entrepreneurs were perhaps important in driving through change at different stages of this process, they harnessed policy repertoires that had grown relatively organically out of earlier rounds of labour market policy development.

In this way, the dualizing thrust of French unemployment protection reforms in the 1980s and 1990s is being gradually, and in some respects rather seamlessly, displaced by a quite contrary orientation in the new millennium. Certainly, working-age benefit claimants in France continue to receive very different levels of economic support depending on their eligibility for UI, and in this sense there has been only limited benefit homogenization. However, not only has UI been made more accessible to those with irregular patterns of labour market attachment in the 2000s, but working-age benefit claimants are more and more seen as a single group of labour market participants who should be provided support, tailored to their individual circumstances but on the basis of standardized assumptions, from the same set of labour market institutions irrespective of their work record or benefit status. From this perspective the earlier dualization of French unemployment protection looks increasingly like a protracted stage in the as-yet-incomplete development of an integrated benefit-and-service system through which the employment-related risks that characterize post-industrial labour markets can be more adequately regulated.

3.5 CONCLUSION

This chapter has analysed recent transformations in the regulation of the risk of unemployment in France. It has shown that a relatively high level of formal institutional stability has masked significant variations in the primacy of particular policy logics over time. While French labour market policy in the 1990s was characterized by a widening gulf between policies for good and bad contributors and a persistent emphasis on reducing the labour supply of less productive workers, reforms in the (especially late) 2000s have instead emphasized the activation of an enlarged pool of jobseekers, partly harmonizing and coordinating the conditions on which, and institutions through which, different working-age benefit claimants receive public support.

Possibly the most visible driver of this change in policy direction was the growing assertiveness of governments, which weakened the traditional influence of the social partners over norm setting and policy steering in key areas of French labour market policy. As has been argued in this chapter, however, this in turn was possible only because governments were able to harness the transformative potential of initially marginal policy developments that had been enacted as part and parcel of the earlier dualistic adaptation of French labour market institutions. In this way it can be seen that the highly incremental pattern of institutional adjustment that has characterized French labour market policy has been rather ambiguous, serving the interests of particular socio-economic coalitions in the short term but also setting free policy dynamics that would over time help to challenge these.

Understanding the dialectic relationship between the reproduction of the logics dualization and integration in French labour market policy also helps to better understand some of its current contradictions and more clearly appreciate its uncertain future prospects. Because although the dynamic of integration appears at time of writing to have the wind in its sails, and has even resisted the first effects of the global economic crisis, it would be premature to conclude that it has fully supplanted dualizing tendencies. France remains some way from having a fully integrated benefit-and-service system for the non-employed, and the uncoordinated overlap between reforms in UI and SA remains problematic (Cornilleau and Elbaum, 2009). Unlike in the Netherlands (see Hoogenboom, this volume), the social partners retained an institutional foothold in and an influence over French UI even after the reforms of the late 2000s, in which Sarkozy was indeed criticized for conceding too much to their wishes (Cahuc and Zylberberg, 2009). In the context of heightened austerity that is certainly ahead, it thus remains an open question how the ongoing conflict between the logics of integration and of dualization in French labour market policy will play out.

Appendix 3.A Major reforms in provision for the unemployed in France, 1990–2010

Year	Reform
1991	Unemployment Assistance • Removal of eligibility for Allocation d'Insertion (AI) from first-time jobseekers and single-women with dependent children and no employment record
1992	Unemployment Insurance • Creation of Allocation Unique Degressive (AUD) • Introduction of 'degressivity' mechanism, whereby after a specific period of full receipt benefits are periodically reduced over unemployment spell by between 8 and 17% depending on age • Minimum contribution period increased from 3 to 4 months (in last 8) • Reduction of benefit duration for all unemployed, but especially those with more limited contribution histories (6 months in last 12 months), who now receive benefit for 7 months instead of 15–21 (depending on age) previously
1993	Unemployment Insurance • 'Degressivity' mechanism in AUD reinforced
1994	Public Employment Service, Job Search and Activation • Specific effort to target subsidized employment contracts on recipients of social assistance (Revenu Minimum d'Insertion, RMI) to facilitate labour market reintegration
1995	Unemployment Insurance Creation of Allocation de Remplacement pour l'Emploi (ARPE), an early retirement benefit financed through unemployment insurance for those with 40 years' contribution record
1997	Unemployment Insurance • 'Degressivity' mechanism eased, with benefits now reduced every 6 months instead of 4 previously Unemployment Assistance • Tightening of both means-test and contribution requirement for Allocation Spécifique de Solidarité (ASS)
1998	Unemployment Assistance • Significant increase in level of AI and ASS Public Employment Service, Job Search and Activation • Extension of possibility for recipients of RMI, ASS and single-parent benefit (Allocation de Parent Isolé, API) to temporarily receive income from benefits and work together
2001	Unemployment Insurance • Creation of Allocation de Retour à l'emploi (ARE) • Introduction of requirement for ARE recipients to sign a personalized plan for return to work (plan d'aide au retour à l'emploi, PARE) • Suppression of 'degressivity mechanism' • Loosening of contribution requirements for those with shortest contribution records
2002	Unemployment Insurance • Increase in minimum period of contribution from 4 to 6 months; reduction in maximum period of benefit receipt from 30 to 23 months (or 45 to 36 for over-50s)
2004	Social Assistance • Decentralization of RMI • Refocusing of insertion on labour market integration, particularly for long-term claimants of RMI
2005	Public Employment Service, Job Search, and Activation • Law on social cohesion seeks to encourage reinforced cooperation at local level between different labour market policy administrations

(*continued*)

Appendix 3.A (continued)

Year	Reform
2006	Unemployment Insurance • Reinforcement and personalization of activation measures for unemployment insurance beneficiaries Public Employment Service, Job Search, and Activation • Further extension of possibility for recipients of RMI, ASS, and API to temporarily receive income from benefits and work together
2008	Public Employment Service and Job Search • Merger of ANPE and Assedic (delivery-level institutions of UI system) to create Pôle Emploi • Law on the rights and responsibilities of jobseekers reforms job-search and sanctions regime for all jobseekers • Receipt of benefit without job-search requirements (dispense de recherche de l'emploi) scrapped
2009	Unemployment Insurance • Loosening of contribution requirements, with minimum contribution period reduced from 6 to 4 months, in a reference period extended from 22 to 28 months • Benefit duration now based on duration of contribution, between a minimum of 4 months and a maximum of 24 (36 for over-50s) Social Assistance/Public Employment Service, Job Search, and Activation • Replacement of RMI and API with Revenu de Solidarité Active (RSA), including more generous in-work variant acting as permanent subsidy (replacing previous rules concerning temporary receipt of income from benefits and work together) • Reform of insertion to streamline instruments and increase work focus

4

Germany: moving towards integration whilst maintaining segmentation

Irene Dingeldey

4.1 INTRODUCTION

Until the end of the 1990s, the conservative–corporatist welfare states such as Germany were characterized as 'frozen landscapes' (Esping-Andersen, 1996; Manow and Seils, 2000; Voß, 1997), highlighting their reluctance to structural social policy reform (Pierson, 2001*a*). Since then major reforms have taken place in various social policy arenas (Palier and Martin, 2008*b*) including German unemployment policy which has led to controversial interpretations. Some authors claim that the enhancement of protection for German labour market insiders while targeting both benefit cuts and new activation initiatives on outsiders occurred incrementally by policy drift (Clegg, 2007). Others see path-breaking changes (Mohr, 2008) or even paradigm shifts (Oschmiansky et al., 2007). In this chapter, I show that reform reluctance in German labour market policy was overcome, albeit not fully. More concretely, while unemployment protection as a whole has remained segmented, a trend of integration can clearly be identified, most notably applying to unemployed persons outside unemployment insurance. In essence a de facto three-tier support structure was replaced by a two-tier system.

As will be demonstrated, within this trend all three dimensions of 'triple integration' can be identified. A move towards 'benefit homogenization' has occurred as a result of the introduction of a new means-tested and flat-rate form of unemployment assistance (unemployment benefit II; UBII) which merged the former unemployment assistance and social assistance system in 2005. The fact that it is UBII (rather than unemployment insurance) which covers the vast majority of jobless benefit claimants in Germany today is yet another sign of benefit homogenization as discussed in the introductory chapter of this book. As access to incapacity benefits became limited, and UBII now includes persons who have some care responsibilities, a process of risk re-categorization can be identified too. It should be noted that this does not imply a blurring of differences between the two tiers of unemployment protection however, since both remain very distinct from each other. This also includes job-search requirements and activation more generally which has become more pervasive for both insurance and assistance benefit claimants over the past decade but, as the subsequent discussion will show, apply differently in the two systems.

4.2 ECONOMIC AND POLICY CONTEXTS: RESPONDING TO ECONOMIC CRISES BY LIMITING LABOUR SUPPLY

As in many other countries at the time, the economic crisis of 1973–4 caused a sudden rise of unemployment in West Germany also. As a reaction, macro-economic policy subsequently changed and culminated with a policy of strong budget consolidation introduced by the Social Democratic/liberal government at the beginning of the 1980s in the wake of a second hike in unemployment. With the subsequent centre-right Christian Democratic/liberal coalition, the emphasis on supply-side economics continued in 1982 and full employment as a prior macroeconomic goal was substituted by price stability (Schmidt, 2005).

This paradigm shift in economic policy was combined with rather modest retrenchment in labour market policy (Schmidt, 2005). Reforms in unemployment insurance led to both an expansion of social protection for some groups (particularly older workers) and restrictive reforms in line with budget consolidation for others, such as job starters and those with shorter contribution records (Schmid and Oschmiansky, 2005: 262). Replacement rates in unemployment insurance were reduced to 63 per cent in 1983, albeit only for claimants without children (Steffen, 2009). Furthermore, in 1982, entitlement was limited to those who had been employed for a minimum of twelve months (within the previous three years). However, for older workers with long contribution records, the entitlement to insurance benefits was prolonged from twelve to a maximum of thirty-two months in 1987 (for details of legislative changes, see Appendix 4.A; also Clasen, 2005: 195–7).

To reduce open unemployment, decreasing labour supply formed a central element of German labour market policies (Palier and Martin, 2008a: 7). These included working-time reductions such as several early retirement routes which were very popular in the 1980s (Ebbinghaus, 2006; Friedrich and Wiedemeyer, 1998: 236). The number of entrants into old-age pensions due to unemployment had already increased since the 1960s and reached 13.7 per cent for men and 1.8 per cent for women of all pension entrants in West Germany in 1990 (Bäcker et al., 2008a: 368). Labour market exit via incapacity benefit expanded too during the 1980s, albeit more gradually (see below). Partly as a consequence the labour force activity rate for West German men older than 60 years of age declined to 33 per cent and for women of the same age group to 13 per cent by the mid-1990s. In the eastern part of the country, the respective rates were even lower, namely 15.7 per cent and 3.3 per cent (Bäcker et al., 2008b: 418).

Since 1986, another measure allowed unemployed people over the age of 58 years access to unemployment insurance benefit without the need to seek or be available for work, provided claimants agreed to enter full pension receipt as soon as possible (Brussig and Knuth, 2006). Statistically, persons under this regulation were no longer counted as unemployed. By narrowing the boundary of the administrative status and category of unemployment, this policy thus corresponded directly to the notion of risk reconfiguration, as introduced in the introductory chapter of this book.

Another response to high unemployment was the attempt to create a more flexible labour market. Although the actual scope of deregulation and flexibilization remained somewhat modest, legislation facilitated more options for concluding fixed-term contracts, part-time employment, and working-time flexibility. These might have contributed to a relative decline in the prevalence of the so-called standard employment relationship[1] and an expansion in the scope of labour market segments dominated by employment and working-time flexibility that make it more difficult to fulfil eligibility requirements of the unemployment insurance system, or to acquire a benefit level above the poverty line. Flexibilization of the labour market has therefore contributed to the declining relevance of insurance-based benefits (see below).

More generally, other responses to labour market pressures in Germany included the promotion of labour market inactivity or expulsion of some groups without burdening the social transfer system. Most notably the conservative–liberal coalition introduced policy measures to limit migration and introduced programmes aimed at reintegrating migrants into their home countries (Friedrich and Wiedemeyer, 1998). Furthermore, 'innovative' family policy instruments such as the introduction of parental leave arrangement in 1986 were not only intended to improve the reconciliation between work and family life but to decrease female labour supply (Schmid and Wiebe, 1999).[2] This regulation led to an institutionalization of a career break for German mothers that often lasted much longer than three years (Bird, 2001). As a consequence it reinforced the male breadwinner model which was still reflected in numerous welfare state regulations in Germany, such as a tax-splitting system that rewards non-working or only part-time employed partners and a childcare system that offered only part-time places (Dingeldey, 2001; Friedrich and Wiedemeyer, 1998). As a consequence, the scale of female labour market participation, and that of mothers in particular, remained well below the rates in Nordic countries or the United Kingdom by the end of the 1980s (see Statistical Annex, Table A.4).

In sum, the policies of reducing labour supply during the 1980s, and beyond, have contributed to containing open unemployment and thus relieving financial pressure on the unemployment insurance system. German policies during the 1980s included the promotion of policies which allowed claimants to leave the administrative risk category of unemployment. This, in addition to an overall improvement of the economic situation, contributed to a decline in unemployment rates to below 6 per cent by the end of the 1980s (Statistical Annex, Table A.5). As

---

[1] The standard employment relationship is defined as continuous, full-time employment relationship, fully liable to social security contribution and employment protection legislation, including wage setting by collective bargaining agreements.

[2] Due to this arrangement, a benefit of about €300 (which was generally means tested, although means testing became rather strict only after six months) was paid for parents, but used nearly exclusively by mothers, who remained off work during the first twelve months after childbirth. The period of parental leave was prolonged stepwise up to thirty-six months by 1992, while means-tested benefit duration was limited to a maximum period of eighteen months.

a whole, by the end of the 1980s, German policies in response to unemployment were considered to have been rather successful and the unemployment protection system as being in no need of major reform.

4.3 UNEMPLOYMENT PROTECTION IN 1990 AND IN 2010

Unemployment insurance is part of social insurance which characterizes German social policy as Bismarckian (Palier, 2010*a*) or as a conservative–corporatist welfare state (Esping-Andersen, 1990). The main features of this system include the notion of a preservation of social status, implying a strong correspondence between individual labour market performance (and thus contribution record) and individual rights to benefits. Full benefit entitlement within this system is acquired by continuous labour market participation within a standard employment relationship. However, it is also closely related to the idea of a male breadwinner family given that the system allows for derived rights for family members (children and non-working spouses) to, for example, health care or survivors' pensions in accordance with the labour market status of the male breadwinner. Consequently, the basic means-tested benefits of the social assistance scheme protected those with no connection to either the labour market or a (male) breadwinner.

German unification posed a unique challenge to this arrangement and particularly to unemployment insurance. As West German welfare institutions were 'transferred' to the East, continuity was preserved, but problems of system transformation tended to overburden the 'old' structures. The contribution rate for the unemployment insurance (paid jointly by employers and employees) was increased sharply from 4.3 per cent in 1990 to 6.8 per cent in 1991 (Bäcker et al., 2008*b*: 125). This was caused by both a rise of unemployment benefit spending and an enormous extension of active labour market programmes. The latter was part of what has been termed 'Keynesianism against intention' (Bultemeier and Neubert, 1998: 299) aimed at reducing unemployment which in the east was calculated to potentially rise by 35 per cent to an actual rate of 12 per cent in 1991 (Schmid and Wiebe, 1999). Major changes in labour market regulation, however, did not occur before the end of the 1990s.

4.3.1 Unemployment protection at the beginning of the 1990s

In the early 1990s, unemployment insurance (UI) granted an earnings-related benefit replacing 60 per cent of former net earnings (or 67 per cent for persons with at least one child). Both benefits and active labour market programmes were mainly funded through shared contributions by employers and employees to the Federal Employment Office (FEO), subsidized by tax funding from the federal budget. Benefit duration was generally limited to twelve months, but since 1987 unemployed persons older than 42 (53) had been entitled to UI for a maximum of eighteen (32) months (Clasen, 2005: 195; Steffen, 2009). Eligibility required an employment record of at least one year within the last three. UI recipients had also access to active labour market programmes. The so-called 'occupational protection' was removed in 1997, when after the receipt of unemployment benefit for six months any job offer became declared suitable as long as the salary was at least as high as the benefit (Gottschall and Dingeldey, 2000). Furthermore, regulations concerning the suspension of benefit receipt became stricter (Schmid and Oschmiansky, 2005: 266; see also Table 4.1). Both UI and active labour market programmes were run by the FEO, a self-governing agency, within which not only the state but also the social partners had rights of co-determination. Although contributions and benefits are determined by legislation, the FEO enjoyed considerable autonomy in terms of implementation of labour market programmes.

Unemployment assistance (UA) was granted to unemployed persons who had exhausted UI.[3] It was paid as an unlimited benefit equivalent to 53 per cent of former net earnings (57 per cent for persons with at least one child). However, although earnings related, eligibility was subject to a means test. Thus, many long-term unemployed women did not receive UA as their partners income was above the applicable ceiling for means-tested eligibility. UA was tax financed (out of the federal budget), but administered by the FEO. In principle, recipients of UA had access to similar active labour market schemes as UB recipients. However, in practice, claimants of UA often remained outside core labour market programmes such as training leading to qualifications, or participated at a scale which was lower than their proportion of all registered unemployed (Clasen and Goerne, 2012).

A third type of support (not only) for the unemployed was social assistance (SA) which was a means-tested and unlimited flat-rate basic benefit. SA was also tax financed, but paid out of municipal budgets. It could be claimed by all residents without sufficient resources or earned income, including unemployed persons with no or insufficient work records in order to claim UI or UA. It was also possible to top up insufficient levels of UI or UA. Means testing within SA was harsher than in the UA system and any job offer was considered suitable for claimants. Municipalities were responsible for reintegrating recipients into paid work and many offered measures including labour market programmes as there was no formal entitlement to integration measures by the public employment service for SA claimants. With the so-called 'help-to–work' schemes a fairly rudimentary labour market activation system was implemented (Eichhorst et al., 2008: 20) which contained elements of workfare, as the refusal to accept work offers or to participate in employment schemes could be sanctioned. Moreover, employment opportunities offered by municipalities often did not constitute proper employment relationships (that would have renewed access to UI benefits) and provided only a supplement to the benefit (Voges et al., 2000; see also Table 4.1).

Other relevant transfers for working-age persons not in work were disability pensions and several early retirement options. There is no general disability pension in Germany, but the incapacity to either pursue one's previous occupation (*Berufsunfähigkeit*) or general incapacity to work (*Erwerbsunfähigkeit*) establish grounds for public pension support. However, both forms required at least five

---

[3] For a certain period, UA was paid also to those with an employment record not substantial enough for eligibility to UI.

Table 4.1. Major features of unemployment support in 1990 and in 2010 in Germany

	1990	2010
Structure	Three-tier: UI, UA, and SA	Two-tier: UBI and UBII
Overall aim and character	Status-oriented transfer and reintegration	
I. First tier	Unemployment insurance benefit (UI)	Unemployment insurance benefit (unemployment benefit I)
Benefit level	60% of previous net earnings (67% with one child)	60% of previous net earnings (67% with one child)
Benefit duration	12 months	12 months
	18 (32) months for people older than 42 (53) years	24 months for people older than 58 years
Eligibility	Contributions paid for one year within the last three years	One year within the last two years
Obligations and rights	Obligations: being registered at the job centre; applying for jobs; accepting 'suitable employment'; cooperation in reintegration activities	Obligations: being registered at the job centre; applying for jobs; accepting 'suitable employment' during the first six months; thereafter accepting any job as long as wages are at least as high as benefit; cooperation in reintegration activities
	Rights: Placement services	Rights: No formal right to employment promotion measures
	Employment promotion	Individual reintegration contract between unemployment agency and recipients
	Claimants older than 58 are excluded from job-search obligations	
Funding	Contributory: 50% employee, 50% employer Subsidized by taxes	No change
Administration	Federal Employment Office (FEO)	No change
II. Second tier	Unemployment assistance (UA; Arbeitslosenhilfe)	Unemployment assistance (unemployment benefit II)
Benefit level	53% of previous net earnings (57% with one child)	Flat-rate benefit €359 per month for single adult plus supplements for dependants and children plus housing costs
Benefit duration	Unlimited as long as circumstances do not change	Unlimited as long as circumstances do not change
Eligibility	Exhaustion of UI; means test	Means test
Obligations and rights	Obligations: being registered at the job centre; applying for jobs; accepting 'suitable employment'; cooperation in reintegration activities	Obligations for all those available to the labour market: being registered at the job centre; applying for jobs; accepting any offered employment; cooperation in reintegration activities
	Rights: In principle right to employment promotion	Rights: No formal right to employment promotion measures Individual reintegration contract between unemployment agency and recipients

Funding	Tax (federal budget)	Tax (federal budget)
		Tax (municipalities) → housing costs
Administration	Federal Employment Office (FEO)	Joint bodies of FEO and municipalities; exception: 69 municipalities and 23 municipalities with separated task responsibilities
III. Third tier	Social Assistance (SA)	
Benefit level	Flat rate	
Benefit duration	Unlimited	
Eligibility	Need: strict means test	
Funding	Tax: municipal budgets	
Administration	Municipalities	

Source: Dingeldey (2011*b*).

years of contributions to the public pension system and were awarded strictly on medical grounds (see Ebbinghaus, 2006: 142).

At the beginning of the 1990s, the disability pension was an important pathway out of the labour market especially for men, even though the annual number of new entrances to disability pensions was already in decline in West Germany. As a share of all pension entrances, disability-related pensions for men in West Germany fell from 43.9 per cent in 1985 to 36 per cent in 1990 and from 30.2 per cent to 17.2 per cent for women, respectively (Bäcker et al., 2008*a*: 368). Hence, ever since the beginning of the 1990s, the stock of pensioners due to incapacity has been rather stagnant and the number of new entrants decreased slightly (from a peak of about 260,000 in 1997 to around 160,000 ten years later), indicating a trend in contrast to the expansive use of that instrument in many other European countries during the 1990s and beyond, such as in the United Kingdom or the Netherlands (Carcillo and Grubb, 2006).

4.3.2 The system in 2010

A major change in the German unemployment protection system was introduced with the so-called Hartz reforms (named after the chairman of the commission *Modern Services on the Labour Market* which was installed in 2002; see Hartz, 2002).[4] The reforms reorganized labour market services and aimed to increase labour market flexibility. In the aftermath of the commission's proposals, a two-tier benefit system for the working-age population was established in 2005. Since then several revisions have been made but the present system is still widely dominated by the spirit of the Hartz reforms, which introduced several features which correspond to the notion of 'triple integration' as discussed in the intro-ductory chapter of this book, while preserving a division between insurance and assistance benefit claimants.

---

[4] The Hartz legislation is officially named as the First to Fourth Law for Modern Services on the Labour Market, which came into force between 2003 and 2005.

Compared with UI of the 1990s, the current system (unemployment benefit I; UBI) represents a deterioration of social rights in terms of eligibility conditions and a considerable shortening of the maximum duration of benefit receipt for older claimants (see Table 4.1). However, in 2008, the latter was changed again to a maximum duration of twenty-four months (depending on contribution record). In addition, participation in training measures or public job-creation schemes no longer counts towards renewed eligibility for UI (see also Appendix 4.A).

The profile of active labour market programmes has also changed. In principle, UI recipients continue to have access to a variety of active employment promotion including counselling, job placement, training measures, and wage subsidies. However, spending on active measures, particularly on further vocational training, has been scaled down significantly since the early 2000s (Bundesagentur für Arbeit, 2009*a*) and there has been a shift from an emphasis on (lengthy) training schemes to a 'job first' approach and shorter promotion measures (Oschmiansky and Ebach, 2009). Activation requirements have become tighter too. Claimants must utilize 'all possibilities available' for their occupational integration. This includes the participation in placement services and the performance of duties as formulated in a so-called 'integration agreement'. The latter is a kind of contract signed between the responsible case manager within the public employment service and the client. UBI recipients are required to search and accept work that can be 'reasonably expected', which means employment is subject to compulsory insurance contributions, comprises a weekly working time of no less than 15 hours, and generates earnings at least equivalent to the level of unemployment compensation (Eichhorst et al., 2008). Although sanctions in the form of a disqualification period are possible if personal compliance is considered to be insufficient, UBI recipients are not obliged to 'work for benefit'. As before, benefits and activation measures for recipients of UI are administered by the federal employment agency and its 178 local public employment service agencies.

Structurally, even more thorough changes have come about as a result of the creation of UBII which now provides the same benefits and services for two groups who previously were covered within separate programmes, that is, claimants of UA and SA recipients who are 'capable to work', respectively. Financially, this newly created basic security scheme for needy jobseekers consists of two parts. A support benefit (of €359 per month in 2010) for single adults plus supplements for other adults and children living in the same household[5] is funded by the FEO. Supplements for housing costs are covered by municipalities (Eichhorst et al., 2008).[6] In order to administer the different parts of UBII jointly

---

[5] Partners older than 19 years living in the same household receive 90 per cent of that amount. The calculation for children's benefits as a percentage rate of adult benefits (60 per cent for children younger than 7, 70 per cent for children younger than 15, and 80 per cent for those 15 and older) was ruled out to be in breach with the German constitution in February 2010. The Constitutional Court has thus demanded the government to change the benefit calculations for all UBII recipients by 2011. The new calculation for 2011, however, increased monthly payments for adults only by €5 per month. Children will receive a voucher to pay special educational services (Bundesministerium für Arbeit und Soziales, 2010*a*).

[6] Additional measures specifically designed for UBII recipients to overcome barriers of labour market integration include various counselling services in case of debt, abuse of alcohol or other drugs, socio-psychological problems, etc., as well as facilitating access to childcare services mainly provided by the municipalities.

and to integrate labour market services and activation, 356 joint bodies (or consortia) of FEO and municipalities were created, which connect public employment services (PES) and municipal social assistance offices (Eichhorst et al., 2008; Knuth, 2006a; Konle-Seidl et al., 2007: 38). However, sixty-nine so-called *Optionskommunen* have chosen to keep the administration of UBII wholly in municipal hands, eschewing any PES involvement (Knuth, 2006a: 18). Furthermore, in twenty-three communal entities, the local PES agencies cooperate with municipal administrations but do not have formal agreements (Kirsch et al., 2009). In other words, while there has been strong benefit homogenization between two previously separate claimants groups, administrative fragmentation (Dingeldey, 2011a) is likely to continue at least for some time due to a reform which had to accommodate different interests at federal and regional levels (Hassel and Schiller, 2010).

Since the former UA scheme provided earnings-related benefits, it provided benefits above the SA level for most of UA claimants who had earnings above average wages. For many former UA recipients, and particularly singles and couples without children, the introduction of the Hartz reforms therefore implied a lower level of benefit under the new scheme. Becker and Hauser (2006) calculate that about 60 per cent of previous UA claimants faced income reductions due to the reform. On the other hand, establishing access to benefits was easier for those entering the labour market for the first time, as means testing of school leavers and students without work no longer takes account of parental income (as long as parents do not share the same household) as had been the case in the former SA.

In many respects the new UBII system is structurally similar to the previous SA. For example, as had already been the case for unemployed SA claimants, UBII recipients are required to accept job offers as long as earnings are as high as benefits received, which could imply below wages set by collective bargaining agreements. Furthermore, UBII recipients can be required to accept the so-called 'one-euro jobs', an activation measure that does not create a formal employment relationship (liable to social security contributions and paying a proper wage), but provides merely a top-up to UBII. This programme may be used as 'work test' (Wolff and Hohmeyer, 2006) and is structurally similar to 'help-to-work' schemes which were offered to SA claimants before 2005 (see above). In 2009, about 322,000 claimants participated in this programme which thus constituted the dominant activation measure for UBII recipients (Bundesagentur für Arbeit, 2010a).

The creation of UBII allowed particularly former SA claimants access to employment promotion measures which are available for UBI recipients. However, the number of UBII claimants involved in such programmes is below a level which had been envisaged by the government. Evaluation studies show that UBII recipients are always underrepresented in employment promotion measures such as vocational training, for example (Bundesagentur für Arbeit, 2010a). While this can partly be explained with differences in occupational backgrounds amongst the two claimant groups, since the beginning of 2009, UBII recipients have been formally excluded from traditional job-creation schemes within the UBI system. It should be noted though that even for UBI claimants these types of schemes have been significantly scaled down and play now a rather marginal role in German labour market policy as a whole.

In sum, it can be argued that the German unemployment protection system continues to be segmented. Nevertheless, its overall character has changed due to the amalgamation of the previous second and third tiers of support into an encompassing unemployment support scheme which is based on assistance principles and which is now dominant in terms of claimant numbers (see below). Based on a comparison between the previous UA with the current UBII scheme, it might be argued that the division between claimants of insurance benefits on the one hand and recipients of means-tested assistance benefits on the other has been reinforced. However, the creation of UBII has also narrowed the previously entrenched division between former SA claimants and other unemployed groups (Clasen and Goerne, 2011). Thus, from a broader perspective, the introduction of UBII can be interpreted as an incidence of benefit homogenization for persons outside UI, as well as an example of risk re-categorization, as will be discussed in the following section.

4.4 RISK RE-CATEGORIZATION, ACTIVATION, AND A SELECTIVE DEPARTURE FROM THE 'MALE BREADWINNER MODEL'

Reforms of the German unemployment protection system correspond with changes envisaged by the analytical concept of 'triple integration' as outlined in the introductory chapter of this book. In the following, I argue that reforms since the late 1990s have led to a form of 'partial integration', analysing why some but not other dimensions have been integrated.

The changes introduced in German unemployment protection after 2005 have been characterized as indications of a trend from 'Bismarck to Beveridge' (Eichhorst et al., 2008: 25). However, such an interpretation ignores that the established principle of status (and income) maintenance established within Germany as a conservative or Bismarckian welfare state was generally maintained, albeit for a minority of the unemployed. The move towards integration in the German case therefore refers to a continuation of a structural divide of social rights with respect to activation and benefit provision between those in receipt of UI on the one hand and those on means-tested benefits on the other (Dingeldey, 2007, 2010a). As discussed, the merger between former UA and SA, as well as the numerical dominance of UBII claimants, can be seen as a form of homogenization of unemployment protection as a whole. This does not imply a breaking down of the boundary between insurance and assistance which remains marked. For example, between December 2008 and November 2009 only about 11 per cent of former UBI recipients transferred to the UBII system, indicating that a vast majority of the insurance claimants found employment within a year – or did not pass the means test for UBII because of other sources of household income. In contrast, about 40 per cent of UBII recipients were still on benefit after one year (Bundesagentur für Arbeit, 2010b).

Due to economic growth and more restrictive eligibility criteria introduced in 2005, the number of insurance benefit recipients declined considerably

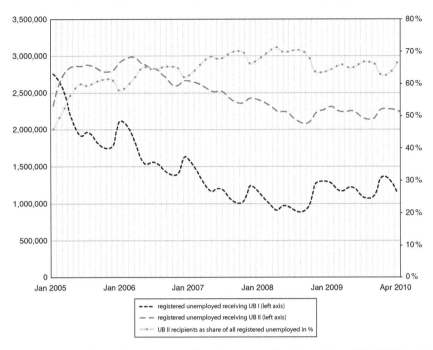

Figure 4.1. Number of persons considered as unemployed receiving UBI, UBII, and unemployed UBII recipients as share of all registered unemployed in Germany

Source: Statistik der Bundesagentur für Arbeit (2010): Arbeitslosigkeit im Zeitverlauf; http://www.pub. arbeitsagentur.de/hst/services/statistik/detail/z.html; downloaded 30 May 2010; Own design.

(see Figure 4.1), notwithstanding a slight rise since 2009 in the wake of the economic crisis. Of all unemployed persons in 2010, around two-thirds received UBII. The dominance of UBII is partly a consequence of administrative re-categorizations brought about by the new system (see Clasen and Goerne, 2011). While many of the former jobless SA claimants were not registered as unemployed, in the wake of the Hartz reforms, 90 per cent of previous SA claimants were classified as fit for work and thus transferred to UBII (Konle-Seidl et al., 2007: 43). Within UBII, unemployment became more broadly defined since it covers all persons 'capable to work', that is, able to engage in paid work for at least three hours daily, and do not have to care for a child younger than three years of age.[7] Moreover, not only people with severe health problems and many lone parents but also the (female) partners of the (long-term) unemployed are now administratively treated as being part of a wider pool of unemployed people. Similar to countries such as the United Kingdom (see Chapter 2), non-working members of the respective claimant households who are deemed to be 'capable to work' may be registered as unemployed and thus are in principle subject to activation.

---

[7] The definition excludes those in full-time education or in employment promotion measures.

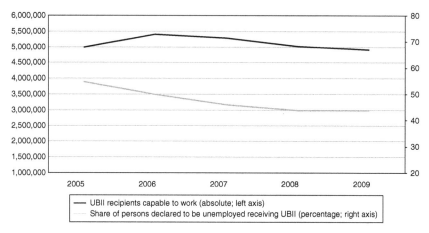

Figure 4.2. All persons considered 'capable to work' receiving UBII and share of UBII recipients who are unemployed in Germany (annual average)

Source: Statistik der Bundesagentur für Arbeit: Arbeitslosigkeit im Zeitverlauf; April 2010; http://www.pub. arbeitsagentur.de/hst/services/statistik/detail/z.html; downloaded 30 May 2010.

On the other hand, the total number of UBII recipients does not only cover those who are unemployed, in a narrow sense, but many others. In fact the total number of UBII recipients in January 2010 (about 5 million persons; see Figure 4.2) included only a minority who were registered as unemployed (44 per cent in 2010). The remainder consisted of parents with children younger than three and other persons (looking after relatives) who are 'able to work' but temporarily not available for labour market integration, representing about one-third of all UBII claimants in September 2009. Other recipients not counted as unemployed were participants in employment programmes and those older than 58, which means that they did not have to be available for the labour market. Finally, a considerable number of UBII recipients have jobs for more than 15 hours per week, and thus are not counted as unemployed, but whose earnings are at a level which is compatible with eligibility conditions (see Figure 4.3). Thus, the introduction of UBII not only widened the risk category of unemployment but also blurred the boundary between unemployment transfers and an in-work-benefit receipt.

While the merger of the former UA and SA increased the number of persons in receipt of unemployment benefit, adverse demographic trends, as well as the heavy financial burden of early retirement programmes, led to a gradual with-drawal of programmes which enabled labour market exit for older workers (see Figure 4.4). For example, the option of occupational incapacity pension was abolished in 2000 and replaced by a less generous disability pension. As a consequence the share of persons entering the public pension system through the pathway of disability transfers has declined from 25.6 per cent in 1995 to 18.6 per cent in 2008 (Deutscher Rentenversicherungsbund, 2009: 51).

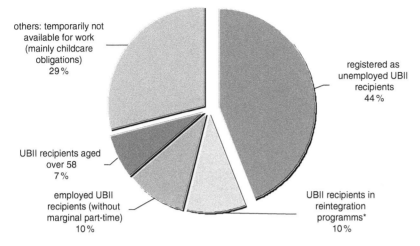

Figure 4.3. Structure of persons considered 'capable to work' and receiving UBII in Germany (January 2010)

Notes: *This includes people in activation programmes not receiving a proper salary.
Source: Statistik der Bundesagentur für Arbeit (2010): Grundsicherung für Arbeitssuchende in Zahlen; http://www.pub.arbeitsamt.de/hst/services/statistik/detail/l.html; downloaded 4 June 2010.

Other early retirement programmes, most notably those based on regulations linked to unemployment or part-time employment,[8] were terminated and finally became less relevant after 2005. This included the end of the so-called *58-regulation* in 2007 (Brussig and Knuth, 2006). The respective share of persons entering retirement pensions via these particular routes (as part of all pensioners) declined to 11.1 per cent in 2008 (Deutscher Rentenversicherungsbund, 2009: 51).

The separation between insurance- and assistance-based unemployment protection has not altered the funding structure for UBI and thus FEO's reluctance to finance employment promotion measures for potentially long-term unemployed. With the introduction of UBII, the government ruled that the FEO was not only responsible to fund employment promotion measures but will also have to pay a further penalty (*Aussteuerungsbetrag*) in case clients were transferred to UBII (Konle-Seidl et al., 2007: 42). Since this proved fairly ineffective as a way to foster employment promotion for those categorized as 'hard to place', the regulation was subsequently changed and the FEO made to finance 50 per cent of all costs of labour market integration for all recipients of UBII (*Eingliederungsbeitrag*) (Steffen, 2009).

---

[8] A part-time employment regulation 'prior to old-age pensions' was introduced in 1996 and regulated within the employment promotion framework. It was supported by collective agreements or single plan bargaining agreements. Originally it was supposed to open up an opportunity to employees older than 55 years of age to gradually reduce their working time (of more than 50 per cent) before full retirement. The rationale for this partial reduction in labour supply was to open up work opportunities for (younger) unemployed or trainees. In reality, the instrument was used as yet another option of early (full) retirement as the majority of those who entered the programme opted for the so-called block version of working-time reduction, that is, full retirement after half of the programme period instead of a combination of work and partial retirement throughout the respective period.

Regulating the risk of unemployment

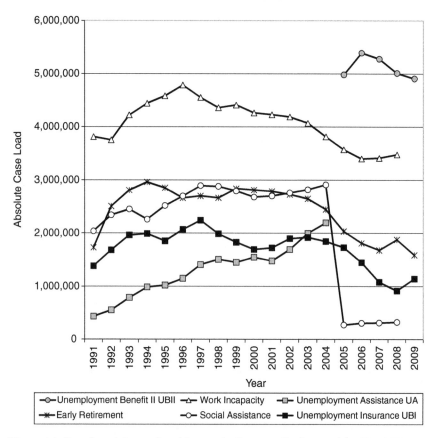

Figure 4.4. Benefit recipients of working age in Germany (in thousands), 1991–2009

Source: see Caseload Annex (Germany).

Within that two-tier-system of unemployment protection, the link between active and passive support has become closer. However, as the insurance-based social security system does not cover long-term unemployed adequately, the introduction of a homogenized UBII was supposed to enhance the employability for the respective claimants groups. In contrast to the previous SA system, UBII – at least in theory – provides access to activation measures and promotes employability also for groups with no prior employment record. This was supposed to help over all lone parents, respectively mothers, and households without earners.

As discussed, work requirements for UBII recipients have been made stricter than for UBI recipients and the refusal of any job offer may be sanctioned more harshly. At the same time, implementation analyses shows that there is still a divide within German labour market policy in the sense that equal access for UBII recipients to employment promotion measures that are offered to UBI claimants has not been achieved. UBII recipients, and among them especially women (IAQ et al., 2009), are underrepresented particularly in employment promotion measures which lead to qualifications and/or promise a sustainable (re-)integration into the first labour market (Dingeldey, 2010*a*; 2010*b*).

Furthermore, the development towards what might be called a more post-industrial labour market in Germany, as well as labour market policy, is closely connected to a selective or partial movement away from the 'male breadwinner model' (Betzelt, 2007; Knuth, 2006*b*). Within UBI, more generous replacement rates continue to be paid to claimants with children while their non-working spouses are not obliged to seek for work. In contrast, within UBII, parents (and especially single mothers) with children older than three are now treated as employable, thereby indicating a departure of a traditional notion within the German welfare system of freeing mothers from the duty to work in order to be able to care for their children. Hence, the enforcement of the 'individual adult worker model' is restricted to only those unemployed households who are in receipt of UBII.

4.5 MAKING SENSE OF THE REFORM TRAJECTORY AND RESPONSES TO THE FINANCIAL CRISIS

The development of unemployment insurance, rather than unemployment protection as a whole, is an example of the institutional continuity in German social policy. One of the reasons for this stability lies in the particular characteristics of the conservative welfare state. The insurance-based system creates individualized social rights to earnings-related benefits, which may be seen as a major obstacle to deep benefit cuts (Clegg, 2007; Palier and Martin, 2008*a*) and an impediment which goes beyond the degree of homogenization of UI described earlier. In other words, turning earnings-related UI into a (quasi) flat-rate insurance model as in Denmark (see Chapter 10 in this volume) or encompassing means-tested benefit system as in the United Kingdom (see Chapter 2 in this volume) would be politically unfeasible. The traditionalist wings both within the Social Democratic and the Christian Democratic parties as well as within the trade union movement can still to be considered as strong defenders of the interests of the core workforce, including status-oriented benefits. Hence, there has never been a 'will to reform' (Cox, 2001) aimed at abolishing the generosity of the German UI particularly for claimants with average and better-than-average former earnings.

However, as discussed, due to the merger of UA and SA there has been a strong trend towards homogenization outside UI, and by implication within German unemployment protection as a whole considering the dominance of UBII amongst jobless benefit claimants. It seems that there were several factors which help to explain this structural change. One aspect was certainly fiscal pressure. When in 2003 the 'modernizers' within the Social Democratic-led government announced the Agenda 2010 suggesting the merger of UA and SA (Schröder, 2003), they reacted to growing problem pressures due to rising unemployment and an increasing budget deficit. A second might be the search to find a response to the growing scale of what are called 'new social risks' in post-industrial societies (Bonoli, 2007) caused by the ongoing flexibilization of the labour market and changes in family composition, namely the increasing number of lone parents (see also Bonoli, 2007; Pierson, 2001*b*). In other words, a broadening of the administrative risk category of unemployment with the creation of UBII as a 'single working-age benefit' may be seen as an answer to this development. Third, the idea of creating a single-benefit system for the long-term unemployed was neither new nor entirely due to the Social Democratic government. Instead, in some respects, the proposal to merge different unemployment benefit regimes under the administrative roof of the FEO was a response to a demand made by the Christian Democrats in prior election manifestos (CDU/CSU, 2002/2006) as well as by many social policy advisers (Schmid et al., 1987) who pointed to inefficiencies due to administrative fragmentation.

The successful introduction of UBII therefore was achieved on the basis of a cross-party consensus (Schlieben, 2007) within major parts of the political elites (Hartung, 2003) – and interpreted as a break of the legendary German reform blockage (Heinze, 1998; Trampusch, 2003). The design of the newly created benefit and its level which was oriented at the SA scheme and therefore introduced cuts for many long-term unemployed, however, caused widespread public protest against the Agenda 2010 which was particularly strong in eastern Germany where unemployment is still higher than in the West. The fact that this opposition remained ineffective may be explained by organizational theory (Olson, 1976), which assumes that within a majoritarian political system a cross-party compromise is easily to be achieved when the costs can be passed on to 'third parties' whose interests are weakly organized.

In terms of the administration of the new UBII system the government's aim of (full) integration was not achieved, however, and the creation of different regional options of benefit and service delivery might be illustrative of an only partially successful reform. The reasons for this include diverging interests within a federal political system, multilevel decision-making structures, and a division of responsibilities between the federal state, the *Länder*, and municipalities (Brussig and Knuth, 2009). As the Christian Democratic parties had the majority in the second chamber at the time when the red–green government proposed the introduction of UBII, it was able to influence the policy output during the policymaking process (Egle, 2006; Poguntke, 2006). Within these negotiations the objective of making the FEO responsible for administering UBI and UBII and establishing Job Centres as one-stop shops for all the unemployed proved impossible to put into practice (Konle-Seidl et al., 2007). Such a reform would have meant removing the responsibility for SA recipients from the municipalities. This was resisted particularly by conservative *Länder* governments interested in keeping municipalities in charge of administering transfer payments and labour market policies for former SA recipients. The outcome of this political deadlock was a muddled political compromise (Knuth, 2006a: 19; Siefken, 2007), that is, the creation of one (dominant) institutional model in which local FEO offices and municipalities work together in a new structure responsible for UBII claimants, as well as allowing municipalities the option of administering UBII on their own.

The general election in 2009 brought about a conservative–liberal coalition government, which had to contest the interventions of the federal constitutional court, which is a rather powerful veto-player within the German political system (Schmidt, 2007: 190). In 2007 the court had declared the new administrative structure as unconstitutional since it did not respect municipal autonomy (Bundesverfassungsgericht, 2007). The resulting threat of having to pass yet another reform by the end of 2010, however, was successfully challenged by cross-party compromise which introduced a partial change of the constitution which allowed the established institutional framework to be maintained (Bundesagentur für Arbeit und Soziales, 2010).

In the wake of the financial crisis at the end of 2008 initially, minor reforms were enacted mainly aimed at a reorganization of employment promotion measures. More prominently the instrument of 'short-time working benefit' (*Kurzarbeit*) was extended (Bundesagentur für Arbeit, 2009*b*). Aimed at avoiding redundancies, this programme makes use of public transfer payments which compensate for the loss of earnings resulting from temporary reductions in working hours. However, while this contributed to the stabilization of general employment successfully, it did not stop unemployment to rise steeply for agency workers (Adamy, 2010), thereby confirming the traditional emphasis on protecting income streams for the core workforce. Most recently, the government announced an austerity package in June 2010, which included restrictions, such as replacing rights to participate in activation programmes with discretionary decision-making or the abolition of benefit supplements. It also entailed cutbacks such as pension contributions, heating cost additions, or temporary support for those transferring from UBI to UBII (Bundesregierung, 2010). As a whole these retrenchments affect particularly long-term unemployed benefit claimants and are likely to affect those who switch between low wage and flexible forms of employment and periods of time out of work and claiming UBII (Hirseland and Ramos Lobato, 2010).

4.6 CONCLUSION

The above analysis confirms that Conservative or Bismarckian welfare states are certainly not reluctant to reform. On the contrary, particularly within the past decade, some countries have introduced far-reaching changes in their social policy landscape. Labour market policy in Germany is a case in point. While maintaining a degree of continuity, especially in the insurance-based domain, this chapter has demonstrated that unemployment protection as a whole looks very different today compared with the early 1990s, which is largely due to major institutional restructuring for those outside the realm of contributory-based benefit and service provision. Of course, German unemployment protection as a whole remains divided. While there has been retrenchment both within UI and UA, differences between the two domains have not disappeared in terms of the nature of social rights, benefit generosity, and access to, and type of, labour market programmes.

This chapter has not been concerned with the debate whether recent reforms have brought about more dualism, or segmentation, within German labour market policy (Dingeldey, 2010*b*; Palier and Thelen, 2010) or less (Clasen and Goerne, 2011). Instead, in line with the analytical interest of this book, it has investigated instances of integration and identified instances of such in all three dimensions. In essence, it showed that an erstwhile fragmented support structure along three institutional, administrative, and financial lines has been replaced by a two-tier system. The replacement of earnings-related with flat-rate benefits within the new UBII scheme can be regarded as complete homogenization for all assistance claimants, notwithstanding its incomplete homogenization in delivery structures. In addition, while maintaining two separate systems, unemployment protection as a whole is now more homogenized than before simply due to the dominance of UBII as a form of benefit for workless people in Germany today. The new tax-based UBII system, however, is also an indicator of risk re-categorization. While broadening the notion of unemployment, it has been designed more widely for what are now referred to as jobseekers, which are all those deemed to be 'capable to work'. Moreover, in line with other countries covered in this volume (such as France and, prospectively, the United Kingdom), it has blurred the boundary between out-of-work and in-work benefits since UBII can also function as a wage subsidy. It is the latter role in particular which connects recent welfare reforms as having contributed to the casualization of employment relationships and a more pronounced segmentation within the German labour market in recent years (Dingeldey, 2010*a*; 2010*b*).

Finally, as in other countries and compared with the early 1990s there is now a much closer link between benefit receipt and job-search requirements and other activation conditions for both insurance and assistance benefit claimants. In addition, there has been a shift away from (lengthy) training programmes towards more short-term 'work first' oriented programmes within the landscape of German active labour market schemes in general, although differences remain in the nature of activation options more readily offered to insurance benefit claimants on the one hand and those typically directed to assistance benefit recipients.

Appendix 4.A Major legislative changes in unemployment protection in Germany, 1982–2010

Year	Measure
1982	Increase in minimum contributory period for unemployment insurance benefit (UB) from 6 to 12 months; and for unemployment assistance (UA) (from 70 to 150 days).
1984	For recipients without children: decrease in UB rate (−5% points to 63%) and UA rate (−2% points to 56%);
1985–7	Stepwise increases in UB entitlement for older worker (older than 42); max 32 months for those older than 53, dependent on individual contribution record.
1994	Decrease in UB and UA rates by 1% point (3% points for those without children). Entitlement to UA limited to one year for those without prior receipt of UB (indefinite before).
1996	Decrease in benefit rate for UA claimants by 3% points per year of claim. Stricter work test imposed on UA recipients (from 1998 also for UB claimants); employment office can request temporary participation in low-paid seasonal jobs.
1998	New suitability criteria (previous qualification no longer relevant; suitability of job offers defined merely in monetary terms; after six months: any job is deemed suitable with net earnings higher than benefit). Proof of active job search required; stricter benefit sanctions. Longer UB durations restricted to over-45-year-olds; max of 32 months only for 57-year-olds. Participation in approved training no longer recognized as equivalent to insured employment (i.e. does no longer establish benefit eligibility).
1998	Introduction of 'reintegration contract' stating responsibilities of jobseeker and employment office. Improved entitlement for claimants who accept less well-paid jobs (and then become unemployed within 3 years) and for those who lose part-time jobs.
2000–2	UA (for those without prior receipt of UB) abolished. Stronger activation focus as part of Job-Aqtiv legislation (job placement, profiling, job-search vouchers, temporary work options, job rotation, training).
2003	Tighter suitability criteria for younger unemployed; new job placement and counselling instruments; new options for business start-ups; temporary work placements.
2004–5	UB (now UBI) duration fixed at standard max. 12 months (from 2006). Extended entitlement to UBI curtailed to max. 18 months – and restricted to claimants aged 55 or older; reference period for required contributions shortened from 3 to 2 years prior to unemployment. Subsidized employment no longer acceptable as benefit qualification period. UA and social assistance (for employable claimants) to merge into a single scheme (UBII). Tighter job suitability criteria for UBII recipients (any legal work and wage level suitable even if below collective wage agreement or standard wages paid in locality). Young unemployed (under 25) only eligible for UBII if they accept offers of training, suitable employment, or other job integration measures.
2006	Enforcement of stricter sanctions in case of non-acceptance of employment offers. Extension of '58-regulation' until 2007 (UBII entitlement without activation requirement for those older than 58).
2008	Increase in UB entitlement for unemployed older than 50 (15–24 months dependent on age and individual contribution record). FEO to finance 50% of all costs of labour market integration for all recipients of UBII (Eingliederungsbeitrag).

2009	Reconfiguration of employment promotion measures (e.g. individual recruitment budgets; curtailment of further training; end of employment promotion measures liable to social security for UBII recipients; extension of sanctions).
	Temporal prolongation of 'short-time compensation' (payable up to 24 months) until end of December 2009; (18 months) until end of December 2010.
2010	End-of-benefit supplement for those passing from UBI to UBII.
	Consolidation of Job Centre reform.

Source: Information derived from Clasen (2005) and Steffen (2009).

5

The Netherlands: two tiers for all

Marcel Hoogenboom

5.1 INTRODUCTION

The unemployment provision system in the Netherlands has been recognized since the 1960s as one of the most comprehensive and generous systems in the world. In the 1970s and 1980s, however, it also became known for its inability to combat benefit dependency and reintegrate benefit recipients into the labour market. In order to improve the reintegration capacities of the system, major reforms have been implemented in the past three decades by various coalition cabinets. Reforms started in the mid-1980s, making the Netherlands one of the forerunners in the process of adaptation of unemployment provision systems to post-industrial conditions. The 'System Revision' of 1987, which is discussed in Section 5.2, only affected the regulations of the unemployment provision schemes, while the reforms of the 1990s turned the administrative organization of unemployment insurance upside-down. In the 2000s, the revision of the administrative organization discussed cleared the path for a partial integration of the administration of unemployment insurance and social assistance, and for the expansion of activation policies.

This chapter claims that the reforms in Dutch unemployment provision of the past three decades amount to a levelling of rights and statuses *within* a still two-tier unemployment provision system. On the one hand, unemployment insurance, which until the mid-1980s was only open to some categories of employees and in that respect was a typically Bismarckian employees' insurance, has been opened up for the large majority of the dependent labour force. On the other hand, since regulations of unemployment insurance have been tightened and benefits duration limited, the risk of dependence on flat-rate and means-tested social assistance has become a reality for the large majority of Dutch employees too. Hence, while the unemployment provision system has remained multi-tier and the benefit levels largely untouched – and in this respect both the formal and actual homogenization of benefit programmes has been limited – a levelling of rights and statuses has taken place. The result is a system that combines Bismarckian and Beveridgian features, and is now composed of a relatively short-term, wage-replacing insurance and a flat-rate social assistance scheme that is open to nearly all employees, increasingly funded through taxation rather than contributions, and run almost exclusively by state institutions.

The relative ease with which the transformation of the Dutch unemployment provision system in the late 1990s and early 2000s was accomplished is striking. I argue here that this can be explained by the rapid loss of legitimacy of the Dutch social partners (especially the labour unions) in the 1990s and a more general process of levelling of statuses in Dutch society in the past three decades.

5.2 THE FIRST WAVE OF RESTRUCTURING: THE SYSTEM REVISION (1980s)

In the late 1970s and early 1980s, the Netherlands, like many other Western European countries, witnessed the rapid collapse of 'traditional' industries like textiles, clothing, and shipbuilding, causing unemployment figures to rise to levels reminiscent of the 1930s Great Depression (Van Zanden, 1997). However, until 1982, the three major political parties in the Dutch political system, generally forced to form cabinet coalitions, were seriously divided on how to combat the economic crisis. The social democrats of the Labour Party (*Partij van de Arbeid*, PvdA) opted for a 'traditional' Keynesian approach of subsidizing ailing industries and stimulating citizens' purchasing power and the Conservative–Liberal VVD (*Volkspartij voor Vrijheid en Democratie*) for a liberalization of the economy and the labour market, while the Christian Democrats (*Christen Democratisch Appèl*, CDA) were unable to choose between either strategy. In 1982, the stalemate was broken when a new Christian Democrat leader, Ruud Lubbers, formed a majority coalition cabinet with the Conservative Liberals, at the same time succeeding in silencing the left wing of his party, which until then had blocked attempts to reorganize welfare state arrangements. Lubbers would stay in office as prime minister until 1994, in 1982–9 in a coalition cabinet with the VVD and between 1989 and 1994 in a coalition with the PvdA.

The domestic policies of the Lubbers governments were almost completely aimed at reducing government spending (Rigter et al., 1995). A vital part of this was a drastic reorganization of Dutch unemployment provision – the so-called 'System Revision' (1987). The first significant revision of the unemployment provision system in more than two decades, it signified a breakthrough of the stalemate surrounding the Dutch welfare state, and more generally socio-economic policy, which had paralysed Dutch politics since the middle of the 1970s.

Until 1987 the Dutch unemployment provision system was composed of three tiers. At the centre of the system was the unemployment insurance scheme WW, a compulsory insurance scheme for employees established in 1949. The WW was a typically Bismarckian employees' insurance, financed from premiums paid by employers and employees and administered by industrial insurance agencies run by the social partners (see below), which in the mid-1980s covered around 45 per cent of the Dutch working-age population (see Figure 5.5). Unemployed workers were granted under certain conditions a benefit of 80 per cent (70 per cent as of 1985) of their daily pay for a maximum of six months. After the benefit period expired, WW recipients and most other unemployed who were ineligible for the WW for lack of a substantial labour history could claim unemployment assistance

(WWV). The WWV, which was established in 1964 and was administered by the municipalities, guaranteed a non-means-tested benefit of 75 per cent (70 per cent as of 1985) of their daily pay for a period of up to two years, financed out of general taxes. Unemployed persons who still had not found a new position after almost two and a half years were entitled to means-tested RWW, a second unemployment assistance scheme financed from general taxation and distributed by the municipalities, at minimum level (for details see Table 5.1).

Throughout the 1970s and early 1980s, dissatisfaction with the unemployment provision system had been growing among the political and civil service establishment. According to politicians from the VVD and CDA, WWV in particular was too generous, and it was claimed that municipalities were not doing enough to encourage recipients to find new jobs. Most political parties also agreed that in the course of time the WW had transformed into an insiders' scheme that was not easily accessible for the growing number of young and female workers, especially in the rapidly upcoming Dutch services sectors. Finally, and probably most importantly, discontent with the functioning of the industrial insurance agencies (*bedrijfsverenigingen*, IIAs), run by the social partners, was spreading rapidly. Not only was it thought that the IIAs were doing little to reintegrate WW recipients into the labour market but it was also an open secret that they were utilizing the disability benefits act, the WAO (see below) – which was also administered by the IIAs and which guaranteed recipients a 70 per cent benefit for an unlimited period of time – to alleviate the consequences of the industrial restructuring (Bannink, 2004; Rigter et al., 1995). By the mid-1980s almost 7 per cent of the Dutch working-age population were receiving a disability benefit.

The 1987 System Revision was the first step towards tackling these problems. By scrapping the WWV and integrating its clientele into the WW, the responsibility for all short-term unemployed was concentrated in the hands of the IIAs. At the same time, qualifying conditions for WW were drastically altered. Rather than linking eligibility to the number of years a person had been working in a certain branch of industry, as in the old scheme, in the new system WW eligibility was linked to the person's general labour history, opening unemployment insurance to a growing number of employees who frequently switched branches or worked part-time. The position of women was also improved by counting some forms of childcare as labour history. Formal job-seeking obligations for recipients were toughened considerably, though an exception was made for employees aged 57.5 years or older (for more details see Table 5.1). As a result, in the following fifteen years unemployment insurance would remain a route to labour shedding for senior employees until this path was finally closed in 2004 (see Section 5.4).

The reform seriously reduced government expenditure for unemployment provision, since about 200,000 recipients of WWV, which used to be paid for from general tax revenues, were gradually transferred to unemployment insurance (WW), financed by contributions from employers and employees. The restructuring of the system also signified a first move away from a policy of labour shedding via unemployment assistance and disability benefits to which labour unions, employers' associations, and to a certain extent the political establishment had tacitly agreed since the early 1970s.

Yet this break with the past was not part of a broader policy of deregulation, as in the United Kingdom and the United States in the same period, but was instead an instrument of what might be called 'protected flexibilization'.[1] The protective shield of the unemployment arrangements was not lowered but altered and extended to categories of employees who had not or only partly been covered previously. Behind this combination of a flexibilization of rights with continued protection was the 'Wassenaar Agreement', signed in the early 1980s between the government, national labour unions, and employers' associations, in which the labour unions promised to accept a programme of wage restraint in exchange for a structural reduction in working hours and job-sharing in all Dutch businesses. This new policy, however, also required an opening-up of Bismarckian unemployment insurance to guarantee the protection of newcomers to the labour market. The System Revision substantially improved the position of the growing number of temporary, flexible, and part-time workers in the tertiary sector (Teulings et al., 1997; Van der Veen and Trommel, 1999), and to a certain extent granted them the same social rights as industrial workers, who in the event of unemployment were increasingly expected to find new jobs. Under the new WW scheme, all benefit recipients were thus legally forced to cooperate in 'employability' assessment and improvement via schooling and training. Furthermore, recipients were obliged to accept 'suitable work', the definition of which was changed to include employment in other economic branches and, after further reforms in subsequent years, employment below one's formal qualifications and previous salary (Van der Veen and Trommel, 1999). Finally, in 1987, the 'secret' legal route from unemployment to disability was barred through abolition of the regulation within the disability benefit act, which in the past had enabled hundreds of thousands of unemployed industrial workers to receive a disability benefit for the rest of their lives (see above, Teulings et al., 1997).

The big problem was that the System Revision left the administrative structure of unemployment and disability insurance largely untouched. Partly due to the reluctance in government circles to antagonize labour unions in a period in which their support for wage restraint was vital for the recovery of the Dutch economy, the social partners' position in the industrial insurances agencies was hardly brought up for discussion (Bannink, 2004). As a consequence, the new policy of protected flexibilization was now put in the hands of the same actors that in the past two decades had proved incapable of developing policies aimed at the reintegration of unemployed and disabled workers. Although in the late 1980s the social partners in the IIAs made great efforts to devise new strategies to improve the agencies' reintegration capabilities (Van der Burgt, 2004), in the early 1990s their (alleged) failure to really 'activate' their clientele resulted in a political backlash against the agencies and, by the end of the decade, their eventual dismantlement (see Section 5.3).

One of the main causes of the inability of the IIAs to adapt to new circumstances was their rootedness in an economic structure that was gradually disappearing. The administrative structure of employees' insurances was created in the late 1940s,

---

[1] Referring to the paradoxical nature of the reforms – the 'liberalization' of social security under the strict supervision of the state – Van der Veen and Trommel (1999: 289) characterize the reforms of this period as 'managed liberalization'. Yet, the authors also signal that the 'process of managed liberalization [took] place under an umbrella of lasting universal social protection'. Therefore, I prefer using the term 'protected flexibilization'.

when about 60 per cent of the Dutch labour force was working in the primary or secondary sector. Consequently, more than half of the twenty-six IIAs – which to a large extent were authorized to set their own regulations – administered the WW for an industrial sector, and combined these IIAs commanded a majority in largely private institutions like the Federation of IIAs and the GAK,[2] entrusted with the coordination of the policies of all IIAs (AWF, 1952–86; Van der Burgt, 2004). By the late 1980s the economic landscape had substantially changed though. Industries like textiles, clothing, and shipbuilding had almost completely disappeared, while upcoming economic branches like banking and insurance, transport, and retail trade were hiring rapidly growing numbers of employees (Van Zanden, 1997). Hence, while in 1956 almost half of the workforce covered by unemployment insurance was employed in one of the industrial branches and just about one-third in the tertiary service sector, thirty years later the ratios had reversed. In 1990, only 27 per cent were employed in industrial branches, compared with 47 per cent in the private sector and 17 per cent in public and semi-public services (schools, hospitals, etc.) (see Statistical Annex, Tables A.1 and A.2). Unlike in industry, where full-time jobs were still standard, in these branches part-time and flexible jobs – many taken by women (CBS, 2009*b*) – were growing rapidly (AWF, 1956, 1990).

5.3 THE SECOND WAVE OF RESTRUCTURING: THE PARTIAL INTEGRATION OF UNEMPLOYMENT INSURANCE AND SOCIAL ASSISTANCE (1990s and 2000s)

5.3.1 The unemployment provision system in the early 1990s

As a result of the 1987 System Revision, the Dutch unemployment protection system had gone from a three-tier into a two-tier system. Now that non-means-tested WWV had been formally abolished, WW and the means-tested unemployment assistance scheme (RWW) together had become the backbone of the system. In order to alleviate the financial consequences of the abolition of WWV for recipients who were transferred to the other schemes, WW regulations had been altered in such a way as to also include in unemployment insurance workers who would not have been eligible under the old scheme. Thus, instead of requiring unemployed persons to have been employed for at least thirteen weeks in the previous year,[3] in the new

[2] In the period 1952–2002, the GAK (Joint Administration Office, *Gemeenschappelijk Administratiekantoor*) was entrusted with the daily administration of unemployment insurance (WW), disability insurance (WAO), sickness insurance (ZW), and several other branch insurances of about half of the IIAs (Van der Burgt, 2004).

[3] For the sake of clarity, in the text the requirements of the old WW have been somewhat simplified. The old WW was composed of two parts, a 'redundancy payment scheme' and an 'unemployment scheme'. The redundancy payment scheme was meant for those employees who were considered to be part of the labour reserve of a specific branch of industry and had been employed in the branch for at least 156 days in the last twelve months. The unemployment scheme was aimed at those employees *not* considered to be part of this labour reserve or whose redundancy payment had expired, and who had been employed for at least seventy-eight days in the last twelve months.

WW a complex system of weeks' and years' requirements was introduced to determine the maximum benefit duration for each recipient. Those unemployed who had been employed in the past year for at least twenty-six weeks were granted a 'loss of wages' benefit that replaced 70 per cent of their daily pay for a period of six months. Subsequently, persons who had been employed for at least three years in the past five could claim a prolongation of the benefit at the same rate for a maximum of 4.5 years, the duration depending on the total labour history (for more details see Table 5.1). For claimants 57.5 or older, a special follow-up benefit was also introduced which guaranteed a non-means-tested income at the minimum level for maximally 3.5 years.

Since it was thought that the changes in eligibility rules would not compensate all categories of employees for the reforms of the System Revision, two additional schemes were introduced. To compensate for the closure of the 'secret' legal route from unemployment to disability, a new scheme was introduced for senior employees who were unemployed and partly disabled but did not qualify for a WAO benefit, the Income Act for Elderly and Partially Disabled Unemployed Employees (*Wet inkomensvoorziening oudere en gedeeltelijk arbeidsongeschikte werkloze werknemers*, IOAW). In addition, to prevent WW recipients (and recipients of other employees' insurances, like the WAO and the Sickness Insurance Act) from receiving a benefit that was lower than the legal 'social minimum', the Social Security Supplements Act (*Toeslagenwet*, TW) was also introduced.

After the WW benefit period expired, an unemployed person could claim RWW for an indefinite period at the municipal social services department. Introduced in 1964, the RWW was formally part of the General Social Assistance Scheme (*Algemene Bijstandswet*, ABW) that was financed from general taxation, guaranteeing all Dutch citizens a minimum income in cases of need (Van der Valk, 1986). Within the administrative system of the ABW, unemployed claimants were, however, treated separately. Under certain conditions they could claim a benefit that was slightly higher than the legally set national ABW benefit. Unlike other social assistance claimants, who dealt with the municipal social services departments directly, in many municipalities RWW benefit applications were referred to a special Advisory Committee composed of representatives of the municipality, the local job centre, the Ministry of Social Affairs, and the national labour unions, who could block negative decisions. Though there is no reliable research on the functioning of these committees, they were known for their leniency towards the RWW claimants.

As part of the System Revision in the late 1980s, the formal activation requirements for RWW were considerably tightened. Whereas these had been rather vague and could easily be circumvented by both municipalities and recipients, after 1987 municipalities were put under considerable pressure by the national government. They were now required to report on their reintegration policies annually and to define obligations for RWW and ABW recipients more explicitly. As a result, municipal social services had to push recipients more actively than before to apply for jobs, to accept 'suitable employment', and to cooperate in

Table 5.1. Major features of unemployment insurance (WW) in the early 1990s and in 2010, and of unemployment assistance (RWW, early 1990s) and social assistance (WWB, in 2010)

	1990	2010
Unemployment insurance		
Legislation	(New) Unemployment Insurance Act (Nieuwe) Werkloosheidswet, WW, 1987)[a]	Idem.
Type	Employees' insurance	Idem.
Membership	Compulsory for all employees, with the exception of civil servants, military personnel, teachers, and personnel of semi-public agencies (e.g. schools, hospitals)	As of 2001, civil servants, teaching personnel, military personnel, and employees of semi-public agencies included[b]
Qualifying condition	Involuntary unemployment	Involuntary unemployment
	'Loss-of-wages' benefit and 'follow-up' benefit: • Eligibility requirement ('weeks' requirement'): having been employed for 26 weeks in past 52 weeks • Labour history requirement ('years' requirement'): having been employed for at least three years (for at least 8 hours per week) in the past five years	*All benefits:* • Eligibility requirement ('weeks' requirement'): 26 weeks in the last 36 weeks[c] • Labour history requirement ('years' requirement'): having been employed for at least four years (at least 52 days per year)[d] in the past five years • No exception for those 57.5 or older
Funding	*Contributory:* 50% employee, 50% employer	50% employer, 50% state (possibly temporary, see text)
Benefit level	*Loss-of-wages benefit:* 70% of previous net earnings *Follow-up benefit:* 70% of legal minimum wage	*All benefits:* • First two months: 75% of previous net earnings • As of third month: 70% of previous net earnings Income above a certain limit is not insured[e]
Benefit duration	*Loss-of-wages benefit:* • Six months • One extra month for every year in employment, with a maximum of 38 months total benefit period • Maximum benefit duration: 5 years *Follow-up benefit:* age 57.5 or older: max. 3.5 years	*All benefits:* • Three months • One extra month for every year in employment • Maximum benefit duration: 38 months (no exceptions for persons aged 57.5–60; for persons aged 60 or older, see IOW)[f]
Obligations and rights	*Obligations:* 1. Being registered at the job centre 2. Applying for jobs 3. Accepting 'suitable employment'	*Obligations:* 1. Being registered at the job centre 2. Applying for jobs at least once a week 3. Accepting 'suitable employment' in the first six months; accepting 'generally accepted employment' thereafter 4. Cooperation in reintegration activities

(continued)

Table 5.1. (continued)

	1990	2010
	4. Cooperation in 'employability' assessment and improvement, via schooling and training	
	Persons aged 57.5 years or older are exempted from the obligations	*Rights*: 1. Reintegration contract between UWV and recipients: reintegration activities suited to personal qualities and conditions 2. Under certain conditions: financial support for starting a business, while temporarily being excluded from job-search requirements

Unemployment assistance (RWW, early 1990s), social assistance (WWB, in 2010)

	1990	2010
Legislation	Special Government Scheme for Unemployed Workers (*Rijksgroepsregeling Werkloze Werknemers*, RWW, 1964)[g]	Work and Income Benefit Act (*Wet werk en bijstand*, WWB, 2004)[h]
Type	Unemployment assistance	Social assistance
Membership	All citizens aged 18 years or older, and registered as job seeking	All citizens aged 18 years or older. For persons aged 18–27 particular conditionality applies (see below)
Qualifying condition	Involuntary unemployment	Idem. *Investment in Young Persons Act (Wet investeren in jongeren (WIJ), 2009)*:[i] • Persons aged 18–27 have to be offered schooling, internship, or job, or a combination by the municipality; refusal means termination of benefit • Exemption for people with disabilities • Lone parents with children aged five or younger only have to accept schooling or internship (not job) in order to maintain their capacities • Temporary exemption for those who want to start up a business
Funding	National government, national tax revenues	National government, national tax revenues, and municipalities 1. I-part ('income'): budget to finance benefits 2. W-part ('work'): budget to finance reintegration activities Municipalities receive earmarked budgets, which are fixed yearly by the national government. Municipalities are permitted to keep financial surpluses of the I-part (not of the W-part), but have to make up shortages in both budgets as they occur.
Benefit level	Nationally determined flat rate. Minimum level depending on (nuclear) family situation and age. Means-tested	Idem. Addition for those unemployed longer than 5 years

Benefit duration	In principle, indefinite	Idem.
Obligations and rights	*Obligations*:	*Obligations*:
	1. Being registered at the job centre	1. Being registered at the job centre
	2. Applying for jobs	2. Applying for jobs
	3. Accepting 'suitable employment'	3. Accepting 'generally accepted employment'
	4. Cooperation in 'employability' assessment and improvement, via schooling and training	4. Cooperation in reintegration activities
		Rights:
		1. Reintegration activities suited to personal qualities and conditions
		2. Under certain conditions: financial support for starting a business, while temporarily being exempted from job-search requirements

[a] *Staatsblad*, 1986, No. 566. Issued: 6 November 1986. Commencement: 1 January 1987.
[b] Assimilation of Civil Servants into Employees' Insurances Act (*Wet Overheidspersoneel onder Werknemersverzekeringen*, OOW), *Staatsblad*, 1997, No. 768.
[c] As of 1 July 2006. *Staatsblad*, 2006, No. 169.
[d] As of 1 March 1995. *Staatsblad*, 1994, No. 955.
[e] For 2010, the threshold was set by the Ministry of Social Affairs at €186.65 per day (www.szw.nl, 17 February 2010).
[f] As of 1 January 2004. *Staatsblad*, 2003, No. 546.
[g] *Staatsblad*, 1964, No. 553. The RWW was issued in 1964. Formally, the RWW was part of the National Assistance Act (*Algemene Bijstandswet*, ABW) issued in 1963. ABW: *Staatsblad*, 1963, No. 284. RWW was nullified in 1996.
[h] *Staatsblad*, 2003, No. 375.
[i] *Staatsblad*, 2009, No. 282. Regulations concerning lone parents and persons who want to start up a business: *Staatsblad*, 2009, No. 284.
Source: See text.

'employability' assessment and improvement via schooling and training (Engbersen, 1990; Van der Veen, 1990).

Despite the steady growth of the Dutch economy in the second half of the 1980s (see Statistical Annex, Table A.3), the changes in activation requirements did not, however, result in a significant drop in the number of unemployment benefit claimants (see Figure 5.1). These disappointing results encouraged the new Lubbers government (1989–94) to turn its attention to the job placement system and the local job centres, which since the late 1920s had been entirely in public hands. Since after the System Revision the IIAs had intensified their activation tasks, it was thought wise to couple these activities to the employment finding system by giving the social partners a say in the policies of local job centres. This is how, with the introduction in 1991 of a new Job Placement Act (*Arbeidsvoorzieningswet-1991*), the job centres and the Central Board of Job Placement, which coordinated local job placement policies, were 'tripartized'. This gave representatives of the national government, labour unions, and employers' associations an equal share in the boards of these institutions (Sol, 2000; Van Gestel et al., 2009). As a result, by the early 1990s the social partners had become jointly responsible for the success of all major parts of the activation policies in the Netherlands.

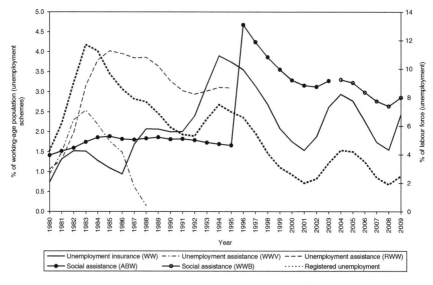

Figure 5.1. Unemployment provision schemes in the Netherlands: caseloads 1980–2009 (as % of working-age population) and registered unemployment (as % of labour force)

Source: See Caseload Annex (the Netherlands).

5.3.2 Transition: the reforms in the late 1990s and 2000s

The social partners were, however, not given the opportunity to prove that their new activation policies were yielding satisfactory results. A series of reports published around 1990 suggested that the number of disability benefit recipients was rising even more rapidly than in the early 1980s, despite the closure of the 'secret' legal route from unemployment to disability. Figures showed that in 1990 almost a million citizens (more than 11 per cent of the working-age population) were receiving a disability benefit, of whom it was assumed that a substantial – but unknown – share did not fulfil the formal disability eligibility standards (Teulings et al., 1997). In the 1980s, the growth of the total costs of disability benefits by far cancelled out the reductions that had been achieved in unemployment provision, partly as a result of the 1987 System Revision. While annual unemployment benefit expenditures had been reduced by more than 25 per cent between 1983 (the height of the economic crisis in the Netherlands) and 1990, the costs of disability benefit spending increased by the same percentage.[4] Consequently, the percentage of the Dutch working-age population receiving income-replacement benefits remained more or less constant for most of the decade despite the System Revision and the substantial economic growth in the second half of the 1980s (see Figure 5.2). When in a 1992 report an independent government auditing institute

---

[4] The costs for unemployment benefits had been reduced by about 1.8 billion euros (from 6.9 to 5.1 billion), or more than 25 per cent, while the costs for disability benefits had risen by 2.7 billion euros (from 10.2 to 13.0 billion), or more than 25 per cent (www.statline.nl 1 December 2009).

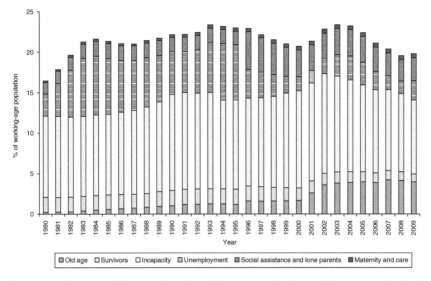

Figure 5.2. Income-replacement benefit recipiency rates for the working-age population in the Netherlands, 1980–2009

Notes: See Caseload Annex (the Netherlands).

concluded that the IIAs' supervision was failing, the Lower House appointed a special parliamentary committee entrusted with investigating the administrative structure of all employees' insurances for the period 1980–92.

The 1993 report of the parliamentary committee had far-reaching consequences for the administration of employees' insurances. The Committee concluded that the IIAs had been mainly concerned with the provision of benefits in a 'socially accepted manner', in other words as efficiently as possible without causing too much inconvenience for benefit recipients. Meanwhile, eligibility procedures had been too leniently applied, fraud-aversion policies were failing, and activation and reintegration measures for benefit recipients were almost entirely absent (Commissie-Buurmeijer, 1992/1993). Under the influence of the Committee's report, a reform process was set in motion that has continued up to the present day, gradually yet thoroughly altering administrative structures and regulations of unemployment provision.

This process was facilitated by the results of the 1994 Lower House elections, which signified the end of seventy-five years of government participation of the Christian Democrats. As one of the historical founders of the Dutch corporatist system – the *Poldermodel* (Hoogenboom, 2004; Visser and Hemerijck, 1997) – Christian Democrats had always been the main proponents of administration of employees' insurances by the social partners. Their electoral loss enabled the formation of the 'Purple Coalition', the first coalition cabinet of Conservative–Liberal VVD and the Labour Party in Dutch history. This alliance was, among other things, made possible by an implicit agreement on a further liberalization and flexibilization of the Dutch economy and of welfare state arrangements, aspired to by the Conservative Liberals, in exchange for the Labour Party's wish that benefit levels remain untouched. It was further agreed that the social partners' role in the administration of employees' insurance would be reduced in steps (Bannink, 2004). In 1995, the Purple Coalition cabinet thus introduced a new Organization Act for employees' insurance that forced the IIAs into a series of mergers and into a close cooperation with commercial insurers. At the same time, the social partners' participation in supervising the social security system was terminated by the abolition of the tripartite Social Insurance Council (SVR) and the establishment of an independent supervisory council, while the social partners' new role in the job placement system was revoked and employment services re-nationalized. In 2002, the involvement of the social partners in the administration of welfare state arrangements was terminated altogether by the complete abolition of IIAs and the transfer of the administration of employees' insurances to a new government agency, the Social Security Agency (*Uitvoeringsorgaan Werknemersverzekeringen*, UWV) (Bannink, 2004).

In the meantime, the Purple Coalition also reformed many social security programmes. In 1996, the Sickness Insurance Act was withdrawn and responsibility for payments of sick employees transferred to employers, who also became (partly) responsible for the reintegration of disabled employees in receipt of a WAO benefit (Van den Hauten, 2003). In the same year, RWW was abolished and recipients were transferred to ABW, a scheme for which eligibility and activation regulations were tightened substantially (Van Gerven, 2008). When in 2000 the Purple Coalition found the results of the new activation activities to be insufficient, plans were made to replace ABW with a new scheme, the Work and Income Benefit (*Wet Werk en Bijstand*, WWB), in which the role of eligibility testing was transferred from municipal social services departments to regional Centres for Work and Income, while municipalities would be forced to outsource the activation and reintegration of benefit recipients to private companies. After its formation in 2002, the new centre-right coalition cabinet of CDA, VVD, and LPF (the party of the assassinated Pim Fortuyn) not only implemented the plans almost unmodified but also broke the Purple Coalition's informal ban on changes in the eligibility requirements, benefit levels, and duration. After 2002, eligibility regulations in the WW, WAO, WWB, and several other social security schemes were significantly tightened, and the duration of WW and WAO benefits limited (Van Gerven, 2008; Van Gestel et al., 2009).

5.3.3 Unemployment provision in 2010

The current unemployment provision system in the Netherlands consists of two separate tiers that are closely connected administratively. Replacement rates in the first tier, WW, have remained more or less unchanged. However, eligibility rules and benefit duration are considerably different compared with twenty years ago. Both the weeks and years requirements have been tightened substantially (see Table 5.1). In addition, the entitlement period of the prolonged wage-replacing benefit has been limited for most recipients from six to three months. At the same time, the scheme's membership has been considerably expanded. While in the greater part of the twentieth century civil servants, teaching personnel, military personnel, and employees working for semi-public agencies had had their own 'redundancy payment' schemes, since 2001 these schemes have been essentially integrated into the WW. Compared to the situation in the early 1990s, in the current unemployment insurance scheme the position of recipients aged 57.5 years or older is far less advantageous. Senior claimants are no longer exempt from job-seeking and activation requirements, and claimants aged 57.5 to 60 now have the same rights and obligations as other WW recipients. Like in the early 1990s, employees aged 60 or older can still claim a disability benefit (IOAW, now called IOW) after their WW benefit expires. The IOW guarantees this category of claimants a benefit equal to the value of social assistance until their retirement without a means test. This however is a temporary scheme that will expire in 2016.

Besides a fundamental administrative reorganization of unemployment insurance which will be discussed more in depth below, possibly the most far-reaching reforms concern the organization of reintegration activities. Whereas in the past all categories of WW recipients were referred by the IIAs to the local job centre for vacancies and activation duties, since 2004 the state agency UWV (which in 2002 replaced the IIAs, run by the social partners), which administers the scheme, concludes a 'reintegration contract' with recipients who are unemployed for more than six months and are deemed to be in need of extra help finding employment. In this Individual Reintegration Agreement (*Individuele Re-integratie Overeen-komst*, IRO), a UWV official and the recipient document the steps needed for reintegration into the labour market, the available budget, and the possible sanctions if one of the parties breaches the contract. Subsequently, the official and the recipient hire one of more than 1,200 certified commercial or public reintegration agencies (which also signs the contract) that are currently active on the Dutch market. The IRO option is also available for disability benefit recipients, but not for WWB claimants or for WW recipients who are unemployed for less than six months. The latter categories are helped by the social services departments (WWB recipients) or the UWV LABOURcompany (WW recipients) in finding a job (De Koning et al., 2008).

Lastly, in 2008–9, the Dutch government abolished employee contributions to unemployment insurance, instead financing half of the scheme from general tax revenues, while employers' contributions remain in place. Though it is still unclear whether the reform will be permanent, the development might be interpreted as another step towards a 'nationalization' of formerly corporatist unemployment insurance. In this respect, it could also be interpreted as a move in the direction of a further homogenization of unemployment insurance and social assistance, with possibly major *psychological* and *political* consequences. After all, while until recently unemployment insurance could be claimed to be the 'property' of employees and employers – since the social partners exclusively administered and financed the scheme – now unemployment insurance, like social assistance, might be considered a 'common good' that not only concerns the social partners but Dutch society as a whole as well.

The second tier within current Dutch unemployment provision system is WWB. The WWB is the successor to general social assistance ABW, which, as discussed, incorporated RWW in 1995. In many aspects, WWB resembles its predecessor, but the financing system, administrative set-up, organization of reintegration, and the position of recipients aged 18–27 within the WWB are quite different. ABW was financed by the municipalities, which were simply reimbursed by the national government by the end of each year. At the beginning of each year, each municipality now receives two types of budgets from the national government which are fixed on the basis of statistical information: a budget for benefits (the 'I' or 'Income part') and a budget for reintegration activities (the 'W' or 'Work part'). To encourage municipalities to work efficiently and to reintegrate WWB recipients into the labour market early, annual surpluses on the I-part budget do not need to be returned to the government, while any reserves on the W-part do. This encourages the municipalities to use the W-part to contract commercial or public reintegration agencies for individual reintegration trajectories. Lastly, in 2009, social assistance rights for persons aged 18–27 were made much more conditional than before. For this group, municipalities are now required to offer training, education, a job, or a combination of these three. A refusal of the young person to accept such an offer might result in a termination of the benefit.

In short, the generosity of Dutch unemployment provision has been subjected to only minor changes since the early 1990s (with the exception of a shortening of insurance benefit duration). By contrast, major reforms have been implemented in relation to activation requirements, job-search obligations, and sanctions, all of which have become more prescriptive. These reforms are also reflected in new administrative structures and procedures of the system as a whole. While in the early 1990s, unemployment insurance and unemployment assistance/social assistance were more or less separate from each other; today the administration of both tiers is highly integrated. This integration was facilitated by the gradual termination of social partners' participation in the administration of unemployment and other employees' insurances, as well as their removal from the job placement system.

5.3.4 Administrative integration

Parallel to benefit provision, the administration of activation arrangements was subjected to major reorganizations that resulted in closer integration. In 2002, the IIAs were abolished and replaced by the state-run UWV. After 2002, the social partners' involvement in the administration of employees' insurance was limited to their presence in the newly formed national Council for Work and Income (*Raad voor Werk en Inkomen*, RWI), which still advises the government on general labour and social security issues, and in the Sector Councils (*Sectorraden*), which were authorized to advise the UWV on a number of subjects concerning administration of employees' insurances in specific economic branches. When in 2006 the Sector Councils too were abolished, active participation of the social partners was completely terminated. This signified the end of more than a century of corporatist administration of social security in the Netherlands.

The second step in the process of administrative integration was the abolition in 2002 of the Central Board of Job Placement and all local job centres, and the creation of the Centre for Work and Income (*Centrum voor werk en inkomen*, CWI), a public agency with about 130 regional branches. Between 2002 and 2009 the CWI coordinated the activation tasks of the UWV and the social services departments, until it was integrated into the UWV and renamed UWV

LABOURcompany (*UWV WERKbedrijf*, see Figure 5.3). Simultaneously, the reintegration activities of the local job centres were put in the hands of private companies that had to compete with each other for 'reintegration contracts' from the UWV and the social services departments. As of 2006, social services departments are also authorized to directly deliver all or part of the reintegration of WWB recipients when the reintegration activities of private companies are deemed unsatisfactory (Koning et al., 2008).

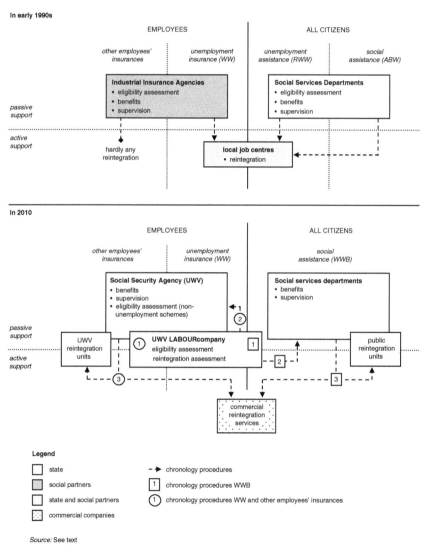

Figure 5.3. Administration of unemployment provision schemes in the Netherlands, early 1990s and 2010

Source: See text.

The partial integration of the administration of unemployment insurance and social assistance has facilitated a further coupling of active and passive support for the unemployed and large procedural changes in administrative agencies. The process for claiming unemployment benefit has been radically altered. In the early 1990s, an unemployed person first claimed for a benefit at an industrial insurance agency (WW) or at a local social services department (ABW) before being referred to the local job centre for information about vacancies. Now, a citizen intending to claim a WW or WWB benefit first has to report to the UWV LABOURcompany, which determines benefit eligibility as well as the person's chances on the labour market and the activities necessary for reintegration. If eligible, the citizen is referred to the relevant agency to receive a benefit and, if deemed necessary, to a commercial and/or public reintegration agency for activation duties (see Figure 5.3).

5.4 COMBINING BISMARCK WITH BEVERIDGE: THE LEVELLING OF RIGHTS AND STATUSES WITHIN A TWO-TIER SYSTEM

5.4.1 Homogenization of unemployment benefit provision

More than fifteen years after the start of the reform process, the Dutch unemployment provision system can still be characterized as a two-tier system. In strict terms, WW is the only benefit scheme left that is explicitly aimed at unemployed workers. However, as a consequence of the abolition of means-tested unemployment assistance in 1995, the social assistance scheme (WWB) now covers large numbers of unemployed workers too. It might even be claimed that WWB has replaced unemployment insurance as the centrepiece of Dutch unemployment provision, since WWB claimants have become much more numerous than WW recipients recently, partly due to tightening WW eligibility regulations (see Figure 5.1). However, in terms of spending, unemployment insurance has remained a vital part of Dutch unemployment provision system, especially in times of rising unemployment. Thus, when spending for social assistance increased by only 8 per cent while unemployment was rising in 2001–5, spending for unemployment insurance more than doubled. As a result, in 2005, the total costs for unemployment insurance and for social assistance were more or less the same (see Figure 5.4).

5.4.2 Risk re-categorization, administrative integration, and activation

The definition of unemployment as an administrative risk category has been altered in two respects. Firstly, already in the late 1980s the coverage of unemployment insurance was extended substantially. WW was as discussed opened up for job-hoppers and part-time workers in the growing service sectors, and as a consequence the percentage of the active working-age population covered by the

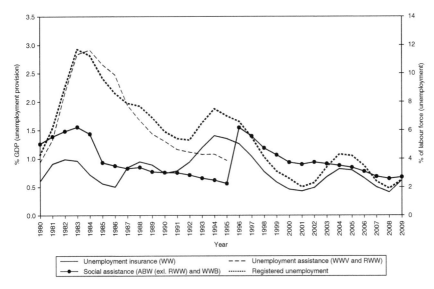

Figure 5.4. Unemployment insurance (WW), unemployment assistance (WWV and RWW), and social assistance (ABW and WWB) in the Netherlands: spending (in % of GDP) and registered unemployment (in % of labour force) 1980–2009

Source: Social Assistance Act: 1980–3: 'Financiële nota sociale zekerheid 1985', Handelingen der Staten Generaal, 1984–5, II, 18612, No. 1–2, p. 99. 1984–95: 'Sociale Nota 1997', ibid., 1996–7, II, 25002, No. 2, p. 149. New Social Assistance Act: Sociale Nota 1998–2002, ibid., 1997–2002, II, resp. 25602, 26202, 26802, 27402, 28001, No. 1–2. Work and Social Assistance Act: 2004–7: Ministerie van SZW, 'Kerncijfers *Wet werk en bijstand*. Resultaten na de evaluatie, Juni 2008', p. 15, www.szw.nl, retrieved, 15 August 2010. 2008–9: Handelingen der Staten Generaal, 2009–10, II, 32123 XV, No. 2, p. 72. RWW: 1980–3: 'Financiële nota sociale zekerheid 1985', ibid., 1984–5, II, 18612, Nos. 1–2, p. 99. 1984–95: 'Sociale Nota 1997', ibid., 1996–7, II, 25002, No. 2, p. 152. WWV: 1980–3: 'Financiële nota sociale zekerheid 1985', ibid., 1984–5, II, 18612, Nos. 1–2, p. 99. 1984–90: 'Sociale Nota 1997', ibid., 1996–7, II, 25002, No. 2, p. 152. WW: 1980–3: 'Sociale Nota 1995', ibid., 1996–7, II, 25002, No. 2, pp. 95–7. 1984–6: 'Sociale Nota 1995', ibid., 1996–7, II, 25002, No. 2, pp. 184–5. nWW: 1987–9: 'Sociale Nota 1995', ibid., 1996–7, II, 25002, No. 2, pp. 184–5. 1990–2000: UWV, 2003: 16. 2001–9: www.statline.nl, retrieved 15 August 2010. GDP: www.statline.nl, retrieved 15 August 2010. The nABW figure for 2003 is an estimate based on the figures for 2002 and 2004.

unemployment insurance scheme grew from 45 per cent in 1980 to 60 per cent in 2000, and to 70 per cent by 2001 when civil servants were also included in the WW (see Figure 5.5). Secondly, due to the integration of unemployment assistance into the general social assistance scheme, 'long-term unemployment' as an administrative category in social security has effectively disappeared. The long-term unemployed are now dependent on the WWB, which covers various categories of inactive citizens who for different reasons cannot or can no longer claim an employees' insurance benefit. Among them are the unemployed with limited labour history, the unemployed whose WW benefit has expired, and former disability benefit recipients who because of tighter eligibility regulations of disability arrangements have lost all or part of their entitlements. All these categories are subjected to more or less the same 'activation' regime. In recent years this regime has also been expanded to categories of social assistance recipients who were formerly exempted from job-search obligations, like single mothers and the unemployed aged 57.5 years or older. In this respect, the introduction of the

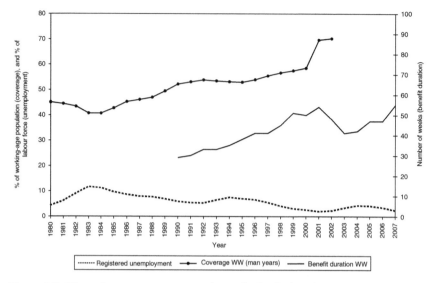

Figure 5.5. Unemployment insurance in the Netherlands (WW): coverage (% of active working-age population), benefit duration (in weeks), and registered unemployment (% of labour force), 1980–2007

Source: WW coverage has been calculated by dividing the absolute number of insured labour years by the total working-age population minus the inactive working-age population, that is, those citizens who are receiving a benefit from one of the income-replacement schemes (see Figure 5.1).

Source: Coverage and benefit duration: UWV, 2003 and 2008; registered unemployment: www.statline.nl, 5 December 2009.

WWB in 2004 signifies a formalization of a process of blurring of the once-clear boundaries between different types of income-replacement schemes for the working-age population that began in the early 1990s.

It would be too bold to claim that the WWB is actually an unemployment assistance scheme, though. Though most of the eligibility rules and activation requirements for the aforementioned categories have more or less converged, the implicit *objectives* of the activation of these categories diverge substantially. While the activation of unemployed workers is exclusively aimed at reintegration into the labour market per se, the objectives of the activation of the (partially) disabled are more ambiguous, largely due to the special history of the WWB bill. As has been explained, in the 1996–2002 period, the WWB bill was designed by the Purple Coalition of the Labour Party and Conservative Liberals for whom the scheme was indeed aimed at the reintegration of various categories of unemployed persons into the labour market, regardless of the cause of their unemployment. The bill was, however, defended and passed in parliament by the centre-right coalition cabinet of Christian Democrats and Conservative Liberals. Especially for the Christian Democrats, the activation of (partially) disabled persons and of some categories of unemployed persons, such as single mothers, not only serves reintegration into the labour market per se but, in a more general sense, also their 'participation' in society, which is deemed vital by the Christian Democrats to advance 'social cohesion'. In this respect, the introduction of the WWB does not entail a clean break with the past in ideological terms, but merely an attempt to make the administration of social security more efficient.

Although Dutch unemployment provision has formally remained a two-tier system, in the past few years the administrative apparatuses of unemployment insurance and social assistance have become partly integrated. Short-term and long-term unemployed still receive their benefits from different administrative bodies, but in order to qualify they have to approach the same agency, the UWV LABOURcompany, which refers claimants as described above (see Figure 5.3). In this respect, passive and active support for the unemployed have become far more integrated than in the 1980s and early 1990s. Where eligibility assessment, provision of benefits, and supervision of recipients were clearly separated from activation and job placement, resulting in inadequate and inefficient reintegration practices, now most vital activities are concentrated in the hands of one agency. Since the concentration of these functions is a very recent phenomenon, it remains to be seen whether it really has improved the reintegration capacities of the Dutch unemployment provision system.

5.4.3 The politics of reforming unemployment protection

All in all, the reforms of the past three decades amount to a levelling of rights and statuses *within* a two-tier unemployment provision system. On the one hand, the formally Bismarckian unemployment insurance, which until the mid-1980s was only open to certain categories of employees, has been opened up for the large majority of the dependent labour force. On the other hand, since unemployment insurance regulations have been tightened and the benefit duration limited, the risk of dependence on flat-rate and means-tested social assistance has become a reality for the large majority of Dutch employees. Hence, while the unemployment provision system has remained multi-tier and benefit levels largely untouched, a levelling of rights and statuses has nonetheless taken place.

What is most striking is the pace at which the transformation of the Dutch unemployment provision system has occurred. In the 1990s, while attempts to reform 'old' unemployment provision systems encountered broad public opposition in countries like Germany and France and often had to be softened or withdrawn (cf. Clasen and Clegg, 2006; Palier and Martin, 2007), Dutch reforms met hardly any resistance and could be accomplished quite easily. How can this 'easy' transformation in the Netherlands be explained? Two possible explanations can be advanced here.

The first is the declining legitimacy of the Dutch social partners, especially the labour unions. In the 1980s and early 1990s, labour unions and employers' associations lost much of their support in society and in political circles as a consequence of their unwillingness or impotence to cooperate in tackling some fundamental problems of the Dutch social security system. The most prominent was the large and growing number of disability benefit recipients and the weak capacities of IIAs to combat inactivity. It is not without reason that the parliamentary committee, which reported in 1993, concluded in its final report that the cooperation of the social partners in employees' insurances administration had turned into a 'paralysing grip' (Buurmeijer 1992–3: 221).

Thus, while in the late 1980s, Dutch employers' associations were willing to carry through far-reaching reforms in the disability benefit system, they were reluctant to persevere and to support government proposals for fear of displeasing the labour unions. In the early 1990s, the unions' unwillingness to cooperate in reforms cost them much of the political backing of their most powerful political ally, the Labour Party (PvdA). With the support of the PvdA, in 1992 the Lower House commissioned the aforementioned parliamentary committee, which in turn cleared the path for the fundamental reforms of the Purple Cabinet of which the PvdA was a prominent member (Bannink, 2004).

Behind the loss of support of the labour unions, and possibly also behind their unwillingness to tackle the pressing problems of the 'old' welfare state, were also fundamental changes in the Dutch economic structure. The transition from an industrial to a post-industrial economy weakened the position of the labour unions. Between 1979 and 1990, trade union membership in the Netherlands dropped from 36 to 24 per cent (Van Cruchten and Kuijpers, 2007). One of the main causes was the relative decline of branches in which labour unions had traditionally high density, and a relative growth of branches of industry in which trade union implantation was and still is traditionally low, like trade, catering, and commercial services. Between 1980 and 1985, as a result of the collapse of 'traditional' industries like shipbuilding and textiles, the largest union FNV lost 20 per cent of its total membership (Van Zanden, 1997); similar losses could be observed in the other unions (CBS, 2006). When the Dutch economy recovered after 1984, the losses were hardly compensated, and although in the 1980s and 1990s the number of female union members more than doubled, interest among new categories of service sector employees in becoming a union member – often young people with flexible and part-time jobs – is low (CBS, 2009a).

Due to the inability of labour unions to 'refresh' their stagnant membership base with new categories of service employees, they were stuck with a rank and file that had much to lose by a reform of the old welfare state schemes. Consequently, when reforms had become inevitable after the publication of the parliamentary committee's report and the formation of the Purple Coalition, the labour unions gradually gave up their resistance to changes in the administrative structure of employees' insurances in exchange for a guarantee of benefit levels and entitlements. When around the turn of the century the Purple Coalition decided on a complete dismantlement of the IIAs and nationalization of employee insurance administration the labour unions fiercely opposed the decision, but by then it was already too late (Bannink, 2004). The dismantlement signified the end to the decades-old participation of labour unions in social security administration in the Netherlands and cleared the path for, among other things, the partial integration of unemployment insurance and social assistance agencies.

In this respect, the 'Dutch miracle' of the mid-1990s – the transformation of the Dutch employment policy from a 'spectacular failure' in the 1980s to an internationally recognized success story only one decade later – could hardly be attributed to a smooth functioning of the Dutch corporatist socio-economic policymaking system, the *Poldermodel*, as some (e.g. Visser and Hemerijck, 1997) claim. Maybe even on the contrary: by the mid-1990s, the *Poldermodel* had come under increasing pressure and the Purple Coalition made no secret of its plans to drastically reform the existing socio-economic policy and the institutional arrangements underlying it (cf. Van Gestel et al., 2009). In view of this, it hardly makes sense to interpret the willingness of the social partners to accept wage-restraint measures and some Purple Coalition reforms in this period as a result of consensual corporatist negations – rather it should be interpreted as an attempt, especially by the labour unions, to rescue at least part of their once-dominant position in the *Poldermodel*. For this reason, as soon as this attempt proved unsuccessful by the early 2000s, relations between labour unions and government and employers' associations worsened, and the Dutch Miracle was never heard of again.

While the first explanation for the relatively easy transformation of the Dutch unemployment provision system concerns the political actors that were directly responsible for the legislative changes, the second explanation addresses accep-tance of the reforms by the Dutch electorate. It may be argued that far-reaching reforms of the unemployment provision system could be accomplished thanks to extremely favourable economic conditions in the 1990s: since economic growth was comparatively high (see Statistical Annex, Table A.3) and the level of tax revenues and social contributions increased, reforms could be accomplished without affecting the generosity and entitlements of the schemes, and since unemployment was extremely low only a small portion of the working-age population was affected. However, it seems that the changes carried through by the Purple Coalition were actually supported by large portions of the Dutch population. One indication is that in the late 1990s support for the welfare state among the Dutch population reached levels not seen since the 1970s (SCP, 2005).

My claim is that the levelling of rights and statuses within the unemployment provision system reflected a more general process of levelling in Dutch society. In the period after 1970, once-clear status divisions within the Dutch working-age population were becoming less rigid or disappeared altogether as a consequence of at least two structural processes. The first was the amazingly rapid spread of part-time work and, closely connected, the strong growth of female participation in the labour market. In 1975, with hardly one-third of the female working-age popula-tion holding a paid job, the Netherlands lagged far behind other Western Euro-pean countries. By 2006 female participation had risen to almost two-thirds, well in line with the Western European average (CPB, 2007: 137; Statistical Annex, Table A.4). About 75 per cent of working women in the Netherlands work part-time, a very high percentage compared to about 40 per cent in the United Kingdom and Germany and 30 per cent in the EU-27 (CBS, 2009b). Clearly, the growing labour market participation of women and the spread of part-time work has undermined the social status of the full-time-job model, since part-time work is relatively widespread among Dutch men too (CBS, 2009b; Statistical Annex, Table A.11).

While the spread of part-time work has blurred status boundaries between various categories of the *employed*, the disqualification of 'social engineering' in social assistance has partly wiped out status differentials between various cate-gories of the *unemployed*. Until the early 1980s, social assistance in the Nether-lands was characterized by a strong emphasis on social engineering, that is, a reintegration of social assistance recipients into *society* rather than into the labour market, somewhat resembling the French social assistance '*insertion* po-licies' (Barbier and Théret, 2001). In the Netherlands this had its roots in the period before 1960, when poor relief and social work were closely connected and largely in the hands of religious organizations (Van der Valk, 1986). When in the 1960s and 1970s, religion in the Netherlands was rapidly losing ground and social assistance and social work came under the authority of the municipalities, social engineering ambitions were simply secularized. While in the past social assistance was aimed at the advancement of social control, now 'emancipation' and 'self-realization' of individual recipients became its central objectives. Yet soon the same democratizing processes that undermined the authority of religious organizations also weakened the endeavours of municipal social workers. As a consequence, in the early 1980s social assistance in the Netherlands was in a crisis (De Haan and Duyvendak, 2002) from which it only recovered when, in the early 1990s, participation in paid employment was discovered by politicians from both the right and the left as an alternative to social engineering. Paid employment, it was (and still is) thought, is the key to the solution of many of the problems citizens at the 'lower end of the social spectrum' are coping with, such as poverty, criminality, poor health, and the like.

To a certain extent, the end of social engineering in the 1990s implied a 'normalization' of the unemployed within the social assistance scheme. They were no longer seen as a special category of unemployed who needed special treatment, but were put on a par with other categories of unemployed – like unemployed workers who formerly had a permanent job and whose statuses in the same period were undermined by the rise of part-time work and whose representatives (the labour unions) were rapidly losing legitimacy. It might be claimed that in combination these developments have contributed to an atmosphere that allowed a rapid levelling of rights and statuses within the Dutch unemployment provision system.

5.5 CONCLUSION

In the past three decades, various reforms have been implemented in the Netherlands in order to improve the reintegration capacities of the unemployment provision system. The system's inability to combat benefit dependency and 'activate' its beneficiaries has been approached through a variety of measures that combined have resulted in a configuration of organizations, regulations, and schemes that seems more integrated and 'logical' than the system that was in place thirty years ago. To a certain extent, the reforms of the past three decades have resulted in a formal and legal homogenization of unemployment and non-employment provision schemes, especially those for disabled persons. Whereas until the early 2000s responsibility for the administration of these schemes was dispersed among a large number of organizations that were run by the national government, local governments, the social partners, or a combination of these, now almost all responsibilities reside with state agencies. Moreover, in the past ten years the Dutch national government has utilized the concentration of authority to homogenize reintegration and activation duties for unemployed and disabled persons.

The homogenization has, however, not gone so far as to really blur the formal and legal boundaries between various social security schemes. As mentioned above, the Dutch unemployment provision system was and still is multi-tier, while disability benefit recipients are still clearly approached as a separate category whose 'activation' requires different measures and has different objectives than that of unemployed persons. In this respect, the current system of unemployment provision in the Netherlands maps only partially onto the ideal–typical framework developed in the Introduction of this volume. Though in the past three decades unemployment insurance and social assistance have grown towards one another, the result is not fully homogeneous provision. But nor does the continuing existence of two benefit tiers mean that the Netherlands has a dualized system of unemployment protection. Rather, the result of three decades of reform is a more or less integrated two-tier system that covers the large majority of the Dutch labour force (see Appendix 5.A).

In the meantime, it remains an open question whether the current Dutch unemployment provision system is really more able than its predecessor to effectively reintegrate unemployment benefit recipients into the labour market. So far, the current reintegration policies of the UWV, the social services departments, and the commercial and public reintegration companies have scarcely been evaluated. The information that is available seems less than encouraging though. In 2008, the Nicis Institute published a report in which it is concluded that the new reintegration policies have increased benefit recipients' chances of finding a job by only 3 per cent, while a successful reintegration into the labour market costs taxpayers on average about half a million euros (Nicis, 2008). Meanwhile, the majority of clients of private and public reintegration agencies are negative about the services provided by these agencies (Van Echtelt and Hoff, 2008), while most of the municipalities have decided to terminate the contracts with private agencies and to keep most of the reintegration services in-house (Mallee et al., 2008).

Similarly, it remains unclear whether the new unemployment provision system as a whole, which was built in a period of extremely low unemployment figures, is really sustainable, in both a practical and a political sense. Although the Dutch economy suffered heavily in the global financial and economic crisis after 2008, so far the new system has hardly been tested by a serious rise in the number of unemployment provision recipients. When the crisis began, the Dutch government almost immediately decided to reactivate an old regulation within the unemployment insurance scheme, which opens the possibility of granting employees a part-time unemployment insurance benefit (*deeltijd-WW*) without losing their jobs, on the proviso that they are offered extra schooling by their employer. Partly for this reason, in the first two years of the economic crisis unemployment figures in the Netherlands – and thus the number of unemployment insurance and social assistance recipients – remained relatively low (Ministry of Social Affairs 2009/2010; Statistical Annex, Table A.5). However, since the economic crisis has also resulted in high government deficits, which in the near future have to be reduced in order to comply with EU regulations, it is expected that sooner or later this scheme will have to be terminated. Only then will it become clear whether the new system can really reintegrate large numbers of unemployed persons into the labour market and, maybe more importantly, whether the reforms of the past fifteen years truly rest on broad public support. By that time not only the 'difficult' categories of unemployed, who long comprised the majority of benefit recipients, but also middle-class employees will experience the activation regulations and the shortened benefit duration of the new Dutch unemployment provision system.

Appendix 5.A Major changes in unemployment provision in the Netherlands, 1987–2009

1987	System Revision:

- Unemployment assistance WWV abolished.
- *Unemployment insurance (WW)*:
  - Redundancy payment benefit abolished.
  - Introduction of new benefit structure: 'loss-of-wages' benefit (70% of previous net earnings, max. 5 years) and 'follow-up benefit' (recipients aged 57.5 years or older, minimum level, no means test, max. 3.5 years).
  - Introduction of labour history requirements regulations: 'weeks requirement' (having been employed for 26 weeks in past 52 weeks), and 'years requirement' (having been employed for at least three years (for at least 8 hours per week) in the past five years).
  - Introduction of Social Security Supplements Act (TW): compensation for loss of income as a result of System Revision.
  - Introduction of Income Act for Elderly and Partially Disabled Unemployed Employees (IOAW): benefit at minimum level, no means test.

1991	*Unemployment insurance (WW)*: revision of labour history years requirement: year only counts if claimant has worked 52 days during that year.
1991	Employment-finding organization made tripartite by inclusion of labour union and employers' association representatives in national board (CBA) and regional job centres (RBAs).
1994	*Unemployment insurance (WW)*: revision of labour history requirements:

- Years requirement: four years in past five years.

1995	*Social assistance (ABW) and unemployment assistance (RWW)*:

- RWW abolished.
- Introduction of New Social Assistance Act (nABW):
- Three benefit norms:
  - Singles: 50% of legal minimum wage
  - Single parents: 70%
  - Couples: 100%
- Obligation to apply for and accept 'suitable employment' extended to all social assistance recipients, with the exception of single parents with children under 5 years and claimants over 57 and a half.
- Contract between recipient, municipal social services department, and job centre on activation ('trajectory plan').

1995–7	*Unemployment insurance (WW)*: administration reformed:

- Bipartite industrial insurance agencies (IIAs) split up: bipartite IIA boards become advisory 'sector councils', and administrative apparatus IIAs become private administrative agencies (uvi's) which have to compete for administrative orders with other commercial companies as of 2001.
- New tripartite coordination agency that commissions administration (Lisv).

1997	Introduction of general labour deployment scheme (WIW) incorporating several labour deployment schemes for specific categories (youth, women, migrants, middle-aged men).
2001	*Unemployment insurance (WW)*: special redundancy payment schemes for civil servants, teachers, and military personnel incorporated into WW.
2002	*Unemployment insurance (WW)*: administration reformed (SUWI):

	• Merger of all uvi's into one public administrative office (UWV).
	• Tripartite coordination agency Lisv abolished, competences transferred to UWV.
2002	*Social assistance (nABW)*: administration reformed (SUWI):
	• Tripartite job centres abolished.
	• New regional agencies (CWIs) entrusted with eligibility testing, employment finding and activation tasks.
2003	*Unemployment insurance (WW)*: follow-up benefit abolished.
2004	*Social assistance (nABW)*: replaced by new scheme (WWB):
	• Introduction of new financing system: budget for benefits ('I' or 'Income part') and budget for reintegration activities ('W' or 'Work part').
	• Municipalities obliged to outsource activation to commercial companies.
2004	Labour deployment scheme (WIW) abolished.
2004	*Unemployment insurance (WW)*: introduction of Individual Reintegration Agreement (IRO) between recipient, UWV, and commercial and/or public activation agency.
2006	*Social assistance (WWB)*: obligation of municipalities to outsource activation to commercial companies partially lifted.
2006	*Unemployment insurance (WW)*:
	• Revision of labour history weeks requirement: 26 worked weeks in past 36 weeks.
	• Benefit level raised to 75% for the first two months of unemployment (after two months: 70%).
	• Maximum benefit duration reduced to 38 months.
	• Introduction of special follow-up benefit at minimum level for recipients aged 60 years or older (IOW).
2008	Temporary activation of scheme for part-time unemployment insurance benefit (WTV, deeltijd-WW).
2009	*Unemployment insurance (WW) and social assistance (WWB)*: merger of UWV and CWIs into new agency (UWV WERKbedrijf) entrusted with claims assessment for WW and WWB.
2009	*Unemployment insurance (WW)*: employees contribution (temporarily?) abolished.
2009	*Social assistance (WWB)*: social assistance rights for persons aged 18–27 made conditional (WIJ act):
	• Municipalities required to offer training, education, or a job, or a combination.
	• Refusal of young persons to accept offer might result in termination of benefit.

Source: Bannink (2004), Rigter et al. (1995), Sol (2000), UWV (2008), Van der Veen (1990), Van der Veen and Trommel (1999), Van Gerven (2008), and Van Gestel et al. (2009).

6

Belgium: a precursor muddling through?

Johan J. De Deken

6.1 INTRODUCTION

Belgium can be considered to be a somewhat atypical case in the context of the analytical frame used in this book. Its unemployment protection system has never really provided status confirming earnings-related benefits and has never operated as a two-tier system to protect the wage-earner working-age population, even if there has always been a form of means-tested social assistance. Attempts to encourage a readjustment of occupational orientations and to retrain recipients of unemployment benefits have so far been limited to prime age unemployed with a wage-earner status rather than extended to recipients of other working-age benefits. The inclusive nature of unemployment compensation, the lack of equivalence between benefits and previous earnings, the encompassing nature of unemployment insurance, and truly residual nature of social assistance can be seen as a form of (early) benefit homogenization which made it less necessary to pursue a policy of re-categorization during the 1980s. The broad definition of unemployment precluded practices of administratively reallocating jobless people from unemployment insurance to other working-age benefit schemes such as work incapacity schemes. The encompassing coverage of unemployment compensation also means that the target population for activation schemes is almost exclusively situated amongst the claimants of unemployment insurance benefits, and that it makes less sense to extent behavioural requirements that are imposed upon the officially recognized unemployed towards beneficiaries of other working-age benefits. There is, however, one major exception to all this: the continued substantial use of early retirement and the lack of effective activation of older unemployed workers.

6.2 ECONOMIC AND POLICY CONTEXT: DEINDUSTRIALIZATION, MASSIVE LABOUR SHEDDING BUT NOT INCREASING THE PRECARIOUSNESS OF EMPLOYMENT

During the 1970s and 1980s, Belgian industry was particularly hard hit by the oil crisis that exacerbated the problematic consequences of a declining traditional industry (Cassiers et al., 1996). The country's economy had been very reliant on a manufacturing industry that was comparatively energy-intensive and therefore particularly sensitive to energy price shocks. If during the 1960s Belgium had been one of the most industrialized countries in the world, during the 1970s it experienced some of the most dramatic declines in manufacturing jobs in the OECD area. The potential social consequences of this sudden and massive job shedding could have been particularly disruptive because of the total dependence on traditional industrial employment of entire cities and regions. The problem of the transformation of the nature of the unemployment risk from frictional to structural joblessness was more pronounced in Belgium than in most other countries.

Even though the share of the tertiary sector in total employment increased from 45 per cent in 1960 to over 62 per cent in 1980, and to 76 per cent in 2008, this transition towards a post-industrial economy was less accompanied by a rise in precarious forms of employment than elsewhere in Europe. Compared to many neighbouring countries, the incidence of non-standard forms of employment, such as temporary contracts and part-time employment, has been traditionally low in Belgium, and their expansion only modest over the past three decades (Schmid, 2010: 121). The share of self-employed as a percentage of the working-age population, which in Belgium was traditionally above the EU average, substantially declined during the period 1998–2008. Cross-national studies for the OECD area for the 1980s and 1990s consistently showed Belgium as having one of the lowest poverty rates for the working-age population (Atkinson et al., 1995). The country appeared to be remarkably successful in containing the social consequences of structural unemployment.

The fiscal crisis in the advent of the oil crisis did not translate into a neo-liberal turn in significant cuts in social benefits in Belgium. Nevertheless, during the 1980s, centre-right coalition governments replaced previous Keynesian policies with more supply-side policies, seeking to counter the rise in unemployment by reducing direct labour costs. The main policy instrument relied upon was to impose wage moderation, and to shift the costs of financing unemployment insurance from employers towards employees. In addition, the automatic link between wages and inflation was abolished and a so-called 'wage norm' replaced the central wage agreements whenever the social partners failed to come to an agreement. The state initially sought to offset the social security deficits by increasing its share in the financial burden, but this in turn aggravated the fiscal crisis that had originated in the politics of linguistic pacification and gradual devolution of the central state.

As in many other continental welfare states, early retirement became one of the main instruments to facilitate industrial restructuring and alleviate the social consequences of structural economic adjustment (De Deken, 2002; Ebbinghaus, 2006). Initially, schemes were set up as an extension of the unemployment insurance schemes. As will be demonstrated below, statutory unemployment benefits are relatively low in Belgium and many of the workers who lost their jobs during the late 1970s and 1980s were sole breadwinners with few formal qualifications or very specific skills. They tended to live in regions that had strongly depended upon traditional industrial employment. Statutory unemployment benefits were insufficient to protect those households from poverty during prolonged spells of unemployment. The early retirement schemes that were established during the late 1970s increased the gross replacement rate of out-of-work benefits from 60 to 80 per cent (De Deken, 2002: 30) and initially helped to keep registered unemployment below the EU average. However, subsequently the state became incapable to finance these more generous replacement rates because of the massive job shedding which created strong fiscal pressure as a result of spending on the meagre statutory benefits (De Deken, 2009). That is why recourse was taken to finance the top-up benefits via sectoral welfare funds (*fondsen voor bestaanszekerheid – fonds de sécurité d'existence*) (SWF) set up by industry-wide joint committees.[1] Early retirement packages thus were attractive for both employees (because of the higher replacement rates and the diluting of work incentives) and their employers (because of externalizing costs of laying off their superfluous workforce and weakening trade union resistance against mass redundancies). As such the schemes might have speeded up the post-industrial transition and induced job shedding.

Facilitating labour market exit of older workers was encouraged also due to the rise in youth unemployment. A so-called 'replacement condition' that required employers to replace the early retiree by a job-seeking person under the age of 30 was first introduced in minor statutory schemes but later extended towards the industry schemes. This was successful to some extent, as the share of youth unemployment in total unemployment declined from 40 per cent in 1975 to 24 per cent by 1995. On the other hand, the labour force participation of older workers, that is, those aged 55 or more, dropped to single digits (and thus became the lowest in the OECD). By contrast, the labour market position of prime-aged male workers remained fairly stable with the vast majority of employees continuing to be able to rely on reasonably well-paid jobs (Marx, 2007: 126). And as we argued, low-wage work and precarious employment contracts were less prevalent among Belgian men than in many other OECD countries. However, long-term unemployment, especially in Wallonia and amongst migrant workers in the Brussels region, became structural, and remained so even during the economic upswing of the 1990s. Overall, the employment–population ratio in Belgium remained one of the lowest in the OECD area with 56 per cent in 1994 and 62 per cent in 2009, even though the negative deviation from the mean narrowed appreciably from 8.2 points in 1994 to 3.2 points by 2009 (OECD, 2010a: 271).

---

[1] In the Belgian neo-corporatist system, these funds are established by negotiations at the level of industrial sectors between the trade unions and the employers associations. Their main task consists in administering various social benefits (including training, measures to promote security in the work-place, and various extra statutory transfer payments such as early retirement benefits) granted in specific industries.

6.3 UNEMPLOYMENT COMPENSATION IN BELGIUM

Even though the Belgian system of unemployment compensation is formally contributory and has an element of earnings relatedness to it, it hardly qualifies as a genuine insurance system. It was only during the 1970s that the system introduced a degree of earnings relatedness in its benefit structure (Palsterman, 2003). Nevertheless, even afterwards, statutory Belgian unemployment insurance remained almost unique in its reliance on needs-based criteria, that is, a contributory system without equivalence between benefits and contributions (De Lathouwer, 1997). It should be noted that this never implied the use of means testing, however, as the determination of needs had always been inferred indirectly from the household status and the age of the unemployment benefit claimant, as well as the labour market status of other members of the household. Unemployment protection is based on a single tier, that is, there is no dedicated unemployment assistance scheme, and almost everyone entering a wage-earner relationship is entitled to unemployment insurance, even school graduates. For those who are not eligible, that is, primarily the self-employed or those who took up dependent employment after school but failed to hang on to it long enough to acquire entitlement to unemployment insurance, there is a kind of residual means-tested minimum income guarantee (*leefloon – revenue d'intégration*) (MIG), which is part of the social assistance system.

Since the reforms of the 1970s, overall benefit generosity hardly changed and continues to depend upon three factors: the length of the unemployment spell (benefits are more generous during the first twelve months of employment), the family situation (heads of households are entitled to more generous benefits than singles), and the age of the beneficiary (seniority supplements are granted for those aged 50 and over). The difference between minimum and maximum benefits has always been small and has deteriorated over time. In 1975, it was 25 per cent for breadwinners, dwindling to only 14 per cent two decades later. For single persons the wedge is still about 28 per cent, but this, too, hardly indicates the existence of an insurance system based on equivalence. As a consequence, replacement rates deteriorate fast as claimants move up the pre-unemployment income ladder (see Appendix 6.A). The seniority supplements, paid to the unemployed above the age of 50, who were employed for at least twenty years prior to becoming unemployed, can substantially increase the replacement rates offered during the second period up to 82 per cent for heads of households.

Belgian unemployment insurance benefits are very rarely supplemented by means-tested social assistance or housing benefits. Thus, in an OECD study on the year 2002, Belgium came out on top in terms of the replacement rates of its unemployment benefit scheme offered during the first five years of unemployment. However, once entire benefit packages for unemployed persons are taken into account, that is, after adding means-tested social assistance supplements and housing benefits paid in other countries on top of unemployment insurance, Belgium only occupied a middle position (OECD, 2004). In addition, while the generosity of benefits changes for some claimants over time (see Appendix 6.A), benefit duration is in principle unlimited. This is one of the main reasons why the Belgian system scores, in comparison with other OECD countries, very high in overall benefit spending and generosity.

Table 6.1 offers an overview of the current conditions of unemployment insurance. Unlike for other countries covered in this book, for Belgium it does not make much sense to compare the conditions in 2010 with those prevailing during the 1990s as (apart from costs of living adjustments of the minimum and maximum benefits), eligibility criteria, benefits levels, and entitlement conditions did not change during the past two decades.

Until the 1970s, when unemployment insurance only provided flat-rate benefits, the scheme was financed on a tripartite basis, with employers, employees, and

Table 6.1. Unemployment insurance: eligibility criteria, benefit levels, entitlement in 2010

Membership	All employees and young persons who are unemployed after completing their education
Waiting period	None
Qualifying period	Period varies according to the age of the insured person between 312 working days during the previous 18 months, and 624 working days over the previous 36 months
Level	Depending upon age and the household situation of the claimant: gross benefit per day granted 26 days per month (monthly amount):
	• *Partners with dependants*: 60% of reference earnings. During first 6 months min. €38.75 (€1007.50), max. €50.92 (€1323.92). As of 6th month of unemployment max. reduced to €47.46 (€1233.96). From second year onwards max. reduced to €44.35 (€1153.10).
	• *Single persons*: in the 1st year of unemployment 60%. During first 6 months min. €32.56 (€846.56), max. €50.92 (€1323.92). As of 6th month of unemployment max. reduced to €47.46 (€1233.96). From 2nd year onwards 53.8%, min. €32.56 (€846.56), max. €39.76 (€1033.76).
	• *Partners without dependants*: 60% in the 1st 6 months of unemployment, min. €24.40 (€634.40), max. €50.92 (€1323.92). As of 6th month max. reduced to €47.46 (€1233.65). From 2nd year onwards 40%, max. €29.56 (768.56), or fixed amount €17.20 (€447.20) or €22.58 (€587.0) (latter amount if both partners live from a benefit and partner's benefit does not exceed €29.56). OR
	• *Waiting allowance* (for unemployed school graduates): Partners with dependants: €37.76 (€. Partners without dependants (household with only replacement incomes): Age below 18: €9.54, over 18: €15.34. Single persons: Age below 18: €10.52, 18-20: €16.53, 21 and over: €27.38.
	• Unemployment benefit plus age supplement after 1st year of unemployment to older workers (over 50) with employment of at least 20 years:
	• *Partners with dependants*: min. €40.62 (€1056.12), max. €48.67 (€1265.42).
	• *Single persons*: min. €33.99 (€883.74), max. €44.35 (€1153.10) depending upon age category.
	• *Partners without dependants*: min. €27.61 (€717.86), max. €40.65 (€1056.90) depending upon age category.
Maximum duration	No limit (except for certain cases of 'abnormally' long-term unemployment spell; see text).
Obligations	To be available for the labour market and accept 'suitable' employment (suitable being defined in terms of commuting time (less than 4 hours per day), learned occupational skills (only during first 6 months), wage level (not less than the unemployment benefit + commuting costs); actively seeking work.
Taxation	Benefits are liable to 10 per cent income tax, but most unemployed are exempt from this (only those cohabiting with an earning partner and receiving first period benefit have to pay the tax). Benefits are not liable to social security contributions.

Source: Own calculations based on the annual social security reports of the Ministry of Social Security (Algemeen Verslag van de Sociale Zekerheid, 1967–95).

the state each providing about a third of the necessary funds. Subsequently, employees and employers took over most of the share, but with the economic crisis that followed the first oil price shock of 1973 and the related massive job shedding in industry, expenditure on unemployment benefits increased fivefold and the state assumed most of this financial burden. State subsidies peaked during the 1980s when almost 80 per cent of the unemployment insurance budget was funded by general taxation. When during the 1980s, the Belgian state needed to reduce its budget deficit as part of its EMU effort, the main source of funding unemployment benefits was again shifted from the central state towards wage earners in the form of the so-called wage-restraint contributions (formally made by the employers, but paid out of funds that originated in employees relinquishing wage increases). During the 1990s, wage restraint paid for more than 40 per cent of the unemployment insurance budget.

In addition, in order to cope with the steep increase in the number of people claiming benefits, from the mid-1970s onwards, unemployment insurance became increasingly financed out of ad hoc transfers from other branches of the social security system that were still running surpluses (in particular the child allowances scheme). Towards the middle of the 1990s, this so-called Fund for Financial Balance in Social Security (FFBSS) footed about 20 per cent of the unemployment bill (Figure 6.1).

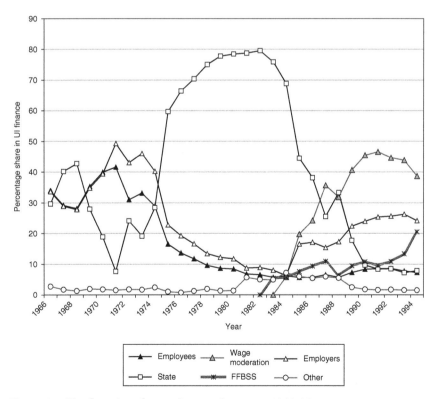

Figure 6.1. The financing of unemployment insurance, 1966–94

Source: Own calculations based on data from the Ministry of Social Affairs (various issues of Algemeen verslag over de sociale zekerheid Brussels: Ministerie van Sociale Voorzorg, 1967–95).

In 1995, the government in effect formalized the ad hoc transfer that in the past was carried out via the FFBSS balancing fund. Under the new system, the National Office for Social Security (NSSO) collected a single integrated social insurance contribution, which it subsequently redistributed on the basis of the expenditure needs of the different branches of the social security system. Since the introduction of this new system, the distribution of the financial burden of social security has remained relatively stable. In 2008, employers paid about 36 per cent, employees about 21 per cent, and the so-called wage moderation levy another 6 per cent. The share of general revenue accounted for 11 per cent, while other sources, in particular VAT, have seen a slow but steady increase from 7 per cent in 1995 to 14 per cent in 2006 (De Deken, 2011*a*, forthcoming).

Finally, Belgian unemployment protection hardly qualifies as a typical continental unemployment insurance scheme for another even more important reason. If during the 1970s there had been a contribution assessment ceiling in place as the logical pendant of maximum benefit levels, this upper limit was gradually increased and subsequently abandoned in 1982.

6.3.1 Administration: tripartism under devolution

The actual payment of unemployment benefits is delivered by the so-called payment bodies. These include one public fund and three auxiliary funds that are linked to the three national trade union federations (Christian, Socialist, and Liberal). As a default, an unemployed person will receive his or her benefit from the public fund, but he or she has always also been able to opt to receive benefits via an auxiliary fund. The auxiliary funds can be compared with insurance brokers: they give advice, help the unemployed with completing their dossiers, and also offer legal assistance in the event of a conflict with the administration of the National Employment Office (NEO). Most unemployed rely upon an auxiliary fund: in 2005, 44 per cent claimed their benefits via a fund linked to the Christian trade union federation, 38 per cent via a fund linked to the Socialist trade union federation, 6 per cent via a fund linked to the Liberal trade union federation, and only 12 per cent via the public fund. The unions and their auxiliary funds have no influence whatsoever on the decision of granting unemployment benefits. A far cry from the traditional 'Ghent' system, benefit eligibility is not limited to union members and trade unions do not choose the kind of insurance policy they administer and have no say in the conditions for entitlement or benefit levels. As demonstrated above, not only union members foot the bill of the insurance scheme. Finally, it is the state, together with both social partners (employers' associations and trade unions), who determines how the scheme is organized and administered. Entitlement decisions are solely made by the NEO administration which is partly dependent upon information provided by the regional employment offices: the VDAB in Flanders, the FOREM in Wallonia, the BGDA-ORBEM in Brussels, and ADG in the German-speaking municipalities in the eastern part of the Walloon region. These regional offices all have a bipartite governance structure similar to that of the NEO. The NEO continues to be responsible for the financial management of employment policies, while the regional offices are responsible for job placement, vocational training, and the reintegration of the unemployed into the labour market (for more details see De Deken, 2009).

6.3.2 Sanctioning and activation policies

Formally, the unemployment benefit system requires beneficiaries to be available for the labour market. In practice this rule is rarely enforced. Many long-term unemployed are simply considered to be incapable to hold a job, and in some other countries would have ended up in a disability scheme. There was, however, a clause in the unemployment benefit code that very often led to a suspension of benefits. This so-called Article 80 suspended the eligibility for a benefit for those unemployed who had been unemployed for an 'abnormal' length of time (see below) and cohabited with a partner in paid work. The assumption was that these unemployed were no longer willing to look for a job. Introduced in 1991, although earlier versions of the unemployment insurance code contained similar articles, the clause was modified in 2004 and integrated into the system of activation.

In order to be suspended, the unemployed had to have had in an 'abnormally' long spell of unemployment. This was initially defined as amounting to twice the average duration of unemployment in a given district (controlling for age and gender of the unemployed). In 1996 this was reduced to a factor of 150 per cent.[2] In addition, he or she needs to cohabit with an earning partner. In that case the claimant is expected to be able to fall back on the income of the spouse, and an unemployed school graduate (without any employment record) is expected to rely on the income of the parents with whom he/she lives. Unemployed persons above the age of 50 with a work history of more than twenty years have always been exempt from this possible suspension. In essence, Article 80 introduced a form of means testing for a particular category of unemployed.

6.3.3 Benefit re-categorization – not a Belgian phenomenon

It can be argued that the inclusiveness and indefinite nature of the unemployment insurance has made the role of functionally equivalent benefits for workless people, such as social assistance or disability benefits, less relevant than in many other countries discussed in this book either in the expansionary phase during the 1980s or in the subsequent phase of reining in such schemes from the 1990s onwards. In addition, such benefits are granted on a far stricter basis than elsewhere, and thus can be seen as fulfilling a merely residual rather than parallel or alternative role.

---

[2] As a consequence, the maximum benefit period for those to whom Article 80 applied could vary from two years (for men under 36 in the district of Arlon) to over two years and six months (for women younger than 36 in the district of Oostende), to six years and ten months (for men over 46 in the district of Tongeren), and eight years and nine months (for women over 46 in the district of Mons) (De Lathouwer et al., 2003: 8).

Of course, those who do not qualify for unemployment insurance benefits in principle fall back on the means-tested social assistance scheme, the so-called MIG, which is administered by the local government. Given the inclusiveness of the insurance system, this concerns primarily the self-employed, however, or the few wage earners who do not meet the qualifying period and whose income does fall under the administrative poverty line. For low-income groups, the benefits granted under this scheme are not that different from the minimum guaranteed benefits within unemployment insurance: depending upon the household category, beneficiaries of long-term unemployment insurance receive the same amount as social assistant recipients (e.g. single parents) to about 15 per cent less (as is the case for singles), provided, of course, they pass the means test (simulations reported in Bogaerts et al., 2009).

Invalidity benefits are granted by different branches of the social security system and different regulations apply for manual workers and salaried employees and length of absence from work due to sickness or incapacity. The sickness insurance scheme takes on the responsibility of paying compensation to incapacitated employees when the guaranteed wage period paid by the employer is over. Incapacity benefits have maintained a stronger equivalence between contributions and earnings than unemployment insurance. However, even here, the gap between maximum and minimum benefits has narrowed over time (Cantillon et al., 2003: 19).

The long-term incapacity scheme offers by far the most attractive working-age benefits (the amounts granted, depending upon the household category, are about 25–40 per cent above long-term unemployment insurance benefits) (Bogaerts et al., 2009), but this does not seem to have led to the abusive practices of shifting unemployed from unemployment insurance to incapacity benefits. Until recently, there has been no indication that the different working-age benefits operated as communicating vessels, that is, there is no reason to believe that a systematic shift occurred in the benefit dependency of non-working persons of unemployment insurance towards sickness-invalidity benefits or to social assistance benefits. Figure 6.2 shows that the number of unemployment beneficiaries clearly fluctuates with the economic cycle (and in the first year there appears to have been an outflow from unemployment in activity). By contrast, the trend of the other working-age benefits seems to follow more or less the growth rate of the labour force and of the working-age population. The caseload of disability and sickness benefits has seen a slow but steady increase, whereas the number of claimants of benefits paid for incapacity caused by work accidents or by occupational diseases has seen a moderate decline since 2001.[3]

---

[3] These numbers include both accidents that resulted in temporary and permanent disability. The level of benefits depends on the degree of disability. These figures do not take this into account and hence much exaggerate the caseload (a more thorough discussion of this problem can be found in Chapter 15).

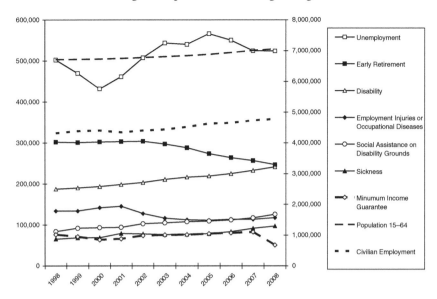

Figure 6.2. The development of working-age benefits (left axis in 1,000 of beneficiaries) compared to the growth of the population aged 16–64 and employment growth (right axis in 1,000 persons) between 1998 and 2008

Source: see Caseload Annex (Belgium).

6.4 REFORM TRENDS

6.4.1 The retreat of Bismarckian elements as a form of early benefit homogenization

As we argued, benefit differentiation according to need inferred from the household situation has always been one of the hallmarks of the Belgian unemployment benefit system. In response to an increased heterogeneity of the labour force (including a shift from industrial wage labour to salaried employment in the service sector), reforms during the early 1970s had sought to introduce some degree of earnings relatedness in the benefit structure (to accommodate the needs of the growing group of white-collar employees), but at the same time these reforms established a distinction between 'heads of households' (those providing for dependent persons: children or non-working spouses) and 'non-heads of households' (replacing the existing discrimination between men and women that in view of emancipation became untenable). During the 1980s, the relative growth of secondary earners amongst the unemployed prompted a further categorization of benefits by splitting the class of 'non-heads of households' into 'singles' and 'partners' (the latter including a person who lives together with another person who has an income above a certain threshold – including transfer incomes). The first two categories of claimants remained entitled to full, albeit differentiated, benefits. The third, though, saw its benefits drastically reduced to quasi flat-rate amounts after the first year and a half of unemployment, resulting in the very low replacement rates (see Appendix 6.A).

In 1986, the government introduced stricter rules for suspending benefits for beneficiaries with an 'abnormal' long spell of unemployment. The adoption of Article 80 in 1991 in the unemployment insurance code was primarily intended to terminate entitlement to benefits of partners.[4] But even after this tightening of the rules, the system remained exceptional by international standards in terms of average benefit duration, as singles and heads of households can only have their unemployment benefits suspended in the case of proven fraud. As discussed, this is one of the reasons why comparatively few unemployed are referred to the social assistance scheme.

In short, because Belgian unemployment protection has always been characterized by a strong emphasis on income protection and poverty prevention, there never was much of a need for further benefit homogenization during the 1980s. The hesitant steps of the early 1970s towards a more earnings-related system were abandoned in the face of financial imbalances caused by the massive labour shedding following the first oil crisis. Priority was given again to poverty prevention and minimum income protection. By selectively manipulating the indexation mechanism, minimum benefit levels maintained their real value more than average and maximum benefits. The link between wage increases and benefit increases had already been abandoned during the late 1970s, while during the 1980s both benefits and wages were not adjusted for inflation. At the same time, minimum guaranteed unemployment insurance benefits and social assistance benefits were exempt from most cuts and even saw selective increases.

In other words, the declining differentiation within unemployment insurance in terms of minimum and maximum benefit levels, as well as reforms which ensured an inclusive character of the system, might make Belgium (in a similar way as Denmark, see Chapter 10) a 'precursor' of benefit homogenization at the time when the 'earnings relatedness' and differentiation within unemployment protection in other countries became more pronounced.

6.4.2 Shifting boundaries between unemployment and other risk categories – a tale of early retirement

Because of relatively low eligibility thresholds and lenient entitlement rules, unemployment as an administrative risk category has always been comparatively broad in Belgium. That is one of the reasons why the caseload of other working-age benefits such as those granted for work incapacity, and those approved in the framework of means-tested social assistance remained quite marginal when compared to the number of recipients of statutory unemployment benefits. This might also help to explain why there never were similar debates of harmonizing or even converging different administrative risk categories. Incapacity benefits always have been granted purely medical grounds and there is no compelling evidence to suspect that they may have been used as a programme with the

---

[4] As well as the category of school graduates who enjoy an interim benefit, that we have left out of the discussion.

purpose of supporting those unemployed who are difficult to reintegrate into the labour market.

Leaving aside schemes which facilitate career breaks and provide 'time credits' for temporary absence from employment (for details see De Deken, 2011*a*), there is one major exception, however: the massive use of various forms of early retirement as a tool for labour shedding. Such schemes saw a considerable expansion in the advent of the first oil crisis, and it was only towards the end of the century that some labour market exit routes started to be phased out gradually. The transfer of unemployment into early retirement was partly indirect, however, as some early retirement routes were, in one way or another, part of the unemployment benefit system.

Figure 6.3 documents the caseload of the three main exit routes for older workers. The EBP and ERP schemes were set up in the context of the statutory pensions system which are financed and administered by the federal pension administration. The CBP and SBP schemes augment unemployment insurance benefits with supplementary benefits paid out of industry welfare funds (*fondsen voor bestaanszekerheid* or *fonds de sécurité d'existence*) and hence are to a significant extent financed by the employers and administered by the social partners. The unemployment benefit scheme itself exempts older beneficiaries from job-seeking requirements.

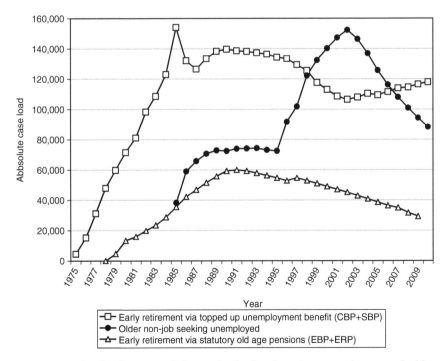

Figure 6.3. The development of the caseload of early retirement schemes and older unemployed exempted from job search, 1975–2010

Source: Own calculations based on annual reports of NEO and of RVP-ONP.

A few years after its introduction, the EBP/ERP exit route was phased out again in order to relieve the state budget as to make it possible for Belgium to comply with the conditions for European monetary union. The third, that is, the route for older unemployed persons, began to be scaled back in the context of activation policies in the wake of the European Employment strategy (see below). In essence, the third option (CBP and SBP) might be regarded as part of the unemployment insurance scheme too, but these programmes are backed by collectively agreed redundancy arrangements and are thus the joint responsibility of employers, employees, and the state. The first type of exit, by contrast, is more granted on an individual case-by-case basis and thus the conditions of entitlement can be more easily adjusted to new administrative guidelines.

6.4.3 Activation – from labour demand to labour supply

In order to limit moral hazard, entitlement to unemployment benefits is almost invariably made conditional upon being available to the labour market and being willing to accept a job. Even if the Belgian unemployment benefit system was never really based on the notion of equivalence between contributions and benefits, it always did entail another core feature of a social insurance model: the protection of entitlements by linking the obligation to accept a job from the labour exchange to the right to refuse jobs deemed inappropriate relative to the qualifications of the beneficiary. In contrast to social *assistance*, unemployment *insurance* typically does not require beneficiaries to accept any type of job. Even if during the past years a series of activation policies have weakened this right, the idea of appropriate jobs continues to be an important hallmark of Belgian unemployment insurance.

Current legislation endows NEO's local employment offices with a considerable degree of discretion for judging what might be considered an appropriate job, but there are a number of formal criteria that guide this assessment, such as skill level relative to formal qualification, remuneration relative to the unemployment benefit, daily commuting time, atypical working time, and liability to social security legislation. In the past decades, those criteria have hardly changed except for school graduates, who up to 1991 enjoyed a stronger protection with respect to their formal qualifications during the first six months of unemployment (see CCE, 2009; de Loose, 2004). Three aspects of the definition of 'appropriate employment' in the unemployment code prevent a drift of those out of work towards precarious jobs: the jobs have to be liable to social insurance, the employment conditions must be in accordance with the collectively negotiated wage agreements of the sector, and the net wage cannot be lower than the benefit that the unemployed is entitled to.

More broadly, although Belgium scores well above the OECD average in terms of expenditure on active labour market programmes, until a decade ago this activation was largely limited to various forms of subsidized employment in the non-profit sector. But since the turn of the century, Belgium has been quite innovative in implementing innovative measures to extend this kind of job creation by subsidizing employment in for-profit enterprises. Initially, such wage subsidies were limited to various reductions in social security contributions of employers recruiting young unemployed (the *Rosetta* Plan launched in 1999) or long-term older unemployed (the *Activa Plan* adopted in 2002). But as of the year 2000, a service voucher scheme (*dienstencheques – titres-services*) started to be rolled out that was very successful in creating jobs in local personal services. The main idea behind this scheme is to allow both non-governmental organizations and for-profit enterprises to provide services at prices that can compete with the clandestine and underground economy. The scheme is financed out of the budget of the NEO because one of the main goals is to create employment for low-skilled, long-term unemployed. The scheme allows households to purchase special subsidized vouchers, which they can use to pay for 'local community services' such as household tasks (e.g. cleaning), and some tasks at the margin of childcare, and care for the elderly and the sick (e.g. transport of disabled persons).[5] Initially, the service voucher jobs were only provided by the local employment agencies of the 'social economy', but later on the scheme was extended to include also profit-based providers, that now form the main bulk of providers (for more details, see De Deken, 2011*a*; Palsterman, 2010).

Even more than was the case with the traditional public job-creation programmes, the service voucher scheme has allowed creation of employment in the sector of personal services that is by definition suffering from low productivity, without relying on extending precarious employment contracts to cope with the inherent 'cost disease' problem in this sector. Rather, the scheme uses public subsidies to compensate for the lack of productivity. Thus, in 2007, about 67 per cent of the workforce of the accredited service firms had an open-ended contract (Henry et al., 2009). The main problem of the service voucher scheme is how financially sustainable it is as a job-creation strategy: if the scheme does more than legalizing part of the black economy, the increased tax returns will soon be outstripped by the exploding costs of the NEO subsidies. Moreover, as the commercial temporary work agencies often only offer non-standard employment,[6] the development of a non-precarious low-skill service sector still primarily depends upon the public and non-profit providers. In other words, to the extent that the scheme is successful in going beyond the realm of the 'old' job-creation programmes in the public and non-profit sector, it may end up enlarging atypical precarious employment contracts.

In the advent of the 1997 European Employment Strategy (EES), labour market policies began to be focused more on labour supply. Even though the job-creation programmes of the past, the local service initiatives, and the new service vouchers system had been set up in part with the intent to improve the labour market skills of low-skilled unemployed, during the 1990s there was also a trend towards more individual career guidance arrangements and a more strict monitoring of the job-search behaviour of the unemployed became apparent. Because eligibility for unemployment benefits became more conditional upon participation in activation programmes, the new system required a better coordination between the various governance levels and agencies that had evolved after the devolution of labour

---

[5] About 90 per cent of the vouchers are currently used for cleaning tasks (Palsterman, 2010).
[6] Not only do they have the highest number of part-timers but they also offer a fixed-term contract to six out of ten workers (Cour des Comptes, 2009).

market policies. For that purpose the federal and regional governments concluded cooperation agreements in 2004, and established a national information database for social security as the platform for exchanging information between the various federal and regional institutions. Under the new administrative system, regional employment offices are obliged to inform the NEO about unemployment benefit claimants' participation in activation schemes. In the event that the NEO considers individual efforts of job seeking or participation in a training scheme as insufficient, it can instruct the payment body to suspend benefit transfer. The auxiliary unemployment funds of the trade unions have to put this decision into practice, but also offer their members legal advice and support in the event that they intend to contest the sanction of suspension imposed by the NEO (De Deken, 2009).

In the wake of these activation schemes, the policy of benefit (paragraph 80; as discussed above) was replaced by a new rule with a potentially broader target population, including in principle all long-term unemployed claimants. While those over the age of 50 have remained exempt, the system no longer differentiates by the average length of unemployment spells in the district where claimants live. As a result, the new rules led to a complete reversal in the gender ratio of those suspended from benefit. Until 2004, about 90 per cent of those sanctioned were females, particularly those who cohabited with an earning partner, involuntary part-time workers, and temporary employees. After 2004, new rules excluded those who were deemed to make insufficient efforts to find a job, and in practice seemed to suspend benefits primarily for those who entered the system after their studies without having any work experience whatsoever (Bauwens, 2009: 430). As Figure 6.4 shows, this not only led to a somehow paradoxical decline in the total number of suspensions but also redressed the gender balance.

The sharp decline of the total number of suspensions suggests that by enrolling in the activation schemes the unemployed who in the past would have seen their benefit suspended are now able to avoid this fate by participating in various activation schemes. It might also be that Belgium is becoming more like its neighbouring countries which force some of its long-term unemployed into precarious employment, thus making it more difficult to establish eligibility to unemployment insurance benefits and reinforcing a trend towards 'dualization'. The fact that the number of fixed-term contracts and part-time employment have recently been growing in number may point in that direction.

Some applicants of the MIG are also subjected to activation measures. These measures, which during the past decade employed about 20,000 applicants per year, are administered by the municipal social assistance offices (MSAO).[7] In about a third of all cases, it is the MSAO itself that operates as the employer. Most of the

---

[7] Comparing this figure to the total number of beneficiaries of the minimum income guarantee is of limited value as most recipients of that benefit (about 400,000 per year) are not fit for the labour market or receive their mean-tested benefits as a mere supplement of other forms of income (e.g. from self-employment). As we already pointed out, the minimum income guarantee plays a truly residual role in the total package of out-of-work benefits for the working-age population. One can compare, though, 20,000 activated social assistance recipients with the 280,000 job-seeking unemployment insurance benefit claimants (out of a total job-seeking unemployed population of close to half a million) who in 2007 were processed by the unemployment insurance activation scheme; and with close to 100,000 unemployed who are annually accommodated by the various schemes of direct job creation in the non-profit sector.

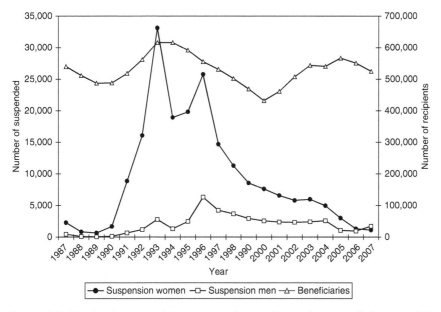

Figure 6.4. The development of the number of unemployed whose benefit is suspended (left axis) and of the total number of UB recipients (right axis)

Source: Own calculations based on RVA-ONEM Statistical Yearbooks

other employers in these programmes are part of the so-called 'social economy' of non-profit organizations and public administrations. These forms of activation might therefore be considered as a continuation of the subsidized employment of the demand-side activation policies of the 1980s.

The reintegration of recipients of incapacity benefits, paid by the employment injuries scheme into the labour market, is initiated on medical grounds, but for actual career guidance and training claimants are referred to the regional employment offices and have to enter special tracks in the above described system. As such there seem to have been attempts to move towards an administrative merger of active support schemes for the beneficiaries of unemployment insurance and of incapacity schemes. But recipients of MIG of the social assistance scheme do not seem to be part of this referral process, even if they too sometimes end up in activation programmes that were set up for beneficiaries of unemployment insurance.

6.5 MAKING SENSE OF THE BELGIAN TRAJECTORY

The incremental reforms of the past three decades were primarily inspired by cost containment. In order to achieve this goal, what little there existed in terms of a link between contributions and benefits was abandoned. While the real value of maximum benefits eroded, wage earners with an income above the median have been made to pay higher contributions by lifting the contribution ceilings that used to exist. As a consequence, it has been argued that for a steadily growing part of the wage-earner population, the gap between what they contribute and what they may reasonably expect to gain has become so large that this may well undermine the legitimacy of the unemployment insurance system. Some observers have argued that this actuarial unfairness ought to have provoked a revolt of middle-and higher-income groups (Shokkaert and Spinnewyn, 1995), but so far the erosion of the insurance principle has remained 'pretty much a non-issue' (Marx, 2007: 155). One reason for the continued tacit support for the given system may lie in its opaqueness and its transformation by stealth. The fact that unemployment contributions are no longer earmarked but lumped together with other social security contributions, including those for health care, makes it difficult to get a precise idea of what one pays into the system and what one is entitled to. There might also be a tacit support amongst middle-income groups that is related to the 'improper' use of the unemployment benefit system as a kind of career interruption scheme for secondary female earners (Marx, 2007). But it was precisely in this area that some of the more drastic reforms have been implemented (in particular the suspension of benefits under Article 80). However, at the same time as the illicit use of unemployment benefits for voluntary withdrawal from the labour market was discouraged, a number of new sabbatical schemes saw the light that extended maternity leave to other forms of care (De Deken and Offe, 2001).[8]

A second set of explanations for the comparable lack of radical reform can be related to the role of the trade unions and the employers' associations in the administration of social security in general and unemployment insurance and early retirement schemes in particular. Given the composition of their membership basis, it does not come as that much of a surprise that the trade unions have been fiercer in their opposition to such issues as the possible curtailment of benefit duration than in countering the aforementioned lack of actuarial fairness (Kuipers, 2006). After all, if scarce resources need to be allocated, benefit duration for the many serves the interests of the bulk of their members better than high replacement rates for the few. The unions have influenced the reform process only to a limited extent via their formal involvement in the benefit administration (which, as we argued, is only vaguely related to what in the international literature is referred to as the 'Ghent system'), but rather via their position in the 'Bismarckian' parity control of social security and their leverage in the neo-corporatist system of tripartite consultation. The unions and employers' associations have a direct control over the schemes that top up unemployment benefits to facilitate early retirement, that serves both the trade union clientele and employers' interest in boosting the productivity of their enterprises without carrying the brunt of the costs of shedding labour. Compared to such countries as the Netherlands, both trade unions and employers could more easily externalize the costs of early labour market exit, because no important second pension pillar with a related financial autonomy exists that could foot the bill (Hartlapp and Kemmerling, 2008). The social

---

[8] In 2010, about 6,400 persons enjoyed a full-time sabbatical, whereas about 66,000 reduced their working time in exchange for a partial career-interruption benefit; and another 60,000 persons enjoyed a full-time benefit for parental leave or the care-palliative leave schemes (*Source*: Annual Statistics of the NEO, www.rva.be, 22.5.2010).

partners were only directly responsible for financing the supplements to unemployment insurance benefits, not the entire early retirement package.

Even though Belgium is, in essence, what the Varieties of Capitalism approach calls a Coordinated Market Economy (Hall and Soskice, 2001), wage bargaining is more fragmented than in more ideal typical countries such as Germany and the Netherlands. Collective wage agreements are negotiated in several hundred joint committees and subcommittees, some covering quite small branches of the economy with only a few hundred employees. The coordinating role of central trade union federations and employers associations is complicated by several ideological, sectoral, and more recently regional, cleavages. Even if at the central level an agreement might be reached on broader macroeconomic or social questions (such as wage restraint or the phasing out of early retirement), there are many ways for the bargaining partners at the local level of the joint committee to defect from the agreed line of policy. This might explain the resilience of the CBP and SBP bridging pension schemes.

The fragmented, complex, and conflict-ridden political system also impedes the kind of unilateral state action that one could observe in the United Kingdom and in the Netherlands. Devolution has led to a system of governance in which competencies and responsibilities are distributed in a way that almost inevitably precludes a high degree of policy consistency (Hemerijck and Marx, 2010). This does not necessarily have to hamper a functioning policy practice, but it does make it difficult for the government to legislate radical social policy reforms. To the extent that changes were implemented, they were more the result of muddling through, initiating marginal changes, and apparently technical alterations or non-interventions, which at some point mounted up to more substantial changes and sometimes also produced beneficial if not always intended outcomes. To the extent that more drastic measures were initiated, they were the result of pressures imposed by external circumstances. During the 1980s, such pressures came in the form of the need to maintain budgetary restraint, necessary for defending the hard currency that would help to boost productivity and preserve Belgium's position as an exporting country. It was also a precondition for the country to be able to join the European Monetary Union. Towards the end of the 1990s the external force started to manifest itself in the form of the 'peer review' and 'benchmarking' of the open method of coordination and the EES (Hartlapp and Kemmerling, 2008).

6.6 CONCLUSIONS

Because of its different development during the 1970s, the Belgian case is hard to fit into the triple integration framework that was identified in the introductory chapter of this book and which refers to policies pursued since the early 1990s in several countries. However, the reason might simply be that Belgium can be considered as a 'precursor', especially in terms of benefit homogenization. Unlike elsewhere, the unemployment benefit system never evolved into a dualist two-tiered system of unemployment insurance and unemployment assistance. Access to what formally is a social insurance scheme is relatively easy to establish, even for school graduates with no employment history. Benefits are only very weakly earnings related and their level depends upon inferred need. For most claimants there is no limit on the duration that they are entitled to a benefit. Thus, in contrast to many other countries in this book, there always was a kind of a single-tiered system for that part of the working-age population that was in (or about to enter) a dependent employment relationship. By contrast, social assistance in Belgium is not a substitute or alternative programme but a truly residual system providing means-tested benefits to those who are not part of the wage-earning population, as well as a small minority of former wage earners who fail to meet the eligibility of an otherwise very inclusive unemployment insurance scheme.

The decline of manufacturing industries and the transition towards a service sector economy started early, but because of the existence of strong encompassing trade unions, this did not, until recently, result in a significant growth of atypical or casual employment. As a consequence of being hit early on by massive structural unemployment, hesitant attempts during the 1970s to develop a more differentiated, that is, earnings-related, unemployment insurance system that could have resulted in a genuine two-tiered system were aborted. The country was in a way ahead of other countries in establishing (or probably better in maintaining) a single-tier, and comparatively inclusive and fairly homogenized, system of unemployment protection.

Because of this character, there never was an attempt to transfer jobless persons from unemployment insurance scheme towards other working-age benefits, such as incapacity benefits or social assistance. There is one exception, though. While unemployment protection remained encompassing, the principal instrument of post-industrial labour shedding was early retirement. During the 1980s, a considerable number of redundant workers left the labour force by drawing a statutory old-age pension early, thus shifting caseloads towards the old-age pension system. During the 1990s, this particular route was phased out, and the remaining form of early retirement was one which topped up unemployment insurance benefits with supplements negotiated at industry level. There have been recurrent attempts to close down these early exit routes, but some of those routes have proved to be remarkably resilient. It is the very low activity rates of older workers that remain the Achilles heel of the Belgian labour market. The fact that older de facto retired workers continue to receive unemployment insurance benefits (while not being subject to job-seeking conditions) is also the main explanation why the total caseload of the unemployment benefit system, in comparison to other European countries, remains colossal in spite of the fact that unemployment rates, as reported in labour force surveys, have moved closer to the EU average. The other main group that is covered in Belgium but excluded in unemployment insurance systems in most other countries are school graduates who cannot find a job. Only those who do get a job after graduating, but end up being unemployed soon afterwards, are excluded as they cannot access the system under the school graduate clause, while also failing to meet the qualifying period. In short, the inclusiveness of Belgian unemployment protection makes it both more homogeneous and provides less of an impetus of benefit re-categorizing than elsewhere in Europe.

The worsening employment situation that followed the banking crisis of 2008 seems to have reduced the sense of urgency to deal with the low inactivity rates of older workers by forcing them (or their employers) to remain in (or be kept in), or return to, paid work. If during the first decade of the twenty-first century even the take-up rate of unemployment insurance-based early retirement had finally started to stagnate (and even showed the first signs of a decline), in the year 2009 one could again observe an increase. However, like in neighbouring Germany and the Netherlands, the main instrument to cope with the sluggish demand for labour has consisted of schemes granting temporary economic unemployment benefits. One reason for the strong growth in the latter is the fact that, following the national collective wage agreement 2009–10, temporary agency workers have for the first time been incorporated into this scheme.

With respect to the third dimension of the triple integration framework, one can observe that in the wake of the 'peer pressure' of the European Union's open method of coordination and EES, Belgium may have introduced or reinforced various activation measures aimed at getting the unemployed back to work, and increase labour force participation particularly of elderly workers. However, the political dynamics of a central state under devolution have prevented a degree of administrative merger which has been observed in other European countries. In fact, at first sight one might be tempted to conclude that the opposite has happened, that is, that by devolving active support and activation policies to the regional governments, while maintaining passive support policies and the possibility to impose sanctions by suspending or cutting benefits a competence of the federal state and its administration, the institutional fragmentation has been amplified. However, one could also interpret this administrative reform as having created, possibly unintended, an intriguing division of labour between the federal bureaucracy holding the 'stick' and the regional administration providing the 'carrot' of labour market policies (De Deken, 2009). This intricate structure is, in part, held together by the social partners who are still organized on a federal basis and who are involved in all these levels of government by traditional 'Bismarckian' parity-based governance structures. In addition, the trade unions fulfil the role of 'brokers' and 'ombudsmen' for the unemployed. On the other hand, the continued call for devolution by most Flemish parties, prompted by an apparent unwillingness of the French-speaking part of the country to follow the gospel of activation, might lead to dissolution of the social insurance system, one of the few remaining backbones of national unity and federal solidarity.

In addition, since compared with other countries much less use has been made of 'alternative' working-age benefit schemes, there may have been less need for creating a one-stop shop for claimants of different working-age benefit programmes. The case remains to be made to integrate these different groups into one administrative structure. An increase in precarious non-standard employment could be such a reason, but so far there are no clear trends in that direction.

In brief, Belgium can be considered to form a precursor muddling through: since the system was already quite homogeneous there was no need to accentuate this feature during the 1990s and beyond; and there was little risk of reconfiguration because the unemployment benefit system already caters to a variety of working-age risks and uses a logic of institutional layering to fulfil additional functions. There was no grand administrative merger because the stakeholders are well entrenched in the governance system and the linguistic cleavage may have marred politics with a joint-decision trap that forced policymakers into a kind of bricolage that inadvertently produced an innovative division of labour.

Appendix 6.A Net replacement rates in 2005 of statutory unemployment benefits for households without children and a recipient aged less than 50 years

Family status	First 12 months (%)	13th–17th month (%)	As of 18th month (%)
Half the APW			
Single	70	70	70
Heads of households	77	77	77
Cohabiting partner on minimum wage	63	46	40
Full APW			
Single	57	57	57
Heads of households	60	57	57
Cohabiting partner on minimum wage	56	42	26
Twice the APW			
Single	37	34	34
Heads of households	37	37	37
Cohabiting partner on minimum wage	25	25	15

Source: Own calculations based on legislation applied to the OECD average production worker wage for (conversion from gross to net was done by means of a simulation programme of the social secretariat ADMB available on www.admb.be).

7

Switzerland: a latecomer catching up?[1]

Cyrielle Champion

7.1 INTRODUCTION

Until the late 1980s, unemployment was not really a social issue in Switzerland. Thanks to a flexible, minimally regulated labour market and high responsiveness of foreign and female workers to economic fluctuations, Switzerland remained an island of economic prosperity and full employment throughout the 1970s and 1980s. The number of working-age people living on the receipt of benefits was generally very low. In fact, in the 1980s the social security system for working-age people still presented some characteristics of an underdeveloped system, and social policymaking at this period was generally synonymous with expanding the coverage and generosity of social programmes. One of the best examples is unemployment insurance (UI), which became mandatory only in 1982.

The 1990s, however, marked a turning point in the Swiss labour market situation when the economic crisis resulted in unprecedented levels of unemployment. Even if the extent of the 'welfare-without-work' problem has been always less severe in Switzerland than in other countries (unemployment rates have never durably exceeded 5 per cent), the sudden appearance of unemployment was a major shock. Combined with emergent budget deficits, this new situation led to a number of reforms in the different branches of the Swiss social security system.

This chapter briefly discusses the most significant labour market transformations in Switzerland since the 1990s. The main reforms of the social security system for working-age people from the 1990s onwards will be examined in a second section. By social security system for working-age people, I refer here not only to UI, which constitutes the first and most important unemployment compensation scheme, but also to general social assistance and disability insurance. Not only have these two benefit schemes become increasingly important in terms of caseloads, but they have also developed as the two major forms of income support for the unemployed who have exhausted their entitlement to UI benefits. Finally, I will show in the third section that, while it has long been acknowledged that joblessness has become a cross-institutional problem, reforms did not pave the way for greater benefit

[1] I would like to thank the editors and authors of this volume, especially Giuliano Bonoli, for very helpful comments on earlier versions of this chapter. Financial support from the Swiss National Science Foundation (grant number 100012–126528) is also gratefully acknowledged.

homogenization or administrative integration. It is argued that the fragmentation of the Swiss social security system, and more particularly the divisions of responsibilities within the federal government and between the federal and the cantonal levels, can explain a large part of the still fragmented approach of the Swiss reform policy.

7.2 THE EMPLOYMENT CRISIS OF THE 1990s AND THE EMERGING CHALLENGE OF POST-INDUSTRIALIZATION

Contrary to most of its European neighbours, Switzerland witnessed an exceptional labour market performance up to the early 1990s. Although unemployment first rose in the 1970s after the first oil crisis, Switzerland was still largely preserved from mass unemployment that hit Europe at that time. Throughout the 1980s, the unemployment rate never exceeded 1 per cent, and employment rates remained very high in comparative perspective. This economic stability led several authors to consider Switzerland as a *Sonderfall*, or a special case (Flückiger, 1998; Obinger, 1998).

Accordingly, Switzerland did not undergo major changes in economic and social policies during the 1980s. To some extent, it can be argued that much of the adjustment undertaken by other European countries was not needed in Switzerland at that time (Bonoli and Mach, 2000). First, considering the Swiss macroeconomic model, Switzerland already possessed many liberal characteristics allowing for high labour market adaptability and competitiveness. In particular, a low degree of employment protection and a decentralized wage-bargaining system, in which collective agreements are negotiated mostly at the sectoral or company level, have always ensured high mobility in the labour market and high wage flexibility (Eichhorst and Konle-Seidl, 2005; Straubhaar and Werner, 2003).

Second, the apparently strong resistance to the economic recessions of the 1970s and 1980s was to a large extent due to high cyclical responsiveness of labour supply (Bonoli and Mach, 2000; Fluckiger, 1998). In particular, specific foreign labour regulation based on temporary work permits that enabled the restriction of work permits in recessionary times, as well as the cyclical withdrawal of female workers from the labour market, played an important role as cyclical shock absorbers. Thus, the economic and social repercussions of the recessions of the 1970s and 1980s were mainly supported by foreign workers and working women, leaving the core labour force largely unaffected (Bertozzi et al., 2005; Bonoli and Mach, 2000).

Subsequently, the Swiss unemployment protection system did not face any particularly strong pressure until the early 1990s. In fact, whereas the first steps towards retrenchment were undertaken in European countries in order to deal with increasing benefit expenditure, Switzerland experienced a relative expansion of its unemployment protection system in the late 1970s, when following the first oil crisis, a first temporary decree made UI universal and mandatory in 1977. This was followed in 1982 by the adoption of the federal UI law. Previously, UI was voluntary, and only about 20 per cent of all workers were covered by an UI plan (Obinger et al., 2005). Partly for this reason, the Swiss welfare state has long been described as a 'welfare laggard' (Armingeon, 2001; Obinger, 1998).

Its position of latecomer in the field of unemployment protection as well as its then exceptional labour market performance at the time allowed Switzerland to develop a relatively comprehensive and generous UI system. First, benefit levels were fixed at a high level, which made the Swiss UI one of the most generous among OECD countries. This generosity in benefit levels was, however, compensated by relatively short benefit duration and strict job-search requirements and controls. Already in the 1980s, UI claimants had to visit the public employment office every week and provide evidence of regular applications (about ten applications per month) (OECD, 1996). Moreover, even if the preferred strategy was the direct integration into the labour market, the first law on UI allowed for activation measures, such as training courses and subsidized employment. However, in the context of low unemployment rates, there was only sporadic recourse to such measures (Maeder and Nadai, 2009).

Up to the 1990s, UI remained the principal pillar of the Swiss unemployment protection system. Unemployment assistance schemes were non-existent. Thus, once claimants had exhausted their entitlement to the UI benefits, they had no other option but to rely on social assistance provided by the Cantons. However, the low rate of long-term unemployment made claims for social assistance rare and other exit options, such as disability benefits or early retirement,[2] even more unusual. As a whole, only a relatively small number of Swiss working-age people were living on welfare.

7.2.1 Labour market changes since the 1990s

The economic downturn in the early 1990s marked the collapse of the Swiss employment miracle. Unlike in the 1970s and 1980s, the economic crisis for the first time resulted in a sharp increase in the unemployment rate (see Statistical Annex, Table A.5; also Figure 7.2). This abrupt change is commonly explained by the abandonment of the buffer function exerted by women and foreign workers. Owing to a change in Swiss immigration policy, many work permits were gradually transformed from temporary to permanent ones during the 1980s. Furthermore, in contrast to the situation prevailing after the oil crisis in the 1970s and 1980s, women no longer withdrew from the labour market in the early 1990s. Indeed, during this period, the female employment rate remained stable (see Statistical Annex, Table A.4). Finally, it also seems that the generalization of UI affected the behaviour of laid-off workers. Whereas a large majority of redundant workers did not register as unemployed at the beginning of the 1980s, this was no longer the case a decade later (Bertozzi et al., 2005; Bonoli and Mach, 2000; Flückiger, 1998).

Ever since the crisis of the 1990s, full employment as it was experienced until the end of the 1980s has not returned. Switzerland has, however, still one of the highest employment rates in Europe with almost 90 per cent of the working-age

---

[2] The Swiss social security system offers only few opportunities to take early retirement. Since 1997, the basic public pension system has made it possible to retire before full retirement age, but under unfavourable conditions. The scheme has, however, rapidly grown in significance, especially among women (see Figure 7.2).

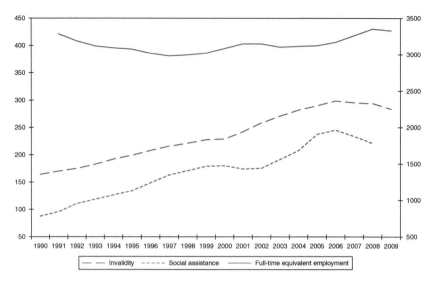

Figure 7.1. Employment (full-time equivalent jobs, in thousands, right axis) and receipt of social assistance and disability insurance (in thousands; left axis), 1990–2009

Source: OFS, STATEM for figures on full-time equivalent employment; OFS, Statistiques de l'AI for figures on disability insurance; OFS (2009) for social assistance (1990–2004: recalculations on the basis of a social assistance index as federal statistics only exist since 2005).

population. Moreover, after a decline of employment in the 1990s, Switzerland experienced steady employment growth in the 2000s (see Figure 7.1). For a large part, job creation has occurred in the service sector, while employment in industry has remained relatively stable over the past decade.

The expansion of the service sector has gone hand in hand with an increase in non-standard employment. In particular, the proportion of people working part-time (i.e. less than 90 per cent of an organization's maximum weekly working time), women in most cases, has massively expanded since the 1990s, rising from 25 per cent of the working population in 1991 to 35 per cent by 2009 (OFS, SLFS; see also Statistical Annex, Table A.9). Other, more precarious forms of employment have also expanded. Between 1991 and 2009, the proportion of people working under fixed-term contracts almost doubled (OFS, SLFS), while the number of temporary agency workers almost tripled over the same period of time (Swiss staffing statistics).

However, the expansion of non-standard employment has not been a major public policy issue for two reasons. First, part-time employment is still predominantly voluntary. In 2008, only 6.5 per cent of all part-time workers claimed that they would like to work more (OFS, SLFS). Second, given the generally weak level of labour market regulation, temporary employment is not really used as a means to circumvent stricter regulations of permanent contracts (Engellandt and Riphahn, 2005). Indeed, in terms of protection against dismissal or access to social benefits, temporary employment is not so different from regular employment. As a result, temporary employment remains predominantly a transitory form of employment that most people leave within one year (SECO, 2010*a*).

More relevant than the growth of atypical employment has been the sharp rise in the number of jobless people who seem to remain excluded from the labour market. In fact, the growth in employment has been accompanied by a steady increase in benefit dependency, particularly during the 2000s (see Figure 7.1). While employment recovered after the economic downturn of the 1990s, the proportion of working-age people in receipt of either social assistance or disability benefits continued to rise.

The early 1990s thus marked a rupture in the Swiss labour market. For the first time since World War II, Switzerland faced social and economic problems which had been familiar in other European countries since the 1970s. After the early 1990s, unemployment had become a structural phenomenon. Even more dramatically, the rise in unemployment has been accompanied by a sharp rise in non-employed working-age people in receipt of benefits for whom work no longer seems to be available. Even though the Swiss labour market still performs very well by international standards, this unprecedented situation, coupled with an economic growth almost constantly below the OECD average, has given rise to growing concerns that the Swiss socio-economic model was in crisis (Berclaz et al., forthcoming; Bonoli and Mach, 2000; Gärtner and Flückiger, 2005).

7.3 REFORMS IN THE SWISS SOCIAL SECURITY SYSTEM FOR WORKING-AGE PEOPLE

In this section, I review major changes introduced in the three main benefit schemes for working-age people, namely UI, social assistance, and invalidity insurance, since 1990. On a general level, it can be said that, whereas pressures have prompted substantial reforms, reforms have largely concentrated on redefining eligibility and entitlement conditions, as well as reinforcing the orientation towards employment, without fundamentally altering the structure of benefit provision. In fact, the most striking change in the three-pillar structure is that the three main benefit schemes have grown significantly in importance. Figure 7.2 illustrates the sharp increase in recipients of unemployment, social assistance, and incapacity benefits between 1990 and 2008, as well as their relative importance compared to other income-replacement benefits.

Two specificities of the Swiss social security system need to be noted. First, the Swiss social security shares important features with Bismarckian countries given that UI and invalidity insurance provide generous earnings-related benefits. At the same time, some liberal traits are visible in invalidity insurance, which relies extensively on compulsory semi-private occupational provision (for an assessment of the classification of the Swiss regime, see Häusermann, 2010).

Second, federalism has strongly shaped the structure of the Swiss social security system, as the Cantons have always retained substantial powers in this field (Bertozzi et al., 2008). Not only are the Cantons involved in the implementation of most social insurance schemes but they have also kept regulatory powers in

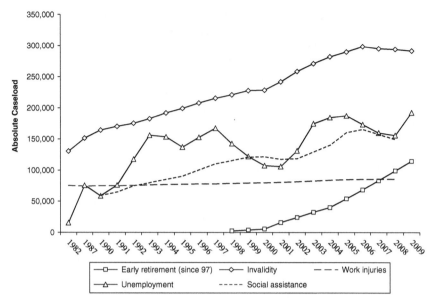

Figure 7.2. The development of the main income-replacement benefit caseloads, 1982–2009

Note: see Caseload Annex (Switzerland).

some fields, such as social assistance. The result is a clear-cut split of responsibilities between the federal level and lower tiers of government. While the two social insurance programmes are regulated at the federal level, social assistance is entirely regulated and funded by the Cantons, with a strong involvement of the municipalities in its implementation in some Cantons.

The Cantons are also empowered to establish unemployment assistance benefit schemes if they wish. However, unlike social assistance, the federal constitution does not oblige them to establish such a scheme. Thus, unemployment assistance remains at the total discretion of the Cantons, and there exists an even greater diversity of schemes across Cantons (Bertozzi et al., 2008; Obinger, 1999). In 2006, twelve out of twenty-six Cantons had introduced a kind of unemployment assistance scheme, mostly in reaction to the steep rise in long-term unemployment in the 1990s (OFS, 2007). Most of these schemes are means-tested, time-limited, and often require beneficiaries to participate in active measures to requalify for UI benefits.

7.3.1 Unemployment insurance

The most important scheme for unemployed people is federal UI. As a standard social insurance programme, it is financed out of employer and employee contributions and, if in deficit, subsidized by federal taxation. It is regulated and funded at the federal level. At the local level, the implementation is characterized by a division of competencies, with forty-three cantonal and social partner-run funds sharing responsibility for the payment of benefits, and regional placement offices (RAV/ORP) in charge of job-search monitoring and allocation of active labour market programmes (ALMPs; Bertozzi et al., 2008).

UI has been subject to several reforms since the 1990s, when unemployment started to grow significantly and the financial situation of the UI fund began to deteriorate. The most important revisions took place in 1993, 1995, 2002, and 2010. As pointed out by Häusermann (2010), these reforms have consisted of two strands, often linked together in reform packages: the first of these involved parametric changes, which were aimed at cost containment by altering eligibility and entitlement conditions, and the second was the introduction of more activation policies. By contrast, benefit levels have remained fairly unchanged, and UI still provides generous benefits.

As for cost containment, the first response was to raise contribution rates. In 1993, employers' and employees' contribution rates rose from 0.4 to 2 per cent of the insured salary, equally distributed between the employer and employee. As this increase proved insufficient to cover continuously growing expenditures, contributions increased to 3 per cent in 1995, on a temporary basis. In the face of declining unemployment, this emergency measure ended in 2003. The most recent reform includes another increase in contribution rates, which now amount to 2.2 per cent.

More important, however, were measures which have sought to make entitlement more dependent on previous work records and age in order to tighten eligibility criteria, especially for young unemployed persons and those with repeated spells of joblessness. These measures were the common denominator of all reforms implemented so far. In 1995, a five-day waiting period was introduced, which could extend up to 120 days for young people without completed training (Perret et al., 2007). In parallel, the possibility for the long-term unemployed to requalify for UI benefits after participating in a federal-funded labour market programme was abolished, thus putting an end to the de facto unlimited duration of receiving UI benefits (Merrien, 2001).

In 2002, a second reform increased the qualifying period from six to twelve months within a period of two years, and reduced the duration of benefits from twenty-four to eighteen months, unless unemployed persons had a contribution record of more than eighteen months or were older than 55 years of age. This reform, and more particularly the tightened access to benefits, was mainly justified in light of Swiss–EU bilateral agreements on the free movement of persons entering into the workforce. Yet, it also led to workers with unstable employment careers being excluded from benefits (Gärtner and Flückiger, 2005). Finally, a new reform was accepted by popular vote in September 2010, after it went through several rounds of debates in parliament and was challenged in referendum by trade unions and the Social Democrats. At the centre of the reform lies the objective of restricting benefits for those with a weak attachment to the labour market, and more specifically young people. On a general level, a contribution period of twelve months gives entitlement to only twelve months of benefits instead of the former entitlement of eighteen months. For young people under 25, the maximum benefit duration has been further limited to nine months. In addition, for people having just completed training the duration of benefits has been reduced to four months while a six-month waiting period has been introduced (Table 7.1).

Concerning activation, the most important reform took place in 1995, which restructured the system profoundly, giving priority to labour market integration (Berclaz and Füglister, 2004). It comprised three main aspects: a further development of ALMPs, the tightening of jobseekers' obligations and requirements, and the administrative reorganization of employment services.

Subsequent to the reform, the scope of federal labour market programmes has been considerably extended. New programmes, such as training allowances and encouragement of self-employment, have been introduced in addition to already existing measures. Besides, in order to enhance the effective number of programmes, substantial additional funds have been made available at the federal level and quotas adopted which require a minimum number of activation measures to be provided in each Canton. At the same time, behavioural obligations were made more stringent. In this regard, the notion of 'employability' has become the driving principle of activating unemployed people (Bertozzi et al., 2008; Maeder and Nadai, 2009). To remain entitled to UI benefits, unemployed people are now required to be 'able and ready for work', that is, capable of fulfilling the requirements of a regular job and ready to accept any suitable

Table 7.1. UI benefits: eligibility and entitlement criteria; generosity (since 2011)

Membership	Mandatory for all employees
Waiting period	Between 5 and 20 days, depending on family situation and previous annual income: • 5 days for people with dependent children or with an annual income less than CHF 60,000 (€41,000) • Between 10 and 20 days for people without dependent children and with an annual income of more than CHF 60,000, depending on income levels • 120 days (6 months) for persons exempt from contributions (women with caring responsibilities, graduates, and school leavers)
Qualifying period	12 months of contributions within a period of 2 years preceding unemployment
Benefit levels	Depending on the family situation: • 80% of the insured salary for persons with dependent children • 70% for others Maximum insured salary: CHF €6100 per month (€8900)
Maximum Duration	Depending on age and contribution periods: • 4 months for persons exempt from contributions • 9 months for young people under 25 and without dependent children • 12 months for persons with a min. 12-month contribution period • 18 months for those with a contribution record of 18 months or more • 24 months for those over 55 years old and with a min. 24-month contribution period
Obligations	To register as unemployed; to be capable and available for work; to attend monthly interviews with job counsellors and comply with job-search requirements (usually 6–10 job applications a month); to accept a 'suitable' job, defined in terms of commuting time (max. 4 hours/day), prior earnings (min. 70% of previous insured income) and qualifications (in line with training and prior occupation, except for unemployed under 30 years old)

Source: OFS, Swiss Labour Force Survey (SLFS), various issues.

work or participate in integration measures if required. The introduction of this condition has profoundly redefined eligibility for UI benefits, as a jobless person can now lose her entitlement to UI benefits if she is deemed unemployable by her case manager.

This new emphasis on employability went hand in hand with tighter job suitability criteria and sanctions. Unemployed people can be forced to accept jobs involving up to four hours travel daily; salaries as low as 70 per cent of previous wages; and even, after a certain period, jobs with lower qualifications. With the last reform, the notion of suitable work has been further broadened for young people under 30 years old, who can now be forced to accept any vacant jobs irrespective of training and prior qualifications. Any refusal to accept a suitable job or participate in activation measures, as well as other administrative misbehaviours, such as the non-compliance with job-search requirements or the non-attendance at interviews, can be sanctioned by benefit suspensions of up to twelve weeks. Benefit sanctions have existed in Switzerland since the introduction of mandatory UI in 1982. Yet, since 1995, they have become more frequently applied. International comparisons show that in the 1990s Switzerland was, with Norway and Finland, one of the European countries with the highest annual number of sanctions (Grubb, 2000).

Finally, in order to support this activation policy in a more efficient way, regional placement offices (RAV/ORP) were established. These were set up by the Cantons, but are essentially financed by the federal UI fund. All claimants in receipt of UI benefits have to register at the ORP and are assigned to a case manager (employment counsellor) who monitors job-search activities, provides access to activation measures, and enforces sanctions if need be. Unemployed people have to meet with their counsellor at least once a month. Finally, it should be noted that job-search assistance provided by the ORP is legally open to all jobseekers, provided they are deemed capable of working. However, only jobless people in receipt of UI benefits are, in principle, eligible for federally funded activation measures (Bertozzi et al., 2008).

7.3.2 Social assistance

Social assistance acts as the last resort safety net for the whole population, assuring a minimum income to those who are not covered by social insurance schemes or to employed people whose income is insufficient to cover basic needs. In this context, social assistance serves as the last option after unemployed people have exhausted their entitlement to UI. In 2008, the share of unemployed people among all social assistance recipients over 15 was 34 per cent (OFS, 2010).

The organization of social assistance varies across Switzerland, as the legislative regulation falls within the competence of the Cantons. Thus, legally speaking, there are twenty-six separate social assistance schemes in Switzerland, with varying types of support and benefit levels according to cantonal legislation. In practice, however, a certain homogenization in social assistance procedures and benefit levels is achieved through guidelines formulated by the Swiss Conference for Social Assistance (CSIAS/SKOS), which brings together representatives of the different levels of public authorities and the most important private social organizations. Even though the CSIAS guidelines are not binding as such, with few exceptions the Cantons generally comply with them.

Before the 1990s, social assistance played a marginal role in Switzerland, mainly due to low unemployment and also a strong stigma associated with dependency on social assistance.[3] However, benefit levels were generous in comparative perspective. According to Eardley et al.'s calculations (1996) for 1992, the net replacement rate after housing costs was 51 per cent of the net income of a Swiss average production worker for a single person and 113 per cent for a couple with two children, respectively.

In the early 1990s, the increasing number of long-term unemployed persons having exhausted their right to unemployment benefits prompted the Cantons to initiate reforms in the field of social assistance. The first and most common response was to introduce integration measures. One important impulse for this was the 1995 UI reform and its new emphasis on activation (Gärtner and Flückiger, 2005: 118). However, the approach pursued by the Cantons was somewhat 'softer' than with UI, as in most Cantons (and in particular in Latin Cantons), the main objective was not labour market integration, but 'social reinsertion', coupled with the introduction of a greater reciprocity within social assistance, which implies the subordination of benefit payments to behavioural obligations (Merrien, 2001; Stofer et al., 2005). Finally, an additional implicit objective is worth mentioning, which is to allow beneficiaries to requalify for UI benefits after the completion of subsidized work in the public sector. However, this possibility has been closed down in the most recent UI reform.

In 2005, the CSIAS guidelines were revised with a view to reinforcing incentives for participating in integration measures. The level of benefits was slightly reduced and financial supplements introduced for those willing to participate in integration measures, thus making the level of benefits partly contingent upon recipients' reintegration efforts (OFS, 2005). Even if heavily criticized especially in the Latin cantons, the new guidelines have been nonetheless adopted everywhere.

7.3.3 Invalidity insurance

Like social assistance, the number of recipients of disability benefits has risen substantially over the past two decades (see Figures 7.1 and 7.2). However, disability insurance remained off the welfare reform agenda until the late 1990s. It was only in the mid-2000s that the first really substantial legislative changes were introduced. Reforms in 2003 and 2007 altered the conditions of access to disability pensions and 'reactivated' the principle of labour market integration. Upon its creation in 1960, the disability insurance benefit scheme was meant to be guided by the principle of 'integration having priority over pension'. In practice, however, this was rarely accomplished. While comprehensive labour market measures and training programmes were always part of the invalidity insurance scheme, their use was limited until the 2000s.

---

[3] Social pressure on social assistance claimants has always been strong, especially in small rural municipalities, where services and benefits may be delivered by local councillors (Obinger, 1999).

Innovations in the field of activation included the introduction of placement services specifically targeted at disability benefit recipients, the implementation of an early detection and intervention system (to help workers with health problems to remain in their job), as well as new programmes to facilitate labour market re-entry of long-term beneficiaries. Since 2008, taking part in early intervention measures has become a prerequisite for all new claimants. By contrast, the system of obligations and sanctions has remained much more lenient for long-term beneficiaries. In theory, benefit receipt is conditional upon the duty to cooperate and participate in activation measures if required. In practice, however, a refusal to take part in an activation measure cannot be sanctioned by benefit curtailments (Bertozzi et al., 2008). In order to implement the new work-focused approach, cantonal disability offices have been established and given full responsibility for activation measures, job-search monitoring, and benefit payment (OECD, 2006*a*: 151). To some extent, they can be considered as a functional equivalent of PES for recipients of disability benefits.

Finally, in addition to the reinforcement of activation principles, several measures were adopted in order to restrict access to disability insurance benefits. The definition of work incapacity has been tightened, so that eligibility to disability benefits is now limited to people whose work incapacity can be clearly attributed to health problems. Moreover, contribution requirements were raised from one to three years,[4] and a six-month waiting period was introduced.

7.4 ANALYSIS OF THE SWISS REFORM TRAJECTORY IN THE LIGHT OF A TRIPLE INTEGRATION

7.4.1 The reform process in the light of a triple integration

Benefit homogenization

At its creation in the 1980s, UI was built on the basis that only few people relied on benefits. The system could afford generous benefits while being relatively unde-manding with respect to contribution levies and eligibility conditions. The deteriorating economic situation at the beginning of the 1990s led to rapid growth in benefit caseload and expenditures, prompting the government to undertake several waves of reforms since the early 1990s. In this regard, making UI more exclusive has emerged as the most favoured solution. By contrast, the question of benefit generosity has remained largely off the political agenda since an attempt to reduce the benefit level (by 1–3 per cent, depending on previous benefit levels) in 1997 was subjected to a referendum and finally rejected by a slight majority in popular vote (Bonoli, 1999). As a result, the replacement rate has not been modified since 1993 when it was reduced from 80 to 70 per cent of previous earnings.

---

[4] The disability insurance scheme is based on a three-pillar model, of which the first pillar aims at providing universal minimal coverage in the event of disability. Contribution requirements are thus relatively lenient from a comparative perspective.

When looking at changes in eligibility, entitlement, and generosity over the past two decades, no clear trend towards a dominant benefit can be observed. Instead, reforms of the UI system have followed many Bismarckian countries until the early 2000s, that is, preserving the rights of core workers while reducing those of workers at the margins of the labour market (Clasen and Clegg, 2006). However, the trend is slightly less pronounced than elsewhere. Indeed, the Swiss UI has traditionally displayed a relatively inclusive character, even though it has been strongly questioned by the most recent UI reform. Exemptions from the usual contributory requirements still exist for women with caring responsibilities and young people who have completed vocational training, who are thus entitled to UI benefits, albeit under more severe conditions. In addition, in terms of benefit caseloads, UI still remains the most important tier of the Swiss unemployment protection system, even though the importance of social assistance has grown substantially since the 1990s. In this regard, on should bear in mind that a significant part of the rise in social assistance caseloads is not directly linked to UI reforms, but has to be attributed to a substantial rise of lone parents whose income is insufficient to cover their basic needs (Bertozzi et al., 2005).

Shifting boundaries between unemployment and other risk categories

Whereas UI has become a somewhat more 'exclusive' benefit system in terms of social rights, reforms in social assistance and disability insurance since the 2000s have redefined the informal boundaries between unemployment and non-employment in two ways. There has been a move towards a convergence of statuses due to a progressive extension of activation measures to social assistance and disability benefits in the 2000s. However, significant differences still exist in the type of integration measures and the degree of obligations within UI on the one hand, and the two other benefit schemes on the other. Integration measures developed within social assistance do not necessarily aim at labour market integration, and activation is still far from being systematically applied in either social assistance or disability insurance. For example, it has been estimated that only about half of jobless social assistance recipients participated in an integration measure in 2008 (CSIAS, 2009). Generally speaking, one peculiarity of the Swiss road to activation is that it is with UI that the activation approach has been developed most strictly (e.g. Berclaz et al., forthcoming; Eichhorst and Konle-Seidl, 2008).

A second trend is that reforms have sought to reduce access to non-employment benefit schemes. In social assistance, this happened mainly through the creation of labour-market programmes in the shape of contribution-paying temporary jobs lasting just long enough to re-establish eligibility for UI benefits (Bertozzi et al., 2008).[5] Within invalidity insurance, the most recent reform has considerably tightened eligibility conditions and emphasized a work-focused approach. Its explicit objective was to diminish the number of new benefit claimants by 20 per cent, and it is most likely that people who are refused a disability pension will swell social assistance caseloads. A recent study of benefit transfers between 2004 and

[5] This possibility was abolished by the most recent UI reform.

2006, that is, before the latest reform, shows that about 30 per cent of all people who were refused access to invalidity pension ended up living on social assistance (OFAS, 2009: 105).

What is particularly remarkable is that these patterns of risk reconfiguration have never been the result of a coherent and comprehensive strategy to formally redefine the boundaries between unemployment and non-employment. Rather, reforms in each benefit system have largely pursued their own objectives, favouring particularistic financial considerations at the expense of the global coherence of the system of benefit support for jobseekers (Bertozzi et al., 2008; Burkhard, 2007; Membres du groupe national de coordination CII, 2004). As a result, reforms have considerably exacerbated problems of jobless people transferring between the different branches of the social security system.

The first criticisms against those perverse effects in terms of benefit transfers emerged on the political arena in the late 1990s. To a large extent, they were expressed by the Cantons concerned about shouldering the costs. However, no serious reconsidering of the overall structure of the Swiss social security system had materialized before 2007, when a parliamentary initiative launched by Social Democrats proposed to completely redesign the Swiss welfare state, and to create one single-benefit scheme for all unemployed persons of working age. Not surprisingly, it was clearly defeated in the first round of parliamentary debates, as the bourgeois majority in the lower chamber of parliament was opposed to embarking on such a 'utopian' reform. Moreover, the Social Democrats themselves were divided as to whether they should support the initiative or not. Arguments that were put forward notably emphasized the high probability of policy failure due to the difficulty of integrating schemes governed by fairly different rules and principles, the lack of clear evidence regarding the necessity of such a radical reform, and the vagueness of the initiative concerning the main features of the single-benefit scheme.[6] From the beginning, it seemed obvious that the reform was doomed to early failure. Nevertheless, the initiative had the merit (and perhaps this was its main objective) to launch the debate around the institutional arrangement of the Swiss social security system, as attested by similar parliamentary requests submitted subsequently. Through force of circumstance, an investigation is being currently made by the federal administration in order to evaluate the feasibility of different options and models in the Swiss context. However, it seems very unlikely that it will end up in one concrete reform proposal in the next few years.

Administrative integration

Just as a more coherent system of benefit support for jobseekers has not materialized, so the development of activation has not yet led to a greater administrative integration. Within UI, the provision of passive and active support is still dealt with separately. Whereas the payment of benefits is performed by a range of funds managed by Cantons or social partners, placement and employment services are

---

[6] For instance, no mention was made of whether social assistance should be included in the single-benefit scheme. Following parliamentary requests were somewhat more precise in this regard, as they only considered integration of federal social insurance programmes.

carried out by the ORPs. However, this division of labour has remained largely a 'non-issue'. Part of the reason for this is probably that the delivery of UI benefits is the only domain where social partners hold administrative responsibilities in the Swiss social security system. Part of the reason is also that this division has never prevented the ORP from enforcing financial sanctions for those not complying with their duties.

Perhaps more importantly, the progressive extension of activation programmes has created a strong segmentation of activation policies for different categories of jobseekers (Wyss and Ruder, 1999). In fact, the current activation approach can be described as a three-tier system: whereas the ORPs are responsible for administrating placement and employment services primarily for claimants of UI benefits, the Cantons provide activation services for social assistance recipients, while Cantonal Disability Offices are responsible for activation services for the disabled unemployed.

Following growing criticism about the inefficiencies of such a segmented activation system, first steps were made towards a better coordination with the establishment of collaboration agreements between the three main organizations in the early 2000s. The objective was to promote a quicker reintegration of the most hard-to-place jobless benefit recipients through the definition of an individual integration plan agreed to by all three organizations and a pooling of activation measures. Concretely, this means that jobless people can benefit from activation measures funded by benefit schemes other than the one from which they receive cash benefits (Champion, 2008; Galster et al., 2009).

Three successive versions of collaboration guidelines have been elaborated since then. The most recent one, introduced in 2005 (CII/IIZ-MAMAC), is also the most comprehensive. Indeed, it is the first of its kind that compels the three organizations to cooperate with each other. As Bonvin and Rosenstein (2009: 10) argue, the introduction of collaboration procedures 'illustrates this political ambition toward more coordinated and integrated policies'. However, even the latest version remains a rather one-off collaboration on a case-by-case basis, and its implementation still depends largely on the goodwill of the Cantons. Moreover, it is questionable whether collaboration really reflects a political will to move towards a more integrated system. Looking at parliamentary debates, it seems that collaboration has been recently used by the government as an instrument to turn down political claims for a deeper reorganization of the social security system.

7.4.2 Explaining the Swiss reform trajectory

As shown in the previous discussion, it appears that the Swiss reform trajectory shows a rather contradictory picture. Somewhat surprisingly, given the generally slow Swiss pattern of welfare state change in the industrial era (Häusermann, 2010; Obinger, 1998), important reforms in the social security system were introduced from the 1990s onwards, particularly in the sense of a general reorientation from a passive to a more work-focused protection system for working-age jobless people. Interestingly, from a comparative perspective the activation emphasis emerged simultaneously with the first cost-containment measures in each benefit system. This applied to UI first and then expanded to social assistance and disability insurance in the 2000s. However, there has been no clear step towards triple integration, that is, the gradual generalization of activation has not been accompanied by reforms towards a greater homogenization of benefit support or administrative integration. Instead, the differentiation between UI and social assistance has somewhat deepened, and the complexity of administrative arrangements was even enhanced due to the parallel development of labour market programmes and employment services for the different categories of benefit recipients. Even though concerns about the necessity for stronger coordination of the social security system have been increasingly expressed since the early 2000s, reform efforts have to date remained quite weak.

How can one make sense of this paradoxical reform trajectory? It is no exaggeration to say that cost containment has been the driving force for all reforms of the past two decades. While benefit systems were still marked by surpluses in the 1980s, their rapidly deteriorating financial situation in the 1990s created a sense of urgency to assure the long-term financial sustainability of the welfare state. Stabilizing the financial situation of benefits has therefore been a primary concern, and it at least partly explains why benefit restrictions have actually been possible in all benefit systems. However, even though the necessity for financial consolidation has been recognized by all political parties as well as trade unions, there has been little agreement on the most adequate means to achieve it. While left-wing parties and trade unions have been generally in favour of increasing contributions and taxes to limit deficits, bourgeois parties and economic interests have always advocated more restrictive and less generous benefits. Thus, reforms have been most often undermined by political conflicts, watering down most government's initial proposals. In the cases where the bourgeois majority managed to impose some controversial reforms, the existence of the popular referendum provided trade unions and the left-wing minority with an additional device to block them, albeit with varying degrees of success.

In such a political context, it is not surprising that reforms undertaken so far have not undermined the core insurance principles of unemployment and disability insurances. However, it is more difficult to figure out why activation could be embraced so 'swiftly' (as compared to cost-containment measures), at the same time as the first important retrenchment initiatives. In this regard, two factors help to understand why the reinforcement of activation has encountered somewhat less political resistance than cost-containment measures.

The first factor relates to the fact that the broad features and principles of the current activation approach were already in place well before caseloads began to rise drastically and the problem of long-term unemployment emerged. Benefit fraud has been a recurring concern in Swiss social policy, which is why unemployment and disability insurances have included a strong emphasis on labour market reintegration ever since their creation. Both schemes were equipped with various labour market and training programmes and a specific focus was put on work incentives, especially in UI. In this respect, tough job-search requirements as well as benefit sanctions already existed and were strictly applied in the 1980s. When labour market problems emerged in the 1990s, these measures quickly proved insufficient to cope with the rapid increase in the number of benefit recipients; but they constituted a valuable basis for the later reinforcement of activation, as all political actors were somehow already 'socialized' to the idea that benefit receipt is both a right and a duty.

The second factor that facilitated the development of activation over the past two decades has to be seen in the strategic use of activation as a compensatory device to gain sufficient political support for the implementation of cost-containment measures (Häusermann, 2010). In a political system which gives trade unions and left-wing parties broad leeway to block reforms, too drastic reforms always run the risk of being challenged in popular referendum, whose outcomes are uncertain. In this context, combining cost-containment measures with expansive elements tend to weaken the opposition, if not foster broad compromise and avoid popular referendum. In the field of unemployment protection, the development of activation, and more particularly the introduction of new labour market programmes, played precisely this compensatory role.

Such a reform strategy was at the heart of two important reforms, namely the 1995 UI reform and the 2007 disability insurance reform. In 1995, while the need to rapidly reform UI was recognized by all actors, negotiations were stuck in a stalemate as trade unions and employers' organizations fundamentally diverged on how to achieve this. Negotiations were thus blocked until a compromise was found which envisaged a reinforcement of ALMPs. The final bill thus included elements that ensured the support from all actors. Trade unions and left-wing parties welcomed the considerable scope of additional funds allocated to ALMPs, while a limitation of benefit entitlements and increased work conditionality ensured the support of the right. Passed by parliament, this bill was not challenged by a referendum (Bonoli, 1999; Giriens and Stauffer, 1999).

In 2007, when it came to reforming disability insurance, the government used a similar strategy. It prepared a bill that included both cost-containment measures and new instruments to favour labour market participation. The strategy failed to achieve the consensus needed to avoid the popular referendum. Nevertheless, the left-wing parties and trade unions were divided over whether to support the reform or not, and so seemed to be the population. The bill was eventually accepted by popular vote, but reasons for accepting it were apparently various. A study of voting behaviour shows that about 10 per cent of its proponents mentioned improved labour market integration for disabled people as the main reason in favour of the reform (Milic, 2007). In sum, the Swiss political institutions had not only a constraining impact on reforms but also contributed to the reorientation of the social security system towards a more work-focused approach. Moreover, the use of activation as a strategic tool to overcome the left-wing opposition helps to explain why in Switzerland the emphasis on activation went hand in hand with the first major cost-containment measures.

Beyond the difficulties of reforming social insurance programmes that contrast with a swifter development of activation, a last point requires further explanation, which is why a comprehensive reorganization of the Swiss social security system, both in terms of risk re-categorization and administrative integration, has not yet emerged in spite of growing pressure in this direction. Here, I would like to highlight two factors: the legacy of the multi-tiered welfare state and the concomitant weakness of the Swiss government in the field of social policy.

First, due to federalism, the Swiss social security system has developed as a 'fragmented welfare state' (Obinger et al., 2005), consisting of several juxtaposed benefit schemes governed by different rules and principles and whose regulatory and financial competencies fall within different tiers of government. In this respect, a particularity of the Swiss case is that legislation, funding, and implementation of social assistance are the entire responsibility of the Cantons and municipalities. This specific jurisdictional arrangement has to date hindered any comprehensive policy approach in two ways. On the one hand, the division of financing responsibilities between the federal state and the Cantons has made solutions such as cost shifting attractive. On the other hand, the fact that the federal state does not possess the legal authority to impose social assistance reforms on the Cantons makes it difficult for the federal government to initiate encompassing reforms. Any change in this situation requires a transfer of competence from the cantonal to the federal level through a constitutional amendment, which in turn requires a popular vote (Obinger, 1998). Moreover, integrating federal social insurance programmes is in itself potentially very tricky, as they differ substantially in their eligibility and entitlement rules, benefit, and behavioural requirements. Any reform of this kind is thus likely to meet with strong political oppositions. It is for these reasons, among others, that the aforementioned 2007 parliamentary initiative to create one single-benefit scheme for all the unemployed of working age was abandoned at the very early stages of the policymaking process.

Finally, encompassing reforms are made all the more tricky as there is not a strong government committed to embark on a profound overhaul of the system. The Swiss federal government is generally described as a weak government, unable to impose policy and initiate major reforms (Bonoli, 2004). In the field of social and labour market policy, this weak leadership is further diluted by the fact that there are two separate ministries in charge of disability insurance on the one hand, and UI and labour market policy on the other. This dual political responsibility has been often criticized as hampering a broad vision to emerge and inhibiting initiatives to undertake comprehensive reforms (Membres du groupe national de coordination CII, 2004). Indeed, so far neither of these two ministries has shown willingness to engage in a fundamental overhaul of the social security system for working-age people.

In this context, it is not surprising that Switzerland has preferred to embark on the path of collaboration rather than the more arduous path of the integration of benefits and services. Collaboration allows for the sharing of resources, more particularly in the field of activation programmes, but otherwise has its limits. Collaboration may actually lead to major accountability problems, as the organization which pays for it is not always the one which implements activation measures. Moreover, it does not resolve the problem of jobless people being merely transferred between the three most important working-age benefit schemes (Bonoli, 2008).

7.5 CONCLUSION

Until the 1990s, Switzerland could be described as a latecomer, both because of its comparatively good labour market performance and marginal unemployment protection system. However, for better or worse, Switzerland has 'caught up' since then in many respects. On the one hand, Switzerland has lost part of its exceptional labour market performance and is now confronted with similar unemployment and inactivity problems as its European neighbours. On the other hand, Switzerland, despite not being an EU member, has followed the same broad tracks of reform, not least with regard to activation. Indeed, not only cost containment but also activation was at the core of all reforms in the three main working-age benefit schemes, namely UI, social assistance, and disability insurance. At different points in time and with different degrees of obligation, reforms developed the supply of ALMPs, and made benefit receipt more conditional on participation in activation measures and job-search efforts. In this respect, changes have been profound, eased by compromise-driven political strategies and a traditionally strong weight put on labour market reintegration.

However, while other continental European countries are now turning towards more integrated approaches to regulating the risk unemployment (see Chapters 3, 4, and 5 in this volume), Switzerland is still lagging behind in this respect despite growing pressure. The progressive extension of activation has not been accompanied by a greater benefit support homogenization or policy coordination. On the benefit side, reforms have above all aimed at tightened access to unemployment and disability insurance benefits. However, the benefit landscape has not been dramatically changed and the distinction between assistance- and insurance-based benefits has remained largely intact. On the organizational side, the development of activation in all benefit schemes has resulted in a fairly segmented system of activation, with each organization developing its own activation programmes for its own benefit clientele. Overall, the Swiss reform pattern has been one of a fairly fragmented approach.

As shown in this chapter, the multi-tiered character of the Swiss social security system may account for a large part of this reform trajectory. The institutional division between federally regulated insurance-based benefits and regional regulation of social assistance can be considered as one of the main obstacles to any initiative to integrate labour market assistance and income support for the different categories of jobless people. As Minas (2009: 16) argues, 'reforms are less developed and less uniform in countries with regional social assistance regulation. The role of other supporting factors for crossing sectional boundaries and building integrated services such as political will, support of relevant stakeholders at the various territorial levels and resources seem absent in these countries.' In the Swiss case, the situation is even trickier as a dual political responsibility on labour market and social affairs, as well as a complex political system, inhibit the emergence of a broad political commitment to embark on a fundamental overhaul of the system.

Nevertheless, the idea of reorganizing the social security system for working-age people towards a more coherent and integrated system is slowly emerging in the political arena, mainly pushed forward by the cantonal governments bearing the costs of reforms at federal level and from a minority fraction within the Social Democrats. However, the chances for a concrete reform to be adopted in the coming years seem to be very slim. In Switzerland, the debate on reforming the social security system is still marked very much by the idea of cost containment through parametric changes and restrictions of benefits. This is particularly visible in the UI reform accepted by popular vote in September 2010, whose principal objective was to reinforce the principle of insurance. And this is also visible to a certain extent in the next disability insurance reform which is in preparation. Both reforms were planned even before the financial crisis took hold. In this sense, they are not a direct consequence of the financial crisis, even though the short-term effects of the crisis on unemployment rates, which rose abruptly in 2009 (see Figure 7.2), as well as the perspective of growing budget deficits, have influenced the political debates and probably facilitated popular acceptance for the reform. More generally, there is little evidence that the crisis may in the end result in a reversal of the pattern of reforms in the Swiss social security system, which is still predominantly geared towards parametric and fragmented cost-containment measures.

Appendix 7.A Major reforms to social security system for jobless people in Switzerland (UI, social assistance, disability insurance), 1990–2010

Year	Measure

1992   First revision of the law on UI:
- Benefit levels raised to 80% of previous earnings for all unemployed people.

Third revision of the law on disability insurance:
- Setting up of cantonal disability offices acting as one-stop shops for the payment of benefits and allocation of rehabilitation measures.

1993   Urgent federal resolution within UI:
- Maximum duration of benefit entitlement prolonged from 250 to 400 daily allowances, but at the same time made dependent on previous contribution periods (Contribution periods of 6, 12, and 18 months give entitlement to, respectively, 170, 250, and 400 daily allowances).
- Stricter definition of a 'suitable job' (at least 70% of previous earnings and up to 4 hours daily commuting time).
- Benefit levels cut from 80 to 70% of previous earnings for the unemployed without child-raising responsibilities.

1995   Second revision of the law on UI:
- Introduction of a 5-day waiting period which can be extended up to 120 for those under 25 years old and without completed training.
- The maximum benefit duration made dependent on the age and participation in ALMPs:
  - 150 daily allowances for those under 50 years old;
  - 250 for those aged between 50 and 60;
  - 400 for those above 60;
  - 520 for those in receipt of disability benefits or participating in an activation measure.
- Minimum contribution period to requalify for benefits after a jobless period raised from 6 to 12 months, therefore abolishing the possibility to requalify for benefits by participating in federal-funded labour market programmes in the shape of public job schemes. The result is a de facto shortening of duration of benefits.
- Establishment of RAV/ORP in order to make employment services more efficient (previously performed by municipalities).
- Introduction of new federally funded ALMPs, such as training allowances and start-up incentives.
- New system of control of job-search efforts: monthly interviews instead of 'stamping'.
- Maximum benefit suspensions in case of non-compliance extended from 40 to 60 working days.

1998   Revision of the CSIAS guidelines on social assistance:
- Introduction of 'reintegration contracts' implying beneficiaries' participation in social and professional measures.

2002   Third revision of the law on UI:
- Minimum contribution period raised from 6 to 12 months (in past 2 years) for all unemployed (except for people exempt from contributions).
- Participating in a federal labour market measure does no longer prolong the duration of benefits. The maximum benefit duration is reduced from 520 to 400 daily allowances, except for the unemployed above 55 years old or in receipt of disability benefits.
- Possibility given to the Federal Council to raise the maximum benefit duration to 520 daily allowances in regions with high unemployment rates.

2003   Fourth revision of the law on disability insurance:
- Abolition of pension supplements for spouses.
- Invalidity pensions granted only if working incapacity exceeds 40%.
- Introduction of one supplementary type of partial disability pension (3/4) for people with a working incapacity between 60 and 70% (in the past, a working incapacity above 66% gave right to a full pension).

- Establishment of regional medical services to provide more uniform and impartial assessments.
- Upgrading of active job-placement services for disabled people through an extension of the role of cantonal disability offices.

2005 Revision of the CSIAS guidelines on social assistance:
- Reduction of benefit levels, compensated by more generous supplements for those participating in activation measures.
- Introduction of earnings disregards to encourage beneficiaries to take up work or increase their working time.
- Reinforcement of sanctions: benefit reductions up to 15% in cases of non-compliance and mistakes.

2007 Fifth revision of the law on disability insurance:
- Tightening of eligibility criteria for disability pensions: minimum contribution period to be entitled to disability pensions increased from 1 to 3 years; stricter medical criteria; introduction of a waiting period of 6 months.
- Introduction of early detection and intervention measures for new benefit claimants in order to sustain employment.
- Introduction of new activation measures for long-term pension recipients to prepare them for moving back into work.
- Introduction of the obligation to take up the measures proposed.
- Introduction of earning disregards to encourage work; introduction of wage subsidies for employers who decide to hire disabled people or keep them in employment.

2010 Fourth revision of the law on unemployment insurance:
- Contribution rates raised from 2 to 2.2% of the insured salary (up to CHF 126,000 a year), and to 3.2% for higher annual incomes, divided equally between employees and employers.
- The duration of benefit entitlement more closely linked to contribution periods:
  ○ 260 daily allowances (1 year) for a 12-month contribution period;
  ○ 400 daily allowances (1.5 year) for a min. 18-month contribution period;
  ○ 520 daily allowances (2 years) only for those above 55 years old and with a 24-month contribution period.
- The maximum duration of benefit entitlement limited to 200 daily allowances for the unemployed under 25 years old, and to 90 for those with contribution exemptions (young people having completed training and women with caring responsibilities).
- Abolition of the possibility to raise the maximum benefit duration to 520 daily allowances in regions with high unemployment rates.
- Increase in waiting periods up to 20 days for unemployed without dependent children and with an annual income superior to CHF 60,000; and to 120 days for those exempt from contributions.
- Abolition of the principle of status maintenance for the unemployed under 30 years old (i.e. can be forced to accept jobs irrespective of prior qualifications and earnings).
- Subsidized employment programmes in the public sector no longer requalifies for UI benefits.

Source: Gärtner and Flückiger (2005), OFS (2005), OFS, Statistiques des assurances sociales suisses (1999–2008), Perret et al. (2007), and SECO (2010*b*).

8

Italy: limited adaptation of an atypical system

Matteo Jessoula and Patrik Vesan[1]

8.1 INTRODUCTION

In the 'industrial age', most European countries set up multi-tiered unemployment compensation systems, based on a first contributory tier providing unemployment insurance benefits (UI) for a limited duration, a second tier of unemployment assistance (UA) for the unemployed who fail to fulfil contribution requirements or have exhausted entitlement, and finally a general social assistance (SA) scheme with a safety net function. Next to income support, some countries also developed fairly extensive active labour market policies (ALMPs) aimed at promoting employment.

Against this background, Italy has traditionally displayed some peculiarities: low investment in labour market policies, with underdeveloped active measures and a single-tier contributory unemployment compensation system providing adequate protection to a limited share of unemployed. This policy framework, however, increasingly came under pressure in the late 1990s, after a U-turn in both macroeconomic policy and employment relations, resulting in the abandonment of Keynesianism and a shift towards more flexible labour markets. Both factors created pressure for reorganization and enlargement of unemployment protection schemes as well as a shift towards more active measures. As we show below, however, attempts over the last two decades to develop a more effective system of unemployment protection, better adapted to increasingly 'post-industrial' labour market conditions, have been only very partially accomplished. We argue that the limited adaptation of Italian unemployment protection is the result of an incomplete learning process resulting from the combination of a number of unfavourable conditions for reform: scarce economic resources, cognitive factors that until recently reduced problem pressure, and path-dependent dynamics cutting across policy sectors, linked to the relative power of the various social groups. In addition, when important reforms have been introduced, implementation has

---

[1] Each section of this chapter has been discussed, written, and revised by the two authors. However, for the purpose of attribution, Matteo Jessoula has written the introduction and Sections 8.2 and 8.4, while Patrik Vesan has written Section 8.3 and the conclusions.

often been weak because of low institutional capabilities and the persistence of traditional organizational habits at delivery level.

Section 8.2 presents the economic and policy context for recent developments in the Italian case. Section 8.3 then provides an overview of the main trends and developments in the period between 1990 and 2010, before Section 8.4 draws out the main factors that help understand the Italian policy response in the face of labour market change. A brief final section concludes.

8.2 FROM LATE INDUSTRIALIZATION TO POST-FORDISM: THE PERSISTENCE OF THE SOUTHERN MODEL

Industrialization occurred later in Italy than many other European countries, between the late 1950s and the 1960s. This ensured growth rates remained relatively high even after the first oil shock (Statistical Annex, Table A.3), which mostly prompted spiralling inflation. During the 1970s the competitiveness of the Italian economy was nonetheless preserved, essentially through recurrent devaluations of the national currency – the so-called 'competitive devaluations' – that reduced relative labour costs and thus favoured exports. This strategy was accompanied by an interventionist approach by successive governments, intended to preserve full employment at least of male breadwinners. State-owned enterprises were developed and the labour market – mostly characterized by full-time permanent contracts – was highly regulated, with the job protection strengthened in 1966 – when firing was restricted by law to well-motivated cases – and again in 1970, when the Article 18 of the Workers Statute obliged firms with more than fifteen employees to reintegrate fired workers if dismissals were declared illegal in court.

Between World War II and the early 1980s, few public resources were devoted to tackling unemployment. The formal unemployment compensation system comprised a single-tier UI with rather strict eligibility rules and providing extremely low benefits; there was neither a UA nor a SA tier. Special schemes providing generous wage replacement benefits (CIGO and CIGS: *Cassa integrazione guadagni ordinaria* e *straordinaria*) in case of (partial or total) working-time reduction *without* definitive dismissal had been introduced in 1945 and 1968, but these mainly concerned workers employed in medium–large firms in the industrial sector. As for ALMPs, they were virtually non-existent.

Together with the highly regulated labour market described above, this policy framework reveals that Italian policymakers' priority has long been to keep workers in employment – whether by limiting dismissals or subsidizing temporary wage reductions – instead of promoting the insertion of people in a more fluid labour market (Jessoula and Alti, 2010). This orientation is further confirmed by the functioning of placement services, which became a state monopoly in 1949. These services functioned through very rigid, and largely ineffective, bureaucratic procedures: jobseekers had to register with the local employment office and periodically confirm their status in order to stay on a placement list, their position on which depended on various criteria (i.e. professional sector, productive category, family income and dependants, and duration of registration on the list). With some exceptions,[2] employers were not free to choose workers to hire, but could only give notice of job vacancies and wait for the automatic assignment of jobseekers by the public authorities.

This institutional setting also favoured a marked divide between 'insiders' – in the Italian context employees in medium–large and unionized firms who enjoyed strong job protection and were entitled to CIG – and 'outsiders', that is, people generally excluded from regular employment and any kind of public income support. A third group of workers – recently labelled as 'mid-siders' (cf. Jessoula et al., 2010), and typically stably employed in one of Italy's many 'micro-firms' – could rely on a lower level of job protection and very limited income security through ordinary UI, which actually provided a flat-rate vital minimum only. However, gaps in the Italian unemployment protection system were long, partly filled by some peculiar institutional and social practices as well as by misuse of alternative social policy measures. Most importantly, in line with the Southern European model of welfare, the family was crucial in providing a last resort safety net for those not employed, as were charitable Catholic institutions. In addition, irregular or informal work provided economic sustenance, however precariously, to many of those registered as unemployed, especially in southern regions. Mostly in the same areas, where the agricultural sector was still relevant and permanent contracts were not widespread, invalidity pensions were also extensively used as disguised unemployment subsidies, at least until 1984 when eligibility rules were tightened.

Unemployment rates remained quite low in Italy until the second oil shock (1979), when the economy entered a prolonged phase of stagflation – four years of recession coupled with very high inflation rates – and a delayed process of deindustrialization was set in motion. In the early 1980s the latter started to 'bite', and unemployment increased steadily (see Statistical Annex, Table A.5). This induced policymakers to complement their traditional policy instruments with new measures. In line with many other European countries the 'labour reduction route' was followed, with early retirement schemes being introduced in 1981 and massively exploited for the rest of the decade, and pre-existing rules for seniority pensions that allowed workers to retire at very young ages. In addition, the special CIGO and CIGS schemes were called upon to play a major role as 'shock absorbers', limiting open unemployment while compensating workers for the temporary loss/reduction of income (see Figure 8.4). However, as the coverage of these schemes was limited and benefit provision was conditional upon a bargaining process between the government and the social partners, 'insiders' employed in unionized sectors were the main beneficiaries of such interventions.

The policy response was not entirely defensive, however, and the increasing labour market difficulties of the early 1980s also brought some innovative ideas into the policy debate with the aim of stimulating growth and boosting employment. The automatic indexation mechanism for wages[3] was made less generous in

---

[2] Employers sometimes eluded this rule by recurring to alternative procedures (Ichino, 1982).

[3] The so-called *'scala mobile'* mechanism automatically linked wage growth to increases in the consumer price index, and turned out to be a source of spiraling inflation rates.

1983 and 1984 in order to reduce labour costs, while the partial liberalization of fixed-term contracts as well as the introduction of three new types of (flexible) employment contracts in 1984 – part-time, 'solidarity contracts',[4] and a new 'work and training' contract for young people (*contratto di formazione e lavoro*) – represented a first breach in the tradition of extreme labour market rigidity. This limited liberalization was accepted by trade unions only as a strategy for tackling specific labour market problems, and was tightly circumscribed to apply only to some categories of workers (mainly youth and women) or situations (industrial crises), with unions furthermore maintaining control over the application of the new rules through collective bargaining (Vesan, 2009). In this period a first step towards a more 'active' labour market strategy was also taken, with the introduction of a new programme labelled 'socially useful jobs' (LSU – *lavori socialmente utili*, L. 390/81). The aim was to reintegrate the long-term unemployed by obliging benefit recipients to engage in jobs created by the state, subnational governments, or non-profit organizations, according to what could be considered an embryonic 'workfare ideology' (Fargion, 2001), However, as argued below, these socially useful jobs were soon transformed into a masked social shock absorber. Finally, while other activation programmes were introduced to promote youth employment and entrepreneurship in this period, they were mainly conceived as 'extraordinary' measures to counteract the contingent employment crisis, rather than as part of a purposeful recalibration of the Italian employment system towards activation.

In sum, the measures adopted in the 1980s, though sometimes innovative with respect to the traditional policy menu, did not substantially modify the established Italian employment policy model as well as its interaction with the broader economic context. Macroeconomic policy orientations were still predominantly Keynesian – allowing a soaring public debt and annual deficits around 10 per cent – while labour market and unemployment policies were not significantly reorganized, despite an ongoing and accelerating process of deindustrialization.

8.3 CHANGE WITH ONLY PARTIAL ADAPTATION: THE LONG (AND SLOW) MARCH OF THE ITALIAN UB SYSTEM

Though the transition to a predominantly service-based economy was largely complete by the early 1990s, a proper post-industrial labour market, characterized by increased levels of flexibility and more frequent transitions into and out of as well as across employment, did not emerge until the late 1990s in Italy. This in fact occurred only when the deepening of European integration severely limited the potential to employ most of policy strategies that Italian policymakers had pursued in order to (indirectly) tackle the problem of unemployment in earlier decades (Ferrera and Gualmini, 2004). With competitive devaluations, notably, ruled out by the 'EMU track', after 1992 governments were forced to adopt more

---

[4] 'Solidarity contracts' are plant-level collective agreements through which it is possible to reduce working time, usually in order to avoid employment losses. The state provided compensation for non-worked hours.

innovative policy strategies to reduce labour costs and foster employment. Early initiatives included the abolition of the automatic wage indexation mechanism (1992) – which completed the reform process launched in the previous decade – and the pursuit of wage moderation through the negotiation of a number of social pacts (signed in 1992, 1993, 1996, and 1998).

Subsequent reductions in labour costs were mainly achieved through a rather selective flexibilization of the labour market, based on favouring the spread of 'atypical jobs', targeted on new entrants to the labour market and generally lower paid and less protected in terms of access to social benefits than open-ended, full-time forms of employment. This occurred after 1997 when, through the 'Treu package', the centre-left government led by Prodi introduced temporary agency work contracts, also favouring the recourse to part-time work and the development of ALMPs. In 2003, another reform (the so-called 'Biagi law') prompted a further and more comprehensive flexibilization of the labour market, abolishing the restrictions on the use of different types of atypical contracts, but leaving un-changed the level of job protection of standard workers. Figures indicate the growing importance of atypical jobs subsequently, as well as their major contribution to total employment growth. Between the mid-1990s and 2007, atypical employment almost doubled to represent about 20 per cent of all employment (8.0 per cent part-time, 11.9 per cent fixed term) (see Statistical Annex, Tables A.10 and A.11). Furthermore, between 1995 and 2001, more than 60 per cent of new job contracts were atypical (Ministry of Labour and Social Protection, 2001), and in 2006 more than half the increase in employment took the form of non-standard contracts (CNEL, 2007).

In the period between 1997 and 2010, a post-industrial labour market has thus gradually emerged in Italy. This process has unfolded, however, across two distinct periods, characterized by very different economic and (especially) em-ployment conditions. Between 1997 and 2007, labour market indicators displayed broadly positive trends, notwithstanding some deep-seated weaknesses in the Italian economy. Both employment and unemployment rates significantly im-proved, and particularly the latter sharply decreased. In 2007 the Italian unem-ployment rate was 6.2 per cent, substantially lower than the EU-15 average. The decline in both youth unemployment (15–24) and long-term unemployment was also significant (see Statistical Annex, Table A.6). By contrast, a second phase – between 2008 and 2010 – has been characterized by the abrupt disappearance of positive labour market trends as a consequence of the financial and subsequent economic crisis. Italian GDP fell by 1 per cent in 2008 and 5 per cent in 2009, and unemployment increased sharply once more.

8.3.1 The industrial legacy: an insurance-based UB system

In the early 1990s, the Italian system of unemployment protection was organized around UI and CIGO/CIGS, the wage compensation funds for working-time reduction.[5] Introduced in 1919 and reformed during the fascist period and in

---

[5] Next to ordinary UI, special occupational schemes provided income support in unemployment to some groups of workers in the agricultural and the construction sectors. In this chapter, we focus on the main measures only.

1949, over subsequent decades ordinary UI basically maintained unaltered qualifying conditions: eligibility requires at least two years of insurance seniority and fifty-two weekly contributions in the two years before employment (see Table 8.1, first column). The first relevant change in this scheme was made in 1988, when previously flat-rate benefits (800 lire per day, that is around €0.4) were replaced by earnings-related benefits, albeit with the replacement rate initially set at a very

Table 8.1. The Italian unemployment benefits system, 1990–2010

Previous system (until 1998)	Current system (2010)
Ordinary UI (outside agricultural and construction sector)	
• *Eligibility requirements*: only dependent workers with at least 2 years of insurance seniority and 52 full-weekly contributions in the 24 months before the onset of unemployment.	• *Eligibility requirements*: the same as before.
• *Duration*: 6 months.	• *Duration*: 8 months, 12 months for over-50s.
• *Replacement rate*: 30% of the previous wage.	• *Replacement rate*: 60% up to 6 months; 50% for the following 2 months; 40% for further months, with ceilings.
UI with reduced eligibility (UIR)	
• *Eligibility requirements*: at least 2 years of insurance seniority and at least 78 working days in the year the benefit is claimed for.	• *Eligibility requirements*: the same as before.
• *Duration*: number of effective working days in the year before the request of the benefit, up to 156 days.	• *Duration*: number of effective working days in the year before the request of the benefit, up to 180 days.
• *Replacement rate*: 30% of the previous wage.	• *Replacement rate*: 35% for the first 4 months, then 40%, with ceilings.
Mobility allowance	
• *Eligibility requirements*: All employees with an open-ended contract in CIGS-recipient firms, and at least 12 months of firm seniority.	• *Eligibility requirements*: the same as before
• *Duration*: 12, 24, 36 months, depending on the age. Under specific circumstances, the duration can be extended up to 10 years for workers aged more than 50 years old in order to reach the retirement age (mobilità lunga).	• *Duration*: the same as before
• *Replacement rate*: 80% for the first 12 months (same level of the CIGS), then 64% (80% of the CIGS).	• *Replacement rate*: the same as before.
Wage compensation funds in case of temporary suspension from work	
Ordinary wage replacement benefits (CIGO)	
• *Eligibility requirements*: employees in manufacturing sector (excluded craft and service) who work in firms which have reduced or suspended their activities because of temporary economic crisis or unexpected events (e.g. bad weather conditions).	• *Eligibility requirements*: the same as before
• *Duration*: 13 weeks with possibility of extension up to 12 months in 2 years.	• *Duration*: the same as before
• *Replacement rate*: 80% of the total remuneration for non-worked hours between 24 and 40 hours a week, with ceilings.	• *Replacement rate*: the same as before

(*continued*)

Table 8.1. (continued)

Previous system (until 1998)	Current system (2010)
Extraordinary wage replacement benefits (CIGS)	
• *Eligibility requirements*: employees, with at least 90 days of firm seniority, who work in firms – with more than 15 employees – that have reduced or suspended their activities because of relevant crisis, restructuring, reconversion, or bankruptcy.	• *Eligibility requirements*: the same as before
• *Duration*: 12 or 24 months depending from the causes, with the possibility of extension up to 48 months in case of restructuring.	• *Duration*: the same as before.
• *Replacement rate*: 80% of total pay for hours not worked, from 0 to 40 hours per week, with ceilings.	• *Replacement rate*: the same as before

low level (7.5 per cent of previous earnings). In the same year a new benefit was also introduced – 'UI with reduced eligibility' (UIR) – characterized by looser qualifying conditions and even lower benefit levels than ordinary UI. Benefits are in fact calculated taking into account the actual days of employment (with a ceiling of 156 days per year), and paid in a lump sum during the year following the onset of unemployment. At the beginning of the 1990s, benefits for the unemployed were thus distinctly ungenerous. By contrast, the special schemes providing wage compensation benefits (CIGO and CIGS) to limited categories of workers in the event of (partial or total) working-time reduction without definitive dismissal had gross replacement rates of 80 per cent.

In 1991, the menu of passive measures was enriched with the introduction of the 'mobility allowance'. This was an unemployment protection scheme that could be extended – depending on the age of the worker and the territorial area – to forty-eight months, and provided generous benefits in case of collective dismissals (replacement rate: 80 per cent for the first twelve months). The eligibility conditions were the same as for CIGS and, similarly to the latter, the scheme required a specific procedure with the involvement of social partners and public authorities. Therefore, the mobility allowance was available only for a share of employees in medium and large firms and service activities, excluding the vast majority of Italian workers employed in small firms. Finally, the duration of the mobility allowance could be extended up to ten years through ad hoc ministerial decrees, in order to allow older workers to reach the minimum age for retirement (long-lasting mobility allowance, the so-called *mobilità lunga*).

In sum, in the mid-1990s the Italian unemployment benefit system was still based on a single UI tier, articulated on two main groups of schemes. On the one hand, UI and UIR offered meagre protection to the unemployed, with low recipiency rates due to the rather strict eligibility conditions. On the other hand, there were schemes providing quite generous income compensation – though conditional upon a bargaining process between public authorities and social partners – in the event of temporary working-time reduction (CIGO and CIGS) and income support in case of collective dismissals (the mobility allowance). Due to the underdevelopment of the regular first pillar, these schemes played a major role in supporting income, but with especially uneven distributive outcomes given that only employees in certain firms could benefit. As we will see below, although this overall configuration has largely remained unchanged in the two decades since, it is nonetheless possible to observe some variation in both the institutional settings and distributive orientations.

8.3.2 Towards (somewhat) fairer and more inclusive unemployment protection

Due to the single-tier structure of the Italian unemployment protection system, there can be no Italian equivalent to the forms of cross-tier benefit homogeniza-tion visible in some of the other countries covered in this volume. Nevertheless, over the last two decades there are signs of a sort of creeping homogenization process within the insurance tier, and specifically with reference to a less-differentiated treatment of some categories of workers. Some legislative changes have impacted on both the generosity of the various forms of income protection and, to a limited extent, the inclusiveness of the system (see Appendix 8.A).

Both UI and UIR have become more generous in terms of replacement rates and benefit duration. Between 1993 and 2007, the incremental upgrading of ordinary UI benefits has been particularly robust: the maximum duration has been extended from six to eight months, and the benefit level has increased from 30 to 60 per cent of the previous average daily wage for the first six months. For UIR, the maximum reference period for calculation of benefits has been extended from 156 to 180 days per year, and the replacement rate has been graduated (between 35 and 40 per cent of average yearly based daily wage). Finally, the 2008 budget law (Law 244/2007) saw a shift to a system where replacement rates in UI decrease with unemployment duration (60 per cent for the first six months, 50 per cent for the last two months), and benefits duration varies in accordance with recipient's age.

The incremental upgrading of ordinary UI has contributed to less unequal treatment for recipients of this benefit compared to that for workers entitled to the special scheme CIGS. As shown in Figure 8.1, average net replacement rates of UI and CIGS converged markedly after 1980, and especially between 1990 and 2000. This convergence has also resulted from the actual generosity of CIGS diminishing due to the introduction of the ceilings applied to benefits, the nominal replacement rate having remained unchanged.[6] Consequently, such convergence of net replacement rates has led to a partial reduction of the

---

[6] Law 427/1980 introduced a ceiling for CIGS wage compensations linked to the wage indexation mechanism (the so-called '*scala mobile*' allowance) that was gradually reduced from 1983 to the beginning of the 1990s, when it was definitively abolished. After 1994, CIGS benefit ceiling has been linked to the consumer price index for blue- and white-collar families, according to some simulations (Picot, 2009), pushing the net replacement rate to around the 60 per cent of the average wage for two household types (cf. Figure 8.1). Moreover, taking into account the ceiling applied in 2010, an unemployed with a previous monthly gross wage of €1,900 will receive – for both ordinary UI and CIGS in case of total suspension from work – a maximum gross compensation of €892, corresponding to a replacement rate of about 47 per cent.

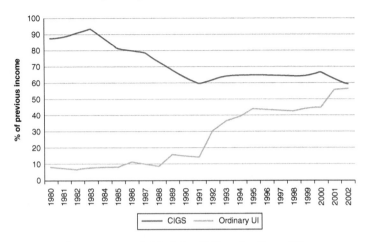

Figure 8.1. Net replacement rates (NRRs*) for CIGS and ordinary UI

Note: *NRRs are unweighted averages for two household types: a single person living alone, and a couple with a single earner and two dependent children.
Source: Picot (2009) and Scruggs (2004).

protection gap between different categories of workers. It is the aforementioned mid-siders who have possibly benefited most from this change, though the insiders in large firms in unionized sectors – albeit penalized by the ceiling effect – remain the most protected category of unemployed workers in Italy, due to the longer duration of CIGS.

As well as becoming more generous, the UI scheme has also become more inclusive. In recent years, the overall recipiency rate for all unemployment benefits has significantly increased, from less than 14 per cent in 2000 to 38 per cent in 2008.[7] Considering the raw number of beneficiaries of the different insurance schemes (Figure 8.2), it can be easily seen that the increase is mostly due to the recipients of ordinary UI.

It should be noted that the increase in absolute recipients occurred in a period of declining unemployment (except for a limited growth in 2008). The increasing inclusiveness of the Italian unemployment benefit system has been a by-product of a number of factors: a higher replacement rate has made UI benefits more attractive, thus increasing the take-up rate, while the longer duration of benefits raised the total amount of UI beneficiaries because of a bigger overlap in the reference year between new and old recipients (CNEL, 2010). The parallel growth in employment and the spread of fixed-term contracts has also plausibly led to a higher number of unemployed fulfilling eligibility requirements for ordinary UI (Anastasia et al., 2009).

Despite the higher inclusiveness of the Italian UB system, the overall recipiency rate, however, remains low compared to other European countries, and estimates

---

[7] Our calculation is based on Eurostat data. The index compares the total number of beneficiaries of out-of-work income support measures (excluding CIG beneficiaries) to the total number of unemployed (annual average).

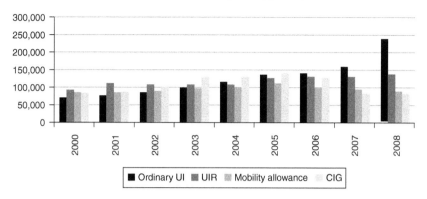

Figure 8.2. Unemployment benefits recipients: main measures, annual average stocks, 2000–8

Note: CIG indicated the sum of CIGO and CIGS beneficiaries.
Source: Authors' calculations from Eurostat and the Italian Ministry of Employment and Social Affairs' monitoring reports.

of the number of employees without access to any financial support in unemployment ranges from 1.6 to 2 million (Banca d'Italia, 2009; Berton et al., 2009). In particular, a large share of atypical workers still have no access to any kind of income protection due to the rather strict eligibility conditions in ordinary UI, while labour market entrants and the long-term unemployed are disadvantaged by the absence of second and third-tier schemes.[8] In order to fill some of these gaps, in 1998 the centre-left Prodi government attempted to introduce a 'Minimum insertion income' (Mii), initially as a three-year pilot scheme. This measure – designed as a non-categorical, means-tested, tax-financed SA measure, addressed to all the people under a predefined poverty threshold, and including an activation component – was indeed innovative with respect to the traditional passive and contribution-based Italian labour market measures. The initiative was, however, scrapped by the new centre-right government in 2004 (cf. Jessoula and Alti, 2010), and further attempts to introduce a national-level SA scheme have thus far failed.[9]

Against the background depicted above, it is easy to understand why the issue of adequate income protection came to the fore in 2008–9 when, due the dramatic economic crisis, Italy for the first time faced a severe employment crisis in the context of a post-industrial labour market. Aiming to tackle the rapidly deteriorating employment situation, the centre-right government led by Berlusconi in 2009 adopted some emergency measures (see Appendix 8.A). One strategy relied on the extensive recourse to CIGO/CIGS, as well as the modification of these

---

[8] Among the main categories of non-standard workers, more than 38 per cent of fixed-term workers, 48 per cent of temporary agency workers, and about 19 per cent of part-time workers with a permanent contract have no access to any kind income support in case of unemployment (Berton et al., 2009).
[9] In a few regions, social assistance schemes similar to Mii are, however, currently being implemented.

schemes' ordinary rules (the so-called *ammortizzatori sociali in deroga*, social shock absorbers 'in derogation') through extended duration and relaxed eligibility requirements. At least in principle, these measures may thus contribute to partially reducing the occupational segmentation of unemployment benefit support, allowing some categories of workers usually excluded from ordinary CIG benefits and mobility allowances to be entitled to these relatively generous schemes. A second, less important, strategy aimed at improving income protection for project workers (i.e. economically dependent workers, cf. Pedersini, 2002). As a three-year pilot scheme, lump sum benefits initially equal to 10 per cent (then 30 per cent) of the previous annual wage were introduced. However, the innovative potential of this measure has been limited due to the (extremely) low benefit level and, especially, very strict eligibility conditions, which allow only a limited share of project workers to get access to this rudimentary form of protection (Banca d'Italia, 2009).

To sum up, before the 2008–10 crisis, changes in the unemployment protection system aimed at reducing some of the disparity in unemployment protection between the insiders and workers in non-unionized small firms, an issue that had long been on the agenda. In the midst of the economic crisis, national policy-makers then reacted with some 'retouches at the margin'. These, however, appear rather inadequate, since the provisions adopted remain temporary and provide only meagre income protection for a limited number of unemployed workers. The recourse to social shock absorbers in derogation was also conceived as an emergency solution, aimed at provisionally filling some gaps in the coverage of unemployed, rather than as a rights-based measure, which would have represented a more major innovation in the Italian system of unemployment support (Jessoula et al., 2010; Sacchi et al., 2011). Though the system has become somewhat fairer and more inclusive, then, a systematic strategy of comprehensive unemployment benefit reform – repeatedly invoked as an aspiration by Italian governments since the late 1980s (Vesan, 2009) – has not seen the light of day, and many traits of the old 'status confirming' arrangements remain in place.

8.3.3 Managing the risk of unemployment: a partial abandonment of the labour reduction route

While changes in the benefit system have only shifted the distributive orientation to a limited extent, in the last ten to fifteen years the boundaries of unemployment as social risk have also been moving, thanks to reductions and changes in a number of schemes previously used to provide exit routes out of the labour market. Though not completely abandoned, the labour reduction strategy has since mid-1990s been pursued much less intensively than in the past.

Possibilities for early exit have been restricted through the tightening of the eligibility conditions for seniority pensions, as well as diminishing recourse to the early retirement measure introduced in the early 1980s, and its definitive phasing out in 1991. Between 2000 and 2008, the average annual stock of early retirement beneficiaries has significantly decreased from about 165,000 beneficiaries to only 38,000 (Figure 8.3). While some of this decline has been offset by reliance on other schemes that can offer alternative exit routes from the labour market,

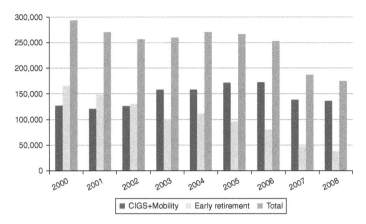

Figure 8.3. Beneficiaries – annual average stocks, 2000–8
Source: Authors' calculations from Italian Ministry of Employment and Social Affairs' monitoring reports.

such as CIGS and the mobility allowance, Figure 8.3 demonstrates that the increase in these measures has been much more modest (on average, +1,200 people per year) compared to the sharp reduction in the stock of early retired (on average, −16,000 people per year). It should also be remembered that only a limited number of beneficiaries of CIGS and the mobility allowance – which are not formally early exit schemes – will eventually withdraw from the labour market. During the 2000s, and for the first time in three decades, the average age of labour market exit for both men and women thus increased in Italy, from 60 and 58, respectively, to 61 for both. Inactivity rates among older people declined steadily during the decade (Statistical Annex, Table A.7).

Recent trends in the usage of special wage compensation schemes (CIG), at least until the recent economic crisis, also seem to confirm the reversal of early exit strategies. These schemes have always played an important role in containing the social impacts of economic recessions, providing wage support in case of temporary layoffs, while keeping people in employment. Nonetheless, as maintained by several studies (e.g. Carabelli, 1995), these wage compensation schemes were often used more as labour-shedding tools than labour-hoarding ones. This was particularly true during the 1980s, when they were massively used to facilitate collective dismissals in strongly unionized workplaces. Through CIG, these workers could often remain formally employed without actually working for many years and, in some cases, until the age required for (early) retirement. Since the mid-1990s, however, important changes can be observed (Figure 8.4). Firstly, the recourse to these schemes has drastically declined. Furthermore, the use of the ordinary scheme (CIGO) has increased relative to the use of the special scheme (CIGS), which more often represented a pathway towards early retirement than CIGO. Finally, although the use of CIG picked up again after the onset of the economic crisis in 2008, the evidence suggests that in this context – and different to the 1980s – the scheme has been used (at least so far) to keep workers in employment and prevent further unemployment growth, in line with its original function as well as with EU guidelines for responding to the crisis.

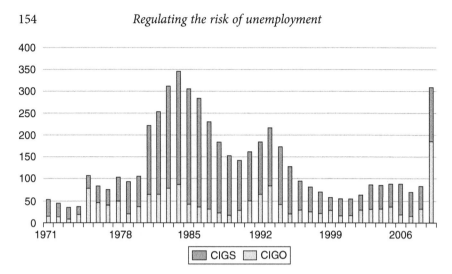

Figure 8.4. CIGO and CIGS schemes. Beneficiaries (full-time equivalents, hours effectively suspended from work), thousands of people, 1971–2009

Note: The last column also considers CIGS 'in deroga'.
Source: CNEL (2010).

A final shift in the boundaries of the risk of unemployment that can be high-lighted relates to a further programme addressed to jobseekers: the so-called socially useful jobs (LSU). As mentioned above, this programme was introduced in the eighties with the aim of activating unemployment benefit recipients, and in 1991 Law 223 explicitly required beneficiaries of short-term compensation and mobility allowance to be engaged in LSU. In fact, rather than promoting working opportunities, LSU were often used as pseudo income protection schemes to respond to short-term social protection needs, like similar 'occupation' schemes in other European countries (Bonoli, this volume). For example, when in 1994 some 300,000 beneficiaries of the mobility allowance risked being left without any kind of support due to their benefit expiring, the then government used LSU to provide extended income protection for this group of unemployed workers (Fargion, 2001). Such usage caused a rapid growth in the cost of LSU (Figure 8.5), which were de facto transformed into a further social shock absorber for the already better protected categories of workers. Between 1999 and 2008, however, expenditure on LSU has contracted sharply, and the number of beneficiaries has fallen by 84 per cent. Attempts to empty the LSU 'reservoir' have been pursued through the adoption of several incentive measures, aimed either at transforming LSU workers in fixed-term or permanent employees in local/regional administra-tions or – more oddly for a programme initially created to activate the unemployed – by encouraging beneficiaries into early retirement.

To sum up, the boundaries of unemployment as administrative category also show some important signs of change in a more expansive direction in recent years. While it is probably too early to argue about a definitive reversal of the traditional Italian labour reduction strategy, it is clear that a number of policy instruments that conventionally encouraged people into administrative statuses other than unem-ployment (or 'real' employment) are being less intensively used than in the past.

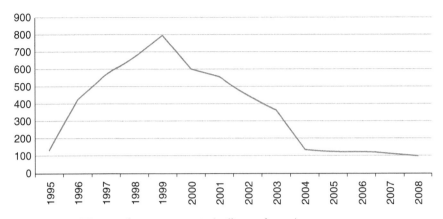

Figure 8.5. LSU, expenditure, 1995–2008 (millions of euros)

Source: Authors' calculations from Eurostat and the Italian Ministry of Employment and Social Affairs' monitoring reports.

8.3.4 From a passive approach to activation: structural reform but weak implementation

If the emergence of a post-industrial labour market has not led to truly path-breaking developments in the UB system, more change can be observed in related labour market policy fields. Since the adoption of the watershed Treu reform in 1997, Italian policy has placed greater emphasis on activation, and a number of changes have been introduced in ALMPs, the organization of the public employment services (PES), and in the link between active and passive measures.

Regarding ALMPs, it is important to distinguish three different phases between 1997 and 2010. In a first period, broadly from 1997 to 2003, governments attempted to overcome the traditionally passive approach to unemployment in Italy by investing heavily in active measures. The traditional predominance of passive policies was thus limited, moving Italian labour market policy towards a more balanced 'policy mix' which sought to facilitate the insertion – especially of disadvantaged groups – in the labour market, in accordance with the guidelines of the European Employment Strategy (Graziano, 2007). Figure 8.6 shows that between 1995 and 2003 – a period of declining unemployment rates – a partial reshuffling of the labour market policy menu occurred, with active measures actually reaching the level of passive expenditure in 2003.

In 2004 the positive trend in ALMPs came to an abrupt halt and has subsequently been reversed. The main reasons for this can be found, on the one hand, in the increase in UI beneficiaries illustrated above and, on the other hand, in the drastic reduction in expenditure on tax incentives for employment. This suggests a (partial) return to the traditional pattern of predominance of compensatory measures for the unemployed. Finally, a third phase can be identified with reference to both funding and management of social shock absorbers 'in derogation', used to tackle the recent economic crisis. These emergency unemployment benefits have been partially financed (about 30 per cent of the total budget) through the European Social Fund (ESF), which usually

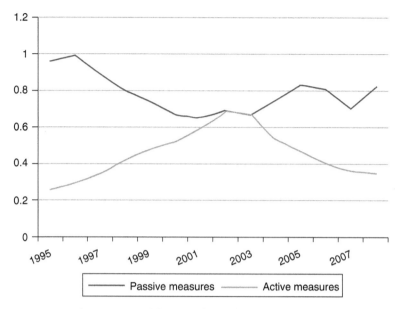

Figure 8.6. Expenditure in active labour market policies and out-of-work income support measures 1996–2006. Public expenditure as percentage of GDP

Note: Total expenditure on passive measures also includes early retirement and socially useful jobs.
Source: OECD Statistics, http://stats.oecd.org/index.aspx?, last updated: 25/07/2010.

provides for ALMPs and is managed at the regional level. This has entailed two important novelties. On the one hand, regional governments have played an unprecedented role in the bargaining on the above-mentioned 'emergency' CIG and mobility allowances, reinforcing their discretion in the domain of unemployment benefit provision, albeit with the risk of further widening territorial disparities in the implementation of such measures. On the other hand, the requirements of the European Commission are that benefits financed through ESF funds must be accompanied by the participation of workers in activation programmes, and must be systematically monitored and evaluated. This represents an important novelty that may in principle promote a greater integration between active and passive labour market policies. However, as we will discuss below, the implementation of these measures is often hampered by the limited ability of many regional and local employment services to actually provide suitable activation programmes for the unemployed.

Alongside the ambivalent developments in the field of ALMPs, over the last two decades other important changes have been seen in the governance of placement services. First, the public monopoly of employment services was abolished in 1997, allowing private actors – for the first time since 1949 – to enter the placement market. The adoption of this crucial reform was also favoured by the need to anticipate the intervention of the European Court of Justice, which, at the end of the same year, ruled against the prohibition on private labour market intermediation services in Italy. The process of liberalization was then completed by law 30/2003 (the so-called 'Biagi law'), which has paved the way for the constitution of a mixed public–private employment service system. Secondly, since 1997 a decentralization of competencies has been pursued, with the transfer of control over ALMPs and placement services to regional and local governments, and a reinforcement of the monitoring function of the state. This was part of a broader administrative decentralization process that involved several policy sectors (the so-called 'Bassanini reform', L.59/1997). In the field of labour market policy, the additional rationale behind decentralization was that assistance to jobseekers could be better tailored to the peculiarities of local labour markets. The abolition of the state monopoly on placement and the decentralization of PES can be read as two dimensions of a turn away from the old, centralized, and bureaucratic logic of labour market policy to embrace a more responsive and customer-oriented approach.

While this was at least the ambition, in reality the decentralization of PES has only partly led to anticipated improvements. There are substantial regional disparities in PES performance, hampering effective implementation of a nationwide activation strategy. The radical changes in the organization of the PES require not only time to be effective but also specific competences which in many places are largely absent, because the PES severely lacks both human capital (high quality personnel) and infrastructure (information technologies in particular). To make matters worse, deficits are most acute in those areas characterized by particularly difficult labour market conditions, making it more difficult for PES to provide effective job brokerage or offer tailored assistance to the unemployed where it is most needed.

Finally, there have also been changes regarding the link between passive and active measures, through the formal introduction of conditionality principles in the management of unemployment benefits. Laws in 2000 and 2002 (Legislative decree 181/2000 and Legislative decree 297/2002) detailed the behavioural requirements of unemployed people, in addition to the duties of the PES in supporting them. Eligibility for benefit receipt has been tied to some 'conditions of conduct' (Clasen and Clegg, 2006) that are specified in a 'client-deal' (*patto di servizio*) between the PES and jobseekers. The placement office should offer timely training or work opportunities that are suitable to the actual situation of unemployed people, with respect to some geographical and professional criteria (such as the distance from recipients' residence, the type of employment relationship and its duration, or the competences required). In return, recipients cannot reject 'suitable' offers to avoid the pain of losing their status of unemployed and, consequently, the related benefits.

This adoption of stricter conditionality criteria seems, however, to be more apparent than real, again due to implementation deficits. Enforcement of the rules remains lax and sporadic, and jobseekers services and the provision of unemployment benefits are loosely articulated, since they are still managed by two separate institutions operating at different levels: the regional PES and the national Social Security Institute (INPS). Devolution of the PES and ALMPs more generally has not been accompanied by an appropriate reorganization of the governance of the unemployment compensation system. Attempts have been made to increase the coordination between PES and INPS in some provinces, relocating their different services in the same building. But the scope of this attempt remains limited, since there is not yet a real integration of missions and functions of the two institutions.

In conclusion, Italian labour market policies moved significantly in the direction of activation in 1997–2003, though implementation problems have hampered the consolidation and effectiveness of this new policy orientation and recent trends in expenditure on ALMP and unemployment benefits, respectively, casts some doubt on whether the activation strategy remains a governmental priority.

8.4 AN UNCOORDINATED ADAPTATION TO POST-INDUSTRIAL CONDITIONS: THE POLITICS OF AN INCOMPLETE LEARNING PROCESS

During the 'golden age', Italy developed an insurance-based unemployment protection, without ever introducing either unemployment assistance or a general minimum income safety net. Resources devoted to ALMP have also traditionally been limited. As illustrated above, this system provided only a low level of economic support to a limited share of workers, and only relatively privileged groups in the industrial labour market workers could enjoy more generous income protection in case of the reduction or suspension of activity due to temporary economic crisis or restructuring processes. Since the late 1990s, growing pressures stemming from the liberalization of the labour market and prolonged economic stagnation have strongly affected the Italian unemployment structure, even more than in the past challenging the capacity of the Italian welfare state to support jobseekers. Despite the elements of benefit homogenization, risk reconfiguration, and activation outlined above, these pressures have, however, not led to a truly encompassing reconfiguration of the Italian system of unemployment protection. Where comprehensive reform proposals have been brought forward they have, significantly, failed to be fully followed through on.

The fate of the Law 223 of 1991 is in this respect telling. In 1991, the government defined new limits for the duration of CIGS, with the aim of bringing CIGS back to its original purpose, namely providing short-term wage compensation. A second major innovation at this time was the adoption of a specific procedure for collective dismissal, whereby redundant workers were required either to attend training programmes or participate in other activation measures in order to gain access to the mobility allowance (Fargion, 2001). These attempts to break with traditional policy logics were undermined, however, when a few years later various legislative decrees were adopted that watered down the innovations previously introduced (ibid.). A second opportunity was missed when, in the wake of the 1997 labour market policy reforms, the centre-left government launched a wider-ranging restructuring of the unemployment support. A commission of experts (the Onofri commission) was appointed, charged with the task of drafting encompassing reform proposals. The Onofri commission recommended the adoption of a three-tier model of unemployment support as well as reforms to the organization of benefit administration, to better articulate it with the newly devolved PES. However, with the exception of its proposals for the introduction of an experimental minimum income scheme, the Onofri Commission's recommendations were all sidelined. A final opportunity for far-reaching reform passed under the centre-right Berlusconi II government in 2002, when the proposals for redesigning the Italian system of unemployment support were made with Bill 848 and the 'Pact for Italy', a tripartite agreement between the government, employers representatives, and two of the main union confederations. Once again these proposals were never implemented, due mainly to financial constraints and the fierce resistance of the third major union confederation, Cgil. The latter had in fact refused to sign the social pact and vigorously opposed the reform plan, which contained an indirect linkage between the restructuring of unemployment benefits and increased labour market flexibility through the revision of Article 18 of the 1970 Workers' Statute (Jessoula et al., 2010; Vesan, 2009).

Since the 1990s there has in fact been a lack of real coordination, both between changes in the regulation of employment and changes in labour market policy and between different areas of labour market policy. When policymakers responded to the economic and employment shocks of the early-to-mid-1990s by containing early exit and pursuing flexibility 'at the margin', the unemployment protection system was not adapted to face the predictable consequences of these changes. When ALMPs were developed in the late 1990s, the management of passive and active measures was not tightly coupled, with the provision of unemployment benefits remaining in the hands of the central government while ALMPs and placement services decentralized. And when the employment crisis hit in the late 2000s, only temporary 'emergency measures' were adopted.

This lack of policy coordination and issue linkage might be interpreted as a failed activation of the so-called 'virtuous learning cycles'. The literature on learning (e.g. Visser and Hemerijck, 2001) identifies a number of conditions that are crucial for the activation of policy-learning dynamics: the perception of strong anomalies that delegitimize the existing policy paradigms or instruments, as well as the perception of the costs of non-reform; a willingness to search for new solutions that is suggested by either internal or external focusing events, or stimuli, and spills beyond expert communities, also catching the attention of contending political parties and impacting on the societal debate more broadly; the presence of financially sustainable and politically sound policy alternatives; and consensual or cooperative modes of interaction among relevant stakeholders, or at least a certain degree of governmental decision-making capacity, in order to avoid reform stalemates. A number of analysts have illustrated how in at least certain periods over the last two decades the presence of some of these conditions – notably the perception of the shortcomings of the Italian labour market, policy alternatives percolating from the supranational level, and cooperative modes of policymaking – has prompted a learning process that has led to a U-turn in Italian labour market policy (Ferrera and Gualmini, 2004). However, we would argue that this deviation from the traditional policy path has only been *partly* realized, notably because some of the necessary conditions for more complete learning were in fact missing.

Firstly, the persistently critical condition of Italy's public finances has represented a major obstacle for both the construction of a fully fledged unemployment benefit system and development of ALMPs, which both required additional resources. Redistributing resources across different welfare sectors, and particularly switching resources from the 'big spender' pension system to unemployment support and active measures – what Ferrera et al. (2000) have called 'welfare recalibration' – proved to be almost impossible in the Italian case, due to the opposition of entrenched interests. Secondly, it must be noted that the actual emergence of a post-industrial labour market – and especially the growth of atypical employment – was a gradual process, which only became fully visible to major stakeholders and policymakers around the mid-2000s, a period that was characterized by positive overall labour market trends, with decreasing unemployment and increasing employment. This limited problem pressure contained the costs of non-reform, both socially and politically. But although this changed with the economic crisis after 2008, a more thorough reform of unemployment protection has still not – to date – proved possible.

This indicates that for the activation of policy-learning dynamics – and, ultimately, for policy change – it is not only policymakers' 'puzzling' and issues of financial affordability that matter but also power resources. Recalibration was – and remains – difficult because the groups that would have benefited from a more robust UB system and/or more developed ALMPs have far fewer power resources than the groups who would lose. The idea of transferring resources from old-age protection to the unemployment protection system came up hard against the resistance of the unions, who were concerned with protecting the pension entitlements of retirees and older workers who form the bulk of their members (Jessoula 2009, 2010). Similarly, when expansive reform of unemployment protection was linked with the reduction in employment protection, it provoked the outright opposition of the most powerful union, Cgil (Vesan, 2009). Furthermore, the resources that were made available for improving unemployment support were 'captured' by the more numerous and better-represented groups in the labour market. This has resulted in the strengthening of UI, and to a lesser extent UIR, as well as the preservation of the central role played by CIG, while neither UA nor SA schemes that could provide support to atypical workers and outsiders were established. At least with respect to the failure to institutionalize SA, the predominance of the centre-right coalition, which has governed the country for seven out of the last ten years, has also been a contributory factor. The centre-right explicitly favours the model of a 'welfare society' in which the family continues to play a major redistributive and income support role (Ministry of Labour and Social Protection, 2003, 2009), and thus has repeatedly opposed the generalization of the minimum insertion income to the whole national territory (Jessoula and Alti, 2010).

Finally, with respect to the development of ALMP and the enforcement of the link between passive and active measures, policies borne of a real 'normative recalibration' (Ferrera et al., 2000) – inspired not least by the European Employment Strategy – have encountered considerable problems at the level of implementation. One of the main obstacles that has hampered the effective translation of activation principles on the ground has been the difficulty of offering suitable jobs or valuable training courses in the areas where unemployment is particularly high. Moreover, despite rhetorical calls for a greater responsibilization of unemployment benefit recipients, local authorities often have clear incentives not to enforce the conditionality principles in order to avoid potential conflicts with their political clienteles. Finally, the resilience of the old bureaucratic style in job placement management has also played a role in the slow and partial implementation of activation measures, in particular in those provinces where PES have limited institutional capabilities.

8.5 CONCLUSIONS

Due to late industrialization, Italy experienced a delayed transition to a service-based economy, fully completed only by the early 1990s. In order to tackle the negative consequences of deindustrialization, governments first followed the so-called labour reduction route, through the introduction of early retirement options and (later) mobility allowances, as well as the exploitation of seniority pensions and special schemes for wage compensation. The gradual emergence of a fully fledged post-industrial labour market occurred at an even later stage, after a U-turn in Italy's economic strategies was induced by tighter European constraints. Since the watershed 1997 employment reform, labour market flexibilization has increased 'at the margin' through the spread of atypical jobs for the new entrants to the labour market, and transitions in and out of employment, as between jobs, have increased.

Against this background, the adaptation trajectory of the Italian unemployment protection system has displayed signs of change alongside considerable continuities. The single-tier unemployment protection system, with contributory UI and UIR schemes and the special programmes CIGO and CIGS, has undergone a number of incremental interventions, leading to a less-differentiated treatment of various categories of workers. In particular, UI/UIR benefits have become more generous, and their inclusiveness has increased. A move away from the traditional passive approach to labour market policy has also been pursued, with the less intense exploitation of the labour reduction route, the expansion of ALMPs in the period 1997–2003, and the abolition of the state monopoly on placement services to attempt to set up a modern customer-oriented PES. These developments were mostly driven by a policy-learning process in the shadow of European constraints, which channelled ideas and policy solutions circulating into the supranational arena in the national debate.

In spite of these changes, tailoring the Italian unemployment protection system to post-industrial conditions is a task that largely remains to be accomplished. Steps taken in that direction have either been partial, or have not been followed through on the ground. In the unemployment protection system the reduction in the security gap has particularly benefited workers employed who can access ordinary UI, but the failure to introduce UA and SA schemes means most atypical workers are still without income protection in case of unemployment. Similarly, the sharp reduction in expenditures on active measures after 2003 does not fit well with the growing number of short-time, fixed-term employment relationships which are typical of a post-industrial labour market. Effective implementation of innovative procedures aimed at promoting jobseekers' reinsertion by local PES has varied greatly across the country, while the enforcement of the conditionality principle has been constrained by incomplete integration between PES and benefit administration.

This lack of policy coordination has been the consequence of a numbers of factors which have either stalled learning processes, or hampered their full translation into concrete policy changes. Certainly, the persistently critical condition of Italian public finances have not been conducive to the adoption of reform efforts that would be partly expansionary in the Italian case, due to the underdevelopment of unemployment benefits previously. Problem pressures were also limited for much of the 2000s by relatively good employment performance. When these pressures have become more evident, however, political calculation has pushed towards the adoption of rather conservative measures, in order to benefit mainly the most powerful groups in the labour market. Power imbalances and path dependency have to date also ruled out the possibility of finding further resources through recalibration between different social policy sectors. While responses to the economic crisis after 2008 included some (at least in principle) innovative measures, policymakers mostly relied on temporary and ad hoc emergency interventions to fill the protection gaps in the unemployment benefit system. It remains to be seen if the more innovative of these measures will turn out to be 'institutional seeds' (Ferrera, 1993) from which a more thorough adaptation of Italian unemployment protection to post-industrial labour market conditions can grow.

Appendix 8.A Major changes in unemployment benefits in Italy (1990–2010)

Law no. 223/1991	• Introduction of a new unemployment benefit scheme: the mobility allowance
Law no. 236/1993	• Ordinary UI: replacement rate increased to 25% of previous wages; duration (six months) and eligibility requirements unchanged.
Law no. 451/1994	• *Ordinary UI*: replacement rate increased to 30% of previous wages; duration and eligibility requirements unchanged.
Law no. 388/2000 (2001 budget law)	• *Ordinary UI*: replacement rate increased to 40% of previous wages; duration increased to nine months only for workers aged 50 and over; eligibility requirements unchanged.
Law no. 80/2005	• *Ordinary UI*: replacement rate increased to 50% of previous wage for the first six months (40% for the following three months and 30% for the remaining months); duration increased to seven months for workers under-50 and to ten months for workers over-50; eligibility requirements unchanged.
Law no. 247/2007 (2008 budget law)	• *Ordinary UI*: duration increased to eight months for the under-50s and twelve months for the over-50s; replacement rate increased to 60% of previous wage for the first six months (50% for the following two months and 40% for the further months); eligibility requirements unchanged. • *UI with reduced eligibility*: replacement rate increased to 35% of previous year daily average wage for the first 120 days, 40% for the following; maximum duration increased to 180 days; eligibility requirements unchanged (at least two years of insurance seniority and at least 78 days of work in the year).
	Anti-crisis measures
Law no. 2/2009	• *Social shock absorber 'on derogation'*: extension of the duration and the eligibility requirements for CIG and mobility allowance, defined by regional pacts. These benefits are also eligible for workers not covered by the regular CIG and mobility allowance. • Una tantum compensation for some categories of atypical workers (independent project workers): 10% of the previous annual wage. In order to be eligible, project workers must be unemployed for at least two months, earn between 5,000 and 20,000 euros per year and have at least 1 month of contribution in the reference year and 3 months of contribution in the previous year.
Law no. 191/2009 (2010 budget law)	• Una tantum compensation for some categories of atypical workers: replacement rate increased to 30% within a ceiling of 4,000 euros per year.

9

Spain: fragmented unemployment protection in a segmented labour market[1]

F. Javier Mato

9.1 INTRODUCTION

The aim of this chapter is to review how Spain has dealt with the risk of unemployment during the last twenty years, and to analyse the adaptation of Spanish labour market institutions to what has been called 'post-industrialism' in European labour markets (Clasen and Clegg, 2006, 2007) within the analytical framework of 'triple integration' as discussed in the introductory chapter of this book. Spain shared the economic pressures common to all European countries during the period under study, it has been a member of the EU throughout this period, and Spanish governments have embraced the European Employment Strategy since its launch in 1997. However, recent economic and social developments in Spain have created a very special case for the analysis of labour market institutions and unemployment policies. The changes that form the basis of this book are typical of post-industrial labour markets, and have coexisted in Spain alongside challenges to labour market policies that have arisen from the country having the highest unemployment levels in Europe during most of the period under consideration.

High rates of long-term unemployment, together with the growth of fixed-term employment since the mid-1980s, have seriously tested the unemployment protection system. As will be shown, all of this might make Spain an exceptional case in which trends of integration have coexisted with pressures which led to fragmentation in a context of influences of a still-present agricultural past, insufficient levels of economic and employment growth, and an unemployment protection system built only in the 1980s as a component of what was then a developing welfare state.

The structure of this chapter is as follows. Section 9.2 provides a brief overview of the socio-political and economic context prior to 1990, with attention being

[1] I would like to thank Jochen Clasen and Daniel Clegg, as well as the participants at the RECWOWE meeting held in Edinburgh in March 2010, for helpful comments. This research benefited from interviews with PES directors in Asturias José Luis Álvarez Alonso, José Berciano, and Juan Carlos Granda, and with Prof. Miguel Ángel Malo.

paid to the particular setting of the unemployment protection policy in Spain during the 1980s. This was the period during which the foundations of the modern unemployment protection system were laid, coinciding with the political transition to democracy. Section 9.3 contrasts the basic components of the unemployment protection system between 1990 and 2010. Section 9.4 is devoted to analysing system changes in the context of the notion of triple integration (see the introductory chapter to this volume). It shows that there has been little benefit homogenization and limited shifts towards activation. It also argues that if the unemployment protection system boundaries have changed, it is in the direction of narrowing unemployment as an administrative status, especially by facilitating bridges towards retirement. In the concluding section the chapter addresses the question why a more thorough process of triple integration has not emerged in Spain thus far.

9.2 THE SOCIO-ECONOMIC, POLITICAL, AND POLICY CONTEXT PRIOR TO 1990

The comprehensive overhaul experienced by the Spanish political system in the late 1970s and 1980s marks a necessary point of departure of this policy analysis. Understanding the rapid process that allowed the country to leave behind political repression and economic ultra-regulation, and to become one of the eleven European countries that formed the Economic and Monetary Union, is key to the contextualization of the changes which occurred in the unemployment protection system. The so-called *Transición* brought about the legalization of political parties from the entire political spectrum, free elections, a democratic Constitution, and a decentralization of the political system that gave the regions an increasing role in politics and policies. The economic crises of the late 1970s and early 1980s hit the Spanish economy hard and, in addition to stagflation, specific challenges emerged as the result of the country's relative isolation and heavy market regulation. The extraordinary social costs of adapting to a new market-led and internationally open economic environment can be seen in the growth of unemployment from around 5 per cent in 1976 to over 20 per cent by the mid-1980s (see Statistical Annex, Table A.5). Spain entered the EU with the highest level of unemployment of all the member states. This was due to both labour shedding and the arrival of the baby-boomers as a new and fast-growing working-age population that could not be absorbed by the labour market.

After entering the EU, and with a stable political environment, the Spanish economy benefited from the virtuous international economic context between 1985 and 1991, helping to create over two million jobs. However, it would be difficult to overstress the scale of the unemployment problem that developed in Spain during the 1980s and that still continues today, compounded by an uneven distribution of joblessness with female unemployment which peaked at 31.6 per cent in 1994, and was never below 20 per cent between 1982 and 2000. At the same time, long-term unemployment was the highest in Europe, often consisting of more than half of all unemployed persons (Statistical Annex, Table A.6), while

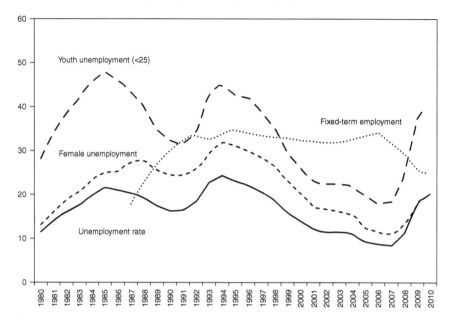

Figure 9.1. Standard unemployment rates and temporary employment rates in Spain (1980–2010)

Source: Own calculations using Labour Force Survey data from the Instituto Nacional de Estadística. Figures show yearly averages.

youth unemployment never dropped below 30 per cent, with peaks of 48 per cent in 1985 and 45 per cent in 1994 (Figure 9.1).

Two other features of the Spanish labour market prior to 1990 should be mentioned: a high degree of employment protection and the prevalence of collective bargaining (Bentolila and Toharia, 1991). Approximately, 90 per cent of all employment contracts were permanent, with fixed-term contracts for seasonal employment left to tourism or agriculture. The strong regulation of the Spanish labour market was the legacy of full employment during the authoritarian regime, which in turn was partly the result of international migration. The *Transición* brought about a profound change for heavily regulated Spanish industrial relations system at the time. Previously, the main objectives had been to maintain political control while keeping wages low and employment stable. Democracy led to a more open and western model. Devising and implementing a new system of industrial relations became inevitable in the context of enduring levels of mass unemployment, high inflation, and political instability.[2]

Democratization also affected the Spanish welfare state, which developed from underdeveloped version of the Bismarckian model (Guillén, 2010) to a system characterized by universal and public health care, expanded pension benefits (contributory and non-contributory), and comprehensive public education

---

[2] For detailed assessments of the Spanish labour market during the *Transición* and the 1980s, see Miguélez and Prieto (1991), Bentolila and Toharia (1991), and Jimeno and Toharia (1994).

(Mangen, 2001). A remarkable feature of this development was the decentralizing or regional devolution process that created a complex, multi-tiered system. Democratic Spain's seventeen Autonomous Communities received broad competencies in health care, education, social services, housing, and labour market issues. It was during the early 1980s that an unemployment protection framework was created, which still exists today. It is based upon the typical two-tier structure combining insurance and assistance benefits for registered unemployed persons (see below). Reforms also included the creation or maintenance of special unemployment assistance schemes designed to address specific social problems, such as agricultural unemployment in the southern regions of Andalusia and Extremadura, as well as processes of industrial adjustment such as coal mining. The former are structural features of the unemployment protection system and apply to a large group of beneficiaries, while the latter were special schemes facilitating paths towards retirement.[3]

In 1984, labour market regulation was profoundly reformed which had long-lasting effects on the volume of temporary jobs, and on the unemployment protection system. Under extreme economic conditions and mass unemployment, the reform introduced greater flexibility by allowing firms to offer fixed-term contracts even if there was no economic need for this. As a result, economic growth during the second part of the 1980s was accompanied by a steep increase in temporary employment to more than 30 per cent of all jobs by the end of the decade.

The fixed-term employment rate remained at about 30 per cent and thus twice as high as the EU average throughout the last two decades (see Statistical Annex, Table A.10). This generated a highly segmented labour market with large insider–outsider differences, and negative consequences for unemployment insurance coverage for outsiders.[4] In addition, a large-scale 'secondary labour market', in which unemployment spells and unstable working trajectories are the norm, generated extraordinary fiscal pressure for the unemployment protection system. For the most of the past twenty years, Public Employment Services (PES) have had to deal with over one-third of the working-age population, managing benefits and addressing activation objectives.

9.3 UNEMPLOYMENT PROTECTION: 1990 AND 2010 COMPARED

The 2010 Spanish unemployment protection system resembles in many ways the two-tier structure which existed in 1990. However, a new contributory scheme was created for the self-employed. In addition, unemployment assistance

---

[3] These schemes mean special treatments with regard to the general system of collective redundancies that existed – and still exist – and through which administrative approval is given to firms facing critical periods, and whose workers access unemployment protection, either on a temporary or on a permanent basis.

[4] See Amuedo-Dorantes (2000), Toharia and Malo (2000), Segura (2001), Dolado et al. (2002), and Malo et al. (2006).

expanded, and the programme specific to agricultural workers divided into two separate arrangements. The management of the system regarding benefit claims still relies on a national government agency, which is now called *Servicio Público de Empleo Estatal* (the national PES). However, the progressive devolution of national government competencies in the registration of vacancies and in job searches led to the creation of regional PES during the late 1990s and early 2000s. This section focuses on each tier of the unemployment protection separately, contrasting its structure as it was in 1990 with current parameters.

9.3.1 Unemployment insurance

The pivotal programme that still forms the current unemployment protection system today is unemployment insurance for employees (the so-called employee's insurance). In 1990 it paid out benefits at a sliding scale in accordance with previous contributions. The rate of benefit was expressed as a decreasing proportion of the average wage earned during the six months prior to unemployment, starting at 80 per cent and reduced by ten percentage points every six months. A benefit floor was set equal to the minimum wage, and different benefit ceilings applied dependent on family conditions at 170, 195, and 220 per cent of the minimum wage (see Table 9.1 for details). Also dependent on individual contribution records the maximum periods for which benefits were paid ranged from three to a maximum of eighteen months for contributors (Table 9.1). Other unemployment insurance conditions included the registration as unemployed and, in principle, a duty to accept adequate employment and/or training courses offered by the PES. However, in practice these obligations had no significant effects given that the scale of the jobless population allowed employers ample discretion for selecting the preferred candidates regardless of benefit status and the intermediation role of PES.

In 2010, unemployment insurance was basically the same as twenty years earlier, with the exception of a new scheme which was introduced for the self-employed. However, in the recession between 1992 and 1994 the minimum contribution period was increased from six to twelve months and a number of benefit cuts were made (see Appendix 9.A for details). The sliding scale of benefits was reduced to one-third of the contribution time, and the replacement rate reduced by ten points during the first year of unemployment (for details, see Table 9.1). For the jobless without children the benefit floor was also lowered but left unchanged for others. Unemployment benefits are now subject to income tax, and social security contributions are only partially subsidized, the rest being discounted from benefit amounts. Prompted by a financial imbalance in the unemployment insurance budget (Arango, 1999; Gutiérrez and Guillén, 2000) and the need to curb overall public expenditure in order to meet the Maastricht criteria (Guillén, 2010), the changes introduced during 1992–3 were significant, restricting both eligibility and generosity.[5]

---

[5] The 1992–3 reforms also affected the capitalization of benefit for the unemployed becoming self-employed, an option that was removed. However, it was taken up again in 2002, and hence it is currently functioning (Appendix 9.A).

Table 9.1. Main features of the unemployment insurance schemes, 1990–2010

	1990	2010
Type	Employees' insurance.	Employees' insurance. A new self-employed insurance plan was passed in 2010.
Membership	Compulsory for all employees except tenured civil servants. Members of co-ops included.	Idem.
Qualifying conditions	• Involuntary unemployed and having contributed for six months during the previous four years. • Seasonal employees included during off-season. • Partial unemployment (involuntary reduction of 30% of working hours) included. • Returning unemployed migrants without UI at destiny, who qualified before leaving Spain.	• Involuntary unemployed and having contributed for 360 days during the previous six years. Other 1990 conditions remain. • *Self-employment programme*: mínimum contribution of 12 months out of the previous 48 months.
Funding	Contributory, pay-as-you-go system. The government decides the contribution rates of employers and employees, as well as its own tax-based contribution to the system.	Idem.
Benefit level	Starting benefit at 80% of the previous wage, then 10% less every six months. Benefit floor at 100% of MW, including two bonuses. Benefit ceilings at 170% of MW (no children); 195% of MW (one child); 220% of MW (two or more children). Benefits exempt from Income Tax. Social Security contributions added to the benefits.	Starting benefit at 70% of the previous wage during the first 180 days; 60% thereafter. Benefit floor at 75% of MW (no children); 100% (others), including two bonuses. Benefit ceilings at 170% of MW (no children); 195% of MW (one child); 220% of MW (two or more children). Benefits subject to Income Tax. Social Security contributions added to the benefits only partially. • *Self-employment programme*: benefit proportional to previous Social Security monthly contributions. Ranges between €426–570 per month (or between €532 and €1,198 with two children).
Benefit duration	Sliding scale from 3 to 24 months, ratio ½ of contribution time.	Sliding scale from 4 to 24 months, ratio 1/3 of contribution time. • *Self-employment programme*: sliding scale from 2 to 12 months, ratio 1/6 of contribution time.
Obligations	• Being registered in the job centre. • Accepting adequate employment, training, or orientation proposals by the PES (first non-compliance suspends benefit; second ends it).	• Being registered in the job centre. • Signing an 'active agreement' compromising acceptance of 'adequate employment'. • Adequate employment defined as the former occupation or other that fits the individual 'insertion itinerary'. Adequate commuting maximums defined as: distance, up to 30 km; time, up to 25% of working time; cost,

(continued)

Table 9.1. (continued)

	1990	2010
		up to 20% of wage. The unemployed for over one year must accept any PES proposal as long as the wage covers the MW plus commuting costs.
Rights	• Possibility to capitalize the benefit for those going into self-employment. • Benefit can be suspended during a work contract inferior to six months.	• Possibility to capitalize the benefit for those going into self-employment. • Benefit can be suspended during a work contract inferior to 12 months. • Benefit is compatible with part-time employment or training grants.

Another difference between the current unemployment insurance regime and that of 1990 is the activation criteria which were introduced in 2002. Nowadays benefit claimants are required to sign an 'active agreement' comprising active job search and acceptance of 'adequate employment' offered by PES (see Table 9.1 for details). Finally, introduced in 2010, there is now also a contributory programme aimed at the self-employed who become unemployed, supporting persons who have paid Social Security payments as self-employed workers for a minimum of one year during the previous four years. Benefit duration is estimated as one-sixth of the contribution time, with a maximum of twelve months. Benefit amounts are proportional to previous Social Security monthly contributions (see Table 9.1).

9.3.2 Unemployment assistance

In 1990, unemployed persons with family dependants who had exhausted eligibility for unemployment insurance were entitled to unemployment assistance for up to six months, with a possibility of extension up to a maximum of thirty months. The amount of benefit paid was dependent on age and family conditions (see Table 9.2 for details). Benefits were exempt from income tax and included free medication in the public health-care system. However, age and family conditions not only affected benefit levels but also eligibility. Thus, a jobless person over 45 was eligible even without dependents, as long as they had exhausted at least twelve months of unemployment insurance. Moreover, the unemployed over the age of 52 and those eligible for a retirement pension were allowed to receive unemployment assistance for an indefinite period, that is, until they reached the retirement age at 65.

In contrast, few young people qualified for assistance. Entering the labour market as an unemployed person did not constitute benefit eligibility, and only those who had contributed sufficiently could receive unemployment insurance, which was key to subsequently receiving unemployment assistance under the conditions previously outlined. Educational status or level neither inhibited nor granted any rights to benefits.

Table 9.2. Main features of the unemployment assistance schemes, 1990–2010

	1990	2010
Type	Unemployment assistance	Idem.
Membership	Citizens between 18 and 64 years old.	Idem.
Qualifying conditions	• Involuntary unemployed who have exhausted UI or who, not being eligible for UI, have contributed for at least 3 months. In either case, eligibility requires having family dependents. • Involuntary unemployed who have just re-entered the labour market from the following situations: ○ Returning migration without UI ○ Imprisonment (minimum 6 months) ○ Complete disability • Involuntary unemployed over 52 without dependents, who qualify for a retirement pension except for age reasons. • Involuntary unemployed over 45 who exhausted a minimum of 12 months' UI. • In all cases, income must be below MW.	*Standard programme*: • Involuntary unemployed who have exhausted UI and have dependents. • Involuntary unemployed over 45 who have exhausted min. 12 months' UI. • Involuntary unemployed, with no right to UI, who contributed at least 180 days or just 90 days if they have dependents. • Involuntary unemployed who re-enter the labour market from situations of migration, imprisonment, or complete disability. • Involuntary unemployed over 52 without dependents, who qualify for a retirement pension except for age reasons. • Involuntary unemployed over 45 who exhausted a minimum of 12 months' UI. • In any case, eligibility requires having an income below 75% of MW. *Renta Activa de Inserción (RAI)*: • Involuntary unemployed over 45 who exhausted min. 12 months' UI, who have dependents, and whose income is below 75% of the MW. • Victims of domestic violence. *Temporary Programme* (PRODI, 2010): • Involuntary unemployed who have exhausted either UI or UA, with no further right to benefit, and with household-per-capita income below 75% of MW.
Funding	Contributory, pay-as-you-go system. The national government decides the contribution rates of employers and employees, as well as its own tax-based contribution to the system.	Idem. The regional governments finance the activation itineraries offered to the unemployed.
Benefit level	• Cash benefit: €225 per month, that is, 75% of the MW, plus two bonuses. The benefit is increased for those over 45 with two dependents (€300), or with three or more dependents (€375). • Social Security medication added to the benefit.	*Standard programme*: • Cash benefit: €426 per month, that is, 80% of the Multiple Effects Income Public Indicator (IPREM) with no bonuses. The benefit is increased for those over 45 with two dependents (€639), or with three or more dependents (€798). • Social Security medication universalized and thus excluded from UA. *Renta Activa de Inserción* and *Temporary Programme* (PRODI, 2010): €426.

(*continued*)

Table 9.2. (continued)

	1990	2010
Benefit duration	Initially six months, with six-month extension periods up to a total of 24 or 30 months, depending on age and family conditions. Those over 52 get the benefit until reaching retirement age.	Initially six months, with six-month extension periods up to a total of 30 months, depending on age, family conditions, and other circumstances. Those over 52 get the benefit until reaching retirement age. *Temporary Programme* (PRODI, 2010): 6 months with no extension. *Renta Activa de Inserción*: 11 months.
Obligations and rights	*Obligations*: being registered in the job centre. Accepting adequate employment or training offered by the job centre: rejection suspends benefits.	*Obligations*: being registered in the job centre. Signing an 'active agreement' compromising acceptance of 'adequate employment' (see UI): rejection ends benefits. UA benefit incompatible with RMI. *Rights*: UA is compatible with temporary and part-time employment under certain conditions.

The 'standard' unemployment assistance programme which operated in 1990 still persisted in 2010, but is now accompanied by two additional schemes directed at the long-term unemployed. A reform in 1992–3 reduced the eligibility income level from 100 to 75 per cent of the minimum wage, and lowered the maximum benefit entitlement for unemployed without dependents. Bonuses or supplements were excluded from benefits and the working time required for establishing benefit eligibility for returning migrants was increased from six to twelve months. Benefits of part-time employees who became unemployed were reduced and application procedures tightened. However, some revisions made benefit eligibility easier and improved the protection of unemployed persons older than 45 without dependents, and beneficiaries older than 52 who may now maintain their partial benefits if they engage in additional paid work in support of their pension entitlement. Overall, however, changes introduced in the early 1990s made standard unemployment assistance more restrictive.

A programme for the long-term unemployed was introduced in 2000. The means-tested so-called *Renta Activa de Inserción* (RAI), or Active Integration Income, is directed at those aged 45 and older who have exhausted other unemployment benefits and have family dependents. Victims of domestic violence are also included in this programme. When it was created, the RAI introduced the requirement of signing an 'activity agreement' with the PES (similar to unemployment insurance claimants), which meant accepting an individual activation route. Apart from training or job-search orientation, the unemployed would have to accept 'adequate employment', specified in accordance with occupational background, qualifications, physical competences, and wage levels commensurate with respect to the relevant industry. The RAI grants a cash benefit of 75 per cent of the minimum wage for a maximum of eleven months, payable three months after the start of the activation process (the latter rule has since been abolished). In essence, RAI basically extended unemployment support for a particular group of jobless people.

Since 2009 yet another programme has been in place in support of long-term unemployed persons. The so-called *Programa Temporal de Protección por Desempleo e Inserción (PRODI)* or 'temporary programme for unemployment protection and integration' was part of a stimulus package introduced by the Spanish government in response to the recession. The PRODI consists of a new means-tested benefit for the unemployed under 65 who have exhausted other benefit rights and whose families have no other source of income. It was meant to be temporary scheme for a period of six months but it was renewed twice, albeit by excluding those claimants who had already benefited from it.[6] Compared to the RAI, the Temporary Programme had a shorter benefit duration (six months as opposed to eleven) but was less restrictive, since it included jobless persons under the age of 45 who may have been unemployed for just six months (i.e. the minimum duration before unemployment insurance expires). In addition, the unemployed who terminate PRODI could still access RAI, but the reverse was not allowed. Thus, an unemployed person eligible for both schemes would choose PRODI first. For the very long-term unemployed the RAI represents the final stage of protection before having to turn to social assistance under the regional Minimum Integration Income programmes (see below) – unless they are over 52, in which case indefinite unemployment assistance can be granted, provided the individual is eligible for a future retirement pension.

An important additional component of unemployment protection which existed already in 1990 was related to rural and agricultural unemployment. Twenty years ago a special programme called *Subsidio Agrario* covered Andalusia and Extremadura, two large southern regions heavily hit by unemployment. These regions were the source of large majorities for the PSOE (the Spanish Socialist Party), and a potential locus of social unrest, given the highly mobilized left-wing unions active at the time. As part of this scheme, day labourers over the age of 52, working for 60 days in one year, could receive benefits (at a rate of 75 per cent of the minimum wage) for up to six months as long as they did not have other sources of income. The benefit duration was directly related to the number of days worked, but the scale used was more favourable to older workers than to young people, unless the latter had dependents. This programme was perceived as a way of counteracting the social problems imposed not just by chronic unemployment but also by rural poverty, and by the difficulty of effective land reform in areas with extreme income inequality, severe working conditions, and abundant clientelistic practices (González, 1990).

In 2002, subsidies for the southern regions were extended to the rest of the country, but eligibility became more restrictive and only experienced agricultural day-labourers can now benefit. However, a new scheme has been in place since 2003 which is directed at day labourers from Andalusia and Extremadura who are not eligible to the subsidy due to the restrictions introduced. This programme is

---

[6] At the time of writing, PRODI was due to end in February 2011 and the Spanish government announced that no further renewals would occur.

called *Renta Agraria* or Agricultural Income. Both programmes are very similar in terms of monthly benefit amounts (up to €426) and duration (up to six months) whilst family and age criteria persist. The minimum number of days worked per year which established right to benefit has been reduced to thirty-five. In 2010 only, the minimum number of days was shortened further (to twenty) in a restricted area heavily hit by the recession. Another novelty is that the beneficiaries must also sign the 'active agreement', just as with recipients of other unemployment programmes.

9.3.3 Assessing changes in unemployment protection

The past two decades have brought about significant changes to the Spanish labour market and to the institutions and policies related to unemployment protection. In an economic environment characterized by persistent and unevenly distributed mass unemployment, labour market liberalization aggravated problems associated with the generalization of temporary employment, affecting about 30 per cent of the employed. In this context, as discussed, there were two major trends in the unemployment protection system. First, the unemployment insurance scheme remained structurally unchanged, with the exception of the cuts introduced in the early 1990s. Second, unemployment assistance has expanded and diversified especially during the last decade when the RAI and the Temporary Programme were created, and when access eased for a larger fraction of the unemployed, such as people re-entering the labour market from abroad, from prison or from disability, or the victims of domestic violence. This suggests a movement from a conservative Bismarckian-type system towards a more solidarity-based one where diverse and new means-tested benefits have been put into place as the system matured. Social problems arising from long-term unemployment help to explain the introduction of additional assistance programmes in Spain.

However, unemployment insurance remained important and became even more important over time, as Figure 9.2 suggests. In 1990 the number of recipients of unemployment insurance and unemployment assistance were roughly the same with about half a million unemployed (or 22 per cent of the caseload) each. The agricultural scheme assisted almost 300,000 people (about 13 per cent of the total number of unemployed). In total, these three schemes covered about 55 per cent of all registered unemployed. Coverage in both main unemployment benefit schemes grew in the early 1990s, was reduced after 1993 due to the above-mentioned cuts, and then remained fairly stable for the rest of the 1990s. During the 2000s a steady rise in unemployment insurance took place while unemployment assistance remained in the region of 20 per cent of the beneficiary rate. As a result, before the recession in 2009 the number of insurance recipients was far greater than the number of recipients of assistance benefits. These trends could be partially explained by the strong creation of employment that characterized the Spanish economy between 1995 and 2008, increasing the proportion of employees with work experience and insurance contributions and thus those eligible for unemployment insurance. At the same time, fixed-term job growth made it fairly likely that a great number of workers in the secondary labour market would have

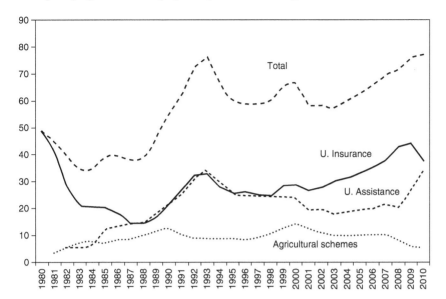

Figure 9.2. Beneficiary rates of unemployment protection programmes in Spain (1980–2010)

Note: All rates are estimated according to the total number of registered unemployed. Figures show yearly averages.

Source: Own calculations using data from the *Ministerio de Trabajo e Inmigración*.

experienced one or more spells of unemployment, and high job rotation may have counteracted the effects of policy developments.

Unemployment assistance in Figure 9.2 includes the various schemes discussed above, that is, the RAI which has operated since 2000, and the new Temporary Programme PRODI. The latter has provided cover to vast numbers of the unemployed who were running out of benefit, roughly to a quarter of the number of beneficiaries of the standard assistance programme in 2010, and it is the introduction of PRODI in 2009 which led to a closing of the gap in caseloads between unemployment assistance as a whole and unemployment insurance. The latter, in turn, decreased in 2010 as unemployment duration rose and many insured jobless exhausted their benefit.

Overall, the divided nature of unemployment protection reflects, and perhaps contributes to, the prevailing labour market segmentation in Spain. Following dualism-based analyses (Rueda, 2007), fixed-term employees tend to experience unstable work trajectories, moving from jobs into unemployment insurance and vice versa. This allows opportunistic behaviour by both employers and employees (Arango, 1999; Arranz et al., 2009; Recio, 1994). There is a remarkable rate of job turnover among both temporary employees and workers holding permanent contracts in Spain (García Serrano and Malo, 2010; Recio, 1994: 62). However, the segmented character of the Spanish labour market is institutionally enforced by protecting the core labour force also via unemployment insurance. As discussed, the insured jobless are better off than the unemployed without protection or those who rely on assistance. Therefore, unemployment insurance could be seen as a scheme for the 'upper secondary' labour market, while unemployment assistance beneficiaries represent a 'lower secondary' group among the working-age population, worse-off than both permanent employees and employees whose contributions allow them to receive insurance. Further down the protection ladder are young people coming out of the educational system. The absence of protection for the unemployed insofar as they lack the necessary work experience makes them dependent on other sources of income and, above all, on residential support from their family.

The emergence of new assistance schemes, such as the RAI in 2000 and the PRODI in 2009, illustrates the ineffective structure of social protection for those who have been jobless for longer periods, and thus highlights the restrictive nature of unemployment insurance. In addition, the extension of unemployment protection was in keeping with the large social and political support for unemployment policies in Spain. In the International Social Survey Programme (ISSP) conducted in 1996–7, Spanish public opinion showed the highest support for increased unemployment benefit spending and the lowest support for cuts within a sample of advanced capitalist OECD countries (Fraile and Ferrer, 2005). Even the significant public expenditure adjustment passed in 2010, which diminished public investment and cut the salaries of public servants by 5 per cent, left unemployment support almost intact.[7]

9.4 TRIPLE INTEGRATION IN SPAIN?

Following the framework outlined in the introductory chapter of this volume, this chapter turns to the notion of 'triple integration' and examines to which extent the three dimensions of integration might be observable in Spain. The previous analysis suggested that there have been adjustments during the past two decades, but no far-reaching structural reforms which would point towards the adoption of a wholesale integration. Nevertheless, the Spanish case shows some interesting and specific developments in all three dimensions which deserve attention.

9.4.1 Unemployment benefit homogenization

As outlined in the introductory chapter of this volume, benefit homogenization refers to the two tiers of unemployment support becoming structurally more similar to each other or, while remaining distinct from each other, one tier would become increasingly dominant as a form of unemployment protection. As discussed, and demonstrated in Figure 9.2, the generosity of unemployment insurance has declined but the scheme has maintained its wage-related character throughout the period under consideration, with further differentiation dependent

---

[7] Unemployment has appeared systematically as the main socio-economic concern of the Spanish population over the past few years, and is mentioned by about 80 per cent of the respondents during periodic surveys by the *Centro de Investigaciones Sociológicas*.

on family status. Moreover, neither unemployment insurance nor unemployment assistance has become the dominant tier. During the last two decades and with the exception of the last part of recessionary periods – when insurance exhaustion generated large flows into the assistance programmes – more individuals were in receipt of unemployment insurance than of any other relevant scheme.

In sum, no trend towards benefit homogenization can be identified in Spain either in terms of structural similarity or domination of one scheme. If anything there has been further segmentation within unemployment protection as a whole due to a proliferation of separate programmes within unemployment assistance itself. The extension of agricultural benefits initially enjoyed only by the southern regions to the rest of Spain may suggest a process of homogenization. But the politics of southern rural agriculture also explains the creation of yet another scheme, the above-mentioned *Renta Agraria*. On the other hand with few exceptions, in 2010, most beneficiaries on unemployment assistance schemes, which includes participants in the RAI and PRODI, received a benefit equal to €426 per month. Therefore, the proliferation of unemployment assistance schemes did not lead to further differentiation in terms of transfer payments.

In conclusion, it could be argued that the reforms introduced in Spain during the last two decades brought about some homogenization in the lower range of unemployment assistance support. However, the social rights enjoyed by the better-off workers with regular employment continue to contrast with those of others who have to rely in one of a number of assistance schemes. The segmented Spanish labour market is reflected in the fragmented Spanish system of unemployment support.

9.4.2 Risk re-categorization?

Risk re-categorization refers to the blurring of the boundaries of unemployment protection and other forms of working-age benefit schemes, making the latter more like the former, or making unemployment benefit more inclusive by reverting policies which, in many countries, were used to facilitate temporary or permanent exits from the labour market in the 1980s or even before. In Spain there has hardly been any reversal of these types of policies. Instead, publicly supporting exit routes from the labour market remained firmly in place, especially for unemployed persons above a certain age, albeit without reducing open unemployment.

As discussed in Section 9.3, for unemployed aged at least 52 who have a right to a retirement pension, that is, workers who have paid social security contributions, unemployment assistance can be paid until retirement. Persons in this group may be considered as de facto 'pre-retired' since they receive benefits until retirement, but they continue to be registered as unemployed and in recent years local authorities and PES officials have approached some claimants with activating programmes. Rather than phasing out this option of 'pre-retirement', the period of benefit eligibility has even been extended compared with 1990. For example, an adult unemployed with full benefit rights, that is, including unemployment insurance and most favourable family conditions, was able to remain in the system from the age of 47, receiving a total of twenty-four months' insurance and thirty-six months' assistance benefits until the age of 52, when eligibility was achieved for indeterminate unemployment assistance until retirement (Toharia, 1995). In 2010, a person in an equivalent social position was hypothetically able to depend on the unemployment protection system from the age of 45 years and 7 months.[8]

While older unemployed persons remain thus included in unemployment protection, even though many might have practically retired, most younger persons remain excluded. With the exception of disability and the minimum integration income (RMI) developed by the regions during the 1990s (see below), access to working-age benefit requires previous work experience and social security contributions (see Table 9.1). In the 1980s, both the minimum working age and compulsory schooling age were raised to 16. There is no right to unemployment insurance benefit for jobless young persons leaving education.

The above illustrates a paradox in Spain. During the past decades, older workers became progressively perceived as having left the labour market but are supported by unemployment benefits, while younger people actually in search of employment have access to, if anything, merely marginal means-tested programmes. This imbalance is an expression of the 'familial' character of the Spanish welfare regime which disadvantages young people in terms of social rights and in the labour market as is reflected in the disproportionate reliance on fixed-term contracts (García-Serrano et al., 1999; Garrido, 1996). In the absence of an explicit family policy, young people are supposed to be supported by intra-family resource sharing (Flaquer, 2004). It is the family which takes on the role of the welfare state in this respect (Moreno, 1997), while the design of welfare state policies, such as unemployment protection, differentiates in accordance with age and family conditions. In this sense, rather than risk re-categorization unemployment support is not more inclusive but contributes to the status quo which transfers responsibility for younger unemployed to the family rather than public policy.

As indicated, there are other benefits for working-age persons in Spain which are not considered as supporting the jobless. Modelled on the French RMI, the *Renta Minima de Inserción* was initiated by the Basque government in 1988 and has thereafter been adopted in all of the seventeen Spanish Autonomous Communities. Thus, by the mid-1990s a new 'solidarity-based' component of the working-age jobless protection system had been in place. In spite of being nominally concerned with integrating the beneficiaries into work, the effective functioning of RMIs does not require recipients to be registered as unemployed and its management does not rely on the unemployment or PES centres. Instead the schemes rely on regional arrangements and are usually run by social services. Legal provisions also differ, with some regions adopting the RMI as a subjective right and others a programme-based approach (Martínez Torres, 2005). There are considerable differences across regions which are linked to funding capabilities

---

[8] Hypothetically, a claimant could get twenty-four months of unemployment insurance, followed by thirty months' standard unemployment assistance, plus six 'special subsidy' unemployment assistance, plus eleven months' RAI, and six months' PRODI, resulting in seventy-seven months, which is the time between 45 years and 7 months and the 52-year-old limit, after which UA becomes indefinite until retiring.

(Arriba, 2009).[9] In general, however, restrictive conditions of access to benefits apply, especially regarding a minimum legal residence period required in the region, making RMI hardly an effective general social safety net (Ayala, 2000). Thus, the RMI resembles an encompassing but low-level assistance system, in which up to 70 per cent of the beneficiaries are currently women and which is characterized by the lack of a realistic activation approach (Rodriguez Cabrero, 2009).

The RMI regional programmes also mark the boundary between social services and unemployment assistance, especially the RAI. In addition, while the number of RMI beneficiaries has grown in recent years there has not been a process of the RMI replacing the dominance of unemployment support schemes, as Figure 9.2 indicated (see above).

In Section 9.2 the rural and agricultural unemployment schemes were discussed because of their not insignificant number of beneficiaries (see Figure 9.2), most of whom are located in the southern regions. Indeed, for many years the number of beneficiaries of the agricultural scheme exceeded the registered agrarian unemployed in the majority of the regions covered (Watson, 2008). The extension of the existing agricultural subsidy to the entire country in 2002 was accompanied by narrowing entitlement criteria, thus excluding day labourers or workers who had been employed in other sectors previously. However, this has not depressed coverage as the number of individuals in receipt of some of the existing schemes for rural unemployment has roughly remained the same since the early 1990s, that is, just above 200,000 people per year.

Finally, it should be pointed out that, as in other countries, there are sickness and disability benefits in Spain, but the take-up is somewhat lower than in most countries. Gruber and Wise (2007) place Spain at the bottom of a group of ten countries, with contribution-based invalidity pension beneficiaries growing with age to reach a maximum of 7 per cent of the oldest cohort, that is, men aged 64. The number of male and female contribution and non-contribution-based recipients of disability programmes was fairly constant during the last decade at around 1 million people. In 2010 this means that the number of disability pension beneficiaries was about one-third of that in receipt of unemployment support.

Disability and illness are covered by Social Security in two separate contributory types: temporary and permanent. Accessing either the permanent disability scheme or going back to work is decided upon when the Temporary Programme is exhausted (after generally eighteen months). Permanent disability benefits are followed by retirement pensions when the individual reaches retirement age. A specific route exists for unqualified workers over 55 who are eligible to receive disability benefit until they reach retirement age and, as in other European countries at the time, in the 1980s both programmes were frequently used as bridges towards early retirement (Boldrin et al., 1999). Conditions to enter the temporary scheme were subsequently tightened, however, and it is now uncommon for people over 55 to access permanent disability (Boldrin and Jiménez-

---

[9] The different values of benefits among the Spanish regions is a problem that goes beyond the RMI programme, and also occurs in centrally created programmes that were subsequently decentralized (Ayala et al., 2001).

Martín, 2007). It can be argued that policies in the field of disability benefits are the one instance of risk re-categorization in Spain which is similar to other countries in which claimants were increasingly transferred from disability and other programmes to unemployment benefit. However, in Spain there is no evidence of people having previously shifted from unemployment into disability benefit support. On the contrary, the growth of unemployment support systems and the more generous benefits paid to unemployed have always made it more attractive for potential claimants to rely on unemployment insurance and assistance.

9.4.3 Activation

Throughout the past two decades, active labour market policies (ALMPs) have had a relatively modest profile in Spain. In a context of labour shedding and the large number of benefit claimants within unemployment protection, active labour market programmes were not a priority. Indeed, it was only after Spain's joining the EU in 1986 that the profile particularly of labour market training activities rose noticeably (Mato, 2002) and by 1990 expenditure on active programmes was close to the EU-15 average. As unemployment support, active labour market schemes were significantly cut back in the midst of the recession between 1992 and 1994 but spending picked up again afterwards and stayed slightly below the EU-15 average (Ramos et al., 2010; see also Statistical Annex, Table A.14).

Given high unemployment, the low profile of ALMP might surprise but may be explained in the light of labour market dualism. Rueda (2007) argues that governments which consider labour market insiders as their core constituencies are more worried about employment protection policies than about training and similar policies which tend to benefit outsiders. Partisanship associates the former stance with social democratic and the latter with conservative governments. Socialist governments held office for twelve out of the last twenty years, and the centre-right was able to govern with an absolute majority for only four years during that period, which may help to explain that employment protection rather than ALMPs or activation dominated the policy agenda. When reforms did take place, the main issues were usually the reduction of dismissal costs and work contract modifications. The most recent labour market reform, adopted in 2010, showed yet again that employment protection was the core issue, leaving both unemployment support and activation measures unchanged. The main labour unions, whose core constituencies are also insiders, have also shown much greater concern over employment protection than ALMPs.

This does not mean that activation measures have not been debated or implemented. After all, successive Spanish governments supported the Lisbon agenda and, accordingly, introduced activation measures and job-search conditions, such as 'active agreements' (see Table 9.1). However, to properly assess the extent of activation mechanisms in Spain, institutional changes in the PES structure and the role of regional authorities must be taken into account. As part of the decentralization process, the PES was transferred from national to regional level during the late 1990s and early 2000s. With the exception of the Basque

Autonomous Community, all of the regions are now responsible for labour market intermediation and ALMPs carried out within the PES.[10] However, the responsibility for unemployment insurance and assistance programmes has not been decentralized, even if the benefits are physically delivered in the same PES offices.

The PES has always been the organization in charge of managing information, as well as controlling access to labour market programmes and related benefits. The activation process introduced during the past decade has thus given regional authorities greater competences, and induced a degree of competition among regions which shaped variation in service modernization and innovations such as 'one-stop centre' designs and the spread of online intermediation resources.

However, the decentralization and modernization of PES has contributed little to fostering activation. Connecting unemployment benefit receipt with active job search is difficult where the responsibility for these tasks is divided between national and regional administrations, respectively. Regional authorities lack incentives to demand benefit claimants to be more actively engaged in job-searching activities and are unlikely to enforce participation in active measures, unless it is a formal condition for the continued receipt of benefit. An unemployed person who does not comply with activating measures may be disqualified from benefit receipt, but for this to happen regional authorities need to report the person's behaviour to the national authorities and the unemployment protection system. If this is done the subsequent administrative process takes a long time and, if disqualification is confirmed, generates savings for the national government rather than the regional authority. Thus, regional PES officials have little to gain for adopting a more enforcing perspective.

Figure 9.3 shows the proportion of exits from the different unemployment schemes caused by benefit disqualifications. In the last decade this proportion was very low (between 3 and 4 per cent) with moderate increases in 2006 and 2007 which might indicate the influence of labour demand in some sectors, or a trend towards activation to some degree, or both. It is noticeable that compared with unemployment insurance, disqualifications are slightly more likely in unemployment assistance scheme and less likely in the agricultural programmes. It could have been expected that the RAI might have led to a stronger rise in disqualifications after its introduction in 2000 which included the need to sign an 'active agreement'; and that standard assistance and insurance schemes, which adopted the agreement in 2002, would have shown a similar rise, but neither seems to have happened.

There is no firm evidence of activation mechanisms having led to higher rates of transitions from unemployment into work. Existing studies concluded that receiving unemployment support does not affect job-search effort or exit from unemployment (Garrido and Toharia, 2004; Toharia et al., 2010). However, other analyses indicate that this depends on the type of benefit received and thus on differences in typical claimant profiles. Exit rates in particular seem to be more influenced by socio-demographic characteristics of claimants groups than by the intensity of activating efforts. For example, the probability of exiting unemployment for those in

---

[10] The transfer of active labour market policies to the Basque government has been delayed due to political differences as to the amount involved, but it is expected to take place in 2011.

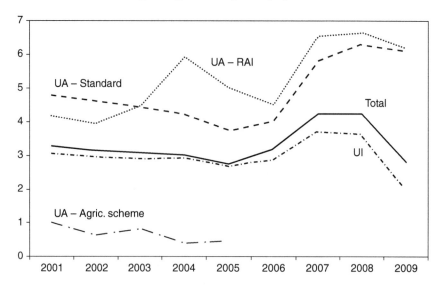

Figure 9.3. Rates of disqualification from unemployment protection programmes in Spain (2001–9)

Note: Figures show the yearly disciplinary and precautionary disqualifications divided by all yearly exits from each unemployment scheme, in percentage terms.
Source: Own calculations using data from the *Ministerio de Trabajo e Inmigración*.

unemployment insurance is much higher than for those in unemployment assistance, but slightly lower than for jobless who are not on benefit. Within unemployment assistance, beneficiaries over the age of 52 show the lowest probability of entering employment, similar to beneficiaries of RAI (Toharia et al., 2006).

The rather poor results of the RAI, the first piece of the system where the activation approach was explicitly introduced in 2000, can be explained by its origin and development. Initially, RAI represented the adoption of activation principles in Spain since it explicitly required active search behaviour as eligibility criterion for benefit claimants. However, later the scheme principally supported a population with low labour force attachment and currently assists groups of unemployed with low job prospects, not dissimilar to claimants of the regional minimum income programmes (see above). Thus, the RAI is perhaps the best example for activation which in Spain stands more for a rhetorical trend than an actual strategy. The activation process has led to some changes, such as defining more precisely the content of what can be considered 'adequate work', but overall activation initiatives in Spain have remained modest (García-Serrano, 2007).

9.5 CONCLUSIONS

Mass unemployment has shaped the Spanish economy and Spanish society throughout the last two decades. Significant economic growth and successive labour market reforms have not prevented Spain from continuing to be the

European champion of unemployment. The concentration of joblessness among young people and women, as well as long-term unemployment, has been accompanied by an acute and persistent level of temporary employment, leading to a clear case of labour market segmentation throughout the period. In this structural context, the use and functionality of the unemployment protection system warrants analysis, given the transition towards a post-industrial labour market and the specific pressure generated on unemployment protection and the PES by having to deal with almost one-third of the total labour force for many years.

The analysis of changes in the different components of unemployment support in the past twenty years suggests a remarkable endurance of basic system features. Overall conditions have been maintained in eligibility and generosity of both the unemployment insurance and the assistance components. Nevertheless, there were some changes driven by two factors. First the financial constraints of the system during the early 1990s recession triggered numerous cuts and retrenchment but left the main system components intact. Second, the enduring level of long-term unemployment throughout the 1990s and beyond was the main cause particularly for the creation of two new programmes, the RAI (in 2000) and the PRODI (in 2009), the latter in response to the latest economic recession.

These reforms have ensured that benefit coverage among the unemployed is fairly high but also firmly divided. The maintenance of a relatively generous unemployment insurance scheme may be functional for a segmented labour market which includes a relatively privileged group with stable employment or short spells of unemployment between jobs. Given the higher benefit levels received, longer total benefit duration, and the higher probability of finding work, it has been suggested that claimants of unemployment insurance belong to an 'upper secondary' labour market. All others, and particularly the long-term unemployed, rely on unemployment assistance which has a higher coverage than twenty years before but is increasingly fragmented in nature.

In terms of its overall structure there has been no homogenization within unemployment benefit support in Spain. Unemployment insurance and unemployment assistance cover roughly the same proportion of the unemployed, and the respective system characteristics have not become more similar over time. Perhaps with the exception of disability benefits, there have been no instances of risk re-categorization in Spanish labour market reforms either. If anything, unemployment as a risk category has become narrower since changes have facilitated rather than closed labour market exit routes for older workers via unemployment benefit receipt as a de facto early retirement vehicle. Younger persons continue to be excluded from unemployment benefit while family status and age are conditions which determine benefit rights, favouring the maintenance of the family wage and 'male breadwinner' model in unemployment protection. In addition, since unemployment assistance is rather low, the family is a non-trivial contributor to the maintenance of young jobseekers who tend to enter temporary jobs and belong to the 'lower secondary' labour market.

Even activation has been more limited than in other European countries, despite a shift in this direction within the public discourse. The lack of actual policymaking is partly due to problems of coordination between regional and national officials who work in the PES, as well as the relative low profile of ALMPs within political parties and labour unions and, of course, the scale of the unemployment problem which makes it difficult to devise personalized trajectories aimed at integrating large numbers of jobless people into the labour market. Thus, at least at the time of writing, activation seems to be more of a rhetorical device than a serious policy shift.

Appendix 9.A Major reforms to income maintenance systems in Spain (1990–2010)

	Unemployment compensation	Other social insurance schemes for working-age population
1992	• *Tightening of UI*: increase in minimum contributory period from 6 months in the previous four years to 12 months in the previous six years; decrease in the replacement rate, down to between 70 and 60% of previous wage, depending on the length of contribution; reduction in duration by lowering ratio to contributory period from 1:2 to 1:3. • Reduction in UA duration, depending on family dependents. Maximum duration down from 30 to 21 months. • Suppression of the lump sum payment option for the unemployed becoming self-employed.	
1993	• Reduction in the minimum UI benefit amount conditioned on not having family dependents, from 100% to 75% of MW. • UI recipients' Social Security contributions change from being totally to partially subsidized. • UA amount is marginally reduced, excluding MW bonus from baseline. • Tightening of the incompatibility of all unemployment benefits with self-employment.	
1994		• Pre-retirement subsidies for over-60-year-olds are made available to a greater number and situation of firms in crisis. • Maximum duration of temporary illness benefits reduced from six to two and a half years.
1995		• Introduction of regional minimum income programmes, which started in the Basque country in 1989, is now complete.
1997	• The minimum number of days worked per year to be eligible for the agriculture subsidy in Andalusia and Extremadura is lowered to 35.	• Disability pensions are converted into retirement pensions for beneficiaries over 65.
2000	• Introduction of a new active integration income (Renta Activa de Inserción) programme, a means-tested scheme for the long-term unemployed for over-45-year-olds with family dependents who exhausted UI and UA.	
2001		• Reduction and convergence with UI of temporary illness benefits for workers whose contracts end while being ill.
2002	• UI recipients are required to sign an 'active agreement', compromising active job search and acceptance of 'adequate employment' defined according to contract features and to commuting time, cost, and distance.	• Temporary illness benefits extended to include self-employed workers.

(continued)

Appendix 9.A (continued)

	Unemployment compensation	Other social insurance schemes for working-age population
	• Reintroduction of the option to partially receive future benefits at present, addressed to the unemployed who become self-employed.	
	• Unemployment compensation is made more flexible, allowing lump sum payments, some regional mobility grants, and compatibility with some forms of work.	
	• New unemployment assistance scheme created for agricultural workers (Renta Agraria), an extension of the one existing in Andalusia.	
2003	• Regional PES takes over labour market intermediation functions from the national PES.	
2004	• Increased MW remains reference indicator for income limits as to entitlements, but new indicator is created for benefit amounts, which has moved thereafter below MW.	
2005		• Working-age recipients of non-contributory pensions for disability are allowed to work, maintaining the benefit during four years conditioned on wage level.
2006	• The Renta Activa de Insercion scheme, renewed annually since 2000, becomes part of the unemployment protection system.	
2007		• Access to permanent disability benefits is tightened via increased waiting periods, while benefit amounts in the lower range are homogenized.
		• Improvement of maternity and parental leave conditions and introduction of paternity leave.
2009	• New temporary scheme (PRODI), means-tested, with a six-month benefit for the unemployed who extinguished their benefits.	
2010	• New unemployment insurance scheme for the self-employed.	

10

Denmark: ambiguous modernization of an inclusive unemployment protection system

Jørgen Goul Andersen

10.1 INTRODUCTION

Shortly before the economic crisis of the 1970s, Denmark had modernized its unemployment protection system to become one of the most generous in the world. Unemployment insurance was open and inclusive, and replacement rates were extremely high. After some cuts in maximum benefits, these features were largely maintained throughout the deep economic crisis of the 1980s and the long-lasting economic upturn between 1993 and 2007. Combining liberal employment protection with generous social protection and activation to ensure re-employment, the Danish model of 'flexicurity' (Beskæftigelsesministeriet, 2005) became celebrated internationally as a source of inspiration (e.g. European Commission, 2008; OECD, 2007a).

Alongside these relatively stable traits the structure of social protection for non-employed people was comprehensively modernized and increasingly integrated between 1990 and 2010. First, the system was transformed to address problems of structural unemployment, mainly via activation, and shortly afterwards to reverse labour shedding and unintentional labour market exit mechanisms. As unemployment declined (see Statistical Annex, Table A.5), job availability requirements were tightened, and activation was redirected towards a 'work first' strategy. The target of employment efforts was gradually broadened from the unemployed to other groups of working-age benefit recipients.

Until the end of the period, this happened without serious deterioration of social rights. There were cuts for particular groups of social assistance recipients (de facto affecting mainly immigrants). But this was the exception. The main instrument to improve economic incentives was a tax deduction for the employed. Further, tighter 'conditionality' (Clasen et al., 2001) in terms of stricter conditions of availability and activation requirements served as an alternative to lowering benefits or shortening benefit duration more drastically.

In Denmark the reforms did not involve an integration of social rights for different claimant groups. Different schemes remained in place, and unemployment benefits continued to be the dominant transfer among ordinary unemployed (see Appendix 10.A). If anything, unemployment benefits occasionally served as an implicit standard for adjusting other entitlements. This was in accordance with the inclusionary tradition of unemployment insurance, not unlike in Belgium (see Chapter 6 in this volume).

Also in accordance with this tradition, unemployment benefits and social assistance were indexed by wage increases from 1990. This remained unchallenged throughout the subsequent two decades, but due to technical details indexation is marginally below 100 per cent. As this is not quite negligible in the long run, the level of maximum unemployment benefit (benefit ceiling) has slowly declined relative to wages, and nearly everybody receives the maximum amount. Thus, unemployment insurance lost its 'industrial-achievement' logic by being gradually transformed to a de facto flat-rate scheme – and in this way became more homogenized, as outlined in the introductory chapter of this volume. While this provided a solid protection against poverty, the maximum became less sufficient for workers with average incomes or above. This generated some interest for supplementary insurance provided via the unions.

Employment efforts were gradually extended to marginal groups on the labour market, modelled on activation efforts for 'core groups' in receipt of unemployment benefits. In that sense one could speak about an integration of different risk categories. Moreover, this was followed by administrative integration for all groups of non-employed in municipal job centres, in accordance with the 'one-shop' philosophy. It had been argued that the division between people receiving unemployment benefits and social assistance was arbitrary, but ironically, the administrative reform was implemented at a time when socio-economic differences between these two categories were the largest ever recorded (Harrits and Goul Andersen, forthcoming; Rosdahl and Petersen, 2006). By 2010, all working-age benefit claimants were divided into three matching groups across administrative lines: those ready for employment, those ready for employment effort, and a residual group labelled 'temporarily passive'.

More generally, against a background of an unusually smooth process of post-industrialization one could speak of quiet and incremental modernization at least until around 2005–7. In spite of massive outsourcing of jobs, Denmark did not experience large regional disparities, oversupply of unskilled labour, growth in 'precarious' employment, or social marginalization. Moreover, the Danish trajectory was based on a consensual political process. In contrast to the orthodoxy of the 'new politics of the welfare state' (Pierson, 1994, 1998), policy change was possible, and economic prosperity rather than crisis was the main driver of change.

In recent years, however, politics and policymaking has become less consensual. By 2010, in the context of increasing unemployment, the maximum duration of unemployment benefits was drastically shortened from four to two years. As will be discussed below, the 2010 reform may be indicative of more fundamental path-breaking in Danish labour market policy.

10.2 ECONOMIC AND POLICY CONTEXT

Unlike the other Nordic countries, Denmark had ended up in dire economic conditions in the wake of the 1973–4 oil crisis. High inflation, large budget deficits, and current account deficits became chronic problems, and for two decades unemployment oscillated around the 10 per cent rate. Under Social Democratic governments (1975–82), an unusually broad range of Keynesian economic instruments were applied in the attempt to reduce unemployment (Goul Andersen, 2002*a*), seemingly with little success. When in 1982 a Conservative led-coalition government took over, it assigned priority to competitiveness, fixed the currency rate, focused on low inflation, and successfully branded itself on 'economic reconstruction'. It failed initially, however, due to excessive private consumption, but in 1986, the government was forced to implement credit restrictions in a package known as the 'potato cure'. This cure increased unemployment even further but it did solve Denmark's chronic balance of payment problem and arguably provided the preconditions for a new 'golden age' of growth and welfare between 1993 and 2007 (Goul Andersen, 2011).

Denmark did not really suffer from deindustrialization and globalization at any time. The 1970s brought a massive decline in manufacturing, due to low competitiveness. Between 1982 and 1992, however, there was no further decline (see Statistical Annex, Table A.1), and for the subsequent decade the decline was rather limited. Whole industries disappeared (such as the textile industry, shipyards, etc.) but they were replaced by new ones, thus helping to maintain low regional disparities, and generational replacement reduced the number of unskilled workers more than the number of unskilled jobs (Andersen, 2006).

In the context of mass unemployment of the 1980s, youth unemployment and long-term unemployment increased (see Statistical Annex, Table A.6) but remained lower than in nearly all other European countries outside Scandinavia (Goul Andersen and Jensen, 2002). Except for jobs for schoolchildren, a secondary employment sector did not emerge.[1] Women were already strongly integrated in the labour market by 1980 and began to shift from part-time to full-time work. The number of involuntarily part-time employed has remained low and, unlike in many other EU countries, fixed-term employment has never been prevalent. In contrast to the European trend, it even declined further during the 1990s and beyond (Eurostat, 2003, 2010). In short, 'precarious' employment has never been a big problem in Denmark.

As elsewhere in Europe, Danish governments sought to reduce open unemployment by stimulating early retirement and other measures to reduce labour supply. Most important in this respect was the introduction of voluntary early retirement (called *efterløn* – 'after wage') in 1979. Workers were given the opportunity to withdraw from the labour market from the age of 60 in return for an early retirement allowance equivalent to unemployment benefits. Other labour supply reductions included longer holidays and collectively agreed shorter

---

[1] In Denmark, students and older schoolchildren typically have a side job. They constitute the majority of workers in much retail trade, which could give the impression of a part-time, low-wage 'proletariat'. Schoolchildren and students also explain why Denmark has extraordinarily high employment rates in international statistics.

working weeks. Further, there was a rapid increase in the number of disability pensioners until the mid-1990s (Clement, 2000; see Appendix 10.A).

Danish policies of the 1970s and 1980s were successful in terms of preventing social marginalization among the unemployed. In this respect, Danish findings were the best in Europe (Goul Andersen, 1996, 2002b; Wheelan and McGinnity, 2000). In spite of the incentive structure, labour force participation nonetheless remained high and long-term unemployment comparatively low.

The coincidence of high unemployment and accelerating wage increases in 1987 fuelled the emergence of a consensus of unemployment having become 'structural' in nature (Albrekt Larsen and Goul Andersen, 2009; Arbejdsminister-iet et al., 1989; Birch Sørensen, 2008; Udredningsadvalget, 1992; Goul Andersen, 1993; Torfing, 2004). There was also some concern for welfare dependency, although more as a social problem than as a moral hazard (Socialkommissionen, 1993). As will be discussed below, this can be seen as the overture to encompassing policy changes which began in the early 1990s.

During the 1980s, however, unemployment protection changed only marginally, and among persons registered as unemployed, the proportion receiving unem-ployment benefits, rather than social assistance, remained surprisingly stable until 2010 (between 85 and 90 per cent; Statistics Denmark, S. E. Arbejdsmarked, various issues; see also Appendix 10.A).

As in other countries, Danish social protection used to be sharply divided between unemployment insurance on the one hand and social assistance on the other; and in administrative terms, between the state and municipal responsibility. Both schemes had been thoroughly reformed shortly before the crisis in the 1970s. Unemployment insurance had become unusually generous and inclusive, whereas social assistance was designed as a flexible instrument to deal with a small residual group with complex problems beyond unemployment.

Ever since 1907, Danish unemployment protection has been organized in accordance with the so-called 'Ghent model' of a voluntary and state-subsidized insurance organized by trade union-affiliated unemployment funds. It was initi-ally a liberal model with rather low replacement rates, but major reforms in the late 1960s and early 1970s made the scheme more 'Social Democratic' since the state took over the 'marginal risk of employment'. Contributions became a fixed amount unrelated to unemployment. Accordingly, at times of rising unemploy-ment, benefits became almost fully tax-financed.[2] Moreover, the replacement rate was raised to 90 per cent of previous earnings, while the ceiling (maximum absolute benefit level) also rose considerably. Benefit duration was fixed at 2.5 years, with uniform entitlement for all members, regardless of contribution record. After the oil crisis in the early 1970s, membership of unemployment insurance funds rose from 35 per cent of the labour force to 66 per cent by 1982 (Pedersen and Huulgaard, 2007: 406, 408).

Even though expenditures rose dramatically, the Danish adaptation to mass unemployment was to extend the maximum duration of benefits in order to

---

[2] From 1973 to 1974, state financing rose from 62 per cent to 87 per cent as expenditures quadrupled, due to rising unemployment and due to a 20 per cent increase in the ceiling of the benefit (Jørgensen, 2007: 174, 417).

prevent claimants from potentially dropping out. In the early 1980s it became possible to requalify twice for a period of 2.5 years, via participation in a job offer programme with seven to nine months of subsidized employment, typically in the public sector. By implication, the maximum entitlement to UI was extended to nearly nine years, and requalification for another full round only required six months of ordinary employment. Conservative-led governments after 1982 managed to cut the maximum by freezing it for about three years (1982–6),[3] which was only partly compensated by 1988. In fixed prices, the maximum in 2009 remained below the 1982 level. The government also increased members' contributions slightly, but failed in attempts to implement a more comprehensive reform.

Looking back, due to a combination of higher replacement rates and extended maximum benefit durations, Danish unemployment insurance had been transformed into one of the most inclusive and most generous systems in the world (Goul Andersen, 1996). For an average worker, replacement rates declined significantly between 1975 and 1990, albeit from a very high level. In return, the maximum benefit duration had become almost unlimited.

10.3 UNEMPLOYMENT POLICY BETWEEN THE EARLY 1990s AND 2010

The speed of reforms accelerated in the 1990s. Several major labour market policy changes were implemented between 1993 and 2005, and subsequently almost annually. In order to put these in context, this section contrasts main regulations as they applied in 1990 with those in 2010 (see Table 10.1).Except for financing and administration (see below), some of the main characteristics remained either unchanged, or they had little impact on social rights because of the context of low unemployment. However, labour market conditions became much less benign after 2008, and far-reaching reforms were implemented in recent years (2010 in particular), which might put the inclusiveness and generosity of Danish unemployment protection, as well as the so-called 'flexicurity' model, into serious doubt.

10.3.1 Unemployment insurance and activation: main parameters and trajectories

Unlike in Sweden (see Chapter 11 in this volume), Danish unemployment insurance has remained highly inclusive and uniform in terms of contributions and entitlements. No variation was introduced according to contributory records, no reduction in benefits according to duration of unemployment, and no adjustment

---

[3] See Hansen (2002: 36); for the long-term decline in compensation rates, see also Korpi (2002), Korpi and Palme (2003), Green-Pedersen (2002: 70–4), and calculations by the Ministry of Employment (Beskæftigelsesministeriet, 2009).

Table 10.1. Major regulations in unemployment insurance, 1990 and 2010

	1990	2010
UI model	Ghent model (voluntary, state subsidized)	Ghent model
Eligibility for UB	Membership: 1 year Employment condition: 26 weeks of full-time work within last 3 years	Membership: 1 year Employment condition: 52 weeks of full-time work (1924 hours) within last 3 years[a]
Availability	To start in an appropriate job within two weeks Active job search (in principle)	1. To start a job immediately 2. Active job search (to be documented) and: • CV (updated on internet) • confirm availability weekly (internet) • respond to any contact from employer 3. Agreed plan for job search within one month (type of job, region, etc.). This may include up to 4 hours of commuting time, occasionally more. 4. Participation in any meeting required by Job Centre, UI Fund, or other actor. 5. Availability reconsidered every third month. 6. Not resigned from a job twice within 12 months without acceptable reason. 7. Sanctions: If considered unavailable, 300 hours of ordinary employment within 10 weeks required to requalify.
Activation measures	None (but acceptance of job offer to requalify after 2.5 years)	Activation measures can include guidance, education, practice, or subsidized work. In principle duty to short-term activation any time. Right and duty to activation after 9 months according to job plan elaborated and signed by the Job Centre. For claimants under 30: right and duty to activation after 13 weeks. For those over 60 after 26 weeks. Claimants under 25 typically required to take transfer to vocational education if they do not have one (transfer to ordinary students' benefits after six months). Others under 25 (with completed a vocational education) have right and duty to six months of activation. Unemployed between 25 and 30 have a right and duty to six months of continuous activation.
Benefit duration	2.5 years. Requalification twice via job offer (6–9 month). Thus, up to 9 years maximum duration.	2 years within a 3-year reference period.
Requalification	After 26 weeks of ordinary (unsubsidized) work.	After 52 weeks of ordinary full-time work (1924 hours) within three years (from 2012).
Waiting days	None	None

Benefit levels	90% up to a ceiling; approaching flat rate for the majority	90% up to ceiling (195,528 DKK in 2010 = €26,250). De facto flat rate for nearly everybody.
Gross compensation[b]	Male skilled worker: 61% Female unskilled worker: 77%	Male skilled worker: 59% Female unskilled worker: 73%
Contributions	Combined for UI insurance and early retirement Tax deductible up to 56%	Separate contributions (since 1998). Tax deductible up to 33% (2009 tax reform: 25% by 2019).

[a]Membership of unemployment insurance fund is required while qualifying for the employment condition. For part-time insured, the requirement is 1258 hours of employment.

[b]http://www.ft.dk/dokumenter/tingdok.aspx?/samling/20091/almdel/amu/spm/6/svar/659171/753391/index.htm

Source: Goul Andersen (2002a); Arbejdsmarkedsstyrelsen. In particular, http://www.ams.dk/Regler-og-satser.aspx, and http://www.ams.dk/Regler-og-satser/Satser.aspx; Ministry of Employment. In particular, http://www.bm.dk/Love%20og%20Regler/Gaeldende%20love%20og%20regler.asp; Homepages of several unemployment insurance funds (for an overview, see http://www.ak-samvirke.dk/default.aspx?func=article.view&menuAction=selectClose&menuID=1717&id=1740); https://www.borger.dk/Emner/arbejde-dagpenge-orlov/Sider/default.aspx

of contributions to unemployment.[4] However, over time, unemployment benefits developed into a de facto flat-rate transfer. Even though the formal replacement rate remained 90 per cent nearly, all claimants receive the maximum due to a rather low ceiling.[5]

Membership in UI funds declined from 79 per cent in 1994 to 74 per cent in 2008 (Due et al., 2010: 17, 177–8), but there are no indications that this was caused by tighter regulations, for example, in the employment condition (see Table 10.1). More likely this is due to a decreasing unemployment risk, as well as to substantially higher levels of net (after tax) contributions.

Since the 1993 reform, participation in activation programmes no longer counts for requalifying. In addition, having been unchanged for many years, the requalification requirement will be raised to fifty-two weeks from 2012 onwards, making unemployment insurance slightly less inclusive. Maximum benefit duration was reduced from seven to four years between 1993 and 1998. As this happened in a context of economic prosperity, the impact was negligible. However, in 2010 the duration was suddenly halved to two years. This had little immediate impact as long-term unemployment had almost been eliminated by 2009 (see Statistical Annex, Table A.6). In a context of prolonged economic crisis, however, effects could be quite different.

[4] In 2010, contributions were usually 400–500 DKK per month (€55–60), consisting of a fixed contribution to the state (301 DKK), a fixed pension contribution (5 DKK), and the remainder a contribution to administration. Even though there is some competition, variations in fund contributions are small.

[5] In 2010, maximum UB was 195,520 DKK annually (€26,300) and applied to all unemployed with prior earnings of above 236,000 DKK (€31,700). This wage level is equivalent of 60 per cent of average earnings for full-time employed, or 68 per cent of average earnings for manual workers (based on 2009 gross wages – including labour market pension contributions – for Danish Employers' Asociation. See DA, 2010). Benefits and wages are subject to rather high income taxes since social contributions or payroll taxes are almost non-existing. See also Clasen et al. (2001), Hansen (2002), and calculations by the Ministry of Employment (2009) for the Danish parliament.

Otherwise, most significant changes over the past two decades include stricter conditionality in terms of availability requirements and activation. In 1990, being registered as unemployed and not refusing appropriate jobs was sufficient to satisfy job seeking criteria. By 2010, requirements had been specified and tightened (see Table 10.1 for details). Unlike in Sweden, the unemployment insurance fund is involved in the administration as it has to consider the job availability of claimants once every three months.

As tougher requirements or shorter duration constitute retrenchment, we find a positive association between prosperity and retrenchment in the Danish case. However, a shortage of labour power at all skill levels helps to explain why the government was keen to push people into employment – and why this was accepted.

As mentioned, labour market policies have been associated with what later became known as the Danish 'flexicurity' model, portrayed as institutional complementarity between flexible employment protection legislation, generous social protection, and activation to bring people back to work (Bredgaard et al., 2008; Madsen, 2008, 2010). However, reforms in 2010 (see below) might seriously undermine this equilibrium. Generosity should be seen as a combination of benefit levels, eligibility, and benefit duration. Danish eligibility rules are by no means lenient, and the replacement rate of unemployment benefits has not been particularly generous since the mid-1980s (for an average worker, the gross replacement is close to 50 per cent).[6] The maximum benefit duration was affected by a radical shortening in 2010 which was the first reform in decades with the potential of excluding a substantial number of people from unemployment insurance and transferring them to social assistance.[7]

Also the 'activation' dimension has been changed, albeit in a more gradual fashion. From Danish experience, three ideal types of activation might be distinguished: activation as social security, as improvement of human resources, and as a disciplinary device (Goul Andersen, 2010; Larsen, 2009). Between 1990 and 2010, Danish activation policy developed from (largely) the first type to a mix between the second and the third type. Activation of long-term unemployed was initially introduced as a job offer programme in 1979, aimed at facilitating requalification for UI and thus preventing a transfer to social assistance (Kvist et al., 2008). To a lesser extent, it served requalification goals.

After some experiments with active schemes in the 1980s, a comprehensive programme was introduced for long-term unemployed in 1993–4, and Denmark competed with Sweden about being the country spending the highest proportion of GDP on active labour market policy (ALMP) (OECD, 1998, 2008). To address the problem of structural unemployment, activation schemes were aimed at developing human resources (Bredgaard and Larsen, 2006; Larsen, 2009). Unemployed persons and their caseworker were supposed to jointly decide, based on the

---

[6] See also footnote 5. For an average full-time worker in the private sector the gross figure was DKK 395,000 in 2009, including contributions to pension savings. Of course, for the lowest paid workers, Danish benefits remain comparatively generous.

[7] It was also agreed to change the reference period for benefit calculation from three to twelve months, but as this recycled idea from the 1980s had lost most of its practical importance (Regeringen, 2010: 7), it was given up in the autumn.

job preferences of the unemployed, on an 'individual plan of action' with specification of the appropriate means, including the possibility of educational leave.

During the 1990s, activation became gradually to emphasize both rights and obligations, and educational leave was terminated as an option. In 2002, 'individual plans of action' were renamed 'job plans', and increasingly a 'work first' strategy was adopted. This included application of activation programmes as a disciplinary device aimed at stimulating job search, without abandoning the human resource approach completely, however. By 2010, activation had become a duty throughout the unemployment period, and a 'right and duty' after nine months of unemployment, with special rules for people of different ages (see Table 10.1).

In the broader sense (as specified in Chapter 1 of this volume), activation policies[8] shifted from long-term to short-term measures, from education to 'work first', and from a lenient approach to tighter conditionality. This development should be put in the context of a change from mass unemployment to a shortage of labour. While not deteriorating social rights, economically at least, the impact is likely be quite different under conditions of full employment than in a context of economic and labour market crisis. This applies to persons in receipt of unemployment insurance, and even more for the rules for social assistance recipients.

10.3.2 Social assistance, benefits for other working-age persons, and administrative reform

Between 1990 and 2010 the total number of social assistance recipients (employable and others) did not decline as fast as unemployment (Appendix 10.A). Apart from claimants aged under 20, social assistance recipients were not a target group for activation until 1990. This changed more radically in 1997, as symbolized by the name of the new 'Law of active social policy' which replaced the law on social assistance from 1976. By 2010, social assistance claimants are requested to participate in activation measures, and have a 'right and duty to activation' after twelve months, and after thirteen weeks for claimants under 30.

Within social assistance, retrenchment took place after 2001, but was explicitly targeted at immigrants or at groups in which immigrants constituted a majority.[9] The *2002 Law on immigration* introduced a new social assistance scheme (start assistance/introductory allowance)[10] with lower rates for newly arrived immigrants (this could include returning Danish citizens) from non-EU countries[11] who had not stayed legally in the country for seven out of the last eight years. Typically, the 'start assistance' is more than 30 per cent below ordinary social assistance rates (largest

---

[8] In a Danish policy context, 'activation' refers to the measures of guidance, education/courses, job training, etc. The term equivalent to 'activation policy' in Chapter 1 would be 'the active line'.

[9] Proportions were explicitly calculated in the documents. Immigrants constituted three-quarters of families where both spouses received social assistance (Regeringen, 2005).

[10] This is the same scheme, but the 'introductory allowance' refers to participation in a mandatory introduction programme.

[11] EU regulation makes these rules inapplicable to people arriving from EU countries, and there are similar exceptions to Nordic citizens.

discrepancy for families with children). It is officially aimed to improve work incentives, and a small employment effect has actually been identified (Huynh et al., 2007), but is negligible considering its social consequences.

Other cuts in social assistance have been introduced in order to make sure that people would always have an incentive to take a low-wage job. Families where both spouses receive social assistance face benefit cuts of about €135 per month after six months, and a ceiling was imposed for families with extraordinary expenses (reduction of up to €350 per month for some families). In 2005 the most far-reaching reform required claimants in households where both spouses receive social assistance to engage in ordinary (unsubsidized) employment for at least 300 hours during a two-year period, including claimants with low employability due to health problems, etc.[12] By 2008, as a political compensation to the Danish People's Party for the so-called Metock verdict of the European Court of Justice (Regeringen, 2008), this was extended to all married social assistance recipients, and the work requirement was raised to 450 hours.

Other efforts to increase employment were targeted at early retirement, disability, and sickness benefits. In 1990, people who were insured against unemployment were normally also entitled to the voluntary early retirement allowance ('efterløn') from the age of 60, receiving an allowance equivalent to unemployment benefits. By 2010 the contribution condition had been raised to thirty years, and contribution rates were slightly increased. In addition, persons who retire before the age of 62 receive only 91 per cent of unemployment benefits and have deductions (by 50–55 per cent) for pensions – not only for occupational pensions (this applies irrespective of age) but also for personal pensions.

Similar to other countries, Denmark experienced increasing number of people leaving the labour market based on receipt of a disability pension until the mid-1990, often without any attempts of rehabilitation (Clement, 2000; see also Appendix 10.A). Sometimes such benefits were granted to relatively young people on the basis of 'social criteria'. This problem was acted upon by changing municipal co-financing of disability pension in order to remove incentives to transfer long-term social assistance recipients to disability pension.

From 1998 onwards, comprehensive changes in rules and procedures were introduced, guided by ideas of the 'inclusive labour market' (Bengtsson, 2009; Bredgaard, 2004; OECD, 2003a: 129) and concomitant with the growth of 'corporate social responsibility'. The so-called 'flexible jobs' were propagated as an alternative to drawing disability pension for people with reduced work capacity (see Appendix 10.A).[13] Typically, this implies employers receiving a subsidy in return for hiring and paying normal wages to employees with reduced working hours and/or less demanding work. Since 1998, any application for disability

---

[12] Social assistance recipients were divided into five 'matching groups' according to employability (based on qualifications, language skills, health problems, psychiatric problems, drugs, or alcohol abuse). The least employable group (about one-fifth) was exempted, whereas the other groups were all subject to this requirement. This includes matching group 3–4 with very low employability, comprising more than one-half.

[13] Flexible jobs typically allow people to work shorter hours and/or with less demanding tasks while still maintaining an ordinary wage and in principle maintaining the same rights as ordinary employees. The subsidy is normally 50–66 per cent.

pension should only be processed as the last resort, after all possibilities of treatment, activation, and rehabilitation have been considered. As a consequence the number of people working in permanently subsidized 'flexible jobs' has grown significantly. It is debatable to what extent this reflects deadweight losses and moral hazard. The number of claimants of disability pensions did not decline as expected, but growth was at least halted in spite of a considerable growth in the size of the most vulnerable age groups (45–64 years old) and slightly improved benefits for disability pensioners.

Manipulating reimbursement for municipalities in order to stimulate the use of active measures has been systematized since 2001, with rules having become equivalent if not identical for different groups of the non-employed. This applies to people in receipt of sickness benefit, too. In 1997, municipalities became obliged to elaborate action plans for sickness benefits claimants after eight weeks of sickness. Later, this was followed by an explicit conversion to a 'work first' approach, which includes requiring claimants to participate in work-focused interviews about job opportunities. In short, similar to developments in other European countries covered in this book, a growing work-focused orientation can be identified for all working-age groups in receipt of public transfers.

Finally, there has also been an administrative integration of non-employed benefit claimants in Denmark. The idea of a 'one string' system for persons receiving unemployment benefits and social assistance, respectively, is not new (e.g. Socialkommissionen, 1993) but never advanced onto the legislative agenda. From 2001 the Liberal–Conservative government steered towards a unitary administrative structure, but was reluctant to take the first step. A window of opportunity emerged in 2005, however, in the wake of a large municipal reform which replaced fourteen counties with five regions and reduced the number of municipalities correspondingly.

Traditionally, municipalities were responsible for social assistance and the state for claimants of unemployment insurance (from 1993, organized as a regionalized state administration supervised by corporatist labour market boards). Inspired by job centre reforms in the Netherlands and the United Kingdom (Carstensen and Pedersen, 2008), the municipal reform was a chance to create a unitary type of administration for all categories of non-employed. In 2005 it was decided to bring the two lines of administration under a single roof within ninety-one municipal job centres. Except for fourteen municipalities with a completely unitary administration, better cooperation was formally aimed at in the administration of the two claimant groups which remained divided. However, case studies indicate that the level of actual cooperation remained fairly limited, while job centres became more centralized (Breidahl and Seemann, 2009).

In the negotiations over the 2009 state budget between the government, the Danish People's Party, and a tiny neo-liberal splinter party (Liberal Alliance), it was unexpectedly decided to transform the job centres to a unitary organization. This also included a radical change of the funding of unemployment benefits.[14]

---

[14] Ironically, the far-reaching reform was not even discussed in the closed negotiations between the parties (Breidahl and Seemann, 2009), and initially, it also went unnoticed in the press (Christiansen and Klitgaard, 2009).

According to this reform, in force from 2010, municipalities have become economically responsible for paying out unemployment benefits, but are reimbursed by the state in accordance with performance indicators (thus creating a structure which is similar to social assistance claimants; see above). The unemployment rate is one performance indicator, but as this is largely beyond the control of the municipality, activation is a more relevant incentive for municipalities acting rationally (Nørgaard, 2009). For insured unemployed, municipalities receive 75 per cent reimbursement of the costs for claimants who participate in an activation programme, 50 per cent for claimants who are 'passive', and no subsidy if unemployed are not in activation at a time when they are supposed to, according to the law. Municipalities have thus a strong incentive to activate people as much as possible, provided they can find cheap solutions, preferably via private providers. In response to concerns over municipalities seeking useless activation measures which (as expected) were raised almost immediately in the media, the minister of employment announced in the autumn 2010 that the new incentive structure would be reconsidered in due course.

10.4 MAKING SENSE OF TWENTY YEARS OF LABOUR MARKET REFORM

As discussed in the previous section, there have been significant changes in all three dimensions of 'integration' outlined in the introductory chapters of this book. Similar to Belgium, Danish unemployment insurance had already been 'homogenized' in the 1980s, and became even more so due to a diminishing 'earnings relatedness' of the system with benefits becoming flat rate for most employees due to a decline in the ceiling relative to wages. Until 2010, the unemployment insurance system remained highly inclusive, but under less benign employment conditions the shortening of entitlement to unemployment insurance might lead to claimants transferring to social assistance and potentially creating more of a two-tier structure. There has been a dramatic change towards very tightly defined conditions of benefit eligibility and the adoption of a 'work first' approach for people receiving unemployment benefits. Activation has been applied deliberately as a work test, and the opportunities for education have been markedly reduced. However, perhaps an even more remarkable trend is the introduction of activation for unemployed social assistance claimants, as well as for other groups of non-employed. In this respect, one can speak of integration across different categories which have remained separate, while labour market exit routes have been made less attractive or abolished for some groups. In turn, this ties in with administrative integration which in Denmark refers to a process of an increasingly widening responsibility placed upon municipalities, embodied by a philosophy of steering municipalities via economic incentives for transferring claimants from benefit receipt to activation programmes. In this final section, some of the main factors will be discussed which have contributed to these developments.

Putting reform initiatives into context, economically three stages need to be distinguished. The long recessions from 1986 to 1993 raised unemployment to unprecedented levels since World War II, followed by fifteen years of economic and labour market recovery. However, the final years of this period were characterized by extraordinarily high levels of revenue (from oil and taxation of pension returns), a housing bubble, excessive borrowing, and (counterproductive) expansionary fiscal and monetary policies. Even before the financial crisis of 2008, Denmark had one of the lowest economic growth rates in the OECD (see Statistical Annex, Table A.3) and the subsequent recession, including the growth of unemployment, was deeper than in neighbouring countries. Even though state deficits and unemployment remained below EU average, the recession in 2007–9 thus represents a dramatic break.

Also politically, three stages can be identified: Conservative–Liberal minority governments (1982–93), Social Democratic centre-left coalitions (1993–2001), and a Liberal–Conservative government (supported by the anti-immigration Danish People's Party) since 2001. Because of extraordinarily high unemployment, the Social Democratic coalition initially introduced a policy mix of activation and tighter conditionality on the one hand, and instruments which continued with the existing emphasis on social protection and reducing labour supply on the other, supporting older unemployed people, early retirees, and persons interested in taking parental, educational, and sabbatical leave. Sabbatical leave was short-lived, however, and parental leave was reduced and later replaced by prolonged maternity leave.

Educational leave was finally abolished in 2000, marking the termination of the social protection path and a policy of de facto or de jure narrowing the administrative category of unemployment (see Appendix 10.B). At the same time what in this book is labelled activation (tighter conditionality; stronger incentives to enter work) gathered strength after it had started in 1993. This was influenced by paradigmatic shift towards regarding unemployment as basically structural in nature, nourished by neoclassical economic thinking resembling those presented by the OECD (1994). However, the Danish solution to the problem of unemployment was guided by a human resources approach. Discrepancies between minimum wages and productivity were responded to by enhancing employability, skills, and qualifications. Matching problems caused by regional disparities were prevented by transferring decision-making in ALMPs to the county level, based on cooperation with the social partners in regional labour market boards.

Since unemployment declined faster than expected, the new labour market policy approach appeared to be highly successful even though it was later revealed that activation measures (mainly education), according to micro-level studies, seemed to have few if any short-term effects on the individual's transition to employment.

10.4.1 Entitlements and generosity

At any rate, cross-party agreement was possible as Social Democrats were willing to tighten up on conditionality as long as this did not exclude substantial numbers from unemployment benefits. For example, the gradual reduction in the maximum entitlement to unemployment benefit (to four years) was based on broad compromises between the Social Democratic coalition government and the Conservatives (1995) or nearly all bourgeois parties (1998). In terms of social rights, the impact was negligible partly because of the economic upturn, and partly because potentially vulnerable groups of elderly workers were protected against losing their unemployment benefits.

It might seem remarkable that the Liberal–Conservative government after 2001 did not seek to reduce benefit generosity. This can partly be explained by the Liberal Party's strategy to attract support from the working-class and lower-middle-class voters who would normally support the Social Democrats. Their 'winning formula' was to combine strict immigration policies with centrist welfare policies. The Danish People's Party developed this into outright welfare chauvinism and became the party with the largest proportion of manual workers among its voters. In the elections during 2001–7, the Liberals, Conservatives, and the anti-immigration Danish People's Party obtained more than 50 per cent of the votes among blue-collar workers (Andersen and Goul Andersen, 2003; Goul Andersen, 2006, 2008). To prevent the Social Democrats from pulling these voters back, the government was aware that it needed to avoid conflicts on welfare.

In the autumn of 2008, however, the government needed to change the political agenda and overcoming an underlying structural imbalance in the state budget caused by tax relief measures in 2007. A newly appointed Labour Market Commission was asked to come up with preliminary proposals almost before it got started. At that time, the Social Democrats might have accepted shorter benefit duration in return for raising the benefit ceiling which was regarded by some trade union leaders as a cause of declining membership in unemployment insurance funds.

When the fundamental economic climate change became obvious in the wake of the turmoil in world financial markets, the Social Democrats became less willing to compromise, and in 2009 the government itself rejected the final proposals from its Labour Market Commission even before they were published. However, things changed suddenly in May 2010 when the government negotiated with the Danish People's Party over a 'reconstruction plan' aimed at reducing the state deficit. After a few days the Danish People's Party presented an almost entirely different plan which unexpectedly included a reduction of benefit duration to two years. The government immediately consented. It would be an exaggeration to describe the reform as accidental. But the timing was surprising, and it broke with the 'winning formula' of the government. At any rate, it was the first severe cut in benefit generosity that had not been carefully targeted at immigrants.

One other important factor in the political process which emerged already at the time when the Social Democrats were in office is the absence of the trade unions or social partners in the preparation of legislation. The social partners had participated in the consensus building around ALMP in the early 1990s. But with one minor exception, they were not involved in the preparation of the frequent reforms from 1993 onwards. This de-corporatization has been typical of Danish politics in the last two decades (Christiansen and Nørgaard, 2003). Important reforms are often adopted in budget negotiations without much preparation (Loftager, 2004). Occasionally fast-working expert commissions are appointed, for instance with the purpose of softening resistance. It apparently makes decision-making more smooth when it is undisturbed by too many actors, too much information, too much media attention – and too much time.

Until 2005, reforms affecting ordinary unemployed receiving unemployment benefits were normally decided in broad political compromises. The job centre reforms, the reduction in duration of benefits to two years, and the reforms for social assistance recipients constitute an exception.

10.4.2 Extending the target of employment efforts and mainstreaming education

Very much in accordance with the notion of risk re-categorization in terms of widening the administrative category of unemployment which has been observed in countries such as the United Kingdom, Germany, or France (see Chapters 2, 3, and 4 in this volume), in Denmark also the separation between various groups of non-employed became less distinct in terms of benefit eligibility. Until 1993, it was informally accepted that full employment would no longer be achievable, but it would at least be possible to avoid social marginalization due to insufficient economic resources, and Denmark was indeed very successful in this respect. During the subsequent two decades, these assumptions were reversed. Full employment had become the norm, and non-employment was both a social and economic problem.

Inspired by communitarian ideas, policies introduced by New Labour in the United Kingdom, and a long period of prosperity, the dominant political discourse had changed and was institutionalized in a language of 'active' and 'passive'. In this context, employment efforts (and requirements; see below) were extended to groups beyond the core of unemployment benefit claimants.

The changes in policies directed at older benefit claimants are illustrative. The 1993 labour market reform was accompanied by the introduction of the 'transitional allowance' (see Appendix 10.B). When this was abolished in 1994, unemployment benefit claimants aged between 50 and 59 were omitted from the restriction of the duration. The 1998 reform abolished the right to unlimited duration of benefits for the 50- to 54-year-olds, and the 2006 welfare reform for the 55- to 59-year-olds. At the same time, those aged 58 and 59 became subject to ordinary activation requirements. In short, there has been a complete mainstreaming for workers above 50 who were previously considered less employable. At the other end of the age spectrum, there has also been a gradual mainstreaming, albeit in the sense of transferring unemployed younger persons towards ordinary education. This also reflects life course change. Most people receive an education, and young people in Denmark have been particularly late starters, completing their education at a relatively high age. There have never really been any strong conflicts about this 'double mainstreaming'. Young unemployed persons are expected to have an ordinary education if at all possible, while older workers are now assumed to work just like everybody else.

Mainstreaming of work/education requirements also extended to other categories of non-employed. Young claimants of social assistance have been pushed towards education, and social assistance recipients with 'other problems than unemployment' have been included in activation programmes. Moreover, married recipients of social assistance lose entitlement to social assistance unless they manage to obtain 450 hours of ordinary employment (in a two-year period). This was opposed by the Social Democrats, even in the softer version from 2005, but mainly because it was extended to matching group 4 (with 'strongly reduced employment possibilities'). Otherwise, we find a rather surprising degree of cross-party consensus even here. Parallel developments as regards people with long-term sickness absence or on their way towards claiming a disability pension were also commenced when the Social Democrats were in office. Still, there was more emphasis on the social welfare gains, and the Social Democrats have typically objected when those involved could run the risk of losing benefits.

10.4.3 Conditionality and administrative integration

The discussion so far might give the impression that the Liberal–Conservative government merely extended Social Democratic activation policies. This would be an exaggeration, but in 2002 and 2006 the Social Democrats supported that conditionality for unemployed was taken one step further in the context of ever more benign employment conditions. The Social Democrats have a strong preference for maintaining an inclusionary unemployment benefit system, but increasing employment rates is a joint preference for all parties; and in the context of prosperity, the Social Democrats could go quite far as regards conditionality. Changes that involved cuts in benefits, on the other hand, were typically opposed, and the Social Democrats also opposed change in the administrative structure.

Still, a distinction should be made between formal rules and actual implementation. Even though the Social Democrats have supported most of the rules, they are not necessarily in favour of their implementation. There may still be too little evidence to arrive at a firm conclusion, but it is indicated that there has been quite a bit of a 'conversion' (Streeck and Thelen, 2005a) in Danish unemployment protection policy since 2001. Institutions appear stable but nonetheless seem to have been transformed since rules are more strictly followed than before, due to closer supervision, more sanctions, and the enhancement by economic incentives. The administrative apparatus has silently been redirected towards a tight 'work first' orientation.

This also helps to explain the Social Democrats' resistance against the job centre reforms. With these reforms, the social partners were even deprived of their formal position in the implementation of ALMP. This is in accordance with the government's long-standing preferences for reducing the influence of the social partners, as well as diminishing the impact of professionals (social workers; job officers). Reforming administrative structures is a classical means to obtain more central control over policy implementation and this helps to explain the government's preference for integrated job centres or 'one-stop shops'. The main instruments to strengthen state control have been stricter with more detailed guidance, coupled with steering via incentives.

Whereas interpreting these government preferences seems straightforward, it is more intriguing to explain why the Social Democrats were willing to go as far as they did, and as regards job centres, to explain how and why the bourgeois parties developed this instrument. In both instances ideational explanations to supplement traditional explanations in terms of class interests are necessary. The Social Democrats had learned from the 1970s that an image of being 'economically responsible' was indispensable, but the party was also influenced by New Labour and by the dissemination of communitarian ideas in the 1990s. For the bourgeois government, 'one-shop' reforms in the United Kingdom and the Netherlands was a much welcomed inspiration to realize its political goals of limiting the influence of both the social partners and professional social workers. But the 'idea' of job centres had to be translated to the language of 'individual treatment' which had become part of the common national discourse in the field (Carstensen, 2010). In principle, the administrative integration, both in the sense of job centres and the new cross-cutting matching groups, could be a stepping stone towards the introduction of a single benefit for working-age people. However, at the time of writing there are no indications of this. The government does not seem to harbour any preferences for such a move and would lack the political power to move in this direction.

The change in economic context also needs to taken into account here. Tightening availability requirements was politically feasible and made economic sense when there was shortage of labour power. By 2010 this was no longer the case, and in summer and autumn of that year there was massive media criticism of what was seen as 'meaningless activation'. Thus, adapting rules in line with the business cycle would seem more logical and this has, implicitly at least, occurred until 2005 as nearly all changes introduced up to then could be seen as alignments with changing economic surroundings and benign employment opportunities which prevented any discernible negative impact on social citizenship. In fact, if anything, unemployment insurance became even more inclusive in terms of coverage. However, even in case of a change in government it does not seem very likely that the reforms adopted since 2005 could be reversed or be adjusted very much to the changing context which has become much less benign. This leaves Danish labour market policy in a rather ambiguous state.

10.5 CONCLUSIONS

In the light of the three dimensions of integration discussed in the introductory chapter of this book, this chapter reviewed changes in Danish labour market policy between 1990 and 2010. As shown, benefit generosity remained largely intact until 2010. Throughout the period there were no cuts in benefits, except for particular groups of social assistance claimants (de facto composed largely of immigrants). A decline in the benefit ceiling relative to wages has made the unemployment insurance system more homogeneous in terms of benefit rates. Almost everybody receives the maximum amount of unemployment benefit, which provides solid protection against poverty but represents a rather low replacement rate for people who had been on average or higher wages before becoming unemployed. Benefit coverage has remained high and thus prevented the emergence of a dual structure in a quantitatively significant sense. Duration of benefits was reduced from eight or nine years to four years in the 1990s, but the exclusion from unemployment remained rare in a context of economic prosperity. However, in 2010, the maximum benefit duration was reduced to two years, and requalification requirements became tighter. In the aftermath of the economic boom, this had no immediate impact, but conditions of the unemployed could deteriorate substantially under conditions of a prolonged recession.

In return for maintaining generous benefits, conditionality requirements have been tightened considerably. Until 2005, this happened largely in the context of political consensus. However, as in the instance of cuts for social assistance recipients in 2005 and after, and similar to the shortening of benefit duration in 2010, recently introduced job-seeking rules were carried through unilaterally by the government, with the support of the Danish People's Party. This seems to jeopardize the Danish 'flexicurity' model. Collective negotiations in 2010 which included a protection against dismissals, favourable for people with long tenure, pull in the same direction.

Moreover, conditionality and job-search efforts were gradually extended: from core groups to the more vulnerable 'ordinary' unemployed persons, to all groups of social assistance claimants, and increasingly to people receiving sickness benefits and those potentially transferring to disability pension receipt. Gradually the distinction between different groups of non-employed has been blurred as employment efforts and duties were extended to ever new segments of working-age benefit claimants. The administrative harmonization was strengthened by the formation of 'one-shop' job centres in 2007, and continued in 2010 with the (administrative) introduction of common matching groups across all categories of working-age benefit recipients.

To some extent, one could speak of continuity in policy, at least until 2005. This should be seen against a background of what could be called harmonious deindustrialization. Regional disparities remained of a minor nature, new jobs were created more rapidly than old jobs disappeared, and the qualification levels within the labour market improved very rapidly due to generational replacement. There has been no tendency towards relatively deteriorating employment conditions for unskilled workers, and there was no growth in precarious jobs. Like elsewhere, the Social Democratic government between 1993 and 2001 largely accepted the idea of unemployment having become structural, but this was tackled by improving qualifications and tightening conditionality rules rather than cutting benefit levels. The Liberal–Conservative government from 2001 to 2010 largely continued this strategy, but with much more emphasis on 'work first' and on tightening conditions.

Until the end of the period, policy changes can be regarded as having been largely adjustments to improving employment conditions. Besides, reforms appeared, in principle at least, reversible. By contrast, some of the most recent reforms appear irreversible while the economic crisis has deteriorated employment prospects. Besides, the qualification gain from generational replacement is coming to an end. This makes the prospects of full employment despite deindustrialization much less promising than previously. All of this leaves the future of the traditional inclusive and encompassing unemployment protection system rather open at this point in time.

(If not otherwise indicated, full-time equivalents per year.)

	Unemployed receiving UB[a]	Unemployed receiving SA[a]	Activation for UB recipients (est.)[b]	Activation for SA recipients (est.)[c]	SA recipients *not* seeking job and *no* employment efforts[d]	Rehabilitation total	Flexible jobs[e]	Early retirement + transitional allowance[f]	Disability pension	Sickness + maternity benefits[g]
1990	225	47	...	...	55	(35)	–	101	250	74
1991	249	47	...	...	76	(35)	–	104	254	69
1992	365	53	...	...	79	(35)	–	110	256	71
1993	294	55	...	...	87	(35)	–	116	266	72
1994	288	55	...	...	49	(35)	–	119	266	74
1995	245	43	...	...	48	(35)	–	138	273	79
1996	209	37	...	...	45	(35)	–	167	270	83
1997	187	33	...	...	48	(35)	–	171	274	86
1998	154	29	73	42	50	35	(6)	177	274	86
1999	131	27	67	45	49	39	(10)	181	270	86
2000	128	22	62	47	57	38	14	181	263	91
2001	124	21	64	48	61	36	19	179	260	96
2002	124	21	61	48	65	34	25	181	265	100
2003	147	24	37	47	62	32	30	186	265	120
2004	149	27	44	37	69	29	36	187	265	123
2005	132	25	40	35	66	26	42	166	253	128
2006	103	21	32	35	58	25	47	145	238	131
2007	75	19	33	33	53	17	49	140	234	141
2008	39	12	23	36	45	15	55	138	235	140
2009	81	16	33	45	56	14	56	131	237	132

[a] Changed definition from 2008 (see Statistiske Efterretninger. Arbejdsmarked, 2009: 2), reducing figures by some 15,000. Unemployed receiving social assistance include matching categories 1–3 (of 5) among social assistance recipients, plus social assistance recipients without matching but registered by the employment office as job-seeking.

[b] ALMP minus flexible jobs (subsidized employment for potential disability pensioners, introduced by 1998).

[c] *Source*: Statistiske Efterretninger. Sociale forhold, sundhed og retsvæsen, various iss.

[d] Social assistance less jobseekers, activated and rehabilitation. 1990–2006 based on statistics on income replacement (indkomsterstattende ydelser, Stat.10 year review), dominant support (dominerende ydelse). This statistic includes all recipients but not those activated. Figures 2007–10 based on statistics on 'Social assistance etc'. From these figures we have subtracted the number of persons on rehabilitation. 1990–7 we have *assumed* that the number of people on rehabilitation is 35,000. For 2007–9 we have more exact figures from the statistics on 'People without ordinary employment'. Our underestimation is 6,000, 12,000, and 8,000, respectively, for 2007–9.

[e] Flexible jobs are subsidized employment for potential disability pensioners, introduced by 1998. Figures include protected jobs ('skånejobs') which constitute 6,000–7,000 in the period 2000–9. Until 2006, figures are reported to be underestimated by about 1,000. (*Source*: 'Persons without ordinary employment'. Statistiske Efterretninger. Arbejdsmarked, various iss.)

[f] Voluntary early retirement from age of 60 till pension age (65 years), but 67 years until 2004, indicated as data break). 2002ff changed calculation increases the figure by about 2 per cent. (1990–4 from 'Indkomsterstattende ydelser' Stat.10 year review, 2000: 54). 1994–6 including 'transitional allowance' (pre-early retirement) for 50–59-year-olds long-term unemployed. This scheme peaked with 46,000 in 1996 when it was terminated for entry. It was phased out in 1996–2006.

[g] In 2002, parental leave (not included in this statistic) was replaced by prolonged maternity leave. From 2002, maternity leave counts some 60,000 full-time persons. Figures excluding maternity leave for 2007–9 was 83,000, 81,000, and 75,000, respectively.

Note: All figures only include working-age recipients (until 2004, working age was 18–66 years). Figures in parantheses are estimated.

Appendix 10.B Major reforms of Danish labour market policy, 1990–2010

Year	Reform (occasion)	Risk re-categorization (reducing/expanding labour supply)	Activation (and conditionality)
1993	Labour market reform I	• Educational, parental, sabbatical leave[a] • Transitional allowance (pre-early retirement for 50–59 years old)[b]	• Duration UB 7 years. No requalification through activation • Individual action plans • Right to activation after 4 years • Regionalized ALMP
1994	Check-up (1995 budget compromise)	• Sabbatical leave phased out • Parental and sabbatical leave compensation reduced • Unlimited right to UB for 50–59 years old	• Right and duty to activation after 4 years • Stricter availability requirements and sanctions
1995	Labour market reform II (1996 budget compromise)	• Transitional allowance closed for entrance by 31 January 1996	• Duration UB 5 years • Right and duty to activation after two years • Employment requirement raised to 52 weeks • Accept 'appropriate job' after 6 months • Accept 4 hours daily commuting time • Duty to education for unemployed under 25 after 6 months
1998	Labour market reform III (1999 budget compromise)	• Unlimited UB abolished for 50–54 years olds • Educational leave only 9 weeks (for unempl.) • Reform voluntary early retirement	• Duration UB 4 years • Right and duty to activation after one year. • Accept 'appropriate job' after 3 months
2000		Educational leave terminated	
2002	Integration package		• Start assistance for immigrants
2002	Labour market reform IV (more people in work)		• Flexible activation, more contact • Savings on activation reserved for tax credit • Tighter control with availability • Duty to accept job immediately • Harmonization of rules for UB and SA recipients (accept job immediately; job search during activation; 'intensive contact'; harmonization of sanctions; stronger control) • Cuts in SA for particular groups to ensure work incentives
2005	Integration package (a new chance for all) – for all SA recipients		• Repeated activation for (nearly) all SA recipients • More duty to education • Five matching groups

			• Employment requirement (300 hours for married partners); SA recipients in matching group 1–4
2006	Welfare reform agreement	• Prolonged benefits for 55–59-year-olds abolished • Activation for 58–59-year-olds • Higher age brackets for early retirement and pension (from 2019)	• Right and duty to activation after 9 months • Job interview and job plan after 4 weeks • Control availability every 3 months • Update CV and check weekly
2005/7	Job centre reform I (municipal reform; impl. 2007)		• Municipal administration for UB + SA, but separate administration with cooperation
2008	Job centre reform II (2009 budget compromise)		• Unitary administration for UB + SA • Municipal financing of UB with reimbursement dep. on performance (activation and employment)
2010	Common matching categories for non-employed		Three groups: (*a*) ready for employment; (*b*) ready for employment efforts; (*c*) temporarily passive

[a] Parental and educational leave were already introduced in 1992, but with unfavourable conditions and low take up.
[b] Introduced for 55–59-year-olds in 1992, but take up was very low.
Notes: Grey cells indicate broad coalitions between the Social Democrats and Conservatives and/or Liberals.
Source: Goul Andersen and Pedersen (2007), and reform agreement texts available from www.fm.dk (Ministry of Finance).

11

Sweden: ambivalent adjustment

Ola Sjöberg

11.1 INTRODUCTION

Among the various institutional forms of unemployment protection, the kind found in Sweden – voluntary state-subsidized insurance, or the 'Ghent system' – is rare in a comparative perspective. Its basic institutional characteristics are that membership of an unemployment insurance fund is voluntary, but that benefits are heavily tax subsidized. Historically, this system was based on solidarity among employees in professionally circumscribed areas, and a close link existed between the trade union and the unemployment fund that assisted workers in case of unemployment. Though trade unions are interest organizations and the unemployment insurance funds are private organizations performing government authority tasks regulated by law, voluntary state-subsidized insurance has been an important support for the organizational strength of Swedish trade unions in the post-war period (Rothstein, 1992; Visser, 2006), as well as for a central trait of the 'Swedish model', namely the regulation of labour markets through collective agreements. But it is a system of unemployment protection that has been under continuous attack. Its introduction in Sweden in 1935 was not uncontested, and proposals to introduce universal and compulsory unemployment insurance have been recurrent ever since. During the last two decades cuts in unemployment benefits have also been seen by all governments as a way of reducing state expenditures and strengthening the economic incentives to work.

This chapter describes and analyses the development of unemployment protection in Sweden, with a special emphasis upon developments since 1990. After an overview of important economic and policy developments in post-World War II Sweden, it describes changes in the unemployment benefit system and other benefits for individuals of working age between 1990 and 2010. With reference to the analytical framework of this volume, developments are discussed in relation to three fundamental characteristics of unemployment protection systems, namely the specification of unemployment protection as a social right, the boundaries of unemployment as a risk category, and the relationship between active and passive labour market policies.

With regard to each dimension, it will be argued that recent developments in Sweden have been particularly ambivalent. While there has indeed been a certain homogenization of benefit levels, mainly due to maximum benefits not keeping pace with wage increases, there has also been increased differentiation in the overall benefit package in case of unemployment, mainly as a consequence of unequal access to and generosity of collectively and privately negotiated unemployment benefits, which are of growing importance in Sweden. Though there has been an attempt since the early 1990s to revive the traditional work-line approach and greater emphasis on the role of unemployment benefit as a 'transition insurance', active labour market policies (ALMPs) are at the same time increasingly targeted on those whose right to unemployment insurance has expired, for whom they may serve as an extended form of income security. Regarding the boundaries of unemployment as a risk category, finally, there has actually been increased differentiation between a core of unemployed, consisting of those who had a stable attachment to the labour market before they became unemployed, and others, resulting in decreasing numbers of unemployed people being in receipt of formal unemployment benefits. The formal boundaries between different risk schemes for working-age people have also been reinforced. But in parallel there have also been moves to harmonize levels and principles of protection across different income protection schemes, regarding, for example, benefit levels. It is suggested that these trends might be understood in with reference to a tension between the general embrace of a new economic policy paradigm and continuing political and ideological differences in the realm of unemployment and labour market policy.

11.2 THE SWEDISH LABOUR MARKET MODEL THROUGH CRISIS AND RECOVERY

Current reforms and debates about economic and welfare policy in Sweden take place in an institutional landscape that in important respects was established over a half-century ago. Firstly, voluntary state-subsidized unemployment insurance was introduced in Sweden in 1935. Originally, members of an insurance fund could decide the amount of benefit they would like to have in case of unemployment, and pay fees accordingly. The state subsidy varied inversely with benefit levels, and as a consequence membership fees for those wanting a relatively high level were substantial. Because of this the establishment of new insurance funds was slow, and in 1940 only 20 per cent of the Swedish Trade Union Confederation (LO) members belonged to one (Edebalk, 2008). In 1941, a substantial improvement of the state subsidy, however, provided stronger incentives for the unions to set up new funds, and in 1945 the funds were also joined together in a common organization, the Swedish Federation of Unemployment Insurance Funds, improving their collective ability to influence the development of unemployment insurance policy.

Secondly, from the late 1950s to the early 1970s, the so-called Rehn–Meidner model was a lodestar for Swedish economic policy. An economic policy programme as well as a theory of wages, profits, inflation, and growth, it combined four objectives: full employment, price stability, economic growth, and equity (Erixon, 2008; Milner and Wadensjö, 2001). Its cornerstone was a solidaristic wage policy with equal pay for equal work irrespective of the profitability of companies, which together with a restrictive economic policy resulted in excess profits for the most profitable companies and closure of the most unprofitable ones. Through extensive ALMPs such as occupational training programmes and programmes to improve the matching on the labour market the benefits of structural change could be fully exploited while the costs of such changes were shifted from the workers involved to the society as a whole. Though unemployment benefits had to be low enough to induce workers to move to the expanding sectors of the economy (Agell, 1999; Rehn, 1985), mobility was primarily achieved by means of extensive ALMPs. Due to its effect on income-distribution, growth, and the position of organized labour, wage competition through reduction in unemployment benefits was not seen as a viable strategy (Erixon, 2000). If anything, well-developed income maintenance schemes were an important component of the Rehn–Meidner model, insuring workers against the risks associated with desired structural change.

By international standards, the Rehn–Meidner model worked well in combining strong growth with low unemployment and an egalitarian wage distribution. By the late 1960s, however, discontent was growing with both the drawbacks of structural change and the apparent persistence of inequalities (Junestav, 2007). A more difficult position for older workers on the labour market also brought the question of universal and compulsory unemployment insurance onto the political agenda. Although voluntary insurance had gradually expanded to cover a larger proportion of the workforce, in 1970 almost half of the workforce still had no protection in case of unemployment (SOU, 1971: 42). However, a government committee set up in 1966 (the so-called KSA committee) rejected any form of universal earnings-related system (SOU, 1971: 42), and opted instead for a solution where those not qualifying for regular unemployment benefits would be covered by a flat-rate scheme (KAS), with benefit duration considerably shorter than in the earnings-related system. This system, together with changes in earnings-related benefits such as longer duration of benefits and making benefits taxable and counted as pensionable income, was introduced in 1974, and persisted basically unchanged until the early 1990s.

In the early 1990s, Sweden was hit by the most severe economic recession since the 1930s. Between 1990 and 1993, employment declined by 13 per cent and unemployment rose from less than 2 to over 8 per cent (see Statistical Annex, Tables A.4 and A.5). As a paradigm shift in economic policy in the 1980s had seen an overarching role assigned to low inflation as opposed to full employment (Jonung, 1999), the budgetary strain caused by increasing unemployment and decreasing employment in the early 1990s was not met by economic stimulus. The 1991 election was won by a centre-right coalition emphasizing deregulation, privatization, and structural reform. However, with acute problems for the Swedish economy piling up, in 1992 the government began talks with the Social Democratic opposition to attempt to resolve the crisis, resulting in several austerity packages. Between 1993 and 1998, various crisis packages were launched, in which cuts in income maintenance programmes were a central ingredient.

Moreover, labour market policy in the 1990s came increasingly to be based on the hypothesis that a significant part of unemployment was structural and caused by inefficient labour markets. One important strategy of both the centre-right and the Social Democratic governments was thus to reduce reservation wages by reducing unemployment compensation generosity (for an account of these changes, see next section and Appendix 11.A). According to the centre-right-wing government that was in power from 1991 to 1994, 'unemployment insurance is an economic safety net of last resort and must give clear indications that the unemployed do not have a free choice between being unemployed and finding work' (Proposition, 1993/4: 209, my translation). The Social Democratic government that came into power in 1994 continued to emphasize the need to strengthen the economic incentives to participate in paid work by tightening qualification conditions and curbing benefit levels (e.g. Proposition, 1996/7: 107; SOU, 1996: 150). However, from 1994, tax increases supplemented expenditure cuts in order to get the budget in balance, which was achieved in 1998 after a period of very strict fiscal restraint. At the end of the 1990s and early 2000s, the Social Democratic government partly restored some of the benefits that had earlier been cut, made investments in the public sector (especially at the municipal level), and introduced measures to combat unemployment. Economic growth was now strong and employment increased during the first half of the 2000s, though unemployment was still higher in 2006 than it had been in 1990. A symbolic occurrence was that employment in the private service sector outgrew employment in manufacturing industries at the end of the 1990s (SOU, 2001: 79).

Following elections in 2006, a coalition of non-Socialist parties formed a majority government after twelve years of minority Social Democratic rule. To a greater extent than before, non-Socialist parties had presented themselves as a united alternative, the Alliance, with a common political programme during the election campaign. In a sense, the Alliance attacked the Social Democratic party from the left, arguing that the government had failed to create new jobs and maintain full employment. In their manifesto, they promised to revive the Swedish work approach. Their policy proposals prior to the election focused on three areas: making work pay (to be achieved through reductions in income tax and in unemployment insurance benefits); making it easier and less costly for employers to recruit staff (partly achieved through increased opportunities to offer temporary contracts); and making it more profitable to start and run especially small- and medium-sized companies.

11.3 CHANGES IN UNEMPLOYMENT AND OTHER BENEFITS FOR INDIVIDUALS OF WORKING AGE BETWEEN 1990 AND 2010

At first glance, the basic characteristics of the Swedish unemployment insurance were the same in 2010 as twenty years earlier.[1] At both points the system consisted of two non-means-tested tiers: a voluntary earnings-related benefit and a flat-rate basic allowance. To be eligible for earnings-related unemployment compensation an

---

[1] The review of changes in unemployment compensation schemes is primarily based on Olli Segendorf (2003) and Arbetslöshetskassornas samorganisation (2008, 2010).

unemployed person must fulfil three conditions: a *basic condition* that requires the unemployed to be able and willing to work, registered at the employment office and actively search for job; a *work condition* that stipulates the length and intensity of work before unemployment; and a *membership condition*, meaning that the unemployed has to be member of an unemployment insurance fund for a certain period to be eligible for benefit. The flat-rate benefit is available to unemployed who meet all except the membership conditions. Despite the apparent institutional stability, however, the two large waves of reforms to the unemployment protection system in Sweden since 1990s – in the aftermath of the recession of the early 1990s and when the centre-right government gained power after the election in 2006 – mean that the conditions facing an unemployed person in 2010 are rather different to those they would have faced twenty years earlier (Table 11.1).

Table 11.1. Main characteristics of unemployment compensation in 1990 and 2010

	1990	2010
Type	Voluntary state-subsidized	Voluntary state-subsidized
Waiting period	0	7 days
Qualifying conditions	*Membership condition*	*Membership condition*
	Member of an insurance fund for at least 12 months	Member of an insurance fund for at least 12 months
	Work condition	*Work condition*
	75 days (at least 3 hours) over a period of at least 4 months	80 hours/month for at least 6 months in the 12 months immediately preceding unemployment, alternatively 480 hours during six consecutive calendar months and at least 50 hours in every single one of those months
	Unemployed who only meet the work condition (i.e. not the membership condition) is entitled to basic allowance (KAS)	
		Unemployed who only meet the work condition (i.e. not the membership condition) is entitled to basic allowance
Financing	No relation between membership fees and unemployment. Average fee = € 4/month	Higher unemployment among members in insurance fund increases membership fee. Average fee = €32/month
Benefit levels	90% of gross wage (benefits taxable), up to a maximum of €46/day	Day 1–200, 80%; day 201–300, 70% of gross wage (benefits taxable), up to a maximum of €63/day
	Basic allowance: €16/day	Basic allowance: €30/day
Benefit duration	300 days (55 years or above: 450 days). In principle unlimited, since participation in active labour market policy measure qualifies for new period of benefit	300 days (450 days for unemployed with children under 18)
	Basic allowance: 150 days (55 years or above: 450 days)	Basic allowance: 300 days (450 days for unemployed with children under 18)
	Part-time unemployed: 150 days	Part-time unemployed: 75 days
Sanctions	25 days suspension for those who voluntary quit their employment	45 days suspension for those who voluntary quit their employment. Refusal to accept suitable job offer may lead to reduced benefits

Source: Olli Segendorf (2003) and Arbetslöshetskassornas samorganisation (2008, 2010).

Besides reductions in gross replacement rates from 90 per cent to 80 or 70 per cent, dependent on the duration of unemployment, two sets of reforms have had fundamental ramifications for the actual replacement levels individuals achieve if they become unemployed. Firstly, in 1993 the automatic adjustment of the benefit ceiling to changes in wage levels in manufacturing was removed. Since then, increases have been at the discretion of the government, and the ceiling has been increased only twice, in 1997 and 2002.[2] Secondly, the income before unemployment upon which benefit is calculated has also been changed. In 1990, benefits were based on average working time, and thus average income from work, during the last four months before unemployment. Moreover, average working time was based on the working time an individual was *supposed* to work according to his or her employment contract, not actual working time, meaning that absence from work that reduced income, such as sickness, did not affect benefit levels. In 2007, however, benefits became based on earnings during the twelve months preceding unemployment, even if the claimants had actually worked for less than twelve months.

In 1990, the maximum duration of unemployment benefits was 300 days (450 for unemployed older than 55), and the unemployed over 60 years of age whose earnings-related benefit period had expired were eligible for the flat-rate benefit. In practice, however, the duration of earnings-related benefits had since the late 1980s been unlimited because participation in active labour market measures qualified individuals for a new benefit period. In 2001, this possibility was removed, and in 2007 formal benefit duration was changed to 300 days for all claimants, except for those with children under the age of 18 years for whom duration was set to 450 days. For part-time unemployed, duration was reduced from 150 to 75 days in 2008.[3] Generally, qualifying conditions have become more stringent since 1990 (see Appendix 11.A), for example, through the introduction of a five-day waiting period in 1993 (extended to seven days in 2008).

Other conditions governing eligibility for unemployment benefits were also a great deal stricter in 2010 than 1990. In 2007, the possibility to receive unemployment benefits during summer breaks from (usually higher) education was removed, and the only remaining possibility for students to be entitled to unemployment benefits was to complete or definitively discontinue their studies. The same year the possibility to qualify for the basic allowance through periods of study, which had been introduced in 1974, was removed. Job-search requirements have also been made stricter. Since 2000 a person receiving unemployment benefits must be ready to take on any suitable job after 100 days of compensation even if it means working in another line of work or relocating elsewhere in Sweden. Although the possibility to limit search for the first 100 days was theoretically a slackening of the previous rule, it was in fact a partial adaptation to an established practice where the demand on the jobseeker in these respects

---

[2] The increase in 2002 also involved an additional rise in maximum benefits for the first 100 days of unemployment, a provision that was removed in 2007.

[3] Part-time unemployed must fulfil the same conditions as other unemployed to be eligible for benefits (i.e. the basic work and membership condition). One additional condition is that there is working time to replace, that is, that working time before (part-time) unemployment is longer than during current part-time unemployment.

generally was on a much lower level, and thus had the effect of requiring job-seekers to look for work more flexibly than before. In 2007 this regulation was itself removed, and all claimants became obliged to search for jobs all over Sweden and in all professions in order to maintain eligibility for unemployment benefits.

Beside the reduction in replacement rates, the reform that caused most controversy in 2007 was the increase in membership fees for the unemployment insurance funds. This reform reversed a long-term trend towards an increase in the level of state subsidy and a progressive disconnection between fees and unemployment levels in a fund's sector (Ds, 1999: 58; Edebalk, 2008). Average fees increased from €9/month in 2006 to €30/month in 2007, and the difference between the lowest and highest monthly fees reached €20, having been only €3 in 1990 (Arbetslöshetskassornas samorganisation, 2007). According to the centre-right government, principal motives for the reform was to increase the system's insurance character, making the costs of unemployment more visible and concrete, and to affect wage setting, by providing incentives for unions not to demand wage increases that would lead to increased unemployment (Ds, 2007: 47).

Between 1990 and 2010, fundamental reforms were also instituted in other income maintenance schemes in Sweden (see Appendix 11.1). The able-bodied unemployed who do not qualify for unemployment benefits are mainly directed to means-tested social assistance, administered and paid out at the municipal level, which is the programme of last resort in Sweden for individuals who cannot meet basic living costs. During the 1990s, increased demands were put on social assistance recipients to take part in training or work-related activities. When the possibility to requalify for unemployment benefits through participation in active labour market measures was removed in 2001, the unemployed were transferred to a newly instituted programme called the activity guarantee programme after their 300 days of unemployment benefits had expired.[4] The primary motive was to break the vicious circle in which many long-term unemployed were caught, where periods on unemployment benefits were followed by participation in active labour market programmes to requalify for a new period of benefits. In 2007, this programme was in turn replaced by the so-called job and development guarantee, to which all unemployed are referred to after 300 days of unemployment (450 for unemployed with children under 18, 200 days for unemployed aged 18–24), and where the participant is paid at a gross replacement rate of 65 per cent. The programme has three phases. The first phase, for up to 150 days, mainly consists of job-search activities with the help of special job coaches. In a second phase of up to 300 days, the unemployed participate in programmes such as job training, work experience, placements, or subsidized employment. After 450 days, participants will be placed with an employer.

A number of reforms in the 1990s also effectively reduced the possibility of early exit from the labour force. In 1992, the granting of early retirement benefit for labour market reasons was ended, though until 1997 it remained possible for older individuals to be granted early retirement on a combination of labour

---

[4] The unemployment office could still grant an unemployed person an additional period of 300 days of unemployment benefits if it was believed that would promote reintegration in the regular labour market.

market and medical grounds. Partial pensions were also phased out gradually in the 1990s, and in 1993 the criteria for injuries to be classified as work-related became much stricter. A series of changes in the 2000s also aimed to create a coherent insurance system for all benefits awarded on the basis of reduced work-capacity, replacing previously existing early retirement benefits for individuals over 30 and temporary disability benefits for those under 30 with sickness compensation and activity allowance, respectively. The period 1990–2010 was a turbulent period in sickness insurance more generally, with reforms following basically the same pattern as in unemployment benefits: cutbacks in benefit levels and stricter qualifying conditions in the first half of the 1990s, followed by a period when benefits partly were restored to their pre-crisis characteristics, and then a period of more radical change after the 2006 election. In 2007, a so-called rehabilitation chain was introduced, where the work capacity individuals on sickness insurance is assessed three times, with different criteria: for the first 90 days, in relation to the sick person's normal employment; for days 91–180, in relation to any task of their employer; and after day 180, in relation to the whole labour market. The work capacity of sick unemployed (i.e. those unemployed receiving sickness insurance benefits) is for its part now assessed in relation to whole labour market from day 1.

11.4 RE-REGULATING THE RISK OF UNEMPLOYMENT IN SWEDEN, 1990–2010

In 1990, 732,000 full-year people, equivalent to around 15 per cent of the population 20–64 years of age, received some form of social benefit in Sweden.[5] Although this share was approximately the same in 2008, the period between saw major changes both in the total number of people on social benefits and the relative proportions receiving different benefits (Figure 11.1).

Between 1990 and 1993, there was a sharp increase in the number of people receiving unemployment compensation, and not until after 1995 was this development reversed. Between 1997 and 2001, the number of people receiving unemployment compensation was more than halved, but in the early 2000s this downward trend ceased and was turned into a marked increase until another strong decline started after 2006. The number of people in active labour market programmes displays a similar development, with a very marked increase between 1990 and 1996, and thereafter a decrease except for the early 2000s. The proportion of people on sickness cash benefits displays a wave-like development over time, with a continuous decline between 1990 and 1997 and a dramatic increase thereafter, around the same time as the share of people on unemployment compensation started to decrease. That sickness absence decreases when unemployment increases is a pattern found repeatedly in Sweden,

---

[5] Caseloads are measured in the so-called full-year persons to increase comparability between compensation systems. Full-year persons equal the number of individuals that could be supported during one whole year with full benefit. Thus, two persons who have been on unemployment benefits for six months equal one full-year person.

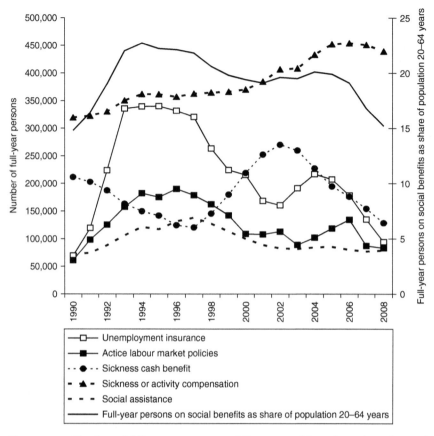

Figure 11.1. Number of full-year persons on different social benefits and as share of population 20–64 years

Source: See Caseload Annex (Sweden).

but only in a few other European countries, such as Norway and the Netherlands (Larsson et al., 2005). It was not until 2008 that the proportion of people
on sickness benefit was back to its 1996 level. The proportion of people
receiving sickness or activity compensation (formerly early retirement and
temporary disability benefit) increased slowly but continuously between 1990
and 2005. These are continuations of a longer term trend whereby the number
of people who do not work because of reduced work capacity had increased
continuously since the 1970s (SOU, 2006: 86). Although the proportion of
people who received support in the form of social assistance may seem to
have been rather stable throughout the period discussed here, it nearly doubled
in relative terms between 1990 and 1997. After 1997 the proportion people on
social assistance decreased steadily and at the end of the 2000s was back at the
levels prevailing in the early 1990s.

11.4.1 Unemployment as a risk category

The decreasing number of claimants of unemployment compensation between the mid-1990s and 2008 was a partly a consequence of improved labour market conditions. However, since the mid-2000s the proportion of unemployed in receipt of earnings-related unemployment benefits has also decreased substantially (Figure 11.2). In 1990, the share was 71 per cent, with 63 per cent receiving earnings-related benefits and 8 per cent receiving flat-rate benefits. The share with earnings-related benefits increased to 72 per cent in 1998, but has since decreased substantially, especially after 2004. This has not been matched by an increase in the share of unemployed with flat-rate benefits, and as a consequence

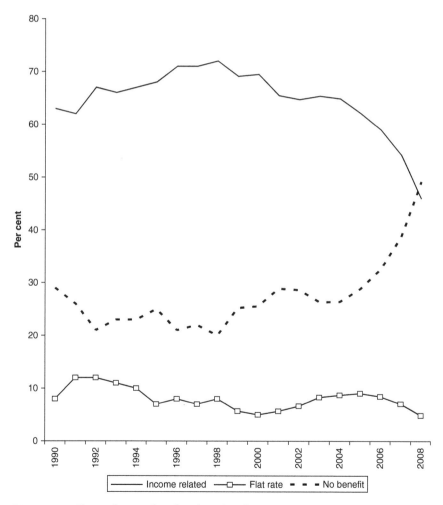

Figure 11.2. Share of unemployed with and without unemployment benefits (earnings related and flat rate)

Source: Regnér (2000) and IAF (2009).

the share of unemployed with no benefits, which fluctuated between 20 and 30 per cent in the period 1990–2005, increased to almost 50 per cent in 2008. These average figures hide considerable variation according to, above all, age, but also country of birth. Among the young unemployed (aged 18–24), only around 22 per cent had some sort of unemployment compensation (earnings related or flat rate) in 2008, and in comparison to older unemployed a higher share of those – around one-third – received only the flat-rate benefit. Among the unemployed born outside the Nordic countries, around 40 per cent received earnings-related or flat-rate benefits in 2008 (IAF, 2009).

There are three main reasons for the decrease in the proportion of unemployed in receipt of unemployment benefits in the second half of the 2000s (IAF, 2009). First, improved labour market conditions changed the composition of the unemployed stock, and the proportion of new entrants without a right to unemployment compensation has increased. Second, an increasing share of active labour market measures have been directed to unemployed people who were previously on unemployment compensation, but whose right to it has been exhausted. This means that a smaller share of unemployed without any benefit rights are offered some sort of active labour market measure than in the past, which in turn means that this group has come to constitute a relatively larger part of the (open) unemployed. Third, changes in rules governing eligibility for unemployment compensation have contributed, though it is very difficult to make a precise estimate of the importance of such changes given the practical impossibility of separate them from changes in the composition of unemployed. However, the most important change in this context was the abolition in 2007 of the possibility to qualify for unemployment benefits through periods of study, a change that affected mostly youths: in 2006, around one-third of the unemployed aged 18–24 had qualified for unemployed benefits in this way, and 18 per cent of the total stock of unemployed (IAF, 2007a, 2007b). The second most important reform was the abolition of the possibility to receive unemployment compensation during school holidays, something slightly less than 10 per cent of registered unemployed, again mainly youths, enjoyed in 2006. The implementation of stricter work conditions was of lesser importance. Had these rules been applied to the pool of unemployed in 2006 they would have affected about 1500 people in receipt of unemployment compensation, or less than 1 per cent of registered unemployed. Other institutional changes in 2007 – changes in the calculation period, the abolition of extended benefits and increase in waiting days – probably only had a very minor impact (IAF, 2009).

One question that re-emerged in the wake of falling benefit coverage during the economic recession of the early 1990s was the introduction of compulsory unemployment insurance. In 1994 the centre-right government introduced such a scheme, abolishing the membership condition for unemployment benefits and allowing other actors, such as private insurance companies, to be insurers (Proposition, 1993/4: 80, 209). However, this reform was never fully implemented, and after the election in 1994 the newly elected Social Democratic government restored the system to its pre-existing design. However, the Social Democrats also saw low coverage rates in times of high unemployment as a problem, and in 1998 a general and coherent unemployment insurance scheme was introduced. In this new scheme, those who had fulfilled the qualifying conditions were eligible for income-related benefits, whereas those who were not affiliated to an insurance fund or those who were affiliated to a fund but who did not yet fulfil the qualifying conditions got a basic amount. The new insurance (i.e. also the flat-rate benefits) was administered by the unemployment insurance funds. In addition, a new insurance fund, the so-called alfa-fund, was introduced. This fund should primarily be a transfer fund for those not yet members of a 'regular' insurance fund. This reform had, however, very little effect on coverage and recipiency rates.

Before the election in 2006, the question of introducing compulsory unemployment insurance was once again at the forefront of political debate, with the centre-right Alliance having made the introduction of such a scheme an important electoral pledge. However, a condition was that it would not involve higher state expenditures, and as a consequence the contributions from the insured (including those who had previously chosen not to be a member of an unemployment insurance fund) had to be substantial (SOU, 2008: 54). Once elected, the centre-right government deemed that this would imply a tax that counteracted their ambitions to increase the economic incentives to participate in paid work, and sidelined the project. Before the election in 2010, the Liberal Party once again argued for a compulsory insurance scheme, and although the Conservative Party – which became the dominant party in the coalition government after the election – in principle favours such a system, the same financial constraint has hindered any progress on the idea. The position of the Alliance on this issue is further complicated by the fact that the Centre Party wants to combine unemployment and sickness insurance in a single coherent insurance scheme with flat-rate benefits (Andersson and Andersson, 2007).

Unemployment insurance fund membership has meanwhile decreased sharply since 2006, a development largely attributable to increasing membership fees: between September 2006 and June 2008, total members to the unemployment insurance funds decreased by 13 per cent. This has most likely further reduced the proportion of unemployed who receive the earnings-related benefit, since those who discontinued their unemployment insurance fund membership, or abstained from joining an insurance fund because of higher membership fees, are liable to have higher unemployment risks. Fund membership decreased most among the young (aged 16–34), the old (aged 55–64), and those with low incomes, and relatively more in blue-collar worker funds (Kjellberg, 2010).

The negative relationship between the number of people on sickness and unemployment benefits up to the early 2000s (see Figure 11.1), along with a strong positive relationship between unemployment and the proportion receiving sickness benefits at the regional level, led some to conclude that the sickness insurance scheme was being deliberately used as a disguised labour market programme in regions with high unemployment (e.g. Edling, 2005; Larsson et al., 2005). During this period, the National Insurance Act indeed stipulated that when evaluating capacity for work, considerations were also allowed to be made to age, education, place of settlement, and prior work experience. This regulation was removed in 2008, but even before then the policies of the Swedish Social Insurance Agency stated that if the insured was under 60, only very substantial non-medical reasons could be considered when assessing eligibility for sickness benefits (RAR, 2002: 17). The empirical evidence to support the hypothesis of significant regional variation in the application of the Social Insurance Act is also limited (Statskontoret, 2006).

Important steps were nevertheless taken in the 2000s to remove the financial incentives to apply for sickness as opposed to unemployment benefits. Although the replacement ratio was the same in both systems for most of the 1990s, the income upon which the benefit is based, however, differs: in the case of unemployment, benefit is based on the income during a period (currently twelve months) immediately preceding unemployment, whereas sickness benefits are based on present income. More importantly, however, the maximum benefit in the sickness insurance scheme has been about 35–40 per cent higher than for unemployment insurance benefits since the mid-1990s, and when maximum sickness benefits were increased in 2006 this difference increased to around 70 per cent. Furthermore, collectively bargained supplements are often higher in the case of sickness. A reform in 2003 set maximum benefits for unemployed who had been granted sickness benefits to the same level as in the unemployment compensation system. This effectively narrowed the difference in compensation levels between the two systems and thereby minimized the economic incentive for the unemployed to apply for sickness benefits. By harmonizing benefit levels between different income maintenance schemes, the expectation is that the objective needs and conditions of individuals will determine the system from which they will receive help (SOU, 2006: 86). Although it has been argued that a complete harmonization between different income protection systems would increase economic efficiency in the short run, the fact that different systems cater to different risks mean that such harmonization perhaps is neither possible nor desirable (Hägglund and Skogman Thoursie, 2010).[6] Throughout the 1990s and 2000s, qualification conditions have also been different between sickness and unemployment compensation systems. Whereas it takes approximately one year to qualify for earnings-related unemployment benefits, all employed individuals, no matter of their work record, are qualified for earnings-related sickness benefits. Newcomers on the labour market that are at risk of becoming unemployed may therefore have an incentive to seek compensation from sickness insurance instead of unemployment insurance.

The Swedish response to the problem of working-age benefit dependency has more generally fallen short of wholesale risk re-categorization. Certainly, as a consequence of the dramatic increase in number of people on social benefits in the early 1990s, increased attention was directed towards individuals with complex social problems, such as the unemployed with reduced work capacity. A number of governmental committees concluded that the inability to address the problems of these individuals partly could be attributed to increased 'sectorization', in other words the fact that such cases were handled by several organizations and public support systems with partly conflicting goals and activities (Lindqvist, 1998; Proposition, 1996/7: 63; SOU, 1996: 85, 113; 2000: 78). Increased attention was also paid to groups whose designation implied that they were no-one's

---

[6] However, between 2002 and 2007, the maximum benefit in the unemployment compensation system was €68 for the first 100 days (€63 thereafter), and maximum benefit for individuals moving from unemployment to sickness benefits was €68 also after the first 100 days.

responsibility, such as 'able-bodied but not fit to be employed' (Fridolf, 2001). The Commission of Inquiry on Social Insurance, launched by the Social Democratic government in 2004 with the aim of analysing how to create a durable social insurance system, concluded that 'it is remarkable that today there is no public authority or other agency with the aim of increasing the total number of people in paid work' (SOU, 2006: 86, 131, my translation).

These committees came to the conclusion that addressing the needs of individuals with complex social problems was best accomplished by a two-pronged strategy; on the one hand separating risks, and on the other intensifying cooperation between different public authorities. Thus, since the mid-1990s it is the administrative separation of risks and making the distinction between different social insurance schemes more clear, not blurring the traditional boundaries between the risk of unemployment and other income maintenance schemes, that has been emphasized. To direct people to the right support system – unemployed to labour market policy and the unemployment insurance, and sick to the health-care system and sickness insurance – has been seen as essential for monitoring the development of different forms of social problems and thereby being able to prioritize between different areas of welfare policy, as well as directing people to the support systems that are best equipped to deal with their problems (Proposition, 1996/7: 63; Sjöberg, 2001; SOU, 2006: 86).

11.4.2 Unemployment protection as a social right

As shown earlier, formal replacement rates in unemployment insurance were lower in 2010 than in 1990. As important for the economic position of many unemployed is the fact that benefit ceilings have lagged behind both wage increases and benefit ceilings in other income protection schemes. While ceiling in most of the latter schemes have continued to be related to the base amount linked to the price index, the automatic indexation of the unemployment benefit ceiling was abolished in 1993. If maximum unemployment benefits had continued to be tied to wage increases among manufacturing workers, they would have been around 40 per cent higher in 2008.

Figure 11.3 depicts the development of gross replacement rates and maximum and average benefits and basic allowance as per cent of an average production workers wage over the period 1990–2008.

Between 1980 and 1993, maximum unemployment benefits fluctuated between 73 and 89 per cent of the average wage in the manufacturing sector. Since the gross replacement rate was 91.7 per cent up to 1987 and then 90 per cent up to 1992, this meant that the benefits for an average worker were lower than the level specified in percentage terms. Still, in the period 1990–2, an average worker received around 87 per cent of his or her previous wage in case of unemployment. The fact that a relatively large proportion of unemployed had earnings well above the ceiling meant that the average replacement rate was between 73 per cent during this period. Since 1993 both maximum and average benefits have decreased substantially, and were around 60 and 51 per cent, respectively, by 2008. The basic allowance has, however, been rather stable during the whole period

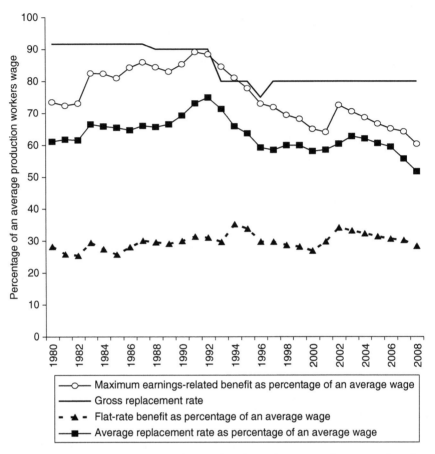

Figure 11.3. Gross replacement rate, flat-rate benefits, and average and maximum benefits, 1980–2008

Source: IAF (2010).

1980–2008 at around 30 per cent of an average productions workers' wage, leading to a gradual convergence in benefit levels received in the public system.

Trade unions fear that the continuous decrease in maximum benefit levels will further reduce the role of unemployment benefits as a form of income replacement, and effectively transform it into a flat-rate basic allowance (Andersson et al., 2008; TCO, 2010). In 2009, 87 per cent of all unemployed benefit claimants who previously worked full-time received less than 80 per cent of their previous income in unemployment compensation, corresponding to an almost linear increase from around 25 per cent in 2002 (Arbetslöshetskassornas samorganisation, 2009). The gradual drift to a flat-rate system is in part explained by a greater emphasis on economic incentives and cost containment among all political parties in the 1990s and early 2000s. The late 1980s witnessed an ideological change where the traditional Social Democratic policy was attacked not only from the right but also from the labour movement itself. Parts of the Social Democratic government argued for reforms in areas such as taxation policy and allowing private alternatives in sectors traditionally reserved for the public sector, whereas other parts of the party as well as the Swedish Trade Union Confederation was seen as defenders of the traditional Swedish welfare model. The debate before the election in 1991 largely focused upon the effect of the public sector on economic growth and the need to increase flexibility and the role of economic incentives on the labour market, a debate where the defenders of the traditional Swedish welfare state model were on the defensive (Hadenius, 2008). Rather than being seen as providing a safety net in times of crisis, the welfare state and unemployment compensation came to be seen as a major cause of the crisis (Lundborg, 2000). However, before the election in 2010 the Social Democratic party joined both white- and blue-collar unions in articulating demands for higher benefit ceilings, a campaign summarized in the slogan 80/80 – that 80 per cent of the unemployed should get 80 per cent of the former wage in compensation.[7]

It could perhaps be expected that the relative reduction in maximum benefits would primarily be a matter of concern for white-collar unions. However, although a larger proportion of their members have incomes above the ceiling, the risk of becoming unemployed is generally higher for blue-collar workers, who therefore more gain from a public system where risks and resources are more widely pooled. Moreover, as maximum benefits have not kept pace with wage increases, an increasing share of blue-collar workers also receive less than 80 per cent of their former wage in the event of unemployment. Besides the obvious effects on the income and living standards of their unemployed members, both white- and blue-collar unions are concerned that lower replacement rates will lead to lower real wages as their members are forced to accept job offers below their qualification level, something that might also increase the mismatch between the unemployed and available vacancies. They also argue that lower replacement rates will make their members more reluctant to accept structural changes in the economy, leading to higher unemployment and/or lower growth in real wages in the long run, and that it might have an adverse effect on labour supply by reducing the so-called entitlement effect, that is, the incentive to qualify for unemployment benefits through work. Consequently, there are strong reasons for both blue- and white-collar workers to demand that the benefit ceiling is raised.

While benefit rights have been homogenized in the public system, the broader picture is, however, more complex. The gradual deterioration of average and maximum unemployment benefits has increased the importance of benefits provided through collective agreements as well as private unemployment insurance schemes. The vast majority of wage earners in Sweden are covered by collective agreements, which give them higher replacement rates than in the public benefit system. For state employees as well as white-collar workers in the private sector, these agreements generally include rights to unemployment benefits which replace lost earnings also above the benefit ceiling (in some cases up to a

[7] Before the election in 2010, the white- and blue-collar unions launched a joint website – http://akassan.kampanjen.nu – where one could sign a petition which would be handed over to the government demanding higher ceilings in unemployment insurance. 122,562 people had signed this petition.

Table 11.2. Conditions for receiving complementary benefits through collective agreements in case of unemployment, and proportion covered by and fulfilling conditions in agreements

	Conditions Period of employment	Age	Proportion employees covered by and fulfilling conditions of agreement
State	12 months (36 months temporarily employed)	–	90%
Local authorities	Lump sum payment: 36 months	25	Lump sum payment: 72%
	Periodic compensation: 120–210 months depending on age	45	Periodic compensation: 40%
White collar, private sector	5 years	40	46%
Blue collar, private sector	50 months	40	39%

Source: Sjögren Lindquist and Wadensjö (2007, 2010).

certain amount), while employees in the municipal sector and blue-collar workers often receive a lump sum, usually determined by their former wage and/or age/ period of employment. Some collective agreements also prolong the duration of unemployment benefits. According to a recent survey (Sjögren Lindquist and Wadensjö, 2010), the proportion of employees covered by and fulfilling the eligibility conditions (in terms of age and length of employment) varies between around 40 per cent for blue-collar workers in the private sector up to 90 per cent among state employees (Table 11.2).

In 2004, eight unions offered members private unemployment insurance, a figure that had increased to thirty-two by 2009 (Sjögren Lindquist and Wadensjö, 2010: 13). This means that in 2009 close to 2.5 million union members had access to complementary unemployment insurance. Premiums paid to this type of private unemployment insurance increased from close to €1.3 million in 2001 to over €20 million in 2008, while benefits paid out from this type of scheme increased from close to €1.5 million to over €1.6 million in the same period. That this form of private insurance might, however, be difficult to sustain in times of high unemployment is shown by the fact that the Swedish Building Workers' Union discontinued the cover offered to their members in 2010 on the grounds that the insurance was too expensive for the union to finance (Byggnadsarbetaren, 2010). In addition, an unknown, but presumably very low, number of wage earners have a personal private unemployment insurance (i.e. unrelated to membership in a union). Although the growth in non-public unemployment insurance is not trivial, in 2005 (the latest year for which data are available) over 95 per cent of total earnings-related benefits paid in case of unemployment still came from the public system (Sjögren Lindquist and Wadensjö, 2007, 2010). Nevertheless, there is a trend towards increasing importance of private insurance arranged by unions or benefits through collective agreements in the overall unemployment compensation package.

11.4.3 Passive and active labour market policy

During the economic crisis of the 1990s, placement in active labour market programmes became the main short-run policy instrument to counteract the rise in open unemployment. Around 55,000 people participated in labour market in 1990, increasing to nearly 200,000 in the mid-1990s (see Figure 11.1). During this period, 'active' policy was to an increasing extent guided by the social policy objectives of providing income support for the unemployed (Regnér, 2000). As discussed, the duration of unemployment compensation was 300 days for the majority of the work force, but eligibility could be renewed through participation in active labour market programmes. There is ample evidence that placement in active labour market programmes were systematically used to this end (Carling et al., 1996; Sianesi, 2001), and that the resulting 'carousel' effect was an important factor making the active programmes less effective in promoting the transition to ordinary work (Forslund et al., 2004).

When the possibility to requalify for unemployment benefits though participation in active labour market measures was removed in 2001, this signalled (at least rhetorically) an important reorientation of ALMP. Different job-search activities have become an increasingly important part of ALMP in the 2000s (Figure 11.4; Statistical Annex, Table A.11), and although still high by international standards,

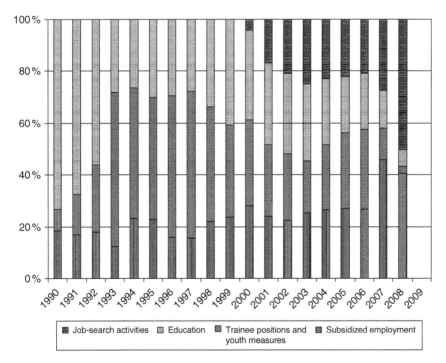

Figure 11.4. Distribution of participants in different active labour market programmes, 1990–2008

Source: Own calculations based on Regnér (2000), Olli Segendorf (2003), and Sibbmark (various years).

overall expenditure on ALMP has declined sharply (Statistical Annex, Table A.10). This development that was further pronounced when the centre-right government gained power in 2006 and launched an economic policy with stronger emphasis upon the matching of unemployed with available job vacancies (Proposition, 2008/9: 97). Since 1990, the relative importance of educational measures has also decreased substantially.

The main argument of both Social Democratic and centre-right governments for restricting unemployment benefit duration and putting more emphasis upon job-search activities has been to strengthen the role of unemployment compensation as a 'transition insurance', a short-term financial assistance aimed at facilitating the transition between jobs. The activity guarantee and the job and development guarantee that succeeded it were especially targeted at the long-term unemployed, and the argument was that their programmes of intensive job-search activities coupled with financial incentives would help avoid lock-in effects in long-term unemployment. The job and development guarantee had grown to be the largest ALMP programme by 2009. With so many participants, it has, however, been questioned to what extent the activities within this programme can be rendered meaningful, and whether it therefore is really a forceful labour market policy initiative to facilitate the return to the regular labour market among long-term unemployed, or simply a way of providing economic support for those whose right to unemployment benefits has expired (Finanspolitiska rådet, 2009; IAF, 2009).

Faced with rising costs as a result of higher social assistance caseloads, and lower incomes due to reduced tax receipts, in the 1990s many local authorities began to develop municipal activation policy programmes where the long-term unemployed and recipients of social assistance in particular were required to take part in compulsory training schemes or work-related activities in order to remain eligible for social assistance. The National Board of Health and Welfare opposed this development, arguing that no-one should be denied social assistance even if they refuse to accept offers of employment or training, particularly where wages were not agreement-linked or where normal labour market insurance was not provided (Bergmark, 2003). This tension between local practices and central guidelines eventually reached the Supreme Administrative Court, which in the mid-1990s ruled that social assistance recipients were required to participate not only in government activation programmes but also in programmes arranged by the municipalities (Bergmark, 2003). In the 1990s, the municipalities' role in labour market policy was further strengthened through the creation of local labour market boards. Besides initiating and coordinating local labour market policy projects, in many municipalities these boards have also had influence over the budget and work of the local employment offices and the allocation of funds from the EU.

In 1998, the Social Service Act was also revised, though to an important extent the amendments to this Act were an adaptation to a local practice already evolved in the municipalities (Johansson, 2001; Ulmestig, 2007). In the introduction to this government bill, it was argued that if in principle social assistance should be regarded as a social right, each individual nonetheless has the obligation to contribute to society according to his or her ability. Labour market programmes at the municipal level have a long tradition in Sweden. The main difference between these programmes and the programmes that emerged in 1990s was the emphasis upon conditionality, whereby eligibility for means-tested social assistance benefits was tied to programme participation. Moreover, while before the 1990s municipal activities in this area were to a large extent targeted at some subgroup of social assistance benefit receivers, and often aimed at employing them in various forms of subsidized employment in order to re-establish entitlement for regular unemployment insurance benefits, the new activation programmes generally encompass all recipients of social assistance that are able to work.

It has been argued that the increased emphasis upon activation measures and the changing role of the municipalities and the state in labour market policy in the 1990s also brought about an increased differentiation between the unemployed close to employment and those more on the margins of the labour market. Whereas the former group was a priority for national labour market policy with programmes of comparatively high quality, the latter group was to an increasing extent directed municipal programmes, with lower quality and lower cost per participant (Ulmestig, 2007).[8] Thus, though activation has been emphasized (or rediscovered) in Sweden since the 1990s, ALMPs have to an increasing degree come to be divided into two more or less separate parts: traditional active labour market measures administered and financed by the state on the one hand, and local measures administered by the municipalities on the other (Regnér, 2000; Salonen and Ulmestig, 2004).

11.5 CONCLUSIONS

The period since 1990 has been turbulent for Swedish labour market policy in general and unemployment protection in particular. Two large waves of reforms can be identified: the first in connection with the economic crisis in the early 1990s, and the second after the centre-right Alliance gained power following the 2006 election. During this period, unemployment compensation became less generous (in terms of benefit levels and duration), eligibility rules became stricter (in terms of qualifying conditions), and coverage decreased. In this concluding part of the chapter, I will discuss important factors that help explain the reform trajectory in Sweden, as well as what these reforms imply for the Swedish labour market model.

The immediate trigger for the labour market reforms in the early 1990s was the economic recession and the need to curb the costs of the public welfare system. However, crucial for understanding these reforms is the change that occurred in the 1980s when low inflation and price stability, as opposed to full employment, was assigned the primary goal of Swedish economic policy (Jonung, 1999). The budgetary strain cased by increasing unemployment and decreasing employment in the early 1990s was therefore not met by stimulating the economy, since it was

---

[8] This is, however, not an uncontested conclusion: other analyses have indicated that the unemployed people receiving social assistance participate in national labour market programmes as much as short-term unemployed in receipt of unemployment compensation (Löfbom, 2007).

believed that this might jeopardize the fight against inflation. Instead, cuts in public expenditures, or budget restructuring as it came to be called, became the central tools for economic recovery. Furthermore, within the Social Democratic Party a divide emerged in the late 1980s between those arguing that increased flexibility on the labour market was a necessary condition for maintaining Sweden's competitiveness on the global market, and the defenders of the traditional Swedish welfare model. Though on return to office in the late 1990s the Social Democrats at least partly restored some unemployment benefit cuts, most of their 'reconstitution measures' concerned other parts of the transfer system, such as family policy. Both the Social Democratic party and the centre-right parties have increasingly come to argue that unemployment insurance must play the role of a transition insurance, providing temporary economic help in case of unemployment. While all political parties in Sweden have long embraced the work approach, this has come to today have a rather different meaning than before the recession of the early 1990s. Now, control and discipline, manifested through increased monitoring of people's working capacity and restricted access to unemployment benefits, are emphasized at the expense of employment as a social right and work as a mean to increase people's opportunities and life chances.

Thus, fundamental changes in the rules of the game, that is, the change to a low-inflation policy, an acute economic crisis in the early 1990s, a weakened and divided Social Democracy, and an ideational and ideological change involving increased emphasis on the role of economic incentives among all major political actors, are important factors explaining the reform trajectory of unemployment protection in Sweden since the early 1990s. That important political and ideological differences nonetheless remain with regard to unemployment compensation is demonstrated by the debates before the elections of 2006 and 2010. 'Making work pay' was the mantra of the centre-right Alliance ahead of these elections, and before the election in 2006 in particular they made no secret that major cuts in the system of unemployment protection, increased contributions from the insured together with substantial cuts in income taxes, were the major means to achieve this. Rather remarkably, the Alliance went to the polls and won the election by promising reductions in a major social insurance scheme during the height of an economic boom. The reforms implemented after the 2006 election, however, provoked massive opposition from the unions, for whom reduced replacement rates and increased financing fees and the differentiation of these fees between different unemployment insurance funds were perceived as an attack on the traditional Swedish model. During the 2010 election campaign, in a political landscape where the differences between political parties in many areas appear to be smaller than ever before, unemployment protection once again emerged as a key issue dividing the political parties from each other. The Social Democrats, Left and Green parties – fighting the election as a Red–Green cooperation – promised to increase replacement rates and the benefit ceiling substantially and to reduce the level of fees paid by the insured. However, some tensions were visible even within the Red–Green coalition: whereas the Left Party expressed that their ambition is to increase the replacement level to 90 per cent and to further increase benefit ceilings, the Green Party declared that they in the long run want to introduce a new compulsory insurance covering both sickness and unemployment (Svenska Dagbladet, 2008).

The ambivalence of Sweden's adjustment trajectory in unemployment protection thus reflects a deeper ambivalence in the political debate. While the main political actors have embraced a new economic paradigm, the debate on unemployment protection remains centred on and organized around the institutions of the traditional Swedish model. As a result, although the basic institutional format – voluntary state-subsidized insurance – remains intact, it has increasingly been emptied of its substance. It may well be that a turning point has already been passed where it is practically impossible to reverse this development, as the economic and political costs of increasing benefits and ceilings are too high, and the legitimacy of the system has been eroded to such an extent that promises to improve benefits are hard to make credible. If so, whether a new institutional settlement for unemployment protection could emerge in its place, or whether public protection of the unemployed would simply decline in salience, remains highly uncertain.

Appendix 11.A Major reforms to income maintenance systems in Sweden (1990–2008)

	Unemployment compensation	Other social insurance schemes for working-age population
1990		• Possibility to get 3/4 and 1/4 sickness benefit
1991		• Reduced RR (replacement rate) in *sickness insurance*: day 1–3: 65%, day 4–90: 80%, day 91: 90%. Combined RR (public + collective agreement) must not exceed 90%
		• Possibility to be granted *early retirement* for labour market reasons removed
1992		• *Sick pay* introduced: first two weeks of sickness benefits paid by employer
1993	• Reduced RR from 90 to 80%	• One waiting day introduced in *sickness insurance* and RR reduced to 80% from day 91
	• 5 waiting days (re)introduced	• Increased demands for an injury to be classified as work related in *work injury insurance*
	• Maximum benefit increased, but automatic adjustment of maximum benefits removed	• Disability compensation can be received on a 25%, 50%, 75%, or 100% basis, where the fraction is determined by the degree of loss of work capacity
1994	• A universal insurance introduced by centre-right-wing government but repelled by Social Democratic government after September election	
1995	• Restrictions in possibility to be part-time unemployed	
1996	• Reduced RR to 75%	• RR in *sickness insurance* reduced to 75% during whole period
	• Only work qualifies for benefits	• A uniform RR at 75% of previous income is introduced in compensation systems relating to sickness and rehabilitation

(*continued*)

Appendix 11.A (continued)

	Unemployment compensation	Other social insurance schemes for working-age population
1997	• More stringent sanctions in case of refusal to accept suitable job offers, voluntarily quitting a job, or fraudulent behaviour • Increased RR to 80% • Changed work condition	• *Sick pay* period prolonged to 28 days • Possibility to get *early retirement* for 60–64 years old for labour market reasons removed (only strictly medical grounds)
1998	• Maximum benefit increased • A new comprehensive UI system introduced with two parts, (*a*) basic allowance and (*b*) income-related benefits. A new fund, the Alfa fund, pays basic benefits to unemployed not member of an insurance fund	• RR in *sickness insurance* increased to 80%
1999		• *Sick pay* period reduced to 14 days • Combined RR (public + collective agreement) may exceed 90% • Possibility to be granted *early retirement* for labour market reasons removed (only strictly medical grounds) • New social service act with increased activation requirements for *social assistance* recipients • *Partial pension* phased out • Stricter qualifying conditions in *early retirement*
2000	• Activity guarantee introduced for long-termed unemployed, with in principle unlimited duration • Increased demands to actively search for jobs	
2001	• Unemployed must establish a plan of action with employment office to be eligible for UI • Increased demands to take on any suitable job. • Participation in labour market programme can no longer be used to fulfil the work criteria when applying for unemployment compensation • Sanction in the form of temporary decrease of benefit is introduced if the unemployed reject suitable job/activation offer • Increased maximum benefit for the first 100 days	
2002	• Maximum benefit increased • Part of the membership fee to the insurance funds becomes deductible	

2003 • Maximum benefit reduced for unemployed who becomes sick

• RR in *sickness insurance* reduced to 77.6%

• *Sick pay* period increased to 21 days
• *Early retirement* becomes *sickness compensation (for* individuals of at least 30 years of age) and *temporary disability benefit* becomes *activity allowance (for individuals up to 30 years of age)*. Both benefits become part of sickness insurance system (before part of old-age pensions)

2004 • A new public authority – Swedish Unemployment Insurance Board – takes over supervision of the unemployment insurance system from the Swedish Public Employment Service (AMS)

2005

• *Sick pay* period decreased to 14 days
• RR in *sickness insurance* increased to 80%
• The 21 regional social insurance agencies were joined with the National Social Insurance Board into one public authority

2006

• Maximum RR in *sickness insurance* increased

2007 • Decreased RR: day 1–200: 80%, day 201–300: 70%, from day 300: 65% (70% for unemployed with children below 18, for this group the duration is 450 days)

• RR in *sickness insurance* decreased to 79%

• Higher maximum benefit for first 100 days removed

• Maximum RR in *sickness insurance* decreased

• Increased financing fees for the UI funds, leading to increased membership fees
• Calculation of UB based on 12 months prior to unemployment, irrespective of whether unemployed worked or not
• The time that may be omitted from the 12 months upon which benefits and work condition is calculated is reduced from seven to five years
• Stricter work condition
• Possibility to get UB during school holidays removed
• Possibility to restrict search area for the first 100 days removed

2008 • Waiting days increased to 7

• RR in *sickness insurance* decreased to 76.5%

• Period of part-time unemployment reduced to 75 days

• Maximum duration in *sickness insurance* set to 1 year. Rehabilitation chain introduced where work capacity is assessed three times: day 1–90: sickness benefit if unable to perform usual tasks, day 91–180: sickness benefits paid if unable to perform any task at employer, day 181–365: sickness benefits paid if unable to perform any work on whole labour market

Source: Försäkringskassan (2005), Olli Segendorf (2003), and Arbetslöshetskassornas samorganisation (2008, 2010).

12

Hungary: fiscal pressures and a rising resentment against the (idle) poor[1]

Anil Duman and Ágota Scharle

12.1 INTRODUCTION

Hungarian labour market processes were dominated by the economic transition for most part of the 1990s, which involved rapid restructuring and the establishment of adequate institutions to assist the unemployed and respond to other newly emerging needs. This chapter briefly reviews this first stage of institution building before moving on to examine the hypotheses of triple integration, as outlined in the introductory chapter of this volume. Sections follow the same outline as in other country chapters. The results are mixed. We find some indication of the unemployment benefit system moving towards integration in all three dimensions, being strongest in the homogenization of insured benefit and unemployment assistance. In terms of risk re-categorization and the administrative merger of unemployment and social benefits, changes so far appear to have affected goal setting and rhetoric and not much of that has trickled down to the daily practice in local job centres.

12.2 ECONOMIC AND POLICY CONTEXT

12.2.1 The transitional recession

In Hungary, labour market processes had been dominated by the transition from planned to market economy throughout the early 1990s. Political changes in Central and East European countries were followed by dramatic changes in their economies over the early 1990s.

Output fell by 15–25 per cent and there were large shifts in the ownership structure, in the sectoral composition of GDP, and in firm-size distribution. In the

---

[1] We would like to thank the editors, Pieter Vanhuysse and participants of the Recwowe working group, for their helpful comments on the earlier versions of this chapter.

gloomiest three years between 1990 and 1993, the cumulative fall in real GDP amounted to 18 per cent (EBRD, 2000: 4).

As some early commentators and the retrospective analyses of microdata have convincingly shown, this was due to the loss of export markets (an aggregate demand shock), followed by disruptions in supply caused by shifts in relative costs and relative demand in response to price liberalization and the removal of subsidies (Blanchard, 1998; Blanchard et al., 1995; Carlin and Landesmann,1997; Gomulka, 1998; Kornai, 1993). In this sense the recession was far more Schumpeterian than Keynesian,[2] and the only effect of macroeconomic policy was to hasten or delay the fall in output and the start of recovery.

In Hungary, the variation in output decline across sectors was rather large and the correlation between relative sector price and output change was high already in 1990, which may indicate an earlier start in restructuring than in other Central and Eastern European countries. The shift was, in rough terms, away from industry and especially heavy industry and towards services. Between 1990 and 1994, the share of industry in total employment fell from 36 to 33 per cent, and services grew from 54 to 58 per cent (Ehrlich et al., 1994). Restructuring also entailed a change of ownership structure. The share of the private sector in producing the GDP as well as in total employment grew at a modest pace during the 1980s, and quickly gathered speed in the first years of the transition.[3] Foreign direct investment was large and accounted for most of this growth from the second half of the 1990s.

Prior to 1989, labour force participation and employment were rather high in Hungary. Female participation was close to 75 per cent and male participation exceeded 80 per cent of the population aged 15–54/59 in 1985. During the transition, unemployment shot up in 1991, peaked in 1993, from when on was very slowly decreasing, while employment dropped from over 71 per cent in 1990 to below 55 per cent by 1993 and continued to decline until 1997 (see Figure 12.1; see also Statistical Annex, Table A.4).

The overall decline in economic activity had a strong impact on certain groups of workers, such as low-skilled workers employed in manufacturing and traditional industries, women, the elderly, the Roma, and young labor market entrants. At the time of the mass layoffs, the low qualified were most at risk of losing their job. In 1992, almost half the ILO-defined unemployed only had primary qualifications, and about one-third of them had lower secondary education. Those closer to retirement age constituted most of the long-term unemployed: their chances of re-employment were very small (Micklewright and Nagy, 1998).

The contraction of demand discussed above naturally led to cuts in employment. The subsequent rise in unemployment could have been temporary, lasting until aggregate demand picked up again. However, with considerable restructuring also taking place, structural unemployment emerged as well. Much of the

---

[2] A Schumpeterian explanation of the recession would stress the importance of structural changes (shifting relative costs and relative demand) and view it as a mix of creation and destruction, while a Keynesian explanation would put the emphasis on falling aggregate demand.

[3] Reforms in the early 1980s introduced enterprise contract work associations allowing private economic activity outside the planning mechanism. For more details, see Marer (1986: 251–2) or Kornai (1992: 435–44).

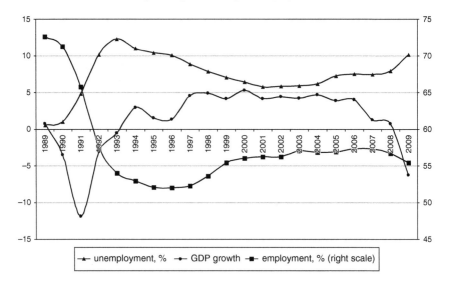

Figure 12.1. Economic growth, level of employment, and the unemployment rate, 1989–2009

Source: Central Statistical Office (Labour Force Survey for the employment and unemployment rates, population aged 15–64).

reallocation of the labour force took place through differential increases in rates of unemployment across sectors, while few new jobs were created (Jackman and Pauna,1997).

12.2.2 The policy response: reducing labour supply

The adjustment of labour supply to the decline in labour demand followed two channels. Besides the rise in unemployment, which was especially sharp for men, labour force participation fell significantly during the 1990s, especially among women (see Statistical Annex, Table A.7). Government-supported pension poli-cies intended to mitigate the effects of declining labour demand appear to account for most of the decrease in participation. Most people leaving the labour market became eligible to some social provision, such as old-age pension, disability pension, or maternity allowance. By 1995, the share of benefit recipients among the working-age population reached 31 per cent (see Table 12.1).

The use of pension schemes for the reduction of open unemployment started in the mid-1980s, when the mild reforms of the planned economy threatened to increase open unemployment. The government decided to tackle this on several fronts: offering state subsidies on early pension schemes and introducing unem-ployment insurance (see Section 12.3). Coming into office in 1990, the new democratic government continued and expanded this practice, fearing that the

Table 12.1. Percentage receiving benefit in population aged 15–64

	UI	UA	Pensions (below 64)	Disability benefits	Parental leave	Total
1990	0.4	0.7	15.9	1.8	3.6	22.5
1995	2.3	3.7	17.5	3.2	4.4	31.3
2000	1.8	2.4	19.7	3.5	4.4	31.8
2005	1.5	2.3	18.1	3.6	4.3	30.0
2010	2.8	2.5	15.9	2.8	4.0	28.0

Note: UA (unemployment assistance) includes career starters allowance (pályakezdők segélye), and two types of unemployment assistance (jövedelempótló támogatás, rendszeres szociális segély), as reported by local councils. Pension includes disability pensions. UI (unemployment insurance) includes insurance-type unemployment benefits (járadék).
Source: Authors' calculations based on data from the National Statistical Office, the National Employment Office, and the Pension Fund.

transitional recession would lead to unmanageable levels of unemployment and along with it misery and social unrest (Vanhuysse, 2004).

In order of importance there were four main early-pension programmes: a disability pension, a disability benefit, an early retirement benefit, and a pre-pension. In 1990, these four schemes accounted for 51 per cent of all entries into pensions, while the share of old-age pensions was 40 per cent. By 1992, the share of early-pension schemes increased to 65 per cent, and that of old-age pensions dropped to 26 per cent (see also Figure 12.2). The share of these four schemes slightly declined after 1997, when the pre-pension was abolished and eventually dropped to pre-transition levels by around 2005.

Disability pensions had been available since before the Second World War,[4] while disability benefit[5] in its current form was introduced in 1983. Their eligibility rules remained unchanged during the transition, but the evaluation of claims was rather generous until 1998, when the government finally decided to tighten both the rules and the practice of evaluation committees.

An early retirement pension was introduced in 1988 and extended in 1991.[6] It was available for persons no more than five years below retirement age, with at least thirty years of service time for men and twenty-five years for women (Scharle, 2002). Until reaching the retirement age, the state financed Employment Fund covered up to 50 per cent of pension expenditure, while the employer covered the rest. This subsidy was only available if the firm was shutting down, was making a loss, or carried out mass lay-offs. It was typically used by firms undergoing privatization (Széman, 1994). Finally, between 1991 and 1997, the

---

[4] Compulsory funded old-age and disability pension insurance was introduced in 1928 and was replaced by a pay-as-you-go system in 1951, which was gradually extended to cover the total population (including agricultural workers) by 1975.

[5] Various benefits (labelled disability benefits in Table 12.3) are paid to claimants not satisfying either the service years or the loss of work capacity condition of the disability pension. The benefit is flat rate if service years are insufficient and wage related if the claimant has sufficient work history but only between 40–67 per cent loss in their work capacity.

[6] Initial rules required thirty-five years of service for men, and stricter rules applied for the state-funded part.

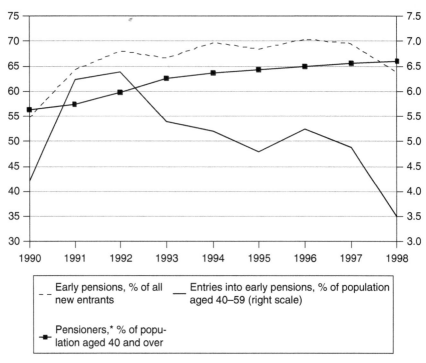

Figure 12.2. Change in non-standard pension claims 1990–8

Note: *Includes all types of pension and benefit granted on the basis of pension insurance (old-age and disability pension, disability benefit, see footnote 5 for further details). For women, the standard retirement age was 55 until 1997, when it was raised to 57 years (and then gradually raised to 62 by 2009). For men, it was 60 until 1998 when it was raised to 61, and to 62 in 2000.
Source: Authors' calculations based on data from the National Statistical Office and the Pension Fund.

pre-pension was available to long-term unemployed people with less than three years to reach retirement age, and having the required service time.[7]

Excluding disability benefits, the level of all three pension schemes was calculated according to the general rules of old-age pensions, making them much more generous than unemployment transfers. Also, early retirees enjoyed an advantage over others in their age cohort as the years they still had to go until retirement age were ignored in the calculation of their pensions. This was partially eliminated in 1998, when the pre-pension scheme was replaced by a flat-rate pre-retirement unemployment benefit. This benefit was set at 80 per cent of the minimum pension and was conditional on cooperating with the local job centre. It was available to those who had exhausted their eligibility to all other types of unemployment benefit and had only five years or less to reach retirement age (Scharle, 2002). This benefit was eliminated in 2005.

---

[7] It was also available to persons who had received unemployment insurance benefits for at least 180 days, had no more than four years before reaching retirement age when the benefits expired, and were not legally entitled to any other form of jobless assistance.

At a much smaller scale, parental leave was also extended to keep mothers at home and out of the workforce. In 1990, parental leave was available until the 3rd birthday of the child and was conditional on prior employment. It had two phases: an earnings-related allowance in the first two years, and a flat-rate benefit in the third. An extended paid leave was introduced in 1993 for mothers with three or more children, paying a flat-rate benefit until the 8th birthday of the youngest child. Initially, both flat-rate benefits were conditional on prior employment, but were made universal in 1999.[8] Bálint and Köllő (2008) show that parental leave benefits increasingly became an alternative to social assistance for uneducated young women with little or no employment history.

To summarize, both early pensions and parental leave benefits seem to have served as functional equivalents to unemployment benefits during the transition years. From the perspective of the triple integration framework (see introductory Chapter 1), this may be interpreted as an attempt to narrow down the risk category of unemployment as much as possible – almost exclusively to the able-bodied, prime-age male breadwinner.

Allison and Ringold (1996) report a similar preference for soft measures to cut the workforce in other Central European countries. During the early 1990s, the number of persons on disability pension increased significantly in Slovakia, Poland, and the Czech Republic (see Chapter 13) and old-age pension receipts also showed a marked rise in Slovakia and Poland. In Hungary, there seems to have been a wide political consensus about the aim to build a market economy at a minimum social cost in terms of job loss, rise in inequality, and social tensions (Vanhuysse, 2004). This translated into opening access to all types of provision that facilitated exits from the labour market, ignoring long-term costs.

Though this policy may be rightly questioned in view of the long-term consequences for the balance of the pension fund, there was some justification for it. The transition entailed considerable technological change and it could be argued that this made much of the human capital of older workers obsolete and their retraining did not seem viable given that labour demand was expected to be declining further.[9] However, Balla et al. (2008) show that the preference for benefits over wage subsidies and active labour market measures to facilitate the re-employment of low-productivity workers was an important factor contributing to the persistence of high unemployment. The political gain, however, was clearly positive. As Vanhuysse (2006) argued, early pension policies successfully divided and pacified the large group of workers threatened by unemployment, thereby preventing any serious opposition to emerge against the transition into a fully functioning market economy.

The prevailing growth-oriented mindset of socialist central planners may have also played a role. Successive governments have focused their efforts and attention primarily on macroeconomic growth incentives and regarded employment as a

---

[8] There was an interlude in 1996, when the earnings-related benefit was abolished, but the prior employment condition of the general flat-rate benefit was lifted as part of an austerity package. The extended paid leave for mothers of three children was left unchanged until 1999, and the earnings-related benefit was reintroduced in 2000 (Bálint and Köllő, 2008).

[9] Older people were overrepresented among the registered long-term unemployed and, as Galasi and Nagy (1999) demonstrated, between 1992 and 1996 the reemployment probability close to retirement was only 10–15 per cent of the reemployment probability for those aged 21–25.

residual issue in the sense that the level of employment depends on the level of output and hence on growth. While the institutional foundations of competition in the goods market (such as price liberalization, protection of private property, or a public agency to monitor free competition) were laid with much care during the early 1990s, the role of labour market institutions, social policy, and active labour market programmes had been neglected. As we show in Section 12.4, this would only change towards the year 2000, when politicians began to notice that employment had grown at a much slower pace than GDP.

12.2.3 Re-establishing public administration

Since unemployment was virtually non-existent in the socialist era, in the early years of the transition employment policy was dominated by building new institutions to provide unemployment protection. This coincided with a decentralization of government functions in 1990, mostly in response to the political demands of increasing self-governance and to prevent the resurgence of the old regime, which resulted in small and weak local municipalities. While the employment service remained under the control of central government, the management of schools, local infrastructure, and social assistance were devolved to local councils.

Institutional reforms of the central public administration focused on strengthening the executive power of the government (against parliament) and within that the prime minister (Brusis, 2006; Goetz and Wollmann, 2001). This has improved the efficiency of executing government decisions, but not the quality of those decisions. Despite early legislative efforts and some degree of professionalization in key policy areas,[10] successive governments have so far failed to establish a non-partisan professional civil service (Meyer-Sahling, 2009). Coordination across related policy areas, such as social policy and employment policy, has been weak, and clear goal setting, impact evaluation, and adjustment of policies are often missing (OECD, 2007b; Verheijen, 2006).

12.2.4 Changes since the 1990s

The transitional recession and a brief episode of an austerity package in 1996 were followed by steady and relatively high growth in output, but very little increase in employment after 1999 (see Figure 12.1; also Statistical Annex, Table A.4). Before the global crisis in late 2008, the employment rate stood at 57 per cent (age 15–64), which was seven points below the EU average and lowest among the former socialist new member states. As Table 12.2 indicates, over a quarter of the working-age population lived on some kind of social benefit; the majority of recipients were inactive and most of them absent from the labour market for extended periods or permanently.

---

[10] Notably those affected by EU accession or other international commitments, such as fiscal policy (Goetz and Wollmann, 2001). Even in these areas, Meyer-Sahling (2009) recorded a large gap between civil servants' attitudes and personnel practices (examined in the framework of the European Principles of Administration).

Table 12.2. Population aged 25–64 years according to transfer and labour market status, 2006 (%)

	Employed	Unemployed	Inactive	Total
No transfer	62.4	2.5	5.2	70.1
Unemployment insurance (UI)	0.0	1.0	0.5	1.6
Unemployment assistance (UA)	0.0	0.7	0.6	1.3
Parental leave benefits (gyed, gyes, gyet)	0.3	0.1	4.0	4.5
Pension	2.5	0.2	19.3	22.0
Other transfer	0.1	0.0	0.4	0.5
Total	65.3	4.5	30.1	100.0

Note: A person is classified here, and in what follows, as unemployed with reference to the ILO definition: if he or she actively seeks employment and is available to start work within the next two weeks. The three main parental leave benefits include an insurance-based benefit (gyed), a flat-rate benefit (gyes), and an extended paid leave (gyet).
Source: Cseres-Gergely and Scharle (2008), based on data provided by the CSO labour force survey.

Table 12.3. Activity and transfer status by level of education for people aged 25–64, 2006 (%)

Education	Activity and transfer status							
	Working	Unemployed	Inactive + UA	Inactive + PLB	Inactive + Pension	Inactive, other transfer	Inactive, no transfer	Total
Primary or less	47.7	8.9	2.3	6.5	21.0	1.0	12.5	100.0
Lower secondary	73.9	5.9	0.5	4.0	10.0	0.5	5.2	100.0
Upper secondary	77.9	4.0	0.2	5.1	6.4	0.3	6.1	100.0
Higher education	87.5	2.0	0.0	5.0	2.4	0.0	3.0	100.0
Total	72.7	5.2	0.7	5.0	9.6	0.4	6.4	100.0

Note: UA, unemployment assistance; PLB, parental leave benefits (gyed, gyes, and gyet).
Source: Cseres-Gergely and Scharle (2008) based on the CSO labour force survey.

The above simple facts suggest that the initial choice of a policy mix dominated by passive (rather than active) labour market measures has proved difficult to reverse,[11] and has become a hindrance to growth. Welfare payments, in combination with the wider system of redistribution, contribute greatly to the persistence of a low equilibrium characterized by low employment and a high burden of taxes and contributions. High tax rates curb economic performance and thus impede economic growth. Long-term unemployment or inactivity among the working-age population in turn leads to long-term poverty, the propagation of poverty from generation to generation, and social exclusion (World Bank, 2001.) And thus the vicious circle closes, in as much as these social disadvantages generate the need for further welfare spending.

The above described 'welfare trap' is especially deep for the less educated who make up over 20 per cent of the population aged 25–64. Less than half of them are in employment, a fifth receives some form of pension-like support, and a tenth is unemployed (see Table 12.3).

---

[11] Vanhuysse (2006) argues that this is partly due to a feedback mechanism whereby the initial expansion of the group of early pensioners makes it politically costly to cut spending on pensions.

12.3 UNEMPLOYMENT PROTECTION IN 1990 AND IN 2010

In the socialist regime, social provisions were supplied primarily through in-kind benefits, price subsidies, full employment, and a compressed wage distribution that was to a large extent controlled by the state. Some social assistance was available to the needy but was meant primarily for the elderly, as working-age adults were expected to be earning their keep through work.[12] There was no provision specifically designed for unemployment or in-work poverty; as such problems were considered to be treated at the root, by full employment and decent wages.

The need for introducing such provisions was first recognized in the mid-1980s, when the government decided to increase the autonomy of state-owned firms in managing production and allowed the establishment of small private firms. It was understood that these measures would allow market forces to start operating and this would inevitably lead to some open unemployment. An unemployment insurance (UI) benefit scheme was introduced in 1986. In this scheme, the firm paid the benefit for the first few months, then the central government, and finally the local municipality.

This scheme, however, was never used by a large number of workers, as it was replaced by another in 1989, well before unemployment increased considerably. The new scheme was also based on the insurance principle (contributory record required), but benefits were paid out of the central budget (i.e. there was no dedicated contribution to UI until 1991). The benefit rate was proportional to previous earnings and decreased gradually from 70 to 45 per cent during a spell of unemployment (for more detail, see Appendix 12.A, Tables 12.A.3 and 12.A.4). As the final step to complete the establishment of a two-tier benefit system, a means-tested, flat-rate unemployment assistance (UA) was introduced in 1992 for claimants who had exhausted eligibility for the insurance benefit (Nagy, 2002). Initially, UI was paid for a maximum of two years, while UA was open-ended until 1995, when it was limited to two years. UA was granted to claimants who exhausted UI if their per capita family income was below 80 per cent of the minimum pension; the benefit rate was set equal to this threshold.

Both UI and UA were regulated by the central government and, as of 1991, financed by compulsory contributions from employers and employees to a separate fund which was managed by the government (Keune, 2002). The public employment service (PES) was set up in 1986, but at the time it was primarily intended to facilitate job exchange, since unemployment was well below 1 per cent. The PES network was subsequently strengthened considerably, when registered unemployment grew from below one to over 10 per cent within two years after 1991.

---

[12] Three such schemes existed before 1990: the regular social assistance, the one-off social assistance, and the regular or one-off assistance for parents. All were means-tested and administered by the local municipality. The first of the three was used primarily to aid old people who had no pension. This scheme was merged with UA in 2000 and thus became a means-tested assistance conditional on work test. This also meant that the working-poor were no longer eligible for it and no assistance was put in place for them. (Note also that there is a housing benefit, but its amount is very small compared to the regular social assistance.)

Table 12.4. The main criteria of UI and UA in 1990 and 2010

	1990	2010
Type	State financed but tied to prior employment	Employees' and employers' contributions
Membership	n.a.	Compulsory to all employees and as of 2005, to the self-employed
Qualifying condition	Involuntary unemployment	Involuntary unemployment
	UI: 18 months of employment in past 3 years	UI: 12 month of employment in past 4 years
UA: prior cooperation of at least 1 year with job centre, family income below 90% of minimum pension
Benefit level and duration	UI: 70% of prior earnings for 6 months; 60% for 6 months; 45% for 12 months	UI: 60% of prior earnings for 3 months (maximum); 60% of minimum wage for 6 months (max); 40% of minimum wage for 3 months (max)
UA: 100% of minimum pension (39% of minimum wage), unlimited, with annual review
Obligations	UI: registering/cooperating with job centre; applying for jobs; accepting offer of 'suitable' job or training	UI: registering/cooperating with job centre; applying for jobs; accepting offer of 'suitable' job or training
UA: as UI and acceptance of 'public work' of 90 days/year

Source: See Appendix Tables 12.A.3–12.A.6.

Other welfare programmes for the working-age population, such as disability pensions, maternity leave, or parental leave benefits, were less affected by the transition to a market economy, as they had already been important parts of the socialist welfare regime. In 1989, the main welfare programmes were all insurance based, as typical of a Bismarckian system. Universal and means-tested schemes introduced during the past twenty years include the above-mentioned UA and a flat-rate maternity allowance introduced in 1996, which was changed from means-tested to universal in 1999. Lastly, a new insurance-based rehabilitation allowance was introduced in 2008. It is granted to new claimants of the disability pension or disability benefit whose work capacity can be partially or fully rehabilitated. The benefit rate is roughly the same as the disability pension[13] and it is granted for the duration of the rehabilitation programme but only up to a maximum of three years. The current welfare regulations are summarized in Table 12.5.

Only the unemployment schemes and the new rehabilitation allowance require registration and cooperation with the PES. As a result, the coverage of registered

---

[13] It is set at 120 per cent of the disability pension, given the service years and degree of lost work capacity, but is subject to compulsory pension contribution, so that the net amount is roughly the same as the pension.

Table 12.5. Regulations on the main social welfare programmes in 2010

Programme	Can be claimed while in employment?	Tax allowances
Unemployment insurance/jobseeker's allowance	No (availability for work must be proved*)	
Unemployment assistance	No (availability for work must be proved*)	
Old-age pension	Yes	Yes (lower health insurance contribution)
Disability pension	Limited	
Disability benefit	Limited	
Rehabilitation allowance	Limited and availability for work must be proved	
Gyed: paid to families with children up to the age of two, 70% of the gross wage but maximum twice the minimum wage (either partner can claim)	No	
Gyes: flat rate, may be claimed by families with children up to the age of two	Yes (after child reaches the age of one) (no restriction on working hours)	Yes (lower health insurance contribution)
Gyet: support for parents raising three or more children, where the youngest child is eight or younger	Yes (4 hours a day)	

Note: *Claimants are required to accept suitable job offers or community work as proof of availability for work. Support may be denied if the claimant does not cooperate. See Appendix 12.A, Table 12.A.1, and Table 12.A.2 for the evolution of caseloads.
Source: Authors' update of table 1.5 in Cseres-Gergely and Scharle (2008: 39).

unemployment has been very low: though the majority of the non-employed, working-age population receives some benefit, only 13–16 per cent are registered with the PES. The large majority of the registered unemployed are receiving some form of benefit or allowance, but many of them – about 40 per cent according to labour force surveys – are not actively looking for work (Fazekas et al., 2008: 198). At the same time, about a third of the genuine jobseekers are not registered with the PES. This suggests that the PES is not very effective at activating the unemployed and that the services they offer (beyond administering benefit claims) are poor, or at least perceived to be of poor quality by jobseekers.

The eligibility conditions of all types of unemployment benefit are relatively undemanding in terms of behavioural requirements (Koltayné, 2002; OECD, 2001, 2007*a*), and their enforcement varies greatly across local job centres (Bódis and Nagy, 2008). For example, individual job-search efforts do not need to be documented, and participants in active labour market policies (ALMPs) are exempt from continuing job search and attending interviews with the PES. Personal attendance at the job centres for verifying unemployed status is usually required every one to three months in Hungary, which is much less frequent than in many other countries (OECD, 2007*c*).

12.4 ANALYSING MAJOR REFORMS

This section reviews the five major episodes of welfare reform in the past twenty years and their political context, with a focus on the divergence or integration of unemployment benefits (for a summary, see Appendix 12.B).

12.4.1 Transition years (1989–92)

Unemployment insurance was established in anticipation of growing unemployment as a result of structural reforms in the mid-1980s, preceding the collapse of socialism and the planned economy. The first major step in employment policy after 1990 was the adoption of the Act on Job Assistance and Unemployment Benefits in 1991, which established a single-tier unemployment benefit system with additional provisions for older workers. It introduced a two-phase UI scheme, the pre-pension, and assistance for school leavers (the latter was abolished in 1996). As discussed in Section 12.3 above, a second tier was added in 1992. The Act was viewed as a necessity to handle the high levels of unemployment emerging at the beginning of the transition – a challenge that the socialist administration had never experienced and hence was not equipped to face. Due to this consensus, there was no opposition to the reforms proposed and all political parties supported the Act.

12.4.2 Reducing generosity (1991–2000)

Unemployment insurance was adjusted frequently during the first half of 1990s, and most of the reforms were aimed at reducing the generosity of the system. As shown in Tables 12.A.3–12.A.4, the prior employment condition was the only element of the UI scheme that was not tightened during this period. Between 1991 and 2000, the maximum duration was cut from two years to 270 days; the replacement rate from 70 to 65 per cent of gross earnings (with a temporary rise to 75 per cent between 1993 and 1997); the maximum UI benefit from three times to twice the minimum wage (1992); and the benefit floor and ceiling not adjusted for inflation between 1993 and 1996, at a time when price levels rose by around 20 per cent a year (Nagy, 2002). The eligibility conditions of the UI scheme did not change until 2000.

With the increase in long-term unemployment, the share of UA claimants reached 45 per cent of all unemployment benefit recipients and has ranged between 50–60 per cent since then (IE, 2009). At the same time, UI and UA converged in terms of average payments. When the UA scheme was introduced in 1992, on average benefits amounted to less than half the average UI benefit, but reached 64 per cent by 1997. The average UI benefit dropped from 56 to 36 per cent of the average net wage (Nagy, 2002). This was mostly a result of the above-mentioned drop in the real value of the benefit floor and ceiling. Nagy (2002) shows that the benefit amount was determined by the ceiling in 35 per cent of UI benefit claims in 2000, as opposed to 2 per cent in 1992, while the floor was applied in ever fewer cases (7 per cent in 2000 vs 43 per cent in 1992).

The gradual retrenchment in unemployment protection was met with little resistance. Part of the explanation for this may lie in the early divide-and-pacify policies, which provided other, often more generous types of support (early pension, disability pension, maternity leave) to claimants who had a sufficiently long enough employment history, thereby helping to prevent the emergence of discontent among social groups with a significant bargaining power. Trade unions were also too weak to raise their voice. They had been weakened by the dismantling of large state-owned firms and lost their former powers to influence government decisions via the communist party. In the new legislative framework, social partners are solely involved in pre-legislation discussions about unemployment support, rather than implementation or administration (Neumann, 2007).[14]

The deep and abrupt welfare cuts of the so-called Bokros package in 1996–7 were not so easily accepted. For the UI scheme, the replacement rate was reduced from 75 to 65 per cent, its two phases merged into one, and the ceiling was further reduced in real value (there was a small nominal rise, but not enough to make up for the lack of adjustment in the preceding five years). The pre-pension was replaced by the considerably less generous pre-retirement unemployment benefit, the earnings-related paid parental leave was abolished, and the insured flat-rate paid parental leave was replaced by a means-tested assistance (with no prior contribution required). In response, the unions went on strike, the minister for welfare resigned, and MPs of both the ruling coalition and the opposition parties raised their voice against the welfare cuts but the austerity package was nevertheless passed amid the looming financial crisis (Antal, 2000; Kelen, 1996).[15]

12.4.3 The supply incentive experiment (2000–2)

With a conservative coalition (Fidesz – Hungarian Civic Union, joined by the Small-holders Party) coming into power, a comprehensive 'welfare to work' reform was adopted in 1999. The government's programme for 1998–2002 underlined the need to reduce state redistribution and costly means-tested welfare systems, and support self-help (Fidesz, 1998: 5). According to official rhetoric, the programme was justified by the need to support people who are willing to help themselves and the government's responsibility to safeguard the interests of the tax-paying citizen (Fidesz, 1998: 3; Lakner, 2005). The main goal was to increase incentives for the unemployed to actively seek employment. Measures included the introduction of activation plans, cutting the maximum duration of UI, the merger of UA with the regular social assistance, and doubling the minimum wage in two years.

---

[14] An exception is the administration of active labour market policies in which social partners have special committees and significantly influence the work and expenditure of public institutions.

[15] The welfare cuts of the austerity package were criticized mostly on the grounds that they were disproportionate, their fiscal gains small, and their targeting ill-defined, which would hurt the poor and not only wealthier families, as was propagated.

In 2000, means-tested UA was merged with the more general social assistance scheme (see footnote 12) and made available regardless of prior work history.[16] The benefit level was cut from 80 to 70 per cent of the minimum old-age pension. The new scheme maintained the character of a UA support in that eligibility was conditional on cooperation with the job centre or the local welfare agency. In addition, the work test was considerably strengthened in an effort to focus more on activation and workfare (Frey, 2001). Most notably, eligibility for the new scheme was dependent on claimants engaging in thirty days of public works (prior to accessing benefit) which was paid at a rate no lower than the minimum wage.[17] This development made UI and UA more similar in terms of job-search criteria, but more distinct in all other respects and particularly in terms of generosity. Between 1997 and 2006, the average amount of the UI and UA schemes diverged, mostly because the UA had not been fully adjusted to inflation and wage increases. While UI transfers were typically around 40 per cent of the average net wage, the average UA dropped from 26 to 16 per cent of the average wage during the period (IE, 2008).

The administration of the new UA was devolved to local governments in 2000, who were reimbursed by the central government for most of their expenditure on UA. The fact that dedicated grants could not be used for other purposes (Semjén, 1996) created a disincentive for the local governments to strictly enforce job-search regulations for UA. In addition, many municipalities (especially in villages) merely paid out benefits, lacking the adequate expertise for the provision of genuine employment-oriented assistance to the long-term unemployed. One year after the introduction of the new work test, half of all municipalities had not organized public works at all, which was mostly due to the lack of administrative and managerial capacity (Fazekas, 2001). On the other hand, larger municipalities benefited from the reform as it provided a new source of funding for public works and extended the eligible types of work to any activity that 'served the public interest'.

As a whole, the 'welfare-to-work' reform resulted in a divergence between UI on the one hand and UA on the other in terms of eligibility and in administering support. There was little or no integration of risk categories either, since the reform focused rather narrowly on the registered unemployed. Other than implementing the gradual increase of the standard retirement age as set out in the pension reform of 1997 (drafted by the previous government), there was no attempt to extend labour market integration efforts to a wider group of benefit claimants.

Another element of the 'welfare-to-work' reform was a rise of the minimum wage in 2001–2. The prime minister promoted this as an incentive for people to seek employment via increasing the gap between wages and welfare (Kertesi and Köllő, 2003). In political debates over the plan, politicians also referred to the

---

[16] Except that the claimant had to prove that they had cooperated with the local job centre or municipality for at least twelve months within the past two years (as proof of their long-term unemployment).

[17] This rule applied to all able-bodied, working-age claimants.

moral obligation to grant decent wages for all workers, the need to approximate local wages to Western levels, and to suppress informal employment (Cserpes and Papp, 2008; Orbán, 2001). The government tended to downplay the potential labour demand effect noted by economists and also the European Commission (JAP, 2001), but introduced some measures to compensate employers.[18] Besides the genuine belief that it would raise employment, the minimum wage hikes may have been intended to appeal to middle-class voters and perhaps also to increase public revenues (Kaufman, 2007).

Reactions to the workfare measures were rather mixed. Employers, experts, and opposition parties stressed the potentially negative effects of the increase in minimum wage on labour demand. The Socialist Party accused the government that the minimum wage rise was intended mainly to boost government revenues (Kovács, 2001). The largest trade union federation of socialist orientation (MSZOSZ) worried about potentially adverse employment effects (Cserpes and Papp, 2008; Kertesi and Köllő, 2003),[19] while public employees protested because the rise removed much of the wage advantage of skilled workers and professionals in public health care and education. The new UA conditions also attracted fierce criticism by the socialist and liberal opposition, stating that the proposal was based on prejudice against the poor (and the Roma), ineffective, and would thus hurt the long-term unemployed especially in underdeveloped regions where there were few opportunities to work (Parliament, 1999). However, public opinion strongly approved of compulsory public works for UA recipients though not of the benefit cuts. The support for the new work test was so strong that the overall acceptance of the reform was positive (Köllő, 2002).[20]

Subsequent impact analyses of the reform identified few favourable results. A simulation of budgetary impacts showed that the minimum wage increases were unlikely to reduce unregistered employment and their net effect on the budget was expected to be negative. The employment effect was proved definitely negative by detailed empirical analyses (Kertesi and Köllő, 2003).[21] Galasi and Nagy (2002) also showed that the tightening of UA did not significantly increase re-employment probabilities, while it substantially reduced the income of the long-term unemployed.

---

[18] These included a 4 per cent cut in social security contributions (implemented over two years) and a temporary relief fund for low-wage sectors.

[19] Unions were also alienated by the tactics of the government in introducing the minimum wage rise. In November 2000, the parliament adopted an amendment to the Labour Code authorizing the government to set the minimum wage where the process of negotiations with the social partners did not yield agreement. Social partners feared that the new rule would weaken the social dialogue in this area. Indeed, the first rise in 2001 was passed by government decision, without the consent of the social partners (Cserpes and Papp, 2008; JAP, 2001).

[20] International attitude surveys suggest that – as in most post-socialist countries – disapproval of income inequalities and support for publicly financed welfare provisions is much stronger in Hungary than in the old EU member states (Murthi and Thiongson, 2008). However, most people would prefer to allocate benefits on the basis of merit, rather than needs (TÁRKI, 2002).

[21] For an overview of the impact analyses and the ensuing debate over further increases in the minimum wage, see Benedek et al. (2006).

12.4.4 Combining welfare and activation (2002–8)

After the 2002 elections, the new socialist–liberal government was mainly concerned with correcting relative wages in the public sector (as the wage distribution had been distorted by the minimum wage rise). One of their first measures was a 50 per cent wage rise for persons employed in the public health-care and education sectors, while the minimum wage was only raised by the level of inflation. Besides a minor alteration of the UI scheme in 2003,[22] there was no change in the unemployment benefits until late 2005. Learning the lesson of the unsuccessful supply-side measures of the previous government, the Socialist administration re-established the Ministry of Labour and concentrated more on demand-side policies, such as targeted wage subsidies. In 2005 the re-elected coalition – possibly inspired by EU recommendations – redesigned the benefit system with an aim to provide strong incentives for job search, but at the same time adequate levels of income support. UI was renamed as 'job-search' provision, and behavioural conditions were futher tightened (Frey, 2006: 208). To encourage early exit from benefit receipt, the new UI was made heavily front loaded in 2006 (see Table A.12.4) and a re-employment bonus was introduced.[23] The new UI had three phases: a wage-related first phase and a flat-rate second and a third phase with declining rates of support. The maximum duration was reduced by ninety days but the average benefit amount increased considerably in the first phase as both the floor and the ceiling of UI were raised, which compensated for the drop in the replacement rate from 65 to 60 per cent. Opposition parties mainly supported the expansion of ALMPs but challenged the government to make the activation measures more concrete.

In April 2006, the UA became a minimum income scheme, and the benefit amount dependent on equivalent family income (rather than per capita income). As intended, the redesigned allowance was more effective in reducing poverty, and especially child poverty, but also raised concerns about widening the unemployment trap, as there was no phasing out or disregard for those entering a job. It also generated tensions in some municipalities, where officials considered the provision too generous, in some cases based on prejudice against large Roma families. In response, the allowance was capped in December 2006, fixing its maximum level equal to the minimum wage (Firle and Szabó, 2007).

Aided by EU support under the Phare and HRD programmes, the PES was reorganized into a regional system (as opposed to the former network of county headquarters) and gradually started to introduce new, client-oriented services designed to support individual job search. To support job exchange and monitoring, a national information system was established, accessible by all local PES offices, and PES staff received training to implement internal quality assurance and evaluation (Galasi, 2004).

---

[22] To 'correct the negative effects of the 1999 amendment', the government reintroduced the second phase of the UI, with special, more favourable conditions for those with less than five years before retirement age (see Tables A.12.3 and A.12.4; also Frey, 2003: 176).

[23] Those getting back to work before exhausting benefit would receive 50 per cent of the benefit amount which would have been due for the rest of the benefit duration.

The strengthening of activation has been on the agenda of the PES since the late 1990s and especially since Hungary joined the European Union in 2004. Activation plans as a tool to increase motivation for job-search were introduced in 2003, which had a positive effect on job search efforts (Galasi and Nagy, 2009). There is some evidence, however, that such activation efforts have mainly affected UI recipients. Bódis and Nagy (2008) find that the drafting and enforcement of activation plans have remained a largely formal exercise, and especially so in the case of UA recipients. In the labour force survey, one in two UI recipients reports to have visited the local job centre within a month, compared to one in four UA recipients.[24] This apparent difference in the implementation of behavioural requirements for the two groups suggests there is no clear tendency towards the administrative integration of unemployment benefits.

Finally, activation was gradually extended to claimants of other working-age support. Wage subsidies and training programmes were gradually extended to cover disabled persons, less-qualified workers, older workers, and mothers re-entering the labour market. The boldest of such measures was the introduction of a rehabilitation allowance in 2008. As already mentioned in Section 12.2, this was granted to new claimants of the disability pension or disability benefit whose work capacity can be partially or fully rehabilitated (as assessed by a committee of health and employment experts). Recipients of the allowance must cooperate with the PES and participate in trainings or other rehabilitation services as required by the PES. The impact of the new measure has been limited so far, partly because the supply of personalized rehabilitation services is scarce and partly because the global crisis has reduced employment prospects.

12.4.5 Responding to the global crisis (2009–10)

The global financial crisis reached Hungary in late 2008. Within a year, unemployment rose from 8 to 10 per cent, and employment (in the population aged 15–64) dropped from 57 to 55 per cent. The government responded by cutting employers' social security contributions, increasing subsidies for job retention schemes, and further tightening the UA benefit (see below, and for more details Cseres-Gergely and Scharle, 2010). The crisis weakened the Hungarian currency, also because it coincided with political turmoil erupting in early 2009. The political crisis ended with the resignation of the prime minister and the announcement of an austerity package in April 2009, designed to regain foreign investors' confidence. The package included some long overdue but politically difficult measures, such as abolishing the so-called '13th month pension', raising the retirement age to 65, and reducing the maximum duration of paid parental leave to two years. It also included a general 10 per cent reduction in government

---

[24] By law, both UI and UA recipients should visit the local job centre at least once in three months. The National Employment Office recommends that UI recipients are called in more frequently: at least once a month. The LFS data suggest that in practice, the average frequency of visits is two months for UI and four months for UA recipients (calculation by Ágota Scharle based on the second quarter of the Hungarian Labour Force Survey of 2005).

staff, which was applied to the PES as well, not considering the obvious increase in the demand for their services.

Changes made to UA were similar to those in 2000, except more severe. Recipients of the old UA were divided into two groups: those considered able to work, and those too frail to do so. For the latter group, the benefit amount remained unchanged and the work test was removed. For the former, the benefit amount was flattened and considerably reduced and the work test extended to ninety days of public works a year, paid at least at a rate equivalent to the minimum wage. Long-term unemployed aged over 55 were automatically put in the 'frail' category, thereby narrowing the risk category of the unemployed. The cut in the UA benefit amount widened the gap between UI and UA recipients further, particularly since many of the newly unemployed were better-paid skilled workers laid off from crisis ridden manufacturing firms. The two groups converged, however, in terms of job-search requirements and also in benefit administration as able-bodied UA recipients are now served by the PES instead of the municipalities. Public works remained a municipal responsibility and available funds were considerably increased.

The austerity measures were clearly a response to the financial crisis and the structural dysfunctions of the Hungarian economy which had caused a slowdown even before the global crisis. The tightening of UA, however, had been on the agenda since its controversial redesign as a minimum income scheme in 2006. In one interpretation, the amendment in 2009 was a political deal with the powerful lobby of mayors (Kis, 2010).[25] In return for their consent to the austerity measures, mayors were allowed to use the UA for regulating the (idle) poor and especially the Roma, and for filling gaps in their budgets via public works funds, which were not closely scrutinized by the central government. The tightening may have also served to appease the growing public discontent over the inefficiency of Roma integration policies (and a gloomy economic prospect) and to prevent the further growth of support for the far-right.[26]

12.5 CONCLUSIONS

In terms of the triple integration hypothesis (see Chapter 1), we may summarize the changes in the unemployment benefit system as follows. There was some homogenization of unemployment benefit support caused mainly by the gradual cuts in the generosity of the UI scheme. However, the reform of late 2005 was rather mixed in this respect since it reduced entitlement while increased the replacement rate in the UI scheme, which may be interpreted as moving back towards the traditional separation between insurance-based and means-tested support. This is also underlined by the fact that neither scheme has become

---

[25] The 3,176 mayors who are elected directly in each village, town, and city may hold a seat in parliament as well, and many of them do, which clearly increases the power of their lobby.

[26] Established in 2003, Jobbik ('The Movement for a Better Hungary') burst onto the political scene by winning three of the twenty-two Hungarian seats at the EU elections in 2009.

dominant in terms of coverage.[27] At the same time, the generosity and entitlement to the means-tested scheme were increased, which brought the average level of payments closer to the insured benefit. The latest reforms of 2008–9 reversed this trend, so the gap between UI and UA widened again.

A need for risk re-categorization, that is, making parallel programmes for working-age claimants more like unemployment support, or making labour market exit routes less attractive, has been propagated by international experts since the mid-1990s, but Hungarian governments have been very slow or inconsistent in taking such advice. Early measures merely aimed to reduce the generosity of working-age benefits in 1996–7, while easing access (to early pension, parental leave) at the same time. This was later reversed by curbing access to pre-pension and disability schemes in 1998. Efforts of broadening unemployment as a risk category also included parental leave recipients who became eligible (but not required) to participate in some active labour market programmes but the extension of a work test requirement to the incapacity benefit was only introduced in 2008. Registration at the local job centre has been kept as a condition of claiming UA, though it is often merely an administrative formality. The latest rearrangement of the UA, however, has again narrowed the focus of the PES by removing older workers from the unemployment register.

The idea of an administrative merger of distinct support systems for working-age benefit recipients has been widely discussed in the past few years but most of these plans are still waiting to be implemented. The new rehabilitation scheme with a work test introduced in 2008 was a first major step in this direction since it moved the main responsibility of dealing with this client group from the health and pension insurance agencies to the public employment service. The ministries of welfare and labour were merged in 2006, and the national headquarters of the PES have assumed some new roles related to social provisions. However, at the local level no merging of welfare and PES functions has taken place so far. Indeed, there are signs of diminished integration, as indicated by the strengthened responsibility of local governments in managing public works programmes for UA recipients.

In summary, the suggestion of integrating working-age benefits or their administration has been a frequent element in policy debates, but has not materialized yet in the actual design and implementation of employment policy. Rather than responding to structural changes or distortions in the labour market, policymaking has been largely dictated by the politically determined cycle of overspending and fiscal squeeze, and more specific short-term political aims, such as the recent attempt to appease public discontent by regulating the 'idle poor'. Most labour market reforms would necessitate complex deals and potential gains can often be reaped only by the next government. This reduces governments' intrinsic motivation to initiate reforms, while civil society, the media, and fiscal watchdogs are still too weak to hold them accountable. Even when a hard-fought political decision is made, implementation may fail on the restricted or uneven ability of public administration to adequately design a new policy and ensure its proper implementation.

---

[27] At the time there were about 160,000 people on UA and 100,000 on UI.

Appendix 12.A Additional tables (Hungary)

Table 12.A.1 Registered unemployed by type of benefit received (%)

	1990	1995	2000	2005	2008
Unemployment insurance	100	38.4	44.8	42.0	34.3
Job-search assistance	–	–	–	6.9	13.7
Means-tested UA	–	49.1	36.9	–	–
Means-tested SA	–	–	13.2	49.1	50.1
School-leavers' allowance	–	6.7	0.0	–	–
Pre-retirement UA	–	–	2.9	2.0	1.8
Pre-pension	–	5.8	2.2	–	–
Total receiving some assistance	100	100	100	100	100
Those not receiving any assistance (% of the registered unemployed)*	10.3	22.6	29.5	33.8	35.8
Registered unemployed (thousand persons)	47.4	507.7	390.2	409.5	442.3

Source: The Hungarian Labour Market 2001–9.
Note: *The increase in non-recipiency is partly explained by the phasing out of the school-leavers allowance in 1996, and partly by the tightening of UI and UA rules. In 2007, the share of those aged below 30 was 40 per cent among non-recipients, and 24 per cent among the other registered unemployed.

Table 12.A.2 Other non-employed working-age population by type of benefit received (in thousands)

	1990	1995	2000	2005	2008
Old-age pension (korhatár alatti öregségi és hozzátartozói)	41.1	27.3	94	173.4	261.7
Disability pension (korhatár alatti rokkant)	232.6	332.3	418.7	465.7	432.8
Other disability benefit (egyéb mmk)	126.4	222.7	240.3	251.8	225.5
Insured maternity leave (gyed)	154.9	128.5	54.0	87.1	93.9
Flat-rate parental leave (gyes, gyet)	94.7	175.7	245.4	208.7	207.6
Sick leave (táppénz, napi átlag létszám)	272	173	112	102	90
(A) Non-employed together (unemployed+inactive) (thousand persons)	1,969	3,245	3,009	2,936	2,945
(B) Working-age (15–64) population (thousand persons)	6,849	6,835	6,841	6,815	6,794
(A/B) Non-employed working age (%)	29	47	44	43	43

Source: The Hungarian Labour Market 2001–9, CSO Labour force survey (for working-age population), and Yearbook of Welfare Statistics, 2008.

Table 12.A.3 Changes in the entitlement conditions of insured unemployment benefit

Year of introduction	Prior employment condition	Duration		Waiting period after	
		Minimum	Maximum	Voluntary quit.	Severance pay
1989	18 months/3 years	24 months	24 months	smaller benefit	None
1991		180 days		3 months	
1992	12 months/4 years	135 days	18 months		same as
1993				6 months	months
1997		90 days	360 days		of severance
1998				3 months	pay
2000	200 days/4 years	40 days	270 days	(90 days)	None
2006*	365 days/4 years	73 days	360 days		

Note: *November 2005, no change until June 2010.
Source: Nagy (2002) and Frey (2010).

Table 12.A.4 Changes in the generosity of UI

Year of introduction	Benefit in proportion of previous gross wage (and maximum duration)			Calculation of average earnings	Benefit	
	Phase 1	Phase 2	Phase 3		Minimum	Maximum
1989				Base wage in last month + monthly average of additional earnings in last year	1989: none	Phase 1: 300% of minimum wage;
1990	70% for 6 months	60% for 6 months	45% in the second year		0.8*min w	Phase 2: 200% of min w
					min w	300% min w
1991	70% for 360 days	50% for 360 days	–			
1992	70% for 360 days	50% for 180 days		Average earnings in four calendar quarters before job loss	min w	200% min w
1993	75% for 90 days	60% for 270 days	–		8,600 HUF	Phase 1: 18,000 HUF; Phase 2: 15 000 HUF
1997	65% (no phases) for 360 days (270 days after 2000)				90% of min pension (22,230 HUF in 2005)	180% of min pension (44,460 HUF in 2005)
2003	65% for 270 days		85% of min wage for 180 days			
2006*	60% for 91 days	60% of min wage for 179 days	40% of min wage for 90 days		60% of min wage (37,500 in 2006)	120% of min wage (75,000 in 2006)

Note: *November 2005, no change until June 2010. **This column gives the length of the first, typically more generous phase of UI, compared to the total duration of UI benefit (given in Table A.12.3).
min w, minimum wage; min p, minimum old-age pension.
In Hungarian, phases 1 and 2 were called 'munkanélküli járadék' until 2005, when it was renamed to 'álláskeresési járadék'. Phase 3 is called 'álláskeresési segély'. Phase 3 is insurance based. Eligibility conditions are either 200 days (140 days for those less than five years before pensionable age) of prior employment or exhaustion of phase 2.
Source: Nagy (2002) and Frey (2010).

Table 12.A.5 Changes in the entitlement conditions of the unemployment allowances

Year of introduction	Prior employment condition	Means test		Activation criteria/ work test
Before 1989	SA – none	–		SA – none
1992	UA – exhausted eligibility for UI; SA – none	UA – monthly (per capita) family income is below widows' minimum pension	SA – monthly income is below widows' minimum pension	UA – min. 18 years old, capable of work, unemployed, not in receipt of UI benefit; SA – none, may work limited hours
1993	UA – exhausted eligibility for UI; SA – none	UA – monthly (per capita) family income is below 80% of minimum pension		
1997	UA – exhausted eligibility for UI; SA – 2 years of prior cooperation with job centre		SA – own monthly income is below 70%, per capita family income is below 80% of minimum pension	UA – min. 18 years old, capable of work, unemployed, no UI benefit;SA – cooperation with job centre or family centre
2000	UA – exhausted other allowance or 1 year of prior cooperation with job centre	UA – own monthly income is below 70%, per capita family income is below 80% of minimum pension, no property (except for own housing);SA merged into UA (the new UA was named 'social assistance' but requires a work test)		UA – min. 18 years old, capable of work, unemployed, no UI benefit, take part in 30 days of public works
2006 April		UA – equivalent family income** is less than 90% of minimum pension		
2009		UA – equivalent family income** is below 90% of minimum pension	SA – equivalent family income** is below 90% of minimum pension	UA – public works of at least 90 days/ year, cooperate with job centre;SA – cooperate with family centre

Source: Gábos (1996), Nagy (2002), and Frey (2010).
Note: UA, unemployment assistance (jövedelempótló támogatás); SA, social assistance (rszs).
**Equivalence scale changed (consumption unit instead of per capita). When splitting the UA and SA in 2009, the SA kept its old name 'rendszeres szociális segély' (regular social assistance) and the UA was called 'rendelkezésre állási támogatás' (availability allowance).

Table 12.A.6 Changes in the generosity of SA and UA

Year of introduction	Amount		Duration
	UA	SA	
1992		According to need, up to minimum widow's pension	UA, SA – unlimited
1995 July	80% of the minimum pension (top up to own income)		UA – max. 2 years
			SA – unlimited, annual review
1997		70% of the minimum pension (top up to own income)	UA – max. 2 years
			SA – unlimited, annual review
2000	70% of the minimum pension (top up to own income)		
2006 May	Top up of equivalent income to 90% of minimum pension		Unlimited with annual review of entitlement
2007	Top up of equivalent income to 90% of minimum pension, but maximum the minimum wage		
2009	Flat rate = minimum pension (about 39% of minimum wage)	Top up of equivalent income to 90% of minimum pension, but maximum the net minimum wage	UA, SA – Unlimited with review every 2 years

Source: Gábos (1996), Nagy (2002), and Frey (2010).

Appendix 12.B Major reform episodes in Hungary (1989–2009)

1989–92	easing entitlement conditions in all elements of the welfare system: unemployment insurance, means-tested support for the unemployed, incapacity benefits, early pensions, paid parental leave
1991–2000	recurring reductions in the generosity of UI in 1991–3, 1997, and 2000
1996–7	reduction in generosity in most welfare benefits (UI, early pension, and parental leave), 1998 reduction in entitlement to incapacity benefit and rise in pensionable age, as part of austerity package
2000	widening entitlement (prior work history condition) and reducing generosity in unemployment benefits (both UI and UA), strengthening work test, (but increase in both entitlement and generosity in parental leave), 2001–2: doubling the minimum wage
2006–8	reducing entitlement to insurance benefits (unemployment, incapacity, early pension, old-age pension), increasing both entitlement and generosity of means-tested UA, strengthening work test for UA and incapacity benefit
2009	reducing generosity and strengthening work test of UA

13

The Czech Republic: activation, diversification, and marginalization[1]

Tomáš Sirovátka and Ondřej Hora

13.1 INTRODUCTION

This chapter analyses the development of the social protection of the unemployed in the Czech Republic (and the former Czechoslovakia) since the early 1990s. From the perspective of the framework for analysis that informs this volume, the Czech case presents a number of specificities. With the exception of the closure of some exit routes for elderly workers, there is little evidence of the blurring of the boundaries between the risk of unemployment and other forms of working-age benefit dependency, or of any convergence in eligibility and entitlement rules between unemployment protection and other schemes for non-working populations. Nor is there any trend to benefit homogenization; on the contrary, in the Czech case there is evidence of growing diversification in benefit rights, in several respects: between unemployment insurance (UI) and social assistance (SA) concerning replacement rates and entitlement conditions, and in the approach to different subcategories of the unemployed (e.g. long-term and short-term claimants, the youth). However, a strong trend to activation can be seen in the Czech case, both in schemes for the unemployed and in SA.[1]

In more concrete terms, in the early 1990s the first post-communist Czech governments introduced a two-tiered benefit system, comprising UI and SA. The system was quite encompassing, and though it was not overly generous, it provided an acceptable living standard. Activation elements were originally neglected in both schemes. The UI and SA schemes would later converge, because of rather modest standards in UI and the development of SA into a relatively generous safety net. Since the late 1990s, however, changes in the benefit system have moved in the opposite direction: towards a strengthening of insider–outsider differentiation and the movement of some groups out of the scope of unemployment protection altogether. Over the course of the 2000s strong activation

[1] This study was written with the support of the Ministry of Education of the Czech Republic (MSM 0021622408 'Social Reproduction and Social Integration').

elements have also been incorporated, alongside cuts in benefit entitlements for marginal groups like long-term SA claimants.

The chapter commences by describing the economic and labour market conditions that accompanied the transition to a market economy at the end of the communist era, and the policy measures put in place to treat the immediate social consequences of massive structural change. The subsequent sections then describe the major changes within unemployment protection between 1990 and 2010, and develop the analysis of Czech trends in relation to the analytical framework of this volume. The final part of the chapter discusses the main forces behind the Czech trajectory, emphasizing the importance of three factors in particular: the timing of the transformation process, the political imperative of blame avoidance in the context of the transformation, and finally the economic constraints which have framed the choices of Czech policymakers in this area.

13.2 ECONOMIC AND POLICY CONTEXT FROM THE EARLY 1990s: SLOW TRANSFORMATION, COMPREHENSIVE PROTECTION

In the communist era the Czech economy was oriented strongly towards heavy industry, while services were underdeveloped. Women nonetheless already participated extensively in the labour market, which was in keeping with the regime's appeal to gender equality (Hašková, 2007). Wages were set by the state as nearly equal (small differences between low-skilled and high-skilled professions), with advantages given to specific manual professions (e.g. in mining, metallurgy, mass agriculture). There was a legislative obligation to work, while job positions were assigned by a specific work allocation system. Most people worked in the same firm for lengthy periods of time, or even for all their productive lives. It was not common to be without work for more than a short time period, and hence there was no necessity for an unemployment protection system. For ideological reasons and because of the availability and enforcement of work, poverty was not recognized as a relevant social problem (Sirovátka, 2009).

The situation changed dramatically after the 'Velvet revolution' in November 1989. The conditions of the emerging market economy, privatization, liberalization of prices, the new phenomenon of unemployment, and the necessity to reallocate part of the labour force from inefficient branches of the industry implied that about one-half of the working population changed their jobs between 1990 and 1996; many of them found jobs in the expanding service sector (MLSA, 1999). The transformation also had several economic consequences such as falling GDP and real wages. However, the transformation strategy in the Czech Republic until 1997 was somewhat different from the other post-communist countries, given the emphasis on preservation of employment. As a result of this, it was mainly the least qualified, working pensioners, and Roma minority workers[2] who were made redundant following the initial economic shock (Možný, 2002; Vanhuysse, 2006).

---

[2] The Roma constituted 13.1 per cent of the unemployed in June 1991.

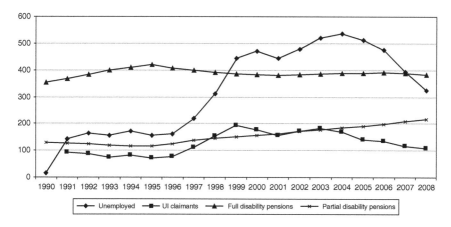

Figure 13.1. Unemployment, recipients of unemployment benefits and disability pensions

Note: Monthly average numbers of unemployed (claimants) and all invalidity pensions (including pensions paid to foreign countries) paid in December of given year.
Source: Unemployment (MLSA, 2009*b*), disability pensions (MLSA, 2003, 2006, 2008, 2009*a*).

In contrast to pessimistic expectations and unlike other post-socialist countries, the Czech unemployment rate stabilized at the level of approximately 3–4 per cent in the first half of the 1990s. The share of long-term unemployed was merely 16 per cent of the unemployment stock (Mareš et al., 2003). This meant that the Czech Republic experienced one of the lowest unemployment rates in Europe at the time, despite undergoing a process of profound economic restructuring (see Statistical Annex, Table A.5 and Figure 13.1).

There were several reasons for this: the delayed transformation of the economy, the development of private entrepreneurship, a problematic privatization of state property including firms; and the role of the so-called 'bank socialism', which was characterized by easy access to the bank loans (sometimes based upon personal relationships) and very loose conditions of pay morale: banks with strong state share tolerated indebtedness of the companies.

An UI system was implemented with originally generous benefit levels in 1990–1, but in 1992 benefit levels were rapidly scaled back. Since the government's overall strategy was to protect jobs, the pressures for improving benefits were feeble and the system remained unchanged. At the end of 1991 an SA system was also established, which was relevant for the unemployed since UI benefits were provided only for a period of six months. In order to alleviate the risks of poverty the SA scheme was relatively generous at first, but became more modest over the following years.

The second main period of the development of the labour market, from 1998 to 2005, overlaps with the governments led by Czech Social Democratic Party ('Česká strana sociálně demokratická'/ČSSD), which won parliamentary elections in 1998 and 2002 and remained in power until 2006. This period was characterized by the privatization of banks, inflows of foreign capital, and more intensive restructuring, including bankruptcies and mass redundancies in the traditional branches of industry (e.g. mining, shoemaking, glass, and textile industry).

The unemployment rate increased rapidly from about 3 per cent at the end of 1996 to about 9 per cent by the end of 2000, and dropped only slightly thereafter. However, in spite of the relatively higher unemployment rate the economy was growing strongly.

The changes in the labour market affected in particular older (or even middle-aged) people with relatively stable previous work careers: if they were made redundant they rarely found a new job, and often opted for early exit. In the 1990s, early exit was easily accessible: pensions could be received for up to two years before regular retirement age with only a temporary penalty on pension (1 per cent reduction for each three months of earlier exit) in case of the unemployed, and three years before regular retirement age with the enduring penalty on pension (0.6 per cent of pension less for each three months of earlier exit) in other cases. The first exit route was closed only in 2001, while the penalty on early exit in the other case was simply increased to 0.9 per cent for each three months of earlier exit.

Between 2005 and 2007, the Czech Republic experienced strong economic growth (between 6–7 per cent of GDP yearly) and unemployment dropped from about 9 per cent to slightly more than 6 per cent and continued to decline even in 2008. Long-term unemployment declined as well. The economic crisis has become apparent only at the very end of 2008, and in 2009 GDP declined by more than 4 per cent and unemployment climbed quickly to above 9 per cent. After 2007 a centre-right government was in power, prioritizing reductions in public spending, a strategy that was continued under the 'administrative government' in 2009 and the government formed following elections in the middle of 2010.

13.3 UNEMPLOYMENT PROTECTION FROM THE EARLY 1990s TO 2010

When looking at the recent development of unemployment protection in the Czech Republic, the period from 1990 to 2010 can be divided into three distinct phases of reform: an early stage of system development (1990–2), a period of relative stability (1993–2003), and a third stage (2004–9) of frequent reform changes,[3] in which many measures implemented had little longer term viability.

At the beginning of the 1990s the former Czechoslovakia adopted a new system of 'social safety net', including unemployment protection, as part of the transformation to a market economy. From the beginning the main part of the social protection system dealing with the unemployed was in hands of Public Employment Services (PES), represented by two levels of governance: Central and Local Employment Offices. The functions of unemployment benefit administration, job mediation, and active labour market policies (ALMPs) were integrated within the PES, which was a section of Ministry of Labour and Social Affairs. While job mediation and ALMPs covered all the unemployed, after 1992 the benefits were

---

[3] The Employment Act was for example changed more than thirty times between 2004 and 2009.

Table 13.1. The dynamics of unemployment protection systems

	Periods	Unemployment benefits	Social assistance benefits
1990–2	Initial period, creation of social safety net	Generous but soon rather modest	Generous, easily accessible
1993–2003	Transformation, soft economic conditions ('protest avoidance')	Modest, some improvements during slowdown	Continuous deterioration
2004–9	Accession into the EU, post-transformation	Modest Further improvements for regular workforce	Rather modest Strong reforms (conditionality, activation, cuts in benefits)

provided only for a short period of time (up to six months). It follows from this that for the large part of the unemployed population another part of the social protection system was highly relevant: social assistance (minimum income scheme), established in September 1991 as a means-tested assistance of the last resort. This scheme is in fact partly parallel to the UI scheme, as unemployment benefits may be topped up with SA if the level of income after unemployment benefit is below the living minimum of the household. In contrast to the UI scheme, SA is administered by municipalities, which are, however, in no way responsible for ALMP measures. This means that there is a dual system in terms of income protection (UI and SA), while job mediation and ALMPs are integrated within PES for all the unemployed, irrespective of whether they are UB or SA claimants. Nevertheless, later some minor activation programmes were imposed on municipalities as a part of activation of the SA claimants (see below).

13.3.1 Benefit entitlements

The UI system was established in 1990 by a government decree and redefined in February 1991 by the Employment Act 1/1991 Coll. ('Zákon o zaměstnanosti'). Since 1993, UI has been funded by employers' and employees' contributions under the control of Czech Social Security Administration ('Česká správa sociálního zabezpečení'). There are no tax subsidies to UI.

The basic characteristics of the original system were in some aspects similar to the system in Germany, which served as a model that time (see Table 13.2). This first benefit in 1990 was quite encompassing and generous, with a replacement rate 60 per cent of the previous income provided for one year for all previously employed, former students/school leavers, and mothers with children up to 3 years of age. A special benefit rate (90 per cent of previous income for the first six months) was paid to employees made redundant for 'structural reasons' (mass lay-offs) (Decree 195/1989 of the Federal Ministry of Labor and Social Affairs).

From February 1991 until the end of 1991 this special rate was changed to 65 per cent, and since August 1991 the maximum benefit level was applied at 1.5 times the minimum wage. Since social assistance was established only in September 1991, the twelve-month duration of unemployment benefits implemented in the original system was particularly important in preventing hardship among the unemployed.

Table 13.2. Basic parameters of the unemployment insurance and social assistance system in 1990 and in 2009

	Year 1990 [Decree of FMLSA 195/1989], and 1991 [Employment Act 1/991 Coll.],	Year 2009 [Employment Act 435/2004 Coll.]
Basic characteristics of the unemployment insurance system		
Distribution logic	Tax funded	Mandatory contribution based (social insurance)
Benefit logic	Replaces previous income at given rate	
Eligibility criteria	Registration at local employment office, 1 year of work in last 3 years (no waiting period)	
Basic benefit period	12 months/6 months since 1992	5 months standard rate (since 2009), longer for older workers
Level of the benefit	60% of income (but max of 2,400 Czechoslovak crowns after 6 months)	65% of net income for first 2 months, 50% for 3rd and 4th month, 45% for rest of benefit period
Special rules related to demographic and economic status of the claimants (categories)		
For school leavers	School leavers are entitled to benefits at fixed rates	School leavers are excluded (1 year of contributions required)
For older workers (above 50)	None	Older workers qualify for prolonged benefit duration since 2004: 8 months (when 50–55), 11 (when over 55 years)
For ALMP participants	70% (since 1991)	Benefit level set at 60% of previous net work income
For recipient made redundant (collective dismissals due to restructuring)	90% of previous income in 1990, 65% in 1991 (for first six months)	None
For recipients with no prior reference income	Fixed amount (all people were included)	0.11–0.15 gross average wage (see Table 13.3)
For repeatedly unemployed (with employment between unemployment spells)	None	Unemployed are eligible for a new benefit period after having worked for 6 months (since 1999), later 3 months (since 2004)
	Year 1991 [Acts No. 463/1991 and No. 482/1991 Coll.]	Year 2009 [Acts No. 110/2006 and 111/2006 Coll.]
Basic characteristics of the social assistance system		
Distribution logic	Tax funded, administered by municipalities	
Benefit logic	Living minimum provided to each person – it consists from the part for personal needs and part for needs of the household. The household's living minimum is the sum of living minimum of its individual members.	Living or existence minimum for personal needs. Special 'supplement for housing' (doplatek na bydlení) is now paid to cover all reasonable housing costs.
Eligibility criteria	Means and income-tested	Means and income-tested Young people living with parents excluded because of parents' incomes

Basic benefit period	Indefinite if other conditions are met	Indefinite, but only existence minimum after 6 months
Institutionally set level of the benefit (fixed rates)	1,200 CZK for single person	3,126 CZK for single person (increase is due to inflation)
Special rules related to demographic and economic status of the claimants (categories)		
People who cannot work for objective reasons (e.g. old age and disability pensioners, people over 65, parents of small children)	Living minimum, not required to look for work	Living minimum + 50% of difference between existence and living minimum, may be increased further to living minimum if specific conditions are met, not required to look for work
	Special benefits for people with heavy disabilities or elderly above 70 years (e.g. telephone, special aids for the handicapped)	dtto
People with special nutrition needs (diet)	600 CZK	650–1,800 CZK depending on the type of diet (since 2003)

Source: Authors, on the basis of laws and decrees included in LexData system.

After this initial phase of institutional establishment, benefit levels and entitlements were, however, successively reduced, something typical for many Central and Eastern European countries (Vodopivec et al., 2003). The most important change in this second phase of policy development in the UI system came into effect in January 1992, when the maximum benefit duration was shortened from twelve to six months and the benefit level was set at 60 per cent of previous net income for the first three months and 50 per cent for next three. Thereafter benefit rates were frequently lowered over time (see Table 13.3).

In 1991 an SA system (designed as a support scheme of last resort for all people without proper basic income – both for those 'able-bodied' and for older and severely handicapped people) was adopted in the Czech Republic. SA includes several kinds of regular and discretionary lump sum benefits, some of which are provided to specific groups or for specific purposes (e.g. benefits for heating to old people, or benefits for the school needs of children). The most important of these benefits is the repeated monthly benefit for people without other 'sufficient' earnings/incomes (see Table 13.2). Each person in a household has the right to a certain amount of the living minimum aimed to cover the personal needs set with respect to the age of the person. In addition, an amount covering 'household needs' (mainly housing costs) is provided to the household.

Until the 2000s, both UI and SA remained essentially unchanged. The only significant change in UI was as part of the 1997 austerity package of V. Klaus, who was Prime Minister in the centre-right government from 1993 to 1997. At this time, UI replacement rates were reduced to 50 per cent for the initial period and 40 per cent for the subsequent one (see Table 13.3). However, as a reaction to growing unemployment in the late 1990s, in 1999 the ceiling for UI benefit was raised from 1.5 to 2.5 times the living minimum (and 1.8–2.8 times the living

Table 13.3. Generosity of unemployment insurance (1990–2010)

Valid since	Basic rate[a]	Reduced rates	If in ALMP	If not employed before benefit	Set minimum/maximum UI amount	Average/maximum UI amount (CSK, CZK)
January 1990	60% of previous net earnings	(Max 2,400 CSK after 6 months)	Same as standard rate	Fixed amount (1,000 CSK)	Min 1,000 CSK/no ceiling,	No information/not defined
February 1991	60% first 6 months	50% subsequent 6 months		Fixed amount at rate of the living minimum	The living minimum no ceiling	1,562/not defined
May 1992	60% first 3 months	50% subsequent 3 months	70% in retraining course	← % of living minimum	No minimum/ 1.5 times more than the living minimum 1.8 times more for ALMP participants	1,351/2,400
December 1997	50% first 3 months	40% following 3 months	60% in retraining course	← % of living minimum	1.5 of living minimum, 1.8 for ALMP	2,534
October 1999					max 2.5 of living	2,529
October 2004		45% for rest of benefit period (3 months)			minimum, 2.8 for ALMP	3,562/10,250
January 2007		months)	60% when in retraining course (0.14 of GAW if not employed)	0.12 (first 3 months) and 0.11 (for rest of period) of GAW	0.58 of GAW, 0.65 in ALMP	4,830/11,389
January 2009	65% first 2 months	50% 3–4 month, 45% for the rest of benefit period (1, 4, or 7 months)	not employed)	0.15 (first 2 months), 0.12 (3–4 month), 0.11 (rest of period) of GAW	No minimum/ 0.58 of GAW, 0.65 in ALMP	5,853/13,307
November 2009 (never valid)	80% first 2 months	50% 3–4 month, 45% for the rest of benefit period (2, 5, or 8 months)	85% when in retraining course (0.14 of GAW if not employed)	0.15 (first 2 months), 0.12 (3–4 month), 0.11 (rest of period) of GAW	No minimum/ 0.58 of GAW, 0.85 in ALMP	5,853/ 13,307

| January 2010 | 65% first 2 months | 50% 3–4 month, 45% for the rest of benefit period (1, 4, or 7 months) | 60% when in retraining course (0.14 of GAW if not employed) | 0.15 (first 2 months), 0.12 (3–4 month), 0.11 (rest of period) of GAW | No minimum/ 0.58 of GAW[b], 0.65 in ALMP | –/13,280 |

[a]Average monthly net wage in previous employment or income in previous entrepreneurship.
[b]GAW = gross average wage in national economy in 1–3 quarter of previous year. GAW is announced by MLSA on basis of CZSO calculations.

minimum for ALMP participants) by the Social Democratic government elected in 1998. The other important changes in UI came into effect with the new Employment Act 435/2004 Coll. in October 2004. This reform improved income support for the regular workforce, while restricting the access to the benefits for the marginal workforce. The UI benefit rate during the second three months was increased from 40 to 45 per cent of net income (in accordance with the demands of ILO treaty no. 168, which requires minimum unemployment benefit to be at least 45 per cent of net income). The benefit period of UI for workers older than 50 years of age was also extended to nine and twelve months for those with contribution periods of twenty-five and thirty years, respectively, not only to reflect an understanding that 'older people have much worse conditions for looking for jobs than younger people' (MLSA, 2004), but also to partially eliminate the penalties on early retirees that were implemented in 2001, when pension reductions for early retirement were increased (see above). On the other hand, in the same reform the entitlement to UI was restricted for people without sufficient previous employment and contribution periods. This measure affected mainly school leavers, who practically lost all entitlement to UI.

Similarly, important changes have been incorporated into SA in 2006, when the benefit covering housing costs was separated from the benefits covering the personal needs of the household's members and a new 'supplement for housing' benefit was established to cover full reasonable housing expenses. Most importantly, in parallel with the living minimum for personal needs provided to the unemployed who cooperated properly with the employment office, children, and elderly people over 65, the existence minimum (at lower rate of about two-thirds of living minimum) has been implemented for the unemployed who did not cooperate properly with the unemployment offices or for the claimants who did not fulfil other commitments like school attendance of children.

A number of changes were seen in UI towards the end of the first decade of the 2000s. Firstly, in September 2008 a reform was adopted shortening the maximum benefit entitlement period by one month, but improving replacement rates for the first two months (to 65 per cent). Regulations concerning older workers were unaffected. Then in March 2009 the centre-right government lost its fragile majority in parliament and resigned, which gave more influence to the opposition in the negotiations around the anti-crisis package being prepared in parliament.

When this was adopted in April, it included increases in UI benefits: the replacement rate was to be increased from 65 to 80 per cent in the first two months, and to 85 per cent in case of those participating in labour market training programmes. The period of benefit entitlement was also to be prolonged by one month, to six, nine, or twelve months, depending on age. However, the new non-political (administrative) government soon accepted the goal of diminishing the public budget deficit as its top priority, and these planned improvements to UI were cancelled in October 2009, just before they came into force.

13.3.2 Job-seeking criteria

Since the origins of UI in 1991, claimants have been required to actively seek work, to be capable and available for work, and to accept job offers recommended by the employment office (Vodopivec et al., 2003). The unemployed who in the last six months left a job without good reason more than once, or were made redundant for misconduct, were denied eligibility to UI benefits (see Appendix 13.A). The SA created in 1991 also included the standard means of the behavioural and family status control (see Appendix 13.A). The entitlement for the benefit provided in social need was not intended to be unconditional, but was meant to be based on an assessment of an individuals' situation, on which a decision about the most proper form of intervention would then be based (Federal Government of Czechoslovakia, 1991).

Important changes of benefit conditionality were initiated first within the UI scheme, but they were adopted relatively late, coming into force only with the new Employment Act in 2004. The explicit objective of these changes was to make people look for work more intensively. Most of the previous conditions remained in place, but they were supplemented with some new disqualifying conditions, notably a stricter definition of suitable work, which might now be temporary work. No reference was any longer made to an individuals' qualification level or family situation when considering whether a job offer is suitable. Failure to take up such offers could lead to removal from the employment office's register of claimants, being in which was a precondition for benefit entitlement. The unemployed could also be removed from the register if they did not cooperate with employment office or if they failed to fill the obligations detailed in their Individual Action Plan (IAP). At the same time, in an effort to promote incentives to work, earnings in temporary jobs were disregarded up to the level of 50 per cent of the national minimum wage when assessing unemployment benefit entitlements (Table 13.4).

Disqualification criteria in UI were further expanded in 2007. People who during the six months prior to registration were made redundant due to severe misbehaviour or violation of working rules, as stipulated in the Labour Code, were henceforth excluded from the employment office register, and illegal work was added to the reasons leading to disqualification. Under the new rules, the unemployed could furthermore only return to the register six months after their initial disqualification (Bukovjan, 2007).

Recently, the reforms in job-seeking criteria have continued both in UI and SA. In 2008 a strong new activation element was introduced within SA. After six

Table 13.4. Special rules for behaviour of benefit recipients in unemployment insurance and social assistance in 1990 and in 2009

	Year 1990 [Decree of FMLSA 195/1989], and 1991 [Employment Act 1/991 Coll.],	Year 2009 [Employment Act 435/2004 Coll.]
Special rules for behaviour of UI claimants		
Unemployment behaviour expectations and control	Unemployed are required to actively seek work	
Previous employment behaviour	Since 1991 people who are sacked for work dereliction or leave work 'on their own will' are denied benefits.	
Disregard on earnings for the unemployed entitled for the benefits	None	Disregard on earnings at level of half of minimum income since 2004 (about 4,000 CZK)
	Year 1991 [Acts No. 463/1991 and No. 482/1991 Coll.]	Year 2009 [Acts No. 110/2006 and 111/2006 Coll.]
Special rules for behaviour of SA claimants		
Special rules for people who did not bring to Social assistance administration the Individual Action Plan done in cooperation with Labour Offices	None	Existence minimum only (before 1.1.2009 also SA workers had to elaborate the so-called activation plans with SA claimants)
Special rules for people who work or are in public service jobs	None	Disregard applied at 70% of benefit, bonus 50% of difference between existence minimum and living minimum
Special rules for people in the evidence of PES	None	Existence minimum + 30% of difference between existence minimum and living minimum
Special rules for people who are in debts in alimony for more then three months	None	Existence minimum only

Source: Authors, on the basis of laws and decrees included in LexData system.

months of SA receipt the claimants are now only entitled to the 'existence minimum', and not the more generous 'living minimum' as before. Only if they participate in public works between 20 and 30 hours per week will they be entitled for the living minimum, and if they work more than 30 hours they receive a bonus amounting to half the difference between the living and existence minima. Municipalities are thus being pushed to use SA as an activation tool, in parallel with the ALMP measures provided by employment offices. The two sectors of activation are, however, not coordinated; according to our own research at a number of employment offices, for example, the mediators working there do not generally know whether the unemployed receive SA benefit at the reduced level.

Since January 2009 the UI benefit period has been shortened from six to five months in order to 'make people to look more actively for work'. Where previously an IAP was voluntary for jobseekers, since 2009 it has also been made compulsory, and employment offices are obliged to offer IAPs to all jobseekers who have been registered for longer than five months. As before, those benefit claimants who do not fulfil their duties (as outlined in the IAP) or refuse to participate in requalification measures might be excluded from the register.

The number of jobseekers excluded from the register of employment offices within a year period gives a good indication of the effects of the implementation of this stricter system of behavioural conditions in unemployment protection. In the 1990s the length of the exclusion from the register was three months. About 10 per cent of unemployed claimants were suspended from benefit for this reason in 1995, and in subsequent years this rate fell to 8 per cent (Homola and Kotrusová, 1998). Since 2004 the suspension period has been prolonged to six months and, as discussed, there are now more grounds in the legislation to exclude jobseekers from the register. As shown in Figure 13.2, the absolute number of claimants excluded for behavioural reasons per year rose from about 30,000 in 1996–7 to 98,000 in 2007, and to 91,000 in 2008, a period in which unemployment was declining.

It is not surprising therefore that between 1991 and 2006 the numbers of recipients of SA gradually increased, while the numbers of people on unemployed benefits declined. Until 2004 this was due to increasing numbers of the long-term unemployed, while after 2004 it was instead because of tighter eligibility rules in UI, especially for the young, the long-term unemployed, and those unemployed dependent on SA but assessed as inactive in their job search and dependent, who were excluded particularly frequently as a result of the above changes in eligibility

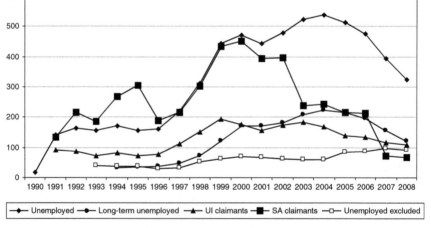

Figure 13.2. Unemployment, long-term unemployed (12+ months), UI claimants, SA claimants, and the unemployed excluded from registers (yearly averages in thousand)

Source: Unemployment: employment statistical yearbook 2008 (MLSA, 2009*b*). Data not available for 1990–2; long-term unemployment: www.mpsv.cz (SSZ); social assistance: MLSA (2003, 2006, 2008, 2009*a*). The data about social assistance were collected once a year in 1993–2002 and represent the number of social assistance recipients who received a benefit at least once a year. Since 2003 the data have been collected four times a year and present an average number of benefits paid per month. Since 2007 the data of administrative database system have been used rather than paper returns.

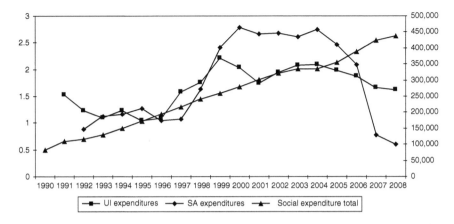

Figure 13.3. UI expenditures and SA expenditures as % of total social expenditures, social protection expenditure total in billions CZK

Note: Data on social assistance from 2007 and 2008 (living and existence minimum + supplement for housing) are not fully comparable with data for previous years.

Source: Unemployment insurance: Employment service of MLSA and MLSA statistics published online at www.mpsv.cz. Data for 2008 are from Budget Fulfilment Report (published by Ministry of Finance). Social assistance: MLSA (2003, 2006, 2008, 2009a). Total social expenditure consists of all social expenditures including, for example, pensions but without health care (*Source*: VUPSV, 2009).

rules (see Figure 13.2). We can also observe (in Figure 13.3 below) that expenditures on SA were substantially reduced due to the reform in 2006 (between 2004 and 2006 they dropped due to decreasing unemployment rates).

13.4 ASSESSING CHANGES IN CZECH UNEMPLOYMENT PROTECTION

In this section, we analyse the Czech reform trajectory in relation to the three dimensions – risk re-categorization, homogenization, and activation – of post-industrial unemployment benefit reform laid out in the introductory chapter of the volume.

In the Czech case, the story within SA is largely one of tightening conditionality, especially after 2004. This relates to unemployment status, eligibility conditions, and activation requirements. Benefit levels, benefit duration, and the coverage of the SA system (and thus the number of claimants) decreased significantly (see above). On the other hand, within UI benefit levels and durations were set at a relatively modest level from the introduction of the system, and this probably explains why only minor changes were adopted on this dimension in the subsequent ten years. However, considerable restrictions of access are nonetheless evident regarding coverage and eligibility. Fewer claimants became eligible for the unemployment benefit. The share of unemployed persons in receipt of unemployment benefits fell from 64.8 per cent in 1991 to 28.1 per cent in 2006 (see Figure 13.1). This trend may be in part explained by the changed economic conditions (fewer people in stable jobs which help to qualify for UI, and more long-term unemployed), and but is partly also a consequence of the measures implemented (restrictions in access to UI benefits).

Some processes of risk re-categorization are evident, but not to the extent of merging of benefit claimant groups. People in different situations have always been perceived and approached as groups with different needs and duties, and this remains largely the case. Certainly, part of the category of elderly workers has been de facto transferred into unemployment protection with the restrictions on access to early exit, but even within UI this groups continues to enjoy more generous entitlements than other groups. This means that the modest risk re-categorization of early retirees which has taken place has been accompanied with differentiation of the entitlements. Inversely, some previously included claimant groups such as school leavers were actually excluded from coverage of UI, a process which can be seen as a form of restrictive risk re-categorization.

Other inactive groups have been left aside in this process: parents caring for children below 4 and disabled people are covered by different social protection schemes (parental benefit, invalidity pension), and no attempt was made in the Czech case to include them in UI or the unemployment category. During the seventeen years between 1990 and 2007, the number of full invalidity pensions paid monthly increased by 10 per cent, while the number of partial invalidity pensions increased in the same period by 60 per cent (see Figure 13.1), circumstances which (among other factors) led to the reform of the invalidity system in 2008.[4] But there are indications of the continuing use of invalidity benefits as an alternative to unemployment benefit. Parental benefit is provided in the Czech Republic until a child is aged 4, the most expansive time period in EU. Administration of parental benefit and other 'social support benefits' (e.g. child benefit) was indeed merged with UI at the street level, and these benefits are now administered by the PES. However, this administrative merger does not indicate any attempt at risk re-categorization for reasons of labour force mobilization, but was instead driven by administrative cost-efficiency considerations: while employment offices took over these tasks from municipalities, they have always been very careful to keep their delivery separate from the delivery of benefits turned to the labour market.

The status boundaries between various beneficiary groups within the system of social protection as a whole remained either unchanged or became even more pronounced, even within the same functional category (e.g. unemployed, people in receipt of disability benefit). Social insurance and social assistance have always been and have remained strictly separated both by function and administration, in spite of the fact that the numbers of the unemployed eligible for SA benefits has become higher over time than the number eligible for unemployment benefits. The eligibility criteria for claimants of UI, SA, incapacity benefits, and parental

---

[4] Data presented are in one aspect disputable. Invalidity pensions are not transposed to old-age pensions in the Czech Republic as it is common in some other European countries and this could lead to the exaggeration of the problem indicated by sole numbers of invalidity pensions (Bruthansová et al., 2002).

benefit are very different. At the beginning of 2000s, more elderly workers have been covered by unemployment protection (restrictions in early exit), but later people above 50 and 55 have been provided with more generous entitlements for UI.

In contrast to the assumption of greater homogenization in social rights for the unemployed, as outlined in the introductory chapter of this volume, in the Czech case we instead find evidence of greater diversification. There is obviously an 'insider–outsider' distinction behind this process. In terms of caseloads, we have shown the increasingly 'residual' role of the UI system when compared to SA during the 1990s. In the period between 2006 and 2009, by contrast, we see the strong efforts to marginalize SA scheme by excluding parts of the recipients completely outside the social protection system and thus reducing overall claimant numbers.

A major trend after 2003 was increasing economic incentives to work, and the efforts to make benefit receipt more conditional on working or work-seeking activity were stepped up both in UI and SA. This activation trend is clearly visible not only in policy and government documents but also in the data on the numbers of claimants sanctioned for failing to fulfil their duties. This trend could be described as mainly negative activation, based essentially on the instrument of repressive sanctions. On the other hand, and in line with limited risk re-categorization more generally, activation in benefit systems other than UI and SA is not evident. For example, people with disabilities are permitted to work while receiving invalidity pensions as long as their health status corresponds to their benefit status. Similarly, parents caring for small children are permitted to work while claiming parental benefit but it is not demanded nor expected and only rarely used in practice (Hašková, 2007; Kuchařová et al., 2006). In fact, the only category of the inactive which has been 'activated' in the Czech Republic were (potential) early pensioners, as the 2001 Pension Act implemented stricter sanctions on early exit due to the expected deficits in the Pension budget and an increasing number of early pensioners.

13.5 UNDERSTANDING CHANGE: GUARDING THE LEGITIMACY OF TRANSFORMATION IN FACE OF THE ECONOMIC PRESSURES

The trends evidenced in Czech unemployment protection are due to coincidence of several factors. First, unemployment protection reforms can be understood in relation to the specific conditions/needs of transformation from socialist to a capitalist economy (the transformation thesis). Second, the reform path has been shaped by the political strategies adopted by the government and the dynamics of public opinion and partisan politics. Finally, it is crucial to take economic conditions into account, in particular the pressure of reducing public budget deficits and promoting long-term economic sustainability.

13.5.1 The transformation thesis examined

The Czech Republic had a very different starting position from most of the other countries analysed in this volume, with the exception of Hungary. There was little previous experience with unemployment protection, and the transformation to a market economy was expected to bring harsh social impacts and imbalances in public finance. The period after 1989 can be seen as the continuation of the 'emergency welfare state' (Inglot, 2008), which aimed to adopt appropriate measures (either temporary or more systemic). It may not be a surprise that some reforms proved to be badly designed or not functional, and have been subjected to subsequent alterations.

The new system of unemployment protection was created in a context of strong political demand for fast solutions. A process of experimentation and institutional learning followed, in which the timing of the transformation process itself played a crucial role. In the initial period (1990–2), unemployment protection and SA were created as systems with broad coverage, lenient eligibility, relatively high generosity, and low demands on jobseekers. However, due to the threat of increasing unemployment and increases in benefit expenditure, the UI system was redesigned as early as 1991, and became less generous. At the same time, SA played an important role as a measure of last resort for those not or insufficiently covered by social insurance. The priority was to achieve full coverage, and to alleviate the risks of poverty with rather 'moderate' but quite accessible benefits.

Since the risk of unemployment was managed effectively thanks to anti-bankruptcy policy, UI and SA remained mainly concentrated on relatively narrow categories of the marginal work force. As a result, UI benefits could be kept at rather low level of generosity with limited popular disquiet. The 'regular work force', which represented the potential source of social protest, was not expected to become unemployed often or for particularly lengthy periods of time.

When in 1997–8 an economic slowdown led to widespread indebtedness, many post-socialist manufacturing firms were declared bankrupt and many workers had to be laid off. The government now felt obliged to help the affected regular labour force to overcome this situation. The ceiling of the UI (maximum benefit level) was raised from 1.5 to 2.5 times more than the living minimum by the Social Democratic government in 1999 in order to provide better unemployment benefits to previously well-positioned workers, while conditionality increased at the same time (see Table 13.3). At this time (like in the initial transformation period in 1991), the UI scheme was recognized in the Czech Republic as the scheme relevant for the 'insiders'. Except for this change, the system remained relatively stable until 2004. During this period, however, the protection of those at the margin of the labour force deteriorated due to delays of revaluation of the living minimum and decreasing replacement rates of SA benefits.

In 2004 the Czech Republic joined the European Union, which greatly helped to attract foreign investment, intensified international trade, and supported the economic boom. Continuing high economic growth during 2005–8 (4–6 per cent GDP per year), and the less intensive restructuring process, contributed to a reduction in unemployment between 2005 and 2008 (Statistical Annex, Table A.5). In the UI system, tighter conditionality and restricted access was imposed while benefits were slightly improved, albeit with differentiations depending on age. This was followed by improved replacement rates for the short-term unemployed, evidently with the aim to protect better the insiders now more reliably identified thanks to stricter eligibility criteria. On the other hand, strong reforms in SA were introduced which deteriorated the access to benefits.

13.5.2 Political process and public opinion

Initially, two social policy goals were explicit: firstly, easing the social burden of, and thus weakening social barriers to, economic reform; and secondly, contributing to the activation of working-age and employable population and improving self-reliance while still guaranteeing a living minimum for everyone (Miller, 1992). Until 1997 the government in the Czech Republic was led by the right-wing Civic Democratic Party (ODS), which contributed to the reduction in the unemployment protection system both in 1992 and 1997, since this government preferred to improve work incentives in general. In practice, it in fact protected the jobs of insiders and provided easy access to SA benefits for the marginal workforce, guided by political considerations of 'protest avoidance'.

This temporal policy was in the early 1990s supported by measures of labour shedding with respect to some groups of workforce (e.g. forced retirements for working pensioners and early pensions and long parental leave for mothers) with the intention to 'clear the market'. Since this strategy succeeded both in guaranteeing a low level of unemployment and a low level of poverty, from the immediate post-communist period until the late 1990s there was little interest in changing the system. However, the increase in unemployment during 1997–9 contributed to the improvements in UI benefits, in line with the protest avoidance strategy. These also led to more differentiation between UI and SA, in line with the aim of dividing potentially influential protest groups (Vanhuysse, 2006).

This process of differentiation continued later with more intensity. In the period between 2004 and 2009, several reform steps were undertaken both in UI and in SA. In the UI system both the reforms adopted by Social Democrats (2004) as well as right-wing Civic Democrats (2007) brought not only more conditionality and emphasis on activation but also better benefits for older workers and the short-term unemployed. In contrast, the reforms in SA were directed towards more conditionality, stricter access, and cuts in benefit levels. The main reforms of SA scheme in 2006 were undertaken under the rule of ČSSD. Some Social Democratic politicians stated that they recognized the need to change the system, which was increasingly seen to lead to long-term welfare dependence. In 2007–8, the new right-wing cabinet continued with further and more radical reforms of SA.

Changes in both schemes were in many aspects inspired by the reform experience in the United Kingdom during the 1980s (see Clasen 2005 and Chapter 2 in this volume), and were accompanied by a strong right-wing ideological ethos (even during periods of Social Democratic government). This can be explained by two factors. First, the central role of the narrow groups of policy experts and policymakers who always helped to maintain continuity in the 'emergency welfare state' during communist and post-communist times (see Inglot, 2008), and who at the end of 1990s accused the SA system of being outdated because of lacking work incentives. Second, under conditions of economic pressure the Social Democratic government perceived the low legitimacy of the SA among the public, and accepted that it, rather than the other parts of the social protection system (pensions, UI), should be a target of cuts.

Although inspired by the UK example, the Czech government nonetheless decided to give more space to the equivalence principle in the UI scheme, which should reward 'the more deserving' unemployed (short-term, with higher previous income and contributions), while other 'less deserving' groups of SA claimants were being activated. The main reason for this was 'moral' and ideological considerations: despite their opportunistic policies, political elites have since the 1990s influenced the public discourse and media by the propagation of strong neo-liberal ideas. This discourse blamed those unemployed who were long-term SA benefit recipients for lack of morals. On the other hand, the recession during 1997–9 convinced policymakers that even the insiders may be hit strongly by unemployment.

In later years, SA came to increasingly be seen by the public as a measure for people 'cheating the system' and avoiding work. Public opinion was especially unfavourable towards Roma, who were regarded as the main group of SA claimants. In research conducted by STEM (2004), 66 per cent of respondents thought that the contemporary level of benefits was not motivating for job search and social benefits should be lower so that people would have to take less qualified work, participate in ALMPs, or move to another region to look for work. It was clear that retrenchments of social assistance would not meet with any public resistance. When the centre-right government coalition introduced the reform of public finance in 2007, making reference to long-term dependency and 'misuse of social system', reforms were undertaken without much public interest and a lack of public debate: the media on the whole supported the reform processes. Trade unions were also unable to influence these reforms. Though they criticized the reforms in UI and SA of the centre-right government in 2007 and 2008, the negotiations between the government and the unions in tripartite bodies were purely formal, and the government did not take on board any arguments raised by the unions.[5]

13.5.3 Economic austerity

A final explanation of the pattern of reforms in Czech unemployment protection relates to economic constraints, and especially the perceived threat of growing public budget deficits. In international comparison, expenditure on UI and SA in the Czech Republic was always rather modest, even during periods of increased unemployment. Nevertheless, in the context of the lower legitimacy of income support for the unemployed compared to the other parts of social expenditure, the

[5] During the Social Democratic government (1998–2006), negotiations with the trade unions were more serious. However, the inclination of the government to improve the UI scheme and let the SA scheme deteriorate was motivated by electoral considerations rather than by the influence of the trade unions.

pressures on public expenditure stemming from the increasing pension and health-care expenditure and other pressures, such as the conditions for adopting the euro, represented influential factors contributing to the changes in the unemployment protection system.

Social spending was first seriously hit as a consequence of economic crisis in 1997 (see Figure 13.3). Because of contribution-based funding of UI, its relatively modest benefit levels, and strict eligibility criteria, the economic cost of the UI system actually never became a serious problem. The real problem was seen in the growing costs of SA system to which more and more people were directed, especially after 1998. The most significant groups of claimants were single people, single parents, and large families (the latter often from the Roma ethnic group) (Sirovátka, 2006). The coincidence of relatively high expenditure on SA since 1999 with the low legitimacy of SA benefits among the public and policymakers created an incentive for preparing the reform of SA implemented in 2006.

13.6 CONCLUSIONS

The reforms of the unemployment protection in the Czech Republic followed a trajectory which differed from many other 'old' EU countries. The original system of UI as designed at the beginning of 1990s was rather modest, while mass unemployment and public protest were prevented more through the deliberate anti-bankruptcy policy of the government, which kept a majority share in bank sector while tolerating mutual indebtedness of ineffective companies. In contrast, the SA scheme was originally designed to be quite generous and easily accessible. The two schemes were in fact 'converging' for a time: unemployment benefits were provided for a short period of six months, with a low replacement rate (60, later 50 and 40 per cent), up to a low ceiling of 1.5 times more than the living minimum for a single person (SA benefit). On the other hand, SA benefits for households with children were close to average wage or even higher (in case of family of four). Subsequently, however, SA was scaled back in a series of small steps, while moderate improvements were implemented in UI whenever unemployment tended to increase and threatened the regular insider workforce. Reforms after 2004 became increasingly radical, with a growing tendency towards differentiation of both schemes in terms of generosity, while greater conditionality appeared as a key feature in both. This saw stricter definition of suitable work and more severe sanctions in both the UI scheme and the SA scheme.

With the exception of a brief period in the early 1990s, then, social rights for the unemployed in the Czech Republic have not become more homogeneous. On the contrary, a clear trend towards diversification can be identified in a number of respects, and particularly with the generosity of UI and SA increasingly diverging. Nor is there considerable evidence of the pool of unemployed people being made wider. Schemes for parents and invalids remained strictly separate from UI and SA, and while older workers were integrated back into the pool of unemployed by the closure of formal exit routes, they continued to receive rather more generous entitlements than other workers, and especially young workers, who were excluded from entitlement to UI and SA altogether.

While trends towards broadening the pool of unemployed and homogenizing their rights are limited in the Czech case, there has been a strong push to implement of the principle of activation. Activating measures have been introduced both in SA and UI, though – in line with the growing differentiation of treatment of different claimants groups – these are stronger and more punitive in the former scheme than the latter. Particularly for the more irregular parts of the workforce, the current Czech system of unemployment protection thus seems to be one of strictest unemployment in Europe, in terms of both generosity and conditionality.

All in all, the rationale behind the recent evolution in Czech unemployment protection seems to be sharpening the distinction between the deserving (short-term unemployed, older workers, regular workforce) and the undeserving (long-term unemployed, younger workers, marginal workforce) parts of the unemployed population. We have argued that the most important factors that have influenced the development of this policy logic have been the nature and timing of the major transformation process related to post-communist transition and the political logic of directing most resources to the most powerful and legitimate groups of claimants, with the latter dynamic intensified since the late 1990s by economic and budgetary constraints.

Appendix 13.A Main changes in job-seeking conditions in unemployment insurance and social assistance in Czech Republic (1990–2009)

	Unemployment insurance	Social assistance
1991	• Exclusion from benefit entitlement if suitable job is refused, the definition of which takes account of health, qualification and skills, age, duration of previous employment, and family situation/ possibilities of accommodation. • Has not lost repeatedly job without good reason or was not made redundant because of misconduct. • Sanction of exclusion from register for a period of 3 months – consequently the complete loss of the benefit entitlements.	• *Income condition*: have to prove circumstances (e.g. that income is less than living minimum) in 8 days. No possibility exists to increase income by own effort: by working, by selling property, etc. • *Disqualifying status conditions*: people not listed in the register of jobseekers (with exception for people 65+, disabled, parents of small children, people caring about disabled and elderly, etc.) including people excluded from registers of employment office due to non-cooperation/misconduct. • Those who evidently do not try to improve their situation by own effort are excluded from SA.
2004	• School (and university) graduates no longer eligible for unemployment benefits unless they fulfil the employment record condition (i.e. 12 months of employment within the last three years). • Stricter definition of 'suitable job': does not take necessarily into account qualification and skills, age, duration of the previous employment, and family situation/ possibilities of accommodation. Definition includes temporary jobs that last for longer than 3 months and amount to 80% of full-time job. • *Work incentive*: disregard of earnings below half of minimum (monthly) wage (temporary or part-time job) • *Sanction*: exclusion from register for the period of 6 months which implies a complete loss of the benefit entitlement. • Compliance with the Individual Action Plan commitments (signing IAP is voluntary).	
2005	• Stricter definition of a 'suitable job' for people unemployed more than 12 months. Claimants have to accept also job offers shorter than 3 months or at least 50% of normal working time.	
2006		• *Qualifying status conditions*: unsatisfactory social circumstances, lack financial resources and if endangered by social exclusion • *Disqualifying status conditions*: listed in the register of jobseekers more than 12 months and have refused to take up short-term employment or to participate in an active

(continued)

Appendix 13.A (Continued)

	Unemployment insurance	Social assistance
		employment policy programme without serious reason. • *Lowered benefits*: existence (subsistence) minimum instead of living minimum applied (based on discretionary decision) in cases where willingness to cooperate with the Social Department in order to improve own incomes by working (or other possibilities) is lacking. Pensioners and parents caring about children below 4 years or dependent person/person older than 80 years accused from this rule. • *Disregard*: only 70% of income from work and 80% of income from sickness and unemployment benefits is taken into account when testing means of subsistence. • Special bonuses which increases the level of the living minimum for jobseekers after 1 year of unemployment, provided they require special assistance with job search (600 CZK) or have proved increased costs of job search (300 CZK). • An activation plan should be elaborated for those who are welfare dependent for more than six months.
2007	• The unemployed person whose job in the past 6 months was terminated for breaking laws in connection to their work are not eligible for the benefit	• *Disqualifying status conditions*: people who refused to take up short-term employment or to participate in an active employment policy programme without serious reason are excluded for 3 months. • Bonuses increasing the living minimum for active jobseekers were cancelled.
2008	• The unemployment insurance benefit is withheld from jobseekers who in previous six months ended suitable employment arranged by the employment office at least at two occasions without good reason.	• Since January 2009 after 6 months of social assistance benefit receipt, the recipients are entitled only to the allowance for living which would be computed with use of 'existence minimum' instead of 'living minimum'. In case that they participate in public service programme (at least 20–30 hours per month), they would be entitled for the allowance for living computed with use of the living minimum. If they work more than 30 hours they would receive a bonus in amount of half of difference between living minimum and subsistence minimum. Similarly, those who are employed on low earnings get this bonus. • Possibility of in-kind benefits or benefits provided to the 'substitute' recipient in cases of their misuse or evident risk of

- Sanction for failing to 'announce duty' within 8 days: unemployed have the legal duty to announce any circumstance which could affect their benefit entitlement (including undeclared work).
- Sanctions for refusing to comply with Individual Action Plan (IAP is obligatory) or refusing participation in requalification programme.

misuse. Mean of benefit payment (by cash, electronic payment, food stamps/vouchers) is decided by the benefit provider (municipality).

- Activation plan cancelled as an instrument used by Social Departments of municipalities. Instead Employment Offices obliged to elaborate activation plans with all unemployed after 5 months and claimants are obliged to show it at SA departments.

Source: Authors, on the basis of laws and decrees included in LexData system.

Part II

Cross-National Perspectives

14

Quantity over quality? A European comparison of the changing nature of transitions between non-employment and employment

Werner Eichhorst, Regina Konle-Seidl,
Alison Koslowski, and Paul Marx

14.1 INTRODUCTION

Recent reforms to unemployment protection systems of the type analysed elsewhere in this volume have largely been justified with reference to increasing employment opportunities. Reforms to these policies and other labour market institutions, it is argued, will make it more likely for unemployed and inactive people of working age to make the transition back into work, harnessing the inclusive potential of post-industrial labour markets. This chapter explores some of the available empirical evidence for such a claim. This analysis also serves to set the stage for a second, related question: is an increasingly inclusive labour market associated with a reduction in job quality, as measured by contract type, for those having most recently made the transition from non-employment to employment? All the countries covered in this volume are included in our cross-national analysis as far as European Labour Force Survey data availability allows. Eight countries are thus fully included in the analysis: Belgium, the Czech Republic, Denmark, France, Hungary, Italy, Spain, and the United Kingdom.

14.2 LINKING UNEMPLOYMENT PROTECTION, ACTIVATION, AND LABOUR MARKET DEVELOPMENTS

As discussed in the introduction to this volume, major trends in contemporary unemployment protection can be understood in relation to a process of triple integration. The case studies in the volume demonstrate that, notwithstanding some variation cross-nationally, there is widespread evidence of moves towards more homogeneous benefit structures, a blurring of the traditional social policy boundaries between the unemployed and other working-age benefit claimants, and a more activating approach to the regulation of unemployment. But while the promotion of more inclusive labour markets through activating labour market and social policies imply that more people should enter the labour market, any expansion in the number of jobs may also be associated with new forms of inequality – or possibly even duality – with respect to the quality of jobs. This may comprise, for example, a wider variety of contract types, more pronounced wage dispersion, and higher barriers to mobility from entry to more stable and better-paid jobs.

Looking at the broad relationship between changes to unemployment protection and developments in labour markets, such a trade-off between quantity and quality of jobs could be the result of any one of three major trends which have occurred in parallel in virtually all European countries: unemployment protection reform, and particularly an increased focus on activation, tertiarization, and increased labour market flexibility. Whether it is labour market changes that have driven the process of unemployment benefit reform, or vice versa, is beyond the scope of this chapter. However, it is reasonable to assume that there is a mutually reinforcing interplay between the growth of the service economy, increasing labour market flexibility, and activating benefit and labour market policies, all of which should lead to a change in certain labour market outcomes. While it may be difficult to accord causal primacy to any one of these sets of factors, empirical analyses can help us evaluate how far labour markets have generally become more inclusive, if more heterogeneous, and what changes there have been in the risk of various non-employed people (not) finding permanent employment over time and across countries.

14.2.1 Activation and its impact on the labour market

Labour market policy across the Organisation for Economic Co-operation and Development (OECD) has moved towards a stronger employment orientation in the past two decades. Activation policies have made passive benefit receipt less legitimate and attractive. The belief is that the road to economic self-sufficiency is taking up a job in order to end benefit dependency. As the contributions to this volume have shown, work support measures like in-work benefits have been implemented in many countries and more integrated services are today offered to job searchers than in the past. Across countries more 'work first' policies have been developed, resulting in less emphasis on extended training programmes or purely 'passive' benefit receipt (see also Konle-Seidl and Eichhorst, 2008). The work requirement stemming from activation policies means that it has become less attractive for the unemployed, including those not actively looking for a job, to claim benefits. As a consequence, the unemployed may either leave the labour force or become genuine jobseekers with lower reservation wages.

In general, both 'demanding' and 'enabling' interventions (or some combinations of the two) promote the exit into regular or subsidized jobs of those who they targeted. However, work requirements and mandatory programme participation do not only affect the fraction of unemployed in activation programmes but also other groups of the labour force, including the unemployed in general as well as the employed – and even the economically inactive members of the working-age population. The employed may be affected indirectly as out-of-work options become less attractive. Wage-bargaining models predict under very general assumptions that this will lead to lower wage demands, as the markup of wages over benefits is reduced. Lower wages will, in turn, be conducive to employment. A necessary condition for this supply-side effect to be present is that there is both a downward pressure on wage setting and an upward move in employment.

From a theoretical perspective, activation may increase wage flexibility by inducing lower reservation wages. Like the lowering of replacement rates, compulsory activation measures such as imposing additional search requirements or mandatory programme participation aim at changing the returns from work relative to benefit receipt. In the end this implies a behavioural change leading to potentially lower reservation wages and higher search efforts, contributing to a strengthening of work incentives (Andersen and Svarer, 2008). Since in-work benefits make employment – even in low-paid jobs – more attractive relative to unemployment, this also facilitates wage moderation. In-work benefits are designed to create work incentives. However, at times when the labour market is weak, they can facilitate continued work attachment for those already in employment, with redistribution and avoidance of poverty becoming more important than employment creation. During a subsequent recovery it can be expected that in-work benefits support outflows from unemployment (see e.g. Immervoll and Pearson, 2009).

14.2.2 Labour market flexibility as a by-product of tertiarization

At the same time, but not necessarily directly related to reforms in unemployment protection and active labour market programmes, the very nature of employment has changed over the last decade. Compared to the situation in 1997 when 27 per cent of all workers in the EU-15 were still employed in manufacturing and 69 per cent in services, by 2009 the service sector made up 74 per cent of overall employment (22 per cent in manufacturing) according to Eurostat data. In most countries, particularly strong growth can be observed in business-related, social, and personal services.

The share of standard, open-ended, full-time contracts, which were the norm for people in manufacturing jobs, has also declined in virtually all European countries. This was not associated with a shrinking number of jobs overall, but rather with an enormous growth of both public and private service sector employment, new types of occupations, and a larger share of flexible or 'atypical' contracts, which are particularly pervasive in the private service sector (OECD, 2001). Notwithstanding differences across countries and service subsectors, it is fair to say that most dynamic parts of the service sector operate outside traditional open-ended, full-time contracts covered by collective agreements, full social insurance coverage, and long tenure. In services, we generally find larger shares of part-time work, fixed-term contracts, self-employment, as well as low pay.

Given the fact that employment rates rose across European countries, this has meant an even larger increase in the absolute number of jobs created by the service sector, which more than compensate for the jobs lost in manufacturing. Hence, there is a strong long-term trend from manufacturing to service sector employment, which makes up for the vast majority of jobs in current European labour markets. Tertiarization is driven by global economic integration, technological change, and, equally important, demographic change, in particular ageing and strongly increasing female labour force participation, which in turn also generates demand for services delivered to households (see e.g. Iversen and Wren, 1998; Regini and Esping-Andersen, 2000; Scharpf, 2000). Technological change and global economic integration tend to be mutually reinforcing, and together accelerate structural change in the economy. This, in turn, makes continued employment in exposed sectors more demanding. Low-skilled workers, whom the manufacturing sector can no longer absorb, face particular difficulties. However, service employment poses different skills demands to manufacturing. Mobility across sectors and occupations generates a major challenge to labour market policies as costly labour supply reduction policies such as early retirement are phased out. Workers with insufficient and obsolete qualifications risk being referred to low-pay and insecure jobs when activated, if the provision of retraining is inappropriate or ineffective. Hence, most entry jobs for labour market entrants and activated non-employed are expected to be provided by the service sector, resulting in a greater heterogeneity of working conditions. The partial deregulation of labour markets has facilitated this.

14.2.3 Partial labour market deregulation and increasing dualization

Labour market deregulation has played a major role in allowing for the creation of service sector jobs and growing heterogeneity in the labour market. Over the last two or three decades there has been a general tendency to deregulate labour markets, in particular with respect to flexible or 'atypical' forms of employment. The motivation for this has been two-fold: first, to create additional jobs by lowering the barriers that employers face when hiring additional staff, in particular small service sector firms; and second to establish a segment of entry jobs which could act as a stepping stone towards 'regular' employment.

The potential for employment growth in an increasingly post-industrial labour market could only be realized by the service sector, with its stronger reliance on external labour market flexibility. Hence, the liberalization of fixed-term contracts, agency work, self-employment and start-ups, as well as the active promotion of job creation in these areas by means of active labour market policies has been on the agenda of all the countries compared here. Comparative institutional indicators developed by the OECD show a general tendency to reduce the level of regulation regarding fixed-term jobs, temporary agency work, and barriers to self-employment (Venn, 2009). In empirical terms, this has facilitated job creation such as agency work, which deviates from 'standard employment'. This is shown in Table 14.1, which also presents evidence that low pay has become more frequent in a number of – if not all – countries over the last decade. Figure 14.1 furthermore shows the evolution of the share of workers with fixed-term contracts (including apprentices) over time. Contrary to some beliefs there has in fact only been a slight increase in the average share of fixed-term employment, from 12.2 per cent in 1998 to a peak of 13.5 per cent in 2007. Fixed-term employment has

Table 14.1. Different forms of non-standard employment

	Wage dispersion D5–D1		Share of temporary agency workers	
	1998	2008	1997	2008
Belgium	1.41	1.38	1.3	2.1
Czech Republic	1.66	1.73	n.a.	0.7
Denmark	1.48	1.57	0.2	0.7
Germany	1.75	1.93	0.4	2.0
Spain	n.a.	1.66	0.5	0.7
France	1.58	1.47	1.3	2.3
Italy	n.a.	1.55	0.0	0.9
Hungary	1.93	1.74	0.8	1.4
The Netherlands	1.66	1.65	2.1	2.9
Sweden	1.37	1.37	0.3	1.3
Switzerland	1.49	1.47	0.6	1.7
The United Kingdom	1.84	1.83	2.6	4.1

Source: OECD for wage dispersion (for Belgium 1999 instead of 1999, and 2005 instead of 2008 for the Netherlands, 2007 for Belgium and France, for low pay); figures only refer to full-time workers; EURO CIETT for agency work (for Italy 1998, Hungary 2002 instead of 1997).

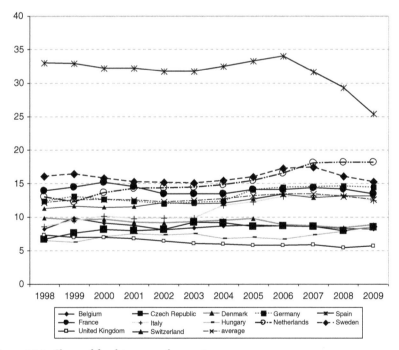

Figure 14.1. Share of fixed-term employment
Source: Eurostat.

subsequently decreased to 12.7 per cent of all employment. The average figures, however, hide a considerable degree of variation at the national level. More heavy reliance on fixed-term jobs can not only mostly be observed in labour markets with strict dismissal protection, such as Spain and Italy, but also in the Netherlands and Sweden. Fixed-term contracts have on the contrary become less important in less-regulated labour markets such as Denmark or the United Kingdom.

While liberalizing non-standard jobs can facilitate job creation, this trend also means that a larger share of workers are not (fully) covered by social insurance or cannot build up a sufficient employment record in order to be entitled to contributory unemployment insurance benefits. Across Europe, substantial shares of unemployed people do not in fact qualify for insurance-related benefits. They may be excluded by law (e.g. the self-employed in most countries, including the so-called 'bogus' self-employed) or de facto because they are less likely to meet contribution requirements or satisfy other relevant eligibility criteria (e.g. temporary or part-time workers). As the various chapters in this volume have shown, the responses to this development have varied cross-nationally and over time. Sometimes policymakers have tried to maintain or even reinforce the link between contributions and benefits, therefore consolidating the exclusion of those with short or interrupted work histories. In other instances, by contrast, access to social insurance benefits has been eased, and dynamically growing categories of employment (e.g. freelancers) have been integrated into the system. At the same time, in many countries, minimum standards, in particular means-tested income protection, have been reinforced institutionally and grown in importance relative to unemployment insurance (see also Hemerijck and Eichhorst, 2010).

14.2.4 What do we know from empirical research? Findings in the literature

There are quite robust findings across countries from micro-econometric studies with regard to the short-term effectiveness of demanding elements such as mandatory participation in activation programmes, job-search monitoring, or reducing maximum benefit duration.[1] Andersen and Svarer (2008) show, for example, that the threat of mandatory participation in activation programmes even has a positive impact on the search effort of those unemployed persons not yet assigned to an activation programme. Threat and screening effects seem to have an important impact on job-finding and benefit caseloads. Evidence on net re-employment effects of voluntary or mandatory programme participation is less robust. However, work first measures are often ineffective in lifting the individuals and their families out of poverty on a sustainable basis (Bolvig et al., 2003; Moffitt, 2008).

Given displacement, substitution, deadweight, wage, and fiscal effects, the macroeconomic effectiveness and efficiency of activation programmes as well as the sustainability of effects are less clear. In particular, some studies point at the fact that activating interventions based on the threat potential and demanding

---

[1] For an overview of the available evidence, see Konle-Seidl and Eichhorst, 2008. For a recent meta-analysis of evaluation studies, see Card et al., 2009.

principle may help move benefit recipients to low-skill, low-pay, and unstable jobs, so that they run the risk of continued partial reliance or repeated return to benefits. Germany is an illustrative case for this type of 'revolving door' effect. The first wave of the German PASS – introduced to monitor the effects of the Hartz IV reform (2005) – shows that within less than a year, 14 per cent of UB II recipients had left benefit rolls. About 50 per cent of those leavers became self-sufficient by taking up a full (78 per cent) or a part-time job of at least 16 hours a week and 5 per cent of leavers took up a subsidized job. About one in four took up jobs below their formal skill level. Gross hourly wages were below €7.50 for nearly half of the leavers. Thirty-six per cent found temporary jobs, 12 per cent temp agency work, and between 32 and 46 per cent of those leaving benefit rolls in 2006 and 2007 entered a 'standard work arrangement'. However, only further waves of PASS will show whether flexible jobs are a springboard to more stable and better-paid jobs for those ending benefit receipt, or whether they rather constitute a revolving door back to benefit receipt (Achatz and Trappmann, 2009).

A similar picture is given by leaver surveys of New Deal participants in the United Kingdom. Around 40 per cent of NDYP (New Deal for Young People) participants who find work claim JSA again within a year. This pattern of recycling between benefits and programmes has been found also in the other New Deals. However, there is no information on the type of jobs found by New Deal leavers. In a survey, the majority (72 per cent) of 'repeaters' who made at least three claims for Jobseeker's Allowance indicated that they had not been able to find 'suitable' work. The main problem was the type of work available rather than not being able to find work at all (Carpenter, 2006).

Surprisingly, little is known, however, about the effects of activation policies on wages. There is a general lack of empirical research on the wage moderation and wage-setting effects of both the demanding side of activation like mandatory programme participation or benefit cuts as well as the enabling side like in-work benefits. Graafland and Huizinga (1998), for example, found that the wage-moderating effect of lower replacement rates is stronger during periods of high unemployment. Kettner and Rebien (2007) were able to show with data from business surveys taken in 2005 and 2006 for Germany that, from the firm's perspective, the unemployed are willing to take more concessions in earnings and working terms after the Hartz reforms than they did in the past. For Denmark, Bolvig (2008) shows that tightening unemployment insurance benefits led to a stronger inflow from unemployment into low-pay jobs, limited upward mobility, and more unstable careers for less-skilled people, who would otherwise have remained on benefits.

Evaluation studies focusing on the transition from unemployment to work rarely focus on the type of job taken up. One exception is a Dutch study by Zijl et al. (2004) showing that, compared to a situation in which there are no temporary jobs, the latter effectively provide a stepping stone for the unemployed towards regular employment – though the study does not study potential side effects of increases in temporary work. More is known about mobility from non-standard to standard employment, and from low pay to medium pay. First, there is evidence of strong differences between countries in mobility from fixed-term to permanent contracts. In countries such as France the risk of longer spells under (renewed) fixed-term contracts is much higher than, for example, in Germany (Blanchard and Landier, 2002; Gash, 2008; Gebel and Giesecke, 2009). This can be seen as a direct consequence of regulatory differentials between permanent and fixed-term contracts. Furthermore, studies on Germany could not find clear evidence regarding a significant stepping stone effect of agency work for labour market entrants in Germany (Kvasnicka, 2009; Lehmer and Ziegler, 2010). Regarding pay mobility, a German study found strong differences by qualification, age, type of job, firm, and occupation (Mosthaf et al., 2010). It seems fair to argue that most studies suggest that non-standard employment has become a permanent feature of post-industrial labour markets as atypical work provides additional flexibility and often lower labour costs, which are particularly important with respect to important segments of the service sector. Countries vary greatly with respect to their reliance on particular types of employment and the likelihood of non-standard workers making a transition to permanent jobs (Eichhorst and Marx, 2010).

These three trends lead us to assume that the formerly unemployed or inactive persons (*a*) tend to enter the labour market more frequently than at earlier points in time and (*b*) are mostly doing so using non-standard jobs as entry points with the prospect of both stabilization of the employment record (sustainability of employment) and upward mobility; the service sector comes in as an alternative or the only job-creating sector relevant for labour market entrants, in particular after longer spells of inactivity or unemployment. The three trends of activating reforms to benefit systems and labour market policies, tertiarization, and labour market flexibility thus lead us towards the following hypotheses, which will be explored empirically in the remainder of this chapter:

> **H1**: Formerly unemployed or inactive persons tend to enter the labour market more frequently than at earlier points in time.
>
> **H2**: This is mostly achieved using jobs associated with atypical employment contracts.

14.3 HAVE LABOUR MARKETS BECOME MORE INCLUSIVE? AN EMPIRICAL ANALYSIS BASED ON THE EUROPEAN LABOUR FORCE SURVEY

There are various ways to approach the question of whether labour markets are more or less inclusive in the late 2000s than they were in the late 1990s and. We might expect to observe a more diverse composition of the labour force given the increased labour market participation of women (OECD, 2008). For the reasons discussed above, we might also expect to see decreased numbers of non-employed. In this chapter, we are particularly interested in whether unemployed and inactive individuals are increasingly likely to make the transition into employment. We are also interested, if we do find a more inclusive labour market, in whether there are also impacts on the quality of employment people move in to, understood in terms of the type of contract they receive.[2]

---

[2] It would also be worthwhile to consider wages levels, the duration of unemployment, and other spells of non-employment, but this is beyond the scope of the current analysis. There is a lack of comparative data concerning wage and income levels. The prevalence of non-standard jobs would be a further route of enquiry.

One way to consider whether labour markets have become more inclusive is to look at transition rates. There is a relative paucity of comparative European Union data from which to calculate transition rates from non-employment to employment. Often incomplete, the main sources which include information on pay, employment, and type of contract type are the European Community Household Panel (1994–2001 for the EU-15) and EU-SILC (2002–ongoing for the since enlarged European Union) (European Commission, 2010*a*). Other than this, transition rate data are drawn from national sources that are not normally directly comparable. The European Labour Force Survey (ELFS), a harmonized collection of Labour Force Survey data as produced by the EU-25 countries, can also be used to compute transition rates, however. It has far greater coverage than any other available data, both in terms of sample size and the number of countries covered over a substantial period of time. For many countries, data are available from 1983 to the current day. This potential for the analysis of trends over time and between countries has been exploited in a number of prior studies (e.g. Mazzuco and Suhrcke, 2010).

Clearly, the harmonization of such a large data set across time and countries is a challenge, and at times comparability between data tables is inevitably compromised (Charlier and Franco, 2001). For our analysis, it should be noted that the construction of the 'annual' data sets is not the same between the two time periods. To take the example of Belgium, the 1997 data is collected in quarter 2 (weeks 14–26 of the year) and there are 80,373 observations. However, in 2007, the Belgian data are collected from observations across the yearly period and there are 111,978 observations. One possibility to ensure 'like with like' comparison would be to look only at quarter 2 data for 2007 (as recorded in the annual data set be2007_y). This, however, yields only 26,578 observations, which is a much reduced sample size. In addition to the annual data, there are quarterly data sets available. However, Eurostat advise that the annual datasets 'be considered as the best sample available to cover all variables and allow all cross-tabulations' including a yearly weighting factor (European Commission, 2010*b*). For our analysis, we thus use the yearly harmonized ELFS data rather than the quarterly data sets, as the latter do not appear to contain the full range of harmonized variables.

In Table 14.2 it can be seen that for most countries, the percentage of the non-employed making a transition to employment does indeed appear to have increased between 1997 and 2007 across Europe, particularly for the unemployed.

In order to control for the nature of the composition of the groups of unemployed and inactive persons making a transition to employment, we turn to a logistic regression model, again using the ELFS. Our first model considers whether a transition is more likely in the late 2000s than in the late 1990s for those of working age (between 16 and 65 years), controlling for other factors (sex, age, education level, country, and real GDP growth rate). The equation to follow describes a logistic regression model. The dependent variable in a logistic regression is the log of the odds ratio.

$$\ln[p/(1-p)] = B_0 + B_i X(year, country, sex, age, education, \text{GDP growth})_i + e \tag{1}$$

In this first model, p is the probability of making a transition from non-activity or unemployment to employment. The vector X_i consists of the following

Table 14.2. Transition rates from unemployment and inactivity to employment from one year to the next (per cent of those unemployed and inactive in the previous year $(t-1)$ making the transition to employment in a given year (t))

Country	Year (t)	% unemployed at $t-1$ making transition to employment	% inactive at $t-1$ making transition to employment
Belgium	1997	17	3
	2007	20	8
Czech Republic	1998[a]	46	14
	2007	34	11
Denmark	1997	36	29
	2007	44	27
France	1997	32	8
	2007	35	10
Germany[b]	1997	(24)	(14)
	2007	(31)	(21)
Hungary	1997	30	6
	2007	31	6
Italy	1997	26	6
	2007	31	6
Spain	1997	32	9
	2007	44	11
The United Kingdom	1997	40	16
	2007	50	16

[a]Key variable for this analysis missing for Czech Republic for 1997, so 1998 data are used.
[b]The German transition rates were not computed on the basis of ELFS data, but were calculated analogously with data from the German Socio-Economic Panel (GSOEP). Due to methodological differences (panel data instead of a retrospective question), the German results are not comparable to the rest of the sample.
Source: ELFS data, weighted. Authors' own calculations.

characteristics: whether the transition was made recently (2007) as compared to 1997, country, sex, age, education level, and the real GDP growth rate.

Whilst the ELFS is a collection of cross-sectional (rather than longitudinal) data sets, this analysis is able to exploit a lagged variable that acquires retrospective information on an individual's situation with regard to activity one year before the survey. This variable captures information as to whether the person was employed,[3] unemployed, or otherwise inactive[4] in the previous year. If individuals indicate that they were either unemployed or inactive in the previous year, and employed in the current year, they are deemed to have made a transition. The variable in question (wstat1y) is not available for every country for every year and suffers from varying degrees of missing data. This is particularly the case for Sweden and the Netherlands, which are excluded from analysis on these grounds. German data for late 1990s were not available either.

[3] Employed is defined in the ELFS as 'carries out a job or profession, including unpaid work for a family business or holding, including an apprenticeship or paid traineeship, etc'.

[4] Inactive is defined in the ELFS as 'pupil, student, further training, unpaid work experience; in retirement or early retirement or has given up business; permanently disabled; in compulsory military service; fulfilling domestic tasks; other inactive person'. Not all categories are collected for all countries.

The independent variable of central interest is the year. Is there a noticeable change between 1997 and 2007? Country dummies are included to capture the difference between countries, with the United Kingdom serving as the reference category. The 'usual suspects' are also included in the model to control for changes in composition. These are: whether the individual is male or not; age measured in years and age squared; and education level coded according to the International Standard Classification of Education (ISCED 97), with low level of education as the reference category. We also control for macroeconomic conditions using the real GDP growth rate.

In order to address the question of whether labour markets have become more inclusive between the years 1997 and 2007, logistic regressions are estimated and odds ratios are reported, to give insight to the odds of someone who was either unemployed or inactive in the previous year, making the transition into any form of employment. The odds ratio is a way of comparing whether the probability of a certain event is the same for two groups. An odds ratio of 1 implies that the event is equally likely in both groups. An odds ratio of >1 implies that the event is more likely than in the reference category in the case of dichotomous explanatory variables, such as country. An odds ratio of <1 implies that the event is less likely than in the reference category.

Table 14.3. Logistic regression: transition from non-employment (unemployment and inactivity) to employment

Transition to employment

	Odds ratio	Robust standard error	z	$P > z$	95% confidence interval	
2007[a]	1.17	0.01	12.82	0.000	1.14	1.20
Male[b]	1.87	0.02	50.12	0.000	1.82	1.91
Age	1.23	0.003	73.95	0.000	1.22	1.24
Age	1.00	0.00004	−83.12	0.000	0.9967	0.9968
High-level education[c]	2.88	0.05	57.82	0.000	2.77	2.98
Medium-level education[d]	1.59	0.02	35.66	0.000	1.55	1.63
Country[e]						
Belgium	0.34	0.007	−50.43	0.000	0.32	0.35
Czech Republic	0.72	0.01	−16.51	0.000	0.70	0.75
Denmark	1.81	0.06	19.18	0.000	1.71	1.92
Spain	0.63	0.01	−23.18	0.000	0.61	0.65
France	0.59	0.01	−24.75	0.000	0.57	0.62
Hungary	0.41	0.009	−40.70	0.000	0.40	0.43
Italy	0.44	0.007	−48.96	0.000	0.43	0.46
GDP growth	0.96	0.004	−10.32	0.000	0.95	0.97

[a]Reference category: 1997.
[b]Reference category: female.
[c]Reference category: low-level education.
[d]Reference category: low-level education.
[e]Reference category: Denmark.
Note: Number of observations = 738,816; Wald chi^2 () = 22,082.23; Prob ⟩ chi^2 = 0.0000; Log pseudo-likelihood = −45,995.1; Pseudo-R^2 = 0.12.
Source: Authors' calculations using the European Labour Force Survey 1997 and 2007.

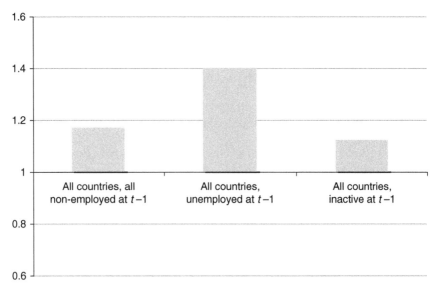

Figure 14.2. Logistic regression odds ratios for the transition to employment from non-employment the previous survey year $(t - 1)$, in 2007 compared with 1997

Note: An odds ratio of 1 implies that the event is equally likely in both 1997 and 2007. An odds ratio of >1 implies that the event is more likely in 2007 than in 1997. An odds ratio of <1 implies that the event is less likely in 2007 than in 1997.
Source: Authors' calculations using the European Labour Force Survey 1997 and 2007.

To begin with, all countries are pooled together and the unemployed and the inactive are grouped together (see Table 14.3). This model suggests that there is a pan-European trend over time towards labour markets becoming more inclusive with respect to increased odds (the odds ratio is 1.17) of a non-employed (unemployed person or inactive) person making the transition to employment. Separate models are run for those potentially making the transition from unemployment and for those potentially making the transition from inactivity. This reveals that the odds ratio for the unemployed is greater (1.40) than for the inactive (1.11) (Figure 14.2).

It is apparent that there is some variation between countries with regard to the trends towards increasing transitions. Only in Denmark was a transition more likely than in the United Kingdom (Table 14.3). All other countries in the analysis were less likely to see a transition. Separate models were also run for each country and for each group (the unemployed and the inactive). The odds ratios are presented for the key variable of interest (2007 rather than 1997) in Figures 14.3 and 14.4. Figure 14.3 shows that the unemployed were more likely to make the transition to employment in 2007 in most countries in the analysis (Belgium, Denmark, Spain, France, and the United Kingdom), with only the Czech Republic and Italy being different in this respect. The data for Hungary were inconclusive. Figure 14.4 shows that the inactive were more likely to make the transition to employment in Belgium, Spain, and France, but less likely in the Czech Republic,

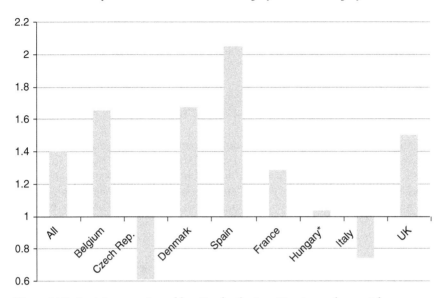

Figure 14.3. Logistic regression odds ratios for the transition to employment from unemployment the previous survey year $(t - 1)$, in 2007 compared with 1997

Note: *Odds ratio not statistically significant.
Source: Authors' calculations using the European Labour Force Survey 1997 and 2007.

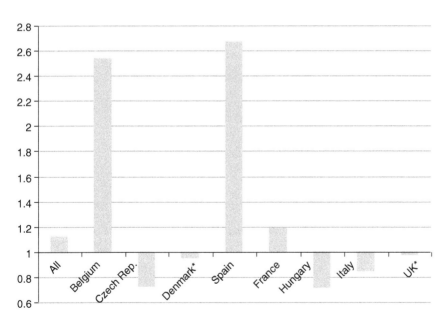

Figure 14.4. Logistic regression odds ratios for the transition to employment from inactivity the previous survey year $(t - 1)$, in 2007 compared with 1997

Note: *Odds ratio not statistically significant.
Source: Authors' calculations using the European Labour Force Survey 1997 and 2007.

Hungary, and Italy. Results for the inactive in the United Kingdom and Denmark are inconclusive as they are not statistically significant.

14.4 THE CHANGING NATURE OF LABOUR MARKET TRANSITIONS

Thus far we have been able to show that in many if not all countries labour markets have become more inclusive for the unemployed, as well as for the inactive. In this section, we employ an innovative approach to explore whether the increase in labour market inclusion with respect to those making the transition from non-employment has been accompanied (at the aggregate level) by an increase in more precarious employment. More insecure employment here is measured by contract type, specifically as non-permanent contracts or self-employment.

With reference to equation (1), in this second group of models, p is the probability, having made a transition, that the transition has been into a permanent as compared to a temporary contract. The vector X_i consists of the following characteristics: whether the transition was made recently (2007) as compared to in

Table 14.4. Logistic regression: transition into permanent contract from non-employment (unemployment and inactivity)

	Transition into permanent contract					
	Odds ratio	Robust standard error	z	$P > z$	95% confidence interval	
2007 (1)	0.93	0.02	−3.00	0.003	0.89	0.98
Male (2)	0.83	0.02	−7.71	0.000	0.79	0.87
Age	1.07	0.006	12.54	0.000	1.06	1.08
Age (2)	0.999	0.00008	−12.87	0.000	0.9989	0.9992
High-level education (3)	0.90	0.03	−3.00	0.003	0.84	0.96
Medium-level education (3)	0.99	0.03	−0.28	0.781	0.94	1.04
Country (4)						
Belgium	0.55	0.02	−14.67	0.000	0.50	0.59
Czech Republic	0.59	0.02	−14.70	0.000	0.55	0.64
Denmark	0.97	0.05	−0.62	0.533	0.88	1.07
Spain	0.11	0.005	−48.54	0.000	0.10	0.12
France	0.25	0.01	−35.40	0.000	0.23	0.27
Hungary	0.82	0.03	−4.87	0.000	0.75	0.89
Italy	0.35	0.01	−33.63	0.000	0.33	0.37
GDP growth	0.94	0.01	−8.50	0.000	0.93	0.95
Agriculture (5)	0.34	0.02	−17.57	0.000	0.30	0.38
Industry (5)	1.05	0.03	1.66	0.096	0.99	1.12

Note: Reference category (1) 1997; (2) female; (3) low-level education; (4) Denmark; (5) Service.
Number of observations = 87,343.
Wald chi^2 () = 4,750.42.
Prob > chi^2 = 0.0000.
Log pseudo-likelihood = −11,001.
Pseudo-R^2 = 0.11.
Source: Authors' calculations using the European Labour Force Survey 1997 and 2007.

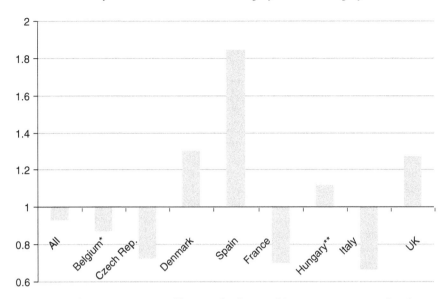

Figure 14.5. Logistic regression odds ratios for the transition to a permanent rather than a temporary contract, in 2007 compared with 1997

Note: *Not statistically significant; **statistically significant at the 10 per cent level only.
Source: Authors' calculations using the European Labour Force Survey 1997 and 2007.

1997, country, sex, age and age-squared, education level, the real GDP growth rate, and sector of employment (agriculture, industry, or service). For each of the countries for which data are available, we exploit again the lagged employment status variable in the ELFS. Logistic regressions, reporting odds ratios, are estimated to give insight to the odds of someone who has made the transition from non-employment to employment in 2007, as opposed to in 1997, making the transition into permanent employment rather than into self-employment or a fixed-term contract. The ELFS data are used as before, with the addition of a variable to control for sector of employment: agriculture, industry, and service. The service sector is taken as the reference category.

As expected, the pooled model containing all countries finds a pan-European trend towards more insecure employment. The odds have decreased slightly (the odds ratio is 0.93) between 1997 and 2007 of making a transition from non-employment into a permanent contract (Table 14.4). However, looking country by country reveals a rather diversified picture (Figure 14.5). With respect to those making a transition from non-employment, those in Denmark, Spain, the United Kingdom, and Hungary (although this coefficient is statistically significant only at the 10 per cent level) were actually *more* likely to find permanent employment in 2007 as compared to 1997. Those in the Czech Republic, France, Italy, and possibly Belgium (although this coefficient is statistically insignificant) were less likely to find permanent employment in 2007 as compared to 1997.

14.5 CONCLUSIONS

This chapter has explored the empirical evidence for the claim that non-employed people in post-industrial labour markets are more likely to make the transition into employment than has previously been the case. Our results show that, as a general trend, post-industrial labour markets have indeed become more inclusive, as the transition rate of the unemployed and the inactive into employment has increased in 2007 compared to 1997. However, in spite of the diminishing differences in their administrative treatment that many chapters in this volume have highlighted, the unemployed and inactive remain distinct groups with regards to transitions into employment. Just two countries (the Czech Republic and Italy) out of the eight considered saw decreased odds of transition over time for the unemployed, controlling for macroeconomic conditions. The picture for the inactive is more mixed cross-nationally. Labour markets have become more inclusive for the inactive in Belgium, Spain, France, but not in the Czech Republic, Hungary, Italy, and possibly Denmark and the United Kingdom.

A second, related question that we asked was whether an increasingly inclusive labour market is associated with a reduction in job quality, as measured by contract type. There is a trend towards more insecure employment for the recently non-employed in the Czech Republic, France, Italy, and possibly Belgium. However, in the other countries considered, Denmark, the United Kingdom, and Hungary, there was the opposite trend towards more permanent employment. One can also observe a slight decline in the otherwise very high incidence of fixed-term employment in Spain. It is likely that these findings in part reflect differences in the stability and institutional set-up of permanent employment.

15

Tracking caseloads: the changing composition of working-age benefit receipt in Europe

Johan De Deken and Jochen Clasen

15.1 INTRODUCTION

The regulation of the risk of unemployment since the 1980s has involved shifts not only between unemployment and paid work, as discussed in Chapter 14, but between different working-age benefit systems as well. Such shifts have been common in most countries, as demonstrated in the national chapters. They can be regarded, at least in part, as having disguised the scale of 'open' unemployment, but they also added fiscal pressure in the medium term. In contrast to the 1980s, it is thus no surprise that most governments claim they are pursuing policies aimed at a reduction in social security spending and benefit dependency. It is more surprising, however, that comprehensive data on the development of the number of benefit claimants (or 'caseloads' in administrative parlance) of various transfer programmes are often not systematically collected, or published, at the national level. Comparative research aimed at tracking the changing composition of working-age benefit receipt cross-nationally is thus seriously hampered.

The lack of relevant data might be due to the complexity of national social security systems, which can be compounded in multi-tier welfare states with divided administrative and financial responsibilities. For example, in Spain the 'Renta minima' social assistance benefits are not administered at the central level but by the seventeen autonomous regions and figures on these benefits cannot be found in national statistics. Moreover, not all social security programmes are part of the public domain. In the Netherlands, for example, early retirement schemes are formally considered to be voluntary agreements that are initiated and run by the social partners at the level of industrial sectors. Even though such agreements end up being encompassing because they are subject to a mandate via the practice of administrative extension, it is hard to obtain comprehensive data for such schemes, because they lack the status of a statutory arrangement.

Some governments have begun to address the problem of benefit complexity by merging functionally similar systems, such as in Germany for example, where unemployment benefit II has been created as a basic income security scheme for all employable persons outside unemployment insurance (see Chapter 3). Others, such as the United Kingdom, are about to introduce a 'single working-age benefit system', even though this is to some extent a misnomer (see Chapter 2). Nevertheless, even in these two countries, persons out of work continue to receive income transfers from a range of schemes that differ significantly in terms of generosity and conditionality, but often overlap in terms of risks covered.

National programmes also differ in the ways in which respective caseloads are documented. In most countries, it is relatively straightforward and has been common to collect claimant data on unemployment insurance benefits in a systematic fashion. For other schemes, particularly incapacity and also early retirement, the availability of administrative data becomes much more problematic, partly due to the existence of parallel systems (e.g. early retirement options within unemployment as well as pension programmes) and the termination of some and introduction of often merely slightly different programmes. Systematically collecting and analysing comparable social assistance claimant data is even more challenging for several reasons. First, in many countries social assistance is administered, and often financed, in a decentralized fashion, leaving considerable space for regional variation. Second, the 'target population' of social assistance can be very wide ('general' social assistance) or specific (e.g. particular social assistance schemes for older people, lone parents, immigrants, etc). In Germany, for example, social assistance used to be an encompassing scheme for persons in need, irrespective of citizenship, age, or labour market status. Since the early 1990s, separate social assistance (or basic security) programmes have emerged for asylum seekers, people of retirement age, and, most recently, persons who are deemed not to be employable.

A third complication is the very nature of social assistance as a residual benefit intended to alleviate poverty rather than to provide a wage replacement. It seems to be impossible in some countries to separate out beneficiaries who receive social assistance in addition to other social security transfers, or to distinguish between social assistance and other means-tested (e.g. housing or unemployment) assistance transfers, some of which might supplement labour market income (that thus only makes part of their income package). National statistics can make it all but impossible to distinguish between those for whom social assistance is a complete substitute for labour market income and others for whom it is merely a supplement. Finally, across countries there are problems of comparability and functional equivalents. For example, as discussed in Chapter 2, almost a third of recipients of unemployment assistance (UBII) in Germany are actually in paid work. These claimants are thus part of the benefit caseload. Elsewhere those with similar subsidized types of (generally low-paid and/or part-time) jobs might receive tax-funded wage subsidies (tax credits) and are thus, as in the United Kingdom, excluded from the social security caseloads claimant count. All of these reasons make systematic research based on claimant data challenging for single countries, and even more so for comparative analyses.

Of course there are some data, and some of the core arguments made in most of the twelve country chapters in this volume were based on these data. Indeed, if we had not been able to illustrate at least broad changes in caseloads across different benefit programmes a key rationale for the book would have been undermined, which is to investigate evidence of 're-categorization' and institutional integration between benefit systems (see also the concluding chapter of this book). As shown in previous chapters, while various branches of national social security system were established to provide income protection against particular risks, in recent years the boundaries between some of these schemes have become less rigid. As discussed, this was to a large extent the consequence of attempts to counteract policies in response to the decline in industrial employment and the development of mass unemployment of the 1980s. 'Labour shedding' via opening temporary or permanent routes out of the labour market had led to steep increases in the caseloads of some benefit programmes. Depending on national institutional arrangements, persons who were deemed to be 'structurally unemployed' were transferred to different types of working-age benefit systems (Erlinghagen and Knuth, 2010). As we demonstrate below, in some countries these claimants remained part of the administrative category of the unemployed. Elsewhere incapacity schemes expanded, or jobless workers exited the labour force via what were often several options for early retirement.

In short, caseload trends are not exclusively determined by changes in unemployment (and employment) but also reflect ways in which the risk of unemployment is politically regulated, as implied by the title of this volume. Thus, if data can be systematically documented, it might be asked whether caseloads might be used as a 'dependent variable' in comparative welfare state research, potentially complementing conventional indicators such as social expenditure and social rights. However, while the latter have been extensively applied, and their respective conceptual and methodological implications extensively discussed (see Clasen and Siegel, 2007), caseload data have hardly figured in cross-national analysis. What are the chances of this changing? Is it conceivable that caseloads might one day become an indicator of social policy change alongside social spending or social rights? The aim of this chapter is to start exploring these questions. In the first two sections, we review the availability and quality of existing data sources and discuss some of the main methodological challenges and problems they are faced with, highlighting issues of reliability and validity. The third and fourth sections make use of some of the administrative caseload data which were collected by authors of the country chapters in this book (see Caseload Annex). As will be discussed below, we have made those data as comparable as possible by re-categorizing some national figures and using a common classificatory scheme. We do not suggest that this procedure has solved methodological problems as discussed in Sections 2 and 3. Nevertheless, the data which has been specifically assembled for the purpose of this book allows us not only to illustrate some interesting cross-national trends but also to extend the exploration into the options for, and limitations of, comparative research based on claimant data.

15.2 THE NEI STUDY AND THE REVISIONS BY THE OECD

The first, and potentially the most comprehensive, attempt to assemble and standardize national administrative data on caseloads in different countries dates back to the late 1990s, when the Dutch Ministry of Labour (NEI) commissioned a pioneering study that covered nine European countries, Japan, and the

Table 15.1. Working-age benefit recipients (% of 15–64-year-olds), and composition in 2004

	B	NL	DK	S	D	F	UK
1980	17	16	20	16	15	14	15
1990	24	20	23	17	18	20	18
1995	25	20	26	23	22	23	22
2004	22	19	22	22	22	23	19
2004 (main categories)							
Unemployment	8	6	5	3	8	5	2
Old-age	5	1	2	1	4	6	4
Incapacity/sickness	5	11	11	15	6	7	8
Social assistance	2	1	2	1	3	3	2

Source: OECD (2003*b*), plus orginial and updated data for 2004 provided by OECD (social assistance includes lone parent benefits; other benefits not listed include maternity, care, survivor).

United States for the period 1980–97 (Arents et al., 2002). The Organisation for Economic Co-operation and Development (OECD) has sought to improve the comparability of this database, and updated it for subsequent years (OECD, 2003*b*). For illustrative purposes, we reproduce the OECD data for some of the countries covered in this volume in Table 15.1.[1]

The table suggests remarkably similar trends of increasing claimant numbers across the seven countries between 1980 and the mid-1990s, followed by only modest declines. The OECD data also show a breakdown of the composition of the total caseload which indicates interesting differences in the prevalence of different beneficiary groups which do not reflect differences in unemployment rates (see Statistical Annex, Table A.5). Using administrative data, the OECD database includes some updates to extend the series of the original Dutch study by a few years, but most figures for the period 2000–4 appear to be based on extrapolations of the earlier series. On the basis of administrative data generated by the authors of the country chapters in this book, we have sought to rearrange and extend the time series of the NEI–OECD database up to the year 2008. It should be pointed out that our aims are less ambitious than those of the original NEI study. Arents et al. (2002) sought to estimate a *total* 'benefit dependency ratio', that is, the percentage of the population which is dependent upon some kind of benefit, which is an endeavour confronted with particular problems (see below). By contrast, we are merely interested in tracing caseload trends, that is, changes in the volume and composition of those working-age benefit schemes which can be considered as alternative or substitute for income from paid work and hence allow recipients to exit the labour force. In other words, we have not sought to collect caseload data on survivor benefits or maternity benefits, and only examined old-age benefits in so far as they allow people to leave the labour market prior to the statutory retirement age.

---

[1] We would like to thank David Grubb of the OECD for allowing us to use the original datafiles and the update for 2004.

The OECD too focused primarily on the working-age population, but, like the NEI study, aimed to estimate a total dependency rate. Such an endeavour invites several major methodological challenges, which, in contrast to what has sometimes been suggested (see, e.g. CESifo, 2003), have at best only been partially resolved. Even though we are not interested in the total benefit dependency rate, and thus avoid some of these methodological problems, we have nevertheless aimed to apply as far as possible the same principles which were adopted in the original NEI study, and have tried to address four major challenges.

The first refers to the problem of *partial benefit receipt*, that is, the beneficiary continues to be employed on a part-time basis and receives benefits which replace earnings in part. Partial benefits are often prevalent in disability schemes and also exist in early retirement and in unemployment benefit schemes in some countries. In order to make caseloads comparable, it might be necessary to transform partial benefits into full benefit years. In some countries, including the Netherlands and Sweden, partial unemployment benefits are already expressed in full-time equivalents. For other countries where such schemes exist, including Belgium, Denmark, Spain, and France, a factor of 0.5 is applied to beneficiaries of part-time benefits. Similar procedures can be applied to part-time early retirement.

Secondly, 'periodic' benefits could be, wherever possible and appropriate, expressed in benefit years. For recipients of unemployment, early retirement, disability, and social assistance benefits, this could be done by annually calculating the caseload of any particular calendar month. For sickness benefits, benefits years could be calculated by dividing the number of days during which a benefit was paid by the maximum number of days for which a benefit can be paid out. This differs from country to country, that is, 260 days in France, 312 days in Belgium, and 365 days in Germany. Not limited to sickness benefits, this problem applies to all schemes in which claimants receive benefits for less than a year, or where benefits are not paid for every day of the week (e.g. unemployment benefits in Sweden are only payable five days a week). One problem is that the information of the number of days benefits were paid is often missing or not available, another that figures only of a particular benchmark month in the year might be collected or accessible. In such instances, the NEI and the OECD used either the number of beneficiaries in December of the year or 'the figures of from whatever month there [was] . . . available data' (Arents et al., 2002: 11). Evidently it is impossible to know whether persons who received a benefit during the benchmark month claimed benefits also for the rest of the year. Moreover, persons who received a benefit during months other than the benchmark month are not included, and the assumption might be that these two effects might somehow cancel each other out. It should be noted that this is a rather big assumption, however, neglecting, for example, seasonal effects. In what follows below, we choose whenever possible September rather than December figures, as seasonal effects are the most likely to manifest themselves in June and December. Nevertheless, other problems of taking monthly figures as an approximation of average annual caseloads remain. For example, a reduction in the average spells of unemployment might explain why trends in benefit expenditure and benefit caseloads diverge (see Section 15.4).

Thirdly, there is a potential problem of *double counting*. One person should count for no more than one full-time equivalent benefit claimant. In practice, however, the fragmented nature of social security administration makes it often impossible to implement this principle in countries where the simultaneous receipt of different benefits is permissible. As part of their efforts to combat benefit fraud, some countries have started to set up integrated databases of different kinds of social security benefits in a single registry. In the future, databases such as the 'datawarehouse labour market and social protection' of the Belgian KSZ-BCSS system might form a valuable tool in eliminating double counts, but the recent introduction of such initiatives make them of little use for developing a historical time series. In the NEI study (Arents et al., 2002), this problem manifested itself particularly in the case of survivor benefits that are often combined with an old-age pension benefit, and for old-age pensions which are supplemented by social assistance. As we are only interested in working-age benefits, the problem of double counts is less relevant here, except for the case-loads of active labour market policies (ALMPs) as in Denmark, for example. At some point in the 1990s, participants of those programmes started to be reported separately, that is, in addition to rather than included in the caseloads of unem-ployment and other working-age benefits (e.g. see Chapter 10, Table 10.2). In the case of Sweden, by contrast, persons enrolled in such programmes seem to be counted separately and the ALMP scheme was used as an intermediate status to requalify for unemployment compensation (see Chapter 11). For both Sweden and Denmark, persons enrolled in ALMP are reported as a separate category, but whereas for Sweden this caseload comes on top of the other categories; for Denmark, we had to subtract those activated UB and SA beneficiaries from those respective categories in order to prevent double counts.

Finally, *payments to couples* should ideally be individualized. Primarily this problem manifests itself in the case of old-age pensions and social assistance which is typically paid on a household basis. Within the countries covered in this volume, a breakdown of benefit receipt between singles and married couples is available only for Sweden. Thus, for all countries except Sweden, the total number of persons who are dependent upon social assistance is underestimated.

15.3 WORKING-AGE BENEFITS AND PROBLEMS OF CATEGORIZATIONS AND RELIABILITY

As indicated, the problems referred to above are particularly acute while attempt-ing to estimate the volume of caseloads over time or the 'total benefit dependency rate'. In what follows, we merely aim to illustrate shifts in the mix of caseloads of different working-age benefit programmes over time and between countries. For this purpose, we consider five broad types of schemes. These are unemployment benefit (which includes participants in active labour market programmes), work incapacity benefit (including statutory sickness pay, sickness, and disability trans-fers), early retirement (permanently exempting claimants from labour market participation), sabbatical and leave schemes (temporarily exempting claimants from paid work), and social assistance as a residual category which often includes persons in need and facing problems other than, or in addition to, lack of employment. These five categories could be distinguished by differences in behavioural requirements imposed on respective beneficiaries. It should be noted, however, that, as discussed in several chapters, such distinctions have become less explicit over time, for example, social assistance programmes (for some claimants) have gradually been transformed into quasi unemployment assistance schemes, or eligibility to disability transfers has become more employment oriented and subjected to regular 'work tests'.

As indicated, despite the increased political salience of 'benefit dependency', it is difficult to obtain reliable comprehensive time series of recipient numbers. Moreover, the quality of readily available data varies not only between countries but also within the same country depending upon the branch of the social security system. At times this seems to be a consequence of the fragmented and complex nature of those schemes. For example, in the NEI and OECD studies, the category of 'early retirement' ignored one of the many early retirement schemes in Belgium, and thus significantly underestimated the caseload in this particular category.[2]

Another problem is the inclusion or exclusion of benefit programmes based on criteria which are not always easy to apply cross-nationally. For example, the NEI study and the OECD claim that they 'only included social security benefits that are regulated by law ... regardless of the way they are administrated and financed' (Arents et al., 2002: 8). Based on industry-wide collective agreements, which are regarded as 'private', the application of this principle led to the exclusion of Dutch early retirement schemes. By contrast, in what follows below, we have included the Dutch early retirement schemes since we did not consider those as private voluntary contracts. Such schemes are concluded in the shadow of the Dutch neo-corporatist system which gives collective agreements a status which is akin to legislation and which backs such schemes up with a procedure of administrative extension (De Deken, 2011*b*). Moreover, it could be argued that the NEI justification for the exclusion of 'private' schemes is inconsistent since it does not rule out non-statutory programmes such as the Danish unemployment insurance system, which is voluntary. According to the NEI, 'not including [Danish unemployment insurance schemes] would render international comparison difficult because one important benefit category ... would not be included ... ' (Arents et al., 2007: 8). We would agree with this statement, but see no reason why it should not be extended to Dutch early retirement schemes.

However, the creation of meaningful comparable caseload data is not only a challenge at international level but also hampered by figures reported by national administrations which appear to be unreliable at times. For example, published by the Dutch national (CBS) statistical office, annual claimant numbers of early retirement benefit suggest some erratic fluctuations. These tend to be attributed to internal revisions, as illustrated by Figure 15.1 and a break in the series in the year 2001 when the number of beneficiaries was revised from 299,000 to 371,000 claimants. Moreover, discrepancies between trends in claimant numbers and benefit expenditure for the respective programme seem difficult to

---

[2] As discussed in more detail in Chapter 6 of this volume, in the 1980s four main early retirement options existed in Belgium, two of which were administered by the old-age pension system (the so-called 'exceptional bridging pension' and the 'early retirement pension'). The two others were essentially run within the unemployment insurance administration (the 'conventional bridging pension' and the 'statutory bridging pension'). The OECD failed to take into account the former.

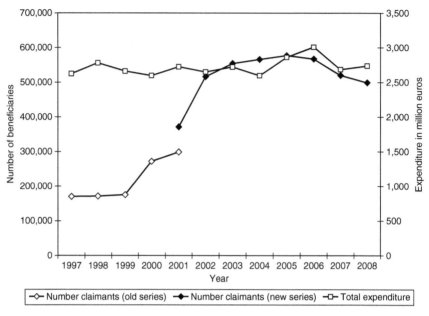

Figure 15.1. The development of caseloads and total expenditure on early retirement schemes in the Netherlands, 1997–2008

Source: Statline Database of the Dutch Statistical Office.

explain. Figure 15.1 illustrates this kind of problem by plotting total expenditure on early retirement benefits in the Netherlands (right Y-axis) to the total number of recipients of benefits (left Y-axis), as reported by the Dutch statistical office. The figure suggests that the benefit caseload more or less trebled during a five-year period, but that the respective benefit spending remained more or less stable.[3]

Of course, a discrepancy between trends in the number of recipients and total expenditure does not necessarily need to imply a measurement problem. It might be caused by other factors, most notably a change in benefit generosity (in terms of level and duration of transfers paid). While this is unlikely to have been the case here, we will return to the relationship between policy change, caseload, and expenditure trends below.

As indicated earlier, of interest in this chapter (and the volume as a whole) are benefits for people of working age, and caseloads are thus expressed as a percentage of the population between 15 and 64 years of age.[4] While this approximates the working-age population in most countries, it can pose a problem for comparisons of the numbers of claimants in early retirement programmes. In most (but

---

[3] To some extent this discrepancy might be related to an increase in part-time early retirement (the CBS statistics do not allow the splitting of the caseload of early retirement benefits into full-time and part-time), but the scale of the deviation in trends is more likely to be related to either a measurement/ reporting problem on the expenditure or the caseload side. In one of its publications, the CBS recognized that a substantial part of the early retirement plans is implemented by companies and these pension funds remained invisible (Gebraad and Pfaff, 2006: 2).

[4] Absolute numbers can be found in the Caseload Annex of this book.

certainly not all) countries the statutory retirement age is still around 65 for men. Women, and in some countries men also, used to enjoy a lower statutory retirement age and some still do. In principle it would be preferable whenever making cross-national comparisons to consider any pensioners below the age of 65 as in the receipt of a form of early retirement benefit rather than standard pension. The NEI–OECD project has made such an attempt for France (see Figure 15.2). For the period 1980–2000, it shows that the number of claimants under 65 in receipt of a statutory pension was much higher than the number of those in receipt of an early retirement programme, that is, the *préretraités* and *dispensés* (older beneficiaries of unemployment benefits exempted from looking for employment). In some countries, however, national data make it hard to distinguish pensioners who are older from those who are younger than 65. Depicting Dutch, Belgian, and French trends, Figure 15.2 illustrates this difficulty of comparing caseload data aimed at covering all those who have retired from paid work and are in receipt of income transfers. It suggests that comparing only recipients of early retirement schemes would be questionable. However, including all claimants of a statutory pension under the age 65 is not without problems either, since this may involve persons who were never part of the workforce. Another challenge for comparative research is the fact that in some countries, such as Belgium, the

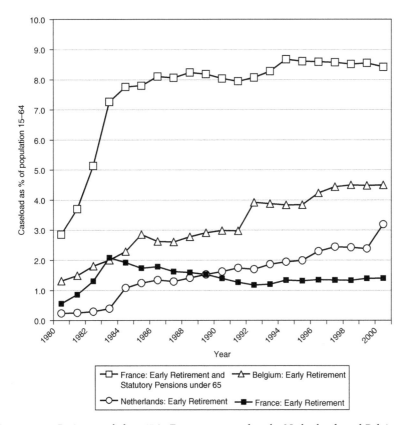

Figure 15.2. Retirement below 65 in France compared to the Netherlands and Belgium

statutory retirement age was raised from 60 to 65 only fairly recently, that is, in the decade after 1997. In other words, proceeding, as we did in Figure 15.2, runs the risk of exaggerating the relative extent of early retirement in France. That is why we decided to create a separate category for France (and Spain) of benefici-aries of statutory pensions before the normal retirement age of 65.

15.4 EXPLORING CASELOAD TRENDS – SOME ILLUSTRATIONS

The aims of the remainder of this chapter are illustrative and explorative in methodological terms. Employing some of the data which were collected by the authors of the country chapters (see Caseload Annex), we highlight selective caseload developments. Despite our efforts, problems of comparability across countries remain (e.g. in terms of early retirement, as discussed above). Assess-ments of total caseload volumes across countries are thus difficult to make. However, our primary interest here is to illustrate trends over time within countries. Moreover, no attempt has been made to be comprehensive at this point. This is only partly due to incomplete data sets for some countries and problems of comparability as discussed above. The main reason is related to the methodological and conceptual purpose of this chapter, however. In what follows we have selected countries in order to be able to illustrate the use, and limitations, of caseload data for comparative analyses in social and labour market policy. Moreover, the focus on caseload trends in only few countries allows us to revisit the main analytical aspects of this book as a whole, and the notion of 'risk re-categorization' in particular (see Section 15.5).

A central premise of this book is that during the past two decades welfare states have sought to reform the unemployment protection systems they inherited from the industrial era. In many countries, these reforms were geared towards reversing earlier policies of 'labour shedding' during the 1980s and early 1990s and to introduce behavioural requirements for the unemployed and other working-age benefit claimants which would encourage the transfer to paid employment. To some extent the success of these policies may be measured in terms of a decline in the caseload of working-age benefit schemes. However, the decrease in claimant numbers in one benefit programme (e.g. unemployment) might lead to a con-comitant growth in others (e.g. disability or social assistance), particularly for some groups such as low-skilled men (Clasen et al., 2006). Such a 'substitution effect' has been noted in several countries and can be gauged from some of the graphs below. In what follows, we map the direction and scale of the change in benefit schemes between 1980 and 2008 in terms of number of beneficiaries. As a first step, however, we explore the relationship between trends in caseload and developments in social spending.

Whereas the caseload data in this chapter are based on the sources described above, the data on benefit expenditure originate from the OECD's Socx database and from Eurostat's ESSPROS database. These two sources are similar in the data they report, but there are differences in the categorization of programmes (Adema and Ladaique, 2009: 51–2; De Deken and Kittel, 2007) and in the fact that ESSPROS, in contrast to Socx, also includes the costs of administering schemes. Where necessary we re-categorized ESSPROS data in line with the five benefit caseload categories discussed above (e.g. by combining sickness benefits with disability benefits into 'work incapacity' benefits – Socx already includes sickness in its incapacity category).

In Figure 15.3, we plotted caseload trends (beneficiaries as a percentage of the population 15–64 – left axis) and total expenditure according to the OECD (in US $, at constant 2000 prices at the 2000 purchasing power parity – right axis) of unemployment benefit schemes in three countries that witnessed different national trajectories during that period.

Figure 15.3 helps to illustrate that, whatever their respective uses, expenditure and caseload data should be regarded as separate indicators since trends in one are not necessarily reflected in the developments of the other. Looking only at Dutch data in Figure 15.3, this point does not seem to be immediately obvious. In the Netherlands the level of benefit caseload and expenditure on unemployment benefit developed more or less in tandem and both are in line with the trend in unemployment rates (see Statistical Annex, Table A.5). This is not the case for the other two countries, however. In Belgium the number of beneficiaries fluctuated broadly in line with the economic cycle and with changes in unemployment rates which remained well above Dutch and British rates during the 1990s and beyond (Statistical Annex, Table A.5). Cross-national differences in unemployment rates

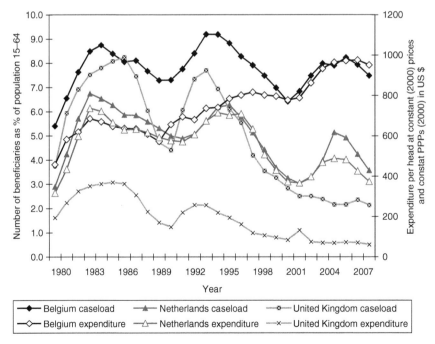

Figure 15.3. Caseload and total expenditure on unemployment benefit schemes between 1980 and 2008 in Belgium, the Netherlands, and the United Kingdom

Source: OECD (2011). Social expenditure – aggregated data. http://stats.oecd.org/Index.aspx

are also reflected in the fact that British caseload data continued to decline in the early 2000s in contrast to Dutch and Belgian claimant numbers which increased for a few years before declining again. Indeed, during the period 2002–5, the UK economy performed marginally better than the Dutch and even more so than the Belgian economy, but it is unlikely that it was completely shielded off from the economic cycle. Hence, the lack of 'responsiveness' of the caseload can be assumed to be related to changes in eligibility conditions.

For Belgium it is striking that spending continued to rise without showing any of the cyclical patterns exhibited by the development of caseloads. This suggests that either unemployment benefits became more generous (which is not very likely) or that the OECD's and the ESSPROS spending categories are broader than our caseload category, that is, that they include spending on beneficiaries who are officially not considered as unemployed. Indeed, there are two schemes which might have contributed to the spending boom: early retirement (which may account for the increases during the first half of the period) and the various paid-leave schemes that started to take off during the second half of the period. As discussed in Chapter 6, the most important Belgian early retirement schemes are financed by the unemployment insurance system, and so are the career break and time-credit benefits. Had the caseloads of these three programmes been plotted next to the OECD aggregate spending data, the inconsistency would have largely disappeared. In other words, the discrepancy between the spending and caseload lines in Belgium is an indicator of a form of a 'risk reconfiguration'. In this particular case this does not imply a trend towards a single benefit for the working-age population (e.g. as is envisaged in the United Kingdom) but a transformation and widening of unemployment benefit into a type of umbrella scheme which incorporates a range of out-of-work benefits for claimants with quite different behavioural requirements.

Turning to the United Kingdom, it is noticeable that the gap between British spending and caseloads is much larger than in Belgium and the Netherlands, respectively. This suggests a considerably less generous unemployment benefit system. However, it does not seem immediately obvious why this gap narrowed so much during the second half of the period. Legislative change is unlikely to be an explanation. As discussed in Chapter 2, the introduction of Jobseeker's Allowance (JSA) in 1996 brought about a halving of the contributory benefit entitlement and thus certainly led to some decline not only in the number of claimants but also in expenditure. A more plausible explanation might be the combination between very low levels of unemployment benefit rates and changes in the composition of unemployment benefit caseloads. It can be assumed that the job growth after the mid-1980s and again after 1993 benefited particularly claimants with shorter unemployment spells. Since caseloads are measured as number of claimants in a particular month, this would mean a faster depletion of recipient numbers than total expenditure since the latter is disproportionately determined by long-term benefit claimants. Potentially there are other, and perhaps better, reasons to do with national data reporting and consistency over time which would yet have to be resolved. For the time being the British trends illustrate our point that it is not possible to simply 'read off' expenditure from caseload date or vice versa.

15.5 FROM UNEMPLOYMENT BENEFITS TO
OUT-OF-WORK BENEFITS FOR THE
WORKING-AGE POPULATION

For a cross-national analysis, an exclusive focus on unemployment benefits can be deceptive if one is interested in assessing the benefit dependency of the working-age population. As we have already pointed out, countries may differ substantially in terms of how they administratively configure the risk of unemployment. In particular, those unemployed who are hard to reintegrate into the labour market are often referred to a range of other out-of-work benefit programmes, which entail different behavioural requirements from their beneficiaries. The most often used alternative exit routes are work incapacity and early retirement. In absence of a long-term insurance type of benefit, hard to employ persons may also end up in social assistance schemes. What complicates things is that in some countries the separation between these three out of work statuses has become blurred. As we have already argued, in Belgium, early retirement and sabbatical leave systems are part of the unemployment insurance system (and hence form a considerable part of this Socx or ESSPROS expenditure category). As discussed in Chapter 3, in Germany, unemployment benefit II can be claimed not only by those who are registered as unemployed but also those who are 'employable', even in a minor capacity, as well as those in low-paid work (see also below).

The category of work incapacity appears to be less marred by discrepancies between trends of caseloads and total benefit spending. In Figure 15.4, we have plotted those

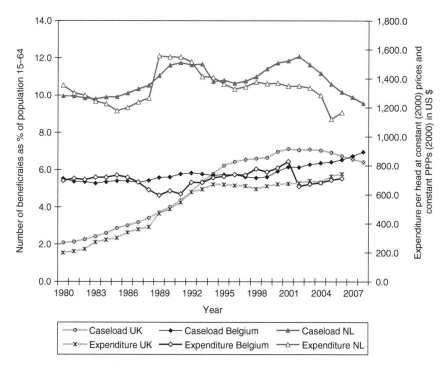

Figure 15.4. Caseload and expenditure on cash benefits of work incapacity benefit schemes between 1980 and 2008 in Belgium, the Netherlands, and the United Kingdom

two trends in a similar way as in Figure 15.3 for unemployment. The two sets of lines are fairly parallel within each country, but differ cross-nationally. In the Netherlands, work incapacity beneficiary numbers followed a cyclical development reminiscent of the caseload of unemployment insurance; in the United Kingdom there has been a steady rise in caseloads; whereas in Belgium the caseload has remained relatively stable.

Following unemployment trends, the cyclical pattern in the Netherlands suggests that work incapacity benefits throughout the period might have functioned as an alternative form of (long-term) unemployment benefit. In the United Kingdom, unemployment declined steadily after 1993 but disability benefit receipt continued to rise. This might be due to a number of reasons, including work incapacity increasingly covering more than the classic types of physiological impairment (see below); policy reforms which appear to have contributed to some transfers from unemployment to disability support for some groups (Clasen et al., 2006); as well as changes in average benefit durations, which might help to explain the divergence between caseload and expenditure trends in the 1990s.

In Figures 15.5 and 15.6, we provide an overview of the evolution of caseloads of different out-of-work benefits in eleven countries at five particular years between 1980 and 2008. For Belgium, Germany, the Netherlands, the United Kingdom, Denmark, and Sweden, we are able to present a time series that covers all (major) benefit programmes for the entire time series. For the remaining countries the data for some programmes are incomplete or are missing altogether. For France, we have no data on work incapacity for 2001 and 2008; for Switzerland there are no data on early retirement for any of the five points in time; for Spain data on social assistance are sketchy or missing; for Hungary some of the data are based on estimates and, as for the Czech Republic, the series only starts in the 1990s (and hence the points in time in the graph are different than in the other countries). In order to improve comparability, we have used the categorization as explained earlier (an exact listing for each country of which benefits are included in which category can be found in the Caseload Annex). Thus, it does not matter out of which branch of a national social security system early retirement, for example, is financed or whether incapacity benefits in a particular country is manifest in sickness, disability, or social assistance schemes (as long as benefits are granted on a medical basis).

What is striking in Figures 15.5 and 15.6 is the common pattern of relatively low out-of-work benefit caseloads in 1980 and the subsequent growth trend (for Hungary the same pattern can be observed for the shorter period 1990–2008). Towards the end of the period only the two Scandinavian countries, the United Kingdom and the Czech Republic managed to reduce claimant numbers that had peaked during the mid-1990s (or in 2000 in the Czech Republic). The Netherlands merely contained the increase, and in Belgium, Germany, and Switzerland the number of working-age benefit claimants continued to rise well into 2008. Given data problems for some countries (see above) and the fact that in almost none of the countries the caseload of work incapacity declined, it is probably safe to conclude that there also was no reduction in the number of recipients of working-age benefits in France. For Spain the reductions accomplished at the beginning of this century seem to have been offset by 2008. Furthermore, a cursory analysis of the mix in those eleven countries suggests some degree of substitution between (low) unemployment caseloads and (comparatively high) work incapacity caseloads: countries with lower caseloads in the unemployment category tend to experience high claimant rates in

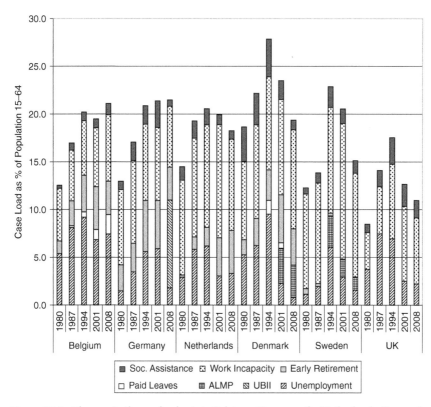

Figure 15.5. Changes in the caseload mix in Belgium, Germany, the Netherlands, Denmark, Sweden, and the United Kingdom between 1980 and 2008

Note: See Caseload Annex.

the work incapacity category (the Netherlands, Sweden, Denmark, Switzerland, and Hungary), and the successes in reducing the caseload of unemployment benefits concur with increasing work incapacity caseloads (the United Kingdom).

This mechanism of 'communicating vessels' also becomes evident on a country-by-country basis. For example, as discussed in Chapter 2 (see Figure 2.1), the caseload of unemployment benefits in the United Kingdom was halved on a long-term basis, but the number of claimants on incapacity benefits almost tripled. Such a dramatic increase is not (only) the consequence of the disappearance of certain types of industrial jobs but suggests a broadening of entitlement criteria or increase in types of work incapacity of a psychological rather than merely physiological nature. In Denmark, one can observe a spectacular decline in the caseload of unemployment benefits between 1994 and 2008, but the number of beneficiaries of work incapacity benefits remained exceptionally high during the same period.

By contrast, in Belgium the number of unemployment benefit claimants has remained high throughout, while the caseload of incapacity benefits has seen only a moderate increase (Figure 15.7).

As discussed in Chapter 6 the transition towards a post-industrial service sector economy seems to have been facilitated by the use of early retirement. The

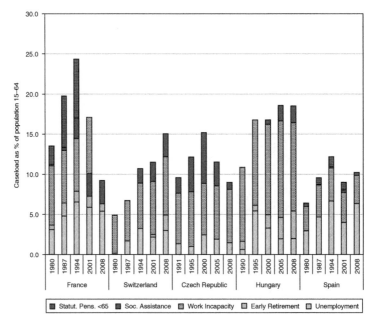

Figure 15.6. Changes in the caseload mix in France, Switzerland, the Czech Republic, Hungary, and Spain between 1980 and 2008

Note: See Caseload Annex. For France and Spain there are no data for statutory pensions under 65 in 2008; for France there are no data on work incapacity benefits for the years 2001 and 2008; for Spain there are no or at best incomplete data on social assistance for any year. For the Czech Republic and Hungary the data are only for the period 1990/1 to 2008.

number of work incapacity beneficiaries started rising only when the Belgian government began to close down this particular exit route. In addition, since 2000 there has been a significant increase in the caseload of the paid sabbatical leave schemes (from below 100,000 to ca. 250,000 case by 2009; see Caseload Annex). This particular labour supply reduction arrangement seems to fit more with the 'cost disease problems' of a service sector economy (Baumol, 2001) than the labour shedding needs of a deindustrializing economy. The benefits of the Belgian sabbatical scheme are financed by the unemployment insurance system, which largely accounts for the divergence between the caseload and expenditure trends which we reported in Figure 15.3.

The Netherlands and Sweden illustrate yet another variation on the principle of communicating vessels. Here, we see not so much a decline of one type of benefit (unemployment) being compensated by an increase in another (work incapacity), but rather what could be described as a delayed shockwave. Trends in unemployment benefits caseload seem to follow the economic cycle, and work incapacity schemes follow suit, albeit with a time lag of a few years.

In some respects, the Netherlands 'pioneered' this use of work incapacity benefits as a way of accommodating redundant workers during the era of the so-called Dutch 'disease' when the country's labour market was plagued by an exceptionally large scale of inactivity. As Figure 15.8 demonstrates, it was only

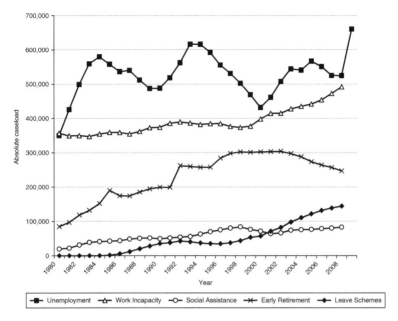

Figure 15.7. Changes in the caseload mix in Belgium, 1980–2008

towards the end of the period under study when policy reforms seem to have facilitated a reduction in the caseload of incapacity benefit receipt. The steep rise in early retirement benefits during the 1990s is a reason to cast doubt on the alleged Dutch employment 'miracle' (Visser and Hemerijck, 1997) of that decade. While the volume of unemployment benefit receipt declined steadily, structural unemployment over time seems to have been accommodated initially by the work incapacity scheme, and since the early 2000s by collectively bargained early exit from the labour market (bearing in mind the discrepancies we discussed earlier between the caseload of early retirement and the spending figures). In other words, these early retirement schemes seem to have taken over the shock-absorbing role that the work incapacity schemes played during the heyday of the Dutch 'disease'. The steep increase in early retirement caseloads between 2000 and 2004 is remarkable. It seems conceivable that this was at least in part a reaction to the Dutch government's plan to close down as of 2006 the early retirement pathways.

Finally, the German case illustrates a number of problems of creating comparable categorizations across countries. However, it also helps to illustrate the relevance of the concept of risk re-categorization which might become a prominent feature in unemployment and labour market policy also in other countries. As Figure 15.9 shows, German unification in 1990 and the collapse of the East German economy manifested itself in steep rises in unemployment, incapacity, and early retirement caseloads. A change in the registration of persons claiming a statutory pension benefit before retirement age masked the scale of the latter for some time. The pension reform law of 1992 led to the re-categorization of persons drawing a standard pension before the statutory retirement age, treating early retirees as 'regular' pensioners and thus reduced the early retirement caseload

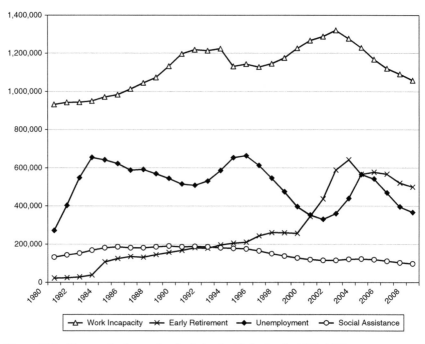

Figure 15.8. Changes in the caseload mix in the Netherlands, 1980–2008

considerably (Deutsche Rentenversicherung, 2010: 169). However, this was masked by the subsequent steady increase of early retirement until about 2004 which indicates the important role this programme played at a time when the German economy was faced with a considerable decline in industrial employment, relatively low economic growth, and mass unemployment (see Statistical Annex, Tables A.1, A.3, and A.5).

Early retirement, and also incapacity benefits, helped to contain the increase in unemployment related caseloads. In Figure 15.9, we expressed the latter, before 2005, in three categories: unemployment insurance, unemployment assistance, and the total of these two (unemployment). A few remarks need to be made. First, a certain percentage of social assistance claimants were registered as unemployed. However, this proportion varied over time as well as across regions. In the absence of systematically collected data we have thus not included unemployed social assistance claimants in the total unemployment caseload which is therefore underestimated. On the other hand, we have included persons in receipt of 'temporary unemployment insurance', officially *Kurzarbeitergeld* (short-term working allowance), which is a temporary benefit for persons in employment whose company, rather than making workers (fully) redundant, reduced their working hours for economic reasons. It is thus a benefit which replaces lost earnings in part and claimants might be considered temporarily (and partially) unemployed. This instrument was heavily used not only in response to the economic downturn in 2008 but also in the earlier periods (see Caseload Annex, Germany).

Plotting trends separately, Figure 15.9 indicates that the means-tested unemployment assistance became increasingly important during the 1990s to the extent

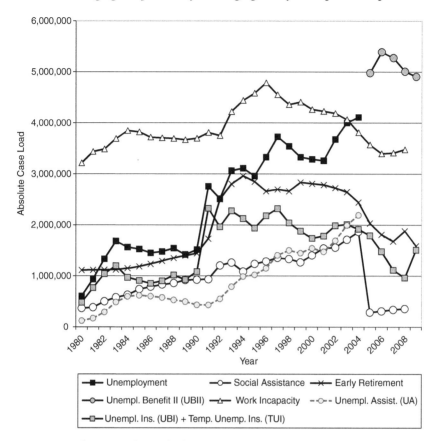

Figure: 15.9. Changes in the caseload mix in Germany, 1980–2008

Note: See Caseload Annex. Unemployment assistance (UA) is also included in the category 'Unemployment'. The series of this category ends in 2005 because the risk reconfiguration that occurred in the wake of the introduction of UBII (see text).

that overall unemployment protection in Germany became increasingly 'dualized' in terms of caseload numbers, or rather heterogeneous if unemployed social assistance claimants are included (see Clasen and Goerne, 2011). However, in 2005 this changed fundamentally. As discussed in Chapter 4 in the context of the most important reform in German labour market policy since the 1960s, unemployment benefit provision was administratively and institutionally altered. Of particular interest for us is the merger between the former unemployment assistance with social assistance (for claimants deemed to be employable) into the new unemployment benefit II (UBII). UBII is conceptually new, however, since it is not (only) a form of unemployment protection. It also covers persons not registered as unemployed but able to work, as well as some groups of persons who are in minor forms of employment (see Chapter 4; Figures 4.3 and 4.4).

UBII may be considered as a type of unemployment assistance, the introduction of which has led to a relative marginalization of unemployment insurance in caseload terms and a dominance of means-tested unemployment support in the modern German welfare state. From one perspective it illustrates a form of risk re-categorization and new orientation within unemployment protection, potentially signalling a shift from unemployment to 'employability' as the more appropriate caseload category in the future. Alternatively, it could be argued that the concept and administrative category of 'unemployment', which historically has been subject to periodic change, is in the process of a major revision, at least in some countries. Unemployment in the industrial era was once a fairly restrictive category applied mainly to workers with regular types of jobs but temporarily out of work. As argued in the introductory chapter, in post-industrial societies the identification of this specific group within total working-age benefit claimants seems to become less meaningful for the purposes of providing benefits and other types of social support. As a result, 'unemployment' and unemployment protection seems to be becoming more integrative in an administrative sense, including those at the margins of the labour market who were previously left out.

15.6 CONCLUSIONS

This chapter has explored the viability of caseload data for comparative analysis while making use of available data to illustrate trends which were discussed in the introductory chapter of this volume, particularly in relation to processes of 'risk re-categorization'. The discussion has shown that the relative paucity of internationally available and comparable time series is not only due to absence or inconsistency of national data sources. There are also substantial methodological challenges especially for those who aim to calculate total benefit dependency ratios and compare those across countries. While certainly of interest, not least politically, considerable efforts would be required to overcome problems such as the registration of the caseload of mandated non-statutory schemes (such as statutory sickness pay in the United Kingdom and Germany) and of regionally administered benefit plans (such as social assistance in Spain), double counting, partial and periodic benefit receipt. Another set of challenges relates to identifying benefit categorizations and conceptual issues, such as drawing boundaries between public and private programmes or functional equivalents between, for example, persons of the same pre-retirement age drawing pensions from different pension programmes. Our discussion has shown that what might appear to be a fairly straightforward task of selecting, allocating, and adding caseload numbers often requires concept stretching, omissions of some data, or compromises, including sometimes even the extrapolation of time series.

This does not mean that caseloads are necessarily an inferior indicator of welfare state change. Indeed, in many respects the use of social expenditure data faces very similar problems. In recent years, information on 'disaggregated' social spending on different areas over time has become more readily available which has allowed more detailed programme-based analyses of developments in comparative perspective (e.g. see Castles, 2008). However, depending on research aims, the use of these data also requires conceptual deliberation and, as with the use of caseload data, rests on contestable assumptions about categorization or functional equivalence. This is underlined by the, at times, considerable degree of discrepancy between what is supposed to be comparable data at the international level (see De Deken and Kittel, 2007).

Neither does this mean that caseloads do not offer any 'added value' over and above social expenditure. The chapter has shown that trends in spending and caseloads of the same programme do not always co-vary. This can be due to changes in employment or unemployment structures, or because of policy reforms which affect the two indicators differently. Provided that methodological problems can be adequately addressed, both are therefore distinctive indicators of welfare state change.

The use of either social expenditure or caseloads as a gauge for trends in and across welfare states needs to be carefully considered. The purpose of this chapter was to contribute to the improvement of such macro indicators in order to go beyond tracing institutional change by merely analysing processes as they evolved in individual countries. It is only possible to draw comparative lessons from such case studies, if the historical narrative is based on the application of concepts that have meaning beyond a particular country. A genuine comparison requires categories that have the same or broadly similar meanings in all the countries under investigation. What this chapter (and the adjunct Caseload Annex) tried to do was to bring to the surface problems that are inherent in any comparative analysis that builds upon process tracing in a set of individual countries. It explored the scope of analysis which existing caseload data allow, documenting institutional change on the basis of tables and graphs expressed in measurement units which, hopefully, do justice to individual idiosyncrasies of particular countries, while acknowledging problems of comparisons across different countries. As such the chapter, and the Caseload Annex, sought to provide a link between using an analytical framework with common categories and comparable definitions of variables on the one hand, and the elaboration of country-specific 'incomparable' aspects of welfare state change on the other hand.

The elaboration of coherent and consistent time series of both caseload data and disaggregated social spending can contribute to such an endeavour. Social spending is likely to be the more appropriate indicator for some purposes. For others the use of reliable caseloads will be more relevant. Reflecting major analytical aims of the book, this is what we have tried to show in this chapter. While processes of benefit homogenization and risk re-categorization affect social spending, it is shifts in caseloads across different programmes which seem the more immediate and thus more appropriate indicator. Assuming that the process of change within national unemployment protection, and working-age benefit provision more generally, has only just begun, we expect caseload based analyses to become more relevant in comparative social policy research. This chapter hopes to have made a small contribution to the discussion not only on the challenges such analyses are faced with but also of their potential.

16

Active labour market policy in a changing economic context[1]

Giuliano Bonoli

16.1 INTRODUCTION

Fighting unemployment and joblessness have been key priorities for policymakers since the early post-war years. While macroeconomic policy was long the main instrument to maintain high rates of employment in many countries, over the last few years a set of tools conveniently labelled 'active labour market policies' (ALMPs) have become the standard approach in this field in a majority of OECD (Organisation for Economic Co-operation and Development) countries. ALMPs have multiple objectives, but generally they aim at removing obstacles to labour market participation. These can be of various origins, including obsolete skills, inadequate behaviour, lack of motivation, bad health, and so forth. ALMPs attempt, with different tools, to address this range of obstacles that can prevent labour market entry.

The active approach in labour market policy has become popular since the mid-1990s often making reference to the notion of activation. However, instances of state intervention in this field have existed before. Sweden is often quoted as a pioneer, thanks to the development of a sophisticated system of ALMPs in the 1950s. In response to the job crises of the late 1970s and early 1980s, many countries developed various types of labour market programmes that go under the rubric of 'active labour market policy'.

It should be noted, however, that ALMPs adopted in different countries and at different times are rather different policies. One important dimension of variation within the universe of ALMPs is the degree to which they invest in the human capital of their clients. As will be shown below, in some countries, ALMPs were at times closely linked to the retraining of jobless people so that they could enter the labour market in expanding economic sectors.

A second important dimension is the extent to which ALMPs do actually expect beneficiaries to re-enter the labour market. While, with a few exceptions, the

[1] This chapter is based on research carried out in the context of the research project 'Adapting Western welfare states to new structures of social risk' (Grant No. 100012-115937/1), financed by the Swiss science foundation. I would like to thank Michel Berclaz and Frank Reber for research assistance.

official and explicit aim of ALMPs is always labour market reintegration, in reality, in many countries, these have been used at times as alternatives to market employment. This was the case, for example, in Sweden in the 1980s or in Germany in the 1980s and after unification. In these contexts, for a large number of non-working individuals, labour market participation seemed a distant prospect, and the policy was used to prevent further human capital depletion or for social purposes rather than with a clear focus on labour market participation. In contrast, since the mid-1990s, under more favourable labour market conditions, governments have tended to abandon this approach in favour of one emphasizing rapid reinsertion in employment, based on a mix of incentives and support for non-working individuals.

This chapter shows that the objectives and tools of ALMPs change among countries and over time. To a large extent the role they play in the labour market is related to the broad economic situation. At times of rapid expansion and labour shortage, like the 1950s and 1960s, their key objective was to upskill the workforce so as to contribute to economic modernization. After the oil shocks of the 1970s, the raison d'être of ALMPs shifted from economic to social policy, and their key objective became the preservation of (some) human capital and social cohesion in the context of mass unemployment. Finally, since the mid-1990s, we see the development of a new function, well captured by the notion of activation, which refers to the strengthening of work incentives and the removal of obstacles to employment, mostly for low-skilled people.

At first sight, the shifting nature of ALMPs can be understood with reference to the changing economic context. This view is broadly accurate, but upon closer inspection, however, it appears that the coupling between economic cycle and orientation of ALMP is not always optimal. Institutional inertia means that when labour market conditions change, it usually takes a while before ALMPs are appropriately reoriented. In fact, while the adoption of a clear employment promotion objective is a common trait of most OECD countries, the countries that have been better able to exploit the mid-1990s–2008 labour market expansion are those that had no or little previous experience with ALMP: among them Denmark and the United Kingdom. Other countries, like Germany or Sweden, were much slower to reorient their already developed ALMP system and take advantage of economic expansion.

This chapter illustrates these claims on the basis of a comparison of ALMPs in six Western European countries: Sweden, Denmark, Germany, France, Italy, and the United Kingdom. It begins by identifying different types of ALMPs that are found across OECD countries. Second, it presents the policy trajectories followed by the six countries, since the beginnings of the policy to the late 2000s. It concludes with some considerations on the role of ALMPs in the broader context of the regulation of the risk of unemployment.

16.2 TYPES OF ACTIVE LABOUR MARKET POLICY

Active labour market policies have different origins. In Sweden, ALMPs were developed as early as the 1950s, with the objective of improving the match between demand and supply of labour in the context of a rapidly evolving economy, essentially by financing extensive vocational training programmes (Swenson, 2002). At the opposite extreme, the term 'active' can been used to describe the approach developed in various English-speaking countries, which combines placement services with stronger work incentives, time limits on recipiency, benefit reductions, and the use of sanctions, the so-called 'workfare' approach (King, 1995; Peck, 2001). In fact, as many have pointed out, ALMP is a particularly ambiguous category of social policy (Barbier, 2001, 2004; Clasen, 2000; Clegg, 2005).

Some authors have attempted to deal with this problem by distinguishing between two types of ALMPs: those which are about improving human capital, and those which use essentially negative incentives to move people from social assistance into employment. Examples of such classifications are found in Torfing (1999) who distinguishes between 'offensive' and 'defensive' workfare. Offensive workfare, which is the term used to describe the Danish variant of activation, relies on improving skills and empowerment rather than on sanctions and benefit reduction, as is the 'defensive' variant found in the United States. Taylor-Gooby makes the same point using instead the terms of 'positive' and 'negative' activation (Taylor-Gooby, 2004). In a similar vein, Barbier distinguishes between 'liberal activation', characterized by stronger work incentives, benefit conditionality, and the use of sanctions, and 'universalistic activation', which is found in the Nordic countries and continues to rely on extensive investment in human capital essentially through training, though he recognizes that a third type might exist in Continental Europe (Barbier, 2004; Barbier and Ludwig-Mayerhofer, 2004).

Dichotomies between human investment and incentive-based approaches to activation are a useful starting point in making sense of an ambiguous concept. However, they probably constitute an oversimplification of the real world and run the risk of carrying value judgements. A different type of distinction is found in Clegg, who identifies two policy mechanisms that can be subsumed under activation: circulation and integration. The idea behind circulation is to improve the chances of an unemployed person to enter in contact with a potential employer, through placement services, for example. Integration, instead, refers to instruments that more directly bring the jobless into employment, like subsidized jobs or sheltered employment (Clegg, 2005: 56).

Here, I also want to depart from the dichotomic and/or value-laden distinction that has dominated debates on ALMPs. I suggest instead distinguishing between four different ideal types of ALMPs, which, like all ideal types, are unlikely to exist in a pure form in the real world: incentive reinforcement, employment assistance, occupation, and human capital investment. The key objectives and tools of each ideal type are presented in Table 16.1.

The first type of ALMPs, incentive reinforcement, refers to measures that aim at strengthening work incentives for benefit recipients. This objective can be achieved in various ways, for example, by curtailing passive benefits, both in terms of benefit rates and duration. Benefits can also be made conditional on participation in work schemes or other labour market programmes. Finally, incentives can be strengthened through the use of sanctions. Elements of incentive reinforcement exist everywhere, but they are particularly strong in English-speaking countries.

Table 16.1. Four ideal types of active labour market policy

Type	Objective	Tools
Incentive reinforcement	Strengthen positive and negative work incentives for people on benefit	• Tax credits, in-work benefits • Time limits on recipiency • Benefit reductions • Benefit conditionality • Sanctions
Employment assistance	Remove obstacle to employment and facilitate (re-) entry into the labour market	• Placement services • Job subsidies • Counselling • Job-search programmes
Occupation	Keep jobless people occupied; limit human capital depletion during unemployment	• Job-creation schemes in the public sector • Non-employment-related training programmes
Human capital investment	Improve the chances of finding employment by upskilling jobless people	• Basic education • Vocational training

The second type, which I term employment assistance, consists of measures aiming at removing obstacles to labour market participation, without necessarily impacting on work incentives. These include placement services, job-search programmes that increase the likelihood of a jobless person establishing contact with a potential employer. Counselling and job subsidies may be particularly useful to beneficiaries who have been out of the labour market for a long time or who have never had a job, or who are often shunned by employers. For parents, an obstacle to employment may be the lack of childcare, belonging to the employment assistance variant. With the exception of placement services, employment assistance is probably the newest type of ALMPs. It is common not only in English-speaking countries (combined with incentive reinforcement) but also in Nordic and Continental Europe.

A third type of ALMP can be labelled as occupation. Its objective is not primarily to promote labour market re-entry, but to keep jobless people busy, also in order to prevent the depletion of human capital associated with an unemployment spell. This type of ALMP consists of not only job creation and work experience programmes in the public or non-profit sector but also training in some cases, such as shorter courses, which do not fundamentally change the type of job a person can do. Continental European countries in the 1980s and early 1990s have been among the main users of this type of ALMP.

Finally, ALMPs can consist of providing vocational training to jobless people or, if needed, basic education. The idea here is to offer a second chance to people who were not able to profit from the education system or whose skills have become obsolete. The provision of vocational training to jobless people is most developed in the Nordic countries.

It would be extremely helpful to operationalize these four ideal types with measurable indicators, and then map their variation across time and space. Unfortunately, available data allow only a very crude approximation of this exercise. There have been attempts to summarize with indicators the key institutional features of activation in different countries (Hasselpflug, 2005; OECD, 2007c). The results obtained, however, are not entirely convincing, and do not match expectations based on more qualitative knowledge of many of the countries covered. This is due to a number of problems, among which the fact that these data sources are based on formal regulation, which can differ significantly from actual implementation. An alternative way to map, at least in part, cross-national variation in ALMPs on the basis of the ideal types discussed above is to use expenditure data on subprogrammes. The OCED provides this information since 1985 for most of its members. Available categories are: public employment services and administration, employment subsidies, job rotation schemes, start-up incentives, training, and direct job creation (cf. Statistical Annex, Table A.15).

These data allows us to operationalize three of the four ideal types presented above as shown in Table 16.1: employment assistance which includes the OECD spending categories 'public employment services and administration, employment subsidies, job rotation schemes, and start-up incentives'; occupation, which includes the category 'direct job creation'; and human capital investment which includes the category 'training'. In this way, we are able to trace the evolution over a twenty-year period of the relative effort made in the different components of ALMP.

ALMPs' spending profiles presented in Figure 16.1 reveal a number of important observations. First, there is obviously a cyclical effect, shown by the decline in overall spending between 1995 and 2005, which can be explained with the decline

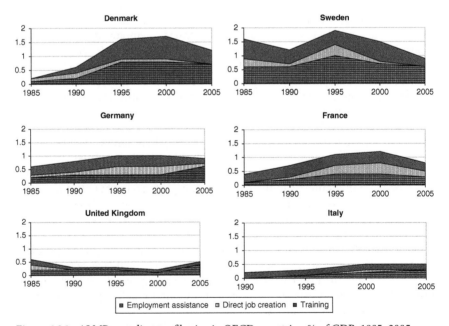

Figure 16.1. ALMP spending profiles in six OECD countries, % of GDP, 1985–2005

Source: Graphs constructed on the basis of data obtained from OECD. Stat (available on www.oecd.org).

in unemployment (especially in Sweden, Denmark, and France). The increase in overall spending in the United Kingdom, instead, calls for a political explanation, as this took place in the context of declining numbers of jobless. Second, if one compares trends over the twenty-year period covered, there is clearly a reduction in the size of direct job creation, which is relatively important in France, Germany, and Sweden until the mid-1990s, but then declines everywhere. Third, over the same period of time, one sees employment assistance gaining importance everywhere, expect perhaps in Sweden where spending on this function is basically stable over time. Spending on training, finally, does not show a clear trend over time (except in Denmark where it peaks in 2000). The biggest variation in relation to training is across countries, not time, with the Nordic countries being the biggest spenders, the United Kingdom the lowest, and the continental European countries somewhere in between.

OECD's spending data needs to be considered with caution since the distinctions adopted by the OECD do not always match national categories, and sometimes information is missing on given categories for several years. The results presented in Figure 16.1, however, are broadly compatible with the expectations put forward above, and with the findings of the qualitative literature, which distinguished between two or three different approaches to activation.

16.3 ACTIVE LABOUR MARKET POLICIES ACROSS ECONOMIC CYCLES

The development of ALMP-spending profiles over time suggests that this area of social policy has undergone substantial change over the last two decades. ALMPs, however, pre-existed data collection by the OECD (which begins in 1985 for most countries). This section looks at the development in this field of labour market policy since the 1950s, when Sweden embraced an active approach in labour market policy. In fact, one can identify three periods in the development of ALMPs in OECD countries. First, in the 1950s and the 1960s, when in the context of labour market shortage, countries developed active policies in order to provide appropriately skilled workers to expanding industrial economies. In this period the key objective of policy was investment in human capital. The second period follows the oil shocks of 1973–5. ALMPs have had to face a considerably more difficult environment, characterized by persistent high unemployment. In this context, in many countries the key function of ALMPs becomes occupation. Finally, since the mid-1990s, labour market policy aims essentially at encouraging and facilitating labour market re-entry of unemployed persons and other non-working individuals. The tools adopted here consist of various mixes of incentive reinforcement and employment assistance.

What precisely happened during these three periods is reviewed next. The account focuses on six countries in Western Europe: Sweden, Denmark, Germany, France, Italy, and the United Kingdom. Each period-section adopts a different order in the presentation of country developments, starting each time with the 'pioneers' of the relevant use of ALMPs and then moving on to other countries.[2]

16.3.1 The post-war years: ALMP in the context of labour shortage

Most experts agree that ALMPs were born in Sweden with the so-called Rehn–Meidner model. Put forward in 1951 by two trade union economists, Gosta Rehn and Rudolf Meidner, this strategy had several objectives: equality in the wage distribution, sustainable full employment, and the modernization of Swedish industry. Equality and full employment were to be promoted through a solidaristic wage policy, which basically meant identical wage increases across all sectors of industry. The egalitarian wage policy had both intended and unintended effects. Among the intended effects was a strong incentive for Swedish producers to invest in productivity-enhancing technologies. If productivity lagged behind, imposed wage growth would push out of the market less competitive companies. This represented a strong push for the modernization of Swedish industry.

But of course, not every industry would be able to keep up with the pace of wage increases agreed centrally. Low-productivity industries were to be priced out of the market as collectively bargained wages increased. It was in order to deal with the workers that would as a result find themselves unemployed that Rehn and Meidner conceived ALMPs. As less-productive companies were pushed out of the market, the workers they made redundant were to be retrained and made available for expanding high-productivity industries (see e.g. Anxo and Niklasson, 2006; Benner and Vad, 2000: 401; Mabbet, 1995: 141ff.; Swenson, 2002: 275).

According to Swenson, however, ALMPs also constituted a response to one of Swedish employers' recurrent problems at the time: shortage of labour. By quickly retraining workers who had lost their jobs, ALMPs ensured a steady supply of appropriately qualified labour. If the idea of setting up an ALMP came from the trade unions, it was clearly acceptable to and possibly desirable for employers as well. In fact, according to Swenson, it was probably them who suggested it in the first place (2002: 275). On the basis of extensive historical research, he concludes that:

> Employers warmly endorsed activist training and mobility measures even before the labor confederation included them as the centerpiece of their plan for economic stabilization and industrial development (the "Rehn-Meidner Model"). . . . Organized employers were not merely resigned to hegemonic Social Democrats and hoping to appease them for special consideration on particular details, for nicer treatment in other domains, or to avoid public disfavor. They knew what they wanted. Sometimes they liked best what they got and got what they liked best. (Swenson, 2002: 11)

The Rhen–Meidner model is a unique feature of Swedish economic history that was not repeated elsewhere. However, the idea of an ALMP in a rapidly modernizing economy characterized by labour shortage was found appealing in other places as well. Sometimes, the tools used were different though, because the

---

[2] Note that the selection of information presented here is based on extensive country case studies, which look systematically at labour market policy developments in the six countries.

starting point was also different. This was the case of Italy, where unemployment was not the result of people being laid off by declining industries, but of labour surplus in the southern part of the country.

During the 1950s and 1960s, two decades of strong growth that Italians remember as the 'economic miracle', Italy was also concerned with a labour shortage problem. Expanding industries in the north needed adequately trained workers. The south still constituted a major reservoir of labour, but essentially unskilled. In order to improve the matching between skill demand and supply, a law on apprenticeship was adopted in 1955. It made provision for on-the-job training and lower salaries for trainees. The scheme, however, did not take off. Employers were generally not allowed to select apprentices, who were sent to them by labour exchange offices, and the trade unions complained that the law was being used to underpay young workers (Gualmini, 1998: 108).

Moves in this direction were also made in the case of France. In 1963, the Gaullist government embarked on a reform of the unemployment compensation system that would have facilitated access to (re-)training for unemployed people. This proposal encountered nonetheless the strong opposition of the trade unions, who feared increased state intervention in the management of unemployment insurance (UNEDIC). In France, unemployment insurance, as the rest of social security, is run jointly by the social partners who have traditionally resisted government intervention in what they consider a 'private' institution (Bonoli and Palier, 1997; Palier, 2002). The result was a watered-down version of the initial proposal. The episode highlighted the tension between an insurance-based unemployment compensations system run by the social partners and a public policy objective: the upskilling of unemployed people in the context of labour shortage. The social partner's and particularly the trade unions' narrow understanding of unemployment compensation as an insurance scheme severely limited the scope for injecting active and training measures into unemployment policy (Clegg, 2005: 176–9).

Only a few years later, Germany was to follow the same path, with the adoption of the 1969 Employment Promotion Act (*Arbeitsförderungsgesetz*). The law was adopted by the short-lived first 'Grand Coalition' government in Germany's post-war history. The CDU–SPD coalition, lead by the Christian Democrats, lasted only three years (1966–9), but played an important role in shaping post-war labour market policy. The coalition came against the backdrop of the 1966–7 recession, after a row over budget broke out between the CDU and the FDP, the parties that formed the previous government. Its approach to social and economic policy anticipated many of the themes that have been popularized by political leaders in the 2000s. According to Alber:

> To combat the economic crisis, the new government intended to shift public expenditure from social consumption to social investment. Various transfer payments were curbed, and for the first time, educational issues were given priority. . . . As a first step towards a more active labour market policy, the competence of the unemployment insurance scheme was extended to include the promotion of vocational training. (Alber, 1987: 14)

The law was largely based on a proposal prepared by the SPD in 1966, at the time still in opposition. It emphasized a new, preventative, role for labour market policy, based on the adjustment of the workforce skills to technological change. The new law instituted the Federal Institute of Labour (*Bundesanstalt für Arbeit*) responsible not only for unemployment compensation insurance but also for continuing education, retraining, employment services for the disabled, job-creation programmes, and for training (Frerich and Frey, 1996). At the same time, a new law on vocational training was adopted, which significantly consolidated the system put in place seventy years earlier (Thelen, 2004: 241).

Contrary to a widespread perception among welfare state scholars, the post-war years were not an era of passive income protection only. Although unemployment insurance was the core instrument of labour market policy in post-war Europe, other initiatives were taken in several European countries to reinforce the active dimension of unemployment protection, essentially through vocational training. This made sense. In a context of rapid economic growth and labour shortage, to retrain jobless people so that they could provide the labour force needed by expanding industries was an obvious thing to do. The developments reviewed above show little consistency in terms of political determinants though. The idea of linking training to unemployment policy came from political parties distributed across the political spectrum: the Swedish Social Democrats, the French Gaullists, Italian Christian Democrats, and a coalition government in Germany. These political forces have little in common, except perhaps a centrist orientation in economic and social policy matters.

16.3.2 Facing the employment crisis: ALMPs in the context of mass unemployment

The economic context of labour market policy changed dramatically after the oil shocks of 1973–5 and the subsequent economic crisis. All of a sudden, labour market policy had to deal with a new problem: mass unemployment. The idea of an ALMP was present in most countries, but the unfavourable economic context meant that labour market policy, no matter how active, could achieve little. Against this background, we see the emergence of a different ideal type of ALMPs, the one I have labelled occupation, which does not really aim at putting jobless people back into the labour market, but more at keeping them busy and slowing down the deterioration of human capital associated with unemployment. This new function of ALMPs developed across countries, but through different channels that reflected previous policy.

In response to the employment crises of the 1970s, Sweden radically transformed its system of ALMP. It is noteworthy that the crisis years (mid-1970s to the late 1980s) did not result in open unemployment in Sweden. This was partly the result of not only the expansion of public sector employment, which took place over the same period of time, but also a consequence of the liberal use of ALMPs. In fact, by providing an occupation to otherwise jobless persons, ALMPs allowed Sweden to keep employment at pre-recession levels (Mjoset, 1987: 430). This was obviously a rather new function for ALMPs, which was adopted by default in the context of a stagnating economy with little net job creation outside the state sector.

What role did ALMPs play during those years? To find out, we have to turn to the evaluation literature. In the Swedish case, from the 1970s onwards, ALMPs resemble increasingly alternatives to market employment. On offer one finds training programmes, relief works, that is, temporary jobs arranged mostly in the public sector. Typically, these jobs were used to renew entitlement to unemployment insurance (theoretically limited to fourteen months). During these years, there was a relative shift away from supply-side measures towards demand-side interventions: that is, job-creation programmes (Anxo and Niklasson, 2006: 360). Micro-level evaluations pointed out that most of these schemes were rather ineffective in terms of favouring labour market re-entry (Calmfors et al., 2001). The original aim of ALMPs, to upskill workers so that they can enter more productive occupations, had somewhat fallen out of sight. Swedish ALMP had clearly moved towards the 'occupation' type described above. During the same period (in 1974), Sweden also adopted a relatively strict employment protection law (Emmenegger, 2009). The 1970s can thus be characterized as a period of departure from the post-war Swedish model, with the country adopting many of the policy options that were being developed in Continental Europe.

With unemployment rising, Germany turned to ALMPs in the second half of the 1970s. These measures were based on the Employment Promotion Act of 1969. In a development that is reminiscent of the Swedish story, the objective of this law shifted from the general upskilling of the workforce to a tool aimed at reducing open unemployment, even though training continued to play an important role. The post-crisis years were characterized by a stop-and-go approach to ALMPs, partly due to the funding mechanism of these measures. Both passive and active unemployment benefits are financed out of the same fund. When unemployment is high, passive expenditure increases automatically, leaving fewer resources to finance active measures (Manow and Seils, 2000: 282). For example, after a sharp increase in the number of beneficiaries of ALMPs from 1,600 in 1970 to 648,00 in 1975, the numbers involved declined to 545,000 in 1982, under budgetary pressures (Frerich and Frey, 1996: 177; Seeleib-Kaiser et al., 2008: 43).

Active labour market policies were back with the return to power of the Christian democrats. The Kohl government, elected in 1982, expanded ALMPs in the context of a 'qualification offensive' based on various labour market and training programmes. Between 1982 and 1987, the total number of participants in such programmes rose from 555,000 to 1.4 million (Frerich and Frey, 1996; Seeleib-Kaiser et al., 2008: 43). Most of these concerned training and employment assistance, but an increasing number of people (some 10 per cent) were on job-creation schemes in the non-commercial sector (ABM). During the second half of the 1980s, Germany had yearly expenses on ALMP of around 1 per cent of GDP, which was above the OECD average. The figure was slightly up from the first half of the decade (around 0.7 per cent of GDP, see Clasen, 2005: table 4.5).

Things were to change with unification in 1991. As former GDR companies underwent restructuring, redundant workers were given access to early retirement and labour market programmes, which again had the objective of limiting open unemployment. Spending on ALMPs peaked in 1992 at 1.8 per cent of GDP. At that time, however, the lion's share of active spending went to job-creation programmes (Clasen, 2005: 61–2; Manow and Seils, 2000: 293). The move was effective in reducing open unemployment. It was not, however, able to prevent a massive surge in the unemployment rate following the recession of the 1990s.

Other countries, which did not develop extensive ALMPs before the crisis, were somewhat slower in introducing active elements in their unemployment policy afterwards. In France, tensions between the government and the trade unions arguably delayed the adoption of such measures (Clegg, 2005). However, starting from the mid-1980s, French ALMP is a rapid succession of different tools targeted sometimes on different groups. In general, their objective is 'occupation', that is, providing an occupation to jobless people rather than labour market re-entry. Typically, much emphasis is put on the notion of 'social insertion' or the possibility to participate to society without being in paid employment (Barbier and Fargion, 2004; Dufour et al., 2003). In practical terms, these measures consist of subsidized temporary jobs in the public or in the non-profit making private sector.

The development of French ALMP started in 1984 with the adoption of the TUC (*Travaux d'utilité publique* – public utility works) for jobless youth by the Socialist government. These were soon complemented in 1986 with the PIL (*Programmes d'insertion locale*) targeted on long-term unemployed and introduced by a Gaullist government. By 1989, these were replaced by CES (*Contrats emploi-solidarité*). In 1988 a general means-tested benefit was introduced (RMI, Revenu minimum d'insertion) which theoretically included an activation component in the shape of an insertion contract signed between the beneficiary and the authorities. In fact, as extensive evaluation of this programme has shown, its ability to move beneficiaries into the labour market is extremely limited (Palier, 2002: 302–3). The French approach to activation is characterized by a strong emphasis on occupation, accompanied by a strong rhetoric of social inclusion or '*insertion*'. This trajectory was confirmed by the Socialist government of the late 1990s (1997–2002). Besides the well-known law, reducing weekly working hours to thirty-five, the government introduced new job-creation programmes, aimed at the young, subsidizing jobs in non-commercial sectors for up to five years (Clegg, 2005: 222).

During the post-crisis years and well into the 1980s and early 1990s, occupation is an important function of ALMPs. Training continues to play a key role, as shown by the spending profiles presented in Figure 16.1 above. However, in such an unfavourable labour market context, training programmes can de facto become more akin to occupation than to effective human capital investment. The evaluation literature suggests that this might have been the case throughout most of the 1980s and early 1990s. This is a result reached in one of the first meta-analyses of evaluation studies of ALMPs, where two OECD economists conclude that many labour market programmes are ineffective or even counterproductive in terms of their ability to bring jobless people back to the labour market (Martin and Grubb, 2001). This may be the result of the predominant orientation of ALMPs (occupation) in the time span covered by the study (1980s and early 1990s).

16.3.3 ALMPs since the mid-1990s: the 'activation turn'

The mid-1990s signalled a new reorientation of ALMP in OECD countries. The economic context has changed. First, after the mid-1990s, labour market conditions in most OECD countries began to improve (cf. Statistical Annex, Tables A.4

and A.5). Second, unemployment was essentially the result of an excess supply of low-skill labour, and low-skill workers found it difficult to earn more from work than what their benefits are worth. The result was the development of a new role of ALMPs, which emphasized stronger work incentives and employment assistance. This reorientation was signalled also by a change in the language used and the increasing reference to the term 'activation'. OECD countries clearly move in this direction, but in a perhaps surprising order. The pioneers of this new phase are clearly not those who initiated ALMP in previous periods. Arguably, the pre-existence of active policies with a different objective slows down the development of activation.

Among the first to embrace the new activation paradigm in employment policy is Denmark, a country which up to then had done relatively little in the field of ALMPs (see Figure 16.1).The Social Democratic government elected in 1993 adopted a series of reforms that transformed the Danish system of unemployment compensation. The 1994 reform removed the possibility of regaining entitlement to unemployment insurance through participation in labour market programmes. It also set a seven-year limit to unemployment benefit. This period was subdivided in two phases: first, a passive period of four years and then an active period of three years. Work availability requirements were also strengthened and individual action plans were introduced (Goul-Andersen, this volume; Kvist et al., 2008: 243; Madsen, 2002). In addition, the reform introduced also the decentralization of employment services, making it possible for labour offices at the regional level to develop labour market programmes suitable for their area.

The reform was based on the recommendations made by a tripartite outfit known as the Zeuthen committee, consisting mostly of representative of both the trade unions and employer organizations. The social partners obtained important concessions, such as an important role in the implementation of labour market measures. At the same time, however, they agreed to reorient unemployment policy in the direction of activation (Kvist et al., 2008: 245).

Subsequent reforms further strengthened work incentives and employment assistance elements. The duration of the entitlement period was reduced first to five years (1996) and then to four years (1998). The 'passive' period was also shortened to two years and to six months for unemployed people younger than 25. After this period, claimants had both a right and an obligation to a labour market programme.

The year 1998 signalled a further acceleration of the trend towards activation. First, policy for youth unemployed took a strong step towards strengthening work incentives and investment in human capital. Measures adopted included a six-month limit on standard unemployment benefit for the under 25 and the obligation to participate in training for eighteen months, with a benefit equal to 50 per cent of the standard unemployment benefit. Second, with the adoption of a 'Law on active social policy', the principle of activation was extended to social assistance claimants (Kvist et al., 2008: 241–3). Like in past reform, together with incentive-strengthening measures, more inclusive instruments are also adopted. This is the case of a programme known as flexjobs, which subsidizes up to two-thirds of labour costs for disabled people, without time limits (Hogelund, 2003).

Other countries followed the Danish lead in reorienting their unemployment compensation systems towards activation. Under Conservative rule, the United

Kingdom had developed an approach clearly based on incentive reinforcement, with a series of reductions in unemployment benefit (Atkinson and Micklewright, 1989; King, 1995). A more significant step in the direction of activation was taken by the new labour government elected in 1997, on the basis of a centrist orientation in social and economic policy which became known as the Third Way. Concretely, a whole range of programmes targeted on various groups of non-employed persons were developed since the mid-1990s. These consist mostly of employment assistance. They are coupled with incentive reinforcement, for instance, with the introduction of a tax credit programme in 1998 (Clasen, this volume; Clasen, 2005; Clegg, 2005). This orientation is further pursued in subsequent years, and is visible in the spending profile of UK's ALMPs, which especially in 2005 put by far most of the emphasis on employment assistance.

Sweden was somewhat slower to reorient its ALMPs towards activation, but since the late 1990s labour market policy places considerably more emphasis on incentive reinforcement and employment assistance than in the past (Sjöberg, this volume). Work requirements have been strengthened so that those who are still jobless after 100 days of unemployment may be required to accept a job anywhere in the country and a wage up to 10 per cent lower than the unemployment benefit (Clasen et al., 2001: 211). The unemployment insurance reform of February 2001 further strengthened the pro-employment orientation of ALMP. This was done through a number of measures. First, the possibility to renew entitlement to unemployment insurance through participation in labour market programmes was abolished. Second, the reform introduced an 'activity guarantee' for long-term unemployed people or people at risk of becoming long-term unemployed. This consists of more individualized activities clearly geared towards re-employment (Swedish Government, 2002; Timonen, 2004).

Germany is another latecomer to the activation paradigm, even though since the mid-1990s policy has clearly adopted this overall orientation (Clasen, 2005; Digledey, this volume). One important step in this direction was the adoption of the so-called Job Aqtiv Act in 2001. The reform included several of the measures that one finds in the standard activation toolbox: stricter monitoring of job search, the profiling of jobless people, reintegration contracts, and wage subsidies (Clasen, 2005: 72).

These changes, however, were not regarded as going far enough by the Schroeder government. In fact, only a few months after the adoption of the Job Aqtiv Act, a new commission was set up and given the task to make proposals for the modernization of labour market policy. The commission was headed by Peter Hartz, a former manager at Volkswagen. Its proposals included several measures, ranging from support to unemployed people who want to set up their own business to the creation of a 'Personal service agency', a temporary placement service for unemployment people. However, the most visible and controversial proposal was the merger of long-term unemployment benefit and social assistance (the so-called Hartz IV reform), which resulted in benefit reductions for many recipients (Fleckenstein, 2008).

The activation paradigm, combining the incentive reinforcement and employment assistance, has clearly gained influence over the years. Combined with an expanding economy until 2008, it has also produced more encouraging results than in previous years, so that more recent meta-evaluations provide a more optimistic picture of the potential of ALMPs (Eichhorst et al., 2008; OECD, 2006*b*). But activation has not reached every corner of Europe. Italy, for instance, is clearly lagging behind in this respect (Samek Lodovici and Semenza, 2008), while France only started moving more aggressively in this direction in the late 2000s, with the merger of employment services and benefit agencies, and the transformation of RMI into RSA (*Revenu de solidarité active*), effective since 1 June 2009 (Clegg, this volume).

16.4 CONCLUSIONS

The above account of policy trajectories in six countries shows that ALMPs tend to adapt to changing economic circumstances. The three periods identified above are characterized above all by very different economic and labour market conditions. The first period, the 1950s and 1960s, is a time of rapid economic growth and labour shortage. Under these circumstances, at least four out of the six countries covered developed an ALMP system geared towards upskilling the labour force, so as to provide adequately trained workers to expanding industries. Steps in this direction were taken by Sweden, Germany, Italy, and France, though only Sweden succeeded in developing a fully fledged ALMP system. During this period, ALMPs were relatively unrelated to the unemployment compensation system. In some countries, Italy for example, the state turned to an apprenticeship system to upskill youth jobless people living mostly in the south of the country. ALMPs complemented unemployment insurance during this period.

In the second period, sluggish growth and industrial restructuring dominated the economic context. ALMPs turned into an alternative to market employment, and provided mostly occupation to jobless people. Even programmes labelled as training tended to fulfil this function more than upskilling during this period, as shown by the evaluation literature. The turn towards occupation concerns countries that had developed ALMPs during the previous period (Sweden, Germany, and France), belonging to different welfare regimes. In this period, ALMPs were considerably more integrated into the broader field of unemployment policy. In a way, they tended to substitute for unemployment benefit.

Finally, in the third phase, better economic and labour market conditions since the mid-1990s pushed countries towards activation. This was also a development that spanned across regimes: in fact, all the countries covered (except perhaps Italy) adopted the activation paradigm in labour market policy, putting emphasis on employment assistance and the reinforcement of work incentives. It is in this phase that the integration between active and passive labour market policy was the strongest. The emphasis on work incentives of this approach required policymakers to coordinate active and passive benefits. This resulted in a situation in which it became difficult to distinguish between the two categories of tools. For example, is an unemployment benefit that decreases over time (and where work incentives increase as time passes) a passive or an active tool?

As shown above, developments in each period are shaped by decisions taken during the previous one. After the oil shocks of the 1970s, ALMPs initially meant to upskill workers were turned into providers of occupation. This is clearly the case in Sweden and in Germany. Other countries, such as Denmark and the United Kingdom, which did not develop ALMPs to a significant extent during the early post-war years, were much slower to expand this field of labour market policy.

Rather paradoxically, the laggards of the second phase became the leaders in the third one. The first countries which turned to activation were Denmark and the United Kingdom, with high profile reforms adopted in 1994 and 1997, respectively. Other countries followed suit, but more slowly. In Sweden, the 2001 reform can be seen as a milestone in this process. For Germany, one could identify the 2004 Hartz IV reform as the tipping point. Quite clearly, countries without an extensive system of ALMPs in place in the early 1990s have an advantage when it comes to reorienting the policy towards the objective of re-entry into market employment. Using ALMPs as alternatives to market employment created expectations among actual and potential beneficiaries, for example, in terms of the ability to renew the entitlement to unemployment insurance. These practices, which are incompatible with the activation paradigm, are difficult to abandon.

ALMPs need to be seen in the broader context of unemployment policy. As such, they do follow changes in the economic context. When labour market conditions deteriorate, the conversion from an employment-promoting to an employment-substituting tool happens first by default, simply because fewer jobs are available. It can then be promoted by policymakers together with other tools that reduce labour supply (e.g. early retirement). Rather paradoxically, adapting unemployment policy to an improved labour market seems more difficult. Tools developed as alternatives to market employment are not necessarily going to help jobless people finding market jobs. On the contrary, they may 'lock' them in the programmes and slow down the process of labour market reintegration. Adaptation to an expanding economy requires a more proactive approach which implies stronger work incentives. This may not always be politically popular.

The place of ALMPs within unemployment policy changes over time, and, in line with the framework developed in the introduction to this volume, one can notice an ever stronger integration between active and passive employment policies. In the early days, the 1950s in Sweden and a few years later in other countries, ALMPs developed in parallel to unemployment compensation, and tended to be seen as part of economic policy. In the second phase, the response to the employment crises of the 1970s and 1980s, ALMPs became an alternative not only to market employment as pointed out above but also to passive benefit recipiency. Finally, since the 1990s, active tools are found within passive benefit, resulting in an almost complete integration of the two policy domains.

17

The transformation of unemployment protection in Europe

Jochen Clasen and Daniel Clegg

17.1 INTRODUCTION

The first part of this book provided an overview of key changes in national unemployment protection schemes in twelve European countries. Each chapter depicted institutional arrangements as they existed in 1990 and 2010. These detailed presentations had a primarily descriptive aim, providing information about features of unemployment protection systems such as eligibility and entitlement criteria, administrative divisions, and job-search conditions. In this respect, the chapters can be seen as complementary to other texts aimed at capturing arrangements and changes in different dimensions of income transfer programmes, whether by identifying differences in benefit generosity (e.g. Scruggs, 2007); examining administrative arrangements and responsibilities (e.g. de Beer and Schils, 2009); or discussing activation conditions (Eichhorst et al., 2008; Serrano Pascual and Magnusson, 2007). In other respects, however, the aim was different, both in terms of the particular analytical perspective adopted and the relatively long time period under investigation, examining key changes in a twenty-year period since 1990. At this time, the end of state socialism in Eastern Europe raised the question how countries such as the Czech Republic or Hungary would deal with the challenges of transition to market economies. The early 1990s were also significant in seeing a steep rise in unemployment in many European countries. A large number of these countries had already experienced mass unemployment in the 1970s and early 1980s, while others (Sweden and Switzerland) were faced with this challenge for the first time since the Second World War.

An underlying assumption was that in the twenty years since 1990 the conditions have been reunited for a paradigmatic shift in the regulation of the risk of unemployment. The growth in overall benefit receipt amongst the working-age population created strong fiscal pressures, and strengthened political resolve to halt or reverse the 'labour-shedding' policies of the 1980s. The steady improvement in employment and decline in unemployment across all but a few of our twelve countries after the early 1990s (see Statistical Annex, Tables A.4 and A.5) has potentially made policies aimed at labour market integration more politically and economically feasible. Finally, from the early 1990s onwards, calls for a more 'activating' approach to the regulation of unemployment risks, entailing switching resources from 'passive' transfers to 'active' employment integration and job-search policies, became more frequently expressed and increasingly powerful at international level, promoted first by the OECD (1994) and later by the EU (1997). Taking account of contextual factors, including the legacy of policies pursued in earlier decades, the investigation of changes in unemployment protection over the past twenty years was aimed at assessing how far this paradigm shift had in fact materialized in different countries by systematically analysing institutional arrangements and policies that so far have only been sporadically or partially scrutinized.

More concretely, we identified the potential for challenges to the logic of 'first wave' adjustment strategies in response to mass unemployment in the 1970s and 1980s, focused mainly on facilitating labour market exit or narrowing the administrative category of unemployment. In areas such as pensions, such policy reversals had already been observed and systematically compared (Ebbinghaus, 2006). Within unemployment protection and labour market policy the continuing dominance of research on activation might be seen as structurally similar, since these studies are also based on an implicit or explicit notion of a change in direction, that is, from a policy that (arguably) emphasized benefit rights and 'passive' benefit receipt in the past to one which now stresses individual obligation and active participation on the part of jobseekers. While this has been a conventional point of departure, however, we argue that it is also a rather narrow one, since changes in this area go well 'beyond activation' in many countries (Clasen and Clegg, 2006). Put differently, we regard activation as merely one aspect of a broader emerging policy trend. As outlined in the introductory chapter, we looked for changes that could be indicative of a more multifaceted and thoroughgoing process of 'institutional integration', embodied not only by activation but also by what we have called unemployment benefit homogenization and risk recategorization.

Having discussed instances of integration across the twelve country chapters, in this concluding chapter we revisit some of the main findings. The first aim is to identify and map types and intensities of change, leading to a tentative grouping of countries in terms of the scale of integrative reform observed. In the subsequent section, we discuss some of the reasons that can help to account for diverse policy profiles and patterns across different national settings. This book was not aimed at analysing the causes of national policy change and reform in any rigorous fashion, and this section will necessarily have to remain somewhat exploratory. A more systematic comparative analysis of the 'politics of triple integration' (see also Clasen and Clegg, 2012) is a task that we hope will find its way onto the research agenda of comparative unemployment and labour market policy analysis in the future.

17.2 MAPPING CHANGE AND DIVERSITY

17.2.1 Unemployment protection – trends towards homogenization

In the introductory chapter, we outlined the three dimensions of 'triple integration', which has served as analytic and heuristic frame for the discussion of change within national unemployment protection systems. One of these dimensions, which we referred to as 'unemployment benefit homogenization', considers changes in traditional unemployment protection schemes, that is, transfer programmes for claimants who are registered as unemployed or generally have to fulfil job-search conditions in order and to be eligible for state support. As discussed in Chapter 1, it is reasonable to expect that adaptation to post-industrial employment structures could be manifest in unemployment protection arrangements that are less differentiated than in the past. Fostering occupational flexibility rather than rewarding stability, unemployment insurance might become less earnings related in character, which means benefit generosity less determined by individual's previous wages. Other indicators of homogenization would be the amalgamation of separate unemployment transfer programmes, as well as diminishing differences in the way separate tiers of benefit support are designed and operate. Alternatively, while separate tiers might remain in place, one tier might become dominant in terms of the number of jobseekers it covers.

Of course, it should be noted that in some countries, such as Belgium and Denmark, the degree of wage proportionality in unemployment insurance was already relatively modest even before the 1990s. Due to the effect of the declining benefit ceiling, Danish unemployment insurance became even less earnings-related during the 1990s – something that also applied to Sweden as far as the public unemployment benefit system is concerned. However, as discussed in Chapter 11, a significant expansion of collectively bargained non-statutory benefit support has compensated for this real decline for many unemployed people. In the United Kingdom, earnings-related benefits were abolished already in the early 1980s, and the share of the unemployed in receipt of insurance-based unemployment support rapidly declined during the decade. In Italy there was some convergence in levels of protection between Casa Integrazione and unemployment benefit. The number of separate transfer programmes for unemployed people declined in Germany, in Hungary, and in the Netherlands. Diminishing structural differences between benefit tiers can be found in the United Kingdom, in Italy, and in Hungary, although in the latter only with respect to the introduction of more uniform job-search criteria. In terms of coverage, the Belgian and Danish contributory schemes remained fairly encompassing, while British means-tested JSA has become the overriding type of unemployment benefit. In Germany, as well as in the Netherlands, unemployment support has become dominated by assistance-based benefits.

However, there are countries which suggest that benefit homogenization is not a ubiquitous trend. Due to the introduction of further assistance programmes, there are now there are now more rather than fewer tiers of unemployment support in Spain. In Switzerland, too, several Cantons have introduced unemployment assistance in addition to general social assistance. In these two countries, as well as in the Czech Republic and Hungary, unemployment protection has remained firmly segmented. Amongst Swedish jobseekers the coverage of unemployment insurance has declined and social assistance increased considerably, emphasizing a shift to more divided (public) unemployment protection. In France, a strong institutional differentiation between insurance and assistance benefits emerged in the 1980s and 1990s, and this has not been unambiguously challenged.

In sum, reviewing the various indicators of unemployment benefit homogenization as a whole, two groups of countries can be identified. One includes Belgium, Denmark, and the United Kingdom, which had already fairly homogenized and encompassing unemployment protection systems at the start of the period under investigation. Germany and the Netherlands can be regarded as having joined this group due to reforms and changes which made their respective systems, as a whole, less differentiated and led to the emergence of dominant tiers. A second group consists of countries where the segmented nature of unemployment protection has remained intact, such as in France, the Czech Republic, and Hungary, or where it has become structurally more fragmented, as in Spain and Switzerland. Sweden and Italy both occupy a somewhat ambiguous position, the former because differences in benefit levels within unemployment insurance diminished but a more segmented unemployment support structure emerged, and the latter because while differences between schemes decreased the rather segmented overall unemployment protection structure remained in place.

17.2.2 Risk re-categorization – broadening unemployment

The second indicator of integration goes beyond unemployment protection in a narrow sense. As mentioned, policies in response to rising unemployment in the 1970s and 1980s followed a logic of decreasing labour supply via facilitating temporary exit from employment through eased access to early retirement benefits, parental leave schemes, or incapacity benefits – or by exempting certain groups of unemployment benefit claimants from the usual job-search conditions. As outlined in the introductory chapter, these policies effectively narrowed the statistical and administrative category of unemployment and contributed to an increase in beneficiary rates in working-age transfer programmes outside unemployment benefit. During the 1990s, however, a reversal of such policies has been observed in many countries.

Several countries have made attempts to close exit routes from unemployment to 'parallel' transfer schemes, thus de facto transferring claimants 'back' to unemployment benefit. Others made benefit eligibility in various non-employment benefits more dependent on job search and employment-oriented criteria. For example, disability and incapacity benefit schemes have been based more firmly on work-related capacity tests in the United Kingdom, Denmark, Switzerland, Spain, and Hungary. Lone parents in the United Kingdom and France, and parents with younger children in Germany, are now generally categorized as unemployed or employable and thus expected to be looking for paid work. In Hungary, parental leave allowances, as well as disability benefits, have become more conditional on job-search conditions, at least formally. Social assistance programmes have become more oriented to labour market integration, and thus more akin to unemployment assistance, in France, Denmark and the Netherlands. Partners of workless social assistance claimants who are also out of work have been required to also register as job seeking in several countries. Access to early retirement programmes were closed, or made more difficult, in Belgium and Denmark, and older unemployed are no longer exempt from job-search conditions in France and Denmark.

In some countries, programmes for working-age groups have merged or become more work oriented. For example, in France the transformation of the RMI into RSA strengthened the articulation between income support and labour market policy, with claimants now having to register with the employment services. Unemployment benefit II in Germany is a new encompassing basic and work-oriented programme for all long-term unemployed as well as others deemed to be fit to enter employment. In the United Kingdom, the government is planning to create what it calls a 'single working-age benefit' scheme, thereby blurring the boundaries between unemployment and inactivity. Moreover, the reform will extend work conditionality to those who are already in work but whose jobs are subsidized. The administrative boundaries between in-work and out-of-work income support have already became more fluid in Germany and France.

In short, there are numerous examples which suggest an emergent trend towards a broadening of the category of unemployment. There are also some exceptions, however, at least in respect to some of the indicators of risk re-categorization. For example, while benefits schemes have certainly become more employment oriented in Sweden, they are not more coordinated. In the Netherlands, unemployment and social assistance programmes have become more similar to each other and more integrated, but this does not extend to incapacity benefit arrangements. Facilitating labour market exit, and the quasi-early retirement of older unemployed persons, continues to be a characteristic feature of labour market policies particularly in Spain and Hungary. Early retirement remains prevalent in Belgium too, despite repeated attempts to close this labour market exit route. However, Belgium already has a rather broad and inclusive administrative definition of unemployment.

17.2.3 Activation – increasing work conditionality and administrative integration

As discussed in the introductory chapter, the third dimension of integration relates to a closer articulation between 'passive' and 'active' labour market policy, both for individual benefit claimants and the administration of relevant policies. This trend, widely referred to as 'activation', includes a stricter work conditionality embedded within eligibility to unemployment benefit, such as more intensive job-search criteria or greater expectations towards occupational mobility (e.g. widening job suitability conditions). It also encompasses a stronger labour supply or 'work first' orientation within active labour market programmes. Rather than lengthy training and qualification schemes, more emphasis would be put on intensive job search, as well as participation in short training or work experience schemes. Such aspects have been discussed in several country chapters, and shifts within national active labour market policy profiles were analysed in Chapter 16.

Activation also involves changes in administrative arrangements in the sense of a closer coordination between the provision of unemployment benefits and employment services. In principle, this could be extended to benefits and services for all working-age benefit claimants, harmonizing or even merging separate programmes at the administrative level. The extent of administrative integration was already fairly advanced in some countries before the 1990s. In many others we were able to identify trends towards adopting such an approach.

The conditionality of unemployment benefit receipt on job search or work activities has become more explicit in almost all countries reviewed in previous chapters. Reforms of this kind were first introduced in Denmark, the Netherlands, and the United Kingdom and followed in the late 1990s or early 2000s by similar measures in Germany, Switzerland, the Czech Republic, Italy, France, Sweden, Hungary, and Spain. Apart from differences in timing, variations are also noticeable in the degree or intensity of activation, as well as the extension to different target groups. In Germany and France, for example, activation requirements became more explicit for (unemployment or social) assistance claimants before spreading to core (unemployment) insurance programmes. The reverse was the case in Denmark. A stronger 'work first' orientation within labour market policy has perhaps been most recognizable in countries such as the United Kingdom, Germany, Sweden, Denmark, and Hungary. In the latter two the intensity of work-related conditionality has become particularly explicit for long-term social assistance claimants. In what some would regard as 'workfare', in Denmark, recipients who are married (and the partner also unemployed) have to engage in ordinary employment of a certain number of hours in order to maintain benefit eligibility (see Chapter 10). In Hungary, social assistance claimants are required to participate in 'public work' schemes.

Trends of greater administrative coordination have been particularly evident in the United Kingdom and the Netherlands, and more recently also in Germany and France. It should be noted that the extent of integration varies, however, in the sense of covering some programmes, for example, leaving out unemployment insurance or incapacity benefit claimants. It is also noticeable that instances of merging administrative responsibilities are typically of a fairly recent nature, although there are some pioneer countries such as the Netherlands and the United Kingdom.

In sum, it appears that countries that have shifted their unemployment protection systems most notably towards a more activating approach include the United Kingdom, the Netherlands, Denmark, Germany, and France. In all other countries, there have been some indications of policy shifts in the same direction. However, rhetoric has often been clearer than actual developments, particularly regarding the area of institutional integration between unemployment and other programmes for working-age benefit claimants.

17.2.4 The shift towards integration – a tentative categorization

The overview of policy trends provided above has been necessarily sketchy, abstracting from the detail of nationally specific developments and trajectories discussed in the country chapters. Nevertheless, it allows us to propose a rough categorization of countries according to the intensity of integrative dynamics in recent reforms to unemployment protection (Table 17.1).

The division of our countries into three loose clusters is based on the evidence found across all three indicators of institutional integration. It should be stressed that the table does not depict differences in existing institutional arrangements, but instead tries to capture the intensity of policy shifts in accordance with our analytical framework. For example, it does not suggest that Germany or the Netherlands no longer have segmented (or multi-tier) unemployment protection systems, but instead that there have been changes in each of the three dimensions of integration, meaning the degree of integration within both countries' unemployment protection systems as a whole is stronger in 2010 than it was in 1990. Belgium is, however, somewhat awkward to classify simply according to a logic of change, given that there has, in fact, been mainly stability across all the dimensions of integration in recent decades. Due to the already encompassing nature of the unemployment category and the homogenized unemployment benefit structure, Belgium is positioned here in the first group, though its specificity must be acknowledged.

It is also worth underscoring that a country's membership in one or other of these groupings is not fixed or immutable. Of the countries in group B, it is possibly in the French case that, after a period in which a logic of institutional dualization long seemed dominant, there is today most evidence of integrative reform dynamics. As discussed in Chapter 3, both activation and risk re-categorization were clearly visible in the French reforms of the 2000s, and by the end of the decade there are even signs of a timid turn to unemployment benefit homogenization. Though the fact that the last reform dynamic is very recent and not yet unequivocally dominant in policy adjustment justifies placing the French case in the intermediate grouping, things may well look rather different if the current pattern of integrative reforms continues into the next decade.

Finally, it should be noted that even in the third group there have been some signs of movement towards a more integrative unemployment protection approach, most notably in the field of activation. However, these four countries have arguably moved least in this overall direction, and in certain respects some countries (Spain, Switzerland) actually manifest opposite trends. In any case, in all four countries unemployment protection continues to be firmly segmented in insurance and assistance-type support, there has been little risk re-categorization and shifts towards activation have remained modest, partial, or mainly rhetorical.

To sum up this section, there is ample evidence from across European countries of substantial institutional change in the field of unemployment protection since the early 1990s, and the triple integration framework helps illustrate variations in the frequency of instances of fundamental and far-reaching institutional restructuring. In many countries the direction of travel seems to be clearly towards an unemployment protection policy that will provide combined packages of benefits and labour market support services in a more integrated manner not

Table 17.1. Trends of institutional integration

A (clearest)	B (modest)	C (least; partly opposite trends)
The United Kingdom	France	Switzerland
The Netherlands	Sweden	Spain
Germany	Italy	Hungary
Denmark		Czech Republic
Belgium		

only to unemployed people but also more generally to other people of working age with a precarious relationship to the labour market. However, as Table 17.1 suggests, there are considerable cross-national differences in the development and advancement of this emergent trend. Before concluding this chapter, we draw on the discussions in the country chapters to outline some of the main factors accounting for the variable progress of triple integration.

17.3 TOWARDS AN UNDERSTANDING OF 'TRIPLE INTEGRATION'

As discussed in the introductory chapter, and implied in the overall title of this book, we associate policies that have fostered more integrated national unemployment protection systems with profound changes in labour market and social structures. Our point of departure was the observation of an apparent complementarity between the industrial employment paradigm and some widely shared features of unemployment protection systems in post-war Europe. The most notable among these was the central place of contributory and often earnings-related unemployment insurance, with complementary but clearly differentiated roles for secondary systems of unemployment benefit support (unemployment and social assistance), for active labour market policies such as job placement and for benefit schemes for other working-age groups not expected to be active in the labour market. On our reading, this institutional and policy framework fits less well with the operation of post-industrial labour markets, in which the vast majority of working-age people are expected to be economically active, where employment trajectories in certain labour market segments are characterized by flexibility, and where people with low skills require greater support and direction to return to employment from periods out of work. Our question was therefore how far countries were adapting to secular shifts in the labour market by transforming conventional unemployment protection arrangements into more integrated benefit-and-service systems directed to all those with precarious positions in the labour market.

The term 'adaptation' of course carries the implication of a somewhat functionalist reading of policy development. In a loose form – which might be called 'open functionalism'[1] – this is something we are happy to concede. It is certainly not our intention to downplay the impact of political and institutional factors on domestic unemployment protection reforms, and the impact of unemployment and labour market policy in mediating structural change in the labour market. The 'labour shedding' policies adopted in most countries during the 1970s and 1980s are proof enough that the creative exploitation of existing institutional structures is just as likely a response to economic challenges as thoroughgoing institutional reform. But if political and institutional factors may filter

---

[1] Open functionalism implies acknowledgement that imperatives of 'goodness of fit' between policies with economic and social structures are an important driver of policy change, even though the creativity of policymakers is inevitably bounded by political and institutional factors. The term was suggested to us by Anton Hemerijck, whom we thank.

understandings of and responses to structural pressures, they do not eliminate them, particularly in the long-term. While Bonoli (2007) is undoubtedly correct in emphasizing that problem pressure itself rarely explains policy change, it is clear that the labour shedding policies seen as a solution in the 1980s increasingly came to be understood as contributing to a problem of 'benefit dependency' in the latter part of the 1990s and beyond (OECD, 2010*b*). This perception was only reinforced by the apparent disconnect between (often fast) declining unemployment rates and stubbornly high beneficiary rates in other working-age benefit systems, most notably for people declared as long-term sick, incapacitated, or early retired (cf. Chapter 15). Many of the policy reforms discussed in the country chapters do need to be seen in the light of problems that existing policies seemed incapable of solving.

As has been discussed above, however, broadly common problems have not yet led to a strict convergence in the basic logics of institutional reform across the cases considered in this volume. Part of the reason for this is to do with the specificities of some national starting points. This is perhaps most obvious in the cases of the Czech Republic and Hungary, where a very particular institutional legacy, as well as the need to mitigate social costs in a context of profound economic transformation, has meant that the question of unemployment protection reform has been posed in rather different terms than in the other countries analysed. Albeit in rather different ways, the atypical profile of the existing unemployment protection systems in both Belgium and Italy has also made their recent reform dynamics atypical. In the former case, the simple fact that unemployment benefit arrangements were not very 'industrial' in the first place, that is, only weakly contributory and geared towards individual wage replacement, meant that benefit homogenization was unnecessary and risk re-categorization less pressing than elsewhere. In Italy, the quasi-absence of unemployment insurance has meant that the recent period has been as much one of tentative policy expansion under tight fiscal constraints as it has been one of institutional reform, even if some functionally equivalent trends to those seen in other cases can be identified.

Another reason for the absence of strong convergence to date is that thorough-going institutional reform is of course fraught with difficulties, and comes up hard notably against the resilience of existing policy structures. A number of examples of the self-reinforcing characteristics of institutional fragmentation are evident in the case studies. This has been common particularly where divisions in unemployment protection and labour market policy map onto divisions of responsibility between different levels of government. For example, while unemployment insurance is usually a national programme funded out of general taxation or social contributions, social assistance is almost always a local or municipal programme, often with devolved or decentralized financing. Though the different levels in such multi-tiered policy systems have strong incentives to try and shift costs onto the other (Schmid et al., 1992), it is rare that any level of government is willing to relinquish policy competence altogether. In federal political systems, furthermore, multiple veto-points provide ample opportunities for unwanted changes to existing institutional structures to be blocked. 'Turf wars' between different levels of government have characterized recent unemployment protection policies in several countries, and have seriously hindered reforms in cases such as Spain and Switzerland.

Other collective actors with possible vested interests in existing policy structures include trade unions, which have historically had strong roles in the governance of unemployment protection policies in many countries. This is most obviously true in 'Ghent systems', where unions' control of unemployment insurance has helped to uphold their organizational strength (Scruggs, 2002; Clasen and Viebrock, 2008). In Denmark and Sweden, accordingly, the unions' desire to preserve the voluntary state-subsidized system has complicated reforms of unemployment protection. But unions' organizational interests were also long an impediment to institutional change in countries such as France and the Netherlands, where they traditionally derived other organizational benefits from jointly co-managing unemployment insurance with employers. How the unions' participation in social governance arrangements affects their substantive unemployment policy preferences depends on the precise nature of their role, whether they need to find common ground with employers and the character of their relations with the state (Clegg, 2011), but as a number of the case studies in the volume discuss it often resulted in their opposition to integrative reforms.

The unions have not only opposed reforms to unemployment protection out of organizational self-interest, however. It is their private sector members, who in most countries consist mainly of often older workers in industrial sectors with stable and relatively secure jobs, who stand to lose perhaps most from the changes currently unfolding, as activation policies increase competition in the labour market and the flattening of benefit structures deprives them of the guarantee of preserved living standards in the event of unemployment. While such workers represent only a small and declining share of the electorate, unionization gives them a disproportionate influence over policy development where unions remain influential. Unions have sometimes also been able to call here on the support of large employers in industrial sectors, who seek to maintain benefit systems that allow them to externalize the cost of workforce adjustment and preserve peaceful firm-level labour relations. It is the influence of this 'industrial coalition' in unemployment protection policies, underpinned in many welfare states by their institutionalized role in social governance, that is held to explain the dualistic reform pattern that characterized, for example, the French and German cases up to the early 2000s (Clasen and Clegg, 2006; Clegg, 2007; Palier and Thelen, 2010).

In the light of these various obstacles, it may seem more pertinent to ask why far-ranging reforms *have* been seen in so many cases analysed in the volume, including ones such as Denmark, Germany, the Netherlands, and later France, where unions have traditionally had institutionalized roles in unemployment protection and/or central–local conflicts of legitimacy have been common in this policy field. One characteristic of many of these countries has been an open or implicit cross-party consensus on reform. Indeed, in line with the 'new politics' literature on welfare state change (Pierson, 2001b), it is noteworthy that partisan differences appear to matter little in explaining recent trajectories of reform across Europe. Major advances towards a more institutionally integrated unemployment protection system have been made under governments of the right, as in France; of the centre-left, as in Germany; and sometimes under both, as in Denmark and the Netherlands as well as the United Kingdom. This has followed not only from the well-known programmatic transformation of many European social democratic parties (Bonoli and Powell, 2004; Lewis and Surender, 2004) but also from shifts on the political right, where traditional Christian Democratic principles appear to have lost some of their electoral appeal in favour of more liberal policy platforms.

Related to this is the fact that many aspects of the current reform agenda in unemployment protection appear to be rather politically marketable, and open up possibilities for explicit political competition over structural reforms; a logic of 'credit claiming' that the literature on the new politics literature assumed had disappeared along with the possibility for welfare state expansion (cf. Bonoli, 2012). Despite their benefits being apparently diffuse and their costs concentrated, we have seen that opposing political parties in many countries have clearly tried to outbid each other over the ambitiousness of their fundamentally rather similar structural reform strategies in unemployment protection in search of the support of the electorate. The United Kingdom since 1997 represents perhaps the starkest example, but is not the only one. The promise of tackling apparent anomalies in existing policy arrangements, such as 'unnaturally' high numbers of disability or incapacity benefit claimants, seems increasingly to be a way that governments try to attract groups in the electorate who are not individually concerned by such measures. Even when such voters have altruistic motives they can be effectively targeted by these messages, as both activation and the flattening of benefit structures are reforms that can be – and have been – packaged in a language not merely of efficiency but also of fairness (Levy, 1999).

The fact that governments need not pursue these reforms furtively also diminishes the influence of social interests in the unemployment protection policy process. For example, as the cases of Denmark and the Netherlands from the mid-1990s and France since the mid-2000s show, the unions' traditional roles in labour market policy has not prevented governments backed by strong electoral mandates from eventually pushing reforms through. In the Danish and French cases, governments were able to lever the unions' agreement for substantial reform with the veiled threat of ending their governance role in unemployment protection, while in the Netherlands the unions were simply evicted from their historic place in the administrative structures of unemployment insurance (see also Clegg and van Wijnbergen, 2011).

A final factor that has facilitated the gradual progression of far-reaching institutional change is the interdependence and potential 'spillovers' between the different dimensions of unemployment protection reform analysed in this book. As a result of this, even initially limited and rather timid reforms have tended to generate new policy problems and anomalies requiring resolution. Specifically, the common drive to activation has often created pressures for risk re-categorization and benefit homogenization over time, as activation in one benefit programme leads to increasing caseloads in another, or competition between activation measures for claimants in parallel benefit programmes leads to calls for their improved harmonization. For example, the gradual extension in the United Kingdom of the New Deals to cover all working-age benefit claimant groups eventually brought onto the reform agenda first their articulated administration, then harmonization of conditionality regimes, and ultimately the creation of an integrated benefit system for all working-age benefit claimants. Likewise, a process that started relatively modestly with the activation only of disability and unemployment benefit claimants in the Netherlands eventually led to the shift from a three- to a two-tier unemployment benefit system, and a standardized activation regime for all people of working age. In France, an activation element initially introduced in social assistance for essentially rhetorical purposes gradually 'worked up' to unemployment insurance, resulting eventually in both the merger of the social partner-run unemployment insurance institutions and the state-run PES and the development of a unified activation regime for all jobseekers.

As these examples show, there is no single linear sequence through which processes of triple integration progress across different countries. But in addition to its economic and party political drivers, the advance of fundamental reform in labour market policy does seem to also be propelled by a self-reinforcing dynamic over time, of the sort that has been identified in the literature on incremental but transformative institutional change (cf. Streeck and Thelen, 2005a). Even in countries such as Spain or Hungary where there has been relatively little integration to date, the somewhat hesitant or merely formal turn towards more activation-based benefit entitlement – partly due to the influence of the EU and the European Employment Strategy – might therefore be expected, at least in the medium term, to lead to more pressure for risk re-categorization and benefit homogenization. If anything, this suggests that yet further convergence on this new institutional template for unemployment protection and labour market policy is likely in the years ahead.

17.4 CONCLUSIONS

This project departed from the observation that reforms to national unemployment protection systems in Europe that until the early 2000s followed a number of quite distinctive logics of adaptation (cf. Clasen and Clegg, 2006) increasingly seem to share a number of common features. Where the apparently common turn to activation in the 1990s once coexisted with very distinctive institutional structures and politico-economic rationales, and clear 'leaders' and 'laggards' in more far-reaching structural reform could be identified, it appeared by the second half of the decade that the situation was changing. Instead, across a range of national contexts some comparable processes of institutional change, apparently reflecting common concerns about adaptation to transformed structures of labour market risk, were evident. Alongside activation, we dubbed these processes risk re-categorization and benefit homogenization, finding in the coincidence of all three a dynamic of the so-called triple integration that was fundamentally reworking the institutional structures and labour market functions of unemployment protection arrangements inherited from the industrial era.

The findings of our collective project show that a strong claim for Europe-wide convergence in unemployment protection would be premature. Reform dynamics in Central and Eastern Europe remain distinctive. In many cases analysed in this book, institutional integration has foundered on the inherent stickiness of established divisions of institutional labour in unemployment protection between central and local governments and social actors. In some, the politico-economic coalitions behind explicitly dualizing or segmenting reforms in unemployment protection remain influential. Nonetheless, it is noteworthy that even in many of the cases where institutional integration has not been achieved, it has been and remains high on political agendas. Tendencies to institutional dualization in unemployment protection reforms have in other cases been arrested and even reversed. And in a number of cases the institutional structures of unemployment protection have indeed been comprehensively overhauled.

While institutional integration is not a universal reality for unemployment protection in Europe, then, it is a clearly emerging trend, and one that we believe is important. Where across Europe the core of unemployment protection was once the provision of replacement incomes to a relatively clearly defined group of integrated 'workers-without-work', today it increasingly centres on the provision of combined packages of benefits and support services to all working-age people in precarious positions in relation to the labour market. As the focus of unemployment protection changes, so too does the underlying definition of what it means to be unemployed. The institutional changes we have described are driven by changing risk structures in labour markets, but are simultaneously defining and cementing them.

It has not been our intention to offer a normative analysis of these changes, and while one contribution to the volume made a tentative first step in looking at the impact of institutional reforms on labour market outcomes, a thorough analysis of the distributive implications of these reforms remains an important task for future research. Clearly, in most cases there have been winners and losers among the economically vulnerable population in the short-term. How the distributive implications of recent changes will impact on political support for public investment in the protection – active or otherwise – of the unemployed in the longer term is obviously difficult to predict, but will be crucial in determining how far the progressive potential of integrative reforms to unemployment protection can be realized.

Economic vulnerability is also a moving target, shaped by macroeconomic contexts and developments. Between the conception of this project and its completion, countries across Europe have seen very sharp rises in unemployment, as a knock-on consequence of the global financial crisis of 2008. While it might have been anticipated that this would result in pressures to redirect resources to more classic forms of unemployment protection, and perhaps even for the reopening of exit routes from the labour market, there is to date little evidence of this occurring. If anything, the trend to structural reforms evident before the crisis seem to have been consolidated by it. Across much of Europe, the political response to mass unemployment in the late 2000s has been very different to what it was in the early 1990s. This is further evidence in our view that the last two decades have seen a fundamental change in conceptions of the risk of unemployment and of appropriate ways of regulating it.

A. Statistical Annex

Table A.1 Employment in industry (% of all civilian employment)

	1960	1965	1970	1975	1980	1985	1990	1995	2000	2005	2009
Belgium	47	47	43	40	35	30	28	26	26	25	23
Czech Republic	–	–	–	49	48	48	46	42	40	40	39
Denmark	37	37	38	32	30	28	28	27	26	24	19
France	38	39	39	39	36	32	29	24	22	21	–
Germany	47	48	49	45	44	41	39	36	34	30	29
Hungary	–	–	–	–	–	–	–	34	34	33	31
Italy	34	37	40	39	38	34	32	34	32	31	30
Netherlands	41	41	39	35	31	28	26	23	20	20	17
Spain	32	36	37	38	35	31	34	30	31	30	25
Sweden	40	43	38	37	32	30	29	26	25	22	20
Switzerland	47	48	46	43	38	36	32	29	26	24	23
United Kingdom	48	47	45	40	38	35	32	27	25	22	20

Notes: For Czech Republic and Hungary, data is available only from 1975 and 1995 (accordingly). Data is missing for France in 2009.
Rounded figures here and subsequent tables (unless otherwise stated).
Source: OECD ALFS Summary tables: Annual labour force statistics.

Table A.2 Employment in service (% of all civilian employment)

	1960	1965	1970	1975	1980	1985	1990	1995	2000	2005	2009
Belgium	45	47	53	57	62	67	69	71	72	73	75
Czech Republic	–	–	–	37	39	40	42	51	55	56	58
Denmark	45	48	51	59	63	65	67	68	70	73	79
France	40	43	47	51	56	61	66	72	74	76	–
Germany	39	41	42	48	51	54	58	61	64	68	68
Hungary	–	–	–	–	–	–	–	58	59	62	64
Italy	34	37	40	44	48	55	59	59	62	65	67
Netherlands	50	51	55	59	64	67	69	74	77	77	81
Spain	26	31	33	40	46	51	55	61	62	65	71
Sweden	44	46	54	57	62	65	67	71	73	76	78
Switzerland	39	41	45	50	55	58	64	67	70	73	73
United Kingdom	48	50	52	57	60	63	66	71	73	76	79

Notes: For Czech Republic and Hungary, data is available only from 1975 and 1995 (accordingly). Data is missing for France in 2009.
Source: OECD ALFS Summary tables: Annual labour force statistics.

Table A.3 GDP growth rate (five-yearly averages – except the last interval)

	1961–5	1966–70	1971–5	1976–80	1981–5	1986–90	1991–5	1996 –2000	2001–5	2006–9
Belgium	5.0	4.9	3.6	3.2	1.0	3.1	1.6	2.7	1.6	0.8
Czech Republic	–	–	–	–	–	–	−0.8	1.5	3.8	2.2
Denmark	5.3	3.7	1.8	2.8	2.7	1.4	2.4	2.9	1.3	−0.1
France	5.8	5.4	4.0	3.4	1.5	3.3	1.2	2.8	1.7	0.4
Germany	4.7	4.2	2.4	3.4	1.4	3.3	2.2	2.0	0.6	0.4
Hungary	4.4	6.3	6.3	3.7	1.8	0.5	−2.2	4.2	4.3	−0.1
Italy	5.2	6.2	3.2	4.5	1.7	3.2	1.3	1.9	0.9	−0.6
Netherlands	5.5	5.3	3.4	2.6	1.2	3.5	2.3	4.0	1.3	1.0
Spain	8.6	6.2	5.3	2.0	1.4	4.5	1.5	4.1	3.3	1.0
Sweden	5.2	4.1	2.6	1.4	1.9	2.6	0.7	3.4	2.6	0.3
Switzerland	5.0	4.2	0.9	1.7	1.5	2.9	0.1	2.0	1.3	1.8
United Kingdom	3.1	2.6	2.1	1.8	2.1	3.3	1.6	3.4	2.5	0.2

Notes: For Czech Republic, data is available from 1991; for Germany – from 1971.
Source: Calculations based on the World Bank data. Available at http://data.worldbank.org/indicator/NY.GDP. MKTP.KD.ZG

Table A.4 Employment to population ratio (all* and women)

Sex	1980 All	1980 Women	1983 All	1983 Women	1986 All	1986 Women	1989 All	1989 Women	1992 All	1992 Women	1995 All	1995 Women	1998 All	1998 Women	2001 All	2001 Women	2004 All	2004 Women	2007 All	2007 Women	2009 All	2009 Women
Belgium	–	–	54	37	53	38	54	40	57	45	57	46	58	48	60	51	61	53	63	56	62	56
Czech Republic	–	–	–	–	–	–	–	–	–	–	71	62	68	59	66	58	65	57	67	58	66	58
Denmark	–	–	72	65	78	71	77	70	76	71	75	67	76	71	77	72	77	72	79	74	77	74
France	65	51	62	50	60	50	64	50	60	51	60	52	60	53	62	55	63	58	64	60	65	60
Germany	66	51	62	48	63	49	64	51	67	56	65	56	65	57	67	59	66	60	70	64	72	66
Hungary	–	–	–	–	–	–	–	–	59	53	53	46	54	48	57	50	57	51	58	51	56	50
Italy	55	34	54	34	53	35	53	36	53	37	52	36	53	38	56	42	58	46	60	47	58	47
Netherlands	55	34	51	35	52	36	60	45	64	51	66	54	70	59	74	64	73	65	76	69	77	71
Spain	54	29	50	28	47	27	51	31	51	33	49	33	53	37	59	44	62	49	67	56	61	54
Sweden	81	74	80	76	82	78	84	82	79	77	74	72	73	70	77	74	75	73	77	74	74	72
Switzerland	–	–	–	–	–	–	–	–	80	69	79	67	80	71	81	72	79	72	81	73	82	76
United Kingdom	–	–	–	–	68	58	73	63	70	63	70	63	72	65	74	67	74	68	74	68	73	67
European Union 15**	62	44	59	43	60	46	62	48	62	50	61	50	63	52	65	56	66	58	68	60	67	61
European Union 19***	62	44	59	43	60	46	62	48	62	51	61	51	62	53	64	55	64	56	67	59	66	60
OECD-Europe****	62	44	59	43	60	46	61	47	62	49	61	49	62	50	62	52	62	53	64	55	64	55

Notes: *All = men and women. **European Union 15 – was the number of member countries in the European Union prior to the accession of ten candidate countries on 1 May 2004. The EU15 comprised the following fifteen countries: Austria, Belgium, Denmark, Finland, France, Germany, Greece, Ireland, Italy, Luxembourg, Netherlan ds, Portugal, Spain, Sweden, United Kingdom. ***European Union 19 – all EU countries prior to the accession of the ten candidate countries on 1 May 2004, plus the four Eastern European member countries of the OECD, namely Czech Republic, Hungary, Poland, Slovak Republic. ****OECD-Europe comprises all European Union Member countries of the OECD, that is, countries in EU15 plus the Czech Republic, Hungary, Iceland, Norway, Poland, Slovak Republic, Switzerland, Turkey. For Czech Republic, data is available from 1995; for Hungary and Switzerland from 1992; for the United Kingdom from 1986 and for Belgium from 1983.
Source: OECD. Labour. Labour force statistics, labour force by sex and age – indicators.

Table A.5 Unemployment rate (as % of civilian labour force)

	1980	1983	1986	1989	1992	1995	1998	2001	2004	2007	2009
Belgium	8.1	13.5	11.9	9.5	10.5	13.0	11.7	6.6	8.4	7.5	7.9
Czech Republic	–	–	–	–	2.8	4.1	6.5	8.2	8.3	5.3	6.7
Denmark	6.9	11.6	5.5	8.2	9.1	7.1	5.5	4.8	5.7	4.0	6.1
France	5.8	7.7	9.6	8.6	9.2	10.3	10.4	7.7	8.8	8.0	–
Germany	3.2	8.0	6.6	5.6	6.7	8.2	9.3	7.9	10.3	8.7	7.8
Hungary	–	–	–	–	9.9	10.4	7.9	5.8	6.2	7.4	10.1
Italy	7.7	9.5	11.2	12.1	10.6	11.7	11.9	9.6	8.1	6.2	7.9
Netherlands	6.2	12.0	10.5	8.4	6.8	7.1	4.3	2.1	4.6	3.2	3.4
Spain	11.5	17.5	21.1	17.3	18.5	23.0	18.7	10.6	11.0	8.3	18.1
Sweden	2.2	3.9	2.9	1.6	5.8	9.2	8.5	5.1	6.6	6.2	8.3
Switzerland	0.2	0.9	0.8	0.5	2.8	3.4	3.4	2.5	4.2	3.5	4.1
United Kingdom	5.7	11.4	10.8	7.2	9.7	8.6	6.1	4.8	4.7	5.3	7.7

Notes: For Czech Republic and Hungary, data is available from 1992. Data is missing for France in 2009.
Source: Calculations based on the OECD ALFS Summary tables: Annual labour force statistics.

Table A.6 Incidence of long-term unemployment* (as % of unemployment)

	1980	1983	1986	1989	1992	1995	1998	2001	2004	2007	2008	2009
Belgium	–	59	66	74	56	61	60	53	49	49	47	44
Czech Republic	–	–	–	–	–	31	31	52	49	52	50	29
Denmark	–	39	24	19	25	32	24	26	21	15	15	9
France	34	36	42	41	34	42	43	38	41	41	39	36
Germany	–	43	50	52	37	46	50	48	51	57	53	44
Hungary	–	–	–	–	21	52	50	48	47	47	49	42
Italy	–	55	65	68	58	63	60	64	46	46	44	42
Netherlands	–	48	–	54	47	52	51	–	36	42	37	24
Spain	30	49	54	51	38	51	48	38	33	24	19	27
Sweden	7	11	6	15	14	31	36	24	21	14	14	13
Switzerland	–	–	–	–	16	31	38	21	32	38	27	26
United Kingdom	–	51	53	47	40	50	38	33	24	28	28	27
EU15**	30	47	52	52	41	49	48	44	41	42	37	33
EU19***	30	47	52	52	39	48	46	44	43	43	37	33
OECD-Europe****	30	47	52	49	39	46	45	40	42	40	35	31

Notes: *Long-term unemployment is defined as that involving people out of work and looking for work for twelve months or more (*OECD. Glossary of Statistic Terms, 2002*); for Czech Republic, data is available from 1995; for Hungary and Switzerland from 1992, for Belgium, Denmark, Germany, Italy, Netherlands and the United Kingdom – from 1983. Data is missing for Netherlands in 2001.
**European Union 15 – was the number of member countries in the European Union prior to the accession of ten candidate countries on 1 May 2004. The EU15 comprised the following fifteen countries: Austria, Belgium, Denmark, Finland, France, Germany, Greece, Ireland, Italy, Luxembourg, Netherlands, Portugal, Spain, Sweden, United Kingdom.
***European Union 19 – all EU countries prior to the accession of the ten candidate countries on 1 May 2004, plus the four Eastern European member countries of the OECD, namely Czech Republic, Hungary, Poland, Slovak Republic.
****OECD-Europe comprises all European Union Member countries of the OECD, that is, countries in EU15 plus the Czech Republic, Hungary, Iceland, Norway, Poland, Slovak Republic, Switzerland, Turkey.
Source: OECD. Labour. Labour force statistics. Unemployment by duration.

Table A.7 Inactivity rate (as % of population)

Age group	1990		1992		1994		1996		1998		2000		2002		2006		2009	
	25–54	55–64	25–54	55–64	25–54	55–64	25–54	55–64	25–54	55–64	25–54	55–64	25–54	55–64	25–54	55–64	25–54	55–64
EU*	22	60	20	61	20	62	19	60	18	60	18	59	17	58	16	53	15	51
Belgium	23	78	22	77	20	77	19	77	19	76	17	74	18	73	16	66	14	63
Czech Republic	–	–	–	–	–	–	–	–	12	61	12	62	12	58	12	52	12	50
Denmark	9	43	9	43	13	46	13	49	13	47	12	43	12	40	11	37	10	40
Germany**	20	58	17	61	17	59	17	56	16	56	15	57	14	57	12	45	12	39
Spain	30	60	28	60	26	62	25	62	24	61	22	59	22	57	18	53	15	50
France	16	67	15	68	14	69	13	68	14	69	14	68	14	64	12	60	11	59
Italy	27	68	28	69	28	70	28	71	27	71	26	71	24	70	22	67	23	63
Hungary	–	–	–	–	–	–	23	81	24	82	23	77	23	74	20	65	20	65
Netherlands	24	69	23	70	21	70	20	69	18	66	16	61	15	57	13	50	11	43
Sweden	–	–	–	–	–	–	11	30	13	33	13	32	12	29	11	27	10	26
Switzerland	–	–	–	–	–	–	13	36	12	33	13	35	12	34	12	32	10	30
United Kingdom	16	47	16	48	17	48	17	49	17	49	16	47	16	45	16	41	15	40

Notes: For Czech Republic, data is available from 1998; for Hungary, Sweden and Switzerland from 1996.
Source: Eurostat. Population and social conditions. Labour market. Employment and unemployment. LFS series – Detailed annual survey results. Inactivity. *European Union: EU10 from 1990, EU12 from 1994, EU15 from 2004, EU25 from 2006, EU27 in 2009; **including former GDR from 1991.

Table A.8 Temporary employment* share (total** and age 15–24)

Age group	1990 Total	1990 15–24	1992 Total	1992 15–24	1994 Total	1994 15–24	1996 Total	1996 15–24	1998 Total	1998 15–24	2000 Total	2000 15–24	2002 Total	2002 15–24	2004 Total	2004 15–24	2006 Total	2006 15–24	2009 Total	2009 15–24
EU**	10	27	11	29	11	31	12	34	13	38	14	39	13	38	14	39	15	42	14	40
Belgium	5	15	5	15	5	18	6	21	8	28	9	31	8	27	9	29	9	30	8	33
Czech Republic	–	–	–	–	–	–	–	–	7	8	8	13	8	14	10	18	9	19	9	19
Denmark	11	30	11	29	12	31	11	31	10	27	10	30	9	25	10	27	9	22	9	24
Germany***	11	34	11	34	10	38	11	45	12	52	13	52	12	51	12	56	15	58	15	57
Spain	30	66	34	74	34	74	34	75	33	73	32	69	32	65	32	65	34	66	25	56
France	11	38	10	37	11	41	13	47	14	54	15	55	14	49	13	48	14	51	14	51
Italy	5	11	7	16	7	17	7	19	9	23	10	26	10	27	12	34	13	41	13	44
Hungary	–	–	–	–	–	–	–	–	7	11	7	13	8	15	7	15	7	17	9	21
Netherlands	8	17	10	22	11	27	12	30	13	34	14	35	14	36	15	38	17	44	18	47
Sweden	–	–	–	–	–	–	12	38	13	43	15	45	16	51	16	53	17	59	15	53
Switzerland	–	–	–	–	–	–	12	44	11	45	12	47	12	49	12	47	14	51	13	52
United Kingdom	5	10	6	9	6	12	7	13	7	13	7	13	6	12	6	11	6	13	6	12

Notes: *Temporary employment comprises work under a fixed term employment contract or a job which will terminate if certain objective criteria are met, such as completion of an assignment or return of the employee who was temporarily replaced (Eurostat. Metadata, 2010); **total age = 15 years and older; for Czech Republic and Hungary, data is available from 1998; for Sweden and Switzerland from 1996 (data missing for Switzerland in 2004); ***European Union: EU10 from 1990, EU12 from 1994, EU15 from 2004, EU25 from 2006, EU27 in 2009; ****including former GDR from 1991.
Source: Eurostat. Population and social conditions. Labour market. Employment and unemployment. LFS series – Detailed annual survey results. Temporary employment.

Table A.9 Part-time employment* share (total** and 15–24)

Age group	1990 Total	1990 15–24	1992 Total	1992 15–24	1994 Total	1994 15–24	1996 Total	1996 15–24	1998 Total	1998 15–24	2000 Total	2000 15–24	2002 Total	2002 15–24	2004 Total	2004 15–24	2006 Total	2006 15–24	2009 Total	2009 15–24
EU**	14	12	14	12	15	12	16	12	17	12	18	12	18	12	20	12	19	12	19	12
Euro area (11 countries)	–	–	–	–	–	–	14	16	16	19	17	19	17	20	18	22	20	25	21	28
Belgium	11	13	12	14	13	13	14	16	16	18	21	22	19	18	22	21	22	21	23	24
Czech Republic	–	–	–	–	–	–	–	–	6	6	5	5	5	4	5	5	5	4	6	8
Denmark	23	40	23	42	21	45	22	44	22	49	22	47	21	50	23	56	24	58	26	59
Germany****	15	5	14	5	16	6	17	8	18	11	19	12	21	14	22	15	26	19	26	21
Spain	5	6	6	8	7	12	8	13	8	14	8	14	8	14	9	15	12	21	13	25
France	12	17	13	17	15	22	16	24	17	27	17	22	16	20	17	22	17	23	17	22
Italy	5	6	6	7	6	8	7	8	7	9	9	11	9	10	13	17	13	18	14	21
Hungary	–	–	–	–	–	–	3	2	4	3	4	3	4	4	5	4	4	5	6	7
Netherlands	32	39	35	48	36	51	38	57	39	62	41	62	44	64	46	67	46	68	48	73
Sweden	–	–	–	–	–	–	25	40	24	40	23	38	21	41	24	49	25	42	27	49
Switzerland	–	–	–	–	–	–	28	18	30	19	31	19	32	20	33	21	33	22	35	23
United Kingdom	22	17	23	22	24	24	25	29	25	32	25	33	25	34	26	35	25	35	26	38

Notes: *Full-time/part-time distinction in the main job is made on the basis of a spontaneous answer given by the respondent in all countries, except for the Netherlands, Iceland and Norway, where part-time is determined on the basis of whether the usual hours worked are fewer than 35 (Eurostat. Metadata. LFS series – Detailed annual survey results); **total age = 15 and over. ***European Union: EU10 from 1990, EU12 from 1994, EU15 from 2004, EU25 from 2006, EU27 in 2009; ****including former GDR from 1991. For Czech Republic, data is available from 1998; for EU area (11 countries), Hungary, Sweden and Switzerland – from 1996.

Source: Eurostat. Population and social conditions. Labour market. Employment and unemployment. LFS series – detailed annual survey results. Full-time and part-time employment.

Table A.10 Expenditure on active labour market policies* as % GDP

	1990	1992	1994	1996	1998	2000	2002	2004	2006	2008
Belgium	1.1	1.1	1.2	1.3	1.2	1.2	1.1	1.1	1.2	1.3
Czech Republic	–	0.3	0.2	0.1	0.1	0.2	0.2	0.3	0.3	0.2
Denmark	1.1	1.4	1.6	1.7	1.7	1.9	1.9	1.7	1.5	1.4
France	0.7	1.0	1.2	1.2	1.2	1.2	1.1	1.0	0.9	0.8
Germany	0.8	1.5	1.2	1.3	1.2	1.2	1.2	1.1	0.9	0.8
Hungary	–	0.6	0.6	0.4	0.4	0.4	0.5	0.3	0.3	0.3
Italy	–	–	–	–	–	–	–	0.6	0.5	0.5
Netherlands	1.3	1.4	1.4	1.4	1.6	1.5	1.6	1.4	1.2	1.0
Spain	0.8	0.7	0.4	0.4	0.6	0.8	0.7	0.8	0.7	0.7
Sweden	1.7	3.0	3.0	2.3	2.5	1.8	1.6	1.2	1.4	1.0
Switzerland	0.2	0.3	0.4	0.6	0.8	0.6	0.6	0.8	0.7	0.5
United Kingdom	0.6	0.5	0.5	0.4	0.2	0.2	0.3	0.5	0.3	0.3

Notes: *Active labour market programmes (ALMPs) – ALMPs include all social expenditure (other than education) which is aimed at the improvement of the beneficiaries' prospect of finding gainful employment or to otherwise increase their earnings capacity. This category includes spending on public employment services and administration, labour market training, special programmes for youth when in transition from school to work, labour market programmes to provide or promote employment for unemployed and other persons (excluding young and disabled persons) and special programmes for the disabled (OECD. Glossary of Statistic Terms, 2002).

For Italy, data is available from 2004; for Czech Republic from 1992.

Source: OECD. Stat Extracts. Labour. Labour Market Programmes.

Table A.11 Composition of expenditure on active labour market policies

	PES and administration			Training			Employment incentives			Direct job creation		
	1990	2000	2008	1990	2000	2008	1990	2000	2008	1990	2000	2008
Belgium	18.4	19.4	17.4	16.1	17.2	13.9	4.6	14.0	39.1	60.9	49.5	29.6
Czech Republic**	58.1	44.4	80.0	3.2	11.1	6.7	32.3	27.8	6.7	6.5	16.7	6.7
Denmark	10.0	19.6	50.0	31.3	52.0	31.1	50.0	24.3	18.9	8.8	4.1	0.0
France	21.5	15.2	28.6	53.8	33.0	35.7	13.8	16.1	14.3	10.8	35.7	21.4
Germany	26.5	21.7	40.3	51.5	46.2	40.3	8.8	7.5	11.1	13.2	24.5	8.3
Hungary***	27.5	29.7	32.1	27.5	16.2	21.4	27.5	16.2	32.1	17.6	37.8	14.3
Italy****	–	15.8	20.9	84.4	47.2	41.9	13.3	43.4	34.9	2.2	9.4	2.3
Netherlands	56.7	53.3	56.4	34.3	13.0	17.1	4.5	5.4	0.9	4.5	28.3	25.6
Spain	20.7	11.1	22.4	39.7	26.4	29.3	20.7	44.4	32.8	19.0	18.1	15.5
Sweden	18.8	16.8	42.0	42.2	46.2	8.9	30.5	32.2	48.4	8.6	4.9	0.6
Switzerland	75.0	31.0	32.8	12.5	50.7	47.8	6.3	16.9	17.9	6.3	1.4	1.5
United Kingdom	33.0	68.2	87.1	64.2	18.2	6.5	1.8	9.1	3.2	0.9	4.5	3.2

Notes: The figures are expressed as % of total expenditure, expressed as % GDP; *PES – 'PES and administration' includes placement, job search support and benefit administration; ** earlier date is for 1991;

*** earlier date is for 1992.

**** no data for 1990, 2000 PES and administration is data for 2004.

Source: OECD. StatExtracts. Labour. Labour Market Programmes. Public expenditure and participant stocks in labour market programmes.

B. Caseload Annex

Johan De Deken

Working-age benefit programmes are categorized in five broad functional categories of working-age benefit schemes, distinguished by differences in behavioural requirements imposed on respective beneficiaries:

- unemployment benefit (which includes participants in active labour market programmes);
- work incapacity benefit (including sickness and disability transfers);
- early retirement (permanently exempting claimants from labour market participation),
- sabbatical and leave schemes (temporarily exempting claimants from paid work); and
- social assistance as a residual category which includes persons in need and facing problems other than, or in addition to, lack of employment).

For a discussion of the underlying logic behind this classification, see Chapter 15. As we argued there, it does not matter out of which branch of a national social security system a benefit in a particular functional category is financed, as the main criterion is the underlying behavioural requirement. For example, a scheme that is categorized under the early retirement function can either be part of the unemployment benefit system of a country or of the old-age pension scheme; or a work incapacity benefit can be administered by the disability insurance branch, the sickness insurance branch (including statutory sickness pay) or the social assistance scheme of a country. The data are standardized on the basis of the NEI principles elaborated in Chapter 15, in particular, benefits have, whenever possible, been converted into FTE benefit years. For seven countries, the Annex contains complete series for all our benefit categories: the United Kingdom, Germany, the Netherlands, Belgium, Denmark, Sweden, and France (with only some problems with early retirement benefits in the Netherlands, and no data on work incapacity in France beyond the year 1999). For four countries, three of which that were not part of the original NEI project, the data are more fragmented or less comparable. For Spain, there are no reliable data on social assistance claimants; while Switzerland, the Czech Republic, and Hungary were not part of the original NEI project. The notes below that explain the exact benefits included in the time series and the sources from where they were retrieved. The tables include the absolute caseload and the caseload as a percentage of the population aged 15–64 (the data for the latter were retrieved from http://stats.oecd.org).

B.1 Unemployment benefits

United Kingdom:

Benefits: 1980–1985, unemployment benefit (national insurance) plus 'income support' for registered unemployed; 1996–2008 'contributory based' JSA plus 'income-based' JSA (rounded figures to nearest 1000).

Sources 1980–2008: data collected by Jochen Clasen from the ONS.

France:

Benefits: unemployment insurance benefits (*assurance chômage*) (including *allocation de base* (AD) until 1992 and as of 1993 *allocation unique dégressive* (AUD); special unemployment assistance benefit (*allocation de solidarité spécifique*) (ASS); unemployment insertion assistance (*allocation d'insertion*).

Sources 1981–7: Pole Emploi Unistatis http://info.assedic.fr/unistatis/
Sources 1988–2008: Pole Emploi Unistatis http://info.assedic.fr/unistatis/

Germany:

Benefits: unemployment insurance benefits (*Arbeitslosengeld*); unemployment assistance benefits (*Arbeitslosenhilfe*); temporary unemployment insurance benefits (officially 'short-term working allowance (*Kurzarbeitergeld*), see discussion Chapter 15; not included are benefits paid during periods of bad weather and in winter (*Schlechtwettergeld* and *Wintergeld*); nor benefits paid to employees whose employer is insolvent and cannot pay wages (*Konkursgeld*).

Sources 1980–90: OECD–NEI database provided by David Grubb of the OECD.
Sources 1991–2008: BfA Arbeitsmarkt in Deutschland. Zeitreihen and Arbeitsmarkt 2009 Amtliche Nachrichten der BfA 58(2).
The caseload of unemployment benefit II (UBII) is listed separately (see Table B.8).
Sources 2005–8: Arbeitsmarkt 2009 Amtliche Nachrichten der BfA 58(2).

The Netherlands:

Benefits: 1980–95: unemployment insurance benefits (*werkloosheidswet*) (WW), unemployment assistance benefits (*rijksgroepsregeling werkloze werknemers*) (RWW) and (*wet werkloosheidsvoorziening*) (WWV); 1995–2008: unemployment insurance (WW) and part of social assistance (*algemene bijstandswet*) (ABW) using OECD estimation method because although the separate counting of unemployment assistance (RWW) within the total of social assistance (ABW) was abolished in 1996, the series presented here estimates, in line with the procedure used in the NEI study, the 'unemployed' component and has deduced it from the category 'social assistance' (this procedure assumes that unemployed share in social assistance has remained the same after 1995 (this procedure explains the different caseloads in this appendix compared to those reported in Chapter 5).

Does not include unemployed aged 57.5 receiving WW or RWW who during the period 1984–2003 were exempted from job search (*vrijgesteld van solliciatieplicht*) (these have been allocated to the category 'early retirement' and this group has been subtracted from the unemployment caseload numbers reported in Chapter 5).

Sources 1980–94: OECD–NEI database provided by David Grubb of the OECD.
Sources 1995–2008: data collected by Marcel Hoogenboom from the following sources: CBS www.statline.nl corrected for RWW transfer to Social Assistance (AWB) using OECD estimating method (i.e. 1995 share of ABW in Social Assistance).

Belgium:

Benefits: full-time unemployment insurance benefits (*uitkeringsgerechtigde volledige werklozen*); part-time unemployment insurance benefits (*uitkeringsgerechtigde deeltijdse werklozen*); unemployment benefits for school graduates (*wachtgeld*) and temporary unemployment benefits (*tijdelijke werkloosheid*). Part-time unemployment insurance benefits have been converted into FTE benefit years by multiplying them with a factor 0.5; temporary unemployment benefits have been converted from days into benefit years by dividing them by 312.

> *Sources 1980–2000*: OECD–NEI database provided by David Grubb of the OECD.
> *Sources 2000–8*: annual reports and online statistical database of RVA www.rva.be. Note that CBP and SBP early retirement benefits though paid by the unemployment insurance scheme and benefits paid to unemployed older than 50 who are exempted from job search are not included in the 'unemployment' category, but are listed in the 'early retirement' category.

Switzerland:

Benefits: unemployment insurance benefit.

> *Sources 1980–4*: data collected by Cyrielle Champion from Annual Statistical Yearbooks of the OFS.
> *Sources 1985–90*: data collected by Cyrielle Champion from Swiss Statistical Encyclopaedia.
> *Sources 1991–2008*: data collected by Cyrielle Champion from ILO-based Unemployment Statistics www.bfs.admin.ch.

Spain:

Benefits: unemployment insurance benefits (*seguro de desempleo*); unemployment assistance benefits (*subsidio de desempleo*); agricultural subsidy (*Subsidio Agrario*); active integration allowance (*renta activa de inserción*); temporary benefits for agricultural workers (*trabajadores eventuals agrarios*).

> *Sources 1980–98*: OECD–NEI database provided by David Grubb of the OECD.
> *Sources 1998–2008*: calculations based on data collected by F. Javier Mato from Estadísticas del Ministerio de Trabajo e Inmigración.

Denmark:

Benefits: unemployment insurance benefits (*forsikrede*); unemployed receiving social assistance benefits (*ikke-forsikrede*).

> *Sources: 1980–93*: OECD–NEI database provided by David Grubb of the OECD, recalculated for 1990–3. As of 1998, those UB recipients enrolled in AMLP are not included in the caseload counts of the 'unemployment' category, but appear in the separate 'ALMP' category.

Sources 1993–2008: data collected by Jørgen Goul Andersen from Statistiske Efter-retninger: Arbejdsmarked.

Sweden:

Benefits: unemployment insurance benefits (*arbetslöshetskassor*); flat-rate basic allowance (*grundersättningcash* or KAS).
Sources 1980–9: OECD–NEI database provided by David Grubb of the OECD.
Sources 1990–2008: data collected by Ola Sjöberg from Statistics Sweden Antalet helårsekvivalenter i åldrarna 20–64 som försörjdes med sociala ersättningar och bidrag, 1990–2009 www.scb.se.
For Sweden, there is also a separate ALMP category (see Table B.6). As in the case of Denmark, those enrolled in AMLP are not included in the caseload counts of the 'unemployment' category.

Hungary:

Benefits: unemployment insurance (*járadék*); two types of unemployment assistance (*jövedelempótló támogatás*); school graduates allowance (*pályakezdők segélye*).
Sources: estimates on the basis of data on benefit receipt by registered unemployed provided by Anil Duman and Ágota Scharle – see Table 12.A.1.

Czech Republic:

Benefits: unemployment insurances benefits (podpora v nezamětnanosti).
Source 1991–2008: MLSA Statistická ročenka trhu práce v České republice. Praha: MPSV, 2009. Data collected by Ondřej Hora and Tomáš Sirovátka.

B.2 WORK INCAPACITY BENEFITS

United Kingdom:

Benefits: short-term incapacity benefits (SIB) and long-term incapacity benefits, statutory sickness pay (SPP); severe disablement allowances; employment support allowances. Since 1992 employers no longer have to register SSP benefits. Hence benefits from that year onwards have been extrapolated from the number of SIB on the basis of the ratio between SIB from the year 1992.
Sources 1980–97: OECD–NEI database provided by David Grubb of the OECD.
Sources 1998–2008: DWP, tabulation tools, time series; from 2000: DWP Quarterly Statistical Summary, August 2009; February figures, long-term incapacity benefits compiled by Jochen Clasen; short-term incapacity benefits and extrapolations of SSP on the basis of data retrieved by the tabulation tool of the DWP http://research.dwp.gov.uk.

France:

Benefits: sickness benefits (*assurance maladie*) (days converted into benefits years by dividing the number of days by 260); temporary invalidity benefit (*allocation temporaire d'invalidité*); industrial temporary and permanent accident and illness benefits (*accidents du travail et maladie professionnelles*); benefits for permanent disabled

(*allocation aux adultes handicapés*); invalidity pension (*pension d'invalidité - secteurs privé et parapublic*); invalidity pensions for civil servants of local authorities (CNRACL); military invalidity pension (*pension militaire d'invalidité*).
Sources 1980–99: OECD–NEI database provided by David Grubb of the OECD.

Germany:

Benefits: sickness benefits (*Krankengeld*) (days converted into FTE benefits years by dividing the number of days by 365); short-term sickness benefits (*Lohnfortzahlung*) (estimated on the basis of *Krankengeld* caseload by means of the Einerhand formula of OECD); disability pensions of manual workers (*Rentenversicherung der Arbeiter*), salaried employees (*Rentenversicherung der Angestellten*), and miners (*Knappschaftliche Rentenversicherung*) includes both total disability pensions (*erweiterte/volle Erwerbsunfähigkeitsrenten*) and partial disability pensions (*teilweise Erwerbsunfähigkeitsrenten-Berufsunfähigkeitsrenten*) (partial disability benefits are converted into FTE benefit years using NEI-OECD conversion formula); social and war victims compensation (Bundesversorgungsgesetz); industrial accidents/injuries insurance benefits (*gesetzliche Unfallversicherung*).
Sources 1980–92: OECD–NEI database provided by David Grubb of the OECD.
Sources 1992–2008: Deutsche Rentenversicherung, Rentenversicherung in Zeitreihen; BMAS, Statistisches Taschenbuch 2010 Arbeits- und Sozialstatistik.

The Netherlands:

Benefits: sickness benefits (*ziektewet*) (ZW); statutory sickness pay (*wet uitbreiding loondoor-betalingsverplichting*) (Wulbz); disability benefits for wage earners (*wet op arbeidsongeschiktheid*) (WAO) and for self-employed (*wet arbeidsongeschiktheid zelfstandigen*) (WAZ); as of 2004 for all (*wet inkomen en arbeid*) (WIA); disability benefits for handicapped youth (*wet werk en arbeidsondersteuning jonggehandicapten*) (Wajong).
Sources: calculations based on data collected by Marcel Hoogenboom from the following sources: ZW: Kroniek van de sociale verzekeringen (Den Haag: UWV, 2008) ZW benefits minus benefits for maternity leave; Wulbz: number is unknown due to the fact that since 1996 employers are obliged to pay the benefits themselves. The number of Wulbz benefits is estimated by multiplying the total number of labour years by the official sickness leave percentage, and subtracting the number of maternity benefits (sickness leave percentages: CBS www.statline.nl); WAO, WAZ, and Wajong: Kroniek van de sociale verzekeringen (Den Haag: Lisv, 2001) and CBS www.statline.nl.

Belgium:

Benefits: sickness benefits (*ziekengeld -ziekteuitkering*); benefits of employment injuries and occupational diseases (*bedrijfsongevallen en -ziektes werknemers*); social assistance on disability grounds (*inkomensvervangende en integratietegemoetkoming gehandicapten*). Not included are statutory sickness pay (*gewaarborgd loon*) paid by the employers during the first (two) weeks of sickness of manual workers (salaried employees).
Sources 1980–97: OECD–NEI database provided by David Grubb of the OECD.
Sources 1998–2008: the annual reports of the RIZIV-INAMI www.riziv.be; annual reports of the FBZ-FMP www.fmp-fbz.fgov.be; annual reports of the FAO-FAT www.faofat.fgov.be. Sickness benefits have been converted from working days into benefit years by dividing the number of days by 312.

Switzerland:

Benefits: invalidity benefits (*assurance invalidité*) and work injury benefits (*assurance accidents*). Not included are sickness insurance benefits (*assurance maladie*).
Sources: data collected by Cyrielle Champion from the Swiss Statistical Encyclopaedia.

Spain:

Benefits: sickness benefits (*incapacidad laboral temporal/transitoria*), disability pensions (LISMI); contribution-based permanent invalidity pension (*invalidez permanente*); non-contributory retirement and invalidity pension (*pensiones no contributivas*) (PNC); assistance-based sickness pension (*seguro obligatorio de vejez e invalidez*) (SOVI).
Sources 1980–99: OECD–NEI database provided by David Grubb of the OECD.
Sources 2000–8: data provided by F. Javier Mato.

Denmark:

Benefits: sickness benefits (*sygedagpenge ved sygdom*); disability benefits (*fortidspension*).
Sources 1980–95: OECD–NEI database provided by David Grubb of the OECD.
Sources 1995–2008: data provided by Jørgen Goul Andersen.

Sweden:

Benefits: sickness benefits (*sjukpenning*); permament disability benefits (*förtidspension*); temporary disability benefits (*sjukbidrag*).
As of 1992, the employer had to pay the first two to four weeks of the sickness benefits. The NEI–OECD simulates this case load using a procedure similar to the one described for Germany (with a formula that takes into account the length of the period the employer had to pay, and ratio sick days by sickness benefit recipient in 1980). We have extended this procedure for the period after 2000.
Sources 1980–2000: OECD–NEI database provided by David Grubb of the OECD.
Sources 2000–8: data collected by Ola Sjöberg from Statistics Sweden Antalet helårsekvivalenter i åldrarna 20–64 som försörjdes med sociala ersättningar och bidrag, 1990–2009 www.scb.se.

Hungary:

Benefits: sickness benefits (*táppénz, napi átlag létszám*); disability pensions (*korhatár alatti rokkant* and *egyéb mmk*).
Sources 1990–2008: data provided by Anil Duman and Ágota Scharle – see Table 12.A.2.

Czech Republic:

Benefits: full disability benefits (*invalidní důchod*); partial disability benefits (*částečný invalidní důchod*). The caseload of partial disability benefits has been multiplied by a factor of 0.5. Does not include sick leave benefits (*nemocenské*).
Sources 1990–2008: MLSA Základní ukazatele z oblasti trhu práce a sociálního zabezpečení v České republice ve vývojových řadách a grafech, Praha: MPSV, various years. Data collected by Ondřej Hora and Tomáš Sirovátka.

B.3 EARLY RETIREMENT

France:

Benefits: older unemployed exempted from job search (*dispensés de recherche d'emploi*) (DRE); early retirement benefits (*préretraite progressive*) (PRP), (*allocation de remplacement pour l'emploi*) (ARPE), (*allocation spéciale du Fonds National de l'Emploi*) (ASFNE), (*allocation conventionnelle de solidarité démission*) (ACSD), (*garantie de ressources démission*) (GRD), (*garantie de ressources licenciement*) (GRL). Because the French statutory pension scheme makes a distinction between a minimum (60) and a standard retirement age (65), persons drawing a statutory pension before 65 are listed as a separate category (see Table B.7).

Source 1980: recalculations based on OECD–NEI database provided by David Grubb of the OECD.

Sources 1981–2008: Pole Emploi Unistatis (http://info.assedic.fr/unistatis/).

Germany:

Benefits: early retirement pension (*Vorruhestand* and *Altersübergangsgeld*); part-time early retirement pensions (*Altersteilzeit*) for which the caseload is weighted by a factor of 0.5; older unemployed exempted from job search (*58-er Regelung*); persons drawing a statutory pension before the age of 65 (*für langjährig Versicherte* and *wegen Arbeitslosigkeit oder nach Altersteilzeit*). This excludes disability pensions.

Sources 1980–90: recalculations based on data from the OECD–NEI database provided by David Grubb of the OECD.

Sources 1990–2008: Forschungsportal der Deutsche Rentenversicherung. http://forschung.deutsche-rentenversicherung.de; Rentenbestand Gesamt – Zeitreihen; BfA Arbeitsmarkt in Zahlen of Dezember 2009; J. Hinrichs, and M. Schäfer Entwicklung des Arbeitsmartes seit 1962, Working Paper No. 152/2006, Konrad Adenauer Stiftung.

The Netherlands:

Benefits: early retirement for private sector employees (*vervroegde uittreding*) (VUT) and (*pre-pensioen*) (PP); for (semi) public sector employees (*flexibel pensioen en uittreden*) (FPU); unemployed aged 57.5 receiving WW or RWW who during the period 1984–2003 were exempted from job search (*vrijgesteld van solliciatieplicht*) (does not include former WAO beneficiaries who after 2004 continued to be exempted).

There are no early retirement figures available for the whole period 1980–2008. The figures in the table for some years are based on rough estimates by Marcel Hoogenboom on the basis of the sources listed below (see also discussion of reliability problems of Dutch statistics on early retirement in Chapter 15).

Sources 1980–95: for private sector (VUT): Ministry of Social Affaires and Employment Sociale Nota 1996, Handelingen der Staten Generaal, 1995–6, II: 24 402, nr. 2.

Sources for older unemployed exempted from job search: OECD–NEI database provided by David Grubb of the OECD.

Sources 1982–7: for (semi-) public sector (FPU): Heroverwegingswerkgroep (1989). Rapport van de Heroverwegingswerkgroep. Vut in de collectieve sector Begrotings-voorbereiding 1990. Deelrapport Nr. 3, Den Haag.

Sources 1996–2008: for all sectors (VUT, FPU, PP) in the period 1996–2000 CBS www.statline.nl.

Belgium:

Benefits: early retirement schemes set up in the context of the statutory pension scheme (*bijzonder brugpensioen*) (EBP) and (*brugrustpensioen*) (ERP); early retirement schemes that top up unemployment insurance benefits for older workers (*conventioneel brugpensioen*) (CBP) and (*wettelijk brugpensioen*) (SBP); older unemployment beneficiaries are exempted from job seeking (*oudere vrijgestelde werklozen*).

    Sources: annual reports of the National Employment Office (NEO) www.rva.be; and of the National Pension Institute (RVP-ONP) www.onprvp.fgov.be.

Spain:

Benefits: because the Spanish old-age pension schemes allows to retire before that statutory retirement age (for a discussion see Arents et al., 2002: c9.2), the OECD–NEI study has calculated the number of people receiving an old-age pension prior to the standard retirement age. As with France this group is listed as a separate category (see Table B.7).

    Source: OECD–NEI database provided by David Grubb of the OECD.

Denmark:

Benefits: pre-pension benefit (*efterløn*), transitional allowance for older unemployed (*overgangsydelse*); part-time pensions (*delpension*) the caseloads of the latter scheme were multiplied by a factor of 0.5 to convert them into FTE benefit years.

    Sources 1980–2001: recalculations based on OECD–NEI database provided by David Grubb of the OECD.

    Sources 2002–8: calculations based on data provided by Jørgen Goul Andersen.

Sweden:

Benefits: part-time pensions (*delpension*) converted into FTE benefit years.

    Source: calculations based on data from OECD–NEI database provided by David Grubb of the OECD.

Hungary:

Benefits: old-age pension before statutory retirement age (*korhatár alatti öregségi és hozzátartozói*).

    Source: data provided by Anil Duman and Ágota Scharle – Table 12.A.2.

B.4 Social assistance

United Kingdom:

Benefits: lone parent support only.

Sources: DWP Quarterly statistical summary (2000–8: May figures; 2009: February figures); 1980s figures: December or May; 1990s figures: http://research.dwp.gove. uk.

France:

Benefits: social assistance (*revenu minimum d'insertion*) (RMI); lone parent support (*allocation de parent* isolé) (API).
  Sources 1980–9: OECD–NEI database provided by David Grubb of the OECD.
  1990–2008: DREES les minima sociaux www.sante.gouv.fr.

Germany:

Benefits: social assistance benefits (*Sozialhilfe*) to persons 15–64 years old.
  Sources 1980–99: OECD–NEI database provided by David Grubb of the OECD.
  Sources 2000–8: Statistisches Bundesamt Sozialhilfestatistik Fachserie 13, Reihe 2.2 and Datensammlung Sozialpolitik www.sozialpolitik-aktuell.de.

The Netherlands:

Benefits: 1980–2003 social assistance (*algemene bijstandswet*) (AWB) minus unemployment assistance (*rijksgroepsregeling werkloze werknemers*) (RWW) – NEI–OECD simulation from 1996 onwards (see notes on unemployment); 2003–4 social assistance (*wet werk en bijstand*) (WWB).
  Sources 1980–95: data collected by Marcel Hoogenboom from the following sources: Kroniek van de sociale verzekeringen (Den Haag: Lisv, 2001), and CBS www.statline.nl.
  Sources: 1996–2003: data collected by Marcel Hoogenboom from the following sources: CBS www.statline.nl.
  Sources 2004–8: CBS www.statline.nl.

Belgium:

Benefits: guaranteed minimum (*recht op maastchappelijke integratie - leefloon*); social assistance on disability grounds (*inkomensvervangende en integratietegemoetkoming gehandicapten*) is not included in the category 'social assistance' but has been added to the series 'work incapacity'.
  Sources 1980–98: OECD–NEI database provided by David Grubb of the OECD.
  Sources 1999–2008: statistics portal of the Federal Ministry for Social Integration www.mi-is.be.

Switzerland:

Benefit: social assistance (*aide sociale cantonale*).
  Sources: data collected by Cyrielle Champion from federal statistics on social assistance (www.bfs.admin.ch). Data are available since 2005, for the period 1990–2004, the number of recipients aged 18–64 is estimated on the basis of the average number of recipients between 2005 and 2007, and estimated recipiency rates between 1990 and 2004 from OFS (2009), Comparaison des statistiques de l'aide sociale et de la pauvreté Neuchâtel: Office Fédéral de la Statistique.

Spain:

Benefit: minimum integration income (*renta mínima de inserción*) is administrated at the level of the seventeen autonomous regions.

> *Sources 1985–99*: incomplete data from OECD–NEI database provided by David Grubb of the OECD.

Denmark:

Benefit: social assistance (*social kontanthjælp*).

> *Sources 1980–9*: OECD–NEI database provided by David Grubb of the OECD.
> *Sources 1990–2008*: data provided by Jørgen Goul Andersen.

Sweden:

Benefit: social assistance (*socialbidrag*) – estimates of full-time equivalent as calculated by the Ministry of finance on the basis of expenditure data. Because social assistance may be combined with unemployment benefit which may overestimate benefit years, but on the other hand, the fact that persons may not receive the full amount of the benefit, underestimates the benefit years.

> *Sources 1980–9*: OECD–NEI database provided by David Grubb of the OECD.
> *Sources 1990–2008*: data collected by Ola Sjöberg from Statistics Sweden Antalet helårsekvivalenter i åldrarna 20–64 som försörjdes med sociala ersättningar och bidrag, 1990–2009 www.scb.se.

Hungary:

Benefits: social assistance benefit (*rendszeres szociális segélye*).

> *Sources 1990–2008*: data provided by Anil Duman and Ágota Scharle – Table 12.A.1.

Czech Republic:

Benefits: living income (*životní minimum*) and, as of 2006, living and existence minimum (*životní a existenční minimum*).

> *Sources 1990–2008*: MLSA Základní ukazatele z oblasti trhu práce a sociálního zabezpečení v České republice ve vývojových řadách a grafech, Praha: MPSV, various years. Data collected by Ondřej Hora and Tomáš Sirovátka.

B.5 SABBATICAL LEAVE

Belgium:

Benefits: part-time and full-time career interruption benefits (*loopbaanonderbreking*), part-time and full-time credit benefits (*tijdskrediet*) and thematical leaves (*thematische verloven*). Data retrieved in benefit days, converted into benefit years by dividing by 312 (and part-time benefits multiplied by factor 0.5).

> *Sources 2000–8*: RVA online database (interactieve statistieken) www.rva.be.

Denmark:

Benefits: educational leave (*uddannelseorlov*); parental leave (*forældreolov*); and sabbatical leave (*sabbatorlov*) benefits.

Sources: Per H. Jensen 'The Danish Leave of Absence Schemes. 1994–9 from Origins Functioning and Effects from a Gender Perspective' who retrieved data from Danmarks Statistik, Statistiske efterretninger Arbejdsmarked (various issues); and 2004: T. Bredgaard and F. Larsen CARMA Research Paper 2006:2 (based on Statistics Denmark *Statistical Ten Year Review*, 2005).

Table B.1 Unemployment

	United Kingdom		France		Germany		Netherlands		Belgium		Switzerland		Spain		Denmark		Sweden		Hungary		Czech Republic	
	Absolute	%	Absolute	%	Absolute	%	Absolute	%	Absolute	%	Absolute	%	Absolute	%	Absolute	%	Absolute	%	Absolute	%	Absolute	%
1980	1,351,000	4	1,065,8026	3	480,72627	1.5	271,354	2.9	349,693	5.4	7,241	0	6,651,55	2.8	174,6834	5.3	59,44188	1.1	–	–	–	–
1981	2,152,000	6	1,326,213	4	765,02174	2.3	402,263	4.2	426,079	6.6	7,261	0	7,008,97	2.9	232,0366	6.9	86,85081	1.6	–	–	–	–
1982	2,522,000	7	1,407,149	4	1,040,2923	3.2	548,074	5.7	498,974	7.6	15,486	0	6,501,39	2.7	250,7207	7.5	106,2487	2	–	–	–	–
1983	2,762,000	8	1,268,721	4	1,196,6966	3	654,388	6.7	558,950	8.5	30,639	1	6,044,02	2.5	270,6685	8	125,2536	2.3	–	–	–	–
1984	2,888,000	8	1,470,354	4	967,87246	3.7	641,567	6.5	579,426	8.7	38,133	1	8,325,66	3.4	264,0434	7.8	118,2678	2.2	–	–	–	–
1985	2,997,000	8	1,570,988	4	908,54663	3.6	621,820	6.3	557,511	8.4	96,042	2	1,025,412	4.1	240,5805	7.1	108,7432	2	–	–	–	–
1986	3,067,000	8	1,655,855	5	850,48236	3.4	587,513	5.9	536,137	8.1	81,877	2	1,069,473	4.3	210,8565	6.2	108,0105	2	–	–	–	–
1987	2,780,000	7	1,762,940	5	901,83953	3.5	590,944	5.8	539,763	8.1	75,633	2	1,067,421	4.2	213,0514	6.2	105,2144	1.9	–	–	–	–
1988	2,253,000	6	1,820,953	5	1,016,674	3.6	568,946	5.6	511,642	7.7	67,996	2	1,068,820	4.2	234,7794	6.8	860,3875	1.6	–	–	–	–
1989	1,768,000	5	1,846,384	5	925,028	3.3	544,662	5.3	487,046	7.3	55,024	1	1,128,798	4.4	255,5891	7.4	70,26963	1.3	47,400	0.7	–	–
1990	1,648,000	4	1,879,668	5	1,083,361	3.4	514,809	5	487,883	7.3	58,503	1	1,304,061	5	262,5622	7.6	69,129	2.2	–	–	–	–
1991	2,268,000	6	2,103,102	6	2,325,048	5	507,696	4.9	518,212	7.8	75,900	2	1,426,325	5.5	286,6352	8.2	119,200	2.2	–	–	92,000	1.3
1992	2,742,000	7	2,273,206	7	1,962,312	4.5	530,245	5.1	561,928	8.4	117,500	3	1,631,446	6.2	308,5927	8.8	223,866	2	–	–	86,000	1.2
1993	2,877,000	8	2,562,753	7	2,275,703	5.5	585,458	5.6	616,149	9.2	156,100	3	1,931,095	7.3	338,7363	9.7	335,607	6	–	–	73,000	1
1994	2,597,000	7	2,460,063	7	2,125,426	5.6	652,779	6.2	616,040	9.2	153,500	3	1,758,978	6.6	333,5981	9.5	339,597	6.1	228,973	3.4	82,000	1.2
1995	2,290,000	6	2,334,786	6	1,938,742	5.3	663,118	6.3	591,770	8.8	137,100	3	1,456,851	5.4	280,745	8	339,943	6	–	–	71,000	1
1996	2,088,000	6	2,415,262	6	2,180,609	6	612,531	5.8	555,198	8.3	152,700	3	1,342,410	5	239,7242	6.8	331,614	5.9	–	–	76,000	1.1
1997	1,585,000	4	2,416,826	6	2,321,081	6.7	546,001	5.1	530,786	7.9	167,300	3	1,240,903	4.6	214,9513	6.1	320,131	5.7	–	–	111,000	1.6
1998	1,347,000	4	2,380,431	6	2,039,872	6.4	473,936	4.4	502,198	7.5	142,700	3	1,130,105	4.2	178,491	5	263,303	4.7	–	–	152,000	2.1
1999	1,248,000	3	2,368,921	6	1,878,6249	6	396,052	3.7	469,236	7	122,000	3	1,051,756	3.9	158,000	4.4	224,224	3.9	174,810	2.6	194,000	2.7
2000	1,088,000	3	2,202,169	6	1,740,6871	5.9	352,276	3.3	431,903	6.4	107,400	2	1,042,665	3.8	150,000	4.2	215,583	3.8	–	–	176,000	2.5
2001	970,000	3	2,268,172	6	1,783,5357	5.9	329,500	3	461,365	6.8	105,900	2	1,099,577	3.9	145,000	4.1	168,165	2.9	–	–	155,000	2.2
2002	974,000	3	2,480,487	6	1,986,2736	6.7	359,027	3.3	507,470	7.5	131,100	3	1,195,392	4.2	145,000	4.1	160,380	2.8	–	–	173,000	2.4
2003	933,000	2	2,711,717	7	2,008,157	7.3	438,163	4	543,818	8	174,700	4	1,204,190	4.2	171,000	4.8	191,225	3.3	–	–	183,000	2.5
2004	853,000	2	2,750,097	7	1,919,1725	7.5	565,000	5.1	540,424	7.9	184,500	4	1,252,612	4.3	176,000	4.9	216,966	3.7	200,246	2.9	169,000	2.3
2005	861,000	2	2,602,638	7	1,791,2122	3.2	542,000	4.9	566,439	8.2	187,400	4	1,280,016	4.3	157,000	4.4	207,350	3.5	–	–	139,000	1.9
2006	945,000	2	2,391,884	6	1,479,8524	2.7	468,000	4.2	550,653	7.9	173,200	3	1,310,500	4.3	124,000	3.5	178,278	3	–	–	134,000	1.8
2007	864,000	2	2,230,929	5	1,115,9839	2	395,000	3.6	524,743	7.5	159,900	3	1,394,886	4.5	94,000	2.6	134,801	2.2	–	–	117,000	1.6
2008	905,000	2	2,186,211	5	962,785	1.8	366,000	3.3	524,384	7.4	155,800	3	1,783,153	5.7	51,000	1.4	94,291	1.6	212,304	3.1	109,000	1.5

Table B.2 Work incapacity

	United Kingdom		France		Germany		Netherlands		Belgium		Switzerland		Spain		Denmark		Sweden		Hungary		Czech Republic	
	Absolute	%	Absolute	%	Absolute	%	Absolute	%	Absolute	%	Absolute	%	Absolute	%	Absolute	%	Absolute	%	Absolute	%	Absolute	%
1980	1,390,414	3.9	2,533,606	7.4	3,215,085	7.9	932,000	10.0	356,960	5.5	198,623	4.7	712,203	3.0	271,712	8.2	527,776	9.9	–	–	–	–
1981	1,438,512	4.0	2,560,216	7.4	3,435,647	8.3	943,000	9.9	349,064	5.4	202,959	4.7	762,766	3.2	296,006	8.9	510,137	9.5	–	–	–	–
1982	1,429,562	3.9	2,578,257	7.3	3,484,649	8.3	944,000	9.8	349,723	5.4	205,812	4.8	884,783	3.7	288,694	8.6	504,005	9.4	–	–	–	–
1983	1,474,307	4.0	2,558,053	7.2	3,692,485	8.7	950,000	9.8	347,047	5.3	210,413	4.8	925,040	3.8	290,851	8.6	510,678	9.5	–	–	–	–
1984	1,586,756	4.3	2,512,506	7.0	3,848,647	9.0	971,000	9.9	354,337	5.3	215,490	4.9	1,003,072	4.1	280,054	8.3	514,208	9.5	–	–	–	–
1985	1,621,672	4.4	2,500,918	6.9	3,821,660	8.9	983,000	9.9	358,937	5.4	219,469	5.0	1,017,144	4.1	298,456	8.8	536,152	9.9	–	–	–	–
1986	1,723,009	4.6	2,481,344	6.8	3,718,174	8.7	1,013,000	10.1	358,685	5.4	223,370	5.0	1,005,995	4.0	314,020	9.2	545,936	10.1	–	–	–	–
1987	1,843,119	4.9	2,416,704	6.6	3,706,345	8.7	1,045,000	10.3	354,146	5.3	225,812	5.0	1,012,420	4.0	335,761	9.8	571,240	10.6	–	–	–	–
1988	1,959,598	5.3	2,427,846	6.6	3,693,560	8.6	1,073,000	10.5	361,603	5.4	229,865	5.1	1,029,618	4.0	339,088	9.9	607,519	11.2	–	–	–	–
1989	2,087,968	5.6	2,436,830	6.5	3,668,137	8.5	1,132,000	11.0	372,668	5.4	235,259	5.1	1,055,552	4.1	378,191	11.0	598,089	10.9	–	–	–	–
1990	2,205,519	5.9	2,464,223	6.6	3,699,091	8.4	1,196,000	11.6	373,842	5.6	239,330	5.2	1,077,568	4.2	340,635	9.8	582,052	10.6	631,000	9.2	–	–
1991	2,430,774	6.5	2,486,505	6.6	3,811,570	6.9	1,218,000	11.7	385,285	5.8	245,100	5.3	1,104,679	4.2	327,302	9.4	563,209	10.2	–	–	430,500	6.3
1992	2,613,632	7.0	2,492,254	6.6	3,751,912	6.8	1,213,000	11.6	389,366	5.8	250,661	5.3	1,107,345	4.2	329,114	9.4	602,239	10.9	–	–	443,500	6.4
1993	2,745,600	7.4	2,480,885	6.6	4,223,755	7.6	1,224,000	11.7	386,049	5.8	258,876	5.5	1,104,948	4.2	337,782	9.6	596,667	10.7	–	–	457,500	6.6
1994	2,921,467	7.8	2,483,430	6.6	4,443,702	8.0	1,131,000	10.7	381,928	5.7	269,167	5.7	1,102,318	4.1	342,107	9.7	619,824	11.1	–	–	468,500	6.7
1995	2,924,221	7.8	2,495,961	6.6	4,584,699	8.3	1,143,000	10.8	384,354	5.7	276,802	5.8	1,107,042	4.1	352,446	10.0	618,110	11.0	728,000	10.7	478,500	6.8
1996	2,920,737	7.8	2,470,921	6.6	4,787,065	8.6	1,128,000	10.6	384,374	5.7	285,945	6.0	1,105,988	4.1	353,000	10.0	592,451	10.5	–	–	470,000	6.7
1997	2,825,905	7.5	2,484,369	6.5	4,554,045	8.2	1,145,000	10.8	376,299	5.6	293,986	6.1	1,130,241	4.1	360,000	10.1	579,138	10.3	–	–	467,000	6.6
1998	2,855,449	7.5	2,541,073	6.7	4,362,456	7.8	1,175,000	11.0	373,339	5.6	300,054	6.3	1,127,664	4.2	360,000	10.1	627,900	11.1	–	–	464,500	6.5
1999	2,860,245	7.5	2,602,256	6.8	4,412,085	7.9	1,226,000	11.4	376,794	5.6	307,297	6.4	1,135,468	4.2	356,000	10.0	692,368	12.2	–	–	460,000	6.4
2000	2,972,935	7.7	–	–	4,265,547	7.7	1,267,000	11.7	397,798	5.9	308,719	6.4	1,140,016	4.1	354,000	9.9	774,390	13.6	771,000	11.3	459,500	6.4
2001	3,023,247	7.8	–	–	4,232,030	7.7	1,288,000	11.8	414,807	6.2	322,691	6.6	1,040,638	3.7	356,000	10.0	817,120	14.2	–	–	461,000	6.4
2002	3,030,902	7.8	–	–	4,190,976	7.6	1,321,000	12.1	415,216	6.1	340,129	6.9	1,041,060	3.7	365,000	10.2	869,681	15.1	–	–	467,500	6.5
2003	3,049,545	7.8	–	–	4,069,278	7.4	1,277,000	11.6	427,740	6.3	353,842	7.1	1,049,855	3.6	385,000	10.8	853,760	14.7	–	–	474,000	6.6
2004	3,041,810	7.7	–	–	3,813,805	7.0	1,229,000	11.2	435,141	6.4	366,096	7.3	1,051,665	3.6	388,000	10.9	822,854	14.1	–	–	480,000	6.6
2005	2,996,824	7.5	–	–	3,572,804	6.5	1,167,000	10.6	441,725	6.4	374,828	7.4	1,059,479	3.6	381,000	10.6	785,514	13.3	819,500	12.0	483,500	6.6
2006	2,949,692	7.3	–	–	3,399,739	6.2	1,120,000	10.2	453,801	6.5	384,149	7.5	1,074,272	3.5	369,000	10.3	755,569	12.7	–	–	489,500	6.7
2007	2,903,745	7.2	–	–	3,413,479	6.3	1,091,000	9.9	472,422	6.7	381,081	7.4	1,098,037	3.6	375,000	10.4	715,372	11.9	–	–	493,000	6.7
2008	2,820,131	6.9	–	–	3,478,944	6.4	1,058,000	9.6	492,031	7.0	379,718	7.3	1,109,503	3.5	375,000	10.4	659,030	10.9	748,300	11.0	491,000	6.6

Table B.3 Early retirement

	France		Germany		Netherlands		Belgium		Denmark		Sweden		Hungary	
	Absolute	%	Absolute	%	Absolute	%	Absolute	%	Absolute	%	Absolute	%	Absolute	%
1980	190,497	0.6	1,111,166	2.7	22,000	0.2	84,906	1.3	52,500	1.6	30,120	0.6	–	–
1981	298,045	0.9	1,113,927	2.7	24,000	0.3	97,012	1.5	63,750	1.9	28,424	0.5	–	–
1982	460,664	1.3	1,118,415	2.7	28,000	0.3	118,187	1.8	72,500	2.2	26,105	0.5	–	–
1983	745,013	2.1	1,122,032	2.6	38,000	0.4	131,926	2.0	81,875	2.4	25,072	0.5	–	–
1984	694,129	1.9	1,148,634	2.7	106,265	1.1	151,623	2.3	91,625	2.7	23,885	0.4	–	–
1985	633,353	1.7	1,183,630	2.8	123,278	1.2	189,506	2.9	96,875	2.8	14,396	0.3	–	–
1986	653,177	1.8	1,233,209	2.9	134,472	1.3	174,262	2.6	100,100	2.9	12,142	0.2	–	–
1987	597,831	1.6	1,293,435	3.0	130,684	1.3	173,446	2.6	98,125	2.9	13,592	0.3	–	–
1988	590,212	1.6	1,350,323	3.1	143,991	1.4	184,951	2.8	99,500	2.9	14,618	0.3	–	–
1989	569,351	1.5	1,398,812	3.2	156,719	1.5	194,089	2.9	97,500	2.8	14,856	0.3	–	–
1990	521,582	1.4	1,446,483	3.3	167,172	1.6	199,047	3.0	101,000	2.9	14,457	0.3	70,547	1.0
1991	474,635	1.3	1,730,449	3.1	180,981	1.7	198,587	3.0	104,000	3.0	14,048	0.3	–	–
1992	441,468	1.2	2,503,517	4.5	177,747	1.7	262,165	3.9	110,000	3.2	18,014	0.3	–	–
1993	452,588	1.2	2,806,782	5.1	195,682	1.9	259,735	3.9	116,000	3.3	18,257	0.3	–	–
1994	504,979	1.3	2,960,534	5.3	204,728	1.9	257,294	3.8	119,000	3.4	18,790	0.3	–	–
1995	496,658	1.3	2,850,839	5.1	210,319	2.0	257,437	3.8	138,000	3.9	14,056	0.3	47,500	0.7
1996	512,090	1.4	2,661,010	4.8	243,469	2.3	283,811	4.2	167,000	4.7	9,307	0.2	–	–
1997	509,698	1.3	2,696,902	4.8	259,999	2.4	297,775	4.4	171,000	4.8	6,598	0.1	–	–
1998	506,726	1.3	2,663,211	4.8	259,064	2.4	301,970	4.5	177,000	5.0	4,032	0.1	–	–
1999	533,476	1.4	2,836,977	5.1	255,948	2.4	300,881	4.5	181,000	5.1	2,933	0.1	–	–
2000	538,907	1.4	2,810,892	5.1	344,724	3.2	302,361	4.5	181,000	5.1	0	0.0	113,900	1.7
2001	527,473	1.4	2,788,338	5.0	435,500	4.0	302,981	4.5	179,000	5.0	0	0.0	–	–
2002	500,454	1.3	2,727,020	4.9	587,973	5.4	303,957	4.5	181,000	5.1	0	0.0	–	–
2003	500,187	1.3	2,646,028	4.8	641,837	5.8	297,266	4.4	176,000	4.9	0	0.0	–	–
2004	481,891	1.2	2,443,980	4.5	566,000	5.1	288,046	4.2	187,000	5.2	0	0.0	–	–
2005	464,833	1.2	2,033,589	3.7	577,000	5.2	273,699	4.0	166,000	4.6	0	0.0	181,361	2.7
2006	444,951	1.1	1,811,147	3.3	567,000	5.1	263,950	3.8	145,000	4.0	0	0.0	–	–
2007	409,804	1.0	1,680,769	3.1	520,000	4.7	256,785	3.7	140,000	3.9	0	0.0	–	–
2008	369,150	0.9	1,879,536	3.5	499,000	4.5	246,884	3.5	138,000	3.8	0	0.0	231,700	3.4

Table B.4 Social assistance

	United Kingdom		France		Germany		Netherlands		Belgium		Switzerland		Spain		Denmark		Sweden		Hungary		Czech Republic	
	Absolute	%	Absolute	%	Absolute	%	Absolute	%	Absolute	%	Absolute	%	Absolute	%	Absolute	%	Absolute	%	Absolute	%	Absolute	%
1980	316,000	0.9	65,437	0.2	368,483	0.9	131,000	1.4	20,000	0.3	–	–	–	–	119,697	3.6	34,849	0.7	–	–	–	–
1981	369,000	1.0	74,244	0.2	384,223	0.9	143,000	1.5	22,131	0.3	–	–	–	–	115,909	3.5	32,413	0.6	–	–	–	–
1982	415,000	1.1	78,256	0.2	500,403	1.2	152,000	1.6	31,266	0.5	–	–	–	–	105,303	3.1	40,649	0.8	–	–	–	–
1983	449,000	1.2	89,001	0.2	577,901	1.4	168,000	1.7	38,949	0.6	–	–	–	–	119,697	3.5	45,392	0.8	–	–	–	–
1984	492,000	1.3	104,362	0.3	629,313	1.5	181,000	1.8	41,286	0.6	–	–	–	–	119,697	3.5	52,925	1.0	–	–	–	–
1985	534,000	1.4	111,499	0.3	738,978	1.7	186,000	1.9	42,525	0.6	–	–	282	0.0	111,364	3.3	56,903	1.1	–	–	–	–
1986	579,000	1.6	119,969	0.3	785,750	1.8	181,000	1.8	43,774	0.7	–	–	1,050	0.0	109,091	3.2	63,055	1.2	–	–	–	–
1987	630,000	1.7	124,380	0.3	829,091	1.9	181,000	1.8	48,602	0.7	–	–	2,226	0.0	113,636	3.3	57,396	1.1	–	–	–	–
1988	695,000	1.9	127,196	0.3	857,913	2.0	186,000	1.8	50,928	0.8	–	–	42,100	0.2	136,364	4.0	57,465	1.1	–	–	–	–
1989	757,000	2.0	465,598	1.3	918,845	2.1	190,000	1.9	51,782	0.8	–	–	37,723	0.1	138,636	4.0	59,443	1.1	–	–	–	–
1990	794,000	2.1	553,101	1.5	925,065	2.1	186,000	1.8	49,479	0.7	59,237	1.3	42,100	0.2	137,000	4.0	71,718	1.3	–	–	–	–
1991	872,000	2.3	621,422	1.7	934,813	1.7	188,000	1.8	51,700	0.8	64,664	1.4	42,100	0.2	158,000	4.5	74,191	1.3	–	–	134,000	2.0
1992	957,000	2.6	713,034	1.9	1,204,622	2.2	186,000	1.8	53,874	0.8	74,606	1.6	43,445	0.2	167,000	4.8	88,128	1.6	–	–	215,000	3.1
1993	1,014,000	2.7	841,589	2.2	1,261,499	2.3	181,000	1.7	56,059	0.8	79,964	1.7	57,960	0.2	177,000	5.1	106,138	1.9	–	–	186,000	2.7
1994	1,040,000	2.8	955,303	2.5	1,085,528	2.0	178,000	1.7	62,599	0.9	85,281	1.8	50,874	0.2	139,000	4.0	121,230	2.2	–	–	269,000	3.8
1995	1,041,000	2.8	988,839	2.6	1,235,242	2.2	175,000	1.7	69,740	1.0	90,575	1.9	47,913	0.2	120,000	3.4	116,885	2.1	–	–	306,000	4.3
1996	1,044,000	2.8	1,052,200	2.8	1,284,994	2.3	165,000	1.6	75,163	1.1	100,378	2.1	66,177	0.2	117,000	3.3	131,389	2.3	–	–	189,000	2.7
1997	1,014,000	2.7	1,107,486	2.9	1,354,018	2.9	150,000	1.4	80,412	1.2	100,173	2.3	63,714	0.2	116,000	3.3	137,902	2.4	–	–	216,000	3.0
1998	961,000	2.5	1,143,509	3.0	1,332,927	2.4	137,000	1.3	83,784	1.2	115,401	2.4	56,900	0.2	114,000	3.2	127,083	2.2	–	–	302,000	4.2
1999	936,000	2.5	1,173,011	3.1	1,267,344	2.3	127,000	1.2	76,386	1.1	120,900	2.5	69,703	0.3	115,000	3.2	113,002	2.0	–	–	433,000	6.1
2000	914,000	2.4	1,121,939	2.9	1,406,172	2.7	118,000	1.1	71,399	1.1	121,568	2.5	–	–	117,000	3.3	99,659	1.7	36,312	0.5	452,000	6.3
2001	896,000	2.3	1,099,205	2.8	1,545,000	2.8	114,000	1.0	63,966	0.9	117,542	2.4	–	–	118,000	3.3	88,759	1.5	–	–	393,000	5.5
2002	866,000	2.2	1,114,756	2.9	1,560,000	2.8	114,000	1.0	66,161	1.0	118,484	2.4	–	–	120,000	3.4	82,623	1.4	–	–	369,000	5.1
2003	853,000	2.2	1,168,689	3.0	1,715,000	2.7	120,000	1.1	74,065	1.1	129,241	2.6	–	–	118,000	3.3	81,536	1.4	–	–	237,000	3.3
2004	823,000	2.1	1,259,528	3.2	1,870,000	3.4	121,000	1.1	75,544	1.1	140,145	2.8	–	–	125,000	3.5	84,455	1.4	–	–	243,000	3.4
2005	790,000	2.0	1,316,797	3.3	287,440	0.5	118,000	1.1	76,257	1.1	160,309	3.2	–	–	117,000	3.3	85,389	1.4	133,104	2.0	216,000	3.0
2006	775,000	1.9	1,315,626	3.3	311,448	0.6	110,000	1.0	78,705	1.1	165,480	3.3	–	–	104,000	2.9	79,915	1.3	–	–	213,000	2.9
2007	766,000	1.9	1,205,158	3.0	340,234	0.6	102,000	0.9	80,402	1.1	157,602	3.1	–	–	89,000	2.5	76,735	1.3	–	–	72,000	1.0
2008	739,000	1.8	1,177,143	2.9	357,724	0.7	97,000	0.9	82,901	1.2	148,909	2.9	–	–	72,000	2.0	78,860	1.3	142,262	2.1	66,000	0.9

Table B.5 Paid sabbatical leave

	Belgium		Denmark	
	Absolute	%	Absolute	%
1984	0		0	0.0
1985	1,610	0.0	0	0.0
1986	5,539	0.1	0	0.0
1987	11,896	0.2	0	0.0
1988	20,405	0.3	0	0.0
1989	28,113	0.4	0	0.0
1990	35,358	0.5	0	0.0
1991	37,735	0.6	0	0.0
1992	42,880	0.6	0	0.0
1993	40,413	0.6	8,700	0.2
1994	37,057	0.6	50,845	1.4
1995	35,046	0.5	82,116	2.3
1996	34,511	0.5	62,900	1.8
1997	37,555	0.6	46,709	1.3
1998	43,597	0.6	42,944	1.2
1999	53,265	0.8	34,201	1.0
2000	57,135	0.8	30,210	0.8
2001	71,239	1.1	20,670	0.6
2002	81,760	1.2	14,310	0.4
2003	97,915	1.4	–	–
2004	110,412	1.6	–	–
2005	121,657	1.8	–	–
2006	131,513	1.9	–	–
2007	138,519	2.0	–	–
2008	144,032	2.0	–	–

Table B.6 Active labour market programmes

	Sweden		Denmark	
	Absolute	%	Absolute	%
1987	–	–	–	–
1988	–	–	–	–
1989	–	–	–	–
1990	60,585	1.1	–	–
1991	98,192	1.8	–	–
1992	125,140	2.3	–	–
1993	157,466	2.8	–	–
1994	181,974	3.3	–	–
1995	174,909	3.1	–	–
1996	189,772	3.4	138,000	3.9
1997	178,473	3.2	123,000	3.5
1998	162,074	2.9	121,000	3.4
1999	142,279	2.5	122,000	3.4
2000	108,704	1.9	123,000	3.5
2001	107,750	1.9	131,000	3.7
2002	112,798	2.0	134,000	3.8
2003	88,893	1.5	114,000	3.2
2004	101,903	1.7	117,000	3.3
2005	118,430	2.0	117,000	3.3
2006	134,136	2.3	114,000	3.2
2007	87,194	1.5	115,000	3.2
2008	83,023	1.4	123,000	3.4

Table B.7 Statutory pensions before standard retirement age

	France		Spain	
	Absolute	%	Absolute	%
1980	787,217	2.3	97,126	0.4
1981	990,902	2.8	103,960	0.4
1982	1,350,598	3.8	105,984	0.4
1983	1,849,864	5.2	115,606	0.5
1984	2,110,058	5.8	140,302	0.6
1985	2,204,369	6.1	162,060	0.7
1986	2,311,712	6.3	183,650	0.7
1987	2,369,158	6.4	199,881	0.8
1988	2,460,857	6.6	229,779	0.9
1989	2,478,225	6.7	245,025	1.0
1990	2,476,177	6.6	256,707	1.0
1991	2,500,340	6.7	265,716	1.0
1992	2,587,563	6.9	280,368	1.1
1993	2,662,350	7.1	296,109	1.1
1994	2,764,642	7.3	317,295	1.2
1995	2,755,835	7.3	334,818	1.2
1996	2,743,751	7.2	343,530	1.3
1997	2,746,704	7.2	340,560	1.3
1998	2,735,480	7.2	318,384	1.2
1999	2,735,725	7.2	287,496	1.1
2000	2,697,418	7.0	268,785	1.0
2001			278,190	1.0

Table B.8 Unemployment benefit II (UBII)

	Germany	
	Absolute	%
2004	0	0.0
2005	4,981,748	9.0
2006	5,392,166	9.8
2007	5,276,609	9.7
2008	5,009,872	9.2

References

Acemoglu, D. and Shimer, R. (2000) Productivity gains from unemployment insurance, *European Economic Review*, 44, 7, 1195–224.

Achatz, J. and Trappmann, M. (2009) Befragung von Arbeitslosengeld-II-Beziehern: Wege aus der Grundsicherung, *IAB Kurzbericht 28/2009*, Nürnberg: IAB.

Adamy, W. (2010) *Leiharbeit und Arbeitslosigkei*, Berlin: Deutscher Gewerkschaftsbund.

Adema, W. and M. Ladaique (2009) How Expensive is the Welfare State? Gross and Net Indicators in the OECD Social Expenditure Database (SOCX), *OECD Social, Employment and Migration Working Papers*, No. 92.

Agell, J. (1999) On the benefits from rigid labour markets: Norms, market failures, and social insurance, *The Economic Journal*, 109, 453, 143–64.

Alber, J. (1981) Government responses to the challenge of unemployment: The development of unemployment insurance in Western Europe, in P. Flora, and A. Heidenheimer, (eds), *The Development of Welfare States in Europe and America*, London: Transaction, 151–83.

—— (1987) Germany, in P. Flora, (ed.), *Growth to limits: the Western European welfare states since World War II*, Florence: European University Institute.

Albrekt Larsen, C. and Goul Andersen, J. (2009) *Magten på Borgen – En analyse af beslutningsprocesser i større politiske reformer*, Aarhus: Aarhus University Press.

Alcock, P., Beatty, C., Fothergill, S., MacMillan, R. and Yeandle, S. (2003) *Work to Welfare. How men become detached from the labour market*, Cambridge: Cambridge University Press.

Allison, C. and Ringold, D. (1996) Labour markets in transition in Central and Eastern Europe 1989–1995, World Bank Technical Paper, No. 352. *Social Challenges of Transition Series*, Washington, DC.

Amuedo-Dorantes, C. (2000) Work transitions into and out of Involuntary Employment in a Segmented Market: Evidence from Spain, *Industrial and Labor Relations Review*, 53, 2, 309–25.

Anastasia, B., Mancini, M. and Trivellato, U. (2009) Il sostegno al reddito dei disoccupati: note sullo stato dell'arte. Tra riformismo strisciante, inerzie dell'impianto categoriale e incerti orizzonti di flexicurity, contribution to the research report 'Il lavoro che cambia. Contributi tematici e raccomandazioni', Camera dei Deputati-Senato-Cnel. Available at www.cnel.it

Andersen, L. (2006) Veje til flere i arbejde, in J. H. Petersen and K. Petersen (eds), *13 løsninger for den danske velfærdsstat*, Odense: Southern Denmark University Press.

Andersen, J. and Goul Andersen, J. (2003) Klassernes forsvinden, in J. Goul Andersen and O. Borre (eds), *Politisk forandring. Værdipolitik og nye skillelinjer ved folketingsvalget 2001*, Aarhus: Systime, 207–22.

Andersen, T. M. and Svarer, M. (2008) The role of workfare in striking a balance between incentives and insurance in the labour market, *CESifo Working Paper 2267*, Denmark: Univeristy of Aarhus.

Andersson, G. and Andersson, M. (2007) Avskaff a-kassan och sjukförsäkringen, *Dagens Nyheter*, July 2.

Andersson, D., Löfgren, A.-K. and Lindblad, J. (2008) *Trygghet och effektivitet, en bättre arbetslöshetsförsäkring. Om vägvalen i sysselsättningspolitiken*, Stockholm: LO.

Antal, L. (2000) A Bokros-csomag, *Beszélő*, 6.

Anxo, D. and Niklasson, H. (2006) The Swedish model in turbulent times: Decline or renaissance? *International Labour Review*, 145, 339–75.

Arango, J. (1999) *La protección por desempleo en España*, Madrid: Consejo Económico y Social de España.

Arbejdsministeriet et al. (1989) *Hvidbog om arbejdsmarkedets strukturproblemer*, Copenhagen: Arbejdsministeriet (Ministry of Labour), 65–76.

Arbetslöshetskassornas samorganisation (2007) *Konsekvensanalys avseende förändringar av a-kassornas finansiering och medlemsavgiftern*, Stockholm: Arbetslöshetskassornas samorganisation.

—— (2008) *Historik över arbetslöshetsförsäkringen 1885–2008*, Stockholm: Arbetslöshetskassornas samorganisation.

—— (2009) *Bara en av tio heltidare får 80 procent*, Report 2009-11-20, Stockholm: Arbetslöshetskassornas samorganisation.

—— (2010) Ändringar i arbetslöshetsförsäkringen 2007–2010. Available at www.samorg. org, accessed 20August 2010.

Arents, M., Cluitmans, M. and van der Ende, M. (2002) Benefit Dependency Ratios. An Analysis of Nine European Countries, Japan and the US, *Final Report, SZW* (Dutch Ministry of Social Affairs), No. 16/153/2000.

Armingeon, K. (2001) Institutionalising the Swiss Welfare State, *West European Politics*, 24, 2, 145–68.

Arranz, J.M., García-Serrano, C. and Hernanz, V. (2009) El uso perverso de las prestaciones: el retorno al empleo anterior, XIII Encuentro de Economía Aplicada.

Arriba, A. (2009) Rentas Mínimas de Inserción de las Comunidades Autónomas: una visión conjunta de su evolu ción y alcance, *Gestión y Análisis de Políticas Públicas*, 2, 81–99.

Atkinson, A. and Micklewright, J. (1989) Turning the screw: benefits for the unemployed, 1979–1988, in A. Dilnot and I. Walker (eds), *The Economics of Social Security*, Oxford: Oxford University Press.

—— —— (1990) Unemployment compensation and labour market transitions: A critical review, *Journal of Economic Literature*, 29, 4, 1679–727.

—— Rainwater, L. and Smeeding, T. (1995) *Income Distribution in OECD Countries*, Paris: OECD.

AWF (1952–1995) *Jaarverslag Algemeen Werkloosheidsfonds*, Den Haag: AWF.

Ayala, L. (2000) *Las Rentas Mínimas en la Reestructuración de los Estados del Bienestar*, Madrid: Consejo Económico y Social de España.

—— Martínez López, R. and Ruiz-Huerta, J. (2001) La descentralización territorial de las prestaciones asistenciales: efectos sobre la igualdad, Papeles de trabajo del Instituto de Estudios Fiscales, *Serie Economía*, 16, 1–39.

Bäcker, G., Bispinck, R., Hofemann, K. and Naegele, G. (2008a) *Sozialpolitik und soziale Lage in Deutschland. Gesundheit und Gesundheitssystem, Familie, Alter, Soziale Dienste*, Bd. 2; 4. überarb. Aufl., Opladen: Westdeutscher Verlag.

—— —— —— —— (2008b) *Sozialpolitik und soziale Lage in Deutschland. Ökonomische Grundlagen, Einkommen, Arbeit und Arbeitsmarkt, Arbeit und Gesundheitsschutz*, Bd.1, 4. überarb. Aufl., Opladen: Westdeutscher Verlag.

Bálint, M. and Köllő, J. (2008) The labour supply effects of maternity benefits, in Z. Cseres-Gergely and A. Scharle (eds), *In focus: social welfare and labour supply*, Budapest: Institute of Economics, HAS.

Balla, K, Köllő, J. and Simonovits, A. (2008) Transition with heterogeneous labour, *Structural Change and Economic Dynamics*, 19, 3, 203–20.

Banca d'Italia (2009) *Relazione annuale 2008*, Rome: Banca d'Italia.

Banks, J., Blundell, R., Bozio, A. and Emmerson, C. (2008) Releasing jobs for the young? Early retirement and youth unemployment in the United Kingdom, in J. Gruber and

D. Wise (eds), *Social Security Programs and Retirement around the World: the relationship to youth employment*, Chicago: University of Chicago Press.

Bannink, D. (2004) *The Reform of Dutch Disability Insurance*, Enschede: University of Twente.

Barbier, J.-C. (2001) Welfare to Work Policies in Europe. The Current Challenges of Activation Policies, *Document de Travail No. 11*, Paris: Centre d'études de l'emploi.

—— (2004) Systems of social protection in Europe: Two contrasted paths to activation, and maybe a third, in J. Lind, H. Knudsen and H. Jørgensen (eds), *Labour and Employment Regulation in Europe*, Brussels: Peter Lang.

—— (2007) Réformer le service public de l'emploi: une fenêtre d'opportunité, *Regards croisées sur l'économie*, 2007/2, 235–43.

—— Fargion, V. (2004) Continental inconsistencies on the path to activation – Consequences for social citizenship in Italy and France, *European Societies*, 6, 437–60.

—— Kaufmann, O. (2008) The French strategy against unemployment: Innovative but inconsistent, in W. Eichhorst, R. Kohnle-Seidl and O. Kaufmann (eds), *Bringing the Jobless into Wok? Experiences with Activation Schemes in Europe and the US*, Berlin: Springer, 69–119.

——Ludwig-Mayerhoffer, W. (2004) Introduction: The many worlds of activation, *European Societies*, 6, 4, 423–36.

—— Théret, B. (2001) Welfare to Work or Work to Welfare, the French Case? in N. Gilbert and R.A.V. Voorhis (eds), *Comparative Study of Evaluations of Welfare to Work Policies in Social Assistance*, London: Transaction Books, 135–83.

Baumol, W. J. (2001) Paradox of the services: exploding costs, persistent demand, in T. Ten Raa and R. Schettkat (ed.), *The Growth of Service Industries: The Paradox of Exploding Costs and Persistent Demand*, Cheltenham: Edward Elgar, 3–28.

Bauwens, D. (2009) La suspension du benefice des allocations de chômage, *Revue Belge de Sécurité Sociale* 51, 2, 391–422.

Becker, I. and Hauser, R. (2006) Verteilungseffekte der Hartz IV-Reform. Ergebnisse von Simulationsanalysen, Berlin: Edition Sigma.

Beer, P. de and Schils, T. (eds) (2009) *The Labour Market Triangle, The Labour Market triangle. Employment protection, unemployment compensation and activation in Europe*, Cheltenham: Edward Elgar.

Belorgey, J-M. (1988) *La gauche et les pauvres*, Paris: Syros.

Benedek, D., Rigó, M., Scharle, Á. and Szabó, P.A. (2006) Increases in the minimum wage in Hungary: 2001–2006, *Ministry of Finance Working Papers*, 16, Budapest: Ministry of Finance.

Bengtsson, S. (2009) *Førtidspension – forskning og politik i samspil*. Danish National Centre of Social Research – SFI. Available at http://www.sfi.dk/Default.aspx?ID=4509

Benner, M. and Vad, T. (2000) Sweden and Denmark: defending the welfare state, in F. W. Scharpf and V. Schmid (eds), *Welfare and work in the open economy*, Oxford: Oxford University Press.

Bentolila, S. and Toharia, L. (eds) (1991) *Estudios de economía del trabajo en España III*, Madrid: Ministerio de Trabajo.

Berclaz, M. and Füglister, K. (2004) National report Switzerland: Policy deliberation in national domains, Workpackage 2, UNEMPOL Project, Universities of Geneva and Leeds.

—— Füglister, K. and Giugni, M. (forthcoming). Political opportunities and the mobilization of the unemployed in Switzerland, in D. Chabanet and J. Faniel (eds), *From acquiescence to protest? The mobilization of the unemployed in Europe*, Houndmills: Palgrave.

Bergmark, Å. (2003) Activated to work? Activation policies in Sweden in the 1990s, *Revue Francaise des Affaires Sociales*, 4, 4, 291–306.

Berton, F., Richiardi, M. and Sacchi, S. (2009) *Flex-insecurity. Perché in Italia la flessibilità diventa precarietà*, Bologna: Il Mulino.

Bertozzi, F., Bonoli, G. and Gay-des-Combes, B. (2005) *La réforme de l'Etat social en Suisse*, Lausanne: Presses polytechniques et universitaires romandes.

—— Bonoli, G. and Ross, F. (2008) The Swiss road to activation: legal aspects, implementation and outcomes, in W. Eichhorst, O. Kaufmann and R. Konle-Seidl (eds), *Bringing the jobless into work? Experiences with activation in Europe and the US*, Berlin: Springer, 121–60.

Beskæftigelsesministeriet (2005) *Flexicurity. Udfordringer for den danske model*, Copenhagen: Ministry of Labour.

Betzelt, S. (2007) Hartz IV aus Gender-Sicht. Einige Befunde und viele offene Fragen, *WSI-Mitteilungen*, 60, 298–304.

Beveridge, W. (1909) *Unemployment: A Problem of Industry*, London: Longmans Green.

Birch Sørensen, P. (2008) Miraklet på det danske arbejdsmarked, *Berlingske Tidende*, 25. Aug., 2008.

Bird, K. (2001) Parental Leave in Germany – An Institution with two Faces?, in L. Leisering, R. Müller and K. Schumann (eds), *Institutionen und Lebenslauf im Wandel*, Weinheim/München: Juventa, 55–87.

Blanchard, O. (1998) *The Economics of Post Communist Transition*, Oxford: Oxford University Press.

—— Landier, A. (2002) The Perverse Effects of Partial Labour Market Reform: fixed-term contracts in France, *The Economic Journal*, 112, 480, 214–44.

—— Commander, S. and Coricelli, F. (1995) Unemployment and restructuring in Eastern Europe and Russia, in S. Commander and F. Coricelli (eds), *Unemployment and Restructuring and the Labour market in Eastern Europe and Russia*, Washington: Economic Development Institute of the World Bank.

Blöndal, S. and Pearsson, M. (1995) Unemployment and other non-employment benefits, *Oxford Review of Economic Policy*, 2, 1, 136–69.

Bódis, L. and Nagy, G. (2008) Empirikus vizsgálatok a munkanélküli ellátások magatartási előírásainak ellenőrzéséről, *Kormányzás, Közpénzügyek, Szabályozás*, 3, 1, 39–47.

Bogaerts, K., De Grave, D., Marx, I. and Vandenbroucke, P. (2009) Inactiviteitsvallen voor personen met een handicap of met langdurige gezondheidsproblemen. Een onderzoek in opdracht van de Vlaamse minister van werk, onderwijs en vorming in het kader van het VIONA-onderzoeksprogramma final report of March 2009, UFSIA, Antwerpen: Centrum voor Sociaal Beleid Herman Deleeck. Available at www.centrumvoorsociaalbeleid.be

Boldrin, M., and Jiménez-Martín, S. (2007) Spanish Pension Expenditure under alternative Reform Scenarios, in J. Gruber and D. Wise (eds), *Social Security Programs and Retirement around the World. Fiscal Implications of Reform*, Chicago: Chicago University Press, 351–411.

Boldrin, M. and Jiménez-Martín, S. (2007) Spanish Pension Expenditure under alternative Reform Scenarios, in J. Gruber and D. Wise (eds), *Social Security Programs and Retirement around the World. Fiscal Implications of Reform*, Chicago: Chicago University Press, 351–11.

—— —— and Peracchi, F. (1999) Social security and retirement in Spain, in J. Gruber and D. Wise (eds), *Social Security Programs and Retirement around the World*, Chicago: Chicago University Press, 305–82.

Bolvig, I. (2008) Low-wage work after unemployment – the effect of changes in the UI System, No 08–11, Working Papers, University of Aarhus, Aarhus School of Business, Department of Economics.

—— Jensen, P. and Rosholm, M. (2003) The Employment Effects of Active Social Policy, *IZA Discussion Paper 736*, Bonn: IZA.

Bonoli, G. (1999) La réforme de l'Etat social Suisse: Contraintes institutionnelles et opportunités de changement, *Swiss Political Science Review*, 5, 3, 57–77.

—— (2003) Social policy through labour markets: Understanding national differences in the provision of economic security to wage earners, *Comparative Political Studies*, 36, 983–1006.

—— (2004) Switzerland: Negotiating a new welfare state in a fragmented political system, in P. Taylor-Gooby (ed.), *New risks, new welfare: The transformation of the European welfare state*, Oxford: Oxford University Press, 157–80.

—— (2005) The politics of the new social policies: providing coverage against new social risks in mature welfare states, *Policy & Politics*, 33, 3, 431–49.

—— (2007) Time matters: post-industrialization, new social risks and welfare state adaptation in advanced industrial democracies, *Comparative Political Studies*, 40, 5, 495–520.

—— (2008) Réorienter les régimes sociaux vers la réinsertion professionnelle, Working Paper de l'IDHEAP, *Politiques sociales*, 2.

—— (2012) Blame avoidance and credit claiming revisted, in G. Bonoli and D. Natali (eds), *The New Politics of the Welfare State* (forthcoming).

—— Mach, A. (2000) Switzerland: Adjustment politics within institutional constraints, in F. W. Scharpf and V. Schmid (eds), *Welfare and work in the open economy*, Oxford: Oxford University Press, 131–74.

—— Palier, B. (1997) Reclaiming Welfare: The Politics of French Social Protection Reform, in M. Rhodes (ed.), *Southern European Welfare States. Between Crisis and Reform*. London: Portland, Frank Cass.

—— Powell, M. (eds) (2004) *Social Democratic Parties in Contemporary Europe*, London: Routledge.

Bonvin, J.-M. and Rosenstein, E. (2009) Accountability procedures and their impact on participation and empowerment at local level: Comparing activation programmes in Switzerland, paper presented at the 7th Annual ESPAnet conference the future of the welfare state: Paths of social policy innovation between constraints and opportunities, Urbino, 17–19 September 2009.

Borgetto, M. (2009) L'activation de la solidarité: d'hier à aujourd'hui, *Droit Social*, 11/2009, 1043–53.

Bredgaard, T. (2004) Det rummelige arbejdsmarked og arbejdsmarkedets rummelighed: Forudsætninger, potentialer og realiter, in P. Nielsen, E. Emmett Caraker and J. Magnussen (eds), *Perspektiver på arbejdsmarked, virksomheder og medarbejdere*, Aalborg: CARMA, 13–43.

—— Larsen, F. (2006) *Udlicitering af beskæftigelsespolitikken – Australien, Holland og Danmark*, Copenhagen: Jurist og 0konomforbundets Forlag.

—— —— Madsen, P. K. (2008) Flexicurity: In Pursuit of a Moving Target, *European Journal of Social Security*, 10, 4, 305–23.

Breidahl, K. and Seemann, J. (2009) *Jobcentret som organisatorisk fænomen*, Copenhagen: Frydenlund Academic.

Bridgen, P. and Meyer, T. (2010) The convergence of a liberal and a conservative pension regime?, in J. Clasen (ed.), *Converging worlds of welfare? German and British social policy in the 21st Century*, Oxford: Oxford University Press (forthcoming).

Brusis, M. (2006) Hungary: a core supreme, in D. Vesselin, K.H. Goetz and H. Wollmann (eds), *Governing after Communism: institutions and policymaking*, Lanham, MD: Rowman & Littlefield, 49–82.

Brussig, M. and Knuth, M. (2006) Altersgrenzpolitik und Arbeitsmarkt – Zur Heraufsetzung des gesetzlichen Rentenalters, WSI-Mitteilungen, 59, 307–13.

Brussig, M. and Knuth, M. (2009) Alternative Styles and Roles for Local Governments, in F. Larsen and van R. Berkel (eds), *The New Governance and Implementation of Labour Market Policies Copenhagen,* DJOF Publishing Copenhagen, 69–94.

Bruthansová, D., Červenková, A, Kolářová, M. *(2002) Vývoj invalidity v České republice a ve vybraných zemích EU,* Praha: VÚPSV.

Bukovjan, P. (2007) Reforma veřejných financí a zákon o zaměstnanosti, *Práce a mzda,* 11, 47–8.

Bultemeier, A. and Neubert, J. (1998) Arbeitsmarktentwicklung und Arbeitsmarktpolitik in Ostdeutschland, in R. Lutz and M. Zeng (eds), *Armutsforschung und Sozialberichtserstattung in den neuen Bundesländern,* Opladen: Leske + Budrich, 287–307.

Bundesagentur für Arbeit (2009a) Analytikreport der Statistik April 2009. Arbeitsmarkt in Deutschland, Zeitreihen bis 2008.

—— (2009b) Der Arbeitsmarkt in Deutschland. Kurzarbeit. Aktuelle Entwicklungen, Nürnberg: Bundesagentur für Arbeit.

—— (2010a) Der Arbeitsmarkt in Deutschland. Jahresrückblick 2009, Nürnberg: Bundesagentur für Arbeit.

—— (2010b) Grundsicherung für Arbeitsuchende. Erwerbstätige Arbeitslosengeld II-Bezieher. Begriff, Messung, Struktur und Entwicklung. Bericht der Statistik der BA, Nürnberg.

Bundesministerium für Arbeit und Soziales (2010a) Pressemitteilung. Gezielte Bildungsleistungen sind ein Riesenfortschritt für die Kinder, Bundeskabinett beschließt Gesetzentwurf zur SGB II Leistungsreform, 16.11.2010, Berlin: BMAS.

Bundesministerium für Arbeit und Soziales (2010b) Pressemitteilung. Bundestag billigt Verfassungsänderung für Arbeitslosenbetreuung aus einer Hand, 17.06.2010, Berlin: BMAS.

Bundesregierung (2010) Solide Finanzen für Wohlstand und soziale Sicherheit. Verlautbarung vom 9.06.2010, Berlin: Presse und Informationsamt der Bundesregierung.

Bundesverfassungsgericht (2007) Hartz IV-Arbeitsgemeinschaften mit Verfassung nicht vereinbar. Pressemitteilung Nr. 118/2007 vom 20. Dez. 2007.

Burkhard, H.-P. (2007) Institutionelle und rechtliche Herausforderungen der IIZ am Beispiel des Projektes 'IIZ-MAMAC', in T. Gächter (ed.), *Rechtsfragen zur IIZ,* Bern: Weblau, 31–40.

Byggnadsarbetaren (2010) Hej då inkomstförsäkringen, 4, 10.

Cabinet Office (2010) The coalition: our programme for government, HM government, May 2010, London.

Cahuc, P. and Kramarz, F. (2005) De la précarité à la mobilité: vers une sécurité sociale professionnelle, Paris: la Documentation Française.

—— Zylberberg, A. (2009) Les réformes ratées du Président Sarkozy, Paris: Flammarion.

Calmfors, L., Forslund, A. and Hemström, M. (2001) Does active labour market policy work? Lessons from the Swedish experiences, *Swedish Economic Policy Review,* 85, 61–124.

Cantillon, B., Marx, I. and De Maesschalck, V. (2003) De bodem van de welvaartsstaat van 1970 tot nu, en daarna, *Berichten/UFSIA,* Antwerpen: Centrum voor Sociaal Beleid.

Carabelli, U. (1995) Italia: profili giuridici, in CNEL, La gestione delle eccedenze in Europa. Un'analisi giuridica ed economica, 3030–379.

Carcillo, S. and Grubb, D. (2006) From Inactivity to Work: The Role of Active Labour Market Policies, *OECD Social Employment and Migration Working Papers,* 5, 1–74.

Card, D., Kluve, J. and Weber, A. (2009) Active Labour Market Policy Evaluation: A Meta-Analysis, *IZA Discussion Paper 4002,* Bonn: IZA.

Carlin, W. and Landesmann, M. (1997) From theory to practice? Restructuring and dynamism in transition economies, *Oxford Review of Economic Policy,* 13, 2, 77–165.

Carling, K., Edin, P.-A., Harkman, A. and Holmlund, B. (1996) Unemployment duration, unemployment benefits, and labour market programs in Sweden, *Journal of Public Economics,* 59, 3, 313–34.

Carpenter, H. (2006) Repeat jobseeker's allowance spells, DWP Research report, 394.

Carstensen, M.B. (2010) The nature of ideas, and why political scientists should care: Analysing the Danish jobcentre reform from an ideational perspective, *Political Studies*, 58, 5, 847–65.

—— Møller Pedersen, J. (2008) Translating jobcentres: The complex transfer of new labour market policy instruments from the UK and the Netherlands to Denmark, paper presented at panel 'Networks and Ideas in Policy Making', 2nd ECPR Graduate Conference, Universitat Autònma Barcelona, 25–7 Aug. 2008.

Casey, B. and Wood, S. (1994) Great Britain: firm policy, state policy and the employment and unemployment of older workers, in F. Naschold and B. de Vroom (eds), *Regulating Employment and Welfare*, Berlin: W. de Gruyter, 363–94.

Cassiers, I., De Villé, P. and Slar, P. (1996) Economic growth in post-war Belgium, in N. Crafts and G. Tonioli (eds), *Economic Growth in Europe since 1945*, Cambridge: Cambridge University Press, 173–209.

Castel, R. (2007) Au-delà du salariat ou en deçà de l'emploi: l'institutionnalisation du précariat?, in Paugam, S. (ed.), *Repenser la solidarité*, Paris: Presses Universitaires de France, 416–33.

Castles, F. (2008) What welfare states do: a disaggregated expenditure approach, *Journal of Social Policy*, 38, 1, 45–62.

Castra, D. (2003) *L'insertion professionnelle des publics précaires*, Paris: Presses Universitaires de France.

CBS (2009a) Organisatiegraad van werknemers 1995–2008. Available at www.cbs.nl/nl-NL/menu/themas/arbeid-sociale-zekerheid/cijfers/incidenteel/maatwerk/2009-organisatiegraad-werknemers-1995–2008-cm.htm, accessed 3 December 2009.

—— (2009b) Nederland is Europees kampioen deeltijdwerken. Available at www.cbs.nl/nl-NL/menu/themas/dossiers/eu/publicaties/archief/2009/2009-2821-wm.htm, accessed 5 December 2009.

CCE (2009) Les incitants financiers à la reprise du travail pour les chômeurs et bénéficiaires du revenu d'intégration en Belgique: hier et aujourd'hui, Documentation No.1486, Brussels: Conseil Central de l'Economie. Available at www.ccecrb.fgov.be/txt/fr/doc09-1486.pdf.

CDU/CSU (2002/2006) Leistung und Sicherheit. Zeit für Taten, Berlin: Regierungsprogramm.

CERC (2005) Aider au retour à l'emploi, Paris: la Documentation Française.

CESifo (2003) Benefit Dependency, *Dice Report*, 4, 68–9.

Champion, C. (2008) La collaboration interinstitutionnelle: Prémices d'une réforme de la sécurité sociale suisse, *Working Paper de l'IDHEAP*, Novembre 2008.

Charlier, H. and Franco, A. (2001) *The EU Labour Force Survey on the Way to Convergence and Quality*, proceedings of Statistics Canada Symposium 2001 Achieving Data Quality in A Statistical Agency: A Methodological Perspective, Ottawa, Canada: Statistics Canada.

Christiansen, P. M. and Klitgaard, M. B. (2009) Som en tyv om natten. Etableringen af den enstrengede arbejdsmarkedsforvaltning, *Samfundsøkonomen*, 5, 5–9.

—— Nørgaard, A. S. (2003) *Faste forhold – flygtige forbindelser. Stat og interesseorganisationer i Danmark*, Aarhus: Aarhus University Press.

Clary, G. (1995) Face à la croissance et la mutation du RMI, *Droit Social*, 1995/9–10, 820–2.

Clasen, J. (1994) *Paying the Jobless. A comparison of unemployment benefit policies in Great Britain and Germany*, Aldershot: Avebury.

—— (1999) Beyond social security: the economic value of giving money to unemployed people, *European Journal of Social Security*, 1, 2, 151–80.

—— (2000) Motives, means and opportunities. Reforming unemployment compensation in the 1990s, *West European Politics*, 23, 2, 89–112.

Clasen, J. (2005) *Reforming European Welfare States. Germany and the United Kingdom compared*, Oxford: Oxford University Press.

—— (2009a) The United Kingdom, in P. De Beer and T. Schils (eds), *The Labour Market triangle. Employment protection, unemployment compensation and activation in Europe*, Cheltenham: Edward Elgar, 70–95.

—— (2009b) Les nouvelles politiques de l'emploi au Royaume-Uni et en Allemagne, *Critique International*, 43, 2, 37–50.

—— Clegg, D. (2006) Beyond Activation. Reforming European Employment Protection Systems in Post-Industrial Labour Markets, *European Societies*, 8, 4, 527–53.

—— —— (2007) Levels and levers of conditionality: measuring change within welfare states, in J. Clasen and N. Siegel (eds), *Investigating welfare state change – the 'dependent variable problem' in comparative analysis*, Cheltenham: Edward Elgar, 166–97.

—— —— (2012) Adapting labour market policy to a transformed employment structure: the politics of 'triple integration', in G. Bonoli and D. Natali (eds), *The New Politics of theWelfare State* (forthcoming).

—— Davidson, J., Ganssmann, H. and A. Mauer (2006) Non-employment and the welfare state: the UK and Germany compared, *Journal of European Social Policy*, 16, 2, 134–54.

—— Goerne, A. (2011) Exit Bismarck, enter dualism? Assessing contemporary German labour market policy, *Journal of Social Policy* (forthcoming).

—— —— (2012) Germany: ambivalent activation, in I. Lødemel and A. Moreira (eds), *Workfare revisited*, New York, Oxford University Press (forthcoming).

—— Kvist, J. and van Oorschot, W. (2001) On condition of work: Increasing work requirements in unemployment compensation schemes, in M. Kautto, J. Fritzell, B. Hvinden, J. Kvist and H. Uusitalo (eds), *Nordic Welfare States in the European Context*, London: Routledge, 161–84.

—— Siegel N. (eds) (2007) *Investigating welfare state change – the 'dependent variable problem' in comparative analysis*, Cheltenham: Edward Elgar.

—— Viebrock, E. (2008) Voluntary unemployment insurance and trade union membership: investigating connections in Denmark and Sweden, *Journal of Social Policy*, 37, 3, 433–52.

Clayton, R. and Pontusson, J. (1998) Welfare state retrenchment revisited – entitlement rules, public sector restructuring, and inegalitarian trends in advanced capitalist societies, *World Politics*, 51, 1, 67–98.

Clegg, D. (2002) The political status of social assistance benefits in European welfare states: lessons from reforms to provision for the unemployed in France and Great Britain, *European Journal of Social Security*, 4, 3, 201–26.

—— (2005) Activating the multi-tiered welfare state: social governance, welfare politics and unemployment policies in France and the United Kingdom, Florence, European University Institute, PhD Thesis.

—— (2007) Continental drift: on unemployment policy change in Bismarckian welfare states, *Social Policy and Administration*, 41, 6, 597–617.

—— (2010) From insurance or insertion to rights and responsibilities: the shifting logics of unemployment protection in France, in A. Nevile (ed.), *Human Rights and Social Policy: A Comparative Analysis of Values and Citizenship in OECD countries*, Cheltenham: Edward Elgar, 83–100.

—— (2011) Solidarity or dualization? Social governance, union preferences and unemployment benefit adjustment in Belgium and France, in P. Emmenegger, S. Häusermann, B. Palier and M. Seeleib-Kaiser (eds), *The Age of Dualization* (forthcoming), New York: Oxford University Press.

—— Palier, B. (2007) From Labour Shedding to Labour Mobilisation: The Staggered Transformation of French Labour Market Policy, paper presented to the American Political Science Association annual meeting, Chicago, August 30–September 2, 2007.

—— —— (2012) Implementing a myth: the growth of work conditionality in French minimum income provision, in I. Lodemel and A. Moreira (eds), *Workfare Revisited*, New York: Oxford University Press (forthcoming).

—— van Wijnbergen, C. (2011) Welfare institutions and the mobilisation of consent: Union responses to labour market activation policies in France and the Netherlands, *European Journal of Industrial Relations*, December 2011.

Clement, S. L. (2000) Dansk forskning om førtidspensionister og medborgerskab, *CCWS Working Paper, 11*, Aalborg: Aalborg Universitet.

Cm 3968 (1998) Fairness at Work, May, London: The Stationery Office.

CNEL (2007) Il Mercato del Lavoro 2006, Roma.

—— (2010) Rapporto sul mercato del lavoro 2009–10, Roma.

Commissie-Buurmeijer (1992/1993) Parlementaire enquête uitvoeringsorganen sociale verzekeringen. Rapport van de commissie. Den Haag, in *Handelingen der Staten-Generaal*, II, 22730, 7–8.

Cordazzo, P. (2003) Les bénéficiaires du RMI: évolution et renouvellement des effectifs (1989–2002), *CNAF Recherches et Prévisions*, 74, 71–9.

Cornilleau, G. and Elbaum, M. (2009) Indemnisation du chômage: une occasion manquée face à la crise?, *Lettre de l'OFCE*, 307.

Cour des Comptes (2006) Rapport publique thématique sur l'évolution de l'assurance chômage, Paris: Cour de Comptes.

—— (2009) Titres-services. Coût et gestion Brussels: Cour des Comptes. Available at www.ccrek.be/docs/Reports/2009/2009_04_TitresServices.pdf.

Cox, R. H. (2001) The Social Construction of an Imperative. Why Welfare Reform Happened in Denmark and the Netherlands but Not in Germany, *World Politics*, 53, 463–98.

CPAG (Child Poverty Action Group) (2009) *Welfare benefits and tax credits Handbook 2009/2010*, London: CPAG.

CPB (2007) Macro Economische Verkenning 2008, Den Haag: CPB.

Crouch, C. (1999) Employment, Industrial Relations and Social Policy: New Life in an old connection, *Social Policy and Administration*, 33, 4, 437–57.

Cseres-Gergely, Zs. and Scharle, A. (2008) Social welfare provision, labour supply effects and policy making, *The Hungarian Labour Market Review and Analysis*, Budapest: Institute of Economics, HAS, 33–49.

—— —— (2010) The Hungarian Labour Market in 2008–2009, in K. Fazekas, A. Lovász, and Á. Telegdy, (eds,). *The Hungarian Labour Market: Review and Analysis*, Budapest: Institute of Economics, HAS, 15–40.

Cserpes, T. and Papp, G. (2008) A 2001 és 2002 evi minimálbéremelés szándékolt és tényleges hatásai, MKIK GVI Kutatási Füzetek. Available at: http://www.gvi.hu/data/research/minimalber_kut_fuz_08_3.pdf

CSIAS (2009) La pratique du mandat d'intégration de l'aide sociale: Synthèse de l'étude de la CSIAS, Berne: CSIAS.

DA (2010) Strukturstatistik 2004–2009, Copenhagen: Danish Employers Association.

Daguerre, A. and Palier, B. (2004) Francia, in M. Rhodes, and M. Ferrera (eds), *Sistemi di welfare e gestione del rischio economico di disoccupazionze*, Milano: Franco Angeli, 195–236.

Damon, J. (2009) Du RMI au RSA, en passant par le RMA, *Revue de Droit Sanitaire et Social*, 46, 2, 213–22.

Daniel, C. (2000) L'indemnisation du chômage depuis 1974: d'une logique d'intégration à une logique de segmentation, *Revue Française des Affaires Sociales*, 54, 3–4, 29–46.

—— Tuchszirer, C. (1999) *L'État face aux chômeurs: l'indemnisation du chômage de 1884 à nos jours*, Paris: Flammarion.

De Deken, J. (2002) Christian Democracy, Social Democracy and the paradoxes of earnings-related social security, *International Journal of Social Welfare*, 11, 1, 22–39.

De Deken, J. (2009) Belgium, in P. de Beer and T. Schils (eds), *The Labour Market Triangle*, Cheltenham: Edward Elgar, 145–73.

—— (2011a) Belgien: Konsolidierung und Wandel durch Institutionelle Überlagerung, in C. Bodegan, S. Leibner and E. Seils (eds), *Sozialversicherung: Wandel, Wirkung, Weiterentwicklung*, Wiesbaden: VS Verlag für Sozialwissenschaften. (forthcoming).

—— (2011b) *Towards and Index of pension privatisation* (fortcomming).

—— Kittel, B. (2007) Social expenditure under scrutiny: the problems of using aggregate spending data for assessing welfare state dynamics, in J. Clasen and N. Siegel (eds), *Investigating Welfare State Change*, Cheltenham: Edward Elgar, 72–105.

—— Offe, C. (2001) Travail, temps et participation sociale, in A. Puchet (ed.), *Sociologies du travail: 40 ans après*, Paris: Elsevier, 53–70.

De Haan, I. and Duyvendak, J.W. (2002) In het hart van de verzorgingsstaat. Het ministerie van Maatschappelijk Werk en zijn opvolgers (CRM, WVC, VWS), 1952–2002, Zutphen: Walburg Pers.

De Koning, J., Gravesteijn-Ligthelm, J., Gelderblom, A., Tanis, O. and Maasland, E. (2008) Reïntegratie door gemeenten: zelf doen, uitbesteden of samenwerken?, Den Haag: Raad voor Werk en Inkomen.

De Lathouwer, L. (1997) Het Belgische werkloosheidsstelsel in internationaal perspectief, in *Economisch en Sociaal Tijdschrift*, 2, 295–338.

De Loose, K. (2004) Emploi convenable versus état social actif: analyse réglementaire et jurisprudentielle 1970–2003, *Revue Belge de Sécurité Sociale*, 46, 1, 179–202.

—— Bogaerts, K. and Van den Bosch, K. (2003) De Impact van Schorsing Artikel 80 in de Werkloosheidsverzekering op Herintrede en Armoede Studievoormiddag van 3 December 2003, Gent: Academia Press.

Deacon, A. (1997) Welfare to Work. Options and Issues, in E. Brunsdon, H. Dean and R. Woods (eds), *Social Policy Review* 9, London: Social Policy Association, 34–49.

Deutscher Rentenversicherungsbund (2009) Rentenversicherung in Zeitreihen Oktober 2009. Bd. 22, Berlin: DRV.

Deutscher Renteversicherung (2010) Renteversicherung in Zeitreihen, Berlin: Deutscher Rentenversicherungs Bund.

Dingeldey, I. (2001) European Tax Systems and their Impact on Family Employment Patterns, *Journal of Social Policy*, 30, 653–72.

—— (2007) Between Workfare and Enablement. The Different Paths to Transformation of the Welfare state, *European Journal of Political Research*, 46, 823–51.

—— (2010a) Activating Labour Market Policy in a Bismarckian Welfare State. Old and New Divisions of Social Rights and Citizenship in Germany, in A. Neville (ed.), *Human Rights and Social Policy. A Comparative Analysis of Values and Citizenship in OECD Countries*, Cheltenham/Northampton: Edward Elgar, 65–83.

—— (2010b) Agenda 2010. Dualisierung der Arbeitsmarktpolitik, *Aus Politik und Zeitgeschichte*, 2010.

—— (2011a) Fragmented Governance Continued: The German Case, in R. van Berkel, W. de Graaf, and T. Sirovatka (ed.), *The Governance of Active Welfare States in Europe*, Houndmills/Basingstoke: Palgrave (forthcoming).

—— (2011b) Der aktivierende Wohlfahrtsstaat. Governance der Arbeitsmarktpolitik in Dänemark, Großbritannien und Deutschland, Frankfurt/New York: Campus, (forthcoming).

Disney, R. and Webb, S. (1991) Why are there so many long term sick in Britain?, *The Economic Journal*, 101 (March), 252–62.

Dolado, J., García-Serrano, C., Jimeno, J.F. (2002) Drawing Lessons from the Boom of Temporary Jobs in Spain, *The Economic Journal*, 112, F270-F295.

Ds 1999:58 Kontrakt för arbete. Rättvisa och tydliga regler i Arbetslöshetsförsäkringen, Stockholm: Fakta info direkt.

Ds 2007:47 En effektivare arbetslöshetsförsäkring, Stockholm: Fritzes.

Due, J., Madsen, J.S. and Pihl, M.D. (2010) *Udviklingen i den faglige organisering: årsager og konsekvenser for den danske model.* LO-dokumentation 1/2010, Copenhagen: LO.

Dufour, P., Boisménu, G. and Noël, A. (2003) *L'aide au conditionnel. La contreparties dans les mesures envers les personnes sans emploi en Europe et en Amérique du Nord*, Montreal, Presses de l'Université de Montreal.

DWP (2003) *The UK Employment Action Plan*, London: DWP.

—— (2008a) *No one written off: reforming welfare to reward responsibility*, Public consultation, July, London: DWP.

—— (2008b) *Raising expectations and increasing support: reforming welfare for the future*, CM 7506, London: DWP.

—— (2009) *Building Britain's recovery: achieving full employment*, Cm 7751, London: DWP.

—— (2010a) *Benefit Expenditure Tables, Pre-budget report 2009*; numbers in receipt of benefit by DWP objective, London: DWP.

—— (2010b) *First release. DWP statistical summary*, 20 January 2010, London: DWP.

—— (2010c) *21st Century Welfare*, Cm7913, London: DWP.

—— (2010d) *Universal Credit: welfare that works*, Cm7957, London: DWP.

Eardley, T., Bradshaw, J., Ditch, J., Gough, I. and Whiteford, P. (1996) *Social Assistance in OECD Countries*, Department of Social Security Research report, 46, London: HMSO.

Ebbinghaus, B. (2006) *Reforming Early Retirement in Europe, Japan and the USA*, Oxford: Oxford University Press.

EBRD (2000) *Transition Report 2000, London*: European Bank for Reconstruction and Development.

Edebalk, P. G. (2008) *Staten, arbetsmarknadens parter och arbetslöshetsersättningarna 1945–1975*, Working Paper 2008:1, University of Lund: Department of Social Work.

Edling, J. (2005) Alla behövs: Blott arbetsmarknadspolitik skapar inga nya jobb, Stockholm: Timbro.

Egle, C. (2006) Deutschland, in W. Merkel, C. Egle, C. Henkes, T. Ostheim, and A. Petring (eds), *Die Reformfähigkeit der Sozialdemokratie. Herausforderungen und Bilanz der Regierungspolitik in Westeuropa*, Wiesbaden: Verlag der Sozialwissenschaften, 154–96.

Ehrlich, É., Révész, G. and Tamási, P. (eds) (1994) *Kelet-Közép-Európa: honnan hová?*, Budapest: Akadémiai Kiadó.

Eichhorst, W. and Konle-Seidl, R. (2005) The interaction of labor market regulation and labor market policies in welfare state reform, *IAB Discussion Paper no 19*, Nurnberg: IAB.

—— —— (2008) Contingent Convergence: A comparative Analysis of Activation Policies, *IZA Discussion Paper no 3905*, Bonn: IZA.

—— Marx, P. (2010) Whatever Works: Dualisation and the Service Economy in Bismarckian Welfare States, *IZA Discussion Paper 5035*, Bonn: IZA.

—— Grienberger-Zingerle, M. and Konle-Seidl, R. (2008) Activation Policies in Germany. From Status Protection to Basic Income Support, in W. Eichhorst, O. Kaufmann and R. Konle-Seidl (eds), *Bringing the Jobless into Work. Experiences with Activation Schemes in Europe and the US*, Heidelberg: Springer-Verlag, 17–68.

—— Kaufmann, O. and Konle-Seidl, R. (eds) (2008) *Bringing the jobless into work? Experiences with activation in Europe and the US*, Berlin: Springer.

Emmenegger, P. (2009) Regulatory Social Policy: The Politics of Job Security Regulations, Bern: Haupt Verlag.

Engbersen, G. (1990) Publieke bijstandsgeheimen. Het ontstaan van een onderklasse in Nederland, Leiden/Antwerpen: Stenfert Kroese.

Engellandt, A. and Riphahn, R. T. (2005) Temporary contracts and employee effort, *Labour Economics*, 12, 281–99.

Erhel, C. (2009) *Les politiques de l'emploi*, Paris: Presses Universitaires de France.

Erhel, C. Mandin, L. and Palier, B. (2005) The leverage effect: The OMC in France, in J. Zeitlin, P. Pochet, and L. Magnusson (eds), *The Open Method of Coordination in Action*, Brussels: P.I.E.-Peter Lang, 217–48.

Erixon, L. (2000) A Swedish economic policy – the theory, application and validity of the Rehn-Meidner model, *Working Paper 2000:13*, Stockholm University: Department of Economics.

—— (2008) The Swedish third way: An assessment of the performance and validity of the Rehn-Meidner model, *Cambridge Journal of Economics*, 32, 3, 367–93.

Erlinghagen, M. and Knuth, M. (2010) Unemployment as an Institutional Construct? Structural Differences in Non-Employment between Selected European Countries and the United States, *Journal of Social Policy*, 39, 1, 71–94.

Esping-Andersen, G. (1990) The Three Worlds of Welfare Capitalism, Cambridge: Polity.

—— (1996) Welfare States without Work. The Impasse of Labour Shedding and Familialism in the Continental European Social Policy, in Esping-Andersen, G. (ed.), *Welfare States in Transition. National Adaptions in Global Economies*, London: SAGE Publications, 66–87.

—— (1999) *The Social Foundations of Post-Industrial Economies*, Oxford: Oxford University Press.

—— Regini, M. (2000) *Why Deregulate Labour Markets?*, Oxford: Oxford University Press.

Estevez-Abe, M., Iversen, T. and Soskice, D. (2001) Social protection and the formation of skills: A reinterpretation of the welfare state, in P. Hall and D. Soskice (ed.), *Varieties of Capitalism*, Oxford: oxford University Press, 145–83.

European Commission (1997) *Employment in Europe 1997*, Luxembourg: Statistical Office of the European Communities.

—— (2008) *Communication from the Commission to the European Council. A European Economic Recovery Plan*. European Commission, 26.11.2008.

—— (2010a) Compendium, July 2010. Available at http://ec.europa.eu/social/BlobServlet?docI-d=4093&langId=en, accessed 31st May, 2010.

—— (2010b) The European Labour Force Survey. Available at http://circa.europa.eu/irc/dsis/employment/info/data/eu_lfs/lfs_main/lfs/dissemination_structure.htm, accessed 28th September, 2010.

Eurostat (2003) *Employment in Europe*, Bruxelles: Eurostat.

—— (2010) *Employment in Europe*, Bruxelles: Eurostat.

Evans, M. and Williams, L. (2009) *A generation of change: a lifetime of difference? Social Policy in Britain since 1979*, Bristol: Policy Press.

Fargion, V. (2001) Creeping Workfare Policies: The Case of Italy, in N. Gilbert and R. A. Van Voorhis (eds), *Activating the unemployed: A comparative appraisal of work-oriented policies*, Rutgers, N.S., New Brunswick, Transaction Publishers, 29–68.

Fazekas, K. (2001) Az aktív korú állástalanok rendszeres szociális segélyezésével és közcélú foglalkoztatásával kapcsolatos onkormányzati tapasztalatok, *Budapest Working Papers on the Labour Market*, No. 2001/9.

—— Köllő, J., Lakatos, J. and Lázár, Gy. (eds) (2008) *Statistical data in The Hungarian Labour Market: Review and Analysis*, Budapest: Institute of Economics, HAS.

Federal Government of Czechoslovakia (1991) *Vládní návrh zákona o životním minimu*, Materiál předložený vládou federálního shromáždění ČSFR, Praha 29. srpna 1991.

Ferrera, M. (1993) Modelli di solidarietà. Politica e riforme sociali nelle democrazie, Bologna: Il Mulino.

Ferrera, M. and Gualmini, E. (2004) *Rescued by Europe? Italy's social policy reforms from Maastricht to Berlusconi*, Amsterdam: Amsterdam University Press.

—— Hemerijck, A. and Rhodes, M. (2000) The Future of Social Europe: Recasting Work and Welfare in the New Economy, Oeiras: Celta Editora.

Fidesz (1998) Az uj evezred küszöbén. kormányprogram a polgári Magyarországért 1998–2002, Budapest: Fidesz – Hungarian Civic Union.

Field, F. (2002) Making welfare work: the politics of reform, *Scottish Journal of Political Economy*, 49, 1, 91–103.

Finanspolitiska rådet (2009) *Svensk finanspolitik*. Finanspolitiska rådets rapport 2009, Stockholm: Finanspolitiska rådet.

Finn, D. (2005) Contracting out and contestability: modernising the British public employment service, in T. Bredgaard and F. Larsen (eds), *Employment policy from different angles*, Copenhagen: DJØF Publishing, 233–49.

—— Gloster, R. (2010) Lone parent obligations. A review of recent evidence on the work-related requirements within the benefit systems of different countries, *DWP research report no 632*, London: DWP.

—— Schulte, B. (2008) 'Employment First': activating the British welfare state, in W. Eichhorst, O. Kaufmann and R. Konle-Seidl (eds), *Bringing the Jobless into work? Experiences with activation schemes in Europe and the US*, Berlin: Springer, 297–344.

—— Knuth, M., Schweer, O. and Somerville, W. (2005) *Reinventing the Public Employment Service: the changing role of employment assistance in Britain and Germany*, London: Anglo-German Foundation.

Firle, R. and Szabó, R. (2007) Targeting and labour supply effect of the regular social assistance, *Working Papers in Public Finance*, No. 18.

Flaquer, L. (2004) Familia y Estado de bienestar en los países de la Europa del sur, *Papers*, 73, 27–58.

Fleckenstein, T. (2008) Restructuring Welfare for the Unemployed. The Case of Hartz Legislation in Germany, *Journal of European Social Policy*, 18, 177–88.

Flückiger, Y. (1998) The labour market in Switzerland: The end of a special case?, *International Journal of Manpower*, 19, 6, 369–95.

Försäkringskassan (2005) Förändringarinom socialförsäkringsoch bidragsområdena 1968-01-01–2005-01-01, Stockholm: Försäkringskassan.

Forslund, A., Fröberg, D. and Lindqvist, L. (2004) The Swedish activity guarantee, *OECD Social, Employment and Migration Working Paper no 16*, Paris: OECD.

Fraile, M. and Ferrer, M. (2005) Explaining the Determinants of Public Support for Cuts in Unemployment Benefits Spending across OECD Countries, *International Sociology*, 20, 4, 459–81.

Frerich, J. and Frey, M. (1996) *Handbuch der Geschichte der Sozialpolitik in Deutschland. Sozialpolitik in der Bundesrepublik Deutschland bis zur Herstellung der Deutschen Einheit*, Munich: Oldenburg Verlag.

Freud, D. (2007) Reducing dependency, increasing opportunity: options for the future of welfare to work. *An independent report to the DWP*, London: DWP, Corporate Document Services.

Frey, M. (2001) Jogszabályok és intézmények, Munkaerőpiaci Tükör, Budapest: Institute of Economics, HAS, 179–97.

—— (2003) A Magyarországi munkaerőpiacot erintő jogszabályi és intézményi változások, in Munkaerőpiaci Tükör, Budapest: Insitute of Economics, HAS.

—— (2006) Changes in the legal and institutional environment of the labour market, The Hungarian Labour Market, Budapest: Institute of Economics, HAS.

—— (2010) The legal and institutional environment of the Hungarian labour market, in: The Hungarian Labour Market, Budapest: Institute of Economics, HAS.

Freyssinet, J. (2002) La réforme de l'indemnisation du chômage en France, *IRES Document du Travail no. 02/01*, Paris: IRES.

—— (2010) Négocier l'emploi: 50 ans de négociations interprofessionnelles sur l'emploi et la formation, Paris: Editions Liaisons.

Fridolf, M. (2001) Samarbete – en arbetsform för de särskilt utsatta, Stockholm: Socialstyrelsen.

Friedrich, H. and Wiedemeyer, M. (1998) *Arbeitslosigkeit. Ein Dauerproblem. Dimensionen. Ursachen. Strategien*, Opladen: Leske+Budrich.

Gábos, A. (1996) A Magyar jóléti rendszer jogi szabályozásának változása 1990–1995 között, *Esély*, 1996, 3, 62–117.

Galasi, P. (2004) The Active labour market policy reform – the second wave: statements and comments, Peer Review. Available at: http://www.mutual-learning-employment.net/ uploads/ModuleXtender/PeerReviews/17/HU_FIN04.pdf

—— Nagy, G. (1999) Outflows from insured unemployment in Hungary, 1992–1996, *Budapest Working Papers on the Labour Market*, 3, Institute of Economics, HAS.

—— —— (2002) Assistance recipients and re-employment following the exhaustion of unemployment insurance entitlement, *The Hungarian Labour Market*, Budapest: Institute of Economics, HAS, 242–63.

—— —— (2009) Presentation at the meeting of the'Kreatív Terezési Munkacsoport' of the National Employment Office, Budapest, 10 December 2009.

Gallie, D. And Paugam, S. (2000) The experience of unemployment in Europe: The debate, in Gallie, D. and Paugam, S. (eds), *Welfare Regimes and the Experience of Unemployment*, Oxford: Oxford University Press, 1–22.

Galster, D., Rosenstein, E. and Bonvin, J.-M. (2009) Assessing integrated employment policies against the capability approach: A Swiss case study, *The International Journal of Sociology and Social Policy*, 29, 11, 637–48.

García Serrano, C. (2007) Las políticas del mercado de trabajo: desempleo y activación laboral, *Política y Sociedad*, 44, 2, 135–51.

—— Malo, M.A. (2010) Los contratos indefinidos y sus costes, *El País*, 31.01.2010.

—— Garrido, L. and Toharia, L. (1999) Empleo y paro en España: algunas cuestiones candentes, in F. Miguélez and C. Prieto (eds), *Las relaciones de empleo en España*, Madrid: Siglo XXI de España, 23–50.

Garrido, L. (1996) La temporalidad, ¿pacto intergeneracional o imposición?, *Consejo Económico y Social de la Comunidad de Madrid*, La duración del contrato de trabajo, Madrid: CES Madrid, 47–74.

—— Toharia, L. (2004) What Does It Take To Be (Counted As) Unemployed? The Case of Spain, *Labour Economics*, 11, 4, 507–23.

Gärtner, L. and Flückiger, Y. (2005) *Probleme des Sozialstaats: Ursachen, Hintergründe, Perspektiven*, Chur: Rüegger.

Gash, V. (2008) Bridge or Trap? Temporary Workers' Transitions to Unemployment and to the Standard Employment Contract, *European Sociological Review*, 24, 5, 651–88.

Gautié, J. (2002) De l'invention du chômage a sa déconstruction, *Genèses*, 46, 3, 60–76.

Gebel, M. and Giesecke, J. (2009) Labour market flexibility and inequality: the changing risk patterns of temporary employment in West Germany, *Zeitschrift für Arbeitsmarktforschung*, 42, 3, 234–51.

Gebraad, J. and Pfaff, J. (2006) *Stabiele omvang VUT fondsen in 2000–2004*, Voorburg: Centraal Bureau voor de Statistiek.

Gilles, C. and Loisy, C. (2005) Allocation spécifique de solidarité: caractéristiques et évolution des allocataires, *DREES Etudes et Résultats, no. 394*, Paris: DREES.

Giriens, P.-Y. and Stauffer, J. (1999) Deuxième révision de l'assurance chômage: Genèse d'un compromis, in A. Mach (ed.), *Globalisation, néo-libéralisme et politiques publiques dans la Suisse des années 1990*, Zurich: Seismo, 105–44.

Glennerster, H. and Hills, J. (eds) (1998) *The State of Welfare*, Oxford: Oxford University Press.

Goetz, K.H. and Wollmann, H. (2001) Governmentalizing central executives in post-communist Europe: a four-country comparison, *Journal of European Public Policy*, 8, 6, 864–87.

Gomulka, S. (1998) Output: causes of the decline and the recovery, *CASE-CEU Working Paper*, No. 8.

González, J.J. (1990) El desempleo rural en Andalucía y Extremadura, *Agricultura y Sociedad*, 229–66.

Gottschall, K. and Dingeldey, I. (2000) Arbeitsmarktpolitik im konservativ-korporatistischen Wohlfahrtsstaat. Auf dem Weg zu reflexiver Deregulierung, in S. Leibfried and U. Wagschal (eds), *Der deutsche Sozialstaat. Bilanzen. Reformen. Perspektiven*, Frankfurt: Campus, 306–39.

Goul Andersen, J. (1993) *Politik og samfund i forandring*. Copenhagen: Columbus.

—— (1996) Marginalisation, Citizenship and the Economy: The Capacity of the Universalist Welfare State in Denmark, in E. O. Eriksen and J. Loftager (eds), *The Rationality of the Welfare State*, Oslo: Scandinavian University Press, 155–202.

—— (2002a) Work and citizenship: Unemployment and unemployment policies in Denmark, 1980–2000, in J. Goul Andersen and Per H. Jensen (eds), *Changing Labour Markets, Welfare Policies and Citizenship*, Bristol: Policy Press, 59–84.

—— (2002b) Coping with Long-Term Unemployment: Economic security, labour Market Integration and Well-being. Results from a Danish Panel Study, 1994–1999, *International Journal of Social Welfare*, 11, 2, 178–90.

—— (2006) The Parliamentary Election in Denmark, February 2005, *Electoral Studies*, 25, 2, 393–8.

—— (2008) Et valg med paradokser: Opinionsklimaet og folketingsvalget 2007, *Tidsskriftet Politik*, 11, 3, 10–26.

—— (2010) Activation as an element of two decades of Labour Market Policy Reforms in Denmark, presentation at International Symposion 'Activation or Basic Income? Towards a Sustainable Social Framework', Hokkaido University, Grand Palace Hotel, Tokyo, Feb. 26, 2010.

—— (2011) From the Edge of the Economic Abyss to Prosperity – and Back Into the Abyss. Danish Economy and Economic Policies 1980–2010, *CCWS Working Paper*, Aalborg: Aalborg University.

—— Jensen, J. B. (2002) Employment and unemployment in Europe: overview and new trends, in J.Goul Andersen, J. Clasen, W. van Oorschot and K. Halvorsen (eds), *Europe's New State of Welfare. Unemployment, Employment Policies and Citizenship*, Bristol: Policy Press, 21–58.

—— Pedersen, J. J. (2007) Continuity and change in Danish active labour market policy: 1990–2007. The battlefield between activation and workfare, CCWS Working Paper 54.

Graafland, J. J. and Huizinga, F. H. (1998) Taxes and benefits in a non-linear wage equation, *MPRA Paper*, 21076.

Graziano, P. (2007) Adapting to the European Empoloyment Strategy?, *International Journal of Labour Law and Industrial Relations*, 4, 543–65.

Green-Pedersen, C. (2002) *The Politics of Justification. Party Competition and Welfare State Retrenchment in Denmark and the Netherlands from 1982 to 1998*, Amsterdam: Amsterdam University Press.

Gregg, P. (2008) Realising Potential: a vision for personalised conditionality and support, *an independent report to the DWP*, London: DWP.

Griggs, J., Hammond, A. and Walker, R. (2011) Activation for all: welfare reform in the UK, 1995 to 2009, in I. Lødemel and A. Moreira (eds), *Workfare revisited*, Bristol: Policy Press (forthcoming).

Grubb, D. (2000) Eligibility Criteria for Unemployment Benefits, *OECD Economic Studies*, 31, 1, 147–84.

Gruber, J. and Wise, D. (2007) *Social Security Programs and Retirement around the World, Fiscal Implications of Reform*, Chicago: Chicago University Press.

Gualmini, E. (1998) *La politica del lavoro*, Bologna, Il Mulino.

Guillén, A. (2010) Defrosting the Spanish Welfare State: the Weight of Conservative Components, in B. Palier (ed.), *A Long Goodbye to Bismarck: The politics of Welfare Reforms in Continental Europe*, Amsterdam: Amsterdam University Press.

Gutiérrez, R. and Guillén, A. (2000) Protecting the long-term unemployed. The impact of targeting policies in Spain, *European Societies*, 2, 2, 195–216.

Hadenius, S. (2008) *Modern svensk politisk historia: Konflikt och samförstånd*, Stockholm: Hjalmarson & Högberg.

Hägglund, P. and Skogman Thoursie, P. (2010) De senaste reformerna inom sjukförsäkringen: En diskussion om deras förväntade effecter, Report 2010/5 to Finanspolitiska rådet, Stockholm: Finanspolitiska rådet.

Hall, P.A. and Soskice, D. (eds) (2001) *Varieties of Capitalism. The Institutional Foundations of Comparative Advantage*, Oxford: Oxford University Press.

Hansen, H. (2002) *Elements of social security (9th ed.) A comparison covering: Denmark, Sweden, Finland, Austria, Germany, The Netherlands, Great Britain, Canada*, Copenhagen: Socialforskningsinstituttet.

Harrits, G. S. and Goul Andersen, J. (forthcoming). *Profilen af længerevarende ledige dagpenge og kontanthjælpsmodtagere under højkonjunktur og lavkonjunktur*, [preliminary title] Copenhagen: Frydenlund Academic.

Hartlapp, M. and Kemmerling, A. (2008) When a solution becomes a problem: the causes of policy reversal on early exit from the labour force, *Journal of European Social Policy*, 18, 4, 366–79.

Hartung, K. (2003) Die lange Reformnacht, Die Zeit, 52.

Hartz, P. (2002) Moderne Dienstleistungen am Arbeitsmarkt. Vorschläge der Kommission zum Abbau der Arbeitslosigkeit und zur Umstrukturierung der Bundesanstalt für Arbeit, Berlin.

Hašková, H. (2007) Doma, vjeslích, nebo ve školce? Rodinná a institucionální péče o předškolní děti včeské společnosti mezi lety 1945–2006, *Gender, rovné příležitosti, výzkum*, 8, 2, 15–26.

Hassel, A. And Schiller, C. (2010) *Der Fall Hartz IV. Wie es zur Agenda 2010 kam und wie es weiter geht*, Frankfurt: Campus.

Hasselpflug, S. (2005) *Availability criteria in 25 countries*, Working paper No 12, Copenhagen: Ministry of Finance.

Häusermann, S. (2010) Reform Opportunities in a Bismarckian Latecomer: Restructuring the Swiss Welfare State, in B. Palier (ed.), *A Long Goodbye to Bismarck? The Politics of Weflare Reform in Continental Europe*, Amsterdam: Amsterdam University Press, 207–32.

Heinze, R. G. (1998) *Die blockierte Gesellschaft. Sozioökonomischer Wandel und die Krise des Modell Deutschland*, Opladen: Westdeutscher Verlag.

Hemerijck, A. and Eichhorst, W. (2010) Whatever Happened to the Bismarckian Welfare State? From Labor Shedding to Employment-Friendly Reforms, in B. Palier (ed.), *A long goodbye to Bismarck*, Amsterdam: Amsterdam University Press, 301–32.

—— Marx, I. (2010) Continental welfare at a crossroads. The choice between activation and minimum income protection in Belgium and the Netherlands, in B. Palier (ed.), *A long goodbye to Bismarck? The Politics of Welfare Reform in Continental Europe*, Amsterdam: Amsterdam University Press.

Henry, A., Nassaut, S., Defourny, J. and Nyssens, M. (2009) *Economie plurielle et régulation publique. Le quasi-marché des titres-services en Belgique*, Gent, Belgium: Academia Press.

Heroverwegingswerkgroep (1989) Rapport van de Heroverwegingswerkgroep. Vut in de collectieve sector, *Begrotingsvoorbereiding 1990. Deelrapport Nr. 3*, Den Haag.

Hills, J. (1998) Thatcherism, New Labour and the welfare state, *CASE paper no. 13*, London: CASE, London School of Economics.

—— (2004) *Inequality and the State*, Oxford: Oxford University Press.

388   References

Hirseland, A. and Ramos Lobato, P. (2010) Armutsdynamik und Arbeitsmarkt. Entste-
hung, Verfestigung und Überwindung von Hilfebedürftigkeit bei Erwerbsfähigen. *IAB-
Forschungsbericht 03/2010*, Nürnberg, IAB.
HM Treasury and DWP (2001) *The changing welfare state: employment opportunity for all*,
London: HM Treasury and DWP.
Hogelund, J. (2003) *In search of the effective disability policy*, Amsterdam, Amsterdam
University Press.
Homola, A. and Kortusová, M. (1998) Politika trhu práce včeskej a slovenskej republike po
roku 1989, in. M. Potůček and I. Radičová (eds), *Sociální politika v Čechách a na
Slovensku po roce 1989*, Praha: Karolinum, 193–229.
Hoogenboom, M. (2004) *Standenstrijd en zekerheid. Een geschiedenis van oude orde en
sociale zorg in Nederland*, Amsterdam: Boom.
Huber, E. and Stephens J. (2001) *Development and Crisis of the Welfare States: Parties and
Poltics in Global Markets*, Chicago: Chicago University Press.
Huynh, D. T., Schultz-Nielsen, M. L. and Tranæs, T. (2007) *Employment Effects of Reducing
Welfare to Refugees*, study paper 15, Rockwool Foundation Research Unit, Copenhagen:
Schultz.
IAF (2007a) *Effekterna av förändringarna i arbetslöshetsförsäkringen*, Report 2007:8,
Katrineholm: IAF.
—— (2007b) *Effekterna av förändringarna i arbetslöshetsförsäkringen*, Report 2007:24
(report 2), Katrineholm: IAF.
—— (2009) *Arbetssökande med och utan arbetslöshetsersättning*, Report 2009:7, Katrine-
holm: IAF.
—— (2010) Arbetslöshetsförsäkringen – ersättningsnivå, högsta dagspenning, genomsnitt-
lig dagpenning och KAS/grundbelopp från och med 1980. Available at www.iaf.se,
accessed 20August 2010.
IAQ, FIA and GendA (2009) *Bewertung des SGB II aus gleichstellungspolitischer Sicht.
Abschlussbericht*, Duisburg, Berlin, Marburg.
Ichino, P. (1982) Il collocamento impossibile, Bari: De Donato.
IE (2008) Statistical data, *The Hungarian Labour Market*, Budapest: Institute of Economics,
HAS.
—— (2009) Statistical data, *The Hungarian Labour Market*, Budapest: Institute of Eco-
nomics, HAS.
IGAS (1992) *Rapport annuel de l'IGAS*, Paris: la Documentation Française.
—— (2004) *Gestion des ages et politique de l'emploi: Rapport annuel 2004*, Paris: la
Documentation Française.
Immervoll, H. and Pearson, M. (2009) A good time for making work pay? Taking stock of
in-work benefits and related measures across the OECD, *OECD Social, Employment and
Migration Working Paper 81*, Paris: OECD.
Inglot, T. (2008) *Welfare States in East Central Europe, 1919–2004*, Cambridge, New York:
Cambridge University Press.
Iversen, T. and Wren, A. (1998) Employment, equality and budgetary restraint: The
trilemma of the service economy, *World Politics*, 50, 4, 507–46.
—— —— (1998) Equality, Employment, and Budgetary Restraint: The Trilemma of the
Service Economy, *World Politics*, 50, 4, 507–46.
Jackman, R. and Pauna, C. (1997) Labour market policy and the reallocation of labour
across sectors, *CEP Discussion Paper*, No. 338.
JAP (2001) *Joint assessment of the employment policy priorities of Hungary*, Report, Hungarian
Government and the European Commission's Directorate-General for Employment
and Social Affairs. Available at: http://www.lex.unict.it/eurolabor/documentazione/stati/
dossier/hungary.pdf
Jessoula, M. (2009) La politica pensionistica, Bologna, Il Mulino.

Jessoula, M. (2010) Recalibrating the Italian welfare state: a too weak politics for a 'necessary' policy strategy?, in M. Giuliani and E. Jones (eds), *Italian Politics 2009*, Oxford: Berghahn Books.

—— Alti, T. (2010) Italy: An uncompleted departure from Bismarck, in B. Palier (ed.), *A Long Goodbye to Bismarck? The Politics of Welfare Reforms in Continental Europe*, Amsterdam/Chicago: Amsterdam University Press, 157–82.

—— Graziano, P. and Madama, I. (2010) 'Selective flexicurity' in segmented labour markets: the case of Italian mid-siders, *Journal of Social Policy*, 39, 4, 561–583.

Jimeno, J.F. and Toharia, L. (1994) Unemployment and labour market flexibility. The case of Spain, Geneva: International Labour Office.

Johansson, H. (2001) I det sociala medborgarskapets skugga: Rätten till socialbidrag under 1980-och 1990-talen, Lund: Arkiv.

Jonung, L. (1999) Med backspegeln som kompass. Om stabiliseringspolitiken som läropro-cess, *Report to ESO – Expertgruppen för studier i offentlig ekonomi*, Ds 1999:9, Stockholm: Fakta info direkt.

Jørgensen, H. (2007) 100 års ledighed, in J.H.Pedersen and A.Huulgaard (eds), *Arbejdsløsheds-forsikringsloven 1907–2007 – Udvikling og perspektiver*. Copenhagen: Arbejdsdirektoratet.

Junestav, M. (2007) Socialförsäkringssystemet och arbetsmarknaden. Politiska idéer, sociala normer och institutionell förändring – en historik, *IFAU Report 2007:4*, Uppsala: IFAU.

Kalleberg, A. (2009) Precarious work, insecure workers: Employment relations in transi-tion, *American Sociological Review*, 74, 1–22.

Kangas, O. and Palme, J. (2007) Social rights, structural needs and social exependiture: a comparative study of 18 OECD countries 1960–2000, in J. Clasen and N. Siegel (eds), *Investigating Welfare State Change*, Cheltenham: Edward Elgar, 72–106.

Kaufman, R. (2007) Market reform and social protection: lessons from the Czech Republic, Hungary, and Poland, *East European Politics and Societies*, 21, 111–25.

Kelen, A. (1996) Purgatórium vagy regula – A Bokros-csomag és a reformpolitika, *Esély*, 2, 37–44.

Kemp, P. (2008) The transformation of incapacity benefits, in Seeleib-Kaiser, M. (ed.), *Welfare State Transformations: Comparative Perspectives*, Basingstoke: Palgrave MacMillan.

Kenworthy, L. (2008) *Jobs with Equality*, Oxford: Oxford University Press.

Kertesi, G. and Köllő, J. (2003) Fighting low equilibria by doubling the minimum wage? Hungary's experiment, *IZA Discussion Paper*, No.970.

Kettner, A. and Rebien, M. (2007) Hartz-IV-Reform: Impulse für den Arbeitsmarkt, *IAB Kurzbericht 19/2007*, Nürnberg: IAB.

Keune, M. (2002) Creating capitalist institutions: labour market governance in Hungary in the 1990s, Working Paper, Florence: European University Institute.

King, D. (1995) *Actively seeking work? The politics of unemployment and welfare policy in the United States and Great Britain*, Chicago: University of Chicago Press.

Kirsch, J., Knuth, M., Mühge, G. and Schweer, O. (ed.) (2009) Können wir nicht einfach gute Freunde bleiben. Getrennte Aufgabenwahrnehmung in der Grundsicherung für Arbeitsuchende bietet keine Zukunft, *IAQ – Report 2009-04*, Essen Duisburg: Universität Essen Duisburg.

Kis, J. (2010) Van kereslet liberális párt iránt, Interview with János Kis by A. Mink and S. Révész, *Beszélő*, 15, 2.

Kjellberg, A. (2010) Vilka 'hoppade av' a-kassan eller avstod från att gå med? En studie av a-kassornas medlemsras, *Studies in Social Policy, Industrial Relations, Working Life and Mobility*, Research Report 2010:3, Lund University: Department of Sociology.

Knuth, M. (2006a) Activation as a Change of the Unemployment Regime. Implications for the German Employment System at large, paper prepared for the ASPEN/ETUI Con-verence October 2006, Gelsenkirchen.

—— (2006b) Hartz IV. Die unbegriffene Reform, *Sozialer Fortschritt*, 160–8.

Köllő, J. (2002) Public opinions on changes in the unemployment benefit system in 2000, *The Hungarian Labour Market*, Budapest: Institute of Economics, HAS, 214–20.

Koltayné, K.T. (2002) Eligibility requirements for the unemployment insurance benefit, *The Hungarian Labour Market*, Budapest: Institute of Economics, HAS, 181–6.

Konle-Seidl, R. (2009) Erfassung von Arbeitslosigkeit im internationalen Vergleich. Notwendige Anpassung oder unzulässige Tricks?, *IAB-Kurzbericht*, 4, 1–7, Nürnberg: IAB.

—— Eichhorst, W. (2008) Does activation work?, in W. Eichhorst, O. Kaufmann and R. Konle-Seidl (eds), *Bringing the jobless into work? Experiences with activation schemes in Europe and the US*, Berlin: Springer, 415–43.

—— —— Grienberger-Zingerle, M. (2007) Activation Policies in Germany. From Status Protection to Basic Income Support, *IAB Discussion Paper No. 6/2007*, Nürnberg: Bundesagentur für Arbeit.

Kornai, J. (1992) *The socialist system: the political economy of communism*, Oxford: Clarendon Press.

—— (1993) Transformational recession: a general phenomenon examined through the example of Hungary's development, *Collegium Budapest Working Paper*, No.1.

Korpi, W. (2002) *Velfærdsstat og socialt medborgerskab. Danmark i et komparativt perspektiv, 1930-1995*, Aarhus: Magtutredningen.

—— Palme, J. (2003) New politics and class politics in the context of austerity and globalization: Welfare state New Politics and Class Politics in the Context of Austerity and Globalization: Welfare State Regress in 18 Countries, 1975–95, *American Political Science Review*, 97, 3, 425–46.

Kovács, L. (2001) Press release of 27 October 2001. Available at: http://www.origo.hu/itthon/20011027kovacs.html

Kuchařová, V., Ettlerová, S., Nešporová, O. and Svobodová, K. (2006) *Zaměstnání a péčeo malé děti z perspektivy rodičů a zaměstnavatelů*, Praha: VÚPSV.

Kuipers, S. (2006) *The Crisis Imperative: Crisis Rhetoric and Welfare State Reform in Belgium and the Netherlands in the Early 1990s*, Amsterdam: Amsterdam University Press.

Kvasnicka, M. (2009) Does Temporary Help Work Provide a Stepping Stone to Regular Employment?, in D. H. Autor (ed.), *Studies of labor market intermediation*, Chicago: University of Chicago Press, 335–272.

Kvist, J. (1998) Complexities in assessing unemployment benefits and policies, *International Social Security Review*, 51, 4, 33–55.

—— Pedersen, L. and Köhler, P. A. (2008) Making all persons work: modern Danish labour market policies, in W. Eichhorst, O. Kaufmann, and R. Konle-Seidl (eds), *Bringing the jobless into work? Experiences with activation in Europe and the US*, Berlin: Springer, 221–56.

Lafore, R. (1996) Exclusion, insertion, intégration, fracture sociale, cohésion sociale: le poids des maux, *Revue de Droit Sanitaire et Social*, 1996/4, 803–24.

—— (2004) La décentralisation du revenu minimum d'insertion, Revue de Droit Sanitaire et Social, 2004/1, 14–29.

—— (2009) Le RSA: la dilution de l'emploi dans l'assistance, *Revue de Droit Sanitaire et Social*, 2009/2, 223–35.

Lakner, Z. (2005) A megszakítottság folyamatossága: változó prioritások a rendszerváltás utáni Magyar szociálpolitikában, Unpublished mimeo.

Larsen, F. (2009) *Kommunal beskæftigelsespolitik. Kommunale Jobcentre mellem statslig styring og kommunal autonomi*, Copenhagen: Frydenlund Academic.

Larsson, L., Kruse, A., Palme, M., and Persson, M. (2005) En hållbar sjukpenningförsäkring, *Välfärdsrådet Report 2005*, Stockholm: SNS förlag.

Layard, R. (2000) Welfare-to-work and the New Deal, *World Economics*, 1, 2, 29–39.

Lefèvre, C. and Zoyem, J-P. (1999) Les contrats d'insertion du RMI: quelle perception en ont les allocataires ?, DREES Etudes et Résultats, 45.

Lehmer, F. and Ziegler, K. (2010) Zumindest ein schmaler Steg, *IAB Kurzbericht 13/2010*, Nürnberg: IAB.

Levell, P., May, R., O'Dea, C. and Phillips, D. (2009) A survey of the UK benefit system, *Briefing note No 13*, London: Institute of Fiscal Studies.

Levy, J. (1999) Vice into virtue: Progressive politics and welfare reform in Continental Europe, *Politics & Society*, 27, 2, 239–73.

—— (2000) France: Directing Adjustment?, in Scharpf, F. and Schmidt, V. (eds), *Welfare and Work in the Open Economy*, volume 2, Oxford: Oxford University Press, 308–50.

Lewis, J. (ed.) (1997) *Lone Mothers in European Welfare Regimes*, London: Jessica Kingsley.

—— Surender, R. (eds) (2004) *Welfare State Change: Towards a Third Way?*, Oxford: Oxford University Press.

Lindqvist, R. (1998) Gränser mellan organisationer – exemplet arbetslivsinriktad rehabilitering, in R. Lindvist (ed.), *Organisation och välfärdsstat*, Lund: Studentlitteratur, 76–104.

Lisv (2001) Kroniek van de sociale verzekeringen, Den Haag: Lisv.

Löfbom, E. (2007) Arbetslöshet och arbetsmarknadspolitik i praktiken för personer med ekonomiskt bistånd, in SOU 2007:2, Från socialbidrag till arbete, Bilaga Fördjupningsstudier, Stockholm: Fritzes, 71–104.

Loftager, J. (2004) *Politisk offentlighed og demokrati i Danmark*, Aarhus: Aarhus University Press.

Lohmann, H. and Marx, I. (2008) The different faces of in-work poverty across welfare state regimes, in H.J. Andrez and H. Lohmann (eds), *The Working Poor in Europe*, Cheltenham: Edward Elgar.

Lonsdale, S. (1993) Invalidity benefits. An international comparison, research report, London: Department of Social Security, Analytical Services Division.

Lundborg, P. (2000) Vilka förlorade jobben under 1990-talet?, in J. Frizell (ed.), *Välfärdens förutsättningar*, SOU 2000:37, Stockholm: Fritzes, 11–50.

Mabbet, D. (1995) *Trade, employment and welfare. A comparative study of trade and labour market policies in Sweden and New Zealand, 1880–1980*, Oxford: Clarendon Press.

Madsen, P. (2002) The Danish model of flexicurity: a paradise swith some snakes, in H. Sarfati and G. Bonoli (eds), *Labour market and social protection reforms in international perspective*, Aldershot, Ashgate.

—— (2008) The Danish Road to 'Flexicurity': Where are we Compared to Others? And How did we Get There?, in R. Muffels (ed.), *Flexibility And Employment Security in Europe: Labour Markets in Transition*, Cheltenham: Edward Elgar Publishing, 341–62.

—— (2010) Denmark, in P. de Beer and T. Schils (eds), *The Labour Market Triangle: Employment Protection, Unemployment Compensation and Activation in Europe*, Cheltenham: Edward Elgar Publishing, 44–69.

Maeder, C. and Nadai, E. (2009) The promises of labour: The practices of activating unemployment policies in Switzerland, in M. Giugni (ed.), *The politics of unemployment in Europe: Policy responses and collective action*, Aldershot: Ashgate, 67–82.

Mallee, L., Mevissen, J.W.M. and Tap, W.R. (2008) Ontwikkelingen op de reïntegratiemarkt, Amsterdam: Regioplan.

Malo, M., Toharia, L. and Gautié, J. (2000) France: the deregulation that never existed, in G. Esping-Andersen and M. Regini (eds), *Why Deregulate Labour Markets?*, Oxford: Oxford University Press, 245–71.

—— Mato, F.J., Cueto, B., García-Serrano, C. and Muñoz-Bullón, F. (2006) La temporalidad en Asturias. Un análisis desde las historias laborales, Servicio Público de Empleo del Principado de Asturias.

Mangen, S. (2001) *Spanish society after Franco. Regime Transition and the Welfare State*, New York: Palgrave.

Manow, P. and Seils, E. (2000) Adjusting Badly. The German Welfare State, Structural Change, and the Open Economy, in F. W. Scharpf, and V. A. Schmid, (eds), *Welfare and work in the open economy*. Oxford: Oxford University Press.

Marer, P. (1986) Economic reform in Hungary: from central planning to regulated market, *Joint Economic Committee*, Washington: Congress of the United States, 223–97.

Mareš, P., Sirovátka, T. and Vyhlídal, J. (2003) Dlouhodobě nezaměstnaní – životní situace a strategie, *Sociologický časopis*, 39, 1, 37–54.

Marimbert, J. (2004) Rapprochement des services de l'emploi: rapport au Ministre des Affaires Sociales, du Travail et de la Solidarité, Paris: Ministère des Affaires Sociales, du Travail et de la Solidarité.

Martin, J. and Grubb, D. (2001) What works and for whom: A review of OECD countries' experiences with active labour market policies, *Swedish Economic Policy Review*, 8, 9–56.

Martínez Torres, M. (2005) Las rentas mínimas autonómicas desde una perspectiva comparada, *Cuaderno de Relaciones Laborales*, 23, 2, 151–89.

Marx, I. (2007) *A New Social Question. On Minimum Income Protection in the Postindustrial Era*, Amsterdam: Amsterdam University Press.

Mato, F.J. (2002) La formación para el empleo. Una evaluación cuasiexperimental, Madrid: Civitas.

Mazzuco, S. and Suhrcke, M. (2010) Health Inequalities in Europe: new insights from European Labour Force Surveys, *Journal of Epidemiology and Community Health*, doi:10.1136/jech.2009.096271.

Meager, N. (1997) United Kingdom. Active and passive labour market policies in the United Kingdom, Employment Observatory, *SYSDEM Trends, No.28*, European Commission, DG Employment and Social Affairs, Berlin: IAS, 69–75.

Membres du groupe national de coordination CII (2004) Manuel pour la collaboration interinstitutionnelle (CII).

Merrien, F.-X. (2001) The emergence of active policy in Switzerland, in N. Gilbert and R. A. Van Voorhis (eds), *Activating the unemployed: A comparative appraisal of work-oriented policies*, New Brunswick: Transaction Publishers, 213–42.

Meyer, J-L. (1999) Des contrats emploi-solidarité aux emploi jeunes: régards sur l'insertion, Paris: L'Harmattan.

Meyer-Sahling, J.H. (2009) Sustainability of civil service reforms in Central and Eastern Europe five years after EU accession, *Sigma Paper*, No. 44.

Micklewright, J. and Nagy, G. (1998) Unemployment assistance in Hungary, *Empirical Economics*, 23, 1–2, 155–75.

Miguélez, F. and Prieto, C. (eds) (1991) *Las relaciones laborales en España, Madrid*: Siglo XXI.

Milic, T. (2007) Analyse de la votation fédérale du 17 juin 2007, gfs.bern and Universität Zürich.

Millar, J. (2008) 'Work is Good for You': Lone Mothers, Children, Work and Wellbeing, *Social Security and Health Research Working Papers*, 60, Kela: Helsinki.

Miller, P. (1992) Aktuální problémy sociální politiky vČSFR, in Měnící se trh práce – výzva pracovníkům voblasti vzdělávání dospělých a sociální práce, Praha, Olomouc: MŠMT a Katedra sociologie a andragogiky FF ÚP, 48–50.

Milner, H. and Wadensjö, E. (eds) (2001) *Gösta Rehn, the Swedish model and labour market policies: International and national perspectives*, Aldershot: Ashgate.

Minas, R. (2009) Activation in integrated services? Bridging social and employment services in European countries, *Working Paper 11*, Stockholm: Institute for Future Studies.

Ministry of Employment (Beskæftigelsesministeriet, 2009) Udviklingen i de maksimale arbejdsløshedsdagpenge. Note for Minister's reply in Parliament. http://www.ft.dk/dokumenter/tingdok.aspx?/samling/20091/almdel/amu/spm/6/svar/659171/753391/index.htm

Ministry of Labour and Social Protection (2001) Libro bianco sul mercato del lavoro, Roma.

—— (2003) Libro bianco sul welfare, Roma.

—— (2009) Libro bianco sul futuro del modello sociale. La vita buona nella società attiva, Roma.

Ministry of Social Affaires (2009–2010) Arbeidsmarkt in crisis, *Handelingen der Staten Generaal,* II, 29544, 213.

Ministry of Social Affaires and Employment (SoZa, 1996) 'Sociale Nota 1996', *Handelingen der Staten Generaal,* 1995–1996, II: 24 402, nr. 2.

Mjoset, L. (1987) Nordic economic policies in the 1970s and 1980s. *International Organization,* 41, 403–56.

MLSA (1999) Národní plán zaměstnanosti České republiky, Praha: MPSV.

—— (2003) Základní ukazatele z oblasti trhu práce a sociálního zabezpečení vČeské republice ve vývojových řadách a grafech, Praha: MPSV.

—— (2004) Nový zákon o zaměstnanosti pomůže snížit nezaměstnanost, Press release of MLSA 08/04/2004.

—— (2006) Základní ukazatele z oblasti trhu práce a sociálního zabezpečení vČeské republice ve vývojových řadách a grafech, Praha: MPSV.

—— (2008) Základní ukazatele z oblasti trhu práce a sociálního zabezpečení vČeské republice ve vývojových řadách a grafech, Praha: MPSV.

—— (2009a) Základní ukazatele z oblasti trhu práce a sociálního zabezpečení vČeské republice ve vývojových řadách a grafech, Praha: MPSV.

—— (2009b) Statistická ročenka trhu práce v České republice, Praha: MPSV.

Moffitt, R. (2008) Welfare reform: the US experience. With comments by Knut Røed, *IFAU Working Paper* 13/2008.

Mohr, K. (2008) Creeping Convergence. Wandel der Arbeitsmarktpolitik in Großbritannien und Deutschland, *Zeitschrift für Sozialreform,* 54, 187–207.

Moreno, L. (1997) The Spanish Development of Southern Welfare, *Working Paper 97-04/ 1997,* Madrid: IESA-CSIC.

Mosthaf, A., Schnabel, C. and Stephani, J. (2010) Low-wage careers: are there dead-end firms and dead-end jobs?, *IZA Discussion Paper 4696,* Bonn: IZA.

Možný, I. (2002) Česká společnost, Praha: Portál.

Murthi, M. and Tiongson, E.R. (2008) Attitudes to equality: the 'socialist legacy' revisited policy, *World Bank Research Working Paper 4529.*

Nagy, G. (2002) Unemployment benefits: forms, entitlement criteria and amounts, *The Hungarian Labour Market,* Budapest: Institute of Economics, HAS, 181–6.

Neumann, L. (2007) Contribution to EIRO comparative study on social partners and the social security system: case of Hungary, *Euroline,* Available at: http://www.eurofound. europa.eu/eiro/2005/09/study/hu0509102s.htm#contentpage

Nicis (2008) Werk is overal, maar niet voor iedereen. Aan de slag met een doelmatig arbeidsmarktbeleid, The Hague: Nicis.

Nickell, S. and Quintini, G. (2002) The recent performance of the UK labour market, *Oxford Review of Economic Policy,* 18, 2, 202–20.

Nørgaard, A. S. (2009) Kommunalisering af det offentlige ansvar for arbejdsløshedsforsikring: Mellem incitamenter og socialsikring, *Samfundsøkonomen,* 5, 37–43.

Obinger, H. (1998) Federalism, Direct Democracy, and Welfare State Development in Switzerland, *Journal of Public Policy,* 18, 3, 241–63.

—— (1999) Minimum Income in Switzerland, *Journal of European Social Policy,* 9, 1, 29–47.

—— Castles, F. G. and Leibfried, S. (2005) Introduction: Federalism and the Welfare State, in H. Obinger, S. Leibfried and F. G. Castles (eds), *Federalism and the Welfare State: New World and European Experiences,* Cambridge: Cambridge University Press.

OECD (1994) *The OECD Jobs Study: Evidence and Explanations*; Part 1: Labour Market trends and underlying forces of change; Part 2: The adjustment potential of the labour market, Paris: OECD.

—— (1994) *The OECD Jobs Study* 1–2. Paris: OECD.

—— (1996) *Labour Market Policies in Switzerland*, Paris: OECD.

—— (1998) *Employment Outlook*. Paris: OECD.

—— (2001) *Employment Outlook*, Paris: OECD.

—— (2003a) *Transforming Disability into Ability. Policies to Promote Work and Income Security for Disabled People.* Paris: OECD.

—— (2003b) *Employment Outlook*, Paris: OECD.

—— (2004) *Benefits and Wages*, Paris: OECD.

—— (2006a) *Sickness, Disability and Work: Breaking the Barriers; Norway, Poland and Switzerland*, Paris: OECD.

—— (2006b) General Policies to Improve Employment Opportunities for All. *Employment Outlook*, 2006, 47–126.

—— (2007a) *Employment Outlook. Paris*: OECD.

—— (2007b) Regulatory management capacities of member states of the European Union that joined the Union on 1 May 2004, *SIGMA Paper*, No. 42.

—— (2007c) Activating the unemployed: what countries do?, *Employment Outlook*, Paris: OECD.

—— (2008) *Employment Outlook. Paris*: OECD.

—— (2010a) *OECD Employment Outlook. Moving Beyond the Jobs Crisis*, Paris: OECD.

—— (2010b) *Sickness, disability and work: breaking the barriers. A synthesis of findings across OECD countries*, Paris: OECD.

OFAS (2009) *Quantifizierung der Übergänge zwischen Systemen der sozialen Sicherheit* (IV, ALV und Sozialhilfe), Berne: Office Fédéral des Assurances Sociales.

OFS (2005) Actualités statistiques de la protection sociale, *Info Social*, 11, 41–3.

—— (2007) Les prestations sociales sous condition de ressources allouées dans les cantons suisses en 2007: Inventaire au 01.01.2007, Neuchâtel: Office Fédéral de la Statistique.

—— (2009) *Comparaison des statistiques de l'aide sociale et de la pauvreté: Concepts et résultats*, Neuchâtel: Office Fédéral de la Statistique.

—— (2010) La statistique suisse de l'aide sociale 2008: Résultats nationaux, Neuchâtel: Office Fédéral de la Statistique.

Olli Segendorf, Å. (2003) Arbetsmarknadspolitiskt kalendarium II, *Report 2003:9*, Uppsala: IFAU.

Olson, M. (1976) Die Logik des kollektiven Handelns, in Dettling, W. (ed.) Macht der Verbände. Ohnmacht der Demokratie, München, Wien: Olzog Verlag, 105–23.

Orbán, V. (2001) Response to questions on his speech opening the autumn sitting of parliament, Available at: http://www.parlament.hu/internet/plsql/ogy_naplo.naplo_fadat?p_ckl=36&p_uln=220&p_felsz=4&p_szoveg=&p_felszig=4

Oschmiansky, F. and Ebach, M. (2009) Der Wandel des arbeitsmarktpolitischen Instrumentariums, in S. Bothfeld, Sesselmeier, W. and Bogedan, C. (ed.). *Arbeitsmarktpolitik in der sozialen Marktwirtschaft – Vom Arbeitsförderungsgesetz zu Sozialgesetzbuch II und III*, Wiesbaden: VS Verlag für Sozialwissenschaften, p. 79–93.

—— Mauer, A. and Schulze Buschoff, K. (2007) Arbeitsmarktreformen in Deutschland. Zwischen Pfadabhängigkeit und Paradigmenwechsel, *WSI-Mitteilungen*, 60, 291–7.

Palier, B. (2002) *Gouverner la sécurité sociale. Les réformes du système français de protection sociale depuis 1945*, Paris, Presses Universitaires de France.

—— (2010a) The long conservative–corporatist road to welfare reforms, in Palier, B. (ed.), *A Long Goodbye to Bismarck?*, Amsterdam: Amsterdam University Press.

—— (2010b) The dualizations of the French welfare system, in Palier, B. (ed.), *A Long Goodbye to Bismarck? The Politics of Welfare Reforms in Continental Europe*, Amsterdam: Amsterdam University Press, 73–101.

—— Martin, C. (eds) (2007) Reforming the Bismarckian Welfare Systems, *Social Policy and Administration*, 41, 6.

—— —— (2008a) From a Frozen Landscape to Structural Reforms. The Sequential Transformation of Bismarckian Welfare Systems, in B. Palier and Martin, C. (eds),

Reforming the Bismarckian Welfare Systems, Malden, USA and Oxford, UK: Blackwell, 1–21.

—— —— (ed.) (2008b) *Reforming the Bismarckian Welfare Systems*, Malden, USA and Oxford, UK: Blackwell.

—— Petrescu, L. (2007) France: defending our model, in Kvist, J. and Saari, J. (eds), *The Europeanisation of Social Protection*, Bristol: The Policy Press, 61–76.

—— Thelen, K. (2010) Institutionalizing dualism: Complementarities and change in France and Germany, *Politics & Society*, 38, 119–48.

Palme, J., Carroll, E. And Sjoberg, O. (2010) Unemployment insurance, in Castles, F. et al. (eds), *The Oxford Handbook of the Welfare State*, Oxford: Oxford University Press.

Palsterman, P. (2003) La notion de chômage involontaire (1945–2003), in *Courrier Hebdomadaire* CRISP, 1806.

—— (2010) Titres-services (I): subventions 'exubérantes' pour quelle efficacité in Démocratie 01/05/2010. Available at www.reveue-democratie.be

Parliament (1999) Debate on draft-law no. T/1756 Egyes munkaügyi és szociális törvények módosításáról, Budapest: Hungarian Parliament. Available at: http://www.parlament.hu/internet/plsql/ogy_naplo.naplo_szoveg? P_CKL=36&p_uln=103&p_felsz=21&p_szoveg=&p_stilu

Paugam, S. (1993*) La société française et ses pauvres: L'expérience du Revenu Minimum d'Insertion*, Paris: Presses Universitaires de France.

Peck, J. (2001) *Workfare states*, New York, Guildford Press.

Pedersen, J. H. and Huulgaard, A. (eds) (2007) *Arbejdsløshedsforsikringsloven 1907–2007– Udvikling og perspektiver,* Copenhagen: Arbejdsdirektoratet.

Pedersini, R. (2002) Economically dependent workers, employment law and industrial relations, Eiro report, EirOnline, Available at: http://www.eurofound.europa.eu/eiro/2002/05/study/tn0205101s.htm

Perret, V., Giraud, O., Helbing, M. and Battaglini, M. (2007) *Les cantons suisses face au chômage: Fédéralisme et politiques de l'emploi,* Paris: L'Harmattan.

Picot, G. (2009) Politics of Segmentation: Party Competition and Unemployment Compensation in Italy and Germany, PhD dissertation, University of Milan.

Pierson, P. (1994) *Dismantling the Welfare State? Reagan, Thatcher, and the Politics of Retrenchment,* Cambridge: Cambridge University Press.

—— (1998) Irresistible forces, immovable objects: post-industrial welfare states confront permanent austerity, *Journal of European Public Policy*, 5, 4, 539–60.

—— (2001a) Coping with Permanent Austerity. Welfare State Restructuring in Affluent Democracies, in P. Pierson, (ed.), *The New Politics of the Welfare State,* Oxford: Oxford University Press, 410–56.

—— (2001b) Post-Industrial Pressures on the Mature Welfare States, in Pierson, P. (ed.), *The New Politics of the Welfare State*, Oxford: Oxford University Press, 80–106.

Plant, R. (2003) Citizenship and social security, *Fiscal Studies*, 24, 2, 153–66.

Poguntke, T. (2006) Germany, *European Journal of Political Research*, 47ff.

Proposition 1993/94:209 Den fortsatta reformeringen av arbetslöshetsförsäkringen.

Proposition 1993/94:80 En allmän och obligatorisk arbetslöshetsförsäkring.

Proposition 1996/97:107 En allmän och sammanhållen arbetslöshetsförsäkring.

Proposition 1996/97:63 Samverkan, socialförsäkringens ersättningsnivåer och administration, m.m.

Proposition 2008/09:97 Åtgärder för jobb och omställning.

Ramos, R., Suriñach, J., Artís, M. (2010) Es necesario reformar las políticas activas de mercado de trabajo en España? Algunos elementos para la reflexión, *Papeles de Economía Española*, 124, 281–300.

RAR 2002:17. Riksförsäkringsverkets allmänna råd om sjukersättning och aktivitetsersättning. Available at http://lagrummet.forsakringskassan.se.

Recio, A. (1994) Flexibilidad laboral y desempleo en España. *Cuadernos de Relaciones Laborales*, 5, 57–85.

Regeringen (2005) *En ny chance for all.* Available from http://www.nyidanmark.dk/bibliotek/publikationer/regeringsinitiativer/2005/En_ny_chance_til_alle/html/full_publication.htm

—— (2008) *Politisk aftale mellem regeringen og Dansk Folkeparti om håndtering af EU-retten om fri bevægelighed efter EF-Domstolens afgørelse i Metocksagen* (2008) 22. September 2008. Available at http://www.nyidanmark.dk/NR/rdonlyres/9B324726-C36D-4750-BDC1-B70FCB8908D5/0/politisk_aftale_22092008.pdf.

—— (2010) *Aftale om genopretning af dansk økonomi.* Available at http://www.fm.dk/Publikationer/2010/Aftale%20om%20genopretning%20af%20dansk%20oekonomi.aspx

Regini, M. and Esping-Andersen, G. (eds), (2000) *Why Deregulate Labour Markets?*, Oxford: OUP.

Regnér, H. (2000) Ändrade förutsättningar för arbetsmarknadspolitiken, in J. Frizell (ed.) *Välfärdens förutsättningar*, SOU 2000: 37, Stockholm: Fritzes, 81–118.

Rehn, G. (1985) Swedish active labour market policy, *Industrial Relations Review*, 24, 1, 62–89.

Research Reports 2010:3, Lund University: Department of Sociology.

Rhodes, M. (2000) Restructuring the British welfare state: between domestic constraints and global imperatives, in F. W. Scharpf and V. A. Schmidt (eds), *Welfare and Work in the Open Economy* (vol. II), Oxford: Oxford University Press, 19–68.

Rigter, D. P., Van den Bosch, E.A.M., Hemerijck, A.C. and Van der Veen, R.J. (eds), (1995) *Tussen sociale wil en werkelijkheid. Een geschiedenis van het beleid van het Ministerie van Sociale Zaken*, Den Haag: Vuga.

Rodriguez Cabrero, G. (2009) Valoración de los programas de rentas mínimas en España. Available at www.peer-review-social-inclusion.eu.

Rosdahl, A. and K. N. Petersen (2006) *Modtagere af kontanthjælp. En litteraturoversigt om kontanthjælpsmodtagere og den offentlige indsats for at hjælpe dem*, Copenhagen: Socialforskningsinstituttet.

Rothstein, B. (1992) Labor-market institutions and working-class strength, in S. Steinmo, K. Thelen and F. Longstreth (eds), Structuring politics. Historical institutionalism in comparative analysis, Cambridge, New York: Cambridge University Press, 33–56.

Rousseau, Y. (2008) Sur la fusion de l'ANPE et des ASSEDIC, *Droit Social*, 2008/2, 151–65.

—— (2009) Le suivi du chômage et des personnes tenues de rechercher un emploi après les lois de 2008, *Droit Social*, 2009/11, 1101–13.

Rueda, D. (2007) *Social Democracy Inside Out. Partisanship & Labor Market Policy in Industrialized Democracies*, Oxford: Oxford University Press.

Sacchi, S., Pancaldi F. and Arisi C. (2011) The Economic Crisis as a Trigger of Convergence? Short-time Work in Italy, Germany and Austria, *Social Policy & Administration*, 45, 4, 465–487.

Sainsbury, R. and Stanley, K. (2007) *One for all: active welfare and the single working-age benefit*, London: Institute for Public Policy Research.

Salais, R., Bavarez, N. and Reynaud, B. (1986) L'invention du chômage, Paris: Presses Universitaires de France.

Salonen, T. and Ulmestig, R. (2004) Nedersta trappsteget. En studieom kommunal aktivering, Report no 1 in social work, Växjö University: Institutionen för vårdvetenskap och socialt arbete.

Samek Lodovici, M. and Semenza, R. (2008) The italian case: from employment regulation to welfare reforms? *Social Policy and Administration*, 42, 160–76.

Scharle, Á. (2002) Pre-retirement allowance Schemes, *The Hungarian Labour Market*, Budapest: Institute of Economics, HAS, 193–6.

Scharpf, F. W. (2000) Economic Changes, Vulnerabilities, and Institutional Capabilities, in F. W. Scharpf and V. A. Schmidt (eds), *Welfare and Work in the Open Economy*, Vol.1 *From Vulnerability to Competitiveness*, Oxford: Oxford University Press, 21–124.

Schlieben, M. (2007) Politische Führung in der Opposition. Die CDU nach dem Macht-verlust 1998, Wiesbaden: VS-Verlag für Sozialwissenschaften.

Schmid, G. (2002) *The Dynamics of Full Employment*, Cheltenham: Edward Elgar.

——— (2010) Non-Standard Employment and Labour Force Participation: A Comparative view of the recent development in Europe, in E. Berkhout and E. van den Berg (eds), *Bridging the Gap – International Database on Employment and Adaptive Labour*, Amsterdam: SEO, 114–54.

——— Oschmiansky, F. (2005) Arbeitsmarktpolitik und Arbeitslosenversicherung, in Bundesministerium für Arbeit und Soziales/Bundesarchiv (ed.), *Geschichte der Sozialpolitik in Deutschland, Bd.7. Bundesrepublik Deutschland 1982–1989. Finanzielle Konsolidierung und institutionelle Reform*, Baden-Baden: Nomos, 238–87.

——— Reissert, B. (1996) Unemployment compensation and labour market transitions, in Schmid, G., O'Reilly, J. and Schömann, K. (eds), *International Handbook of Labour Market Policy and Evaluation*, Cheltenham, Edward Elgar: 235–76.

——— Wiebe, N. (1999) Die Politik der Vollbeschäftigung im Wandel. Von der passiven zur interaktiven Arbeitsmarktpolitik, in M. Kaase and G. Schmid (eds), *Eine lernende Demokratie. 50 Jahre Bundesrepublik Deutschland*, Berlin: Edition Sigma, 357–96.

——— Reissert, B. and Bruche, G. (1987) *Arbeitslosenversicherung und aktive Arbeitsmarkt-politik. Finanzierungssysteme im internationalen Vergleich*, Berlin: Edition Sigma.

——— ——— ——— (1992) Unemployment Insurance and Active Labor Market Policy: An International Comparison of Financing Systems Detroit: Wayne State University Press.

Schmidt, M. G. (2005) *Sozialpolitik in Deutschland. Historische Entwicklung und interna-tionaler Vergleich*, 3. überarb. Aufl., Opladen: Leske + Budrich.

——— (2007) *Das politische System Deutschlands*, München: Beck.

Schröder, G. (2003) Regierungserklärung des Bundeskanzler Schröder vor dem Deutschen Bundestag vom 14.03.2003. Plenarprotokoll 15/32 14.03.2003, Berlin: Bundesregierung.

Schumpeter, J. A. (1954) [1917], *History of Economic Analysis*, Oxford: Oxford University Press.

SCP (2005) *De steun voor de verzorgingsstaat in de publieke opinie, 1977–2002. Een analyse van trends in meningen*, Den Haag: SCP.

Scruggs, L. (2002) The Ghent system and union membership in Europe, 1970–1996, *Political Research Quarterly*, 275, 286–90.

——— (2004) Unemployment Replacement Rate Data Set, in Welfare State Entitlements Data Set: A Comparative Institutional Analysis of Eighteen Welfare States, Version 1.1.

——— (2007) Welfare state generosity across space and time, in J. Clasen and N.A. Siegel (eds), *Investigating Welfare State Change: The 'Dependent Variable Problem' in Compar-ative Analysis* Cheltenham, UK/Northampton, MA: Edward Elgar, 133–66.

SECO (2010a) Die Entwicklung atypisch-prekärer Arbeitsverhältnisse in der Schweiz: Nachfolgestudie zur Studie von 2003, Bern: Staatssekretariat für Wirtschaft SECO.

——— (2010b) Factsheet: Les principales modifications. 4e révision partielle de la loi sur l'assurance-chômage, Bern: Staatssekretariat für Wirtschaft SECO.

Seeleib-Kaiser, M., Van Dyk, S. and Roggenkamp, M. (2008) *Party politics and social welfare. Comparing Christian and Social Democracy in Austria, Germany and the Netherlands*, Cheltenham: Edward Elgar.

Segura, J. (2001) La reforma del mercado de trabajo español: un panorama, *Revista de Economía Aplicada*, 25, 157–90.

Semjén, A. (1996) A pénzbeli jóléti támogatások ösztönzési hatásai, *Közgazdasági Szemle*, 10, 841–62.

SER (1999) Bevordering arbeidsdeelname ouderen, Den Haag: SER.

Serrano, P, A. and Magnusson, L. (2007) *Reshaping Welfare States and Activation Regimes in Europe*, Brussels: PIE Peter Lang.

Shokkaert, E. and Spinnewyn, F. (1995) Fundamenten van sociale zekerheid: solidariteit en verzekering, overheid en markten, in M. Despontin and M. Jhegers (eds), *De sociale zekerheid verzekerd?*, Brussels: VUB Press, 223–68.

Sianesi, B. (2001) An evaluation of the active labour market programmes in Sweden, *Working Paper 2001*: 5, Uppsala: IFAU.

Sibbmark, K. (various years) Arbetsmarknadspolitisk översikt, Uppsala: IFAU.

Siefken, S. T. (2007) Expertenkommissionen im politischen Prozess. Eine Bilanz zur rotgrünen Bundesregierung 1998–2005, Wiesbaden: VS Verlag für Sozialwissenschaften.

Siegel, N. (2007) When (only) money matters: the pros and cons of expenditure analysis, in J. Clasen and N. Siegel (eds), *Investigating Welfare State Change*, Cheltenham: Edward Elgar, 43–71.

Sirovátka, T. (2006) Labour Market Exclusion of the Roma in Post-communist Countries, in T. Sirovátka et al. (eds), *The Challenge of Social Exclusion. Minorities and Marginalized Groups in Czech Society*, Brno: Barrister&Principal, 111–32.

—— (2009) *Czech Republic. Assessment of the situation in relation to minimum income schemes. A Study of National Policies*, Brussels: EC.

Sjöberg, O. (2001) Välfärdsstatens finansiering under 1990-talet, in J. Fritzell and J. Palme (eds), *Välfärdens finansiering och fördelning*, SOU 2001: 57, Stockholm: Fritzes, 17–70.

—— (2008) Labour market mobility and workers' skills in a comparative perspective: Exploring the role of unemployment insurance benefits, *International Journal of Social Welfare*, 17, 74–83.

Sjögren Lindquist, G. and Wadensjö, E. (2007) Ett svårlagt pussel – kompletterande ersättningar vid inkomstbortfall, Report 2007:1 to Expertgruppen för studier i offentlig ekonomi, Stockholm: Fritzes.

—— —— (2010) Avtalsförsäkringars och andra kompletterande försäkringars påverkan på arbetsutbudet, Report to Expertgruppen för studier i offentlig ekonomi.

Smith, T. (2004) *France in Crisis: Welfare, Inequality and Globalization since 1980*, Cambridge: Cambridge University Press.

Socialkommisionen (1993) *Reformer. Socialkommisionens samlede forslag*, Copenhagen: Social Commission.

Sol, E. (2000) Arbeidsvoorzieningsbeleid in Nederland. De rol van de overheid en de sociale partners, Den Haag: Sdu.

SOU 1971:42 Försäkring och annat kontant stöd vid arbetslöshet, Stockholm: Fritzes.

SOU 1996:113 En allmän och aktiv försäkring vid sjukdom och rehabilitering, Stockholm: Fritzes.

SOU 1996:85 Egon Jönsson – en kartläggning av lokala samverkansprojekt inom rehabiliteringsområdet, Stockholm: Fritzes.

SOU 1996:150 En allmän och sammanhållen arbetslöshetsförsäkring, Stockholm: Fritzes.

SOU 2000:78 Rehabilitering till arbete. En reform med individen i centrum. Slutbetänkande om den arbetslivsinriktade rehabilitering, Stockholm: Fritzes.

SOU 2001:79 Slutbetänkade av Kommittén Välfärdsbokslut, Stockholm: Fritzes. SOU 2006:86 Mera försäkring och mera arbete, Stockholm: Fritzes.

SOU 2008:54 Obligatorisk arbetslöshetsförsäkring, delbetänkande av 2007 års utredning.

Stafford, B. (2003) Beyond lone parents: extending welfare-to-work to disabled people and the young unemployed, in R. Walker and M. Wiseman (eds), *The welfare we want? The British challenge for American reform*, Bristol: Policy Press, 143–74.

Standing, G. (1999) *Global Labour Flexibility: Seeking Distributive Justice*, Basingstoke: Palgrave Macmillan.

Statistics Sweden (2009) Antalet helårsekvivalenter i åldrarna 20–64 som försörjdes med sociala ersättningar och bidrag, 1990–2009. Available www. scb.se, accessed 20 August 2010.

Statskontoret (2006) Enhetlig regeltillämpning i socialförsäkringarna, Socialförsäkringsutredningens PM no 13.

Steffen, J. (2009) Sozialpolitische Chronik, Bremen: Arbeitnehmerkammer.

STEM (2004) Informace z výzkumu, trendy, 4/2004: Přijme veřejnost zpřísnění dávek pro nezaměstnané?, Praha: STEM.

Stofer, S., Steiner, B. and Da Cunha, A. (2005) Analyse comparative de l'efficacité des mesures d'insertion, *Aspects de la Sécurité Sociale*, 4, 22–31.

Straubhaar, T. and Werner, H. (2003) Arbeitsmarkt Schweiz: Ein Erfolgsmodell?, *Mitteilungen aus der Arbeitsmarkt und Berufsforschung* (IAB), 36, 1, 60–76.

Streeck, W. and Thelen, K. (2005a) Introduction: Institutional change in advanced political economies, in W. Streeck and K. Thelen (eds), *Beyond Continuity. Institutional change in advanced political economies*, Oxford: Oxford University Press, 1–39.

Svenska Dagbladet (2008) Mp-styrelse föreslår statlig a-kassa, February 25.

Swedish Government (2002) *Sweden's action plan for employment*, Stockholm.

Swenson, P. A. (2002) *Capitalists against Markets: The Making of Labor Markets and Welfare States in the United States and Sweden*, Oxford: Oxford University Press.

Széman, Zs. (1994) Az ipari vállalatok munkaerőpolitikája és az idősek, Esély, 2, 32–41.

TÁRKI (2002) Elemzések a gazdasági és társadalompolitikai döntések előkészítéséhez 38, Budapest: TÁRKI.

Taylor-Gooby, P. (2004) New risks and social change, in P. Taylor-Gooby (ed.), *New risks, New Welfare?*, Oxford: Oxford University Press.

TCO (2010) Svensk A-kassa kvar i strykklass, TCO granskar no 4, Stockholm: TCO.

Teulings, C.N., Van der Veen, R.J. and Trommel, W. (1997) Dilemmas van sociale zekerheid. Een analyse van 10 jaar herziening van het stelsel van sociale zekerheid, Amsterdam: VUGA.

Thelen, K. (2004) *How institutions evolve: The political economy of skills in Germany, Britain, the United States and Japan*, Cambridge: Cambridge University Press.

Timmins, N. (2001) *The five Giants. A biography of the welfare state*, London: Harper Collins.

Timonen, V. (2004) New Risks – Are they still new for the Nordic welfare states?, in P. Taylor-Gooby (ed.), *New risks, new welfare*, Oxford: Oxford University Press.

Toharia, L. (1995) La protección por desempleo en España, *Working Paper 9504*, Madrid: Fundación Empresa Pública.

—— Malo, M.A. (2000) The Spanish Experiment: Pros and Cons of the flexibility at the margin, in G. Esping-Andersen and M. Regini (eds), *Why deregulate? Dilemmas of labour market reform in Europe*, Oxford: Oxford University Press, 307–35.

—— Prudencio, C.A. and Pérez-Infante, J.I. (2006) La ocupabilidad de los parados registrados, Report for the Servicio Público de Empleo Estatal.

—— Arranz, J.M., García-Serrano, C. and Hernanz, V. (2010) El sistema de protección por desempleo y la salida del paro, *Papeles de Economía Española*, 124, 230–46.

Torfing, J. (1999) Workfare with welfare: Recent reforms of the Danish welfare state, *Journal of European Social Policy*, 9, 5–28.

—— (2004) *Det stille sporskifte i velfærdsstaten. En diskursteoretisk beslutningsprocesanalyse*, Aarhus: Aarhus University Press.

Trampusch, C. (2003) Dauerproblem Arbeitsmarkt. Reformblockaden und Lösungskonzepte, *Aus Politik und Zeitgeschichte*, B 18–19/2003, 16–23.

Udredningsudvalget (1992) *Rapport fra udredningsudvalget om arbejdsmarkedets strukturproblemer*, Copenhagen: Udredningsudvalget.

Ulmestig, R. (2007) På gränsen till fattigvård? En studie om arbetsmarknadspolitik och socialbidrag, Lund: Socialhögskolan.

Unemployment Unit (1995) *Working Brief*, Issue 66, June.

UWV (2003) Kroniek van de sociale verzekeringen, Den Haag: UWV.

—— (2004) Kerncijfers Werknemersverzekeringen. Available at www.uwv.nl, accessed 2 July 2009.

—— (2007) Kennismemoranda 2007: ZW-ramingen 2007 II. Available at www.uwv.nl, accessed 2 July 2009.

—— (2008a) Kroniek van de sociale verzekeringen, Den Haag: UWV.

—— (2008b) 'Kennismemoranda 2008: ZW Ramingen 2008-III'. Available at www.uwv.nl, accessed 2 July 2009.

Vail, M. (2010) *Recasting Welfare Capitalism: Economic Adjustment in Contemporary France and Germany*, Philadelphia: Temple University Press.

Van Cruchten, J. and Kuijpers, R. (2007) Vakbeweging en organisatiegraad van werknemers. Available at www.cbs.nl/NR/rdonlyres/0087898E-C7E3-40ED-8885-590390DBF54C/0/2007 k1v4p07artpdf.pdf, accessed 13 July 2009.

Van den Hauten, M. (2003) De werking van incentives. De reacties van werkgevers op de privatisering van de Ziektewet, Den Haag: Reed Business Information.

Van der Burgt, M. (2004) Zoals het GAK. Geschiedenis van een uitvoeringsorganisatie voor sociale verzekeringen (1952–2002), Amsterdam: GAK/UWV.

Van der Valk, L. (1986) Van pauperzorg tot bestaanszekerheid. Armenzorg in Nederland 1912–1965, Amsterdam: IISG.

Van der Veen, R.J. (1990) De sociale grenzen van beleid. Een onderzoek naar de uitvoeringen effecten van het stelsel van sociale zekerheid, Leiden: Stenfert Kroese.

—— Trommel, W. (1999) Managed Liberalization of the Dutch Welfare State. A Review and Analysis of the Reform of the Dutch Social Security System, 1985–1998, *Governance*, 12, 3, 289–310.

Van Echtelt, P. and Hoff, S. (2008) Wel of niet aan het werk, Achtergronden van het onbenut arbeidspotentieel onder werkenden, werklozen en arbeidsongeschikten, Den Haag: Sociaal en Cultureel Planbureau.

Van Gerven, M. (2008) *The Broad Tracks of Path Dependent Benefit Reform. A Longitudinal Study of Social Benefit Reforms in Three European Countries, 1980–2006*, Amsterdam: AIAS.

Van Gestel, N., De Beer, P.T. and Van der Meer, M. (2009) Het hervormingsmoeras van de verzorgingsstaat. Veranderingen in de organisatie van de sociale zekerheid, Amsterdam: Amsterdam University Press.

Van Langendonck, J. (1997) The social protection of the unemployed, *International Social Security Review*, 50, 4, 29–41.

Van Oorschot, W. and Schell, J. (1991) Means testing in Europe: A growing concern, in Adler, M. et al. (eds), *The Sociology of Social Security*, Edinburgh: Edinburgh University Press.

Van Zanden, J. L. (1997) *The Economic History of the Netherlands in the 20th Century. A Small Open Economy in the Long Twentieth Century*, London: Routledge.

Vanhuysse, P. (2004) The pensioner booms in post-communist Hungary and Poland: political sociology perspectives, *International Journal of Sociology and Social Policy*, 24, 1–2, 86–102.

—— (2006) *Divide and Pacify: Strategic Social Policies and Political Protests in Post-Communist Democracies*, Budapest, New York: Central European University Press.

Vanlerenberghe, P. (1992) RMI, le pari de l'insertion: Rapport du Commission Nationale d'Evaluation du Revenu Minimum d'Insertion Paris: la Documentation Française.

Venn, D. (2009) Legislation, Collective Bargaining and Enforcement: Updating the OECD Employment Protection Indicators, *OECD Social, Employment and Migration Working Paper 89*, Paris: OECD.

Verheijen, T. (2006) EU-8 administrative capacity in the new member states: the limits of innovation?, *World Bank Report, No. 36930-GLB*, Washington: The World Bank.

Vericel, M. (2006) La convention Etat-UNEDIC-ANPE du 5 mai 2006: accompagnement renforcé des chômeurs mais pas de véritable réorganisation du service public de l'emploi, *Droit Social*, 2006/9–10, 900–4.

Vesan, P. (2009) Breve storia delle politiche del lavoro in Italia, in F. Berton, M. Richiardi and S. Sacchi, *Flex-insecurity. Perché in Italia la flessibilità diventa precarietà*, Bologna: Il Mulino, 73–108.

Visser, J. (2006) Union membership statistics in 24 countries, *Monthly Labor Review*, 129, 1, 38–49.

——— Hemerijck, A. (1997) *A Dutch Miracle, Job Growth, Welfare Reform and Corporatism in the Netherlands*, Amsterdam: Amsterdam University Press.

——— ——— (2001) Learning Ahead of Failure: A Research Agenda, University of Amsterdam.

Vodopivec, M., Wörgötter, A. and Raju, D. (2003) Unemployment Benefit System in Central and Eastern Europe: A Review of the 1990s, *Social Protection Discussion Paper Series No. 0310*, Washington: Social Protection Unit/Human Development Network/ World Bank.

Voges, W., Jacobs, H. and Trickey, H. (2000) Uneven Development. Local Authorities and Workfare in Germany, in I. Lødemel and H. Trickey (eds), *An Offer You Can't Refuse. Workfare in International Perspective*, Bristol: Policy Press, 71–104.

Voß, G. G. (1997) Zur Entwicklung der Arbeitszeiten in der Bundesrepublik Deutschland. Mitteilungen des Sonderforschungsbereichs 333. Entwicklungsperspektiven von Arbeit, 33–58.

VÚPSV (2009) Vývoj hlavních ekonomických a sociálních ukazatelů České republiky (Bulletin No 24), Praha: VÚPSV.

Watson, S. (2008) The Left Divided: Parties, Unions, and the Resolution of Southern Spain's Agrarian Social Question, *Politics & Society*, 36, 4, 451–77.

Weir, M. and Skocpol, T. (1985) State structures and possibilities for Keynesian responses to the Great Depression in Britain, Sweden and the United States, in B. Evans, D. Rueschemeyer and T. Skocpol (eds), *Bringing the State Back In*, London: Cambridge University Press, 107–63.

Wheelan, C. T. and McGinnity, F. (2000) Unemployment and Satisfaction: A European Analysis, in D. Gallie and S. Paugam (eds), *Welfare Regimes and the Experience of Unemployment in Europe*, Oxford: Oxford University Press, 286–306.

Williams, L. (2009) Fair rewards or just deserts? The present and future of the contributory principle in the UK, *Benefits*, 17, 2, 159–69.

Willmann, C. (2009) L'autonomie des partenaires sociaux en débat: Pôle emploi et la convention d'assurance chômage du 19 février 2009, *Droit Social*, 2009/7–8, 830–41.

Wolff, J. and Hohmeyer, K. (2006) Förderung von arbeitslosen Personen im Rechtskreis des SGB II durch Arbeitsgelegenheiten. Bislang wenig zielgruppenorientiert, *IAB Forschungsbericht 10/2006*, Nürnberg: IAB.

Woll, C. (2006) National business associations under stress: lessons from the French case, *West European Politics*, 29, 3, 489–512.

Wood, S. (2001) Labour Market Regimes under Threat? Sources of Continuity in Germany, Britain, and Sweden, in P. Pierson (ed.), *The New Politics of the Welfare State*, Oxford: Oxford University Press, 368–409.

World Bank (2001) Hungary – Long-term Poverty, Social protection, and the Labor Market. *Report No. 20645-HU*, Washington: The World Bank.

Wyss, K. and Ruder, R. (1999) Mesures d'intégration contre le chômage de longue durée: Forte segmentation, *Sécurité sociale*, 5, 239–45.

Zijl, M., van den Berg, G. J. and Heyma, A. (2004) Stepping Stones for the Unemployed: The Effect of Temporary Jobs on the Duration until Regular Work, *IZA Discussion Paper 1241*, Bonn: IZA.

Zoyem, J-P. (2001) Contrats d'insertion et sortie du RMI: évaluation des effets d'une politique sociale, *Economie et statistique*, 346–7, 75–86.

Index

Lightning Source UK Ltd.
Milton Keynes UK
UKHW050916190223
416869UK00031B/173